PROMISES UNFULFILLED
A HISTORY OF THE FIRST LUTHERAN COLLEGE IN NORTH CAROLINA

iUniverse books may be ordered through booksellers or by contacting:

iUniverse
1663 Liberty Drive
Bloomington, IN 47403
www.iuniverse.com
1-800-Authors (1-800-288-4677)

ISBN: 978-1-5320-9503-0 (sc)
ISBN: 978-1-6632-0038-9 (hc)
ISBN: 978-1-5320-9504-7 (e)

Print information available on the last page.

iUniverse rev. date: 06/22/2020

PROMISES UNFULFILLED

A HISTORY OF THE FIRST LUTHERAN COLLEGE IN NORTH CAROLINA

BEN CALLAHAN

CONTENTS

ACKNOWLEDGEMENTS

The only known attempt to document the history of this institution was written by the late Reverend Michael C. D. McDaniel. During his college years in the 1950's, Reverend McDaniel wrote papers on the history of NC College/MPCI for two of his classes. Reverend McDaniel was a native of Mt. Pleasant and the son of a former instructor at MPCI. His great-grandfather was a brick mason who literally helped build the first three college buildings and became Chairman of the Board of Trustees and his great uncle was the founder and President of the Mt. Pleasant Collegiate Institute. Reverend McDaniel served as Bishop of the North Carolina Evangelical Lutheran Synod from 1982-1991. This narrative of the first Lutheran College in North Carolina is written in his honor and fulfills the author's promise to complete the work he began.

Thanks are due to several persons who have been of great help and encouragement during an effort to tell a story that has consumed twenty years of my life.

First, I would like to thank both the founding and sustaining members of the Eastern Cabarrus Historical Society for their foresight in preserving not only the physical buildings which housed North Carolina College and the Mt. Pleasant Collegiate Institute, but also in collecting, maintaining and providing access to the many documents, photographs, and other historical artifacts associated with these schools. All the images and photographs used in the publication of this book were provided by the ECHS and used with their kind permission.

I owe a debt of gratitude to Mr. Burl McCuiston, a distant cousin and Assistant Director of Instruction/ Research Librarian at Lenoir-Rhyne University, for his assistance in accessing the records of the North Carolina Lutheran Synod, Western Carolina Male Academy, North Carolina College, and Mt. Pleasant Collegiate Institute. Twenty years ago, I promised I would send him a copy of my book, and now I will.

I would also like to express appreciation to Denise McLain, Nick

McEntire, and Vincent Vezza for their support and inspiration during the difficult and stressful task of letting go of my project and moving it toward publication.

Finally, I must thank my wife, Janet, for her patience, knowledge, perseverance, love, affection, and overall support in seeing this venture through. Her continued validation through my constant anxiety over my ability to complete such an endeavor has been incalculable.

PREFACE

This narrative is a chronological and interpretive history of the first Lutheran institution of higher learning in the state of North Carolina. Although several individual North Carolina Lutheran congregations established private academies during the Church's first 110 years in the state, it was not until 1855 that the North Carolina Lutheran Synod opened its first "high school of a collegiate character".

Sited in Mt. Pleasant, NC, the institution was initially established as Western Carolina Male Academy, but later existed as North Carolina College, Carolina English and Classical School, and Mt. Pleasant Collegiate Institute. For sixty-three of its seventy-eight-year history, it was the only post-secondary educational establishment for men supported by the NC Lutheran Synod.

When it finally closed in 1933, the institution had provided over 2,500 men and a few women with the tools they would need to fulfill their promise in life, but the school itself, abandoned by its creators and many of its earlier supporters, perished with many promises unfulfilled.

Largely intended to gather and preserve factual information into a single document, the style of this history is different from the traditional chapter format. Instead, the writer has divided the document into three major "Parts" preceded by an "Introduction" and a "Beginning". Each Part – Business, Academics and Campus Life – is organized chronologically from the opening of Western Carolina Male Academy through the closing of Mt. Pleasant Collegiate Institute. Each part begins with the opening year of the Academy (1855) and proceeds through the business, academic and campus activities of each school. Parts I and II are sub-divided for each of the schools that occupied the campus between 1855 and 1933: Western Carolina Male Academy (WCMA), North Carolina College (NCC), the Carolina English and Classical School (CECS), and Mt. Pleasant Collegiate Institute (MPCI). Part II is further sub-divided by the school's "academic year" which differs from the calendar year in that it began in one calendar year and ended in another. Part III is divided by categories and discussed in somewhat chronological order. This approach necessarily creates a "restart" at the beginning of each part and does create some redundancy; however, it separates the various activities into a more cohesive story in the end.

In creating this account, the writer attempted to strike a balance between telling the story and documenting the facts. Purposefully, most of the work is taken directly from primary sources and includes verbatim quotes that are often quite long and stylistically characteristic of the original writer/speaker. These quotations not only provide information but also serve to transmit the context of the times.

For the sake of readability, many of the quotations were shortened or summarized, but in numerous other cases, the source's full, exact wording is more effective. To preserve these messages for future research, entire dialogues are included in endnotes that the reader may review as desired.

One hopes that these stylistic efforts will make this historical chronicle more understandable and informative as well a valuable reference work.

INTRODUCTION

As early as 1745, German and Swiss immigrants began to arrive in the back country of the North Carolina piedmont. Most of these early settlers initially migrated from Europe to Pennsylvania, and after remaining there a few years, traveled down the Great Wagon Road into western North Carolina. These Deutsche (German) families tended to settle in their own communities and in areas not already claimed by their British counterparts. The communities were first established along the Haw and Yadkin Rivers, but as more immigrants arrived, new settlements developed further to the west and south toward the Catawba River. By 1755, according to a report to the British Board of Trade by Royal Governor Arthur Dobbs, there were "21 families of German or Swiss" descent established between the Yadkin and Catawba Rivers in the counties of Rowan and Anson.[1]

Religion played a major role within these communities. The three largest denominations among the Germans were Lutheran, German Reform and Moravian. The first congregations established were called union congregations where Lutheran and German Reform worshipped together. It is generally accepted by researchers that the earliest union congregations in the state included the Hickory Log Church located near present St. Peter's Lutheran Church in present Rowan County; Dutch Buffalo Meeting House, located near Dutch Buffalo Creek about a mile north of Mt. Pleasant in present Cabarrus County; Pilgrim Church located along Abbott's Creek in present Davidson County, and Frieden's Church in present Guilford County.[2] In the very early years there were no actual church buildings and services were conducted in private homes, barns, or in the open. The early worshippers were served mostly by local Reform & Moravian ministers and the occasional traveling Lutheran clergyman from coastal South Carolina or Virginia.[3]

By the early 1770's, Lutheran members of the union congregations desired a more "stable relationship" with their counterparts in Europe and began to separate themselves from their Reform brethren. Two of the earliest North Carolina Lutheran churches were St. John's in then Mecklenburg (now Cabarrus) County and Zion/Organ Church in Rowan County.

For the first few years after they were established, the Lutheran congregations continued to be served by circuit ministers, but by 1772 they "desired a preacher from the King's German possessions." A joint delegation from St. John's and Organ Churches traveled to England and then to Hanover, Germany to recruit a minister and a teacher. Within a short time their "call" was heard, and in 1773, the Reverend Adolphus Nussman arrived in Charleston, South Carolina, in route to serve the congregations in North Carolina.

The arrival of Nussman was also the first tangible evidence that, at least to many Lutherans, education was as important as religion. Accompanying Nussman was a teacher from Germany, Johann Gottleib Arhends.[4]

Upon their arrival in North Carolina, Nussman and Arhends resided in Rowan County and gave most of their attention to Organ Church, but in 1774, Nussman moved to what was then Mecklenburg County and established his home near St. John's Church. Between 1775 and 1787, Nussman and Ahrends, who was ordained in 1775, remained the only resident Lutheran ministers in North Carolina

Due to the conflict with Great Britain, the German congregations were cut off from their brethren in Europe during many of the war years. It was not until 1788 that Nussman was successful in re-establishing contact with the Church in Germany. One of his first requests was for additional trained and ordained ministers to serve the growing number of congregations. By 1790, three new ministers had arrived from Europe, and along with Nussman and Ahrends, served over twenty congregations in an area of North Carolina stretching east from Forsyth and Davidson counties and westward to the counties of Lincoln and Catawba.[5]

Several of Nussman's activities during the period following the end of the war serve as further evidence that education remained an important part of his ministry and the desires of his Lutheran congregations. After long negotiations, Nussman was able to secure the release of funds gathered from members of several local congregations prior to 1775 and placed in English banks where, during the war, they were in danger of being "confiscated" by the British government. With these funds, Nussman purchased Bibles and catechisms in the German language and quickly distributed them among his parishioners.[6]

Nussman's church in Mecklenburg (Cabarrus) County, originally called Dutch Buffalo Church, and later, St. John's, was generally noted as the "strongest [Lutheran] congregation" in the state. It was also acknowledged that the school established near the church was one of the most successful "academies" in the area.[7]

By 1803 there were twenty-one Lutheran and Union congregations in the state served by four or five ministers. It was in this year that the ministers and congregations in the state established the North Carolina Lutheran Synod. The exact number of congregations joining the Synod in 1803 is not known. According to *The History of the Evangelical Lutheran Synod,* written by Rev. G. D. Bernheim and Rev. G. H. Cox, there were at least thirteen churches represented at the initial organizational meeting held in Salisbury, NC.[8]

In 1820, the Lutheran Church in North Carolina split and congregations were divided between the North Carolina and Tennessee Synods. (Although designated the "Tennessee Synod", congregations were located in both North Carolina and Tennessee.) At the time, there were approximately thirty-six Lutheran and Union congregations in the state served by eleven ordained ministers, five "candidates", and six practicing but not yet ordained "catechists".[9] In 1824, the NC Synod also lost a few congregations to the newly created South Carolina Synod.

In 1830 the Lutheran Theological Southern Seminary, a school for training Lutheran ministers, was established in South Carolina. The school was initially located in Pomaria, Newberry Co. SC, but was moved to Lexington, SC in 1834.[10] This school served as the closest institution of higher education for North Carolina Lutherans. Several ministers were also trained at Gettysburg College in Pennsylvania.

THE BEGINNING

By 1850, more than 100 years after Lutherans first established themselves in North Carolina, there were twenty-six congregations in in the NC Synod, but there was no post-primary Lutheran institution in the state.[11] By comparison, there were at least five chartered colleges and numerous private academies in North Carolina, most of which were affiliated with some religious denomination. These included Davidson (Presbyterian), Trinity College (Methodist/ Quaker), Guilford College (Quaker), and Catawba College (German Reformed).

On the 30th of April 1852, the North Carolina Lutheran Synod convened its annual meeting at Frieden's Church in Guilford County. Motivated by the need to educate their youth in the Lutheran doctrine and to mitigate the exodus of potential ministers to out of state congregations, the President of the Synod, Rev. J. A. Linn's opening address declared:

> "... we have but one subject that we would recommend to your wisdom and discretion, one which we conceive of vital importance to the interests of our Church in North Carolina,... Believing with many others that the resources necessary to the establishment of a High School of a collegiate character, are amply sufficient, and adding to this the general wish of our laity, and their expressed willingness to support such an Institution, the time, we believe, has come when we should nobly act on this subject. ... .
>
> But our object was merely to present this subject to your prayerful and prudent consideration. We have no plan or basis of an institution to present – no suggestion to make relative to a place of location. These considerations should be the result of the united deliberations of this body..."[12]

As a result of Rev. Linn's speech, a "Committee on the President's

Report" was formed and on May 1st, the Committee delivered the following statement to the full Synod:

> "... In regard to the establishment of a high school, as suggested in the Report, your Committee fully concur in the opinion that such a school, established upon a solid basis, at a proper place, would be of great advantage to the Church in or ecclesiastical bounds, and would recommend the taking of some incipient steps, relative to the establishment of such a Collegiate School, if, in the judgment of your body, this measure be deemed practicable. Respectfully submitted: Wm. G. Harter, John D. Scheck, D. M. Wagner"

On the 2nd of May, the secretary of the Synod wrote:

> "... Resolved, That we hold a Convention to meet in Concord, Cabarrus Co., on Wednesday, before the 4th Sabbath in July next, at 11 o'clock, A. M. for the further consideration of the establishment of a High School in the bounds of this Synod, and the maturing of a plan for the same, and that each Congregation send at least one representative to said meeting, and that every friend to said Institutions, be invited to attend said convention."[13]

Thus, a plan for the establishment of a Lutheran educational institution in North Carolina was initiated. On Wednesday, July 22nd, 1852, the Convention authorized by the Synod met in Concord, Cabarrus County, NC and was organized with the election of Officers. Christopher Melchor was elected President; Matthias Barrier, Vice-President, and John Shimpoch, Secretary. All three of these men were from Mt. Pleasant, NC, a small community in eastern Cabarrus County. Melchor and Shimpoch were wealthy landowners and merchants in the village. Matthias Barrier was a farmer and miller from northeast Cabarrus County who had recently moved into Mt. Pleasant after purchasing a fifty-acre tract of land in the village.[14]

As the Convention proceeded, there was considerable discussion regarding the establishment of an Institution within the bounds of the North Carolina Synod. Finally, "on motion it was Resolved, that [the]

Convention proceed to mature a plan for the establishment of a Literary Institution."

On further motion, a committee was appointed to draft a plan for the establishment of the institution. On July 23rd the committee submitted its report resolving to "establish an Institution (hereafter to be named and located) to be exclusively devoted to the classical education, literacy training, and moral improvement of all who may come under its tuitionary and fostering care."

The report went on to call for the raising of a $20,000 endowment for Professorships by selling 100 perpetual "scholarships" at $200 each. A scholarship would allow the purchaser the right to enroll a person in the new school. They would be transferable and could be paid for in cash or by "giving bond with approved securities" due within ten years. Scholarship holders would also be given a discount in tuition rates.

The report continued, recommending the establishment of a Board of Directors under the "advice and control" of the Evangelical Lutheran Synod of North Carolina. The Board would consist of twelve members, six of whom would be ordained ministers of the NC Lutheran Synod. The remaining six members could "be chosen from among the Lutheran membership, or from any other Christian denomination." After $10,000 was pledged the Synod would meet and proceed to call a Professor who would direct the institution. The Board of Directors would have the authority to select additional Professors and fill vacancies. If any "sister Synod" contributed $1,000 or more, that body would be entitled to a seat on the Board and for every additional $1,000, an additional seat was earned.

The temporary Board of Directors was granted thirty days to:

> "select and put in nomination two or more sites as suitable places of location for said Institution and that a Committee of three be appointed at each place by the same, whose duty it shall be to open books for subscription in their respective localities, to raise funds wherewith to purchase suitable College grounds and to erect suitable buildings thereon ... [and] said books shall remain open until 12 o'clock, M., of the first day of December, 1852, at which time, on comparing said subscriptions, all shall

> be annulled excepting the highest, at which place said Institution shall be located."

The Board of Directors was also to appoint "five suitable individuals" as a Building Committee whose duty it would be to make the necessary arrangements and oversee the construction of:

> "a suitable building or buildings for said Institution, and that the dimensions and style of said building or buildings, be so regulated as to correspond in some degree to the amount of the funds raised: Provided, however, that said building or buildings be neither too ordinary to command respect, nor too expensive to involve us in unnecessary cost."

And finally, the Board of Directors was to elect a Treasurer "whose duty shall be to take charge of all monies belonging to said Institution and shall keep them subject to the order of said Board."[15]

Following the presentation of the Committee report, the Convention nominated a temporary Board of Directors for the purpose of establishing its educational institution. The members of this Board were Christopher Melchor, President; Caleb A. Heilig, Vice-President; Mathias Barrier, Secretary; Rev. William Artz, Rev. John D. Scheck, Rev. Samuel Rothrock, Rev. William G. Harter, Rev. Benjamin Arey, Rev. Jacob A. Linn, Mr. Paul A. Seaford, Mr. William C. Means, and Mr. Martin L. Brown.

The temporary Board met in Concord on July 21st, 1852 and placed into nomination five proposed locations for the institution. These were - near Luther's Chapel, Rowan County; Concord, Cabarrus County; Organ Church, Rowan County; Lexington, Davidson County, and Mt. Pleasant, Cabarrus County.

Following the resolution adopted by the Convention, committees were appointed for each of the proposed locations. The purpose of these committees was to "open the books for subscriptions" to raise funds for their specific sites. The "site" committees consisted of the following individuals - near Luther's Chapel – John Sloop, David Linn, and C. L. Partee; Concord – Alfred Brown, D. M. Wagner, and R. W. Foard; Organ Church – Caleb A. Heilig, D. Lents, and Solomon Fisher; Lexington – L. C. Groseclose, Alexander Hege and Alfred Hargrave; Mt. Pleasant – Daniel Barrier, Jacob Ludwig, and John Shimpoch.

The Convention adjourned with two final resolutions.

> "I. Resolved, That the Rev. J. D. Scheck, our Director in the Theol. Seminary at Lexington, SC, be instructed to solicit the co-operation of the Board of Directors of said Seminary in support of our Literary Institution; and that our Delegate to the SC Synod be requested to present this subject to the consideration of that body.
>
> II. Resolved, That the Board of Directors hold their first meeting at Organ Church, on the 2nd day of December next, at 10 o'clock, A. M., for the purpose of organizing; and that the Committees appointed at the several localities now in nomination, be required, then and there, to report to the Board of Directors their respective sums, to be compared by said Board, and the locality determined."[16]

On the 2nd of December 1852, the temporary Board of Directors met at Organ Church in Rowan County to open the "subscriptions" (bids) for the new school. The Board examined the proposals of four of the five previously nominated sites. The subscriptions submitted were Mt. Pleasant, $5,825; Lexington, $4,002; Organ Church, $3,723, and Luther's Chapel, $925. No pledges were submitted from Concord.[17] [See Appendix 1 for Mt. Pleasant pledges.]

Following the examination of the subscription books, the Board resolved that "the location of the contemplated school ... has been fixed at Mt. Pleasant, Cabarrus Co. NC" and that "the sale of fifty scholarships are required before the school can go into operation."[18]

In January of 1853, Board of Directors met at Mt. Pleasant and formed a committee consisting of Rev. Joseph A. Linn, Rev. Mathew Petrea, and Rev. L.C. Groseclose to "make or secure plans or drafts either of wood or brick edifice for the Academy [and] to ascertain the probable costs of each plan and present a report [at the next meeting]."[19] The Board also outlined the proposed curriculum for the new school. The curriculum contained courses on the definition of words, English Grammar, arithmetic, bookkeeping, modern geography, History of North Carolina and the United States, composition, natural philosophy, agriculture, Latin & Greek Grammar, Latin & Greek Reading, and commercial algebra. Students would also be required "to attend English grammar and declamation", throughout the year.[20]

While the Academy Board of Directors was making plans to construct the new school, the NC Lutheran Synod was contacting the "other" Lutheran Synod in the state. Prior to convening its convention in April of 1853, the NC Synod sent a delegate, Rev. John D. Scheck, to meet with members of the Tennessee Synod to solicit their cooperation in establishing "a Classical Institution in North Carolina".[21]

The Tennessee Synod responded that "in the establishment of a Classical Institution by the Synod of NC, that body has the best wishes of this Synod for its success," but:

> "In view of the obligations resting on this body ... this Synod regrets its inability to do more than express the Christian sympathy and good wishes of this body on its behalf. That should such an Institution be established, we hope it may tend to preserve and strengthen the bond of union which should characterize the relation existing between us."[22]

In April 1853, at Newton, the Convention and its various committees submitted their work to the entire assembled NC Lutheran Synod. Synod President, Rev. William Artz, presented in his opening of the Convention a report on the activities of the Synod, the temporary Board of Directors, and the various committees over the past year. At the conclusion of his remarks he stated:

> "... This then is to be considered the commencement of an Institution of learning in the Lutheran church in North Carolina – which has been so long and so earnestly desired. ... That the community in general, as well as the church, are greatly benefited by the encouragement of sound education and religion, the history of similar institutions, long since established by other denominations and other States, bears ample testimony. Let us then urge forward the enterprise now in progress. Funds will be needed and needed now."[23]

During the next few days, the Committee on the President's Report presented the plans for the new educational institution as they had been developed over the past several months.

The report of the Secretary of the July Convention "in reference to the establishment of a Literary Institution in our midst" was read, received, and adopted.

The Constitution of the Board of Directors of Western Carolina Academy was also read and on motion was considered by Articles. The members of the Synod proceeded to amend the Constitution and to adopt it as amended.[24] [See Appendix 3 for the entire Constitution]

It is of interest that Article III of the Constitution stated that Professors, including the "principal Professor", need not be Lutheran, but only members of "some orthodox Christian denomination." In practice, while faculty members were often not Lutheran, all subsequent Principals and Presidents of the Academy and the College, with one short-term exception, were ordained Lutheran ministers.

The Synod dissolved the previously appointed temporary Board of Directors and appointed a new permanent Board. The permanent Board consisted of twelve members, with three groups of four serving three, two or one year terms. The first permanent Board of Directors of the Western Carolina Male Academy appointed by the NC Lutheran Synod included Rev. Samuel Rothrock, Rev. J. D. Scheck, Mr. Christopher Melchor and Mr. Mathias Barrier appointed to a three year term; Rev. J. A. Linn, Rev. W. G. Harter, Mr. John Shimpoch, and Mr. Caleb A. Heilig to two year terms; and Rev. Simeon Scherer, Rev. L. C. Groseclose; Mr. Daniel Barrier, and Mr. Charles L. Partee appointed to a one year term.

The first meeting of the new Board of Directors was set for June 8th, 1853 at Mt. Pleasant "for organization and the transaction of business."[25]

As the Synod took up the question of funding for the new school, one of the first actions was to transfer funds from the "Centenary Fund" which traditionally funded the Synod's Education and Missionary Society. The Synod resolved:

> "that the interest now due to said fund be added to the principal; that to this principal and interest be added a sufficient sum to swell the whole amount to $600 and that said $600 be, and is hereby transferred to the endowment funds of Western Carolina Academy located

> at Mt. Pleasant, Cabarrus County, NC. And that in lien of said amount of $600, this Synod shall be and is hereby entitled to three scholarships in said school – the receipt whereof shall be held by the President of this Synod and his successor in Office."[26]

The Synod referred the task of appointing special agents to collect funds to the Academy Board of Directors.

In addition to matters of funding and construction of the academy buildings, the Board of Directors and the Synod began seeking "a competent person" to serve as Principal of the school.

I

BUSINESS

Having finalized the new school's location and funding, the Synod and new Board of Directors set about the business of bringing the plans to life. As sources allow, Part I of this narrative will describe the "business" of constructing, opening, and maintaining the new Lutheran school from inception to closing and beyond.

WESTERN CAROLINA MALE ACADEMY

In June of 1853, the newly appointed Board of Directors of Western Carolina Male Academy met as scheduled in Mt. Pleasant, NC. The members of the Board set about fulfilling obligations set forth in their proposal for the creation of the Academy and those proposed by the Lutheran Synod, to wit: the raising of "ten thousand dollars of perpetual investment aforesaid secured, to make the necessary arrangements and superintend the construction of a suitable building or buildings for said Institution."[27]

One of the first acts of business was the purchase of land for the Academy. As stated previously, Mt. Pleasant's bid for the school included an offer of a sixteen-acre tract of land by Matthias Barrier. This tract was a portion of a fifty-acre tract in Mt. Pleasant that Barrier purchased from Isaac Moose in 1851. The tract was located about one-half mile north and west of the town square and was dominated by a high prominence overlooking the town. The purchase was approved by the Board of Directors for $81.25, and on the 30th of June 1853, the deed was executed.[28] [See Appendix #2 for the entire deed]

Central to launching the academic institution, the North Carolina

Lutheran Synod formed a "committee of correspondence whose duty it was to begin a search for the 'first Professorship' of the Academy." This committee consisted of Rev. Samuel Rothrock, Rev. John D. Scheck, and Rev. Joseph A. Linn.[29] In May 1854 after the committee was unsuccessful in finding a "first Professor to oversee the Academy," the Synod reviewed the applicants and recommended a call to Reverend William Gerhardt of Pennsylvania. Rev. Gerhardt was a native of Germany who received his Seminary training at Gettysburg Seminary in Pennsylvania and was ordained in 1847. Since his ordination, he served in various educational positions in Pennsylvania and was considered highly qualified for the position of Principal of the new academy.[30]

The Board of Director's second order of business, beyond securing the land, was construction funding. No doubt realizing the economic potential and the status of having an academy in their small community, three local business owners, Jacob Ludwick, J. J. Misenheimer, C. P. Cox and two local doctors, J. L. Henderson and P. J. A. Haines, signed a promissory note (bond) on June 13th, 1853, in the amount of $12,000 to cover the initial expense of construction. Jacob Ludwick was appointed Treasurer of the Building Fund and given the task of collecting the pledges secured as part of Mt. Pleasant's bid for the school. As the record of pledges indicates, there was great enthusiasm among the people of Mt. Pleasant.[31]

The Board of Directors also reviewed proposals concerning hiring a contractor to oversee the construction of the first academy buildings. William Addison Weddington of Concord, NC was selected as the construction superintendent.[32]

Completing the June meeting agenda, the Board of Directors approved plans for the proceedings surrounding the laying of the Academy administration building's cornerstone. According to the Board minutes the "proceedings of the day, Tuesday, July 4th, 1854" were to be conducted as follows:

> "1st The audience will assemble at the Methodist church at the ringing of the Bell.
>
> 2nd The procession to be formed by Double file the orator of the day Clergy and Board of Directors in front next the ladies then all who may wish to form in procession.

> 3rd Immediately after arriving at the corner in which the deposits are to be made a prayer will be offered up by Rev. Samuel Rothrock after which the Articles to be deposited will be designated by Rev. John A. Linn and deposited in the corner by C. Melchor.
>
> 4th After the deposits are made in the corner stone the closing prayer will be offered up by Rev. J. D. Scheck
>
> 5th The audience then remarch to the stand in double file the Gentlemen in front Ladies next afterwards the Board of Directors Clergy and orator of the day.
>
> 6th The President of the Board will then announce the Speaker for the occasion.
>
> Signed Colonel D. Lentz} Marshall
>
> Rev. J. A. Linn, C. Melchor, C. A. Heilig} Committee for arrangements
>
> Dr. J. L. Henderson, M. A. Bernhardt, Lawson G. Heilig, M. Melchor} Asst. Marshals"[33]

On the 4th of July 1854, as part of an "imposing ceremony in the presence of a large assembly," the cornerstone for the Western Carolina Male Academy was laid.[34]

The speaker for the ceremony was Cabarrus County native, the Honorable Daniel Moreau Barringer, a former member of the US House of Representatives, and recent United States Minister to Spain.[35]

> "A schedule of the documents and other articles deposited in the cornerstone of the principal building of Western Carolina Male Academy on the 4th day of July AD 1854 being the first day of the 79th year of the Independence of the United States.
>
> 1st The Declaration of Independence of the United States of America
>
> 2nd The Mecklenburg Declaration of Independence
>
> 3rd The Constitution of the United States of America with amendments annexed [presented] by John House of Gold Hill.
>
> 4th The Constitution of North Carolina presented by C. Melchor

5th The Farmer's Almanac containing a catalogue of the names of the principal officers of the General Government of the United States and the State of North Carolina the names of all the Counties and other important statistics presented by J. A. Linn

6th A Copy of the Weekly Concord Gazette published in Concord Cabarrus County No. Co. [presented] by Colonel J. Shimpock

7th A copy of Sacred Scriptures of the Old & New Testament in the English Language [presented] by Rev. J. D. Scheck.

8th The unaltered Augsburg Confession of Faith and Symbols of the Church published by Rev. Christian H. Schote Leipzig Germany [presented] by Rev. S. Rothrock.

9th The General Synod's Constitution the formula for the Government and discipline of the Lutheran Church and Hymns selected & ??? for public and private worship combined in one volume published by the General Synod for the Evangelical Lutheran Church presented by Rev. J. A. Linn.

10th A Copy of Luther's small catechism [presented] by Rev. J. A. Linn

11th A copy of the Lutheran Almanac for 1854 containing valuable statistical information relative to the American Lutheran Church presented by Rev. J. A. Linn.

12th A copy of the Lutheran Observer dated June 30th, 1854 published Baltimore Maryland [presented] by Rev. J. A. Linn

13th A copy of the Lutheran Standard published in Columbus Ohio [presented] by Rev. Samuel Rothrock

14th A copy of the Evangelical Lutheran published in Springfield Ohio [presented] by Rev. Samuel Rothrock

15th A copy of the Evangelical Magazine published in Easton, PA [presented] by Rev. J. A. Linn

16th A copy of the Constitution and Statutes of Western Carolina Male Academy.

One Dollar [presented] by Colonel J. C. Bernhardt

Half dollar [presented] by C. A. Heilig & Dan'l Barrier

Quarter dollar [presented] by J. A. Linn

One dime [presented] by C. Melchor

Half dime [presented] by M. Barrier

Three cents [presented] by M. A. Bernhardt

American Gold coin [presented] by M. A Bernhardt

American Gold Coin [presented] by Nixon Hopkins

The names of the building committee of Western Carolina Male Academy to viz

Rev. Joseph A. Linn, Mathias Barrier, Daniel Barrier, Paul B. C. Smith, Mathew Petrea"[36]

Very little information concerning the actual construction of the first academy building is available. No blueprints or other construction drawings have been found and the earliest known image of the building comes from an 1859 lithograph. The initial proposal for construction adopted by the Synod called for the erection of "a single three-story building, 75'x 40', to house all of the classrooms, boarding rooms, and other necessary Academy facilities." The Academy building was to be constructed of brick, and according to the Lutheran Synod's wishes. "the dimensions and style of said building or buildings, [were to] be so regulated as to correspond in some degree to the amount of the funds raised. Provided, however, that said building or buildings be neither too ordinary to command respect, nor too expensive to involve us in unnecessary cost." The Synod set a cost ceiling of $7,000.[37]

In addition to the academy building, a "Principal's residence" was to be constructed nearby. The initial plan, first outlined at the Board of Director's meeting in December 1854, was for this structure to be 44' x 20', two stories in height, "with passage in front and back shed with rooms on the same, ... and of corresponding architectural style." Three hundred dollars was to be paid when the house was "raised, weatherboarded and covered," and the balance paid when the house was finished. The entire house was to be plastered except the partition of the am (day) room upstairs. The building committee was to "use their discretion" to have the day room plastered. The plaster was to be of "sand finish."[38]

The design of the Principal's house was altered in January 1855, to be "34' in the front by 26' on the first story, containing an open passage 8' in width in the south side extending the entire depth of the building." The house was to contain two rooms, 17' x 18', each on the first floor, "the upper story to contain 3 rooms with doors leading from landing of [the] stairs to each room. The building to have a front pizyas [sic] of style as in former plans. The building to have a kitchen attached to it the dimensions to be 15' square and one story & half high with pizya [sic] on north side 10' wide."[39]

Due to the scope of the project and its brick construction, it was necessary to recruit masons from areas outside of the Cabarrus County. Several skilled masons were hired from the western counties of Gaston and Lincoln. It is probable that much of the actual labor was carried out by slaves who were likely "rented" from local landowners and businessmen.[40]

While the cost of construction of the Academy was covered by a note obtained from several Mt. Pleasant residents, the Board of Directors and the Lutheran Synod now had to begin the process of soliciting funds to repay the note and to establish an endowment for operation of the school. The Academy Board of Directors had $6000.00 on hand from the pledges made during the initial campaign to locate the school in Mt. Pleasant and $600.00 in dedicated interest from the Synod's Centenary Fund. The Synod then directed the appointment of agents to collect funds.

At its annual meeting in May 1854, at Bethel Lutheran Church in Stanly Co. NC, the Lutheran Synod recommended that:

> "Each Minister of this Synod, by the earliest possible convenience, call on his congregations for subscriptions and donations for Western Carolina Male Academy" [and] "that all the Treasurers of the different Funds under the control of the Synod, and also the President of the Board of Directors of Western Carolina Male Academy, be received as advisory members of this Synod, and that this be a standing resolution."[41]

In addition, the President of the Synod recommended that the body examine "the propriety of withholding from the South Carolina Synod the interest annually sent them for the right of a Director in their Seminary, if it can be done without violating the agreement entered into between them and you. It is absolutely necessary that we should husband all of our resources between this and October next."[42]

By September of 1854, $10,000 was pledged by various means, but the solicitation of funds continued into 1855 as the President of the Board of Directors reported to the Synod in April that there was still a shortage of $2,947. As the Synod and the Board of Directors continued to discuss funding the Board dealt with construction issues. In January 1855, the Board of Directors authorized the payment of $97.22 to M. A. Barringer for guttering of the administration building. There is a record indicating that Rev. Samuel Rothrock and J. D. Scheck were appointed to "correspond with Rev. B. Kurtz on the subject of procuring a suitable bell for the Academy."[43]

It had been anticipated that construction would be completed by January 1855. Due to a shortage of lumber caused by a severe drought, the building was not completed until the fall of 1855.[44]

According to the Treasurer's report in the spring of 1855, $3,858 had been paid out and there was "on hand in cash and good subscriptions $2,778." The outstanding debt amounted to $5,225. The report stated that:

> "The main building will be completed in a few months – plastering is being put on – when it is done, we shall have to make a payment of $3,500, and the balance in October next. The Treasurer of Scholarships has disposed of 50 and collected a part of the money which he invested in State Bonds, under the direction of the Board."[45]

At its April 1855 meeting, the Board of Directors instructed the building committee to:

> "have the work completing the building … prosecuted with greater energy than has been done during the preceding part of this spring and that unless the work be carried forward to the satisfaction of the building committee, the President of the Board [is] authorized to bring suit of damages against the contractor for nonfulfillment of his contract."[46]

In December 1856, a convention of Academy scholarship holders was held at Organ Church in Rowan County "to consult about the best interest of the Institution and if possible, to fall upon a plan to increase the endowment fund." Among other plans it was proposed that "in view of the very low rate of scholarships, each holder of a scholarship, having it in use, should pay six dollars in addition to interest and that this should accrue to the Institution, making the obligation binding as soon as forty of the whole number would sign their names." The plan was to be submitted to Synod at the 1857 Convention.[47]

In April 1856, the treasurer of the building fund reported the "whole amount of receipts (expenses)" as follows:

W. A. Weddington	$	3000.00	T. Tucker & Co.	$	56.50
W. A. Weddington	$	500.00	John Eagle	$	28.00
W. A. Weddington	$	300.00	Jas. M. Henderson	$	25.00
W. A. Weddington	$	1937.21	J. J. Bruner	$	20.00
W. Gerhardt	$	172.32	Mathias Barrier	$	22.75
J. L. Shimpoch	$	137.00	J. A. Linn	$	19.00
M. A. Barringer	$	97.25	S. Rothrock & J. A. Linn	$	2.50
Mathias Barrier	$	81.25	John Shimpoch	$	1.00
Heilig & Bernhardt	$	71.12		$	6,470.90
		Cash on hand		$	68.10[48]

While the Academy gained recognition and appeared to be proceeding successfully, issues of sufficient support from several Lutheran congregations within the state remained questionable.

At the Lutheran Synod Meeting in the Spring of 1857, Jacob Ludwig, the Treasurer of the Building Fund, reported that the total cost of the construction of the Academy building and the President's house was $8,424, of which $625 was still owed to the general contractor, W. A. Weddington.[49] The total indebtedness of the building fund was $3,095.[50]

The financial situation confronting the school was further described by Rev. Gerhardt in his report to the Synod on the status of the institution.

> "... It is now more than two years since you called me to preside over this infant Institution. Ever since, it has been the subject of my prayers, and the object of my concentrated energies. I have labored single-handed, I

have toiled incessantly to establish it; to give it character and prominence abroad; and I trust that my labors have not been altogether in vain. But after all, what can your Principal accomplish without your cooperation? You have planted the Institution, you must nurse it, you must rear it, else it cannot flourish, cannot prosper. Are you interested in it? Are you united in sentiment and effort? Brethren, it is needless for me to tell you your duty in reference to this matter. You know what is necessary. You know your duty. … It is the Institution of the Church, and the Church must sustain it, or itself languish and die. Let Synod and the Church sustain the Institution and it will sustain and dignify the Synod, while the benefits resulting will diffuse themselves over the whole Church. We have, indeed, had opposition to contend with, and principally from our own Lutheran household; but we have, thank God, thus far succeeded. But we need the sympathies and liberal support of the Church. I call upon you, then as you value the Church, as you value the cause of Christ, sustain your Institution, hold it up before your people, secure its many liberal friends and you will perform a noble deed and secure a lasting blessing to posterity."[51]

By the Spring of 1858, due primarily to the continued negative financial situation, there were increasing discussions concerning the chartering of the school as a "regular graduating college" in order to encourage more local support and funding.

While these discussions were apparently initiated by financial hardship, such a consideration had apparently been anticipated much earlier when the language of the Academy Constitution stated:

> "… all the branches usually taught in Academies shall be attended to; **and should the interests of the Institution demand it, suitable provision will be made whereby students may receive Graduating Diplomas, as in any other graduating college** [emphasis added]. In this event, the whole course of instruction in this Department, will occupy four years, each being divided into two sessions."[52]

At their convention in April of 1858, the NC Synod simultaneously addressed the question of the debt and the proposal to convert the Academy to a College. Two reports, one by Board of Trustees President, Christopher Melchor, and another Synod President, Rev. Levi C. Groseclose, detailed the issues to be considered.

Melchor began by citing the existing debt and then declared: "**The Board have requested me to ask the Synod to have our Academy … so as to make it a College"** [emphasis added].

He went on to avow that, "the more advanced scholars we may expect to leave us and go to some higher institution if that is not done. The subject is here submitted to [be given] serious consideration for action. God has commenced this institution for a sacred purpose – to increase the intelligence of your people and to honor your Church …."[53]

Reverend Groseclose reinforced Melchor's comments by stating: "We suggest that this Synod immediately proceed to change Western Carolina Male Academy into a regular graduating College, or advise the Board of Directors to do so … and at once elect a President."

As further endorsement he offered:

> "Such a course of immediate action may be urged by numerous weighty considerations, which must be apparent to all who are acquainted with the present condition, and the future prospects of the Academy. We have talented young men connected with the institution who wish to graduate, and would do so with honor to this or any other school, who will leave us and go where they can enjoy this privilege, unless we afford them the opportunity at our own school. Shall we, then, suffer them to leave us, by an inactivity that would be blameable [sic] in a matter of far less importance? Shall we suffer the latent of our talent sons to be developed by other denominational Colleges, and permit them thus to draw off the affections of our own children from the church, of their fathers to these churches? How much have we not already lost, by educating our sons and daughters in the schools of other denominations? Surely it is time to look seriously at this subject."[54]

During the Synod session, the President's recommendation was considered by the various committees and from these discussions the following resolution was presented and adopted:

"Whereas, we are fully persuaded that a crisis in our Institution has arrived, when a change is absolutely necessary for its future prosperity. Therefore:

Resolved, That the Board of Directors of W. C. M. Academy, be, and are hereby instructed to have the charter of our Institution amended, so as to change it from an Academy to a College with the power of conferring degrees.

Resolved, That this College be named __________, and subject to the control of the Evangelical Lutheran Synod of North Carolina

Resolved that the Board of Directors are advised, if practicable, to elect a President of _____ College at its next meeting, the 20th instant, and the he act as agent to collect funds for it until his services are required in the Institution.

Resolved that the Synod confirm the vote just taken, and that the minority be kindly and affectionately invited to concur with the majority.

Resolved that from and after the attainment of a College charter, the present Board of Directors of Western Carolina Male Academy be and are hereby constituted the Board of College until the next meeting of our Synod.

Resolved that the President elect of our Institution, as soon as he shall have accepted the appointment, be constituted by this Synod ex officio as member of the Board.

Resolved that the thanks of this Synod be tendered to the people of Mount Pleasant and Concord for their truly noble and liberal subscriptions in favor of our contemplated College.

Resolved, that in connection with the thanks of this Synod, voted to Concord for their liberal offer, we, as a Synod, pledge ourselves to cooperation with Concord in

> the establishment of a Female College at that place, and that we await their proposals to be tendered at our next meeting."[55]

Following the adoption of the resolution to have the Western Carolina Male Academy chartered as a "graduating College," there was a new debate concerning the location of the school. During the charter discussions, the Town of Concord, the county seat of Cabarrus County, had expressed an interest in having the school relocated to that community. Several individuals from Concord had pledged substantial "subscriptions" to the College and was given a "note of thanks," by the Synod. It was also recommended that Concord be considered as the location for a "female college" which was being contemplated by the Synod. Although Concord had been one of the sites initially proposed for the Academy in 1852, the site delegation from that town had presented no "subscriptions" during the final selection process.

Apparently, the supporters from Concord were not satisfied with the "thanks" of the Synod and appealed to that body for further consideration as the location for the future College. In order to resolve this situation, the Synod called a special session that met at Luther's Chapel in Rowan Co. NC in August 1858. The purpose of the session was to afford an "opportunity ... to the friends of Concord for them to show why the College should not be located at Mount Pleasant; and that Concord offers superior advantages for the location of the College at that place." After three full days of debate, the Synod voted fourteen to eleven to retain the College in Mt. Pleasant.[56]

The Synod appointed Rev. G. D. Bernheim, the minister at St. John's in Cabarrus County, as "financial agent" to begin raising additional funds for the new college.[57]

The citizens of Mt. Pleasant celebrated the decision in grand fashion as described in an unattributed account.

JOYOUS OCCASION – THE ILLUMINATION OF MT. PLEASANT

> "When the joyful tidings, that the college of the Lutheran Church in North Carolina was located at Mt.

> Pleasant, every man, woman & child in the place seemed to be anxious to celebrate the event in some form or other; as the delegation returned from the session of the Lutheran Synod, already at a distance could college and church bells be heard, and as they approached nearer, the sound of music reached the ear, & the whole village was alive with procession, flag, transparencies of various colors; still later, & the college campus was illuminated with the discharge of Roman candles, the whizzing of rockets, the graceful curves of fireballs. This with the huzzas & cheers of the multitude made the night of 31st Ult. The most pleasing & exciting the village ever witnessed.
>
> Short addresses were delivered by Revs. J. D. S(check), G. D. B(ernheim) and Prof Wm. G(erhardt). The last speaker suggested the propriety of a general illumination on the next evening, this idea was heartily cheered & the citizens returned to their quiet homes.
>
> The next evening witnessed a still more gorgeous display, every little cottage, every habitable dwelling sent forth rays of rejoicing, every pane of glass was made brilliant with light, the college building, & the large dwelling of M(atthias) B(arrier) Esq. presented a grand imposing spectacle, showing how heartily all the citizens participated in the general rejoicing.
>
> Processions, the flaming tar-barrels, the display of fire-works, with music & the ringing of bells, was the order of the second night."[58]

Following the Synod's special session, the Board of Trustees of Western Carolina Male Academy met and voted to seek a charter from the state as a graduating college. A new constitution was written and adopted, and a new charter forwarded to the State Legislature for its consideration.[59]

With the decision to become a College, the Academy Board of Trustees made changes in the school administration. In October of 1858, the Board elected Reverend Daniel H. Bittle as the first President of North Carolina College, and "at the recommendation of the Synod," instructed him to begin collecting funds for the institution.[60] Reverend Bittle was a graduate of Gettysburg College, PA, and Lane Seminary, Cincinnati, OH. Ordained by the Ohio Synod in 1849, he served congregations in several states before becoming an instructor at Roanoke College, VA where he was employed when selected to become President of NC College. His salary was set at $1,200 per year and he was to furnish his own residence. His wife, Susan Bigelow Bittle became the first Principal of Mont Amoena Seminary in Mt. Pleasant.[61] Mont Amoena Female Seminary opened in Mt. Pleasant in 1859, and, ironically, was the "female college" for which Concord had been recommended in 1858.

On the 21st of January 1859, Western Carolina Male Academy was officially chartered by the State Legislature as North Carolina College [See Appendix 4]. The Treasurer of the Board of Trustees reported that the College was financed by an endowment of $20,000, half of which was invested in State Bonds at a rate of six percent. Income for 1859 totaled $1,982, which included a gift of $225, collected tuition of $563, and interest from the endowment of $1,242. 1859 expenses included $1,163 in salaries paid to the faculty.[62]

Coupled with its new charter, the College contemplated enlarging the school's physical plant. At its meeting in February 1859, the College Board of Trustees authorized President Bittle to travel to Baltimore to "procure a draft to enlarge the college buildings."[63]

In April of 1859 the Building Committee of the Board of Trustees advertised in local newspapers that:

> "... the undersigned, ... are desirous to erect two large Halls for use of the College, and would take this method to invite Master-builders, wishing the job, to call at Mt. Pleasant, Cabarrus County, and examine the grounds, specifications, $c., with a view to making proposals. Specifications at the house of L. G. Heilig, Esq. – Committee - John Shimpock, C. Melchor, M. Barrier, L. G. Heilig, D. H. Bittle."[64]

No records of who was awarded the contract or the specifications of the buildings have been found.

The resulting expansion resulted in the construction of two new buildings "behind" and to the north and south of the original college building. These structures, constructed at a cost of $8,000 ($5,000 of which was borrowed from the endowment), were two story brick buildings designated as classrooms and debating "halls." The second floors of the Philalaethian Literary Hall and the Pi Sigma Phi Literary Hall (formerly the Crescent Society) were to be dedicated to "declamation and original composition in which every student was expected to participate."[65]

NORTH CAROLINA COLLEGE

North Carolina College (NCC) opened its first session in September 1859 in the former Western Carolina Academy building. There were sixty-two students in attendance. The business of the first year was unexceptional, but by the fall of 1860, national events were of paramount importance. In November of 1860 Abraham Lincoln was elected President of the United States and by February of 1861, when Rev. Bittle made his report to the Board of Trustees, seven states had seceded from the Union and the government of the Confederate States of America had been formed.

Despite the state of national affairs, Rev. Bittle presented only a few brief remarks to the Board. In his only comments referring to the current national circumstances, Rev. Bittle stated, "... the political situation in our sister state [has] been deemed of sufficient importance on the part of parents & Guardians to withdraw their sons and wards for the present, and in nearly every instance with the assurance that so soon as the difficult be overpassed they will return."[66]

By May the situation had begun to accelerate. Addressing the NC Lutheran Synod, President of the Board of Trustees Christopher Melchor paraphrased Rev. Bittle's brief remarks and added his own observations, stating "that [while] the College appears to be in prosperous condition, the political excitement of our country has caused some students to leave our College and has no doubt kept many others away, but as many have been receiving instructions as could reasonably be expected under the excitement of the times."[67]

During the discussion of the coming crisis, the Synod Committee on Education reported that "there remained a debt on the College of $9,600; to meet this the Treasurer of Building fund has on hand $514.92; outstanding subscriptions $3,500. Whole amount of assets $4014.91. This deducted from $9,600 leaves $5,585.09, unprovided for in any way."[68]

The financial status of the College, while noted, was apparently not foremost on the Synod's mind. In much stronger terms than expressed by Rev. Bittle or Christopher Melchor, the Synod, at the conclusion of its convention, resolved, "That we instruct the Board of Directors of NC College to act with extreme caution in view of the distracted condition of political affairs, and discontinue the exercises of the College, if in their judgment it be deemed advisable."[69]

North Carolina seceded from the Union on May 20th, 1861. Nine days later, Reverend Bittle reported to the Board of Trustees:

> "In the prosperous condition of the College, the present political troubles commenced. The novelty of the cry 'to arms,' the roll of the drums, the stirring notes of the bugle created an excitement among the students, perhaps greater than was necessary, yet dangerous on the part of your faculty to express, lest they might incur censure for a want of proper participation. All we could do was to demand permission from parents and guardians and let them withdraw. Many even went without this and forfeited a regular dismissal. The prospects of the school are as favorable as the present circumstances will allow. …"[70]

Still attempting to keep the school open, Rev. Bittle made three recommendations:

"1st - Add to your institution the military feature; 2nd - By circular make a special appeal [for students], and 3rd - Continue the school at least to Feb 22nd, 1862."[71]

The Board responded to Bittle's remarks by voting to postpone, "the question of suspending the exercises of this institution" until its July meeting. At the July meeting the Board voted on the question of keeping the school open. The outcome was a tie. Four trustees, J. B. Anthony, William Artz, Mathias Barrier, and Samuel Rothrock voted to close the school, and four trustees, Rev. Bittle, Christopher Melchor, John Heilig, and John Shimpoch voted against closure. The school managed to remain open for the time being, but events were rapidly overtaking the situation.[72]

On the sixth and seventh of August 1861 men from the surrounding community met on the NC College campus to enlist in the State Troops of North Carolina and organize a local company. The chief organizers of the group were current and former students. Rufus Barrier, son of Academy treasurer and Board of Trustees member, Mathias Barrier, was elected Captain of the Company. Rufus had been a student at the Western Carolina Male Academy in 1855-56. Jacob File, a local lawyer who had attended the Male Academy was elected 1st Lieutenant. Jonas Cook, a current student at the College and the son of Board of Trustees member, Matthew Cook, became 2nd Lieutenant. The 3rd Lieutenant was Harvey C. McAllister, the brick mason who helped to construct the original Academy building in 1855.[73]

During the first two weeks of August, 82 men enlisted in the "Cabarrus Phalanx" company, so named to reflect the classical education of its officers. On August 19th, 1861, the "Cabarrus Phalanx" members again met at the College and proceeded to the nearby Methodist church where they heard a sermon by the Rev. J. B. Anthony, minister at St. John's Lutheran Church. From the church, the men went to the town square where they enjoyed a meal at Matthew Cook and Jacob Ludwig's store. Following the meal, a "bowie knife" fashioned by a local blacksmith was presented to each man. After the presentation the new soldiers lined up and marched nine miles to the county seat at Concord, NC, where they attended another sermon by a local Lutheran minister. On the morning of the 20th of August, the men marched through cheering crowds to the railroad station and boarded a train bound for their training camp in Warren Co. NC. After they arrived at Camp Mason in Warren County, the company was officially designated as Co. H, 8th NC Infantry Regiment.[74]

Based upon available records, thirteen members of Co. H were former students of Western Carolina Male Academy or NC College [In addition to these thirteen men, at least 104 additional students and former students from the Male Academy and the College enlisted in State and Confederate units during the War Between the States.][75]

At the Board of Trustees meeting of October 2nd, 1861, Rev. Bittle submitted his resignation as President of the College "in view of the calamities of the war." Even with many of its students volunteering for service in the Confederate Army, the Board of Trustees kept the College open. The Board authorized the Treasurer to invest a portion of its endowment in Confederate Bonds, "provided they be deemed good."

A year later, Matthias Barrier invested the College endowment in five Confederate bonds totaling $4,000, two Certificates of Deposit totaling $1,800 and two notes to Jacob Ludwig totaling $6,000. The remaining endowment of $1,858.18 was maintained in a cash account.[76] The Board met again on October 29th, 1861. At this time, the remaining professors of the College offered to donate one third of their salaries toward continuing the school for the next year.[77] This offer was accepted, and the Board voted to continue operation. The Board further approved "a military feature" to be adopted whereby students over 14 would be required "to wear a uniform unless satisfactory reasons [could] be furnished for not so doing." The Board also authorized the publication of a "notice of this institution in six various newspapers in and out of state."[78]

October's measures proved short-lived. In November of 1861, the remaining Professors tendered their resignations "owing to the state of the country and the consequent small attendance of students."[79]

The Synod Committee on Education reported on May 1, 1862 that the school operation was indefinitely suspended, and expenses had, in part, been liquidated. The Treasurer's report stated that the College's current indebtedness was $7,189.56.[80] Students were not charged tuition for the last part of the session. Rev. J. B. Anthony was appointed superintendent of the college grounds and the buildings "to lock up the houses and occasionally to ventilate them and to keep the fence well repaired and keep all intruders off the premises."[81]

Even as the College closed its doors, however, local ministers sought permission from the Synod to utilize the buildings for a "private boarding school." There is no record of either permission being granted or any school being opened. In 1863, the Board authorized Rev. Anthony to rent out the stables and the land west of College Street."[82]

The following letter describes one of the College's most legendary contributions to the war effort. Local lore frequently shares the story of how the Society Hall carpets went to war with their boys:

> "Mr. Neblocke, Barger and Anthony are willing as one to give the carpets in the Society Halls for blankets for the soldiers provided a Majority of the Board will say so. We have no legal right to do so but the necessity of the case requires it please some of you write and send word to

> Rothrock, Linn and Danl Heilig? Asking their consent or to meet at Mount Ples earliest days for consideration upon the subject. The women here can cut up … C. Melchor. P. S. Dreher & Doctor ??? can be notified too.
>
> I endorse the within proposition upon condition that the Societies be reimbursed for the Carpet – Saml. Rothrock. I concur in the above - Jos. A. Linn, P. W. Heilig."[83]

Throughout the war the Board of Trustees and the Lutheran Synod debated the future and the fate of the College. At the Synod convention in May1862, the Committee on Education, in response to the President's recommendation to re-open the College at the earliest possible date, stated, "your committee have no suggestions to offer, but would refer this subject to Synod for deliberation."[84]

During 1862, the Board of Trustees' Treasurer reported income of $1675.00, mostly from rent of the buildings.

In 1863, the College property was used as a "Recruiting Camp" for the 1st NC Cavalry.[85] The Synod kept the school closed but authorized the formation of a Committee "to correspond with suitable persons with a view of securing a proper Teacher, and as soon as the war shall cease, or circumstances permit, to re-open the College."[86]

Also in 1863, the Board of Trustees asked Rev. G. D. Bernheim, a former member of the Board of Trustees and financial agent for the Lutheran Synod, to solicit contributions for the College during his visit to Europe. In return, Rev. Bernheim was allowed to keep his books at the College during his travels. The Treasurer of the College reported to the Synod that the College maintained an indebtedness of "about $7,000," resulting mostly from the construction of the new buildings in 1859 and subsequent improvements, the cost of which was in excess of $20,000. He further reported that this debt could possibly be reduced to $6,000 by applying interest from the endowment "which exceeds $20,000" and by collection on the remaining "subscriptions".[87]

By 1864, the College's indebtedness had been reduced to $5,200, but the College Board of Trustees found itself involved in a controversy surrounding the Synod's Seminary Fund. During the preceding year the Board had declined to pay, "for want of funds," an apportionment to the

Synod Seminary Fund which was to be sent to the Lutheran Theological Seminary in South Carolina. Simultaneously, the Board requested that the Synod consider making a "permanent transfer of its Seminary Fund to the Endowment fund of North Carolina College to afford free tuition to indigent students, having the ministry in view."[88]

The debate concerning this issue is not recorded, but the Synod's Committee on Education recommended that the Synod Treasurer be authorized to pay $180 for three years on the Seminary Fund to be transferred to the Seminary in South Carolina, and the NC College Board pay $60 with interest accruing to the Seminary.[89] In addition, the Committee recommended "that the reunion entered into between the Synod and the Synod of South Carolina in reference to her Seminary Fund, be and is hereby dissolved."[90]

Lastly, the Committee recommended:

> "That the "the offer of the Board of Trustees, granting free tuition to indigent students having the ministry in view, be accepted, to apply the interest of that Fund for that purpose, this Synod having the right to say what students should be thus benefited. Samuel Rothrock, G. D. Bernheim, L. C. Groseclose, Daniel I. Dreher, C. Melchor"[91]

As the Civil War ended in April 1865, members of the College Board of Trustees considered how to reopen the school. In May, at the Synod's annual meeting, the Committee on Education requested that the Synod "determine what may be best [in] introducing measures to reopen NC College," and recommended that a meeting of the Board of Directors be convened as soon as possible to discuss the matter.[92]

Although mentioned only slightly in the minutes, one issue sorely troubled the Education Committee and was to become the most significant difficulty faced by the College for the remainder of its existence. The committee chairman "express[ed] fears as to the loss of funds, owing to the failure of the Confederate currency, in which a considerable amount of the funds of the college was invested."[93]

In October of 1865, the Treasurer's report reflected that $10,000 of the College's total endowment of $20,827 had been invested in Confederate Bonds. Another $10,000 was invested in "Old State Bonds." This report also stated that the expenses for the College during the past year were $1,861.95 and that income was only $1,296.28. There was $291.00 in "cash on hand."[94]

The difficulties created by this lack of funds was reflected in the search for a new President, as described in a letter from a former teacher at the College, L. A. Bikle, who was approached about the position.

Writing to Rev. W. H. Cone, in October 1865, Bikle stated:

> "I received a letter from Bro. Long yesterday morning in which I am requested to write you in reference to the probability of my accepting a position in N C. College. With respect to this matter I have only to say that I cannot return to N. Carolina unless definite assurances are given. A letter reached me several weeks ago from the pen of Bro. Dreher in which I was informed that it was the desire of the Board to give me the buildings and to let me make out of the school all I could. Had such an offer been made before I left NC, I would now be in Mt. Pleasant. If the Board of Trustees of NC College assure me a salary the first year of $500 and expenses back to Mt. Pleasant, or $600 and I pay my own expenses, there will be some probability of my accepting an invitation to return. I wish that I could see you to have a talk about some things connected with the affairs of our College. If you can possibly take time to visit this place, I hope you will do soon. On your return to the Old North State remember me to my friends. Yours fraternally, L. A. Bikle"[95]

Despite the lack of money and the other adversities encountered in a state economically and politically devastated by the war, the Board of Trustees moved forward with plans to open the College at the earliest date possible.

In May of 1866, the Report of the College Board of Trustees stated that the Board had obtained the services of two professors. General James H. Lane of Concord had agreed to "have oversight over the school and serve as Professor of Mathematics" until a President was found. And, apparently having had a change of heart from 1865, Rev. L. A. Bikle became Professor of Ancient Languages.[96]

In the effort to recruit a new President, the Board of Trustees proposed to appropriate $1,000 per year from the endowment fund for a salary. This notion met with some resistance from several Board members as a letter from John Shimpoch and Rev. J. B. Anthony indicated:

> "A protest, July 25, 1866, the undersigned offer this their protest against the appropriation of $1000 in currency per anum of the endowment fund for a salary of the President of this College for the following reasons – 1st Believing that we as a Board have no right to use the principal of said fund in any way or for any purpose that it was understood by the people [who made] the donations that it was to be a permanent fund and nothing more than the interest was to be used or expended; 2nd especially when the fund consists of State Bonds and are so much under par at this time that using it now would be too great a sacrifice and waste owing to the financial depression and crippled resources of the state and by keeping [the fund] as it was designated, and believing that it will gradually and eventually rise to par value again, for these and other reasons, we offer this our protest and ask to have it spread upon the minutes."[97]

The protest was apparently never addressed.

In August 1866 the Board of Trustees met without a quorum and learned that General Lane would not be coming to the College, as he had decided to open his own school in Charlotte. The Board decided to proceed with opening the school with only one teacher, Rev. Bikle.[98]

On the first Monday in August 1866, the College re-opened with thirty-three students and "the prospects for a large increase in the number of students the next scholastic year … promising. If plentiful crops are made this season, the Directors will be enabled to procure the necessary means to pay the salaries of all the Professors that may be required to carry on successfully the operations of the College."[99]

During the remainder of 1866 and into the summer of 1867, the school operated with only one Professor. Sometime after the school opened in August 1867, a part-time "tutor", Mr. B. F. Rodgers, was hired. Rev. A. J. Brown of Blountville, TN declined the Presidency in July of 1867.

Finally, in September of 1867, Rev. Charles F. Bansemer of Mt. Inah, South Carolina accepted the position of President of the college.[100]

In December 1867, Jonas Cook, the newly appointed Bursar of the College, reported the following income and expenses – Income from Tuition, $376; from Room Rent, $23.50; from Incidental Fees, $49.20. Expenses to Blank Book, $.50; to 12 Rev Stamps, $.25; to Prof Bikle College expenses, $7.20; to Salary of Bikle, $300.00; to Salary of Rogers in part, $113.00; 1 ??? Paper, $.30; to John Herrin light wood, $1.50; to J. H. Hahn wood, $12.00, to Jonas Dick cutting wood, 65¢. The balance on hand was $13.30. Unpaid tuition amounted to $86.80, unpaid fees, $4.50 and unpaid incidentals, $14.25.[101]

Upon his arrival, Rev. Bansemer challenged the students and promised to work to obtain the "approbation and full confidence" of the College's patrons. The school continued to struggle financially. In the Spring of 1868, the Synod's Committee on Education reported that income from tuition was not sufficient to meet the salaries of the Professors and Tutor of the College, and that the President of the Board of Trustees "desired the Synod to instruct the Board what to do in this emergency, whether they shall sell the coupons on their State Bonds at a sacrifice of less than fifty percent or hold them until they once more rate at a par value, or whether to send out an agent to collect money in the present impoverished condition of the country."[102]

The Synod responded with two recommendations, neither of which improved the current situation. The first recommendation was to "sell to the best possible advantage the coupons of that Institution and pay from the amount thus realized the salaries of the Professors and Tutor." Secondly, the Synod requested that the College admit the sons of Lutheran Ministers at half tuition rates - a recommendation which actually reduced the income of the school.[103]

By October 1868, Rev. Bansemer was apparently extremely discouraged by the financial situation and the school's overall reputation. He delivered a report that was most critical of the Synod's support for the school and produced a long list of negatives concerning the College.

> "The number of students attending has been small. Collegiate [sic] is considered superfluous by the vast majority of men, sometimes brought into disrespect by

men professing to possess it. [The] reasons the College has not prospered as others after the war [is] partly the result of the past. You had over a large number of students .... They [should] remember you with affection, and turn their eyes even now towards you, but for the fact that there was something radically wrong in the management of your institution. Your teachers were young and all of them inexperienced and not qualified to secure a widespread reputation, as the foundation of permanent prosperity. Thus, you failed to secure a permanent patronage from abroad. Your state was more showy than substantial. To other colleges, young men generally returned after the war. Not so with you.

We have not a full set of professors and there were only 3 college students (the rest were preparatory). Our denomination is not as large, influential, and zealous as the societies with which neighboring Institutions are connected. We are confined to our denominational patronage to a portion of our state. SC and Virginia are not only bound to patronage of their own, but if desirous to go beyond their own respective boundaries, they would probably visit Northern institutions. We are too near our rival colleges. Being so the peculiar state of political affairs, these institutions drew in a great many of their students from the University of NC. There we are utterly unknown. Not one of their students represents our denomination. One of their denominations is a graduate of the University. We neglected to advertise. The dilapidated state of our buildings is [sic] rather discouraging, whereas the interior in other places are attractive.

Our basis of operation is too contracted. We ought so to have gone beyond the limits or our denomination because our numbers are small in selecting Trustees, in inviting examinations, in seeking for advice, etc. As competitors for public favor we must meet our rival institutions on common ground. If we had made our object young men from the Universities of NC, SC, and VA we would have been more successful regarding numbers. It was perhaps unwise to suspend the institution during the war, as it was premature to open it again as a College. Some object to the locality as unfavorable to the development of a scientific spirit. And they speak of the loneliness of the place. The price of the Board and the difficulty to obtain it has had an injurious influence. It is perhaps not so much the existence of fact, as the one-sided representations of them that threaten to raise a barrier between us and public favor. We are informed that letters were written from this place to subvert private interest by placing our institution and its achievements in an unfavorable light. It also has been said that the smaller scholars attending the preparatory department had too much play time allowed them, that their lessons were too long and not sufficiently explained, that they were overlooked, crammed and that very severe punishments were inflicted upon the defaulters.

> The president frequently called the attention of the Board to what appeared to him objectionable in the management of the institution but received no authority to make such arrangements as would for- ever have silenced the above complaints.
>
> In conclusion, I would recommend that steps be taken to enlighten the people on the nature and necessity of a liberal education. Let the ministers appoint meetings to that effect and we will come and deliver the address. That we consider as we have recommended to advertise liberally and extensively. That prominent persons be from time to time invited to attend our examinations. That suitable orators be selected to address the community and students at our commencements on any subject beneficial to the cause."[104]

Bansemer's remarks were obviously meant to shame the Synod and its lack of support for the College. Unexpectedly, his comments led to a very negative response from the student body. Twenty-four members delivered a petition to the Board of Trustees.

> "We the undersigned students of NC College, do sincerely petition you for the welfare and future prosperity of this institution, to remove the present President, Mr. Bansemer and either elect another in his place or let us remain under the exclusive jurisdiction of Prof. L. A. Bikle whom we all esteem as a gentleman and a scholar far more competent to take charge of a school like this than Mr. Bansemer. Many of us would like to come back next session but if Mr. Bansemer is allowed to remain, you have our most pious word that we shall seek an education elsewhere."[105]

Shortly following Bansemer's remarks, the students' petition, and complaints from parents who threatened to withdraw their sons from the school if Rev. Bansemer remained on the faculty, the Board of Trustees asked him to resign as President of the College. Bansemer complied with the wishes of the Board and resigned in December 1868, but he did not go quietly. Two letters written early in 1869 reflected his feelings concerning the actions of the Board. To the Board of Trustees, he wrote:

> "A note dated Dec 11th, 1868 and professing to be a resolution of your body was sent to me by our secretary. If you designed to give me by this a written evidence of your principles, I must say that you have been fully successful in securing your aim and in saying so I perhaps express the opinion which you yourself entertain. I would therefore express my regret on perceiving a cloud which may chill the fond indulgences of your self complacency. For several years' past, you hunted for Presidents throughout the whole land, and everyone to whom you replied infinitely wiser than myself, refused your offer. You know the reason. Do you really think any man so silly as to accept your offer for one year!!! Public opinion may not question your veracity, but men will feel interested to know which of the two you regard as evidence of your character. The letter I refer to is your resolution of Dec. 11. The future is

> prepared to answer ... As your resolutions of Nov 11th have been rescinded, I have but to say, that for your subsequent actions, and for your language used on various occasions, I hold you responsible, as far as my privileges might affect you individually and collectively."[106]

And to the Secretary of the Board, Colonel John Shimpock, Bansemer wrote:

> "You stated at the meeting of the Trustees of NC College on Oct 15th that the citizens of this place did not send their children to the college because they did not like the Faculty and on Nov 11th you verified the above assertion by saying you had heard so. As far as I am personally concerned, I would hereby demand on what authority the above assertions were made. You will please either so mention how many and which of the parents kept their children home on my account; or who is the person of whom you profess to have derived your information. [Please forward] your answer without unnecessary delay otherwise I shall hold you personally responsible for the assertions and its consequences."[107]

Upon the resignation of Rev. Bansemer, the College again found itself with only one full-time professor, Rev. L. A. Bikle, who, once again, was appointed acting President of the College. To finish the session, Rev. Bikle hired his brother, Philip M. Bikle, as Professor of Latin & Greek, and a student at the College, H. T. J. Ludwig, as a tutor.[108]

By the Spring of 1869, the College appeared to be on more positive footing as the Committee on Education reported to the Synod that "the Board [of Trustees] confidently believes this arrangement will rebound to the increased prosperity of the College. The Institution is reported as being out of debt and having ten thousand dollars in old State Bonds. All this indicates a hopeful future for our college."[109]

The Committee commented further that:

> "The exigency of the times demands a higher standard of education, and a more general diffusion of learning. The time has come when the power of an educated mind may wield a great intellectual and moral influence. It may

> not be out of place to state here, for the encouragement of young men seeking an education, that a thorough education is equal to an annuity of from six to twelve hundred dollars or to a fund of ten thousand dollars. Now, any young man of energy and sufficient health may obtain a complete education for fifteen hundred or two thousand dollars. Let fathers note the above and send their sons to North Carolina College, where they will receive a hearty welcome and be carefully educated by our worthy and efficient Professor, L. A. Bikle and his assistants."[110]

At its Convention in May 1869, the NC Synod resolved that "no one seeking admission into our ministry will be received unless his literary attainments are at least equal to … the Sophomore year of some first class College," and in order for future ministers to "be furnished with every facility for preparations," a theological Department was to be created at NC College.[111] No such department was ever created.

By June of 1870, the Board of Trustees was still unable to find a full time President for the College. The position was offered to the first President of the College in 1859, Rev. D. H. Bittle, who was currently residing in Shepardstown, Maryland. Rev. Bittle turned down the offer, stating that, while he was "concerned about loss of ministers from the South," and was interested in a Theological Seminary in 'our southern Church,' he was looking at present at establishing a seminary at Roanoke College and putting his brother [Rev. D. F. Bittle] in charge there before considering the Presidency at NC College."[112]

In August, 1870, the NC Synod, meeting at Luther's Chapel in Rowan County, received the Report of the NC College Board of Trustees which stated that while the number of students attending in the coming year had increased, those registering in the College Department were not sufficient to pay current expenses by $300, nor was the endowment sufficient to be a source of income.[113]

The lack of income notwithstanding, the Board reported that it had agreed to adopt the requested resolutions from the previous Synod which stated "that indigent young men having the ministry in view be instructed at NC College gratuitously, but that they be required to give a note to be paid with interest from date if they fail to enter or if they abandon the ministerial vocation." Further, the Board reported that it had resolved "that from the first of August, 1870, the sons of all orthodox ministers of the gospel be admitted into college at half rates of tuition."[114]

The final statement in the Board of Trustees' report was of a more positive nature. It declared that Prof. L. A. Bikle had accepted the presidency "at a salary of $1000 per annum in currency and the Prof's House to live in free of rent, the pay commencing from January 1st, 1871."[115]

While accepting the Board of Trustees' report, the Synod sent a cautionary message. The Board was instructed that it should "be hereby advised not to elect anyone as President of **our** [emphasis added] College unless they have the strongest assurance or hope that such a President-elect will accept the position when so elected."[116]

The Synod also stated that "due to several changes in the General Synod's operation of the Seminary in Columbia, SC, the NC Synod urges churches not to support the Seminary but advised men interested in the ministry to attend NC College."[117]

The current Board of Trustees was approved and consisted of Rev. Samuel Rothrock, Rev. W. H. Cone, Christopher Melchor, Daniel Barrier, Rev. G. D. Bernheim, Rev. D. I. Dreher, John Shimpock, Mathias Barrier, Rev. L. C. Groseclose, Rev. William Kimball, L. G. Heilig, and Jeremiah Graeber.[118]

In May of 1871, the Treasurer of the Board of Trustees reported that tuition, fees and rent collected for the current session totaled $171.05.[119] They made a further request to the Synod that "in as much as the Board of Trustees of NC College have complied with the request of the Synod in admitting indigent young men having the ministry in view free of charge and the sons of ministers at half-rates, therefore we recommend that this Synod devise some plan for the better endowment of the College."[120]

The Synod Committee on Education, reporting on the costs of NC College, offered for comparison the rates of Roanoke College, which at that time was under the Presidency of David F. Bittle, brother of former NC College President, Rev. D. H. Bittle. At Roanoke, tuition, fees, room and board at the college (which included the mess club) cost $140. If a steward was included the cost rose to $205, and if the student resided with a private family the cost was $234. This was compared to a cost of $147 to $167 dollars per session at NC College.

The Committee on Education, repeating the Board of Trustees' request for financial aid, stated that "our college stands in need of some pecuniary aid to pay the salaries of the Professors and that the Board of Trustees look to the Synod to grant them that aid, in as much as many students are being educated free of charge."[121] The Synod responded by resolving that the Treasurer of the Synod pay the Treasurer of NC College a sum of $150 to be regarded as a loan, returnable to Synod whenever the coupons on the bonds of the State became available.[122]

The Board of Trustees' Treasurer's Report for November 1871 reported that income from the College was $1410.65, and expenses were $1301.20.[123] In early 1872, the Board of Trustees reported that "due to free & half tuition measures, the tuitionary revenue is not adequate to the Salaries of the Professors, the [Board] finds themselves embarrassed in devising ways and means to supply the deficiency of income." Furthermore, "the seeming indifference of the ministers of our church" was a discouraging feature connected with the growing prosperity of the College.[124]

The Synod Committee on Education recommended that the Synod pay the second half of tuition for sons of ministers and that indigent students pay notes to the Synod who in turn would reimburse the College. The Synod agreed to pay $240 to the College for six students in attendance who "had the ministry in view."[125]

By the Fall of 1872, with an increase in students and revenue the College again appeared to be making some progress. President Bikle reported that for the first time since the College reopened in 1866, the income from tuition, rent and fees, $2,545, was sufficient to pay the salaries of Professors and to cover expenses. The Synod recommended that "steps be taken to increase the teaching force as the interests of that institution now demand and funds be appropriated to aid the College treasury as will pay the tuition of all the beneficiaries of this Synod."[126]

The optimism of the 1872-'73 session of the College was abruptly halted by the onset of a national economic crisis known as the "Panic of 1873." Marked as the first global depression and often called the "Long Depression", runs on banks created a short supply of cash and credit, and numerous foreclosures and bankruptcies occurred.[127]

By December of 1873, the Board of Trustees again petitioned the Synod to raise money for the school. The Synod Committee on Education reported that 115 students were registered for the 1873-'74 session, fifteen less than the previous year. The College reported an indebtedness of $800, of which, $300 was due to an increase in the teaching force and salaries of two of the Professors. The Committee recommended that the appropriation made by Synod be large enough to meet at least the most urgent demands of the College, and that an agency be immediately instituted to endow at least one professorship.[128] The Committee further recommended a plan for increasing the endowment of the College by "letting every minister consider himself an agent for the College and obtain as many subscribers as possible and secure the payment of $20 to be paid in four annual installments, that is to say $5 every fall after the crop is gathered for four years. By obtaining 1000 subscribers the $20,000 could be raised. Without an endowment fund our College must remain in a crippled condition. We have no right to expect anything else but fluctuations in the number of students every year."[129]

Portending the events of the coming year, academic year 1874-'75 began with another decline in the number of students. Proposals to raise funds made by the Synod Committee on Education in 1873 had failed to produce any significant income. By October of 1874, the financial situation of the College had acutely deteriorated. Rev. Bikle submitted his resignation on October 7th, 1874.

> "My resignation of the Presidency of NC College – a position I was induced to accept against my better judgment – is now tendered for your Christian consideration and action. From the date of this notification of my intended permanent withdrawal from the College, you will perceive that my connection with it, by a provision of your Constitution, will terminate about the 1st of Apr 1875."[130]

C. H. Fisher also submitted his resignation on October 7th, stating:

> "I resign my position as mower of the College grounds unless I am furnished with a written contract by your body through your secretary and Dr. L. A. Bikle. I can afford and am willing to do the work provided the above considerations are complied with."[131]

On October 29th, 1874, a Committee of the Board of Trustees met with W. E. Hubbert, the Professor of Ancient Languages and Literature, concerning his status and consideration of a medal he had only two years earlier offered to the College student most proficient student in oration and composition. The committee proposed that Professor Hubbert "be relieved from furnishing" his medal due to his "liberal subscription [donation] to our new endowment fund" and that his promissory note for this donation be taken up, and his account credited by $34, the amount still owed on the note.[132]

While Rev. Hubbert was persuaded to remain at the College, the third remaining member of the faculty was not. Prof. H. T. J. Ludwig submitted his resignation on November 3rd, 1874, and as another sign of how critical the situation had become, the Board of Trustees' Financial Secretary, Maj. L. G. Heilig, resigned his position a day later.[133]

In the face of what appeared to be a possible institutional collapse, the Board of Trustees moved quickly to restore its status. On the December 10th, 1874, Rev. J. B. Davis, an instructor at Roanoke College and alumnus of NC College (Doctor of Divinity '73), was offered and accepted the Presidency of the school to begin at the end of Rev. Bikle's term.[134] Rev. James H. Turner of Blacksburg, VA was hired to replace H. T. J. Ludwig as Professor of Mathematics beginning in August 1875.[135]

At the NC Synod Assembly in April and May 1875, the general atmosphere at the College was reflected by the Committee on Education report which stated:

> "NC College is not in as flourishing condition as regards the number of pupils and the extent of its influence as we had hoped it would be. The College is not sufficiently advertised in the secular press. The buildings of the College are in bad repair. The late storm has considerably damaged the College buildings, which have been repaired in part by friends in the neighborhood. The interior of the buildings is in bad condition and it will require an outlay of $400 to $600 to fix it up properly, which must be done this ensuing vacation. Synod recommends that every minister lift a collection in each Church for this special purpose at their next communion season."[136]

In a further attempt to deal with the College's financial situation and the continuing difficulty in retaining faculty, the Synod contemplated alternative methods to operate the college. One proposal entertained a plan to modify the structure of the faculty's employment. The proposal, recommended by the Synod Committee on Church Institutions and Education Committee, stated:

> "Another cause for this want of prosperity is the manner of employing the faculty of the College. They have heretofore been elected by the Board of Trustees with a fixed salary for each one of the Professors, grading these salaries according to the position occupied in the Faculty of the College. We recommend that this plan be changed. Let the Professors that are and may hereafter be elected take the College and by their own energy and worth increase the number of their students and pay themselves out of the tuition proceeding therefrom. The plan heretofore pursued has left undeveloped the latent energy of the corps of Professors whilst it has gradually but surely involved the College in debt, until it now is about $1500. There should be some provisions made to meet this indebtedness."[137]

This proposal, referred to as "farming out" the operation of the College, was not new to the Board of Trustees or the Synod. A similar suggestion had been initially put forward nine years earlier by Rev. Bikle when he was first approached by the Board to reopen the school following the end of the Civil War.

While the Synod did not act immediately on the "farming out" recommendation, a year later it was back before the Board of Trustees, who once again referred the matter to Synod.

Even as a new President took over, the Board of Trustees continued the struggle to finance the school's operation. In September 1875, Jonas Cook, Treasurer for the College, reported that "by order of the Board of Trustees, $10,000 in bonds at a rate of 6% had been issued and 'that against my advice, [the Board ordered]' sold in NY through Mers. Magoven & Co. on June 8th & 18th, four bonds netting $955 and six bonds netting $967." According to Cook's ledger book the College had two cd's worth $900 and cash contributions totaling $351.95. The College had $241.92 in uncollected tuition; income from tuition of $968.45; borrowed funds from various individuals of $1,004; stable rent to L. A. Bikle of $25; $25 from Jesse Cody for violation of the College Charter, and interest from cd's of $.30.[138]

Expenses for the previous year included Prof. L. A. Bikle's salary [paid upon his resignation] -$599.50; H. T. J. Ludwig's salary [paid upon his resignation] -$477.85; W. E. Hubbert's (partial) salary $220.46; Laban Petrea's pay for sweeping $65, and C. G. Heilig's pay for hauling sand and lime $9. According to Cook, total income to date was reported at $1,924.75, with expenses of $1,924.48[139]

In November 1875, the College buildings and campus were severely damaged by another windstorm. The faculty declared November 12th as a holiday to clean up the campus and make repairs to the roofs of the buildings. It is not known if the storm was the reason for the action, but on November 10th, 1875, the faculty had voted to move the school's laboratory from the main building to the "northern" building (Pi Sigma Phi Society Hall).[140]

At the Convention of the NC Synod in May 1876, the President of the Synod and member of the College Board of Trustees, Reverend Samuel Rothrock, recommended in his opening address that all resolutions which heretofore had given free tuition to indigent men "having the ministry in view" be rescinded. It was later resolved that this practice was already actually no longer in place as Synod had been paying the tuition, but it was agreed that the practice would be discontinued hereafter.[141] Reverend Rothrock also proposed that the NC College Board of Trustees be reduced from its current eighteen members to twelve, but the Synod voted against this recommendation.[142]

In August 1876, in yet another approach to encourage attendance at the College, a long editorial/article appeared in the *Concord Register* written by "A member of the Cabarrus County Agricultural & Mechanical Club," advocating for NC College as a way to help local farmers educate their sons in the most modern methods of agriculture and science. "Send your sons to North Carolina College, and we vouch for it, that in a brief period you and they will think as we on the important subject of this paper."[143] Most likely, this article was written by H. C. McAllister, the brick mason who had helped construct the college buildings and served as an officer in Mt. Pleasant's Co. H during the Civil War. McAllister married the sister of College Treasurer, Jonas Cook, and was a prominent citizen in the community. He had recently been appointed to his first term on the College Board of Directors and was very involved in promoting agriculture within Cabarrus County. He was also elected as a County Commissioner later in the year.

The College opened on September 6, 1876, still struggling financially. The Board of Trustees attributed the drop in attendance to "the stringency of the times," and noted that "of the consequent, [there is an] insufficiency of the tuition fees to meet current expenses. The endowment fund is not available, its bonds, which are greatly depreciated, bearing no interest, the indebtedness of the college is gradually increasing from year to year and will amount to $4000 at the end of the present scholastic term."[144]

In October 1876, although he was a member of the College Board of Trustees, former President Bikle declined an offer to return to the College as Professor of Ancient Languages.[145]

Another unsigned article appeared in the *Register* in November stating in part:

> "What are we doing for our boys? Is Cabarrus county awake to her whole duty in this all-important matter, where are our institutions of learning …? Why is it that the capacious of halls of Mt. Pleasant's noble college, sound so vacant …? Why is it that an earnest faculty strive in vain to make this, one of the noblest of Cabarrus county's emblems of greatness, as successful, as its worth merits? … Is there danger ahead, is the sin of gambling and licentiousness dormant and dead in our midst, and intemperance, and debauchery no longer to be dreaded among our boys, has Satan no strong holds into which the boys may be lured, and their God given intellects ruined? Ask yourselves these questions Cabarrus county citizens and if we are not doing our duty by the boys, let's begin now, fill up our school rooms, send a round hundred more to North Carolina College, put the boys to their books, and they will cease to study the arts of the gambler and profligate."[146]

In April 1877, President Davis reported to the Synod that tuition and fees had "not been sufficient to meet expenses for some years." He added that "we cannot afford to close the College" and recommended the appointment of a special committee to "suggest some suitable plan" to raise the necessary funds. The Board of Trustees report noted that the fence around the College needed to be repaired and resolved that it no longer assumed responsibility for expenses "beyond what may be necessary for the protection and repair of the property, after the expiration of the present collegiate year." It was resolved that Synod should create a permanent fund called the College Fund and seek to obtain from "our" people an annual average contribution of not less than 25¢ from each member, "requesting those congregations and those members who are able, to give more liberally than those who are less able."[147]

The Board further recommended turning to the plan introduced to the previous Synod concerning "farming out" of the College, stating:

> "That until the College debt is removed, the Board of Trustees [requests to] be authorized to offer to any faculty of their appointment, the College, with its buildings … free of rent to be conducted in accordance with its chartered design, with such guarantees as the Board may deem necessary for the preservation of the buildings in good condition. Should said offer be declined by the present faculty, the Board [asks to] be authorized to make it to such other competent teachers as shall be willing to accept it."[148]

Two members of the Board of Trustees, Rev. Samuel Rothrock and Rev. W. H. Cone, described the advantages of "farming out" the College. It would "relieve the Board of responsibility for salary, stimulate action, and competency." The Board would not incur additional debt and have time to liquidate its liabilities. Because of their financial stake in the success of the school, the faculty will work to increase patronage. The Board would retain power over the appointment of professors and still be responsible for the protection of the property. The two men noted no disadvantages.[149]

At its convention in early May of 1877, the Synod, once again faced with the possibility of having to close the College, accepted the recommendation of the Board of Trustees agreed to move forward with "farming out" the

College to whomever might be interested. Thus, with the end of the College year in May 1877, Rev. Davis relinquished his position as President of the College and the remaining faculty was dismissed.[150]

The Board of Trustees quickly proceeded to enter into an agreement with a "new" group of instructors, who included former College President, Rev. L. A. Bikle, and former Professor of Mathematics, H. T. J. Ludwig. These two men, along with Rev. Sheppard S. Rahn,[151] formed a new faculty to whom the Board surrendered the College buildings, grounds, and President's house free of rent, with the understanding that "all repairs and insurance on the property, shall be made by the Board out of the customary contingent fees of the College or other funds at their command." The faculty, in turn, agreed "to administer the institution in the manner and purposes of its chartered design, and [to] further guarantee to preserve the buildings, grounds."[152]

In order to finance the new operation of the College, the Board of Trustees, using its State Bonds as collateral, borrowed money from a group of local individuals. Jonas Cook's ledger recorded that a total of $5,647 was borrowed from the following persons - Daniel Melchor, $100; John D. Barringer, $300; Evan Lutheran Synod, $300; A. Heilig, $144; John D. Barringer, $24; John Shimpoch, $210; Daniel Barrier, $500; Samuel Rothrock, $50; Moses Barrier, $100; Joseph A. Linn, $40; Harvey C. McAllister $21.50, and Alexander Foil $1,373. All these men were current or former members of the College Board of Trustees. They were promised a rate of return of eight percent on their loans.[153]

Under the "new" administration in the Fall of 1877, the school catalogue described North Carolina College as:

> "... located at Mt. Pleasant, Cabarrus Co. NC, an incorporated and flourishing village, nineteen miles from Salisbury, thirty northeast of Charlotte, near Concord, on the Central RR, from which place it is easily accessible. The College buildings three in number, afford ample accommodation for students. They are beautifully situated in a rolling, oak country, on an eminence, overlooking the village and vicinity. The grounds are attractive, having recently been much improved by planting trees, cutting out adjoining forest, &c. The main building

has been thoroughly renovated at considerable expense, inside and outside, adding much to comfort as well as to appearance."[154]

An advertisement in local newspapers and other periodicals stated:

> "North Carolina College and Mt. Pleasant Female Seminary, our Church Institutions, located in Mount Pleasant, Cabarrus Co. NC, nine miles from Concord, are in a flourishing condition. Each Institution is managed by able and efficient Professors who are ready to receive any who wish to favor them with their patronage. Any young man or young lady desiring to obtain a thorough education, at more reasonable terms than can be obtained elsewhere, would do well to apply."[155]

During the year, a new fence was erected to enclose the campus grounds and the roof of the main building was repaired. The Board of Trustees paid John M. Freeze $4 for work on the old building; J. Barrier $2.15 for repair of the roof; George. R. P. Miller $2.50 for repair of the roof; Bostian 25¢ for work on the building, and John Lentz $3.32 for two and a half days work and four pounds of nails.[156]

In June of 1878, after repeated attempts to recover the College's endowment funds invested in State and Confederate Bonds before and during the Civil War, the Board of Trustees instructed the College Treasurer, Jonas Cook, to place the certificates on the "New York market" for sale. The sale of the certificates, which held a face value of over $15,000, resulted in income of only $1,922.50. These were the same bonds that the Board had used as collateral to cover loans totaling $5,647 made to the College in 1877 by thirteen individuals from Cabarrus County and the Lutheran Synod.[157]

John Shimpock, President of the Board of Trustees, reported to the Board that the "buildings and Professor's house [had] been repaired. The buildings [were] insured in the sum of $5,000 for one year, and the State Bonds [had] been sold and the proceeds applied to the debt of the College, [which had been] reduced to about $1300." He also reported that J. M. Freeze was paid $23.50 for work done on College Halls and the Moses house [Boarding house] in 1876.[158]

In 1880, the leasing arrangement for the operation of the College and a new fund-raising effort by the Synod provided some relief from the previous financial burdens. However, the school's general situation remained precarious.

The Synod Committee on Education reported in 1880 that a plan to appropriate the College debt to various congregations within the Synod had met with some success. The College received $757.31, but not all congregations had responded. The Committee called for an "investigation" into the reasons some churches did not contribute stating that:

> "There seems to be some indifference manifested on the part of the church with reference to the liquidation of the debt under the plan proposed and approved by the Synod and that as there may be some cause or causes for their spirit of indifference, it calls upon this body to enquire into the matter, and if such cause or causes exist to remove them. ... We think that the reputation of the instructors, and the business qualifications of the Board of Trustees require and demand this investigation as well as the prosperity of the College."[159]

At the end of the 1880 session, the College instituted a new fee schedule. The new structure, while reducing the standard tuition, board and incidental costs, added a fee for instruction in Latin, Greek and Classical Studies. In effect, the new cost arrangement allowed students to live on the campus and attend the pre-college classes for less but attached an additional cost to receive instruction in the "college courses."[160]

Despite the new fee schedule, the few records that exist show that the 1880-1881 session was apparently one of extreme difficulty. Attendance weakened and the number of students in the College Department was greatly reduced. (There were no graduates in 1881-1883). By the end of the '80-'81 academic year, the leasing arrangement had been in place for three years came to an end as Rev. Bikle declined to renew his agreement. The operation of the College once again changed and was returned to the earlier system of funding and direction by the Board of Trustees overseen by the Lutheran Synod.

During the summer of 1881 and into 1882, North Carolina experienced a severe drought which devastated crops and caused serious economic hardship, especially for farmers. The 1881-'82 College session appears to have been again affected by the slowing economy as it opened in a rather confused state.

Although, as previously described, Rev. Bikle did not renew his lease at the end of the previous session, an advertisement dated July 1881 appeared in the *Concord Register* stating that NC College would open for its next session on 8 Aug 1881. The announcement was signed by President Rev. L. A. Bikle.[161]

An article appeared in the *Wilmington Post* in August 1881 which stated that "report has it that Rev. Dr. Bernheim has recently been elected to the Presidency of North Carolina College ... Dr. Bernheim says that the election for a President ... will not take place until the 5th day of October; that he is not certain he will be elected, and also he does not know whether he will accept the position if elected."[162]

There was no College catalogue produced for the 1881-82 session "due to the new arrangement [which] was entered into by the Board of Trustees with the College faculty [which made] a reorganization of the college necessary."[163]

In January 1882, the Board of Trustees elected Rev. G. D. Bernheim as the new President of the College. It appears from existing records that Rev. Bernheim began his work immediately, but he was not inaugurated until May.[164]

At a meeting of the Board of Trustees at the College on May 23, 1882, with both Rev. Bernheim and Rev. Bikle present, the Board received the College buildings from the outgoing faculty without holding them responsible for any repairs to the same. Rev. Bernheim was authorized to collect money and put the College buildings in "comfortable" condition.[165]

The state of the school was summed up in the 1882 report to the Synod by the Committee on Education which stated, "our college has not yet taken her place as high in the rank of colleges in NC as she should nor as high as the Synod should desire her to stand. Her wheels seem to be somewhat clogged by debt and otherwise, so that she has not exerted the influence which she should."[166]

The 1882 - '83 school year began on a positive note, but by the end of the Fall session, the financial situation had deteriorated further. Rev.

Bernheim submitted his resignation on Jan. 4, 1883 and the Board of Trustees voted to suspend classes on April 1.[167]

Meeting at St. Stephen's Church in Cabarrus County in May 1883 to dedicate that congregation's new building, Synod President, Rev. S. T. Hallman stated that "North Carolina College and Mt. Pleasant Female Seminary are commended to the careful consideration of this body with the earnest hope that such action will be taken as is necessary to make the College a complete success. **Should we be unable to do this then close its classic doors forever?**" [emphasis added][168]

The Committee on Church Institutions resolved, "that we will not close or give up NC College, but rally anew to its support." Several possible alternatives were presented to begin to liquidate the debt and to reorganize the school. The Committee began by recommending "that we now and right here begin the work of liquidating the debt, $800, resting upon [the school], by subscriptions payable in one year." This recommendation was immediately acted upon and $312 in pledges was raised by the end of the Synod session.[169]

Another recommendation called for "some suitable arrangement [to] be made to call upon the Church at large in the United States for further financial assistance," and a third proposal called for "pastors [to] preach special sermons on Christian education at least twice during the coming year and present the interests of our institution, and with their people make special and earnest prayer to Almighty God our Heavenly Father for His blessing on our school of learning."[170]

The two remaining proposals made by the Committee were more far-reaching, calling for some fundamental changes in the operation of the College. One recommendation proposed "if not in conflict with the [school] Charters, Mt. Pleasant Female Seminary and NC College be united in one and we make of the College an institution for co-education; and that, in case it conflicts with the Charters, [they] be so amended to avoid the conflict." It was also suggested that steps be taken to secure a few lady teachers. The College Board of Trustees opposed this recommendation and it was not adopted.[171]

The second recommendation, which at the time did not appear as radical as the first, had long-term implications that would prove quite important in the future. This proposal, opposed by the College Board of Trustees as "detrimental to the present NC College," called for the appointment of a committee to confer with similar committees from the South Carolina and Tennessee Synods to:

> "Investigate the chances for consolidation of N. C. College with either Newberry or Concordia College or both, and to consider a place at which to locate such a consolidated institution, and to determine whether it shall be a school solely for males or co-education, ... and that [the Committee] be authorized in case of success to secure offers from places desiring the institution in their midst."[172]

The Committee's final recommendation was that "the Treasurer of NC College [should] be required to report the financial condition of said College at each annual meeting of this Synod" and "that the Board of Trustees take the necessary measures to continue the exercises of the College for the present Synodical year."[173]

At the end of the Synod meetings, the College Board of Trustees was instructed to offer the position of President to Rev. F. W. E. Peschau of Wilmington, NC, resolving:

> "that he have the privilege to select his faculty subject to approval of the Board and that the Board tender Rev. Peschau the College Buildings, grounds, apparatus, & etc. to conduct the exercises of NC College upon certain conditions to be hereafter agreed upon between Rev. Peschau and the BoT." Rev. Peschau, however, declined the position.[174]

Even though the Synod and Trustees had kept the doors of the College open through May of 1883, the rejection by Rev. Peschau forced the Synod not to open the College for the beginning of the 1883-'84 school year. During the interim, School Treasurer Jonas Cook inaugurated a plan for the formation of a "College Benefit Association."

Cook's plan stated that any person could become a member of the Association by the payment of $5 on the first day of January and the first of September in each year, for a term of five years. Membership in the Association entitled the individual to a reduction in tuition of ten dollars per year both in the preparatory and collegiate departments of the College.

Also, any congregation in the Synod could send a student with the ministry in view tuition free.[175]

The Board appointed a financial agent, Rev. J. A. Linn, to canvass the interests of the Association. The association required that 100 members be secured before it would go into operation. In order to secure this number, some "friends of the College" duplicated their membership by a double payment.[176]

Under this new plan, the College produced enough funding to reopen, and by December the College had elected a new President, Rev. G. F. Schaeffer, and secured a faculty. The school opened for a "half-session" on January 1st, 1884.[177]

At the Lutheran Synod Convention at Ebenezer Lutheran Church in Rowan County in April and May of 1884, the Committee on Education reported that the Tennessee Synod had "refused to appoint a committee to confer with the North Carolina College," and that the plan to make the school co-educational was deemed "not advisable at this time."[178] The Synod also endorsed the North Carolina College Benefit Association created by Jonas Cook and encouraged Rev. Schaeffer and Rev. Linn "to visit all of the churches within the bounds of this synod to advance the interests of North Carolina College."[179]

In the Fall of 1884, a newly written description of North Carolina College at Mt. Pleasant, Cabarrus County, NC, described the village location as unsurpassed in healthfulness.

> "Its elevation secures pure, salubrious air, free from malaria. The College buildings are comfortable, convenient, and supplied with excellent water. These are the best guaranties of health, and ought to divest parents of all solicitude in sending their sons to this institution. In view of all the advantages of the College, the mild climate ought to attract students from more northern atitudes [sic], who might thus, in vacation, enjoy the cool summer of their homes, and in winter, escape the rigor of northern winters. From the curriculum of studies, which is inferior to none, the government of the College, the very moderate expenses, the healthfulness and morality of the village, it

will be seen that the College compares favorably with any similar institution in the country."[180]

During the year, various books were contributed to the school. Rev. F. W. E. Peschau gave several volumes, including a copy of *Webster's Unabridged Dictionary,* a large collection of United States and foreign coins, and specimens illustrative of Natural History. Rev. J. M. Anspach of Easton, PA, gave two volumes of *Thieves of Homes.* Author, A. M. Gibson donated his book *A Political Crime-The Great Political Fraud.* Professor Rupp donated Vols I & II of *Coal Flora of Pennsylvania.* A book entitled *Forty Coming Wonders* was donated by M. M. Gillion. The Bureau of Education and other Departments in Washington, DC, furnished many books and pamphlets.[181]

The College purchased a new Richmond stove for $24.67, one coffee pot for 50¢, two oven pans for 35¢ each, one poker and one scraper for 10¢ each. In addition, John D. Barrier was paid $12 for repairs to the President's house and a College boarding house was established at a cost of $4 or less per month.[182]

Rev. Schaeffer received a salary of $508 for the 1884-85 Academic Year. Professor Rothrock was paid $470. Rev. Rupp received $394, and Professor Ludwig's salary was $461. Jonas Cook received payment of $50 for his duties as Treasurer of the College. Rev. Rupp's receipt for one payment of his salary was written completely in Latin.[183]

In the Fall of 1885, NC College Officers included Jonas Cook, Treasurer; Rev. Schaeffer, Financial Secretary; L. H. Rothrock, Secretary of the Faculty; H. T. J. Ludwig, School Librarian, and Dr. J. W. Moose, President of the Alumni Association. The Executive Committee members were Rev. J. A. Linn, Jonas Cook, and Dr. Paul A. Barrier.[184]

The College catalogue stated that there was an "urgent need of [an] endowment and Library Fund. [The] chemical and philosophical apparatus cost more than one thousand dollars and is still comparatively new; the cabinet is fairly well supplied with specimens; its museum contains coins, etc., of rare value, but in all these the College feels the necessity of better equipment."[185]

Only three months into the academic year, President Schaeffer addressed the Board of Trustees and requested that "in view of a want of revenue sufficient to sustain the present faculty, he be temporarily released from the duties of the Presidency." The Trustees, citing inefficient revenue, agreed to temporarily suspend Rev. Schaeffer's contract as of May 1st, 1885 and invited the other members of the faculty to "confer with us as to some arrangement by which the expenses of teaching may be brought within the present revenue."[186]

Reverend Schaeffer's request for leave appears to have precipitated reactions outside of the College community. In November 1885, "eleven members of the ministerium" petitioned Synod President Rev. F. W. E. Peschau to convene a special session of the synod "to consider the interest of NC College." As a result of this petition an "extra session" of the Synod was held in Mt. Pleasant on December 10th, 1885.[187] There are no minutes of this extra session but two topics were surely discussed - Rev. Schaeffer's leave request and the College's financial situation. One known consequence was a proposal for the creation of two endowed professorships of $15,000 each - one for chair of the President and another in honor of Rev. Carl A. Storch, the chief organizer of the NC Synod in 1803.[188]

It appears that Rev. Schaffer's request for leave was postponed. He continued as President through the remainder of the school year, as he was listed as receiving $20 of his salary in March and a *Concord Times* article dated May 20th noted that he returned from his wedding trip shortly before College Commencement. Rev Schaffer delivered the Baccalaureate Sermon at commencement on May 17th and was listed in the 1885-'86 catalogue as President of the College. An advertisement in the *Carolina Watchman,* dated August 6th, 1886, stated that requests for catalogues be made in care of "President Rev. G. F. Schaeffer, Mt. Pleasant, NC."[189]

In May of 1886, the NC Synod met for its regular convention at Union Lutheran Church in Rowan County and received the report of the College Board of Trustees. The Synod delayed any substantive discussions on the financial situation of the College. Instead, they formed several committees to further investigate the problem. The Synod referred Rev. Schaeffer's request for a temporary release to the Education Committee, which recommended it be approved. No record exists concerning the circumstances for the leave or the dates during which it occurred.[190] Some members of the Synod were having second thoughts about the two proposed endowments. A motion was made to reconsider that action and was referred to a Committee consisting of Rev. J. A. Linn, Rev. W.

Kimball, Rev. B. S. Brown, C. A. Rose, H. C. McAllister, and Geo. Winecoff. This committee, less Winecoff, made a several changes to the plan and the plan was then adopted. (See endnote for more detail.)[191] The Synod voted to appoint Rev. Whitson Kimball as "a suitable agent" at a salary of $600.00 per year, to canvas the state to raise the endowment.[192]

In yet another attempt to resolve the funding of the College, the Synod returned to a previous proposal and formed a Committee to confer with Tennessee Synod "in regard to the possibility of merging of our educational work." This proposal had been tabled three years earlier after objections from the NC College Board of Trustees who feared that such a discussion would lead to the demise of the College.[193]

In the Fall of 1886, two College catalogues were printed. Evidently Rev. Schaeffer remained as President of the College, but it is unclear if he taught any classes or received pay. The first printing of the 1886-'87 catalogue lists the same faculty as the previous year, including Rev. Schaeffer as President. There was, however, a paragraph on page five that announced that the Presidency of the College had been accepted by Rev. John G. Schaidt of Knoxville, TN, and that he would begin his duties on August 29th, 1887. The remainder of this "first" catalogue was virtually the same as that of the previous year, except for the listing of students and the calendar of commencement dates and events. The "second" printing states that "since the catalogues (1886-'87) were printed, the Faculty and Officers of North Carolina have been reorganized as here-in dictated."[194]

Jonas Cook's ledger book records only three faculty salaries paid during the year – L. H. Rothrock $432; H. T. J. Ludwig $419, and P. E. Wright $80.[195] The advertisement for the opening of the College was posted by Professor H. T. J. Ludwig.[196]

At the 1887 Synod Convention held at St. Michael's Church, Iredell County, Board of Trustees President Rev. Samuel Rothrock, declared to the assembly that:

> "... the College needs the fostering care of the Synod. ... There is a propensity on the part of some members of the church to send their sons and daughters to some foreign schools at a greater expense than they could be educated at home ... [because they] vainly imagine that the name will give special and peculiar embellishment

> to their graduation. This is an unwise policy and must prove detrimental to the prosperity of our schools at home. United we stand, divided we fall."[197]

It was announced at the Synod meeting that Rev. Whitson Kimball had secured $11,000 in pledges for the College and "prospects are brightening," but that he had resigned his post and a replacement was yet to be named.[198] The Committee on Church Institutions reported that, "while the attendance [at the College] has not been as encouraging as it should have been," the school was accomplishing "commendable work." It was reported that a new code of rules had been introduced and was having "a most salutary effect" on the conduct of the students.[199] The appointment of a new President was announced. Reverend John G. Schaidt of Knoxville, Tennessee would begin his duties at the opening of the Fall session (August 1887) and would also head the Department of Ancient Languages and Literature and give instruction in German."[200]

At the end of the academic year in May 1888, College Treasurer, Jonas Cook, reported that the College showed income of $1,578 ($1,043 from tuition). Salaries paid to faculty included $552 to President Shaidt, $390 to Professor Ludwig, $256.87 to Professor Wright, $47 each to W. A. and J. L. Deaton, and $10 to Lewis Rothrock.[201]

During the summer of 1888 the College Board of Trustees and the Synod finally followed through on a three-year-old proposal to increase the endowment of the school by securing $15,000 in pledges from members of the churches in the state. This promise of funding did not take the form of cash, but, if the pledges were actually forthcoming, they would put the school on a firmer financial footing than it had enjoyed for many years.[202]

Through 1888-'89, the College Board of Trustees was involved in several "business" transactions. John D. Ritchie of Burke County, who died in 1887, bequeathed the College his personal property and 200 acres of land located mostly in Rowan County. During the settlement of the estate, Ritchie's widow requested that the Board release the personal property and half of the land to her. At the June 1889 Board meeting, it was decided to grant Mrs. Ritchie's request and relinquish to her 100 acres "on which she was now living" if she agreed not to contest the estate further. In 1890, Jonas Cook recorded the land in Rowan County in the name of the College.[203]

There was also a dispute with a "Mr. Kistler" concerning interest he claimed was due on a loan he had made to the College. In January 1889, Jonas Cook received a letter from Rev. Samuel Rothrock, Chairman of the Board of Trustees, informing him that he (Rothrock) had paid Kistler $64 interest but that the amount owed was still $6.40 short. Mr. Kistler insisted that the full amount of interest be paid "punctually at the end of every year. In October, Rothrock sent a second letter stating that Kistler was still demanding full payment of interest "or he threatens to send the note for collection." The interest was recorded as paid in full on January 1st, 1890.[204]

In June of 1889, Jonas Cook reported to the Board of Trustees that, based upon his examination of the books from 1883 to the present, the College showed income of $11,421.82 and expenses of $11,508.03 over the past six years. The total liability to date was $3,206 with assets valued at $1,596. The Board requested that Dr. Shimpock obtain funds to liquidate the debt. Cook's report of final financials for 1888-'89 academic year cited income of $1,471 with $908 coming from tuition. Faculty salaries for the year were reported as Schaidt $584, Ludwig $334, and Wright $293.[205]

The Board of Trustees approved the adoption of a student uniform. The uniform was described as "neat, pretty and inexpensive, navy blue sack coat, military vest and metal buttons, with light blue cord on the pants and a military cap with the letters 'NCC.'"[206] No explanation was offered as to why the decision to provide uniforms was made or how much the uniforms cost. Neither is there mention of uniforms in any official College correspondence or in College catalogues. Photos made at about this time show a few students wearing what appear to be uniforms, but most are not. Apparently, the uniform policy was not mandatory or was discontinued after a short time.

In July of 1889, the Board voted to give the school faculty discretionary power to employ additional teaching forces if necessary. Forty dollars was appropriated for payment of anyone who was employed.[207]

The most important matter at the July meeting was the unexpected resignation of Rev. Shaidt. He stunned the Trustees by announcing that he planned to accept a teaching position at Concordia College, a Tennessee Synod school located in Conover, Catawba County, which Schaidt described in letters to friends as "a high grade classical school with about seventy students." Interestingly, the letters he wrote from Concordia were on NC College stationary.[208]

Following Rev. Shaidt's resignation, the Board of Trustees began a search for a new President who could take over immediately, as the coming session was scheduled to open in September. The Board voted to extend an offer of the College Presidency to Alumnus and former Instructor, Wiley A. Barrier, '72, of Charlotte, NC.[209]

Barrier, a former Confederate Cavalry Officer, attended Western Carolina Male Academy and NC College before the war, and, after teaching "out west," returned to Mt. Pleasant as the Principal of Mont Amoena Seminary in 1871. He received his BA Degree NC College in 1872 and was awarded an AM Degree in 1875. He was a part-time instructor and frequent lecturer at the College. He moved to Charlotte in 1874 and opened a male academy called the Macon School. He also served as Mecklenburg County Examiner of Public Instruction. At the time of the offer from the NC College Trustees, Barrier had just been appointed to the NCC Board to fill his late father's vacant position.[210]

Barrier initially declined the position, but the Board of Trustees appointed a committee to speak to him further. Barrier asked the Board for more time to consider the position, but shortly thereafter, made a final decision to turn down the offer. Regrettably, Wiley A. Barrier died in October of 1890.[211]

Within a few weeks of Barrier's decision to decline the Presidency, the Board of Trustees made an offer to Rev. John D. Shirey, who, at the time, served as the minister at Salem Lutheran Church in Rowan County. Shirey accepted the offer to become the next NC College President as of August 1889.[212]

Sometime after Rev. Shirey became President, the Board of Trustees reversed a policy initially adopted in 1876 and voted unanimously, at the recommendation of Synod, to give half rates of tuition to sons of ministers and to students preparing for the ministry.[213]

Jonas Cook's 1889-'90 term ledger book showed income of $2,069, $887 from tuition and $674 from the endowment. Salaries paid to faculty included Pres. Shirey, $351, Prof. C. L. Fisher, $417, and Prof. Ludwig, $237, and back salaries to Rev. Schaidt, $187, and P. E. Wright, $71.[214]

During the summer of 1890 improvements were made to the College buildings. Walls were re-plastered and repainted, broken locks were repaired, and a keyboard was installed. The roofs of the main building, the Pi-Sigma-Phi Hall, and the College well were improved. In addition, a second well was dug and a kitchen added to the President's house.[215] The College newspaper, *The Advance,* admonished incoming students:

> "In as much as the College will be neat and clean when the next session opens, let every student resolve to help keep it in such condition.... Let no pencil marks appear on the walls and let no sweepings from your rooms be deposited in the halls at untimely hours."[216]

In May 1890, the *Wilmington Messenger* reported that "both institutions in Mt. Pleasant are in better and more promising condition than they have been for 20 years or more. They have a larger number of students than they have had for many years."[217]

In October of 1890, the Board of Trustees voted to seek a second mortgage on the school property in order to settle the existing debt. They learned that the school was to receive a $1,000 legacy from the estate of Capt. W. A. Barrierr, who died unexpectedly in October. Barrier had declined the Presidency of the College only one year earlier. Although the Board used the news of this legacy extensively to enhance the financial condition of the school and to encourage others to make similar commitments, the school did not actually receive the money until 1895.[218]

In January of 1891, the Board of Trustees noted that the College currently had no insurance and voted to take steps to obtain $10,000 in coverage.[219]

Notwithstanding a few financial problems during the year, at the end of the 1891 session the Lutheran Synod was so pleased with the progress of the College "due to the good condition the College is now in, the advance made during the last year, and the great evidences of her growing prosperity were so heartily received," that it ordered the President's Report printed and distributed to the public.[220]

Summarizing, President Shirey explained that the drop in enrollment from the previous year was due to the discontinuation of a program of joint instruction of Preparatory Department students and local "common school" students, which was deemed unsuccessful. The common school students were apparently counted in the College earlier enrollment totals.

Of the seventy-nine students attending in 1890-'91, only one-fifth were considered local.

President Shirey further conveyed that the 1891 College finances were much improved over previous years. The endowment fund collected $2,087 of which $2,000 had been "loaned out" (invested) and the interest on the previously invested endowment fund was $846.77. Income from tuition, room rent, and fees totaled $1,425, to which the $1,000 "legacy" from the estate of the late Wiley A. Barrier was added. (The legacy had not yet actually been distributed.)

Rev Shirey was pleased to report that during the Summer the main building and the Preparatory Department were painted and new ceiling installed at a cost of $250. The faculty paid for these improvements.

As he concluded his report, Rev. Shirey cited three "needs that required immediate attention. First, the school must clear its debt. Second, a new building/dormitory was necessary to meet the expected increase in enrollment and to provide more adequate space for commencement exercises (which were now being held at Holy Trinity Church in Mt. Pleasant). The third need was an increase in "legacies and gifts." [See endnote for entire report.][221]

At its 1892 annual meeting, the NC Lutheran Synod reported that "the College continues to prosper." During the year, financial agent Rev. C. L. T. Fisher traveled 720 miles at an expense of $96.55. He canvassed thirty-six congregations, visited fifty-seven families, preached sixty-seven times, and delivered thirty-one addresses. During 1892, Professor Fisher was away from his family for fifty-nine days.[222]

While no collections from individual churches were reported during the year, $2,143.10 was collected on the endowment, all of which had been invested at eight percent. Interest of $687.15 was collected. Receipts from tuition, room rent, incidental fees, etc. amounted to $1,844.00.[223] On one negative, but telling note the Board received a claim from Professor H. T. J. Ludwig for back wages owed. Professor Ludwig's claim apparently involved issues of non-payment or underpayment of contracted salary over several terms.[224]

During 1892 the school made numerous improvements to the physical plant. These included renovations to the Literary Halls at a cost of $182.50 and improvements to the grounds at a cost of $137.09. Fire-escapes were added in every room on the 2nd and 3rd floor of main building (actually rope ladders to be used for descending in an emergency), the Laboratory was completely overhauled, and the Library improved, all at a cost of $228.55. Of this sum, $195 was paid by faculty.[225]

Based on the response to the newly created Business course, the Board recommended the establishment of a Commercial Class. An expenditure of $50 was approved for advertising in newspapers.

Finally, the Synod reported that the Board of Trustees recommended that the College property be insured for $10,000 and that the Synod reimburse the Board for this expense. The College Treasurer, Jonas Cook, reported that the Board could not fund this amount by itself, but that it was able to acquire a policy for $1,000 for five years at a cost of $30.[226]

Despite the optimism of the previous two years, by the beginning of the September 1892 academic year, financial problems again plagued the College. There was a thirty percent decrease in the number of students enrolled from the previous year. In October, the Board of Trustees voted to seek a second mortgage on the school property in order to raise $1,500 to meet expenses.[227]

In March of 1893, the Board of Trustees passed a resolution maintaining that it was "the duty of each member of the faculty to canvas during vacation and to work in the interest of the institution in securing students" and that if they incurred expenses in this duty, they would be reimbursed.[228]

The Board of Trustees met following graduation ceremonies on May 31st, 1893. They announced the addition of seventy-two new opera chairs, a great improvement to the College Chapel. They voted to ask the Synod for help to fund a new roof for the main administration building and asked that leaders of the church assist in raising funds for a new Philosophical apparatus. A committee was formed to advise on the selling of the Ritchie property which had been bequeathed to the College in 1888. The Board received a claim from former College President, J. G. Schaidt, who maintained that he was owed money. Jonas Cook, the College Treasurer, stated that he [Schaidt] had been paid in full. The Board instructed President Rev. Shirey to inform Prof. Schaidt that he was paid in full and that "we kindly leave this matter with himself and Jonas Cook."[229]

Lastly, the Board of Trustees voted to take legal action against anyone who was not paying the interest on their pledges.[230]

At its 1893 annual meeting held at Lutheran Chapel in China Grove, NC, the Synod reported that "not as many students [were enrolled] due principally to the want of appreciation of higher education among our people. The small endowment is … still overworked and underpaid." As Financial Agent as well as President of the College, Rev. Shirey had, during the year, collected $725.61 in interest owed from pledges to the endowment, and $324.93 in principal. His expenses were listed at $70.00. The Treasurer's report further stated that the total amount of principal and interest on the endowment collected to date was $2,723.16 of which $2,540.01 was invested at eight percent.[231]

The Synod passed a resolution to request that during September each church minister include the interests of education in a sermon and take a special collection for NC College to repair the roof of the Administration building. It was recommended that the Synod should "ask the prayers and earnest cooperation of our people in behalf of our College and Seminary and that our pastors press and urge their people the importance of sending their sons and daughters to their own College and Seminary."[232]

In the fall of 1893, the College saw a strong rebound in enrollment, as seventy-one students registered for classes. But the Board of Trustees was confronted with several difficult issues, including the two back salary disputes. Professor Ludwig continued his salary appeal and former President Schaidt requested that the Board settle differences between himself and Board Treasurer Jonas Cook. The Board instructed Cook to continue to work with Ludwig individually and concerning Shaidt, advised Cook to form a committee with one member selected by Schaidt, one by Cook, and one member by the Board.[233]

Cook advised the Board that he had obtained a new mortgage on the College property and with it a loan of $2,000. He indicated that he was seeking additional insurance on the property.

The final issue that confronted the Trustees in 1893 must have come as a surprise as Rev. Shirey submitted his resignation as President of the College. No reason for his request was recorded. The Board reacted quickly, replying:

> "Whereas Rev. Prof. J. D. Shirey in the management of NC College has shown splendid executive abilities, and whereas, to frequent changes in the faculty is not helpful to the best interest of said NC College. Therefore, resolved that this Board does not desire to accept the resignation of said Rev. Prof. J. D. Shirey as President of the Faculty of said College; but does hereby respectfully request him to withdraw the same."

Ultimately, Rev. Shirey agreed to remain in his position and continued to serve as both the President of the College and its Financial Agent.[234]

At its annual meeting in May 1894 at Organ Church in Rowan County, the Synod reported that

President Shirey, as financial agent, spent forty-four days collecting interest on the endowment. During this time, he traveled 956 miles, visited twenty-six congregations and eighty-eight families, preached twenty sermons, and delivered fifteen addresses in the interest of the college and education. For his efforts he collected $92.99 principal on bonds and $604.81 in interest. His expenses were $64.80. To date, $2,816.15 of the endowment was collected was, of which, $2,484.71 was invested at eight percent interest. "Collections have somewhat fallen since last year. We believe this to be mainly due to the scarcity of money." The Synod report recorded that the Treasurer received $146.92 in the effort to raise funds for a new roof on the College and "we hope Synod will supplement this amount sufficiently to enable the Executive Committee to put the roof on during vacation."[235]

The Synod ended its 1894 report with a notation that there were five vacant seats on the College Board of Trustees. Based on the College Catalogues, six new Board members were appointed between May 1894 and June 1895. (See Appendix 13)[236]

In October 1894, the Board of Trustees received a recommendation from the faculty that tuition for Sub-Freshman and Preparatory students be reduced by $10. The Board Treasurer reported that he had tendered a bond in the amount of $15,000 to refinance the College debt and pay its outstanding liabilities. Security on the bond was provided by several local men – H. T. J. Ludwig, John K. Patterson, L. J. Foil, R. A. Shimpock, H. C. McAllister and George E. Ritchie. Another financial matter involved the old issue of half-rate tuition for students possibly bound for the ministry. The Board passed a resolution stating that students who were previously required to execute bonds yearly for the remaining portion of their tuition need not repay the tuition if they remained in the ministry for seven years.[237]

In June of 1895, the Board of Trustees reported that the College stable had been repaired and that the $1,000 legacy of Colonel W. A. Barrier had finally been received. The funds were applied to the College debt.[238]

At its 1895 annual meeting the Synod report stated that a new mansard roof had been installed on the College Administration building. This and other repairs cost $548.22, of which, $158.50, was contributed. The report stated that the financial agent for the College spent 26 days collecting interest on the endowment fund. He visited 19 congregations, traveled 570 miles, called upon 34 families, preached 12 sermons, made 12 college addresses, collected principal bonds of $295.70 and interest of $557.68. His expenses were $39. The financial report ended with a request for local pastors to "urge" bond givers toward speedy payment of bonds.[239]

And finally, the Synod declared "Deportment [at the College] is excellent and attention to study commendable. The institution is in a healthy condition and had it not been for the depression in money matters almost everywhere, we are satisfied there would have been a much larger number of students at the college."[240]

At its meeting in January 1896 the Board of Trustees reported to the Synod that, "No indebtedness has been incurred by the present administration, however, [we] regret that the number of students is not larger."

The Trustees declared:

> "The endowment is too small to enable the institution to compete with other colleges in offering reduced tuition to secure young men of limited means as pupils. No scholarships have been created to enable the faculty to offer worthy, but destitute individuals an education free of cost. Academies have sprung up on every side which offer low board and tuition with which the College cannot in its present condition compete. [There is a] want of interest and loyalty on the part of some of our pastors and laymen

> to Synod's institutions [and] we recommend that Synod ask for a renewed expression of interest and appreciation for the College."

The Board went on to request that the Synod "authorize the Board to place a man in the field to raise money to pay the present indebtedness of the institution, increase the endowment by securing bonds and cash for the same, and to solicit students at home and abroad, and that the pastors cooperate with the agent in securing funds and students." The Trustees appealed to the Synod "that there is a growing disposition on the part of some of those who have given bonds to the endowment fund of the College to repudiate the same ...", and "we urgently request Synod to take some action to impress upon our people the great importance of the endowment and their moral and legal obligation to pay the same." The Trustees informed the Synod that $484.48 in endowment funds monies had been collected since the last report, that the total endowment fund collected to date was $3,745.06 of which $3,209.23 was safely invested, "leaving in the hands of the Treasurer $535.83 for (future) investment."

The Board also asked Synod to consider the construction of a hall "on the grounds to furnish opportunity for students to board themselves at low rates."[241]

In early 1896, the College, Synod and local citizens were stunned when President Shirey suffered a series of strokes that left him partially paralyzed. On April 5th, 1896, Shirey suffered a final stoke and died at his home in Mt. Pleasant. He was buried two days later in Holy Trinity Lutheran Church cemetery in Mt. Pleasant.[242]

The Lutheran Synod honored Rev. Shirey with the following memorial:

> "Whereas, God has seen fit to remove from us our beloved and faithful brother, Rev. J. D. Shirey, D. D., who died April 5, 1896, just after the sun of Easter's morn had risen, be it Resolved, 1. That we murmur not at our heavy loss, but humbly own the hand of God in this instance of his hidden wisdom. Resolved, 2. That we extend sympathy to the son and daughters he has left, but point them to the Gospel for comfort, especially to the consideration that their loss has been but an experience of gain to him in his heavenly home. Resolved, 3. That a page of our Minutes

> be devoted to his memory in recognition of the facts that his long continued services of the church have been always marked by devotion to duty and love for humanity, that his labors in our Synod have been characterized by earnest consecration and have been attended with true success; that his work as president of our college has been self-denying, efficient, and greatly beneficial to the interests of education, and that in all relations of life, he was conscientious, candid, and kind."[243]

Even as the Synod eulogized Rev. Shirey, the Committee on Church Institutions and Education expressed some misgivings about the future of the College. The concern voiced that of the seventy-one students enrolled, only eleven from the entire Synod (less those from "local patronage") were in the college classes. The committee stated: "We must conclude from these facts, that there is a lack of love for, interest in, and devotion to our own institution, on the part of Synod, both pastors and people."[244]

This apprehension within the Synod revealed an apparent growing debate concerning the status the College and generated a final appeal by the Board of Trustees. "It is earnestly to be hoped that Synod will renew her interest in the College and not permit the enemies of the institution within the Synod to bury the College with its late lamented and faithful President."[245]

At its June meeting in 1896, the Board of Trustees announced the appointment of a new President, Reverend Melanchthon Gideon Groseclose Scherer. Rev. Scherer, a native of Catawba County, came to the College after serving as the Pastor at St. James Lutheran Church in Concord. His term was to begin immediately at a salary of $600 per year.[246] The Board acknowledged that the stairway in the main building had been repaired. They affirmed that the College was working to establish a "boarding club" for students to help in alleviating the shortage of rooms on the campus and verified that a $300 pledge was received from the estate of "Mrs. Kestler".[247]

At its October 1896 meeting, the Board of Trustees noted that although they had been unable to sell the John Ritchie land bequeathed to the College in 1888, the land was now rented to Mr. William Holshouser.[248]

At the Synod Convention in 1897, the Board of Trustees stated that the low number of students registered for the year was due to the general depression throughout the nation. The Synod repeated an often heard statement, that there was a "want of general appreciation of the institution on the part of the church." The Synod Committee on Educational Institutions commented "[we can] but wonder that an institution that had done and is doing so noble a work for our church – and doing it at so nominal a cost, should receive such a listless and puny support from those whom it blesses." The Board recommended that the Synod appoint a financial agent to solicit funds on behalf of the College. Rev. Vastine R. Stickley, a member of the Board of Trustees, was appointed.[249]

In 1898, the Board of Trustees indicated that there were students from nineteen of the Synod's fifty-eight churches and three students from other Synods. The Board calculated that if the school had two students from each Synod congregation, the school's financial problems would be solved.[250]

Despite its fragile financial condition in the fall of 1897, the College agreed to loan $1,473.43 from its endowment to its "sister" institution in Mt. Pleasant, the Mont Amoena Female Academy, to help pay that school's debts. The loan was secured by a mortgage on the Mont Amoena property and carried a six percent interest rate.[251]

The decision to loan funds to Mont Amoena appears to have been somewhat short-sighted. In March of 1898 an extra session of Board of Trustees was called to consider insufficient income to pay the professors salaries and "the constantly increasing debt which is upon the institution." The Synod Committee on Educational Institutions added that repairs were needed on the building to keep them safe and recommended a special collection from the member churches be endorsed by the Synod.[252]

To ease the financial situation, President Scherer proposed that he be appointed as the agent for the College and relieved from his classroom duties while he visited congregations during the summer and fall, "presented the claims of the college and asked for help with the endowment." During this sabbatical, his salary would continue, and he would be reimbursed travel expenses. He also requested that three members of the Board of Trustees be appointed to present a financial statement and a list of needs of the college to the Synod, and "solicit that body to cooperate" in making plans "in harmony with this action. He urged the Synod to pledge such cooperation and adopt such plans. The Board resolved that Rev. Scherer be authorized "to collect endowment funds on the best terms to serve the interest of the college."[253]

The College continued to support the local community's economy during 1898. Records indicate that College Treasurer Jonas Cook paid several invoices for work performed at the College during the school year. Three local merchants were paid for material furnished to make repairs. Cook & Foil's Store received $68.20 (Jonas Cook was part-owner of this business). W. R. Kindley was paid $26.20, and C. P. Cox received a payment of $7. Cook also paid local blacksmith James L. Lefler, 40¢ for work done at the College.[254]

At its October 1898 meeting, the Board of Trustees authorized the completion of a petition to the North Carolina Legislature concerning the College's purchase of State Bonds prior to and during the Civil War. It is not clear if the petition was ever submitted, but it provides information concerning the College's funding situation.

> "To the Honorable the (sic) General Assembly of the State of North Carolina, met [???] January AD, 1899.
>
> The petition of the Board of Trustees of North Carolina College, an institution located in Mount Pleasant, N. C. for the education of the youth & owned and controlled (sic) by the Evangelical Lutheran Church in North Carolina, respectfully showeth that, in or about the year 1858, the said Board of Trustees loaned to the Treasurer of the State of North Carolina Ten Thousand dollars taking therefor ten state bonds of one thousand dollars each bearing 6% interest; and again in or about the year 1862 fourteen hundred dollars, taking therefor one bond of five hundred dollars and two certificates of deposit, one for five hundred dollars & the other for four hundred dollars, also of which are herewith more fully set forth. Viz: [Left Blank]
>
> After repeated efforts to collect the interest due on said bonds and finally the bonds themselves & failing; the said Board of Trustees, being fully persuaded that the state would not pay these, sold in the New York market (June

> 8 & 10, 1878) ten of the said bonds Viz. Nos. [blank] realizing therefor only the sum of $1922.50, entailing a loss, together with the unpaid bonds and certificates, to said North Carolina College of the sum of [blank], now while we believe it is next to a sacred duty of the state to foster her charitable and educational institutions. … while we hereby approve and endorse the appropriations made by each General Assembly for the support and maintenance of the same, we must insist that it is a sacred duty 'to owe no man anything,' we therefore respectfully ask your honorable body to reimburse the Board of Trustees of North Carolina College at Mt. Pleasant, NC for the loss the said NCC has sustained by [????] of the failures of the great State of North Carolina to pay said bonds in full. Your [????], as in duty bound will we pray."[255]

At a special meeting in April of 1899, the Board appointed a committee "for the purpose of advising with regard to the interests of the College … and to prepare and present to the Synod a report on the condition of the College." The committee, consisting of Prof. Scherer, Rev. Charles B. King, Charles Miller, H. C. McAllister, and Jonas Cook. The committee was tasked with presenting a full and correct statement of the institution's financial condition, presenting a careful statement with regard to the patronage and work of the College, writing a petition for an appropriation of $ [blank] dollars to meet the pressing indebtedness of the College, and requesting that "in view of the financial condition & limited patronage," that some "instruction be given to the Board as to the will of the Synod as the future management of the institution."[256]

Three weeks before the end of the academic year, President Scherer delivered the following speech to the Synod Committee on Education.

> "... the time has come when Synod must determine as to the perpetuation of the college, or whether its doors must be closed. I believe that if the interests of the College were earnestly presented to the Church, her people would rally to the support of the institution. Please pardon me for making a suggestion that I think is feasible and fair, to wit: Assess the membership of the Synod per member, say

> one dollar per year, for ten years, and let the board grant free tuition to one student from each congregation for same length. At the end of said time the College would be endowed, be out of debt, and at least one hundred young men educated in the Church."[257]

Rev. Scherer's remarks were echoed in the Board of Trustee's Report to the Synod which was delivered by H. C. McAllister, President of the Board.

> "... the time has come when the synod must decide as to the perpetuation of the College, or whether it's doors must be closed. ... If the Synod desires to perpetuate the institution, the time has come when decisive and energetic action must be taken to put it on a more hopeful foundation. It is also felt by the Board that the institution does not enjoy the hearty sympathy and support of the entire church, and that without the full, free and united cooperation of all, both pastors and people, their efforts to advance the work of college education cannot succeed."[258]

McAllister repeated President Scherer's suggestion that the Synod consider assessing each congregation a fee of "perhaps one dollar per year for ten years, and let the Board grant free tuition to one student from each congregation for the same length of time. At the end of this time the College would be endowed, be out of debt, and at least one hundred men be educated in the Church."[259]

In May 1899, a report from a Special Committee of the College Board of Trustees further outlined the school's financial situation. The school debt was secured by a mortgage of $2,363.36 and it had notes (bills) of $474.76 in accounts. Professors salaries of $541.57 were owed from June 1896. Salaries due from 1896, '97 and '98 totaled $284.66 and a deficit of $400 was expected on the present (1899) salaries. Of the endowment, $4, 502.98 (one third) had been collected and the Kestler estate totaled $287.78 plus interest. "This together with the uncollected endowment bonds that are regularly paying interest constitutes the productive fund of the college."

The committee declared that "the revenues from all sources has hitherto been insufficient ... to meet the necessary expenses of the institution. This condition must be remedied in some way, or sooner or later the doors of the College must be closed."

The Board of Trustees asked the Synod for an appropriation of $800 to meet the present pressing indebtedness of the institution. The Board pointed out the low tuition and "the smallness of the patronage which the College receives" and with over 7,000 communicant members, the Synod furnished only thirty to fifty students "to its own institution." The Board also asserted:

> "At present the only hope of putting the institution on a paying basis seems to lie with the churches. There needs [to be] a general awaking on the subject of higher education, a deep and strong conviction of the value and necessity of the College for the future vitality and growth of the Church and an intensifying of the loyalty of our people to their own institution."[260]

In response to the Board's report, the Synod voted thirty-five to four to adopt a resolution to keep the school open and to loan the Board of Trustees $800 at six percent interest. But the resolution was laced with anxiety for the Board. The resolution specified that because of the "discouraging reports", a committee of three ministers and two laymen be established "**to solicit bids for a different location of the college.**" [emphasis added][261]

The Synod's resolution set in motion the process which would, two years later, result in the closing of North Carolina College. Needless to say, the reaction in Mt. Pleasant and among the members of the Board of Trustees was total surprise and shock. But shocked disappointment soon turned into solid determination to keep the school open for as long as possible.

On May 27th, only three weeks after the convention, the Synod Committee on Bids for the Location of NC College (Bids Committee) met in Concord. The members of the Committee included Rev. D. H. Holland, Charlotte; Rev. C. A. Rose [NCC '80] Rowan County; Rev. C. B. Miller, Concord; George E. Ritchie [NCC], Concord, and T. L. Ross, China Grove. The Committee began by adopting three resolutions.

Resolution #1 expressed that the Committee interpreted its mission to be "in the welfare of the College," and "in the execution of its commission we will foster no agitation that will mitigate against the institution, it being our conviction that if the college is to remain in Mt. Pleasant, it will do so with the good will and endorsement of the Synod."

Resolution #2 asserted that the Committee agreed that the Synod had acted within its power in action in regard to removal, but "we [will] take no action in soliciting bids until we have more thoroughly examined the relation of the Synod to the College."

Resolution #3 requested that the Chairman of the Bids Committee (Rev. D. D. Holland) "be authorized and instructed to investigate the legal relation of the Synod to the College, and the Synod's power in the matter of removal."[262]

On June 8th, 1899, a lenthy "editorial" appeared in the *Concord Standard.* This article consisted of a long discussion concerning an apparent declaration by the NC College Board of Trustees that based on the College charter, the school **could not be removed from Mt. Pleasant** [emphasis added]**.** Engaging in a line by line analysis of the charter, the *Standard's* writer maintained that the Board was incorrect in its claim. And, in a less than subtle manner, the article mentioned that Concord was interested in having the College relocated there.[263]

Another, but not unexpected result of the Synod resolution, was Rev. Scherer's resignation (in June) from his position as President of the College. Because Rev. Scherer resigned at such a late date, the Board was not able to find a suitable person to serve as President for the coming year. Instead, a current faculty member, Edgar Bowers, was appointed Acting President. Bowers was the first and only President of the College who was not a Lutheran minister.[264]

The Bids Committee held it second meeting on August, 25th, 1899. The committee concluded that the Synod had "full power and authority to remove the College" and that the Committee would "proceed to execute its commission to call for bids" by publishing same in *The Lutheran Visitor, Our Church Paper, The Charlotte Observer* and the Salisbury, Greensboro, and Winston papers."[265]

At a third meeting on Nov 25th, 1899, the Committee reported that it had received two "communications" in response to the notice. One was a formal bid from Salisbury, NC and the second was an "overture" from the Tennessee Synod on behalf of Lenoir College. The Committee recommended that the Synod call a special meeting to consider their report and to "take under advisement the general interest of the College."[266]

The Tennessee Synod's proposal was basically an offer to combine NC College with the Tennessee Synod's Lenoir College at their campus in Hickory. The Tennessee Synod offered a "gift" of $10,000 in the form of half-interest in the value of Lenoir College, equal representation on the Board of Trustees, and "moral support". (See endnote for entire text of the proposal).[267]

The bid from Salisbury initially included a cash payment of $8,500. A revised bid stated that "the citizens of Salisbury" would pay $20,000 divided into three categories - $5,000 for the movable property, furniture, etc.; $5,000 in a cash endowment fund, and $10,000 in an "unpaid endowment fund." The city would also provide a sixteen-acre site valued at $7,000 "most eligibility located in the corporate limits of Salisbury," on the east side of town and "extend a road from Fulton St. to Innis St. through the College property." The offer was contingent on Salisbury's Building Committee's approval to build a suitable main college building on the site at a cost of $13,000 and the promise to open the school in the Fall of 1900.[268]

In early December the Committee received a request from the citizens of Mt. Pleasant requesting "a hearing with reference to the proposed removal of North Carolina College from Mt. Pleasant." Representing the Mt. Pleasant citizens were H. C. McAllister, President of the Board of Trustees; Jonas Cook, Treasurer of the Board, and Clarence Heilig, a local merchant a and member of the Board.[269]

The Synod was also assured that there was no legal obstacle to retaining the name North Carolina College should an offer be accepted and the school relocated[270]

On December 19th, 1899, a called session of the entire NC Synod met at St. John's Lutheran Church in Salisbury to address "the interests pertaining to North Carolina College." This meeting was attended by nineteen ministers and twelve lay members. The Synod addressed each of the three proposals.

The Bids Committee suggested visiting Lenoir College and offered a set of recommendations stating that while the Synod was "encouraged by the prospect of mutual benefit" to both organizations, the idea of joint ownership "involved possible difficulties," and would best be resolved by forming another Committee to "communicate further with the Tennessee Synod." The NC Synod voted to "defer" these recommendations. The Synod's comment regarding the "protest by certain citizens of Mt. Pleasant" was that this matter "should be filed for consideration when the question of the sale becomes a real issue in the negotiations for removal."[271]

And finally, the Synod requested that "the citizens of Salisbury to hold their bid open for one year" and that in the meantime, the offer would be referred back to committee and NC College continue to operate at its present location.[272] Salisbury's reaction was to withdraw their bid.[273]

In the final analysis, the Synod, claiming that the attendance of the meeting was small, stated:

> "It is the sense of the Synod that it would be unwise to change the location of NC College at this time," and that a "committee of five be appointed to take in hand all bids, overtures, papers, etc. … thoroughly consider, investigate, and digest the same, and report a the next annual meeting of the Synod."[274]

At the Board of Trustees meeting in May of 1900, H. C. McAllister, still President of the Board of Trustees, wrote, "I have the pleasure to report that the college has been kept open another year."[275]

In June, the Board of Trustees nominated Reverend William Lutz for President of the College but he declined when asked to guarantee that no debt would be entailed in his operation of the school. Continuing the negotiations, the Board withdrew its request concerning the debt and guaranteed Lutz a salary of between $800 and $1000. Lutz was also offered his choice of subjects to teach and was allowed control of the school's boarding department from which he could draw revenue. In addition, the Board agreed to conduct renovations to the College buildings in the amount of $200 and to establish a boarding house on or near the campus. New contract in hand, Lutz accepted the position of President of the College on June 20th, 1900.[276]

On July 28th, 1900, the College and the town of Mt. Pleasant were again saddened by the death of a community and College institution. Professor H. T. J. Ludwig died after a short illness at the age of fifty-seven.

Professor "Tom" had been associated with NC College since 1867 and was, by far, the most enduring symbol of the school. The Board of Trustees drafted the following resolution:

> "In Memory of Prof. H. T. J. Ludwig, Ph. D:
>
> Since the last annual meeting of the Board of Trustees of NC College, one of the working force of the College, whom we loved and honored has fallen at his post of duty. On the 28th of July 1900, Prof. H. T. J. Ludwig laid aside the mantle he had borne so long and with such distinguished faithfulness and ability and entered into rest.
>
> As a Board and some of us his former students, we desire to record our tribute of affectionate regard for his person and memory. Prof. Ludwig was Tutor in NC College from 1869-1871. He graduated in the first class turned out by the college. He was elected Professor of Mathematics in 1871 and except for two brief intervals, he filled that position till his death having taught in the college 28 years of his life. He died at the age of 57 yrs. 6 mos. & 11 days. As a teacher he was regarded by students and all who encountered him, as possessed with unusual ability and as very painstaking and earnest in imparting instruction to those under his care. As a man he was modest and retiring in his disposition but genial and sincere in association and true in his friendship. By his faithful labors in NC College and by his lovable character, he has left his impression in the minds and hearts of a large circle of former students and friends. Whereas – a prince among us has fallen, a faithful worker and a large-minded man has departed from among us.
>
> Resolved 1st That in the death of Prof. Ludwig we are conscious of a great loss to the college, to the community and to all his friends.
>
> Resolved 2nd That we as a Board wish to record our sincere and affectionate regard for his abilities & the memory of his name.

> Resolved 3rd That a page in our minutes be set apart as a memorial to him & that his testimonial be published in County & Church papers & a copy be furnished his family."[277]

President Lutz's administration began with immediate financial struggles. At a meeting of the Board of Trustees on the same day as Lutz's inauguration, the Trustees were informed that the John Ritchie lands had still not been sold. The Board voted to offer the land at a price of $550. The Board also instructed the Treasurer to borrow additional funds to pay the salaries of the faculty.[278]

In November 1900, in an effort to maintain some influence with the Synod, the Board of Trustees voted to meet as a body at the Synod Convention in 1901, where they hoped to present a show of confidence in the continuation of the College.[279]

As they prepared for the Synod Convention, the Board noted in April 1901 that agent G. F. McAllister had failed to solicit enough subscriptions to fund needed repairs to the College buildings. As the Board moved to develop a plan to raise the necessary funds for the repairs and to keep the school open, President Lutz presented a list of recommendations that he hoped would accomplish the task.

1) That Junior and Senior College Classes be opened for the admission of women.

2) That the length of the session be shortened to thirty-seven weeks (from the current thirty-eight weeks).

3) That work in the Preparatory Department be divided into four years to better prepare students to enter the Freshman class (thereby increasing enrollment), and,

4) That the faculty be allowed the privilege of offering and conducting a four-week normal course (training prospective teachers) on the College campus during the summer.[280]

Recommendations #1 and #4 were approved by the Trustees, but as events proceeded, neither was implemented.

The College Treasurer reported the following income and expenses for the 1900-1901 Academic Year.

Income	Expenses
Tuition	$ 1,727.72
Salaries	$ 1,850.00
Room rent & incidentals	$ 519.40
Refund to E. L. Ritchie	$ 10.00
Borrowed from Bank	$ 800.00
Janitor Service	$ 61.23
Endowment Interest	$ 315.15
Interest on Note	$ 426.97
Sundries Sold	$ 35.50
Wood	$ 21.97
Total	$ 3,397.77
Sundries purchased	$ 369.30
Total	$ 2,739.22 [281]

In May of 1901, H. C. McAllister, President of the Board of Trustees, opened his report to the Synod with:

> "At your last meeting you by resolution ordered the doors of the college to be kept open without incurring any expense upon Synod. At our [BofT] regular meeting in May (1900) we found ourselves with a college in debt – without a faculty, without a dollar, and without the moral support of Synod. Never in the history of the institution had the board met under like circumstances but realizing that we had a duty to perform, we determined to do that duty as best we could."
>
> We elected Rev. W. A. Lutz, president of NC College, giving him full power to select his faculty, and promised to endorse his every effort to revive the institution. The buildings were thoroughly renovated, and expenses borne by the people of Mt. Pleasant."

McAllister went on to state that the present outlook of the College was encouraging, and "that friends of the institution have reason be hope that in this beginning of a new century, that North Carolina College will fulfill the mission for which it was established."

At the conclusion of his otherwise optimistic report, McAllister delivered this incongruent statement.

> "Now after a service of twenty-five years, during which time I have to the best of my limited ability endeavored to advance the interest of North Carolina College to the welfare of the church, ... tender my resignation as a member of the board of trustees ... ."[282]

His resignation was not accepted.

> "Recognizing the faithful service of the chairman of the board of trustees in the past, and in view of the present financial condition of the college, demanding wise legislation by men fully acquainted with the situation, we deem it unwise at this time to make the change."[283]

Beyond McAllister's resignation announcement, the Synod responded most favorably to the improved circumstances of the College. Expressing their approval in biblical terms,

> "There seems to have been a very resurrection of dry bones. We feel that the thanks of Synod are due President Lutz and his aggressive faculty for their self-sacrificing zeal and pains-taking care, which have brought the college to its present state of prosperity."

The Synod approved and seconded McAllister's announcement that the faculty and alumni were erecting a monument to the honor of Prof. H. T. J. Ludwig, and that there was a desire to amend and change the charter of the college, so as to meet more directly the desires of the church.[284] They also addressed the report of the Bids Committee that was deferred from the December 1899 called Synod session.

The Bids Committee indicated that it had not solicited nor received any additional bids for relocation of the College but the "overture" but had recived no response from the Tennessee Synod. The Synod instructed their President, Rev. C. B. Miller, to:

> "inform the committee of the Tennessee Synod that their overture was received ... with much gratification as an evidence of the increasing unity of sentiment and

> practical endeavor between the Tennessee Synod and this body (NC Synod). [Their overture] received careful consideration … but none leading to any definite action, look to the removal of NC College. That in view of the prosperous condition of NC College in its present location, the Synod does not deem it wise to consider further the plan of uniting Lenoir and NC Colleges."[285]

Lastly, the Synod agreed to Rev. Lutz's proposed change to the term limits for members of the College Board of Trustees. He proposed that the current unlimited terms which had been established in 1877 be returned to the three-year terms specified by the "original charter". According to Rev. Lutz, there was "widespread dissatisfaction in the church" with unlimited terms and he therefore recommended a return to the original three-year terms.[286]

The College managed to open in the Fall of 1901 but the financial situation deteriorated quickly. In late November 1901, Professors Bowers, Johnson & McAllister submitted their resignations. At a called meeting of the Board of Trustees on Dec. 4, 1901, the resignations were read, and the Professors stated that unless the Board could provide quarterly salary payments their resignations would take effect on December 27, 1901.

After discussion, a resolution was offered by Reverend Charles B. King that in order to meet the current expenses of the College, "the Treasurer be authorized to borrow a sufficient amount of money to meet the current expenses of the Professors salaries as may be due from time to time during this session according to [their] contracts."

But only three months later, on March 4, 1902, the Board met to settle with the faculty and to plan to close the school. The Board learned that an anticipated source of income from the sale of the Ritchie lands (which had been in the College's hands since 1889) had been blocked and that the whole tract could now be sold for only $800. The Board voted to sell the land and "after paying the mortgage debt on said lands [the remaining funds] be loaned to the board to be disposed of as follows: pay Prof. Bowers $300; Prof. McAllister $102; Prof. Johnson $123; Prof. Keller $42, and the remainder, if any, to be paid on Prof. McAllister's note."

The Board further agreed that the Board Treasurer:

> "be authorized to execute a note to Rev. Prof. Lutz for the sum of $364 in full settlement of his salary to date, and that the balance of the interest accruing on the invested endowment fund, after the interest of $1,900 (mortgage indebtedness) was paid, would be paid on the debts due former Profs. Scherer, Ludwig, and Setzer, and current Professors McAllister and Lutz, pro-rated, until such debts were liquidated." Finally, the Board appointed Dr. Paul A. Barrier and Clarence G. Heilig to audit the books and settle with Rev. Lutz. The Treasurer was also instructed to make settlement with the late Prof. Ludwig's estate as far was possible."[287]

The action of the Board of Trustees in March 1902 essentially terminated North Carolina College's operation as a graduating College. Upon informing the Synod of the situation, the Board was encouraged to keep the school open until the end of the session. Professors Bowers and McAllister agreed to remain and kept the doors open until May for Freshmen and Preparatory students. The College officially suspended all operations in May 1902.[288]

H. C. McAllister reported to the Synod in May 1902 that, although the College remained open, attendance had dropped to sixty-five students. He conveyed that the Board had accepted the resignation of the President and two professors in order to meet the financial obligations to the faculty and that two faculty members remained until the close of the session. McAllister described "lack of patronage from our own church," the inability to collect the interest due on the endowment, and the failure of "full and hearty co-operation with the President as the reasons for the "difficulties."[289]

The Synod Committee on Education responded that, "we are at a loss to know just what steps to take in this report," and, as usual, recommended forming another committee "relative to NC College." Synod President, Rev. Charles B. Miller's opening remarks were

> "... it becomes our sacred duty to give to this institution, at this time, more than a passing notice. The financial conditions that confront the college, its attendance of students, and the general conditions that

> surround it, conspire to lay a duty at the feet of this Synod which it cannot avoid nor evade. Our education problem has not been solved; and the question as to what should be done in the case of NC College is still before the Synod and presses for an answer.
>
> Let us face this question like men, reason together in the fear of God, and let the judgment of the majority be the will of the whole, touching this all-important issue."[290]

After the McAllister and Miller reports, the members of the NC College Board of Trustees, along with Rev. F. M. Harr of the Holston Synod, and Rev. James A. Arndt of the Tennessee Synod were appointed as advisory members to the Synod.[291]

On May 3rd, 1902, the following special report from The Committee on NC College was submitted to the NC Synod.

> "The vitality of the institution seems to be exhausted. It is with the saddest feelings and with painful remembrance of the labors and prayers of the fathers in behalf of NC College, that we make this acknowledgment. But we deem it our duty to you to inform you of what we regard as the truth, however, unwelcome it may be. In view of these discouraging conditions, having insufficient money, inadequate resources, no encouraging prospects, and no cheering hopes, we recommend that the Board of Trustees be instructed to suspend the operations of the College for one year. …" (See endnote for entire text of recommendations.)[292]

In June 1902, the Synod, in their usual manner, appointed a Special Committee on the Financial Condition of NC College to consider resolutions regarding payment of endowment subscriptions. "The Synod endorses the plan adopted by the Board of Trustees and earnestly advises that those who have given bonds to the endowment of the college, promptly pay the same when called upon to do so by the board." Reverend Vastine R. Stickley was appointed Chairman of this committee and George F. McAllister and William H. Fisher became advisory members.[293]

On June 25th, 1902, the Synod by resolution re-affirmed "its moral obligation to the endowment subscriptions from 1898" and "earnestly advised those who have given bonds to the endowment to promptly pay the same when called upon to do so by the Board." The resolution clarified that the Synod considered the notes given by the Students to the Treasurer of the College:

> "as binding except in those cases coming under and condition by the following excuses of Synod which says 'That any young man receiving aid from the Synod shall execute a bond to the treasurer to pay back in full to synod with interest the amount so severally received by him during the prosecution of his studies in the event he voluntarily abandons the active work of the ministry, is deposed or unites with another denomination before the expiration of seven years faithful services. Such seven years faithful service as a Lutheran minister to be considered canceling his bond.'"

The Synod appointed a Committee to collect the outstanding notes. The committee consisted of Rev. George H. Cox, Rev. Bachman S. Brown, and John A. Cline, assisted by Board of Trustees members, Jonas Cook, M. B. Stickley and John K. Patterson.[294]

The suspension of North Carolina College attracted surprisingly little journalistic attention. No articles appeared in newspapers lamenting the action. The *Concord Times* did state at the end of an article on the closing that "It will be a source of much regret to all our people that the College at Mt. Pleasant is to be closed even for the present."[295]

It is also interesting to note that there were no recorded statements from the Mt. Pleasant Town Board or other citizens about the fate of the College. Perhaps, they too, considered the situation temporary and their attention was elsewhere. The College campus would still be active with a new academy opened by George F. McAllister and local minister, Rev. Levi Busby, and Mont Amoena Female Seminary was still fully operational. Perhaps even more distracting was the fact that the Town was experiencing rapid population growth from the opening of two prosperous yarn mills.

North Carolina College never reopened. It would be twenty years before the North Carolina Lutheran Synod would again have a college under its auspices. The Synod would, however, maintain the "Board of

Trustees of North Carolina College" to oversee the opening and closing of two more schools on the old NC College campus.

THE CAROLINA ENGLISH & CLASSICAL SCHOOL (CECS)

Although the NC Synod suspended operation of NC College, it maintained ownership of the facility and the Board of Trustees remained in place. During the summer of 1902, George F. McAllister, a graduate and former teacher at NC College, and Rev. Levi E. Busby, the minister at Holy Trinity Lutheran Church in Mt. Pleasant, entered into a contract with the Synod to operate a private school on the campus of the College.[296]

The terms of the contract included rental of the buildings for $50 per year, to be applied to an insurance policy of $5,000, and the stipulation that rent money ($25.00 p/yr) currently being collected for the use of some of the College property, be applied to repairs of the buildings.[297]

In August 1903, an announcement appeared in the *Concord Times:*

> "Carolina English & Classical School, Mt. Pleasant, NC. An experienced Faculty and commodious, well equipped buildings. Rev. L. E. Busby, DD & Geo. F. McAllister, AB, Principals. The course of study is thorough. Methods of the best character and discipline firm. Rates of tuition and board very reasonable."[298]

According to the Board of Trustees' Treasurer's report, the school had income of $1,945.30 during its 1902 term and $938.43 during the 1903 term. Expenses were $1950.62 for 1902 and $938.43 for the 1903 term.[299]

McAllister and Busby were the only instructors at The Carolina English and Classical School and the school operated for only one year. Regrettably, Rev. Busby died suddenly from an appendicitis attack on March 5th, 1903, making it necessary for McAllister to make other arrangements for the coming year.

Shortly after Rev. Busby's death, as the English & Classical School opened and closed, the Lutheran Synod met for its centennial celebration at St. John's Lutheran Church in Salisbury, NC. The discussion was not, however, about keeping the school open. The Synod's concern was instead focused on reducing the NC College debt. The Joint Committee on the Financial Condition of the College was re-appointed and tasked to "determine and decide the status of all obligations in connection with notes given by students." Committee and Board of Trustees member, M. B. Stickley was asked to act as financial collector with instructions "to endeavor to collect all notes and accounts due the college, except those exempted by action of the Synod or Board of Trustees."[300]

The Committee filed a lengthy report stating that the Synod had made all its claims related to the College in February 1903. Records still contained a claim from a $700 loan made to the school in 1857 from the Synod's Scholarship Fund. Further claims were for a $150 loan made in 1871, and a loan of $300 made in 1874. Based on recall of the Theological Seminary Fund loan of $1,084 provided for building the Western Carolina Male Academy in 1853, the Synod made what they considered a rightful claim "reserving all rights of the Synod in the premises."[301]

Rev. R. C. Holland, President of the Synod, speaking on behalf of the Synod stated:

> "... in filing these claims, I call your attention to the fact that there is no record in the minutes of the Synod that anything has ever been paid upon any one of them, nor is there any hint of the Synod's relinquishment of any one, or any part thereof. While I have deemed it my duty to present this paper in view of the recent proceedings of the Synod and the board, it is due the Synod to say that circumstances may arise when the Synod, in her generosity, may relinquish the same in the interests of the college."[302]

The Committee's collector, M. B. Stickley, reported that he had sent statements to all parties indebted to the College, but had received only two responses. "One paid his account and the other promised to pay." Stickley presented a list of former students whose notes had previously been cancelled which totaled $804.89. Notes totaling $106.25 were outstanding but subject to cancellation if the student fulfilled his obligation to remain in the ministry for seven years. Stickley reported that notes totaling $507.01 from twenty former students were supposedly barred by the statute of limitations on collection, but he was instructed to continue to try to collect them. Further notes from ten students totaling $137.22 were still legally collectible and were in his hands as of the date of his report.[303]

The Committee also reported that it was their opinion that all the endowment bonds which were previously invalidated by the Civil War were valid claims and should be paid by the parties responsible. Jonas Cook reported that a test case to decide the legality of these bonds may be brought before the court at no very distant day.[304]

The final portion of the account listed the liabilities of the College as described by the treasurer, Jonas Cook. The total of $5,675.43 owed included accounts with Cook & Foil's store in Mt. Pleasant in the amount of $449.01; $1,000 to Julia A. Wheeler which had been secured by a mortgage on the property; $900 to Adolphus C. Barrier also secured by mortgage; back salaries and a note owed to the estate of former professor, H. T. J. Ludwig in the amount $648.83; back salaries to former professors Scherer, Setzer and McAllister in the amount of $315.59; $320.00 owed to Henkel & Co. for printing costs; a $660 deficit from Rev. Lutz's administration; $500 in interest on the above debts, and, finally, $925 owed to Jonas Cook, himself, for his services as treasurer.[305]

On May 25th, 1903, the Board of Trustees met and resolved to borrow funds to pay the college debts. They voted to offer notes on the college at $100 each to anyone who would take the same with the college property as security. The notes were to mature in five years with no interest. The Board further determined that the funds accrued from these notes would be used "for the purpose of holding the buildings and property of NC College for the use and benefit of the Evangelical Lutheran Church NC Synod." Once again the Board sought a new mortgage on the debt.[306]

THE MT. PLEASANT COLLEGIATE INSTITUTE (MPCI)

As the Synod and the Board of Trustees wrestled with the finances of the College, former Professor and recent co-principal of the English & Classical School, George F. McAllister searched for a way to continue the use of the facilities in Mt. Pleasant. During the summer of 1903, he spearheaded the establishment of a fourth and final incarnation of an educational institution on the site.

This time McAllister formed a partnership with Rev. Henry A. McCullough who was the new minister at Holy Trinity Lutheran Church in Mt. Pleasant. Together, the two men "entered into an arrangement" with the NC College Board of Trustees "whereby they were to conduct a school under such name as they might select and of such curriculum as they might determine upon and the Board approve." McCullough and McAllister were to manage the school in the buildings of the College and to have the use of the buildings and appurtenances, and also the income from any invested endowment for a period of five years, unless the Board received instructions from Synod to re-establish the college. They were to keep the buildings in repair and conduct a school approved by the Board.[307]

The resolution establishing the new school specified that:

> "The interest and other incomes now belonging to said college shall be used for the payment of a premium of insurance on the college buildings to the amount of six thousand dollars and other current expenses in keeping in repair the said buildings, and the remainder of any (income) shall be applied to the payment of the professors' salaries. ... be it further resolved that the Board of Trustees of North Carolina College shall not be bound in any way held responsible for any debts, obligations or salaries of the said professors so elected, excepted said professors shall be entitled to a surplus in income to said college that is not applied to that payment of premium on [the] insurance or current expenses."[308]

Another resolution recommended that the new school serve as the "church school for the NC Evangelical Lutheran Synod," and the Board appealed to the Synod for "moral support."[309]

The new school was christened "The Mt. Pleasant Collegiate Institute." During its first year several improvements were made to the campus. These included "fitting up" a reading room, renting a desirable athletic ground (from Jonas Cook), and adding 200 volumes to the library donated by Mrs. Lucy Silverly and Ms. Emily Silverly from the estate of the late Walter Silverly of Oil City, PA. Plans were also made to consolidate the three libraries of the former college into one large library. Steps were begun to recover the residence (the former President's house) and the south wing building (Phililaethian Hall) from serious water leaks.[310]

At the Board of Trustee's meeting in April 1904, it was reported that the real estate belonging to the School located in Rowan County (the Ritchie property) had been sold for $800. A committee was formed to determine how to provide a "Public Hall" for use as a Lecture Hall. Another committee was formed to seek a mortgage of $6,000 to pay the existing $5,311.39 Institute/College debts.[311]

At the end of MPCI's first year, Co-Principal McAllister informed the NC Synod that the year was a success. Income generated from tuition and room rent totaled $524.54 and interest from the NC College endowment had generated $130.69 in revenue. Expenses for canvassing, advertising, repairs, fuel and incidentals totaled $233.35. The Board of Trustees' Treasurer, Jonas Cook, reported operating income of $1,238.12 and expenses of $1,150.43 for the period from June 4th, 1903 through April 25th, 1904.[312]

In the Fall of 1904, Cook reported that the school had receipts of $1,598.37 of which $1,221.19 was from tuition. He further reported that the school buildings had been insured for a value of $5,384 and requested that the Board ask the NC Synod to pay the premium.[313]

At the Synod convention in May of 1904, the Committee on Church Institutions reported that the entire debt of North Carolina College had been funded and that "this should be a cause for great rejoicing." What the report did not say, however, was that the debt had been underwritten by taking another mortgage on the property that would be due in five years.[314]

In May 1905, Principal McAllister reported that new furniture had been purchased with funds from friends. All the classrooms were furnished with modern recitation seats and the preparatory department now had the latest automatic single desks. The interior of the main building was repaired throughout, dormitories renovated, and the halls, reading room, and recitation rooms murescoed. Other improvements included new roofs built by "friends of the community" and books donated by Mrs. Martha A. Dreher from her late husband's (Rev. Daniel I. Dreher) library. In addition to improvements made on the campus, McAllister reported that "a new auditorium built by Cook & Foil over their business will be used by MPCI and Mont Amoena for commencement and other public exercises. It is furnished with modern opera chairs and other needed equipment – seats 600. The two schools furnished the hall for a cost of $1,000."[315]

McAllister also described fund raising efforts to improve the two society halls that were already under way and that educational rallies were planned for St. Paul's, Rowan County; Troutman's, Iredell County; St. Martin's, Stanly County; and Union, Rowan County. McAllister concluded his report with a statement concerning the endowment which he indicated, "is quite limited and we recommend that Synod devise a plan by which an improvement fund can be created to keep buildings in good repair."[316]

At the 1905 Synod meeting, the Committee on Educational Work released a report stating that:

> "The educational work of the Lutheran Church in NC should be completely organized and coordinated. We need one or two colleges doing genuine college work, and a sufficient number of preparatory or fitting schools, which shall be embraced in our school system, so as to do their own work and also serve as feeders to the central college or colleges. Our educational work as now constituted consists of Lenoir College, which is owned and operated by the Tennessee Synod, The NC Collegiate Institute [sic] and Mont Amoena Seminary which are owned and controlled by the NC Synod, and also of Gaston College, a private enterprise recognized by the Tennessee Synod, and Elizabeth College, a private enterprise recognized by the United Synod. We recommend that for the present these schools make every effort to work together peaceably and harmoniously and that our people patronize these schools in preference to those outside of our territory."[317]

The Principal's report to the Board of Trustees and NC Synod in the Spring of 1906 contained little information except that additional classroom furniture had been obtained and a high grade piano, stage furniture and scenery had been placed in the auditorium above Cook & Foil's Store. A very brief financial statement listed receipts from the Institute totaling $1,723.34 ($1,602.04 from tuition, room rent, etc.) and expenses of $232.35. This statement apparently did not include the salaries of the instructors. There was no further accounting information regarding salaries or other expenses.[318]

In November 1906, the Board of Trustees appointed the Associate Principals and a member of the Board to draft and publish a report to the "people of the Lutheran Church" outlining the needs of the Institute. No copy of the report has been located.[319]

The Principals' Report to the Board of Trustees presented a financial statement that reflected a large profit for the year, but it appears that, again, the salaries of the instructors were not included. Receipts totaled $2,553.52 ($2,103.16 in tuition) and only $446.51 in expenses.[320]

Although the College debt was not mentioned in 1906, the Synod was again confronted with financial issues in May 1907 when the Board of Trustees advised that the five year term of the current mortgage would be up during the next year and that the "bondholders will demand settlement of their claims."[321]

The contract that McCullough and McAllister signed with the Synod in 1903 did not call for any of the "profits" that the Institute generated to be allocated to Synod or used to reduce the College debt. The Synod was, in effect, left "holding the bag."

At the recommendation of the Committee on Church Institutions, the Synod resolved to once again "form a committee to be instructed to provide for the debt of the College." The members of the Committee were Rev. Edward Fulenwider, Rev. Virgil Y. Boozer, Rev. Edward. L. Ritchie, Mr. Fred B. Efird, and Mr. John A. Cline. Three members of the Committee were NC College alumni.[322]

Shortly before the beginning of examinations in 1907, Co-Principal McCullough resigned his position, effective May 25th, 1907. Rev. McCullough was replaced by Rev. Jefferson P. Miller, who also succeeded him as Pastor at Holy Trinity Lutheran Church in Mt. Pleasant.[323]

In his report to the Board of Trustees in April, 1908, Principal McAllister stated that in MPCI's five year existence, 401 students had attended the school, twenty-two of whom had completed the course and twelve of these had gone on to enter college. Recalling the plan to consolidate the school's libraries, he suggested that "books could be classified, and proper oversight provided for the one library." He pointed out, however, that two of the current libraries were the property of the Philalaethian (Gerhardt) and Pi Sigma Phi (Ludwig) Literary Societies of NC College and that permission must be given to move the books.

McAllister addressed "the College debt," stating that "**We are concerned about foreclosure"**[emphasis added]. He reminded the Board that heretofore the Principals had solicited funds for repairs from several individuals but "We expect to be relieved by Synod of the necessity for repairs, insurance, and improvements if Synod desires the perpetuation of the work."

McAllister indicated that the cost of furnishing the new auditorium above Cook & Foil's Store remained an issue. The Institute and Mont Amonea had committed about $4,000, and $1,200 was not yet paid. According to McAllister, several pledges solicited by the Principals of the Institute and the Seminary (Mont Amoena) remained outstanding.[324]

The financial report for the year indicated that the school had receipts of $1,314.24 against disbursements of $1,247.04 (including salaries). The Board of Trustees requested that Synod pay the $200 insurance premium and reimburse the school for some minor repairs. The Board also requested that it be allowed to borrow funds from the endowment to pay other debts. The Synod agreed to pay the $200 but resolved to request that local congregations take up a special collection to defray the expenses.[325]

McAllister's final point was a plan to introduce a "military system" at the Institute.[326]

While Principal McAllister's report had mentioned mortgage and debt issues, he had been mostly upbeat about the status of the Institute. Synod President Rev. V. Y. Boozer presented a more discouraging picture. In his address to the opening of the 1908 Synod convention, he stated that while the Synod had hoped to see the debt of the College/Institute (mortgages held by A. C. and Hugh Barrier) retired during the preceding year, this had not happened, that a "crisis" had been reached, and "that the debt must be provided for at once." He went on to recommend that "consideration of this matter be made a special order."[327]

The President's report resulted, as usual, in referring the matter of College debt to a committee. The Committee on Literary Institutions promptly returned a recommendation that "the Synod borrow from the endowment as much as is necessary to satisfy the demands of those who threaten to foreclose their mortgages." The Synod agreed to pay off the debt.[328]

This last recommendation, however, set off a series of events that went far beyond the simple payment of a debt. In the summer of 1908, as Rev. Boozer began the process of borrowing the money from the endowment to pay the mortgages, he was informed that the treasurer of the endowment, Jonas Cook, had already "taken up the note" (paid off the mortgage) and was awaiting Synod's "official note" (authorization) to cover the expense. At this time it was "discovered" that somehow the College Board of Trustees was considered a "separate and independent corporation" and that the Synod had only advisory power with no legal claim to the property.[329]

Realizing that by borrowing the money from the endowment without legal claim to the property, the Synod would, in effect, be left "holding the bag" without collateral, Boozer did not follow through with the Synod's agreement to cover the note. He recommended, instead, that the Synod pass the final responsibility to the Special Committee on the Indebtedness of NC College. But the Synod decided that since the endowment treasurer (Jonas Cook) had already paid the note, they (the Synod) would "issue a note" (assume the debt) "to keep him [the Treasurer] safe from personal liability." The note (loan) was for the term September 6th, 1908 to May 1st, 1909 at six percent interest "at which time it is expected that some provision will be made for the full payment of the institution's indebtedness." In other words, responsibility for final payment would fall to the endowment.[330]

Following this episode of financial musical chairs, the officers of the Synod and the Committee on College Indebtedness requested that the Board of Trustees revise the school charter to "clearly define the institution's relation to the Synod and make the Synod secure in its property rights to the same."[331] Jonas Cook requested that the Trustees be more vested in the operation of the Synod and that a committee to liquidate the debt be formed. The Board appointed a committee to again formulate a plan to liquidate the debt and a second committee to revise the school charter so that it would "more directly define relations between the Synod and the Institute."[332]

On March 8th, 1909 a revised Charter of the Trustees of North Carolina College, Mount Pleasant, North Carolina, was adopted by the

NC State Legislature. The new Charter continued to refer to the Board of Trustees of North Carolina College, and it gave the Trustees:

> "the authority to maintain ... a school for the promotion of religion, morality and learning, and teaching the various branches of science, literature and art," and power of conferring all such degrees or marks of literary distinction as are usually conferred in colleges and universities."

The Charter also stated that the school was to remain in "Mt. Pleasant, Cabarrus County, NC," and that the Board of Trustees would maintain possession of "lands, tenements, money's, goods and chattels" which had been given to the College. They would also have the right to accept and receive all property given to the school and to collect "any bonds, notes, accounts and other evidences of indebtedness" due the former Board of Trustees. The Board retained the right to loan and invest all funds that they now had or any which they obtained in the future.

The Charter further made provision for the NC Lutheran Synod to "make such loans and donations ... as may be deemed advisable," and for the Board of Trustees "to make such conveyances to said synod to secure loans and donations as may be mutually agreed upon by the executive committees of the respective bodies." But the Synod retained "the right to indicate the policies that the board of trustees of said college may adopt in carrying out and furthering the purposes of its creation."

The revised Charter concluded with:

> "that should if at any time the object or purpose for which any funds, donations or gifts were acquired shall fall, the said corporation [Board of Trustees] is hereby authorized to transfer said property to the Evangelical Lutheran Synod and Ministerium of North Carolina ... to be invested and used by said synod in such manner as will carry out the intention of the grantor or donor, in so far as the circumstances and conditions will warrant."[333]
>
> [See Appendix 6 for entire Charter]

On April 22nd, 1909, the Board of Trustees met to organize under the newly adopted charter. Co-Principals McAllister and Miller reported that eight young men would complete the course of study in May, and five former Institute students would graduate from Newberry College and two from Roanoke College in June. Several former students would enter the Theological Seminary.

McAllister and Rev. Miller requested that the Board forward a statement to the Synod asking that body to "secure, if possible, the needed assistance for the Institute", or to have the Synod "take into [its] hands the matter of educational work. It appears from this statement that McAllister and Miller were asking that the Synod either subsidize the operating costs (now borne completely by the two men) or take over operation of the school. [See endnote for the entire request.]

The Board responded to the Principals' request by forming a committee "to lay before the Synod the situation respecting the work of the Collegiate Institute and to make recommendations to the Synod as deemed wise."[334]

The Synod responded, at least partially, by instructing the Board of Trustees "to finance the Institute [so that] the Synod be involved in no larger financial responsibility than may be assumed in the report of Literary Institutions."[335]

On April 28th, 1909, the NC Synod met at Faith Lutheran Church in Rowan County. The financial report of the Institute was presented showing $2,113.98 in receipts, of which $1,745.75 was tuition and fees. Current maintenance expenses totaled $559.70. The report stated that the school required an additional $75 to pay for supplies and necessary repairs.[336]

The Committee on Liquidation of the Debt of North Carolina College reported that it had been able to reduce the outstanding liabilities from $5,805 to $2,365, mostly by collecting unpaid pledges, tuition, and other fees. The Committee, "in the spirit of involvement," proposed that up to $1,000 be pledged as a supplement to the Institute with a request that the Principal give five scholarships to students who planned to go into the ministry. They also recommended that the Principals visit local churches and "foster the spirit of Christian education and a mature larger devotion to the School of the Synod."[337]

This arrangement was the same one that previous Synods had with NC College. In effect, the Synod provided some financial assistance to the Institute, but made sure that it got some return on its investment through the potential gain of five ministers. Hedging its bets, the Synod required each scholarship recipient to sign a contract promising that if they chose not to enter the ministry, they would pay back the money – to the Synod.

In May of 1909, Co-principal Rev. J. P. Miller resigned his position. The Board directed that G. F. McAllister be considered the sole Principal of the Institute. Should he accept the position, McAllister's salary would be $1,000 and would include the use of the President's house if needed. As part of his new duties, he was to begin canvassing for funds to support the Institute (as recommended by the Synod). McAllister accepted the position.[338]

Three weeks after the 1909 Commencement ceremonies, disaster literally struck the Institute. During the night of June 12th, 1909, the Pi Sigma Phi Hall was hit by lightning and completely destroyed. The building housed the Ludwig Literary Society debating room, a library and the school's scientific classrooms and equipment. The Vice Chairman of the Board of Trustees, Rev. Jacob E. Schenk, sent the following correspondence to the other members of the Board, requesting that they meet in emergency session to discuss the situation.

> "On last Saturday night the North Wing Building of the Collegiate Institute was destroyed by fire, having been stuck by lightning. Therefore, the Board of Trustees is called to meet in extraordinary session in Mt. Pleasant on next Thursday, June 17th at 10:30 o'clock. Owing to the vital importance of the meeting, it is earnestly hoped that no member will allow anything not providential to prevent him from attending."[339]

The Trustees met on the 17th and McAllister reported that insurance on the burned building and contents amounted to only $550, and that some plan must be made to replace the lost space and equipment as soon as possible. The Trustees immediately passed a resolution to ask for public help to erect a new boarding hall with a kitchen, dining hall and basement. They appointed McAllister and Board members Rev. Schenk and Rev. Boozer to begin a canvass for funds. The Board specified that the brick from the burned building would be used in the new construction.[340]

Colonel McAllister did not depend entirely on the Trustees or the NC

Synod. Within three days of the fire, McAllister drafted letters to possible donors he felt might be able to aid in funding a replacement building.

In a letter to General Julian S. Carr of Durham, NC, McAllister relatd the finances of the Institute and the circumstances of the Ludwig Hall fire. He appealed to General Carr stating that:

> "We write to you with the utmost confidence knowing something of the generosity and philanthropy which you have customarily displayed. There are on the Board of Trustees, Gen. Carr, a half dozen of your old comrades in arms. They are sorely stricken by this dispensation and would be greatly rejoiced by ~~any~~ assistance rendered to the Institution in whose welfare they are so deeply concerned. I want to appeal to you to come to the rescue of this worthy cause. And I shall esteem it a very great favor if you will be so kind as to designate persons to whom I might successfully appeal in the same behalf. Begging to assure you that what you may do for this cause will be well invested and deeply appreciated. I am sincerely yours. G. F. McAllister."[341]

By June 28th, McAllister had also written a letter to John Alfred Morehead, President of Roanoke College, seeking letters of introduction to "philanthropists to help him raise funds to rebuild the burned building." Morehead declined to provide the requested letters saying that men such as Andrew Carnegie did not care for introductions, but wanted to know specifics such as past record, present outlook and future plans. "If you can prove to them that your cause is worthy and promising by the facts and the evidence in the case, they will help you. They go at this work of philanthropy in a very businesslike fashion. Be careful not to overstate."[342]

Morehead gave McAllister the addresses of Carnegie and Dr. David K. Pearsons, stating that "In your place, I should write these gentlemen a straightforward letter, without letters from anybody, explaining your loss by fire and the crisis upon you and asking for an appointment to call in person."[343]

Colonel McAllister drafted letters to Carnegie and others, but was apparently unsure about posting them. He requested the advice of another College President, James A. B. Scherer, at Throop Polytechnic Institute in Pasadena, California. Scherer was known as a very capable fundraiser. He replied to McAllister that it was his opinion that McAllister's best course was to go on with the development of a high-grade secondary school. Scherer indicated that Carnegie, Pearsons and Rockefeller "were all vigorously opposed to the erection of new colleges and will lend their enormous influence in opposition."[344] President Scherer gave McAllister an address for Carnegie in Scotland and advised that an appeal of $10,000 to relieve your immediate need might be effective if addressed to Andrew Carnegie, Esq. LLD, Skibo Castle, Donrock, Sutherland, Scotland."[345] McAllister eventually sent a letter to Andrew Carnegie, but no funds were received.

McAllister took a different approach in writing to Richard W. Sears of Chicago, IL. He offered Mr. Sears an honorary Director's position and Sears replied in a letter dated Nov. 9, 1909.

> "I have yours of the 3rd, which I have read with care. I believe I can say I can in some degree appreciate the position you are in, and would be glad to in some degree commit myself, but for the reasons I have endeavored to make plain in my former letter, I regret to repeat I must, for the time at least, in justice to myself, hold myself free from any commitment."

Sears took the opportunity to make a sales pitch for his new practice of "mail order" purchasing of houses and building plans "which may be of use to the Institute," and that he would give future consideration to providing assistance to the school. In a letter dated Nov. 30, 1909, McAllister replied that he appreciated very much Mr. Sears' information and requested that he [Sears] possibly send something immediately.[346]

Not limiting himself to individuals or men, McAllister solicited assistance from the United Daughters of the Confederacy. In a letter dated July 3, 1909, Gordon M. Finger, Corresponding Secretary of the UDC, replied:

> "...earlier efforts of our order were directed chiefly toward all kinds of betterment for the Confederate Soldier and preservation of our sectional History; but as the ranks of the soldiers became thinner and thinner and our membership more numerous, we find ourselves

> able to broaden our scope of usefulness, and are now entering on an educational campaign on behalf of worth descendants of Confederate men and women. Most of our larger chapters have a yearly scholarship in a local college or seminary that is awarded to some resident. … By our manner of award, we expect to make it a distinction and an honor to hold one of these scholarships which will redound to the good fame of the institution giving it …"

Incredulously, Mr. Finger ended his letter by soliciting a scholarship for his organization's own purposes.

> "We want to know if your institution cannot put such a scholarship at our disposal. Do you not know some friend of your institution who would be glad to establish a Confederate Scholarship? We shall be glad to hear from you on the subject, as we hope to have beneficiaries enjoy the advantages next session."[347]

In addition to seeking assistance to replace the destroyed building, Colonel McAllister prepared for the upcoming academic session. On June 22, 1909, he drafted a letter to be sent to prospective students and their parents. The letter was notably "upbeat" and presented a wholly satisfactory situation at the Institute. Reality was quite different. McAllister greatly downplayed the effects of the loss of the Pi Sigma Phi (Ludwig) Hall and gave a rather enhanced description of the new Dining Hall. According to McAllister's later report to the NC Synod, a building two stories high, with a dining room, kitchen, pantry, cloak room and basement was planned. Only the dining room and kitchen were completed (in 1911). McAllister also failed to inform the students that he was now the sole Principal of the Collegiate Institute, as Reverend Miller had resigned his position and would instead teach English Bible for one hour per week.[348]

As the 1909-1910 academic year closed, the Institute seemed to have adapted to the loss of one of its major buildings, but, the issue of general finances continued to plague the school. On May 4th, 1910, just two weeks before the end of the 1909-'10 school year, the NC Lutheran Synod met for its annual assembly at 1st Church in Albemarle, NC. At this meeting, Synod President, Reverend Virgil Y. Boozer, in his opening speech, fired the opening salvo of a debate that would ultimately decide the fate of Mt. Pleasant Collegiate Institute.

Reverend Boozer stated that:

> "The little our Synod is doing for the education of her young people is much to her discredit. … Our own people need to be aroused.
>
> A year ago, the Synod, seeing that the future of the Collegiate Institute was problematic, endeavored to quicken interest in the institution, and with a little show of enthusiasm made an appropriation of $1,000 to aid in its support for this session. I regret to have to report to you that that money has not been raised, and so you must during this convention, provide for the payment of this obligation. In my judgment it would be unwise to make a new appropriation with this one unpaid and yet the school cannot do the work expected without financial aid from some source. What is to be done? Must the institution be closed? Everyone will answer, NO! Situated as our synod is, she cannot afford not to have her own institution for the training of her young men. And this institution should be one that will command the confidence of all our people and enlist their sympathy and support. It should have an endowment of money, but that which is of more importance is the endowment of the love and loyalty of its constituency.
>
> This is not to be construed as in any sense a reflection on the institution at Mt. Pleasant, for it has always been noted for the high standard of its work, and now ranks among the best of its class in the State. But for some reason this institution has not prospered, has never enjoyed the loyal support of all our people, and therefore, has accomplished only in part the work for which it was established. All efforts to rally the people around it has failed. In view of all these things, **I believe the time has come for the Synod to seriously consider its removal to some place where it can better accomplish the work**

> **for our young men that is so much needed. Indeed, it is imperative. I therefore recommend that action be taken looking to this end**." [emphasis added][349]

On May 7th, 1910, an article appeared in the *Concord Daily Tribune* with the headline:

> "Collegiate Institute To be Moved." [The Institute] "will probably be consolidated with Lenoir College at Hickory. … the North Carolina Lutheran Synod adopted a resolution, after a heated discussion lasting nearly all day, providing for the consolidation of the Collegiate Institute at Mt. Pleasant with Lenoir College in Hickory.
>
> "A committee which had been appointed to consider that matter … to negotiate with the Tennessee Synod as to the consolidation of the Mt. Pleasant Institute with Lenoir College. The resolution provided that if after sixty days the committee should fail to come to satisfactory terms with the Tennessee Synod … they were to give all cities and towns in within the jurisdiction of the NC Synod a chance to make offers and that the place making the best bid … would get the new college. … It provided, however, for the running of another term at Mount Pleasant, but the adoption meant a removal from Mt. Pleasant."[350]

According to the article, after the report was read Mr. James P. Cook of Concord "made a touching plea for Mt. Pleasant," and stated that he objected to the consolidation with Lenoir College. He stated that Mt. Pleasant:

> "was as good a site as was necessary, citing the State University and other institutions in the woods, [and] that it was not necessary for an educational institution to be in a large place. … He closed by stating that if the college must be moved, in the name of God and in the name of justice, do not throw off on Mt. Pleasant."[351]

Following Cook's remarks, Rev. William A. Lutz of the Tennessee Synod, and, ironically, the last President of North Carolina College, differed with Cook regarding the status of Lenoir College, "causing quite a heated discussion."[352]

In late May 1910, "the commission of the NC Lutheran Synod, officers of the Tennessee Synod, and a committee of Board of Trustees of Lenoir College" submitted a resolution to the full Board of Trustees of Lenoir College. This resolution, which was unanimously adopted, called for a "consolidated college conducted on the fundamental principles and constitution of Lenoir College." It also recommended an agreement between the NC and Tennessee Synods whereby the NC Synod would get one-half interest of the Lenoir College property (valued at $100,000) after assuming half of the current indebtedness of school ($12,000), and the Tennessee Synod would get "one-half interest and control" of the "property of the NC Synod in Mt. Pleasant (valued at $30,000 to $40,000), "free of indebtedness and the further moral and financial support of the NC Synod in the consolidated College."[353]

On May 26th, 1910, the following article appeared in *The Charlotte Observer:*

> "The Consolidation of Lenoir & Mt. Pleasant Seems Certainty – Quite confidence on all sides around Hickory that two well-known Lutheran Educational Institutions will be combined – advocates elated over the outlook. Hickory May 25 – There appears to be a quiet confidence on all sides that a proposed consolidation of Lenoir College and the Mt. Pleasant educational interests will be eventually accomplished. Lutherans are people very tenacious in their opinions and convictions and slow to yield. There is a vigorous and wise leadership on both sides, however, which sees the need of co-operation. The fact that the Tennessee Synod has come so near accepting the original proposition of the North Carolina Synod seems to indicate that it is as anxious as the latter to get together. With Roanoke College in Virginia and Newberry in South Carolina there is a useless duplication of money, properties, teaching force, etc. in maintaining two sets of higher educational interests. With Lenoir for the higher college and Mt. Pleasant as a thoroughly equipped high school, the former might do away with its preparatory department and both institutions thrive."[354]

Amid the debate on the fate of the Collegiate Institute, the College Treasurer reported on May 17th, 1910, that the school had receipts for collected funds totaling $2,282.90, which included $2,185.32 from tuition, room rent and fees. There remained about $500 still due on tuition and fees. Disbursements for the year totaled $2,206.12, including $1,378.02 for salaries. The school was obligated for an additional $725 in salaries for the year, not including the Principal's salary.[355]

Principal McAllister pointed out that the expenses of the school were increasing, and that the Synod needed to continue its "maximum pledge." He also mentioned that the President of the Synod (Rev. Boozer) was opposed to raising the apportionment requested from congregations to help with this funding. McAllister reiterated the need for new equipment, a new building, more dormitory space and a larger endowment, stating that due to lack of space, "students were scattered over the town." Finally, McAllister requested that the Board continue the school and attempt to find a solution for financing a supplement to his salary for his duties canvassing for funds.[356]

On November 9th, 1910, the Committee appointed by the Synod to consider the consolidation of NC College and Lenoir College met in Salisbury, NC. The meeting lasted two days and, according to an article in the *Concord Daily Tribune*, "failed ... to meet the unanimous approval of the leaders and it was decided to maintain a joint support and hearty cooperation with the college at Mt. Pleasant and also the one at Hickory."[357]

On November 17th, Committee member Bascom L. Umberger wrote a letter to the Editor of the *Tribune* clarifying the outcome of the meeting. Mr. Umberger stated that "what transpired at our joint meeting ... isn't ready for publication, however, I can say ... that we will have ready to present to the two synods a proposal that will satisfy the most over-zealous member of either of the two bodies."

The proposal called for the Collegiate Institute:

> "to be maintained at its present location with its present curriculum maintained, Mont Amoena Seminary is likewise to be maintained. The consolidated education properties of the two synods shall be controlled by one joint board to be of equal numbers from each synod. Each synod [would] pool its own property free of debt or

> assume same and enter the joint board with no claims or isms. All … objections are eliminated, and it doesn't seem possible for the most prejudiced or over-zealous to object. It does mean, however, the elimination of great waste, better facilities in Lutheran education in NC and smooth sailing for those anxious to help in advancing same."[358]

On April 17, 1911, *The Concord Times,* reprinted an article that appeared earlier in the *Charlotte Observer*:

> "We are now informed on the best possible authority that no such merger (NC College & Lenoir College) has, in fact, been contemplated. The institute … will continue its existence irrespective of the project. It was expressly excepted by the North Carolina Synod in proposing negotiations, and the plan of consolidation … provides that Mt. Pleasant Collegiate Institute will be maintained by the North Carolina Synod as a synodical school."[359]

Thus, by the Spring of 1911, the immediate survival of the Collegiate Institute in Mt. Pleasant appeared secure. But the final resolution of North Carolina's Lutheran educational institutions was far from over. Over the next two decades MPCI would play a major role in the effort of the two North Carolina Lutheran Synods to reach an agreement on issues that kept them apart for almost a century. They would eventually merge and compromise. The new compromise would change the educational landscape of their denomination for years to come.

In the end, old loyalties were tested and new loyalties formed. Promises were made and promises were broken. One school would survive, the other would not.

For Colonel McAllister, however, the future was now. During the 1910-1911 school year, McAllister wrestled with problems relating to the status of MPCI students attempting to enter a college or university. Because the school was not an accredited Junior College, the class standing of a student going on to college depended not only upon the courses he had completed and his grades, but also on an appraisal by the Professors of the college he hoped to attend. Sometime the class standing even depended upon the performance of a former MPCI student at the college. Two cases illustrated this situation.

A letter from Dr. Henry L. Smith, President of Davidson College in reference to MPCI student, Mr. Crane, informed Colonel McAllister that:

> "The question of advanced entrance at Davidson is left ultimately to the judgment of each Professor who is at the head of his Department. If your students have entered [as a] full Junior at Roanoke and Newberry, I think it not probably that they could do so at Davidson. It might be that taking one extra ticket [class] in the Junior year, and one extra in the Senior, a student could graduate in two years, here, without over work."[360]

Dr. Frank P. Venable, President of the University at Chapel Hill, replying to a request concerning the admission of MPCI graduate and current Instructor, Calvin V. B. Williams, stated that : "We shall be very glad to have Mr. Williams enter the University. He will have no tuition to pay as he is a minister's son. His credits will admit him without examination to the sophomore class." Venable also commented on the status of MPCI alumni Fred W. Morrison, stating that "we are very much pleased with his work. He has taken an excellent stand in his class and is a credit in every respect to Mt. Pleasant Institute. We shall always be glad to have you send us such men."[361]

Few other records of the 1910-'11 school year have been located but the financial statement from May 10th, 1911 listed $2,927.10 collected in receipts, including $2,677.46 from tuition and fees. Salary expenses to date were listed as $1,767.50 with $685.88 outstanding. The Board of Trustees stated in its report to the Synod that creditors were asking to be paid and that they were seeking a loan to pay existing debts. Colonel McAllister was authorized to spend $500 to make necessary "emergency" repairs on the campus.[362]

To raise the $500 authorized to McAllister, Board of Trustee's Chairman, Reverend J.E. Shenk, penned a letter to be sent to Lutheran congregations.

> "Dear Brethren,
>
> 'Please see minutes of Synod 1911, p. 60, 'Report of Committee on Church Institutions.' You will find recommended and adopted the appropriation of $500 for necessary and urgent repairs on the buildings of the

Collegiate Institute, and the appointment of a Committee of Ways and Means to secure the same.

1. In pursuance of duty, the Committee desires to call your prayerful attention to the following facts:

2. The repairs were urgent and upon assurance of the Committee, the Principal went forward with them during vacation and is now carrying the bill which soon must be met. For the first time in several years the main building (dormitory) is attractive to students and commendable to patrons.

3. These improvements were made upon a property of the Church easily worth $30,000 at a low valuation and with a prospect of a largely increased value. Common business foresight would dictate that such a property ought not to deteriorate by neglect of repairs.

4. The Institute is doing a commendable work. The discipline is wholesome. Her graduates command scholarships at our best Lutheran Institutions. Other graduates and ex-students are successful teachers and businessmen.

Best of all from the standpoint of the Church, is the large number of men turned into her ministry – fifteen since organization, part of whom are now in preparation. As a matter of history, North Carolina College furnishes five out of every eleven of her graduates for the ministry. Compare the Institute in this respect with other better equipped schools. Does this not appeal to you, Christian men, as fulfilling her mission to the Church in this line?

Your congregation is asked for $5.00 … for this worthy cause. Please send to Synodical Treasurer marked 'College Repair Fund.' How early will you respond?

Yours fraternally, J. E. Shenk, Chairman"[363]

MPCI entered the 1911-'12 academic year still in debt and seeking help to raise the funds necessary to continue operation.

On November 30th, 1911, another calamity impacting the institute, struck the village of Mt. Pleasant. While the students of the Mont Amoena Female Seminary were performing a play at the Town Auditorium, their school building caught fire and was destroyed. Immediately after the fire, the citizens of Mt. Pleasant vowed to rebuild the school and began a fund drive to that effect. Within two years, $30,000 had been raised and a new Seminary constructed.[364]

Col. McAllister strongly supported the rebuilding of Mont Amoena and actively helped to raise funds for the cause. It must have been extremely distressing to see how quickly the citizens of Mt. Pleasant and Lutherans statewide responded to the call to fund the restoration of the Seminary, while he and MPCI struggled to get support to replace a much smaller and less expensive debating hall and to meet continued financial problems.

One month before commencement exercises, on April 21st, 1912, the Institute and the community were saddened by the death of one of their most prominent leaders, Capt. Jonas Cook. Cook was a former student at NC College and was appointed Bursar of the newly reopened College in 1867. He was appointed to the College Board of Trustees in 1874 and served almost continuously as the Board Treasurer until his death in 1912.[365]

Following Cook's death, Colonel McAllister met with the heirs of his estate to "discuss the further securing of the grounds which had been leased for years," and were used by the Institute as athletic and drilling fields.

McAllister reported on work completed on the "new" boarding hall across College Street which was used as the dining hall. The hallways were wainscoted, plaster repaired and whitewashed. A new stove was added. A two- story porch was constructed in front of the Hall and a single story on the North side. The dining hall portion of the building was painted, and the basement walled with brick. New furniture, including bedsteads for eighteen rooms had been purchased. The $700 in repairs and renovations were paid for mainly with a $500 appropriation from Synod and $50 "donated by a good lady and friend of the Institute."[366]

The financial report for the year listed $2,967.48 in receipts ($2,940.23 from tuition and fees) and $2,317.33 in disbursements, including $1,809.38 in salaries to date. There remained an outstanding debt of $1,500 which the Treasurer recommended against paying from the endowment. Instead, the Board of Trustees voted to borrow $600 from the endowment to pay for repairs and the remainder to be borrowed from "the endowment amount collected from Mont Amoena."[367]

The Institute maintained operations but the debate over its status continued. In January 1912, the Joint Committee on Consolidation met again, this time in Charlotte. Of the fifteen-person committee, only Rev. James Henry C. Fisher, present Principal of Mont Amoena Seminary and a former teacher at NC College, was from Mt. Pleasant. The task of the Committee was to render a report to the special convention of the North Carolina Synod that was to convene on January 16th in China Grove.[368]

Ironically, this same special Synod convention was to consider the fate of Mont Amoena Seminary that had been destroyed by fire in November 1911. Based upon existing newspaper accounts, the Mont Amoena discussion became the focus of the special convention and the issue of the consolidation of NC College and Lenoir College faded into the background. The Mont Amoena debate centered around whether to rebuild the school in Mt. Pleasant or to locate to another town. This question dominated the Lutheran community in North Carolina for much of the first half of 1912.[369]

During the academic year 1912-'13, Colonel McAllister continued to solicit help in funding a replacement for the building destroyed in 1909. He wrote the following letter to the Chicago Board of Trade in January 1913.

> "My attention has been directed to the fact that your Board has provided a fund to be used to encourage the teaching of domestic science and scientific farming in the schools of the South. The institute has a course of Agriculture in its curriculum and has some land for use in experimental work. Unfortunately, however, our Laboratory was destroyed a few years ago by fire. I am exceedingly anxious to re-equip this department of our school, as the importance of industrial and vocational education is coming to be more and more recognized. I am a member of the County Board of Education. As such and as the Principal of this school, I should like to receive information from your Board as to the conditions upon

which you lend assistance to schools for the departments mentioned above. … ."[370]

McAllister reported that during the year a second story was added to the Boarding Hall for use as living quarters for the matron and her family. The Library was renovated, the exterior woodwork of Society Hall painted, and repairs completed on the President's residence. Repairs were still needed to several buildings and the Institute was continuously handicapped by the limitation of equipment. There was a need for a new science facility and for an agent to canvas for funds.[371]

The financial report to the Board listed receipts of $3,017.80 ($2,998.82 from tuition and fees) and disbursements of $2911.50, including $2,111.50 in salaries to date. $115 was donated during the year by "several select friends of the Institute."[372]

The Board of Trustees evaluated a report on the endowment fund. Income from invested funds amounted to $310.70, but disbursement of invested income totaled $393.40 and the shortfall was borrowed from the endowment. It was also stated that the endowment had collected $2,663.61 but that $2,580.91 of those funds had been disbursed or borrowed. Additionally, $1,150 of the endowment had been invested, but $3,165.04 was in "non-productive" funds.[373]

In April of 1914, Colonel McAllister reported to the Board of Trustees that a new well had been dug on the campus near the Boarding house. The buildings were in "fair" condition, but an additional building was still needed. The financial report stated that income for the year was $2,712.69 ($2,563.30 from tuition and fees) and expenses totaled $2082.86, including $1,313.15 in salaries to date. There was a surplus on hand of $629.83. In addition, the "Laboratory Fund" had collected $197.50.[374]

For several years prior to 1914, McAllister had attempted to obtain Junior College status for the Institute. While most "graduates" of MPCI who chose to continue to College were able to enter with some "advanced standing," the process was based more on the individual student than on the status of the Institute.

In 1914, Colonel McAllister began an effort to advertise the Institute's advantages by soliciting testimonial letters from various College Presidents, some of which he planned to print in the Institute catalogues. He received and printed letters from William J. Martin, Davidson College; William

L. Poteat, Wake Forest College; Edward K. Graham, UNC-Chapel Hill; John Alfred Morehead, Roanoke College; William P. Few, Trinity College, and N. W. Walker, State Inspector of NC High Schools.[375]

The letters ranged from a glowing recommendation to at least one outright rejection. President Graham of UNC-CH wrote:

> "I remember with a great deal of pleasure my visit to your school. Everything that I saw impressed me with the earnest purpose and the ability of the directors of the school to conduct it in a high-grade fashion. Some of the best men that we have ever had at the University have had their preparatory training at Mount Pleasant."[376]

President Poteat of Wake Forest College wrote a somewhat less positive letter.

> "I take pleasure in saying that I was most favorably impressed in my brief visit to the Mt. Pleasant Collegiate Institute ... [however] I do not feel justified in making a more detailed statement because of my limited opportunity to observe."[377]

One reply from Charles B. King, President of Elizabeth College in Charlotte, was not published.

> "Your letter of the 6th received. I wish that I could conscientiously give you the kind of testimonial that you desire, but I don't feel that I can do so. I do not approve of your methods of government and discipline; neither can I recommend your boarding department. However, I do not desire to hinder the progress and usefulness of your school. The best course for me is to be silent. My opinions would simply be individual and would not count for much one way or the other."[378]

In May of 1914, the Board of Trustees passed a resolution forming a "Ways & Means Committee" that would be "authorized to prepare a resolution asking Synod's endorsement of a proposal to liquidate all debts of NC College by using the endowment fund." The Board also reported the receipt of funds from the Mt. Pleasant Civil League for use in making improvements and repairs to the campus. Finally, the Board formed a committee to secure estimates on the erection of fire escapes on the campus buildings.[379]

The 1914-'15 school year began with a twenty-five percent decrease in enrollment from the previous year. For the first time in five years, the Institute's enrollment fell below 100 students. Principal McAllister attributed the decrease to the rapid decline in cotton prices (the value of cotton in North Carolina in 1914 fell twenty-five percent from its 1913 level). Due to the drop in enrollment, the Institute faculty was reduced to four instructors.[380]

On Oct. 11th, 1914, the Institute and the community of Mt. Pleasant suffered the passing of one their most distinguished citizens, Harvey C. McAllister. McAllister was the father of MPCI Principal G. F. McAllister, and, as previously noted, played a major role in creating, supporting, and maintaining NC College and MPCI.

At a Board of Trustees meeting shortly after the death of his father, Colonel McAllister declared to the Board of Trustees that "while the outlook for a good year's work is exceedingly hopeful, the prospect of meeting the financial obligations is of a difficult nature." McAllister reported that the Institute received a $12 dividend from its investment in cotton mill stock and that the estimated cost of fire escapes was $90. He also reported that a new pump was needed for the Boarding Hall at an estimated cost of $50 and that the cost of campaigning for new students during the summer (which was his duty) had increased.[381]

At this same meeting, an apparently very frustrated Board of Trustees discussed sending a resolution to the Synod requesting that they (the Synod) either 1) rescind their action of 1902-1903 "temporarily" closing NC College, 2) make the action permanent and "authorize a school similar to MPCI, or 3) make the action permanent, rescind the charter, releasing the Board and disposing of the property.

In qualifying their request, the Board proposed asking that if the Synod chose option #2, that they allow the Board to "borrow from the endowment and further authorize raising of a sufficient amount to provide an adequate equipping of the Institute ..."[382]

After a prolonged discussion, the Board decided against submitting the above resolution and voted instead to "recommend only a forward movement of MPCI, as it is now operated, specifically a definite amount to be raised for more adequate equipment."[383]

Records indicate that during early 1915, Colonel McAllister investigated seeking "Normal School" status for the Institute. As a Normal School, the Institute would be certified to train teachers for the public-school system. In January and February, he wrote several letters to College administrators requesting advice on the necessary steps would be to establish such a school.

Robert Wright, President of East Carolina Training School in Greenville, NC, replied to Colonel McAllister.

> "I consider the more essential subjects to be taught in this normal course, I will say that depends entirely upon who is to do the teaching. There should be something in methods and something in Psychology. I do not believe a person can make a really good teacher without some knowledge of child psychology, following some textbook like Kirpatrick's Fundamentals of Child Study. There, of course, should be work done in lesson plans, in method of the recitation and in Primary Methods. The class of your work, however, is going to depend entirely upon the type of teacher you secure for this work. You ought to have specialists."[384]

N. W. Walker, State Inspector of NC High Schools, to whom McAllister had written in 1914 for a testimonial, replied to several questions. On the number of hours per week which should be devoted to subjects "directly bearing" on preparation for teaching, Walker replied that, "I should think from 3 to 5 periods per week should be given to this in the junior and senior years, covering text book and observation … ."

Regarding a question about what subjects are most essential, Walker said, "I should select some of the easier texts for class use on theory and practice of teaching or elementary education … I should base a good deal of my work on the bulletins containing courses of study mailed out by the State Dept. of Education. In short I should make the entire course as simple and as concretely practical as it could possibly be made."

McAllister also asked what should be required as prerequisite for a Normal certificate or diploma, and could an arrangement be effected whereby such certificate or diploma might be of practicable value to the holder with the State Board of Education." Professor Walker replied that a prerequisite for this teacher training work would require a regular high school course up to the point at which the teacher training courses begin."[385]

McAllister also wrote to Denison F. Giles, Chairman of the NC State Senate Committee on Education, concerning the State's position on establishing district normal schools. Giles replied that while he was very sure that sooner or later a plan of establishing "district normal schools" would come to pass, such a plan would not be adopted by the General Assembly in the current session. He closed by stating that "I am sure that your Institution would not only be a good location but would make a great plant of a State institution of this sort."[386]

There was no further correspondence in McAllister's papers. It appears that the reply from Senator Giles demonstrated to Colonel McAllister that his idea of establishing a Normal School at the Institute was a subject for the future and was not something that could or should be pursued at the present time.

On April 25th, 1915, Principal McAllister delivered his year-end report to the Board of Trustees, noting that:

> "… it has been a hard year financially. With full collections, the income of the institute will scarcely meet the current expenses, not counting a salary for the principal. It is true this is an abnormal year, but the margin is so slight in normal years that it does not enable the management to meet the exigencies of this year. It is apparent, therefore, that there is a limit to the time I could maintain the solvency of the institute under existing conditions. Cost of maintenance increases. To secure and retain competent teachers, better salaries must be paid. It is impossible to raise salaries without more income."[387]

The financial report for the preceding year listed $2,086.77 in receipts including $1,937.37 from Tuition and Fees and disbursements of $2096.77, of which $1,330.60 was salary to date.[388]

At the April 25th meeting, the Board discussed a final version of the resolution it had debated six months earlier. In a much revised and complex statement, the Board, in effect, requested that the Synod allow it (the Board) to borrow the remainder of the endowment to "provide adequate equipment for the perpetuation of the institution," and at the same time conduct a campaign to raise $40,000. The Board further proposed that one-fifth of the money raised be used to repay the endowment for funds previously borrowed. Should an amount in excess of $5,000 be collected, those funds would be used "in placing a new dormitory on the campus, in remodeling the present buildings, and in making such other necessary improvements so as to provide a modern and comfortable plant."[389]

On May 25th, 1915, the Board of Trustees reported that the Synod had authorized the Board to "devise ways and means to raise the $40,000 previously mentioned" and to simultaneously borrow the remainder of the endowment to run the school for the next year.[390]

During the summer of 1915, a Board committee engaged architect Mr. Henry E. Bonitz from Wilmington to submit plans for a new and remodeled administration building. On July 15th, 1915 the Board accepted the committee's recommendations and began discussion of the renovation.[391]

Continuing efforts to raise funds for the Institute, in January 1916, Colonel McAllister used a unique approach to solicit assistance from Henry Ford. McAllister wrote to Ford requesting that he [Ford] send MPCI pamphlets on the "subject of the cigarette," which Ford had recently published under the title, "The Case Against the Little White Slaver." Included in this letter was a "folder" concerning benevolence to the Institute. The letter was filled with flattery of Ford and his efforts concerning the dangers of cigarettes before requesting that Ford read the enclosed folder and "help our cause." (See endnote for the entire letter.)[392]

McAllister received a reply from Ford's Assistant Secretary, Mr. George S. Anderson stating, "Your letter of recent date addressed to Mr. Ford has been handed the writer for reply. The numerous requests received like that contained in your letter makes it impossible for Mr. Ford to grant the same."[393]

In April 1916, Colonel McAllister delivered his annual report to the Board of Trustees informing them that since 1903, 1,200 students had attended MPCI and sixty-nine had graduated (5.7%). Forty-eight of the graduates had completed the college course and entered a College. Fifteen students had entered the ministry or were in preparation to do so. Without any supporting statistics, McAllister stated that: "It is doubtful whether another secondary school in the state can show as large a percentage of its graduates who have graduated from College or as large a number of young men, in proportion to students enrolled, who have entered the ministry."

McAllister described some achievements by MPCI students. A recent graduate served as the presiding officer in a recent intercollegiate debate between two "leading Colleges in a neighboring state." A 1915 graduate was one of the debaters on the winning team and "in fact, was credited by the press report as the winner of the debate."[394]

He informed the Board that the state highway association was proposing a highway to run between Charlotte and Raleigh, via Concord, Mt. Pleasant and Albemarle. "Such a road would put MP 'on the map' in such effectual manner than it has ever been before. This, in my judgment, would inure to the benefit of the schools located here. In fact, it should and perhaps would silence the objections sometimes urged to being off the Railroad."

McAllister also described (without naming) "a wonderful development approaching completion in this section, but a little more than 20 miles from here, which is destined, in all probability to have a far reaching effect on the commerce, industry, transportation and prosperity of Piedmont Carolina." McAllister stated that the project was being completed by Southern Power Company (SPC). The closest SPC project near Mt. Pleasant in 1915-1916 was the hydroelectric plant at Lookout Shoals on the Catawba River.

Following his "updates", McAllister expressed despair over conditions at the Institute. He stated that the work of the Institute had been done "at the least maintenance cost of any Church School in the state," and "it has been done at a sacrifice. ... Better equipment would make possible a larger school and an increase in revenue." He concluded by stating:

> "Present conditions are hard. One man cannot stem this tide. With cooperative faith and burden-bearing it will be possible to surmount present difficulties and bring about a realization of a brighter future. If the cause of Christian Education is to be promoted on the foundations laid by our fathers, there is a challenge, gentlemen of the board, facing us here and now. What shall be the answer?[395]

The 1916 financial report showed receipts for the academic year totaling $2,400.69, including $1,919.28 from tuition and fees. $435.00 was still due from tuition and fees. Disbursements totaled an equal amount with $1,447.75 for salaries to date with $351.75 due.[396]

At its April meeting, the Board of Trustees also discussed the feasibility of wiring the Institute buildings for electricity at a cost of $120 for the Main Building, $40 for the Society Hall, $25 for the Boarding Hall, and $32 for the President's House. The Board voted to proceed with the wiring of the Main building "provided the bill be dated Sept. 1st, 1916," and to confer with Mr. A. N. James (owner of the Kindley Mill and the current provider of electricity to the Town of Mt. Pleasant) concerning wiring the remaining buildings on campus. The Board pledged itself to raise $1,000 for the current expenses of the upcoming academic year.[397]

At its meeting in May, the Board voted to complete the wiring of the remainder of the buildings on campus and to complete the renovations recommended by the architect in 1915, but the renovations were delayed for a year due to lack of funds.[398]

It appears that in the Fall of 1916 Colonel McAllister and his wife, Ethelyn, moved into a house which the Institute catalogue called the "Principal's residence". The old "President's house" located on the campus was "not far removed from the buildings. Students are in easy access to the Principal, should there be occasion to consult him when not in his office. He, too, is in a position at all times to exercise supervision over the entire plant."[399]

At its meeting of October 16th, 1916, McAllister advised the Board of Trustees that the wiring of all the buildings on campus had been completed. The Board voted to pay Mr. (Frank) James a first installment of $120 (cost of wiring the Main building) by Nov. 1st and that a $97 payment on the remaining costs be taken from a "special fund in hands of Prof. McAllister, provided that the amount, at the opportune moment, be replaced to the credit of the said special fund."

The Treasurer reported that $650 of the Board's $1,000 pledge for operating funds was available.[400]

The year-end financial report listed receipts in the amount of $2,896.08 ($2,599.72 in tuition and fees), and disbursements of an equal amount including $1,952.20 in salaries to date. The Board Treasurer also noted that the $120 bill for the wiring of the main building remained outstanding. The Board voted to continue this issue until May. McAllister reported that the increased fees for electricity had been passed to the students. He continued to request an enlarged facility, increased faculty, and other improvements.[401]

The Board decided to consider the hiring of an agent to raise funds to "enlarge and modernize the plant according to plans already adopted."[402]

Board Treasurer J. M. Cook reported on the school's Endowment, "where they are and of what they consist." The report stated:

> "Pledge to Synod for interest on $1001.43, which sum of $101.43 was paid by Jonas Cook, Treasurer of Endowment Fund in full satisfaction of a note held by Adolphus C. & Hugh W. Barrier. A note in hand duly executed by [the] Board of Trustees of N. C. College given & executed on account of the expenditure of endowment fund in paying notes held against NC College by Mrs. Wheeler, J. C. Lingle, & R. W Misenheimer – said note dated April 25, 1916, bears interest from May 27, 1913. Note, in hand, duly executed by Board of Trustee of NC College given and executed on account of expenditure of endowment funds in maintenance of Collegiate Institute – said note dated April 25, 1916 and bears from date — Note yet to be given by Board of Trustees of NC College for amt. of Endowment funds paid out by directors on resolutions of Board of Trustees, for maintenance of Collegiate Institute.
>
> Total endowment fund on hand, as cash, as above reported."[403]

The Board's final action of the April 1916 meetingwas to extend a note to Treasurer Cook "for money spent in the maintenance of the Collegiate Institute."[404]

At its meeting of May 22nd, 1917, the Board of Trustees voted once again to go forward with renovation of the main building using the plans the architect produced in 1915, if funds could be raised. A committee was charged with "the duties of remodeling the main building in so far as it is practical in accordance with the general plans worked out by our architect, and that this committee be authorized to solicit funds, and if necessary to negotiate a loan for this purpose, and that the work of the remodeling be undertaken at once."[405]

The Board Treasurer reported that $684 had been collected on the $1,000 pledge made by the Board in April of 1916. The Board gratefully accepted a pledge of $1,000 from the MPCI Alumni. The President of the Association stated that "some of the money had been collected and the remainder would be paid 'in a couple of years.'" The Board thanked the Association and expressed its appreciation for their splendid spirit of optimism. (Existing records of the Alumni Association show that as of 1921, $650 of the pledge had been collected.)[406]

The Board concluded its meeting with several "suggestions" regarding improvements to the "new" rooms which were to be created during the proposed renovations. It was proposed that the Ladies Aid Societies of the various churches be approached to help to furnish the rooms, and that the rooms be "uniform in their equipment, and to secure this it would be better for each Society to ascertain the cost of furnishing a room and send this donation to the management of the school to be used in furnishing the rooms."[407]

The proposed renovations to the main building and Society Hall were completed during the summer of 1917. Some of the changes were quite significant as described by Colonel McAllister in a letter to local Lutheran ministers addressed as "Sir and Brother."

> "Work is rapidly going forward in the modernization of the Main Building of our plant. It will be completely renewed within and equipped with electric lights (completed in Sep 1916), steam heat, and running water in every room. The first-floor space has been rearranged and is divided into three large recitation (class) rooms, a reception room, an office, and a supply room. The stairway has been moved from the end of the building to the center, which is much more convenient. The Society Hall will be used as the Chapel until the new building (included in the plan for improvement and enlargement) is constructed. The students' rooms on the 2nd and 3rd floors have been made one size; and, by narrowing the hallways,

> each is provided with two built-in closets." Furnishings in the students' rooms were to include "two single iron beds with springs and mattresses, a table with book-cases built in, a chiffonier, chairs, a lavatory and set fixtures."[408]

McAllister indicated that funding for the renovations was raised by a canvass of "some of the strongest congregations," contributions from the Civic League of Mt. Pleasant, and local church Young Peoples Societies (Sunday Schools). There were no cost figures.

Society Hall now housed the Chapel and one classroom but remained unheated. During the winter, the newly installed water pipes and furnace froze and "caused considerable inconvenience with considerable expense to repair."[409]

Continuing into 1918, Colonel McAllister, not so subtlety, stated to the Board of Trustees and the Lutheran Synod his thoughts concerning the present and future condition of the school.

> [While MPCI had] "failed to enroll some students and lost others who had matriculated because of the call of the Government, [the school] had still enrolled a larger number of students than for several years past. This is but a contest, - it seems to me, of what might be reasonably expected were your plans for further improvement and enlargement of the plant realized. … A larger school, a larger faculty, a better course of study, in short, a Junior College of which the whole church might justly be proud, are possibilities which, as I see it, only wait these improvements for their realization."[410]

Advertisements in two periodicals from 1918 show that McAllister addressed his "recruiting" announcements to both the obvious circumstances of World War I and to the probable readership of the peridoicals. An advertisement in the *Salisbury Post* newspaper contained a photo of a cadet read:

> "Three generations of satisfied patrons and the oft-repeated opinions of prominent educators pronounce its [MPCI] location in a distinctly school town in healthful Piedmont Carolina ideal. Modern equipment – electric lights, steam heat and running water in every room. …

> Military system develops physique, secures wholesome government and turns out well poised men."[411]

An announcement in the *Lutheran Visitor* stated:

> "This well-known school for boys and young men holds a unique place among the educational institutions of the Church. Its location in a distinctively school town, 25-minute drive from the railroad, is favorable to good morals, economy, undisturbed application ... Its system of government - the modified military – is conceded to be the best known for boys and young men, for its appeals to manliness, develops self-control and at the same time affords highly valuable military training. Institute men in the Army profit decidedly from their previous military training."[412]

Meeting on Apr 9th, 1918, James P. Cook, Chairman of the Board of Trustees Ways and Means Committee, reported that even with all pledges paid and monies previously received there would remain an unpaid balance of "about $5,000" owed for the recent renovations and improvements. In response, the Board voted to appoint a publicity committee to prepare an "educational folder of cuts of the plant and proposed additions looking towards the raising of the $5,000 indebtedness and towards the increasing of attendance of the Institute." Colonel McAllister's 1917-'18 year-end report listed operating revenues at $3,252.89 and expenses of an equal amount. Tuition and fees totaled $3,159.14. Salaries to date were $2,552.50 and electric and telephone expenses were $164.72.[413]

Shortly before the end of the 1918-'19 school year, Colonel McAllister received a letter from Dr. J. Henry Harms, President of Newberry [SC] College, asking if he would consider the position of President of Newberry when he (Harms) retired. Initially the College had offered the position to Reverend John C. Seegers, who was at that time serving as the Pastor of St. Paul's Lutheran Church in Wilmington, NC. Seegers, a South Carolina native and graduate of Newberry, declined the offer and McAllister was the next choice. Dr. Harms wrote that McAllister "was my choice from the beginning," and advised McAllister that the position carried a salary of $2,000 per year and a house. He also asked that McAllister meet him in Columbia "to talk it over." McAllister replied that while he was flattered by the offer, he was "in the midst of Commencement exercises" (Commencement began on May 25th and ended May 28th) and he needed more time and information before giving an answer. He said that he would like to meet with Dr. Harms.[414]

There is no record of whether or not McAllister and Harms met, or the reasons for his decision, but at some point, McAllister declined the Newberry Presidency. Dr. Sidney Jacob Derrick accepted the position in June and served for twelve years.

In what was proving a very busy summer, in June 1918, Colonel McAllister authorized the loan of the Institute's rifles to a local Reserve Militia unit to be used in drill training.[415] In July he began an effort to obtain status as a Student Army Training Center. McAllister asserted that "the provision made for the strengthening of the military insures the maintenance of the high standards previously set by MPCI."[416] Regrettably, a Sept. 1918 telegram from the Committee on Education in Washington, DC stated that the Institute did not meet the necessary "academic and facilities standards" to receive standing as a Training Center.[417]

Shortly after MPCI was turned down as a training center, the Bailey Military Institute in Greenwood, SC was awarded SATC status. Colonel McAllister began a letter writing campaign expressing his concern over why MPCI did not receive similar consideration. While McAllister's efforts did not result in a change in status for MPCI, they did lead to something of a "debate" involving a United States Senator, the Principal of the Bailey Institute, and several members of the War Department Committee on Education and Special Training.

The exchange of letters is presented to demonstrate the typical "red tape" that often swirled around Colonel McAllister and his efforts to maintain and enhance his school.

On Sept. 30th, 1918, McAllister wrote NC Senator Lee Overman. On Oct. 2nd, Overman replied:

> "Your letter of Sept. 30th, advising me that an SATC unit had been established at Bailey Military Academy in SC, a school very similar to your Institute in curriculum, received. I will take the matter up at once with the Committee on education and special training and insist that if other schools similar in curriculum to yours have

been recognized, the MPCI must also be recognized. As soon as I receive a reply, I will communicate with you again."[418]

McAllister received a reply on Oct. 1st to a letter he had written to Edward Graham of the War Department Committee on Education & Special Training. Graham informed McAllister that his committee awarded the SATC status to the Bailey Institute based upon the word of the Principal, Colonel Bailey, that the school was a "full junior college," and only after closer examination was it discovered that it did not satisfy the requirements. The committee, however, allowed the decision to stand. Graham closed, stating that:

> I do not know what action will be taken in the matter. The situation was created through no fault of mine; it is difficult to correct just now. I make this statement for your own information and will ask you to regard it as confidential. The question of whether an institution fulfills the requirement as to number is not within my jurisdiction."[419]

On Oct. 7th, Albert A. Meras, a member of the Committee on Education and Special Training, replied to Senator Overman in reference to the issue. [McAllister was copied on the letter]

> "I beg to state that units of the Student's Army Training Corps have been established only in colleges and schools maintaining at least two years' collegiate work. Furthermore, institutions must have an enrollment of 100 male students over 18 years of age who have completed at least thirteen credits of secondary school work.
>
> I regret that MPCI was not granted the privilege of maintaining the Students' Army Training Corps because their academic standards were not approved by the Advisory Board of the Committee.
>
> The Bailey Military Institute to which you refer in your letter has been investigated, and we shall be ready to announce the result of the investigation within a few days. We are especially interested in institutes and academies organized on a military basis and have submitted to the

> General Staff a plan for the organization of military training in such schools. Should this plan be approved we shall immediately notify MPCI. We feel sure that it will strengthen the military corps under consideration by supplying a successful and efficient unit."[420]

McAllister received a letter on Oct. 8th from Senator Overman stating that:

> "I will again take up with the Committee on Education and Special Training, the issue, but I am afraid that under the rules laid down by the Department ... our request will be denied. I wrote the Committee a very pointed letter some time ago in behalf of your Institute but have not yet received any assurance that your request ... would be complied with."[421]

Finally, in mid-October, Colonel McAllister received another letter from the Senator with a copy of a letter he (Overman) had received from Mr. R. B. Perry, Secretary of the Committee on Education and Special Training. The letter stated:

> "I beg to acknowledge the receipt of your letter of October 8 inclosing [sic] a letter from Mr. G. F. McAllister, Principal of the Collegiate Institute ... this institution did not appear to meet the requirements of the SATC as to academic standards and facilities and for these reasons a unit was not established there. Upon further investigation, it was decided to withdraw the unit from Bailey Military Institute, to which your constituent refers."[422]

In August 1818, the Board of Trustees received a report from Colonel McAllister indicating that the Synod's $1,000 pledge in the form of monies collected from the various congregations had paid only $395. The Board instructed its chairman, Reverend Martin L. Stirewalt, to "take this matter up with the Executive Committee of the Synod at the earliest possible date to the end that this balance be paid at once by the delinquent congregations." By November, the amount collected was $502.86, and the Board, with the approval of the Synod, was authorized to send out appeals to the delinquent congregations "urging them to pay at once all unpaid balances for the year 1917-18."[423]

The Board was informed that its "$40,000 Fund Campaign", first proposed in 1915 and begun in September 1918, was postponed due to a "$50,000 Campaign" being conducted by the Mont Amoena Seminary. The new date to begin the campaign was set as November 24th, and each member of the Board was asked to help in securing a "capable and willing lay leader in each congregation to head the canvass."[424]

In March 1919, the Board of Trustees met at St. James Lutheran Church in Concord. The Board had been without a Treasurer since the resignation of John P. Cook in April and Colonel McAllister reported that the amount collected toward the Synod Pledge now stood at $597. Board Secretary, Reverend Pleasant D. Brown, was appointed to send out an appeal for the early payment of the pledges. Board Chairman, Reverend Charles R. Pless, was authorized to request that the Synod's annual pledge of $1,000 to the Institute maintenance fund be placed in the regular apportionment to the congregations. The Audit Committee stated that its work had been postponed until a new Treasurer was appointed but that although the premium had not been paid, a new $6,000 insurance policy for the school buildings had been obtained. The Chairman of the Ways and Means Committee reported that approximately $3,850 was collected or pledged as part of the "$40,000 Campaign." He challenged the members of the Board to make a personal presentation to the congregations not yet having responded to the campaign.[425]

On May 8th, 1919, Colonel McAllister wrote his annual report to the NC Lutheran Synod. He began the report by stating that "there had been disturbing factors for the past several years which militated against normal procedure in schoolwork, as well as other items of endeavor." In addition to the war, the extension of the draft to 18 and 19-year-old males effected the recruitment of students by the Institute. Enigmatically, after his failure to obtain Student Army Training (SATC) status for the Institute, McAllister apparently developed a "new" attitude toward the SAT Corps, indicating that "it [SATC] would operate very much to the disadvantage to the Collegiate Institute. ... Viewed in the light of subsequent events and the experience of institutions which secured SATC's, it appears fortunate that a Unit was not established at the Institute."[426]

McAllister went on to say that while "prices of commodities" increased as a result of the war, the Institute had fared better that usual financially. This was due largely to the increased enrollment which produced revenue of $4,485.38 in tuition and fees. Total receipts (revenue) for the Institute in 1918-'19 were $5,367.71 versus $5,331.12 in disbursements. This was the first year since McAllister became sole proprietor that an operating fund surplus existed at the end of the year.

McAllister continued to call for enlarged facilities to increase the patronage of the Institute. "An assembly hall other than the Literary Society Hall, more dormitory space, and Science laboratories are especially needed."

In closing McAllister declared:

> "The outlook of the Institute [has never been] brighter. The enrollment for the session was the largest in years. The attendance has held up better than formerly, more students being in attendance during the Third Term than we have ever had before. Enthusiasm and loyalty characterize the student body. More applications for rooms for the coming session have been filed than ever before at this time. Given the enlarged plant, every indication is that the Institute will increase its enrollment 50 to 100% in two year. Earnestly hoping that your plans for an enlarged and improved plant for the Collegiate Institute will soon become a concrete reality."[427]

The Synod Committee on Educational Institutions reported that: "Both schools [MPCI and Mont Amoena] report splendid work and unusually large enrollment. They report bright prospects but make earnest pleas to Synod that they be supplied with adequate facilities for larger service."

In response, the Synod resolved that "The Boards of MPCI and MAS be requested to hold a joint meeting for the purpose of developing a plan by which a more vital relation may be established between Synod and the Schools, and report back to Synod at its next meeting."[428]

Although this report and resolution appeared to support both MPCI and Mont Amoena, there were apparently some statements voiced during the Synod meeting that Colonel McAllister considered critical of the operation of the Institute. As a result of the "criticism" McAllister, again frustrated and probably angry, penned a very long statement to the Board of Trustees, which he titled "Information for the Board." Having provided a short history of MPCI's creation and history, the statement continued:

> "Reports have been made regularly to the Board and through the Board to Synod. More and more, the Institute came to take the place of the College and Synod at different times endorsed the work of the Institute and resolved that it is in a peculiar sense the school of the Synod and deserves the moral and all the financial support the Synod could give it. At different times Synod did vote appropriations to the Institute both for improvements on the buildings and for current expenses. At no time has Synod authorized the Board to finance the Institute. At no time has Synod reconsidered her act by which the College was suspended. The College Charter is held intact. It has been revised and amended, at the direction and upon authorization of the Board making legal the work of the Institute and securing the Institute any funds belonging to North Carolina College. Later, when the burdensomeness of conducting a school like the Institute by individuals single handed and alone was brought to the attention of Synod, Synod voted $1000 to help meet the current expense of the Institute. This was several times repeated. I do not know by whom the initiatory steps should be taken if the status of the school should be altered. Presumably, however, by Synod. At the last convention of Synod, it was "Resolved, That the Boards of MPCI and MAS be requested to hold a joint meeting for the purpose of developing a plan by which a more vital relation may be established between Synod and the Schools and report back to Synod, at its next meeting.
>
> **At different times and from different sources it has been intimated that there was objection to the manner or arrangement by which the Institute is conducted. I do not know how general this feeling is, or what plan**

> **is proposed by those who find objection to the present plan. I wish to make it clear to the Board that there is no fault or blame attaching to anyone connected with the Institute because of present status. Synod recommended the suspension of the College whose financing it was standing sponsor for, largely because of financial difficulties. It endorsed the arrangement entered into by the Board for the conduct of the Institute and has never as yet authorized the Board to undertake the financing of the institution. I desire to make clear further to the Board that any additional information which I can furnish to help the Board to get a perfectly clear understanding of the present status will be gladly furnished. The information I have from time to time given the Board and through the Board to Synod is all that I have been asked for and more. Under the circumstances, it would seem that the information was as full as could be desired - even more extensive than could have legitimately been asked. Notwithstanding, I learn that the Institute and the Principal were the subject of criticism at the last convention of Synod, because of the incompleteness of information furnished in my report. I would like for the Board to ask me for such additional information as it thinks the Church at large should have, and then stand ready to defend the Institute and its management against gratuitous objections** (emphasis added). In view of issues involved, I should like for the Board to give consideration to such action as it thinks proper to be taken at the forthcoming joint meeting with the Board of Mont Amoena Seminary. The matter of catalogue printing and employment of teachers for the Institute may be involved.[429]

The Board made no public comment on McAllister's report except to vote to "confer with the Chairman of the Board of Trustees of Mont

Amoena Seminary and fix a date for a joint meeting to be held in response to (the) action of the Synod."[430]

Three weeks after McAllister's statement to the Board of Trustees, the NC Lutheran Synod made a major announcement that seemed to allay any anxieties raised in earlier discussions.

On June 19th, 1919, *The Charlotte Observer* newspaper reported that Daniel E. Rhyne of Lincolnton had presented the Mt. Pleasant Collegiate Institute with a gift of $2,500. [He also gave $2,000 to Mont Amoena Seminary]. The article stated that the funds would be used toward enlargement of the Institute but that an additional $5,000 was needed to begin any new construction which in most likelihood would include a new science hall.[431]

Following the announcement of Rhyne's gift, the Boards of Trustees of NC College and Mont Amoena Seminary met at St. James Lutheran Church on June 24th in Concord. Although no minutes of this meeting were made public, the information released to the press confirmed that plans were being made to liquidate the debt of the Seminary and enlarge the Institute.[432]

On July 4th, 1919, *The Concord Daily Tribune* published another major announcement. John S. Efird, part-owner of Efird Manufacturing Company of Albemarle, had donated $5,000 to the Institute's building fund. The *Tribune* article stated that Efird's gift came on the eve of completing a campaign [the $40,000 Campaign] throughout the churches of the North Carolina Lutheran Synod. "Plans are made for the enlargement [of the Institute] but actual commencement is deferred until a larger amount of quick assets are available. … The Institute is hard pressed to meet the demands made upon it and it will be a happy day when the planned enlargement becomes an accomplished fact."[433]

As MPCI continued the 1919-'20 academic session, the Boards of Trustees of MPCI and Mont Amoena met on 19 Nov 1919, again in joint session, to follow up on their June meeting and to complete plans for a campaign to raise $150,000 for the two institutions. According to an article from the *Statesville Landmark*, which was reprinted in the *Concord Daily Tribune*, the two Boards had already appointed a committee to meet with the Lutheran Bureau of New York, with whom they had been in discussions for some time. The campaign was to begin during the first week in February 1920. According to the article, "the situation was thoroughly considered by the joint board and the project plans were heartily approved."[434]

On Jan 21st, 1920, the *Concord Daily Tribune* reported that the fund raising campaign would be headquartered in Concord and that the funds raised would "provide for a larger service" by "supplying the schools [MPCI and MAS] with equipment to complete work planned for them."[435]

A follow-up article on Feb 9th stated that about fifty thousand handbills, circulars, booklets of Appeal and a Workers' Handbook were prepared and distributed by the Lutheran Bureau of New York City. According to one of the booklets, Mont Amoena planned to retire its debt, make improvements and repairs to the plant, build another dormitory and a Principal's residence, purchase more equipment for their laboratories, library, and classrooms, and establish a more secure endowment. The Institute focused on additional dormitory space, a new science hall, remodeling Society Hall, additional laboratory equipment, improving campus landscaping, acquiring additional space for drill and recreation activities, and increasing its endowment.[436]

On Feb 9th, the *Lexington Dispatch* in Lexington, NC reported that the "$150,000 Equipment and Endowment Fund Campaign" had attracted national attention with endorsements coming from the headquarters of the United Lutheran Church in America (ULC) located in New York. According to the *Dispatch*, Reverend Frederick H. Knubel, President of the ULC:

> "The maintenance and proper equipment of our Church Schools is of vital importance both to the successful prosecution of the work of the church, and to the building up of an intelligent Christian citizenship. I can think of no better way in which Christian people can exercise their stewardship … than by making liberal provision to these agencies ... a complete success to the campaign for Mont Amoena Seminary and the Collegiate Institute."[437]

The article mentioned that Rev. Melanchthon G. G. Scherer, the current Secretary of the ULC and a former President of North Carolina College, sent an endorsement. "The institutions are worthy; the cause is worthy; and with all confidence I shall pray for the complete success of the campaign."[438]

On Mar 17th, 1920, the *Concord Daily Tribune* reported that "All present indications from the field show that the campaign for $150,000 for Mont Amoena Seminary and the Collegiate Institute at Mt. Pleasant will be successful." The *Tribune* stated that many congregations were conducting canvasses. St. John's Church in Cabarrus County raised double their apportionment and was looking toward a total contribution of $10,000. St. James Lutheran Church in Concord raised $3,750 at their organizational meeting with John A. Cline making the first subscription and J. P. Cook donating $1,000. St. James was also attempting to make a $10,000 contribution.[439] In April, St. Mark's in Mooresville reported subscriptions of $2,100.[440]

Almost simultaneously with the beginning of the $150,000 Campaign, the Tennessee Synod's Lenoir College in Hickory announced that it had raised $300,000 in pledges from "an earlier campaign" and intended to continue toward a goal of $350,000. This announcement stated that the College received pledges from twenty of its congregations, but did not mention the fact that a $100,000 donation was provided by Daniel E. Rhyne, the North Carolina College alumni who gave $4,500 to MPCI and Mont Amoena one year before.[441]

On April 6th, 1920, Colonel McAllister delivered his annual report to the Board of Trustees. He reported that attendance for the year was the largest in the history of the Institute. The school experienced some cases of influenza but, unlike several other institutions, the outbreak did not require classes to be suspended. He recalled that "Rigorous discipline" was necessary "in only a very few cases," and only one cadet was dismissed for dishonesty. Overall, McAllister stated, "we have not had a finer spirit."[442]

During the financial report, McAllister noted receipts totaling $8,872.05 with $8,373.07 from tuition and fees. Disbursements totaled $8,219.27 with $5,940 paid in salaries to date. The operating budget demonstrated a surplus for the second year in a row ($652.78). The $1,000 Synod pledge had an outstanding balance of $505.33.[443]

McAllister used this opportunity to present an ambitious call for a larger "plant" which now included a new Science building, a new dormitory, an enlarged dining hall, two more Literary Society Halls and an infirmary. The need for a larger athletic field, cement walkways and landscape gardening were also described. McAllister lamented directly to the Board:

> "Oh, for a Denhart or a Rhyne to make it possible to supply pressing needs and even to render ornate the grounds and buildings of an institution that would do a high service to the present and coming generations. Let us devoutly hope that the membership of the North Carolina [Lutheran] Synod will respond in such measure to the call now being made that Synod's school may be provided with a more nearly adequate equipment."[444]

On May 18th, 1920, the Board of Trustees met and discussed securing an athletic field and acquiring the John Foil house near the campus. There was also a discussion of erecting temporary barracks on the campus. The newly appointed Board Treasurer, Gilbert Hendrix, reported that the school insurance policy had been paid at a cost of $90. Several other notes were still outstanding for funds borrowed from the Endowment. The Wheeler, Lingle, Misenheimer notes from 1913/1916 now totaled $1,959.78 and the A. C. Barrier note now totaled $1001.43. There were also three notes due totaling $1,308.15 to the Board of Trustees to pay for maintenance repairs to the College buildings. The Endowment Fund, if and when all notes were paid, would total $4,375.04.[445]

In January of 1921, the Board of Trustees reached an agreement with Mrs. Sarah "Sallie" Weiser of Bluefield, West Virginia to purchase a house and a one-acre parcel of land across North Main St. from the Institute. This house was the former residence of the first President of NC College, Rev. Daniel Bittle, and his wife, Susan, the first Principal of Mont Amoena Seminary. The property was purchased by the Bittles in 1860 from John Shimpock and Mrs. Bittle designed the house still standing on the property. The Bittles remained in the house for only two years after which it was sold back to Shimpock and then passed into several hands before being purchased by Mrs. Weiser in 1906.[446]

The Board of Trustees paid $2,000 for the property, $1,000 of which Mrs. Weiser and her sisters returned to the Institute in the form of an endowed scholarship in honor of her father, Charles H. Fisher. The remaining $1,000 was paid to Mrs. Weiser in the form of war bonds held by the Board, as the Institute did not have enough cash. The Board of Trustees voted to make repairs to the house and instructed the Ways and Means committee to "make the best possible disposition of the building" after it was repaired.[447]

On February 26th, 1921, an announcement was made that would have a profound effect on the Collegiate Institute for the remainder of its existence. The North Carolina and Tennessee Lutheran Synods released a joint statement that the two bodies would unite as of March 2nd, 1921. The two Synods, separated for over 100 years, had finally agreed on a plan that would reunite them. The United Evangelical Lutheran Synod of North Carolina (UELSNC) would now consist of 214 congregations with a membership of 39,456.

Although never publicly stated, there is no doubt that the agreement of the North Carolina Synod to recognize the Tennessee Synod's Lenoir College as the future "Lutheran school" in the state played a large role in creating the new United Synod of North Carolina.

Under the new organization, three educational institutions would be supported – Lenoir College in Hickory with an enrollment of 250 male and female students, the Collegiate Institute in Mt. Pleasant with 175 male students, and Mont Amoena Seminary in Mt. Pleasant with 100 female students.[448]

The new Synod's declared policy was to develop all the institutions within the state, but as time would tell, this promise was undoubtedly unfulfilled. Although the fate of Mt. Pleasant Collegiate Institute in this drama was yet to be decided, it was clear that the next step,begun twenty years earlier with the closure of North Carolina College, was now being taken.

Reverend Michael C. D. McDaniel, future Bishop of the North Carolina Lutheran Synod, wrote in his 1954 college research paper:

> **"It became evident that the aim of the members of the old Tennessee Synod was to improve the position of its institution, Lenoir College, and let come what may to the Institute. [In the years to come] many false promises were made by the Synod and the Board of Directors."**[449] (emphasis added)

In his report to the Institute Board of Trustees in May 1921, McAllister listed the "pressing needs" of the Institute. The school needed another dormitory, remodeling of Society (Gerhardt) Hall, and a new roof for the recently acquired Weiser house. He stated further that "given adequate equipment, the steady growth and development of the Institute would seem to be assured." McAllister's financial report listed receipts of $10,005.55, with $9,255.57 collected from tuition and fees and $749.98 provided by the United Lutheran Church of America. Expenses for the year totaled an equal amount. To date $7,137.78 was paid in salaries. According to McAllister, "there are yet some collections to make and there is a balance due on the amount promised by the ULC. This will enable to Institute to meet all obligations and a have a small working balance."[450]

On May 24th, the Board of Trustees met at the Institute and read a resolution from the Alumni Association stating that "it is the humble sense of the Alumni Association … that the present standard of curriculum be maintained in the Collegiate Institute in the merger of the North Carolina and Tennessee Synods." The Board accepted the resolution and referred it to the Committee on Educational Institutions of the new joint Synod of North Carolina. The Board also received a donation of $350 from the Alumni Association "to be used for such purpose as the Board might designate." It was placed in the Institute Building Fund.

At this time, the Board of Trustees heard a report on the funds collected thus far on the $150,000 Campaign. As of May 24, 1921, pledges of $51,679.57 were made and $14,378.84 collected in cash or US Bonds. Using these funds, the Treasurer of the Ways and Means Committee had paid out $5,878.84 as expenses for the Campaign and $6,691 to pay off notes and interest held against the Institute or the Endowment fund. The total cash and bonds on hand from the Campaign fund was $1,808.06.

Finally, Board Treasurer Gilbert Hendrix reported the status of the Endowment fund. As of May 24th, 1921, including the payoff of notes held against the Endowment, the fund held "productive and unproductive funds" of $4,375.04, of which $3,350 was invested in US Bonds. Payoff of the interest due on the notes and interest from the invested Bonds produced another $1,490.22 in income. A disbursement of $139 was made from the Endowment to pay Insurance on the Institute's buildings. The fund "loaned" $1,000 to the Cabarrus County Building & Loan Association to endow the C. H. Fisher Scholarship.[451]

In October 1921, the Board of Trustees created a committee to take inventory and state the needs of the Institute. Based on this study, they decided that the major need was a new dormitory, and the second most important need was repairs to the other buildings. The acquisition of a new dorm was designated Project One and repairs to the other buildings was classified Project Two.[452]

The Synod Committee on Educational Institutions presented amendments to the North Carolina College Charter of 1909 to the Board of Trustees in November 1921. These amendments were approved by the newly merged NC Synod and basically gave the Synod, through its Committee on Educational Institutions, the power to appoint the future Board of Trustees, control the monies raised by the Board, previously and in the future, and direct this money where they deemed necessary. The new amendments were ratified on Dec. 8th, 1921 by the NC State Legislature. [See Appendix 10 for full transcript of amendments].[453]

Meeting in Hickory in November, and recognizing the "need for a larger equipment," the Board of Trustees agreed to instruct the Executive Committee to proceed with preliminary plans for the erection of a dormitory for the Collegiate Institute.[454]

During commencement ceremonies in May 1922, a major announcement communicated that the Board of Trustees had finalized plans to erect a new dormitory on the north side of the campus which would house 50 students. At a cost of $50,000, the building was expected to be completed by the beginning of the fall term. It was also revealed that Society Hall would be completely remodeled at a cost of $10,000. Plans were already underway to raise funds for the projects.[455]

To publicize the plan for the new dormitory and to keep MPCI before the public in the face of the Lutheran Synod merger and the visible emergence of Lenoir College as the new "Lutheran school," an unattributed article/editorial appeared in the *Concord Daily Tribune* on the same date as the Commencement ceremonies.

> "A careful study of the work of the Mt. Pleasant Collegiate Institute will convince anyone of the real worth of the institution. We believe that no preparatory school or junior college in the South is doing a greater work, and the

> institution today is just starting. In another ten years it will be twice as large and twice as powerful. … There are 150 students enrolled in the school, representing a dozen states (actually 164 students from six states), and the institution is growing so rapidly and steadily that a new dormitory has been approved by the Board of Trustees to be erected at a cost of $50,000. … At commencement this year the largest number of alumni in the history of the school were present, and each one of them showed a keen interest in the future of the school. With the alumni standing solidly back of it, and with the Synod, which controls it, showing added interest in its future, there is no way to keep the institution from taking its place in educational circles. … We repeat that MPCI is just beginning to really live. Its future is most bright."[456]

Even though plans for a new dormitory were in only preliminary stages, the Institute began placing advertisements in local, state and national newspapers during the summer of 1922 indicating that there would soon be available a "new dormitory with all modern conveniences."[457] The Institute catalogue for 1922-'23 stated that a campaign was presently in progress "to raise funds for the erection of a new dormitory."[458]

During the summer and early fall of 1922, "Project Two" was completed. Society Hall benefitted from an "interior renewal" and the installation of steam heat. There was hope that the school would be fully ready to start the new dormitory building by early spring.[459]

The Institute's 1922-'23 catalogue featured a six-building campus "plant." In addition to the main building, the President's residence and Society Hall, the old Boarding Hall was described as a frame structure of two stories that provided "ample space for kitchen, pantries, private dining-room, and a large dining-room sufficient to accommodate the boarding students." The second story was fitted as an apartment for the Boarding House matron.

The other two buildings were former private homes purchased by the Institute and now serving as "barracks" for students and faculty. Barracks No. 2 was the former "Bittle house" purchased from Mrs. Sally Weiser in 1921. It was described as "a large residence just across the street (North Main

St.) from the campus," completely remodeled and converted into a dormitory with rooms for twenty cadets and a teacher. The rooms were described as "large, well-lighted and ventilated, quiet and conducive to good work."

Barracks No. 3 was the former "Blackwelder house" which stood on the corner of North Main St. and Walnut St. across from the Principal's residence. This dormitory had rooms for twelve to fifteen cadets and a teacher. "The grounds afford recreation facilities and have a more or less home-like atmosphere."[460]

On Nov. 17, 1922, twenty months after the merger of the NC and Tennessee Synods was declared, and only one year following the reorganization of the merged Synod's Committee on Educational Institutions, Lenoir College released its own major announcement.

Several newspapers reported that Daniel E. Rhyne donated $300,000 to Lenoir College with the challenge that the school raise an equal amount. The *Hickory Daily Record* stated that "of course, the College will raise the other $300,000. Its friends and the liberal members of the Lutheran Church can't afford to do otherwise."[461] The Board of Trustees of Lenoir College responded to the donation announcement by voting to change the name of the school to "Daniel E. Rhyne College," and drafted a resolution to the State Legislature to that effect. [The name was later changed to Lenoir-Rhyne College.][462]

The Synod responded to Rhyne's gift by pledging to raise an additional $550,000 of which $250,000 would be designated for buildings. By February 1923, the Synod and Lenoir (Daniel E. Rhyne) College had reworked the various pledge announcements to declare an $850,000 Campaign "for the needed expansion of the institution." A letter written by Rev. John L. Morgan, President of the NC Synod, and graduate of Lenoir College, declared:

> "Lenoir College is facing its great historic opportunity. Three years ago it stood on trial for life or death. The loyalty of its alumni and the Lutheran people of North Carolina decided that it must live. ... It is in our power to make it great, or allow it to be a second-rate meagre, struggling, limited institution. ... The North Carolina Synod has authoritively [sic] decided to stand back of Lenoir in meeting the conditions of Mr. Rhyne's gift."[463]

During the discussions of Rhyne's gift and the subsequent funding campaign for Lenoir College, the Synod made no mention of the building campaign for MPCI and, for all practical purposes, the letter by Rev. Morgan confirmed the reality that MPCI's status among the state's Lutheran leaders was quickly becoming a secondary issue.

At its annual Board meeting on May 22nd, Colonel McAllister presented the yearly financial statement. Revenues for the year totaled $9,555.58 with $8,955.58 received from tuition, rent and fees and $600 from the Synod. Expenses for the year totaled $9,299.06 with $7,500 expended for salaries to date and $256.52 cash on hand.[464]

The issue of the new dormitory dominated the Board meeting. Colonel McAllister informed the Board that the concern for more dormitory space remained the Institute's most critical need, followed by additional classroom and laboratory equipment. He stated that that attendance would increase by as much as 50% if such improvements were completed. McAllister also reported that sub-committees had been appointed to speed up collection of pledges toward the building fund, but that many of the pledges were held up pending the actual start of construction.

The ensuing discussion proved crucial to MPCI's future. As the architect's plan for the new dorm was presented, changes were requested. The addition of a third floor and enlargement of the heating plant constituted major alterations from the original plan, and no doubt created much concern and anxiety among the Board. As a result, these "last minute" changes led to a motion that operations for **all institutions** be suspended until new plans could be drawn. This resolution, in effect, delayed not only the completion of the much-needed dormitory, but placed the MPCI fund raising effort at the periphery of the much larger $850,000 Campaign being conducted by the Synod and Lenoir College.[465]

While Colonel McAllister and MPCi supporters no doubt saw the resolution as a setback, some Board members thought otherwise. Roland W. Leiby wrote to McAllister, conveying some of his feelings.

> "I went away from our meeting of the Board at Hickory with a better taste than usual. ... I want you to know that I for one want to see the Institute develop, and I believe that we have given you now more than palliative assurances for a new dormitory. I think I realize your

> feelings regarding the Institute and Lenoir College. It has also given me some concern. Not a few of us were averse to the idea that the Campaign should be solely for Lenoir, but there seemed to be nothing else to do for the time being. If we get a goodly sum from the campaign, I for one am going to pull for some of it to be deflected to the other institutions if it can at all be done."[466]

Throughout the summer of 1923, despite the lack of a new dormitory and the apparent waning support from the Synod, Colonel McAllister continued to work to promote the Institute and recruit students. The following "article" in a New Bern, NC newspaper illustrated his effort.

> "This Preparatory School a Leader – Collegiate Institute at Mount Pleasant one of the best in the south – Parents of students and students themselves who are looking about for a Christian military preparatory school which is classed among the best in the South, need look no further. It has been found in [the] Collegiate Institute at Mt. Pleasant, NC and of which Mr. G. F. McAllister is the principal."
>
> The Collegiate Institute has an established reputation for good work. It offers what young men want – training for efficiency under wholesome conditions; work, and some play and innocent amusement with it. It offers what young men need – thorough, conscientious instruction and careful oversite.
>
> The graduates of Collegiate Institute enter the junior class of leading colleges and the sophomore class of State University without examination and take high rank."[467]

As the school year progressed, the Board of Trustees took action to restart the building campaign by requesting that the Executive Committee of MPCI be allowed to start their own campaign to raise funds for the new dormitory. In January, a campaign for $75,000 was proposed with donors being permitted to make "subscriptions" in three levels. $1000 donors would be designated Vanguard Givers; $750 donors, Senior Givers; $500 donors, Junior Givers; $250 donors, Intermediate Givers, and $100 donors, Primary Givers.[468]

In April a pamphlet entitled "The Collegiate Institute Appeal – A Handbook of Facts and Plans" was published and distributed from the Collegiate Institute Appeals Headquarters located in Salisbury. The pamphlet introduction read:

> "This handbook of facts and plans is an honest though feeble, effort to tell the truth, as the facts reveal them concerning our Institute at Mt. Pleasant, NC. This school is one of the three that we have in the North Carolina Synod, hence we call it "Our Institute." [The other schools were Lenoir Rhyne College and Mont Amoena Seminary] This work was intended to be brief and to the point. Because it is such, we hope that it will be read by everyone. It will acquaint you with interesting facts concerning the work of the Collegiate Institute. Our hope is, that it will in some measure accomplish the purpose for which it is intended – the construction and equipment of a dormitory."

The handbook confirmed that the new united Synod had unanimously approved enlarging the "physical plant at the Institute and had proposed that $75,000 be raised to "construct and equip an additional dormitory at the Institute." The "appeal" for funds would begin in the Spring of 1924 and every congregation "would be asked to make an every-member canvass beginning the fourth Sunday of May and continuing through the first Sunday in June."[469]

The *Salisbury Post* newspaper published the following editorial supporting the fund-raising effort. Under the Title "A Most Worthy Cause", the editorial read:

> "Friends of the Collegiate Institute at Mt. Pleasant are making an appeal for funds with which to strengthen the physical equipment of the school. The school is one of the best in the State. It occupies the plant of the old North Carolina College, which the Lutherans maintained for some years, but the plant has been badly reduced by fires. To modernize and make it better fitted for the competition which it must face, it is necessary that some additions be made to the physical equipment.

> We know this school well. The Superintendent is a man of splendid parts, a well-equipped school man and he has done a wonderfully fine work in this place, though he worked for years under a very discouraging handicap. He could have gone elsewhere, and no doubt bettered his on chances for success, but refusing, he devoted his splendid talents to the building just such a school as his church and a wide territory needed.
>
> Now that he is asking for better equipment he ought to be favored with a generous response. This school deserves better than it has been receiving. The man who made it possible has made sacrifices innumerable to carry on the fine work he began some years ago under such discouraging conditions. Today the good people of the church should rally to his efforts and give the necessary funds for building the Institute on a bigger and a firmer foundation. We say the church should, we believe it will, we know it will. There are many friends of education outside the church responsible directly for this school who will also gladly give something to add to the fund. It is with genuine pleasure that the newspaper adds it endorsement to the school, to the able superintendent and to the special plea being made in its behalf. We feel sure its friends in Rowan will deal generously with it in its hour of need."[470]

The Treasurer's Report for 1924 stated that the Institute's income totaled $11,180.55, with an equal amount of expenses. Salaries to date totaled $8,800. Fuel, lights and power totaled $935.14 and the school paid $325.50 to rent space in the town to board students.

McAllister continued to call for additional dormitory space and for a new science laboratory. He stated that there was only capacity for 46 students to board "on campus."[471]

In July of 1924, Colonel McAllister wrote to all incoming students informing them that "The campaign for funds for the new dormitory and equipment is succeeding. The Secretary reported to the Executive Committee on the 8th that he had on record pledges aggregating $45,000."[472]

The picture was actually somewhat different. On July 31, 1924, William L. Dixon of Charlotte, NC reported to Colonel McAllister that according to the Treasurer's Book, the Institute had $7,723.11 on hand. This included $976.36 from the "$150,000 Campaign;" $4,375.04 in the Endowment Fund, plus $1,290.23 in income; $1,026.48 in the Charles H. Fisher MSF, and $55 in the Alumni Building Fund.[473]

During the summer of 1924, one aspect of the Institute's proposal was realized. Using funds donated by Mr. Carl A. Rudisill, a member of the Board of Trustees and Lenoir College alumni, a larger steam furnace was installed on the campus. The public announcement stated that: "With funds generated by the endowment and an "earlier" fund raising campaign, the water system was also overhauled, and the tank moved to "a more advantageous location on the campus."[474]

The effort to improve and enlarge the campus continued into the fall of 1924. A project begun by the Classes of 1923 and 1924 solicited funds for the construction of a notable set of steps and a walkway leading from N. Main Street to the entrance to the Administration building.[475]

A historical sketch in the 1924-'25 College catalogue outlined that in addition to the new dormitory for which funds were now being raised, it was "hoped that it will be practicable to raise funds to restore the Pi Sigma Society Hall which was destroyed by fire some years ago. ... Friends and former students of Prof. H. T. J. Ludwig, Ph.D., will gladly subscribe to such a fund, it is believed, and make possible the restoration of this Hall as a memorial to a highly honored and much beloved teacher."[476]

In March of 1925, Colonel McAllister reported to the Board of Trustees that a sub-committee was investigating the feasibility of beginning construction on the new dormitory. The committee determined the approximate cost of a "closed job" to be $17,500 and that of a "completed job" to be $31,000 for a total cost of $48,000. Currently, $43,500 was available from several sources including a proposed loan of $15,000 from a local bank. Based on this information, the Executive Committee of the Trustees voted to solicit bids and start construction, with hopes that the collection of outstanding pledges would improve.[477] On March 26th, 1925, the *Albemarle Press* publicized that Mr. James D. Harwood of Albemarle, NC was awarded the construction contract for the new dormitory and that he was preparing "to place a full force of workmen on the job."[478]

McAllister received a statement from W. L. Dixon of Charlotte in March that $420.09 was on hand from the "$150,000 Campaign Fund", and income from the Endowment Fund was $604.53.[479] According to McAllister, however, there was "about $14,000 still due on the $150,000 Fund, two-thirds of which, if collected, comes to the Institute. Some of this, at least, will be collected when the building is done."[480]

In May 1925 the Board of Trustees was informed that $10,000 cash was on hand with another $5,000 due by June 1st from pledges and that another $20,000 was available in the form of a bank loan. With this information, the Board voted to complete the building of the dormitory. The Board approved furnishing the new dormitory, enlarging the Dining Hall and concreting the bathroom floors in the main building through a campaign to solicit funds from Church Sunday schools

The school ended the year with an operating deficit of $500. Income from tuition, fees and the United Lutheran Church fund totaled $9,649.15 and expenses totaled $11,149.35, including $7,975 for salaries.[481]

The long-awaited dormitory was completed during the summer of 1925. The MPCI Catalogue pronounced it one of the best dormitory buildings in the state. The structure, a three-story brick edifice, was designated "the New Building" as no action had been taken to formally name the structure. It provided space for fifty-two students on the second and third floors. The rooms were described as 12'x15' with built-in closets, and each containing its own hand basin (sink) with hot and cold water. Each floor also had a common toilet room "finished in tile and marble with shower baths in each one." One room on each of the upper floors was occupied by a faculty member.

The first floor contained a Social Room, an Assembly Room, and two small classrooms. The Social Room was partially furnished with a $350 donation from Holy Trinity Lutheran Church in Mt. Pleasant. The remaining rooms awaited additional funds from the Sunday School campaign which had, to date, raised $889. At completion, $3,000 in construction costs was owed. In addition to the new dormitory, the Boarding Hall was doubled in size, repainted and "otherwise improved."[482]

In January of 1926, the Board of Trustees authorized borrowing $3,000 to pay the remainder of the construction costs for the new dorm "until pledges come in." In April, Colonel McAllister stressed to the Board the "urgent" need for scientific equipment and laboratory space. The campaign to rebuild Pi Sigma Phi (Ludwig Hall) begun in 1924 was still under way and "very much needed to house Science Laboratories and afford ample classrooms for the Department."[483]

The Institute's financial report for the year reflected income in the amount of $13,455.80 with $11,289.15 collected from tuition, rent, uniforms, books and fees. The United Lutheran Church (National Lutheran Synod) provided $2,166.65 to the school. Expenses were reported as $13,455.80 with $10,000 paid in salaries.[484]

In June of 1926, Mr. John S. Efird of Albemarle wrote to the Board of Trustees :

> "Considering the pressing need for additional equipment at North Carolina College [The Collegiate Institute] ... and the presentation made by the Executive Committee of the plan and purpose to work for the development of the institution, I, John S. Efird agree to give $ - - - - - - - for the erection and equipment of a Science Hall. ... I hereby authorize the Executive Committee to proceed with the consumption of this undertaking at the earliest date practicable."[485]

It appears that after some thought and research, Mr. Efird had a change of heart. On July 17th he wrote:

> "I am advised by different parties that your school cannot last, that it will gradually dwindle away and that the patronage it now receives will naturally be absorbed by grade A schools; and in view of these facts, I feel it would be something like waste of money for temporary purposes and I would like to be permitted to withdraw my pledge. Trusting that I have made myself clear in the situation and asking that you kindly grant my request and awaiting your reply."

Colonel McAllister was certainly surprised and probably terrified over the loss of this promised contribution. Two days after receiving Efird's letter, McAllister replied, and thus began a conversation between the two men which presents a vivid picture of the status of MPCI among a large group of North Carolina Lutheran educational and financial leaders and Colonel McAllister's efforts to overcome the Institute's increasingly negative image and financial difficulties.

On July 19th, McAllister replied to Efird.

> "Your communication of the 17th was duly received. I have read it with painful surprise and disappointment. … I do not know who the parties are that have advised you that the Institute cannot last, that it will gradually dwindle away and that the patronage it now receives will naturally be absorbed by A grade schools. That is but a surmise which you assume as a fact. Present indications do not appear to justify such a conclusion. We are receiving inquiries and applications from a wider area than ever before. … Mr. Efird, I proceeded with entire confidence in your pledge. I sent a newsletter to the Lutheran of Philadelphia, the *NC Lutheran*, the *Charlotte Observer*, the *Raleigh News & Observer*, the *Greensboro News*, the *Winston-Salem Journal*, the *Wilmington Star*, and the *Concord Tribune*. In all these the statement appeared that a good friend had made it possible to improve the scientific equipment of the Institute and that an order had been placed for apparatus for the teaching of General Science, Physics and Chemistry. Moreover, I sent a letter to every student in which I made the statement that we would have Laboratories next session. … While I have the greatest respect for you and would comply with your wishes in every way practicable, I am absolutely estopped from sending out any such ruinous news to the public and to the students. Mr. Efird, in view of the past contributions of the Institute and what it can and will yet do, in view of the devotion and sacrifice of men who have given the best of their lives to the promotion of this institution, I do not see how you can ask me to invite such a calamity on the Institute … **In God's name, do not ask me to do this.**" (emphasis added)

Efird's immediate reply is not known but there was apparently other correspondence between the two men. A letter dated Sept. 4th, 1926 from Efird stated:

> "Your letter of the third is received and I hand you herewith my check for $1000.00 amount of my subscription for science apparatus and laboratory furniture. I trust that you will be able to take care of your bills satisfactorily. I am also pleased to know that you are expecting a good enrollment and I trust that you have before you the very best year of the school's history."

The donation was used to purchase and install apparatus for teaching General Science, Physics and Chemistry and was installed in two rooms on the first floor of the new dormitory. McAllister urged the Board of Trustees to offer a vote of thanks Mr. Efird and "it is hoped too that the Board will lose no opportunity to afford Mr. Efird all assurance of its purpose to work for the better equipment and strengthening of the Institute, to the end that he may carry out his idea of providing a Science Building for the Institute."[486]

In the Summer of 1926, construction was begun on the set of entrance steps and walkway on the front (east) side of the main building. The project was funded by the MPCI classes of 1923 and 1924. The steps were supported by an elaborate concrete façade bordering North Main Street at the edge of the campus and a brick sidewalk which extended to the front door of the Administration building.[487]

The Institute expanded its campaign to raise funds to furnish the rooms in the new dormitory in the Fall of 1926. In addition to appealing to Sunday Schools, they sent a letter and pledge form to other organizations. The letter listed the cost of furnishing twenty-eight rooms as follows:

> "Two Single beds with springs and mattresses; Two chairs; One Rocking Chair; One table with bookcase in ends & with two drawers; One Chiffonier; Shades and Curtains for double window; Two or more suitable Pictures framed - $100;
>
> For Dining Room and Kitchen: Additional Utensils and Furniture for Dining Room of doubled capacity to take care of students who can be quartered on the campus with the enlarged dormitory capacity - $250.

For one Social Room: Two large Settees; One half dozen comfortable Chairs; Two Rocking Chairs; One Table; One large Rug; One Victrola with Records; One half dozen Pictures framed; Shades and Curtains for four double windows - $350.

For Physics Room: Apparatus and Furniture - $750; For Chemistry Room: Apparatus and Furniture - $750.

For Assembly Room (Chapel): One Piano; 200 Folding chairs; Lectern and Chairs for Platform; One half dozen Pictures framed; Shades and Curtains for five double windows - $750"[488]

Colonel McAllister recorded several pledges. The Women's Missionary Society of Augsburg Lutheran Church in Winston-Salem, the Women's Educational League of Hickory, and the Sunday School of St. Mark's Lutheran Church, Charlotte each donated $100 to furnish dorm rooms.[489]

A situation during 1926 involving the Institute's athletic fields was indicative of the complications often encountered by McAllister on MPCI's behalf. It also demonstrated the interwoven relationships that existed among the school and some of its most prominent benefactors.

The issue at hand was the status of the athletic fields that had been used by both NC College and MPCI for many years. The fields were on land originally owned by Jonas Cook, a NC College alumnus, long time College and MPCI Treasurer and very prominent pubic figure. During his lifetime Cook had allowed the College and MPCI to use the fields located east of the Institute directly across Main Street at no charge. Upon his death, his son, John M. Cook, continued to allow free use of the property. John M. Cook was also a NC College alumnus and served as the Treasurer of MPCI until his death in 1924.

For perspective and an understanding of how this family was intertwined with the school, note that Colonel McAllister was the son of Jonas Cook's sister. John M. Cook was the husband of Alma Shirey who was the daughter of former and highly esteemed President of NC College, the late Rev. John D. Shirey. Winona Cook Shirey, the sister of John M. Cook, was the wife of the late Luther Shirey, son of Rev. Shirey. He, too, was a NC College alumnus and had served on the Mt. Pleasant Town

Board. In 1926, Winona Shirey and Karl Cook, the youngest son of Jonas Cook lived in the family homeplace which overlooked the athletic fields.

It is not clear from existing records who initiated the exchange, but it appears that the status of the athletic fields was being discussed by the Cook family heirs. In October 1926, McAllister wrote to John Cook's widow, Alma Shirey Cook, concerning continued use of the fields. McAllister noted that Jonas and John M. Cook had both allowed the College and the Institute to use the fields and that "the Institute gratefully appreciated this kindness."

He expressed that:

> "I have entertained the hope that the Institute might sometime come into possession of this Athletic Field, and still hope that good fortune may fall to the Institute. Last Commencement, the Alumni Association started a movement looking toward the building of a fence around the Athletic Field and the erection of a grandstand. The Secretary of the Association has been conducting a successful campaign for funds for the purpose. We now have pledges and cash nearly enough to build the fence. Of course, we shall not presume to erect the fence without proper authorization from the owners of the land. The fence will not depreciate the property. Rather it would enhance it. At any time, the owners of the land should make disposition of the property, the fence and grandstand would of course go with it."

McAllister continued that he had contacted Jonas Cook's son, Karl, who still lived in the homeplace, who had expressed his willingness to build the fence. McAllister wrote that he intended to visit Karl and his sister, Winnona [(Shirey), and he hoped that Alma would also agree.

> "I need hardly emphasize to you the desirability of an enclosure from the standpoint of our Athletic Association. It is very hard for us to arrange for games on the home grounds and pay guarantees and not get any more than we do from spectators."[490]

Mrs. Cook replied on Oct. 29th, 1926.

> "As I consult B. B. Miller about everything of a business nature, I did so regarding the Athletic Field. I am enclosing his reply for your perusal. Since we do not know when we might have to dispose of the farm, it would seem that a good deal might be involved for both parties. Therefore, for my part, I am unable to make any definite reply until I have had opportunity for a conference with Winona and Karl.

Mrs. Cook's letter included a copy of the letter she received from her attorney, B. B. Miller. The letter stated that in his (Miller) opinion a contract for more than three years must be in writing and allowing the Institute to use the would not "work an impairment of the title," but if the field were "enclosed and held for twenty years," possession "might be construed as adverse and the title (then) impaired." He continued:

> "There should be a definite understanding between the parties about the matter – otherwise embarrassing complication may arise. ... In law a lessee is not permitted to dispute his lessor's title. This is doubtless what Captain Cook had in mind when he required the institution to pay a nominal annual rental."[491]

McAllister reported to the Board of Trustees that he was unable to secure the use of Cook Field.[492]

In November of 1926, Colonel McAllister recommended to the Board of Trustees that a "Pay Off Campaign" be instituted to collect all outstanding pledges to the Institute.[493] The continuing struggle to keep MPCI operational was further highlighted in a letter written in January 1927 to Colonel McAllister from Rev. William J. Boger. Rev. Boger was a NC College alumnus and President of the Board of Trustees. He was also the brother-in-law of the late Jonas Cook. In his letter, Boger stated, reference to the replacement of one of the members of the Board of Trustees, "it looks like someone is trying to put us out of business at Lenoir Rhyne." Boger was referring to the replacement of Rev. Nathan D. Bodie, who was succeeded by Rev. Charles E. Ridenhour. While Ridenhour was an alumnus of MPCI, he graduated from Newberry College and was also a member of the Lenoir-Rhyne Board of Trustees. Boger appears to be implying that the membership of the Board of Trustees was being manipulated to strengthen support for Lenoir-Rhyne, while still seemingly backing MPCI.[494]

In February, the Lutheran Synod met in Salisbury. Colonel McAllister delivered his report to the Committee on Educational Institutions. He stated that while the Scientific equipment donated by J. S. Efird in 1926 "greatly aided MPCI, it was only temporary," in terms of gaining Junior College status. To be approved, The school needed a larger endowment, more buildings, equipment and faculty. "The Board has no resources at its disposal which would warrant any further advances." McAllister further stated that "there remains a subscription of $12,000 from a campaign of some years ago [1925] known as the '$150,000 Campaign,'" which resulted in only $3,000, most of which went to Lenoir-Rhyne College. Absent these funds, there was still a need for additional equipment.

Finally McAllister reported on the "Financial Status of the Institute" stating that the $75,000 Campaign to fund the construction and equipping of the new dormitory had collected, to date, $30,779. Loans totaling $23,000 had been secured to complete the building, but there remained a campaign shortfall of $20,000 which was needed for unfunded expenses.[495]

In April 1927, the Institute reported receipts of $30,847.82 with $27,893.49 collected from tuition, fees, board, room rent, uniforms and books. $662.70 was received from athletic events. Expenses also totaled $30,847.82 with two largest costs being salaries at $10,675 and boarding hall, food and fuel costs at $11,578.12.[496]

The Spring of 1927 brought a major change to the Institute. Mont Amoena Seminary, the female academy and MPCI's sister institution in Mt. Pleasant, was closed. The Board of Trustees voted to allow former female students of the Seminary residing in the community to attend MPCI as "day students." MPCI was about to become a co-educational school.[497]

During the Summer of 1927, the Board of Trustees appointed a committee to inventory the property on the MCPI campus that belonged to Colonel McAllister personally. The list included one clock, six pictures, one complete set of mahogany office fixtures, a typewriter, maps, two desks, two globes, a new set of International Encyclopedias, three wardrobes, two dressers, seven student tables, four army cots, twenty-five chairs in Barracks #2, and all the chairs & stools in the Boarding Hall, four drums, one saxophone, one dresser, all of the knives, forks, spoons, dishes and other table ware, the refrigerator, icebox, scales, jars, electric dishwasher, range, and cooking utensils in the Boarding Hall, all of the guns and sabers, all of the athletic supplies, a flagpole, two lawn settees, two benches, various books, and $100 interest in a piano.[498]

In November 1927, *The Institute News* reported that:

> "Colonel McAllister's new home which was begun in July is completed. It is a two story, nine room, brick veneer building and one of the most beautiful homes in MP. Due to the fact that Mrs. McAllister has been ill with influenza, they have not yet been able to move into their new home. They are hoping to move by Christmas."[499]

In December, Colonel McAllister informed the Board of Trustees that the drop in enrollment from previous years was due to the opening of several new County High Schools and the sub-freshman class was affected by these new schools "providing for more of that contingent."

McAllister noted that the Institute could benefit from a "considerable fund" to be "wisely used" to improve the physical plant, provide for an athletic field and a gymnasium. He closed by asking that: "I sincerely trust that the Board of Trustees will give serious thought to this matter, and by the year 1930, if not before, devise a constructive program for meeting these needs and placing the Collegiate Institute unqualifiedly in first class Junior College standing."

At the same time McAllister recommended a fund to improve the physical plant, he reported that a note of $20,000 (from the construction of the new dormitory) was due and there were no funds to pay it. The Board recommended payment of the interest on the note. He also approached the Board with a request to solicit donations from former students and friends of Professor H. T. J. Ludwig to be used to construct a new hall on the campus as a memorial to Ludwig. According to McAllister, "such a project had been attempted before but was allowed to go by default as a result of the unfortunate condition of the administration of the college at the time."[500]

Reflecting Colonel McAllister's ongoing attempts to keep the school on viable financial footing, he made one last proposal. One that had been debated several times over the years, but had not been implemented. He proposed that the Collegiate Institute consider admitting local women who were **not** previously students at Mont Amoena. He stated that, "Any provision for the future, especially on an enlarged scale for taking care of girls can best be made by arranging for coordinate school quarters at the Seminary building." The Board took no action on this request and, as later records indicate, the proposal was never initiated.[501]

At the Board of Trustees meeting in Mt. Pleasant on May 17, 1928, Colonel McAllister informed the Board that it was necessary to borrow more money to keep the Institute open. He sincerely recommended that MPCI be added to the ongoing Lenoir-Rhyne College fund raising campaign. Colonel McAllister informed the Trustees that he hoped to have the Institute in "1st Class Junior College standing" by 1930. The financial statement for 1927-'28 listed receipts of $34,855. $32,600 was from tuition, room rent, board, uniforms, books and fees and the United Lutheran Church of America contributed $2,083. Expenses of $34,855 included $11,500 for salaries and $11,154.31 for boarding hall, food, supplies and service expenses. Uniform costs were $5,444.51 and advertising, printing and postage expense was $2,059.19.[502]

During the summer of 1928, Colonel McAllister continued the struggle with the Institute's finances. In June of 1928, William L. Burns Vice-President of Cabarrus Savings Bank wrote to Board of Trustees President Reverend W. J. Boger concerning the $20,000 loan that the Board had recently voted to pay only the interest. Evidently, Rev. Boger wrote a "pessimistic" reply.

A letter from Board Member Harry E. Isenhour to McAllister registered that he "did not like the tone of Dr. Boger's letter," and that "such a letter would not help our standing at the bank but would further the aims of **a certain bunch at Hickory** (emphasis added)."[503]

From other correspondence, it appears that the Institute Board of Trustees planned an attempt to acquire some funds from the sale of the now defunct Mont Amoena Seminary. At the time, the Committee handling the sale of this property was negotiating with some citizens in Mt. Pleasant and there was a question over whether the price offered was adequate to help the Institute.[504]

Isenhour wrote:

> "I had a very frank talk with Dr. Morgan [former President of Lenoir-Rhyne College] … His heart and sympathy are with the Institute. He does not like the way things have been going at Hickory and especially the evident desire to the folks up there to get rid of the schools at Mt. Pleasant at any cost. He agreed that having the same board of trustees [for Lenoir-Rhyne and MPCI] was a mistake."[505]

At the same time Isenhour was corresponding with Colonel McAllister, he visited John S. Efird in Albemarle. It should be recalled that Efird and Colonel McAllister corresponded in 1926 in reference to funding a new science laboratory. Earlier, Efird had been very negative about the financial status of the Institute, but after several rounds of letters, McAllister persuaded him to contribute and to further support the school. According to Isenhour, Mr. Efird was very supportive of the Institute and "told me that he had made up his mind to fight for the welfare of the institutions at Mt. Pleasant, even if he had to do it single handed." Apparently, Efird promised to contact Mr. Burns at the Cabarrus Bank, because Isenhour concludes his letter by stating, "I don't believe we will have any great trouble in getting the bank to continue the loan."[506]

The outcome was verified five days later when Isenhour wrote to McAllister commenting that:

> "I am glad to report to you that I had a very satisfactory conference with Mr. Burns. He assured me that it was not the desire of the bank to cause us any unnecessary worry. I put the situation before him and told him exactly what we hoped to do … He promised to allow renewals of the notes as they become due until we can arrange to pay them off."[507]

On October 30th, 1928, in response to the Lutheran Church of America's two year old resolution that called for churches to dedicate the year 1930 to strengthening its educational institutions, the NC Synod met in Salisbury, NC to begin organizing a campaign "in the interest of institutions within their bounds." Earlier in 1928, MPCI Trustees requested that the Synod authorize $100,000 for the Institute, and the

Synod resolved to raise $300,000 for Lenoir-Rhyne College and $100,000 for the Collegiate Institute.[508]

The *Institute News* assured its readers:

> "The amount designated is to be used to pay off and indebtedness of $20,000 and will go far toward establishing the status of the Institute as a Junior College. This action of the Board will pave the way. It is confidently expected and believed, for substantial gifts from friends who have been awaiting an opportunity to do something worthwhile for an institution which has made such a notable contribution to the Church."[509]

In November of 1928, Colonel McAllister wrote to the US War Department in an attempt obtain weapons or monetary aid to purchase new rifles for Cadet drill training. Prior to 1928, the Institute furnished its own weapons (paid for by Colonel. McAllister) which were "rented" to the Cadets for $1.00 a session with a 50¢ refund at the end of the year.

McAllister's request ran into some difficulties. A letter dated November 5th, 1928 from the US Adjutant General's Office indicated that "budgetary consideration" precluded any financial aid to the school, but that there was a possibility that the Institute could obtain surplus rifles and ammunition for target practice. McAllister was directed to contact Major General Lutz, US Army Adjutant General.[510]

A few days later, McAllister received a letter from Major J. R. Brooks, Jr., Director of Civilian Marksmanship. Major Brooks advised McAllister that his office could issue equipment to schools, "primarily for target practice," but it required the students to fire on a target range in order to retain the equipment.[511]

It is not clear from existing records if the Institute engaged in target practice or any discharge of the weapons they were issued. It is known that in the early years students kept their rifles in their rooms, but at some point several of the rooms on the second floor of the Administration Building were converted into an "armory" where the weapons were stored. If target practice occurred, the Chairman of the Board of Trustees was unaware of it.

Colonel McAllister wrote to Board Chairman Boger concerning the matter. He attempted to explain the Institute's "weapons policy" to Rev.

Boger and to assure him that he had the situation under control. He informed Boger that "ever since we have had the military feature in the Collegiate Institute, we have furnished our own guns, etc. These are becoming worn and unusable. Many schools such as ours and gun clubs secure guns from the Federal Government for this use."

He informed Boger that he had applied to the War Department for guns, and that "certain forms must be observed, among them approval of the Chairman of the Board of Trustees. McAllister clarified that "this approval does not involve you or the Board in any way. I will give bond for the proper care of guns and their return when called for by the Government." He assured Boger that:

> "It is not our intention to expand our Military system beyond the purpose (we) originally had in mind when the system was introduced, namely, to give boys needed physical exercise and development and to properly control and regulate the school. We shall have to let the cadets engage in firing the rifles upon occasion, but it is not in our mind to devote much time to that. I am therefore asking you to sign at the indicated place, the application. …"[512]

Boger responded that he had no problem approving the acquisition of the rifles, but he was "hesitant" to okay the ammunition. "I don't know what the Board will say about it. It ought at least to have come before the Exec. Board. I am not sure the Board will approve it. As I see it now without further information, I am frank to say personally I would vote against it." He continued that he wanted to delay the matter until the December Board meeting but did not want to "hinder you getting the guns." Boger agreed to sign the form, but asked McAllister to defer from requisitioning the ammunition until the Board could discuss it. "I do not like to take responsibility where I am not sure of myself."[513]

It is not clear from existing records how this situation was resolved, but the Institute received "new" weapons and Cadets began "target practice." The equipment was received in March 1929, and included 80 .30 caliber M/1917 rifles valued at $2,832; 80 gun slings at $104; 80 M/1917 bayonets at $360; 8 chests for storage of rifles at $45, and 3,600 rounds of .30 caliber M/1906 ammunition at $151.[514]

On December 17th, 1928, H. B. Wilkinson, Institute Treasurer, reported to Colonel McAllister that the school had financial assets of $5,667.29. The Endowment Fund held $4,375 plus $31.84 in income. The C. H. Fisher Fund contained $1,000. The "$150,000 Campaign" fund held $21.90 and another $604 in "undivided" monies. The "$75,000 Campaign" account retained $183.55. There was also $175 uncollected from bonds and stamps[515]

At the Board of Trustees meeting in February 1929, Colonel McAllister discussed that for consideration as a Junior College, the Institute needed $50,000 insurance coverage and that there were no funds available to purchase this coverage. The Trustees voted to request that the Lutheran Synod take over the insurance.[516]

In March, the assets and indebtedness of the Institute (NC College) were conveyed to the Trustees. Assets included 16$^{1/4}$ acres of land valued at $12,000, buildings worth $95,000, equipment worth $13,000, and the Weiser house and lot (former Bittle house) valued at $5,000. Endowment funds totaled $4,250 with income of $125. The Endowment was invested with Cabarrus Bank & Trust ($3,100) and in Liberty Bonds ($2,150 at 4.24% interest). The C.H. Fisher scholarship fund contained $1,000. There were pledges of $150,000 from the "College Campaign" but two-thirds of the interest from the MPCI pledges was uncollected. The Institute also had an outstanding $20,000 loan for which interest was due.[517]

Colonel McAllister informed the Board of Trustees that receipts for the year were $35,435.45 with $33,681 coming from tuition, room rent, board, fees, uniforms and books. Disbursements of $35,435.45 included $11,750 for salaries and $10,655.71 for boarding hall expenses.[518]

In October 1929, Colonel McAllister told the Board of Trustees that the school needed to increase the endowment and that the bathrooms in the main building and new dorm needed repair. Repairs were delayed due to lack of funds.

McAllister also reported that the Institute did not meet the State standard for a fully accredited Junior College. The State University (UNC) and other colleges gave credit for Institute courses, but the State Department of Education did not. McAllister clarified that the situation could be resolved by increasing the teaching force and broadening the course of study.[519] McAllister had learned of the Junior College issue in July in an exchange with J. Henry Highsmith, Director of Division

School Inspection - NC Department of Public Instruction, in reference to an MPCI graduate's application for admission to NC State College. Highsmith informed McAllister that "standard high school graduation is required for admission to colleges in this State and the transcript should show that the student has been regularly graduated." According to the Department of Education records, the Institute had no College rating. Thus, completion of "the course" at MPCI would be considered as a high school diploma only. Highsmith specified that unless there was a clear line of demarcation between high school and junior college courses, and the college work accredited, students would get no additional credit towards advanced entrance into a college except that granted by the colleges individually.

> "Unless a definite course is pursued and definite requirements for high school graduation set up we shall be under the necessity of interpreting that only those who have completed the entire course at the Collegiate Institute will be entitled to admission to college without examination."[520]

Issues continued to mount as Col. McAllister struggled onward with the operation of the Institute. The Synod continued discussions about the future of the school and in October 1929, the United Lutheran Church of America cut its appropriation to MPCI by 60%, an income reduction of $500. McAllister urged the Trustees to protest the action.[521]

Yet another negative financial transaction occurred in October. As described earlier, NC College had loaned Mont Amoena Seminary $1,475 at six percent interest in 1898. While the interest had been paid, the principle remained outstanding when Mont Amoena closed in 1927. Since that time, the Special Committee on the Liquidation of the Mont Amoena Seminary had been trying to dispose of the property. In October, the Committee announced that there was an offer of $12,500 and that pending the sale and settlement of claims, the Institute would receive any remaining balance.[522] The sale did not go through.

In February 1930, an alarming letter from BoT member, H. E. Isenhour forewarned Colonel McAllister concerning Synod actions toward the school:

> "Confidentially, there is a systematic undercover campaign being waged by the folks at Hickory to gradually get all the affairs of Synod concentrated in and around the College [Lenoir-Rhyne]. If I am not mistaken, you will see this come out at Synod this year. Every ounce of influence of those of the "old guard" is going to have to be used over the next few years to keep the administrative offices, officers, etc. away from Hickory. They have launched a policy that is very dangerous to the Synod and one that will have to be met and defeated without very much talk."[523]

In the Spring of 1930, the Board of Trustees, urged by Colonel McAllister and several other supporters of the Institute, decided to conduct their own campaign to raise $100,000. In April, *The Institute News* outlined these needs. In an article entitled "The 1930 Campaign," the newsletter stated that the "first endowment [was] sacrificed to the 'Lost Cause'" (the Civil War), that urgent needs included an increased endowment above the current $5,000, athletic fields (currently rented), a gymnasium, an on-campus auditorium, and restoration of Pi Sigma Phi/ Ludwig Literary Hall.[524]

The Board of Trustees hired former MPCI graduate, Carl H, Monsees, of Carl H. Monsees and Associates of Salisbury, MD, to oversee the campaign. Monsees' contract stipulated that he was to be paid $125 per week plus traveling expenses and 10% of the funds raised.[525]

Monsees' firm produced a pamphlet entitled "The Collegiate Institute, Mt. Pleasant, North Carolina, A Lutheran Preparatory School and Junior College Serving the Entire South Is Now Face to Face With The Question of Existence," making "An Urgent Appeal for Friends and Immediate Funds … It is essential that $50,000 be made immediately available with which to pay off the existing debt, secure positively necessary equipment and to begin an endowment fund." The pamphlet contained a photo of Colonel McAllister with a brief biography and a short history of the beginning of the school. A landscape photo of the campus filled two pages and there was a description of the Institute's current academic program. It concluded with the entreaty, "Shall these doors close, to open no more? Shall these strong walls unsheltered, go down in dust for need of GOLD?"

Or shall the Collegiate Institute, founded on strong traditions, continue its noble work for Christian Manhood – indeed, living Memorials of your help?"[526]

Monsees sent Colonel McAllister two articles from Savannah, Georgia outlining the appeal program. He set a pledge goal of $25,000 to be raised by May 28th. Savannah's quota was $5000. The article contained the remark that "The Collegiate Institute is the Only Lutheran Military Preparatory School and Junior College in the United States … ."[527]

A second article stated that "The Savannah Alumni of the Collegiate Institute, Mount Pleasant, NC will give a card tournament at the Country Club on Thursday, May 22 from 4 to 6 PM and 8 to 10 PM. The proceeds will be used to establish a memorial fund to friends in Savannah."[528]

Local newspapers joined the appeal. On May 27, 1930 the *Concord Daily Tribune* published a long article entitled "The Collegiate Institute's Future Threatened!"

> "The Collegiate Institute at Mt. Pleasant is asking Concord to save its life. Colonel G. F. McAllister has labored faithfully for his institution and the enrichment of education in our state and has become known for the quality of his instruction throughout the United States. He has through these many years of service refused flattering offers to leave and has "stuck to the ship at Mt. Pleasant. The closing of this school would indeed be a loss to Cabarrus County. Mt. Pleasant would become only a crossroad and property would lose its value, thus effecting taxes over the entire county. The money which the Institute and its students spend in Cabarrus would be gone forever. Mont Amoena is already closed. A gradual degeneration is not healthy. An institution which is a part of the life of this county should not be permitted to close for the need of a few thousand dollars. We understand that a few thousand dollars – not more than five at the most – will put Institute on its feet again. … "[529]

Shortly before graduation, when asked about the economic problems facing the historic school, Colonel McAllister responded in a very positive manner, stating that, "The Institute has never had a brighter outlook for service than at present."[530]

Colonel McAllister's 1929-'30 financial statement showed income of $33,225.06. While income versus outflow showed a net balance of zero, the amount collected was a 16.5% decrease from the previous year. Funds from tuition, etc. decreased by 14.7% while Boarding Hall operation expense increased by two percent.[531]

During the 1930 commencement ceremonies, the Board of Trustees Executive Committee met and voted to present a resolution calling upon the NC Synod Executive Board "to agree to assume and pay from the assets of the Collegiate Institute any and all expense, liquidating damages and reasonable enumeration for services to Colonel McAllister in connection with reopening the Institute in September, 1930, provided a loan of $3,500 could be obtained."[532]

Based on the funds projected from the fund-raising campaign and the Board of Trustees' resolution, Colonel McAllister announced on the 28th of May, that "MPCI Will be Continued." McAllister stated that five citizens of Mt. Pleasant had given $200 each, and that Synod would be asked to advance the additional funds necessary to continue the school for another year.[533]

In response to the Board of Trustees' resolution, the Synod Executive Committee indicated that it did not feel justified in considering the petition unless it came from the entire Board of Trustees. As a result, a meeting was scheduled for June 19th, 1930 at the Institute, with the "full" Board of Directors.

Prior to the meeting, H. E. Isenhour warned Colonel McAllister that he should be prepared to address his original (1903) contract with the Executive Committee, and that it may be necessary to "pass an amendment to the agreement" to get the aid he requested. "I think considerable discussion can be avoided by having something definite to offer should the question be raised."[534] Isenhour did not specify what part of McAllister's contract was at issue but it was apparent that the Synod was not going to provide further assistance without changes in the agreement that heretofore had provided them no financial advantage but had, in fact, continued to cost them money.

In the two weeks following commencement and the announcement of the special Board Meeting, a flurry of activity erupted surrounding the fund-raising campaign. As heavy correspondence among the several persons involved in this effort shows, there was much "behind the scenes" work going on to keep the school operational.

Two letters from early June sum up the situation that faced Colonel McAllister and MPCI in 1930. These letters were written as a result of the cut in funding by the Lutheran Church in America in October 1929, to which McAllister had urged the Board of Trustees to respond. It is not clear if McAllister wrote to the United Lutheran Church of America (ULCA) earlier, but nine months after the fact, he penned a very long letter to Reverend Norman J. G. Wickey, Chairman of the United Lutheran Church of America.

McAllister began by reminding Rev. Wickey of his visit to MPCI in the Spring of 1929 when he (McAllister) stressed the need for help and requested that the ULCA consider giving its usual amount to the institute or possibly increasing it. (According to previous financial records, the amount averaged between $1,000 to $2,000 annually.) In a very candid comment McAllister stated, "in truth, Dr. Wickey, it was the cutting down of the appropriation … that proved 'the straw that broke the camel's back' in the finances of the Collegiate Institute," and created the necessity to raise an emergency fund in order to keep the Institute open. McAllister wrote that he was, himself, suffering financial hardship trying to keep the school open and the he "faced the possibility of losing all I had in an effort to tide over a very hard year (due to the depression that was so widespread)." He continued, "I have given 33 years of my life to this work. With what fidelity, zeal, earnestness, and results educational, I leave it to those who know best the work of the Institute to say. At any rate, the Board, the Synod and the friends of this cause do not want to see it abandoned." In closing, McAllister described the emergency appeal:

> "… local friends are manifesting real interest. Just yesterday, a millionaire of Concord, not of our church, indicated interest and said he was going to help. The Pres of the National Bank did the same thing. A visit to a very wealthy man of our church ten days ago elicited the promise to help. The Collegiate Institute is the only Preparatory School and Junior College with Military

> feature in the United Lutheran Church. It has a place in our system, the Church South believes. The attitude of the Board of Education of the United Lutheran Church is of vital significance, ... surely the Board of Education of the United Lutheran Church will not fail to lend encouragement and increased support.[535] (See endnote for the entire letter)

On the same date as Colonel McAllister's letter to Rev. Wickey, Rev. Jacob L. Morgan, the first President of the merged Lutheran Synod of North Carolina and an Ex Officio member of the Board of Trustees, wrote to Wickey. Rev. Morgan began by declaring that while the matter should rightly be left to the Synod Committee on Educational Institutions, he had a personal interest in the Institute. His statement accurately reflected the relationship between MPCI and the NC Lutheran Synod and foreshadowed the impending climax of their twenty-seven-year association.

> "We hope your Board will give prayerful and sympathetic consideration to the pressing needs of the Institute at this time. I am afraid a mistaken notion has gotten into the minds of some of our good brethren regarding the finances of this school. **When Dr. H. B. Schaeffer and myself met with a Committee from your Board to consider the needs of the Institute and of Lenoir Rhyne College last year, some of the Board members advanced the opinion that the Institute was a splendidly paying business and that Prof. McAllister was making good money out of it. I tried then to disabuse the minds of the brethren of such a notion, for I could not see how more than a living could be made out of the school as operated.** [emphasis added]

Rev. Morgan verified the well-known fact that Lenoir-Rhyne was receiving funding while the Institute was left lacking.

> "It has not come to our knowledge that Prof. McAllister has lost money in his efforts to operate the school during the past year. We are advised that he has paid himself only $525 salary for his year's work and that he owes bills and accounts amounting to two thousand or

> twenty-five hundred dollars for the year's operations. … I want to urge your Board to do all it can to come to the rescue of the Institute at this time and restore it if possible."[536] (See endnote for the entire letter.)

In the meantime, the fund-raising campaign "hard targeted" the local (Cabarrus County) community for funds. A pamphlet aimed at the local community began:

"The Collegiate Institute – Is A Business and Cultural Asset to Concord & Cabarrus – Will You Help It Continue and Expand? The Collegiate Institute's appeal to Concord & Cabarrus County citizens is a business proposition with an element of sentiment. On this basis Concord will or will not do its part in the present appeal for help and program of expansion; on this basis the Institute will secure or will not secure the amount it is asking. Whatever the result, it will be Cabarrus' and Concord's answer as to whether or not it is good business to have this institution operating in Mt. Pleasant."

The pamphlet itemized "facts and figures" declaring that the Institute generated about $600 per student per year in income for Cabarrus County and that, multiplied by 100 students the financial impact equaled $60,000 a year. "Does it, or will it make any difference whether this Institution operates or not? Other cities are paying big prices for Institutions of learning, because it is good business to have new money coming in every year …."[537]

Various other articles were printed and reprinted in several newspapers and letters were written to wealthy persons soliciting funds. W. L. Morris, Jr., Chairman of the Cabarrus Fund Raising Committee, wrote a letter to James A. Cannon of nearby Cannon Mills requesting help. "Whatever you find it in your heart to give will be most gratefully appreciated by all interested in seeing this noble work continued."[538]

Another letter from Morris to Rev. Lester D. Miller, the Executive Chairman of the fund-raising campaign, further summarized the effort.

> "For the last two weeks we have been trying to raise sufficient funds to keep the Collegiate Institute from closing. It has been quite a job since we had so few helpers in solicitation and unfortunately our appeal had to come during this period of business depression. We

> have raised to date in the county $2,490 with prospect of reaching $3,000. I, personally, and the other Alumni and Supporters have tried hard to show you in unmistakable terms what we think of your continuing the Institute, and are confidently hoping that your Committee will find ways and means of not only continuing the school, but also putting it on such a basis that it will expand and prosper."[539]

Shortly after the 1930 commencement, a newspaper article entitled "Lutheran School Saved from Closing" described the campaign conducted by Carl Monsees as having been successful.

> "The fate of the institution had been hanging in the balance for several weeks and Colonel G. F. McAllister, the Principal, was unable to state whether the institution would re-open in September pending the outcome of the campaign, but due to the splendid aid given by Mr. Monsees of Salisbury, MD, former Savannanian and alumnus of the Institute, and other friends and supporters the school was saved from closing. Plans are now being laid for a general campaign to be started in Cabarrus Co. NC to be extended in October to a drive for $100,000 among the Lutheran of the Synod of NC."[540]

In June, Carl Monsees wrote to Reverend Miller presenting a rather less optimistic picture of the fund-raising effort. Monsees reported that his campaign had raised $3007.75 in seven weeks. He gave several reasons for the slow progress and detailed sources of the money.

> "1. Our appeal was made too near the close of school to receive the full benefit of 'to keep the school from closing' theme. 2. Three weeks were spent with headquarters in Savannah, GA. ... From Savannah we have received $536.75. 3. At the suggestion of your Committee through Colonel McAllister I returned to Mt. Pleasant a few days before Commencement for the purpose of calling on a few individuals. While doing this the Concord papers were carrying our story. No money resulted from this personal canvass work. But during this period the people

at Mt. Pleasant were solicited and $848 was subscribed. 4. … To make a county appeal was out of the question, consequently attention was given only to Mt. Pleasant, Kannapolis and Concord. At this writing something over $2,400 has been raised in the county. 5. I believe that we have not spent enough time on any of our attempts with probably the exception of Concord."

Monsees maintained that two factors explained the inability to raise more funds – "the present business depression and the large number of uncollected pledges among local churches, "especially Lutheran."[541]

He then gave his take on the future of the campaign.

> "This is the first attempt to secure funds outside of North Carolina, and only three weeks were given to that, a very poor basis on which to make any judgments as to possibilities. We have reached as many non-Lutheran as Lutherans in our appeal… The Lutheran support was negligible. I believe because of the indebtedness of the local church. I have received meager help from the alumni. The Institute has begun a big work for itself. (Synod) Ways and Means should be found to continue this effort."[542]

Finally, Monsees got to what appears to have been the real point of his letter. His statements appear to have been sincere, but the bottom line was that he wanted to be paid.

> "It is embarrassing to me to now accept the conditions of our agreement based on our contract never signed, and yet I am financially unable to operate without remuneration. I sincerely wish that I could. Your operator left Mt. Pleasant with only $350 to care for all expenses. This amount was generously put up by Mr. A. W. Fisher. This amount was soon consumed, and your operator has only … that which has been deposited due to his own efforts, since that time. I have labored like this because our work was to me more than financial remuneration, was a labor a love in which I hoped to be able to reward Colonel McAllister for his personal gift to me and for his

unrewarded service to our church and Christian manhood in general."[543]

The campaign continued but a rumor surfaced that may have had a negative effect on the effort. Rev. Morgan wrote to McAllister:

> "Somehow the idea got started from some angle that there might be an effort to locate the Institute in Georgia, which of course would be looked upon as disquieting for those who want Georgia to come across at the approaching called meeting of Synod and join forces in Newberry College. Dr. Voight seemed concerned. I tried to assure the brethren that no unethical efforts were contemplated which seemed to ease off the matter and I think no harm has been occasioned so far, but I believe we would be misunderstood were we to continue to work that territory."[544]

Two letters located in Colonel McAllister's papers demonstrated that there may have been some truth to the rumor. Mr. A. Bates Lovett, Chairman of the University Council of the Savannah, Georgia Chamber of Commerce wrote:

> "Your communication of the 19th inst. was duly received, and contents carefully noted. From several sources, I have learned of the interest your city has in an institution of learning. Your city and people are to be commended for this and I should say that if the interest is sufficiently general and persists you will get an institution. ..."[545]

A second letter from Thomas M. Hoynes, President of the Savannah Chamber of Commerce, read:

> "We deeply appreciate the thoughts suggested in your letter. The writer cannot forecast at this time just what is going to take place in Savannah, except that we are all convinced that we need additional facilities which extend beyond the high school course. I can only express appreciation and say that this matter is being given careful thought."[546]

As anticipated by H. E. Isenhour, a Special Board meeting convened on June 19, 1930 intent on producing a "definite proposal" for the Synod.

> "... the Executive Committee of the Collegiate Institute to borrow in its name, from whatever source available ... the sum of $3,500 to be used in removing a deficit of $1,500 incurred in the operation of the said Institute for the year 1929-30, and to provide the sum of $2,000 for use in making the necessary preparation of the said Institute for the year 1930-31."[547]

Colonel McAllister provided a financial statement of the status of the Institute. There were $6,241.79 in expenses due, with $1,232.69 in the bank. Unpaid salaries totaled $1,886.05 of which, $1,386.05 was due McAllister. There was also a need to have available "several hundred dollars" for repairs and refurnishing during the summer."[548]

In July Carl Monsees wrote to McAllister suggesting a "plan to force the Synod's hand" into making a decision concerning the future of the Institute. Monsees suggested that McAllister:

> "Struggle through as best you can to open with as large a student body as possible next session and let the campaign of the Synod go ahead, you are doing what you find time to do for it. It will not net you very much if the situation is not changed and someone delegated to sell NC Lutherans on the worthiness of your work. If it does not reach an encouraging figure of at least fifty or sixty thousand dollars, then there is but one thing for you to do and that is lay your plans for evacuation. The matter for discussion and debate is a question of method and procedure. My thinking leads me to suggest that you should resign about January first to take effect at the close of the session. This will give Synod time to consider the matter. If they want to continue you are protected; if they desire to abandon, they will put a price on the buildings and grounds which cannot be more than the loans against them. This amount would be easily subscribed to make the Collegiate Institute an independent private institution. At the same time the new corporation could lay plans for

> fully equipping the school through the sale of stock. This I believe you will need about two months for this operation, hence the necessity of early action."[549]

Within a short time Monsees' plan became more than a suggestion. In the meantime, Colonel McAllister evidently expressed some difference of opinion regarding Monsees' pay for services. In July Monsees wrote reminding McAllister the he and Board member A. W. Fisher had verbally agreed that "whatever the result, expenses were to be paid first and then myself," and that Fisher again agreed about a week later "before we closed at which time I was about to give up."

> "I think it but fair to a man to take his time with no guarantee of results and no prospect of making any big money that he be cared for in a little better fashion than had been the tendency of your committee. ... It just seems a bit out of order to now hear you tell me that you will split with me what moneys are coming in. The case is in your hands, - I shall appreciate whatever amounts you have and see fit to send me. Above all my heart's in the same place."[550]

As the fund-raising campaign continued into August and September, confusion apparently caused Colonel McAllister to write alumni to remind them of the $100,000 campaign. He explained that, while the campaign was conducted jointly with a campaign for Lenoir-Rhyne, "the alumni of the college are planning a separate effort. It is up to the alumni of the Collegiate Institute, therefore, to concentrate their efforts in behalf of the Institute." He described the need for a "modern enclosed athletic field" and that: "He who helps now will render a double service. Let's go. Yours for a bigger and stronger Collegiate Institute."[551]

A letter to Colonel McAllister from his nephew in Winston-Salem revealed a great deal about the prevailing attitude concerning the future of MPCI.

> "I have wanted to write to talk to you for a while about the campaign for the two schools. As you know next Sunday is the day for the effort to be put forth up here [Winston-Salem]. I am just wondering if you can arrange to spend this weekend with us and be here to let

> these folks up here in on the true light regarding the two schools. … I had a short talk just a few days ago with the man in charge of the work up here. I can't say what his attitude is exactly. He asked me if I knew that at least 75% of the students at MPCI were from families outside the Lutheran Church.
>
> The best I could judge he is in sympathy with the movement. … Some others up here, when they discuss the program, seem to me to want to lay it on heavy when talking about Lenoir and are satisfied to barely mention the other part of the program. … .
>
> I don't know what will be said on the floor Sunday, but I would like to be prepared to let these people up here have the light on the whole subject. If I can prevent it, I will certainly not see Lenoir emphasized any more than MPCI. …"[552]

Whatever the effect of the fund-raising campaign and the support from friends and alumni, it appears that the fate of the Institute was determined as early as August 1930. Reverend W. J. Boger, Chairman of the Board of Trustees and the Synod Educational Committee, received a definitive letter from the Secretary of the Board of the United Lutheran Church of America (ULCA):

> "… the [ULCA] Board found it was impossible to increase the grant to the Collegiate Institute … I am very frank to state that there is quite a sentiment that the Institute fills a definite place in the Lutheran educational situation of your Synod … and that it should be merged with other institutions."[553]

It is unclear whether Colonel McAllister had knowledge of the letter from the ULCA, but activity continued around the various fund-raising campaigns. During September and October of 1930, McAllister or someone from the Institute spoke at a different Lutheran church every Sunday concerning the fund-raising campaign,[554] and in February 1931, the NC Synod convened its annual meeting at Beth Eden Lutheran Church in Newton.

It appears that nothing prior to the annual meeting alerted Colonel

McAllister or other MPCI supporters that a major decision was about to be made concerning the future of the school. Early in the meeting, the Committee on Education testified that the general Educational Campaigns had raised $122,254 since 1929, but that only $1,950 had been designated for MPCI. McAllister conveyed that only $1065.75 had been raised by the Institute's independent campaign. As a consequence of these financial statements, the letter from the ULCA, and, doubtless, other circumstances, Rev. Boger requested that the Synod "take some definite action and give some definite instruction concerning conducting this Institution."[555]

On February 11, 1931, the Committee on Church Institutions and Education delivered its recommendation.

> "The Report of North Carolina College presents a serious financial situation and asks for instruction ... We recommend that the Synod assume the payment of the debt of $20,000 and interest thereon ... and authorize the Board of Trustees ... to arrange for the payment of the debt.
>
> **We recommend that the Synod hereby instruct the Board of Trustees for Educational Institutions and the Board of Trustees of North Carolina College to cancel the agreement made by the Evangelical Lutheran Synod and Ministerium of North Carolina in 1903 with the Reverend H. A. McCullough and Professor G. F. McAllister and their successors under which agreement the Collegiate Institute is now operated.**
>
> **We recommend that the Synod instruct the Board of Trustees for Educational Institutions and the Board of Trustees of North Carolina College to discontinue the Collegiate Institute as soon as, ... it seems to be wise, but so as not to involve the Synod in further financial liability of the property as will be in the best interest of the Synod."** [emphasis added][556]

Following the introduction of the resolution, Colonel McAllister addressed the Synod. According to several sources, he "bitterly assailed the body for its consistent policy of aggrandizing Lenoir-Rhyne and neglecting the Institute." Colonel McAllister's "attack" centered on what he termed the Synod's neglect of the school. He cited the report of Dr. Schaeffer, President of Lenoir-Rhyne College, which stated that the funds raised in the educational campaign of the past year totaled $131,000 with only $6,000 pledged to the Institute. McAllister further charged that the funds from the campaign were seriously manipulated such that Mt. Pleasant received little benefit and that this was the first time in twenty-eight years that the Institute had asked for help.[557]

According to an article in the *Concord Daily Tribune*, Committee Chariman, Rev. Boger responded to McAllister "with a vigorus defense" of the recommendation. He declared that "the Institute had lost its standing in North Carolina before the Synod united with the Tennessee Synod," and that there was no unfairness in the distribution of funds.[558]

The Synod proceeded to vote "to liquidate the Institute." (emphasis added)

Although they had voted to terminate their relationship with MPCI, they agreed to keep the school open for the remainder of the current term. *The Concord Tribune* stated that "just what the Synod's action means it is impossible to tell now. …" Supposedly, "the suggestion had been made that as a tribute to his long usefulness to the Church and State, the property should be left with Colonel McAllister, so long as he might want it for a school." To this speculation McAllister replied, "while hesitant about the future, I ask that my friends not to be impatient, that in due time things will be worked out."[559]

Supporters of Colonel McAllister and MPCI immediately voiced their distress over the Synod's decision. Former student, Dr. Zeno L. Edwards, DDS, MPCI, 1914 wrote:

> "I am thoroughly convinced that the Educational Board of the Lutheran Synod is not in sympathy with the progress of the Collegiate Institute. Neither has it given Colonel McAllister the support and cooperation which he had a right to expect and certainly to which he was entitled. Lenoir-Rhyne College, the great institution that it is, seems to be the center of affection of this board even to the exclusion and expense of the Collegiate Institute, which might be appropriately termed the 'Red headed

> stepchild' of the Lutheran Synod. ... Instead of canceling its contract with Colonel McAllister and ordering liquidation of the Institute's property, the Synod should not only deed to Colonel McAllister all of the Institute's holdings but should set up a trust fund upon which he could retire at some future time, in order to show in a small way its appreciation for his many years of service in moulding [sic] character and training young men in Christian education."[560]

On March 3rd, the Synod Executive Committee met in Concord to discuss the withdrawal of support from MPCI. The Committee resolved that the property be conveyed by the NC College Board of Trustees to the Evangelical Lutheran Synod of North Carolina "... as consideration for the payment of said debit [$20,000 mortgage], subject to such indebtedness as may legally exist against the same." Further, they resolvedt:

> "A committee of three be appointed ... to endeavor to lease said property to Prof. G. F. McAllister for school purposes for a period not to exceed ten years, and upon the condition that the lease shall carry and pay the premiums on $20,000 fire insurance on said property in as good condition as it now is, ordinary wear and tear excepted."[561]

In May, McAllister announced that "alumni, friends and patrons are united in a desire to see the Collegiate Institute perpetuated" and that "the Institute will go on." He indicated that a broader course of study would be offered including a scientific and probably a business course. The military feature was to be retained and possibly a Junior ROTC unit organized. Additional teachers were also contemplated. Henceforth the Institute would be governed as an independent, Christian, but non-denominational institution.[562]

Already recruiting, McAllister described the new dormitory as "one of the best dormitory buildings in the state, accommodating 52 students in 12x15 rooms with built-in closets, a lavatory with hot and cold running water. There were also toilet rooms on each floor finished in tile and marble with showers on each floor."[563]

Over the next two months Colonel McAllister negotiated the terms of a contract with the Synod, assembled a new Board of Directors and worked to retain a staff of teachers.

Although the Lutheran Synod no longer supported the Institute and Colonel McAllister was operating the school independently, some members of the Synod Committee on Educational Institutions were not happy with the "deal" given to him. While McAllister had his own Board of Directors, the Lutheran Synod maintained its Board of Trustees to oversee the property. In effect, there were now two Boards of Directors overseeing MPCI.[564]

H. E. Isenhour wrote to McAllister in November:

> "The 'foes of the Institute seem not to be reconciled about the disposition made of the property. It has come to me that members of the Special Committee that affected the lease with you made it appears to the Board at its last meeting that the lease executed was not approved by them. The Board passed a 'foolish' resolution rejecting the lease and instructing the committee to have one executed that was approved by the committee. It is clear to me that it is an effort to "unload" the responsibility on me for the whole matter. I have written the committee and Board Chairman of the facts. I have further told them that the lease would stand as executed unless they could break it by court action. It's rather a dirty deal that is being handed me."[565]

Apparently, when the Committee was not able to repudiate the lease with McAllister, they began to "investigate" the status of the Fire Insurance Policy. McAllister payed for the fire Insurance Policy as "rent" for use of the MPCI buildings. Isenhour wrote to McAllister in December:

> "They [the Education Committee] are demanding that I instruct you to have $20,000.00 insurance put in force on the above date, in compliance with the terms of the lease. Since there appears no way to work this matter out in the way we had contemplated, I would suggest that you have $20,000.00 insurance put in force on the above date."[566]

McAllister's problems did not end with the Synod. In December 1931, he received a letter from the U. S. War Department's Director of Civilian Marksmanship notifying him that according to the War Department equipment inventory, three cleaning rods and one bayonet were missing. If these items could not be located, the Institute would be liable $5.71 to the Director of Civilian Marksmanship.[567]

In May 1932, Colonel McAllister submitted an Annual Report to "The Board of Trustees," It appears that this Board was the one McAllister appointed and not that of Lutheran Synod. According to McAllister total receipts for the past year were $26,167.58, with disbursement, (both paid out and due) totaling $25,305.93.

Although the report showed that the school made a small profit during the year, McAllister said:

> "It goes without saying that this has been a most difficult year to finance a school. Although our catalogued terms are specific, yet with the depression, low prices and bank failures, to have enforced our terms rigidly and without exceptions would have worked too great a hardship upon a number of patrons and possibly caused such a depletion in our enrollment as to seriously menace the ongoing of the school. Consequently, I have extended indulgence and we come to the close of the session with a number of unpaid bills."[568]

McAllister's report demonstrated no indications that the school was in danger of closure. In fact, he mentioned that there was the possibility of creating an Aeronautics course "when conditions again approximate a normal state." As he concluded his report, McAllister provided a lengthy discourse on his "plan" to raise money for the Institute. The plan actually consisted of the often-repeated proposal to employ a financial agent who would work under the direction of the President of the Institute and the Advisory Board, and who would "make contacts which would lead to increased patronage."[569]

Finally, McAllister appealed to his new Board to consider personally underwriting half of the expense of the agent while "the Institute through its treasury will underwrite the other half." It is unclear where such a "treasury" existed and/or if it contained any actual funds. McAllister offered a telling caveat to his request.

> "It is to be understood that the Current Expense Fund raised by such representative will be applied first to his salary, and any remainder to go into the Institute treasury; that if said Fund does not equal the salary and expenses fixed for said representative, the underwriters will be responsible for the remainder. Gentlemen, I believe here is a plan that can be employed to the benefit and development of the Institute. Will you join your faith with mine in putting it into execution?"[570]

Even as the Great Depression gained momentum, Colonel McAllister opened his school for another year in September 1932. While he remained upbeat on the surface, the truth was that the Institute was suffering serious financial problems and the Colonel had been using his personal savings to keep his dream afloat.

McAllister continued his efforts to raise funds to operate the school. He made an appointment with Joseph A. Cannon of Concord and received the promise of a donation of $250.[571]

A letter written to Mrs. Sara Morrison, wife of then US Senator Cameron Morrison, demonstrates the pressure McAllister felt as he sought funding for the school.

> "Dear Mrs. Morrison,
>
> Knowing of your ability to befriend worth causes and of your generosity toward several educational institutions, I am prompted to write you with reference to the dire need at this time of the Collegiate institute.
>
> Due to the accumulated effects of the depression, the Collegiate Institute faces a crisis. It has done, many of the best citizens of the state will tell you, a notable work. Not it faces the necessity of suspension unless aid is speedily available from some source.
>
> Would you give me an opportunity to tell the story of the Institute with a view to becoming its savior? If so,

will you do me the very great kindness naming a day real soon when I may see you."[572]

While McAllister appealed for help from outside sources, he also attempted to collect funds owed by former students. The following letter was sent to those who owed money. How much, if any, money he was able to collect is not known. One example of an exchange of letters reads:

"I want you to know that it isn't my disposition or desire to ignore your letters of request for payment of the balance due you on the part term tuition of Elton [Glover], but just simply for the lack of funds. Your representative Mr. Wagner was just in to see me relative to this matter and I stated to him that the crops would begin to move shortly, and should we be fortunate enough to get fair prices, then perhaps I can pay you a part if not all the balance due ... however, should this depression continue and prices be on a parity with the past season none of us will be able to do much toward the settlement of accounts. ...

P. S. Elton is slated for Elon this year, and he tells me that as usual he has either lost or misplaced the certificate of credits issued by you last year, and he hesitates to make a request for an additional one, but if not to [sic] much trouble will be appreciated."[573]

Colonel McAllister replied:

"... I realize only too keenly the conditions, for the Institute has felt the effects quite as much as individuals. Failure to receive payments of accounts due has rendered it impossible for me to meet obligations. Your account is not so large, and I do hope you will strain a point to settle same soon. You recall, Mr. Glover, that I made out Elton's credits at your request last winter. It takes time to do this work. Our Registrar is not in town currently. As per catalog requirements, transcripts of records after the first are charged for at a rate of $1.00 per. Mr. Glover, I appreciate warmly your expressions of regard. I hope I am deserving of them. Candidly, I must say to you that it looks to me like you ought to settle the balance due on

> "Buddy's" schooling before asking me to furnish credits. Schools cannot survive unless they collect what they earn. If you can finance Buddy in college, you should be able to pay what is due the Institute. This is said in all kindness and I hope you will so consider it. Reciprocating your good wishers, I am,"[574]

McAllister's efforts to keep the school open through the spring of 1933 and beyond extended to the faculty. Seeking their input and possible approval, he presented two alternatives.

Alternative one was simply to "... to give up the struggle and close the school at Christmas for the year."

The second alternative was to attempt "to collect all 'we' could that was owed, seek some outside aid, accept greatly reduced salaries; assure creditors of our intention to settle with them as promptly as possible, and go through the year."

Noting that the effects of the Depression coupled with increased expenditures "incurred in an effort to strengthen our athletics have brought about a crisis which threatens the very existence of the school," McAllister proposed a tentative budget, "submitted for your consideration." The proposal projected a revised budget ranging from a low of $23,130 to a high of $29,250. It was based upon the faculty's agreement to accept lower salaries beginning in January 1933, their willingness to "give at least one month in the summer to canvassing or office work, taking the minimum salary for nine months without board and room," and reducing the teaching force by one position next year. No salary would exceed $1,500 for the entire year.

> "If the same appeals to you as substantially sound, then I would like to know your reaction to the proposition of cooperation as a member of the faculty for next session in a determined effort to put the Collegiate Institute on its feet."

The plan also proposed reducing "our rates from $450 down to $350 or maybe $300," and would require sixty-one to seventy-one full pay boarding students for the entire session for the "Low" and eighty –four to ninety-eight for the "High."

This proposal was presented to the faculty in December 1932.

According to McAllister, the faculty voted to continue the school year and accept the reduced salaries. They also agreed to recommend reduced tuition. Room and board were reduced from $450 per session to $375 for boarding students and from $100 to $75 for day students.[575]

When the Board of Directors met during commencement week on May 18, 1933, there was no hint (at least publicly) that the 1932-'33 school year would be the Institute's final year of operation. In what would be his last report to his Board of Directors, McAllister declared:

> "The problem of finances has been the most difficult with which we have had to deal. A year ago, I reported to you that if all tuition accounts were collected there would be a small balance in the treasury for the session 1931-32. Unfortunately, we were unable to collect all too many of these accounts. The same difficulty of collecting has been experienced this session. ... With a broader curriculum, our operating expenses have been increased. The consequence is that we close the school year with a considerable deficit. It is apparent to the Board that to keep the Collegiate going has been a real task. All enterprises have had a struggle. It seems to me that there never was a time when there was more need for institutions to do the kind of work to which the Collegiate Institute is dedicated. It is our purpose to carry on; and in our efforts for strengthening and development of MPCI, we are counting on your continued interest and cooperation." (See endnotes for entire report.)[576]

The Board of Directors set the opening date for the next session as September 13, 1933.[577]

It is not known exactly when in the summer of 1933 Colonel McAllister decided not to reopen his school. Records among McAllister's papers contain an undated draft of a letter to prospective students with a series of "tally" sheets attached which appear to be an attempt to establish how many students would be enrolling in the coming session. The totals are difficult to determine as the sheets seem to be a running tally and not a final number.[578]

As late as August 17th 1933 McAllister was still searching for a way to finance the Institute, but it appears that he had already made his decision. In a letter to NC Congressman R. L. Doughton, Chairman US House of Representatives Committee on Ways & Means, McAllister expressed a desire to continue the Institute and was searching for "any Federal aid available for private institutions." However, the main thrust of his letter was inquiring about the possibility of future employment with the government.

> "I crave your advice, as I said, in the capacity of friend, Board member and Congressman.
>
> If the worst should come and we are forced to suspend, I have nothing in sight. When I was considering the matter of running the Institute independently, tentative offers were made me to teach at several institutions out of the state. I didn't like the idea of readjustment, and besides, I wanted above all to see the Collegiate Institute go on. So, if there should be a position in some Dept. of Government for which I might be fitted and which you might be able to help me secure, it goes without saying that I would be grateful for your assistance."[579]

There are two undated drafts in McAllister's papers in which he refers to the closing of the school. One, which appears to have been written as a press release, begins, "Now that the Collegiate Institute, after twenty-seven years of service, must close its doors, patrons, friends and supporters are entitled to the salient fact concerning its beginning, its work, and its ending." In this draft, McAllister gives a complete review of the history of MPCI and the circumstances which led to the present situation.[580]

The second draft, which was followed by an letter dated August 31, 1933, was addressed to former MPCI students. It read, in part:

> "It is needless to say that the decision made was arrived at after due and deliberate consideration of all the interests involved, both those affecting the faculty of the Institute and patrons present and prospective. If there had been any safe and practicable way of carrying on, to be sure, we would have been inclined to take advantage of it. But, after every possible plan was considered, it still appeared

inevitable that we would run at a loss. Having come out with a heavy deficit last session and having had such poor success in collecting during the summer, it seemed wholly impracticable, in fact, foolhardy to try to run the school another year. …."

Your patronage and good will for the Institute are appreciated profoundly. One who has been associated with the institution for 36 years you know, must feel most keenly the necessity for suspension. Whether the Collegiate Institute can or will be revived in the future, I do not know. Be that as it may, be assured that I shall always feel a peculiar interest in the welfare of those who have been students here and shall learn with gladness of any success that may come to you."[581]

On September 2, 1933, the *Concord Daily Tribune* announced:

"MPCI Not To Open for New Term. Colonel George F. McAllister has decided not to operate Mt. Pleasant Collegiate Institute this year due to economic conditions. McAllister's statement read, 'Due to conditions over which they had no control, bank failures and low prices of farm products, numbers of patrons were unable to settle tuition accounts the past two years. As a consequence, the Institute had a deficit in operating expenses the past session. Of a considerable amount due the school at the close of the first session, less than 10 percent, had been collected during the summer. … Regrettable as it is to the management of the Institute to make [an] announcement of suspension, there is no reasonable alternative. … I cannot conclude this statement without an expression of appreciation of high regard for the loyal faculty members who have stood by the Institute in its struggles; of esteem and thankfulness to the gentlemen who constitute the Board of Trustees; and of profound gratitude to the friends of the Institute and of mine who have given their moral support, and material aid to the work in which I have been so long engaged.'"[582]

McAllister wrote to the "Creditors of the Collegiate Institute" on September 20th. The first sentence of his letter declared that the school was officially closed on September 2, 1933, eleven days before the previously announced opening. He emphasized "To have undertaken to run on, it would have meant incurring additional indebtedness, and we didn't consider that an honest procedure.[583]

CLOSURE

As the announcement of the closing of the Institute began to circulate, McAllister and his landlord, the North Carolina Lutheran Synod, initiated actions toward paying creditors, liquidating assets, answering requests from former students and completing the various tasks required in such a situation.

The Board of Directors formed by McAllister in 1932 was relieved of its duties, and the Lutheran Synod's "Board of Trustees for North Carolina College" immediately became the operative authority for issues concerning the school.

One of the first issues they addressed was the status of the "Weiser property" (the former Bittle house) obtained in 1921 for use as a dormitory. In 1931, the Board of Trustees obtained a loan of $600 from Emma McAllister, G. F. McAllister's sister, using the Weiser property as collateral. Upon the school's closure, the Board declared they had no funds with which to repay the loan and were therefore offering the property to Ms. McAllister as settlement.[584]

Ms. McAllister accepted the settlement. The settlement included a stipulation that Colonel McAllister was in no way connected to the transaction. He also waived any rights he had previously held as lessee during the last two years.[585]

Colonel McAllister was left on his own in dealing with some creditors. The following exchange with A. Jacobs & Sons, Tailors, Uniforms & Equipment, 128 W. Fayette St., Baltimore, MD, the company that supplied MPCI Uniforms was typical of "closing down" activity.

> "Received your letter of the 31st, and check, which we agreed to settle your account. Rest assured that we were glad to cooperate with you in this respect. Now you know how we cooperate with our customers, and we will be very happy to hear from you if you are ever connected with another military institute. We regret to advise you, but we cannot see our way clear in reference to giving you a Spring suit, as you know we have taken a terrible loss on your account, and the used uniforms you forwarded to us were of no value to us at all, and also cost us almost $5 express charges up to here. Therefore, we know you will not think hard of us by saying no at this time."[586]

Colonel McAllister was held responsible for the government military equipment issued to MPCI in 1929. He had received a list of missing items in 1930 and upon the closing of the Institute and the return of the equipment, there were more "lost" items - four 30 Cal. M1917 rifles. M1917; six cleaning rods, two cases of cleaning oil and brushes; eleven M1917 bayonets; ten bayonet scabbards; thirteen cartridge belts; three breech lock covers; one M1907 gun sling, and firty-nine depressors. McAllister paid the $143.43 debt by money order.[587]

Following payment, apparently by McAllister personally, he asked Congressman Doughton if he might be reimbursed any money if he located and returned the lost items. Doughton, in turn, contacted Capt. G. F. Herbert who explained that not only were the items listed lost, but certain "required reports" had not been submitted. He stated further that:

> "Insofar as the writer [Herbert] knows there is no provision under which Mr. McAllister might get a refund of the amount that he has paid. This office was genuinely sorry that a collection of this kind had to be made from Mr. McAllister as the Collegiate Institute was looked upon as one of the better schools operating under this office during the time that it was active."[588]

Congressman Doughton replied to McAllister, sending him a copy of Herbert's reply and himself declaring, "I regret very much that he [Capt. Herbert] stated that there is no legal way by which the claim can be cancelled."[589]

McAllister did not surrender his lease on the Institute property until November 20, 1934. He requested that he be allowed to sell the "considerable personal property" in the plant and also that he be allowed to store said property on the premises until it could be disposed of. McAllister also requested that he be allowed to continue to obtain water for his personal residence from the Institute water system per an arrangement made when he built his home in 1922.

Although McAllister ceded his lease, he could not separate himself from his beloved school. He wrote, "I shall consider that my responsibility for oversight, care and upkeep of the Institute property will cease." Nevertheless, McAllister continued to offer advice, recommendations and even left open the possibility of reopening the Institute. He "emphasized that it was important to make provision for the proper oversight and care of the plant to guard against 'costly deterioration' and 'unscrupulous trespass.'" He also suggested that, "Housing facilities are at a premium this time in Mt. Pleasant, and I would recommend that some reliable and dependable family be placed in the residence or perhaps in one of the dormitories and authorized to exercise jurisdiction."

Finally, he asserted that:

> "In terminating my lease with it **possibly** [emphasis added] terminating the operation of the Collegiate Institute, I experience a feeling of profound reluctance and regret. I am of the firm conviction that there is a need for the kind of educational work to which the Collegiate was dedicated. ... If I can be of service to your Committee or the Board in working out a plan for the proper care of the Institute plant or disposition of same, I shall be at your command."[590]

The saga of the Mt. Pleasant Collegiate Institute and G. F. McAllister's involvement with the school did not end with the surrender of his lease. Despite his statement that he considered his responsibility for "oversight, care and upkeep," no longer required, he continued to be deeply enmeshed in the school's fate. It was requested that McAllister write a history of the educational work of North Carolina College, and in an ironic twist, there was a short campaign in 1934 advocating that McAllister be considered for the Presidency of Lenoir-Rhyne College. He was, of course, not the choice of the College Board of Trustees.[591]

The Synod obtained a $15,000 insurance policy on the property and buildings and designated A. W. Moose and McAllister to "look after" it. The new dormitory "reception room" furnishings were "returned" to the Aid Society of Holy Trinity Lutheran Church who had originally "donated" them.[592]

The dormitory furniture was sold to Mr. and Mrs. W. J. Jones, Pinelands College, Salemburg, NC for $696.50.[593] The school's pianos were given to McAllister and Mrs. J. H. C. Fisher.[594]

In 1936, the Board of Trustees granted the Town of Mt. Pleasant permission to place a water tank on the property for the sum of $250 and approved McAllister's use any rental income from the two dormitories to pay for necessary repairs.[595]

The "problem" of what to do with the Institute buildings and real estate remained an issue. The property carried a $10,000 debt that required maintenance by the Synod. McAllister was offered and accepted the responsibility of "looking after the property." He never gave up hope that he might somehow recover some of the money he had invested in the school and/or revive interest in the property and become a part of whatever endeavor was attempted by a new owner.

Between 1935 and 1937, there were numerous proposals, offers and even one auction to sell the property. In June of 1935 Dr. W. J. James of Hamlet, N. C. and Rev. Francis M. Osborne contacted McAllister, expressing interest in establishing a "Boys School with special features," somewhere in North Carolina. Although McAllister replied with a description of the facilities and James planned to have Osborne inspect the property, no further discussion was documented[596]

In September 1936 McAllister received a letter from a Walter O. Steinhauser of Atlanta, GA. Steinhauser presented a long resume of past educational positions and stated that he was interested in starting a Junior College in 1937. It is unknown what McAllister replied, but there was no further correspondence.[597]

Records indicate that in March of 1937, McAllister was pursuing two separate "deals" for the property. One proposed transaction involved an auction and sale of the property to a group of Mt. Pleasant citizens. On

March 16, 1937, the Board of Trustees authorized McAllister, "representing certain parties ... [who] would probably purchase all of said property," to proceed with the transaction.[598]

Existing records confirm that at an auction on March 27, 1937 twelve individuals bid on the Institute property which was divided into lots. The property was sold for $13,550.50, some of which was paid in cash. There are no further records of this sale but for some reason these deeds were never finalized and the property remained in the possession of the Lutheran Synod.[599]

Another proposition was initiated by W. Roscoe Slack of New York. Slack listed himself as an "Educational Advisor" with offices on Fifth Avenue in New York. He sought information for an "Educational Foundation" on "schools or colleges that may be purchased. According to Slack, these institutions, if purchased, would be endowed, thus eliminating financial worries. Slack also indicated in a postscript that his client was looking for "a substantial educator seeking a school or college."

Correspondence continued through March and April and into October of 1937. McAllister and Slack discussed the purchase of the Institute property as well as Mont Amoena Seminary property which was also for sale. In the correspondence, McAllister advised Roscoe that a decision needed to be made quickly as there were others interested in both properties. He did not mention that the property belonged to the Lutheran Synod nor did Roscoe further identify his client(s). On October 6, 1937, McAllister pressed Slack for "prior consideration."[600]

Five days later, McAllister suffered a heart attack. He died on October 17, 1937.[601]

George F. McAllister's unexpected death stunned the local community and the alumni of North Carolina College and MPCI. A long front-page article describing McAllister's life and achievements and photograph appeared in the *Concord Daily Herald-Observer* on October 19, 1937. (See Part II endnotes for a full bio.)[602]

Although McAllister's death was a blow to his community and friends, it did not diminish the Synod's efforts to resolve the issue of what to do with the Institute property. On the same day the College Board of Trustees voted to formulate a resolution honoring McAllister, they considered three matters concerning the property. The first was a proposal to "make a home for aged and retired ministers" at NC College." This option was referred to the Board Executive Committee. Secondly, they considered a request that the Executive Committee "procure a caretaker for the property." The third matter was the formation of a "special committee" to "remove such properties from the [Institute] buildings as may seem proper."[603]

In January 1938, the Board of Trustees designated Board member Harry E. Cline the "responsibility of procuring a caretaker and collecting rents." He was given authority to rent houses and to evict undesirable tenants therefrom. Ethelyn McAllister, G. F. McAllister's widow, and her daughter, Virginia, were designated as custodians of the Institute records.[604] In March, Cline reported that he had hired a man to move into the old dormitory (the Administration building) to look after the property.[605]

Little or no activity involving the Institute property was recorded from 1938 to 1941, but in 1941, a series of events occurred that brought together some of the main characters from the school's recent past.

In March of 1941, the North Carolina State Legislature formed a commission to select a piedmont NC site for a "textile training school" to provide vocational training for prospective textile workers in the state. Representative Eugene T. Bost of Cabarrus County was one of the authors of the bill. Bost graduated from MPCI in in 1929 and later received a law degree from Duke University.[606]

Advocates of MPCI saw this as a perfect opportunity to market the Institute property. On April 5, 1941, Bost wrote to College Board of Trustees member H. E. Isenhour inquiring about the status of the property.[607] In May, the Board of Trustees passed a motion granting a committee the authority to sign an option of the North Carolina College property for $5,000 "for the sole purpose of establishing a textile school as authorized by the North Carolina Legislature."[608]

Cabarrus County textile magnate Charles A. Cannon was a member of the Commission, and for a brief time, interest and hope ran high as the selection process wound its way through the inevitable political process.

In July, the *Kannapolis Daily Independent* featured an article stating that "Mt. Pleasant has an excellent chance." The article stated that a group of Mt. Pleasant businessmen, aided by Rep. E. T. Bost, had "engineered" the Cabarrus County offer.[609]

In the end, after a "donation" of $50,000, the site selected for the school was in Gaston County, the home of another of the bill's authors, Rep. Carl A. Rudisill.[610] Rudisill was himself a sizable textile tycoon and an alumnus of Lenoir College. Ironically, he was also a member of the N.C. College Board of Trustees in 1941.[611]

After the textile school selection failure, the Board of Trustees offered the Institute property for sale to the general public. The Auction Company of Walter & Gurley was contracted to inspect, subdivide, advertise and offer the property at public auction. Terms of the agreement were to set a minimum sale price of $10,000, ten percent of which would be paid to the auction company. The advertising and development expense for the auction were to be split fifty-fifty between the contracting parties.[612]

The Board selected H. E. Isenhour, MPCI alumnus and longtime MPCI supporter, to represent the Board in carrying out the provisions of the contract and determining the terms of sale with the bidders. It was decided that the net proceeds of the sale would be paid "to the Treasurer of the North Carolina Synod to reimburse the Synod for sums advanced in paying off certain notes against the property."[613]

On December 13, 1941 the North Carolina College/MPCI property was offered for sale at auction. The property, totaling 16.5 acres and containing two dwellings and three brick buildings was sub-divided into 100 parcels. There were eleven purchasers. The property sold for $7,977 before expenses and net the net proceeds were $6,289.71. [See Appendix 12 for additional auction information.][614]

As the Lutheran Synod closed its books on North Carolina College and Mt. Pleasant Collegiate Institute, one final episode bears recounting. The incident succinctly illustrates the feelings left behind and the promises unfulfilled.

In 1938, the Board of Trustees designated Mrs. G. F. McAllister custodian of the MPCI records. On December 17th, four days after the sale of the property, Dr. P. E. Monroe, President of Lenoir-Rhyne College, traveled to Mt. Pleasant with the intent to "bring back whatever might be left that might possibly be of interest to the board of the old college, Synod or to Lenoir-Rhyne College." Dr. Monroe found a lock on the old library door and was informed by Mr. Hoy Moose that Mrs. McAllister "preferred that no one else go there or take anything else away to Lenoir-Rhyne College." According to Mr. Moose, Mrs. McAllister declared that "all through the years Lenoir-Rhyne had tried to kill the Institute and had succeeded in killing it and her husband."

Monroe concluded:

> "Finding her in this state, I did not try to argue with her but got away as politely as possible. She stated that there was considerable feeling in Mt. Pleasant over the fact we were taking the library here [Lenoir-Rhyne]. ... I do not believe that it would be well to suggest that anybody else go into there to collect historic matter, at least until Dr. Morgan [Board of Trustees President] has a chance to see Mrs. McAllister."[615]

On January 18, 1942, the *Kannapolis Daily Independent* published the following as part of its "Off the Record" column. It seems a fitting epitaph.

> "Sale last week of the Mt. Pleasant Collegiate Institute property removed the last dream of establishment of a great seat of higher learning in Cabarrus County."[616]

One of the earliest known photographs of North Carolina College, probably taken in the 1880's. Note the rail fence at the base of the hill which bordered Main St. The building on the right is Pi Sigma Phi Society Hall. To the left, behind the trees is the Philalethian Society Hall.

Rev. William Gerhardt, Principal of Western Carolina Male Academy, 1855-1859

Rev. Daniel H. Bittle, First President of North Carolina College, 1859-1861.

Mathias Barrier. Sold land for location of WCMA. Served on 1st Board of Directors of WCMA and Board of Trustees of NC College. His home was located next to the College.

Harvey C. McAllister. Brick mason who was employed to construct WCMA buildings. Served as Secretary and President of the NC College Board of Trustees from 1877-1915.

Jonas Cook. Student at NC College 1859-1861. Served multiple terms as Treasurer of NC College Board of Trustees from 1874-1905.

North Carolina College Class about 1889. Professor H. T. J. Ludwig stands to the far left. In front of him appears to be College President, John G. Schaidt. In the center (seated) is Wiley A. Barrier. Seated to Barrier's left is Rev. C. L. T. Fisher, professor of Ancient Languages & Literature.

North Carolina College Class before 1890. Wiley Barrier is again at the center of the photograph. No other persons have been identified.

Henry Thomas Jefferson Ludwig. Photo taken cir 1900 shortly before his death. "Professor Tom" graduated from NC College in 1871 and served as Professor of Mathematics for over 25 years. Ludwig also taught Astronomy, Physics and Business Math, as well as coaching the baseball team.

NC College Class photo was probably taken sometime around 1889. H. T. J. Ludwig standing on the left side with the hat on. Also in this photo are the Fisher brothers who attended NC College in the 1870's and taught there in the late 1880's. On the back row 1st on the right is Wiley A. Barrier.

The Philalethian Debating Society Hall, later renamed Gerhardt Society. The above image first appeared in NC College catalogues in the 1880's.

The Pi Sigma Phi Debating Society Hall, later renamed Ludwig Society. The building was destroyed by fire in 1909.

SOUTH WING. MAIN BUILDING NORTH WING.

1904 Lithograph of Campus

First known photo of MPCI as Military School (cir 1908)

George Franklin McAllister, Principal of Carolina English & Classical School – 1902, Mt. Pleasant Collegiate Institute - 1903-1933

This photo appears to be of students at the Carolina English & Classical School, cir 1902. George F. McAllister is in the first row (standing) third from the right with hat in his hand. The person on the far right may have been Rev. Levi Busby who was co-principal with McAllister at the CECS. He died in 1903.

MPCI Cadets in review 1909-1914

MPCI Cadets in review abt 1917

MPCI Cadets in review 1930

MPCI Cadets – 1925 Photo illustration of different styles of uniforms worn by cadets

Faculty & Cadet Officers - 1919

Cadets pre-1925

Classroom #1 after 1916. This photograph was published in several MPCI catalogs in the 1920's

The College Laboratory was located in the Pi Sigma Phi/Ludwig Society Hall. This building burned in 1909. The photograph appeared in catalogues of NC College prior to 1901.

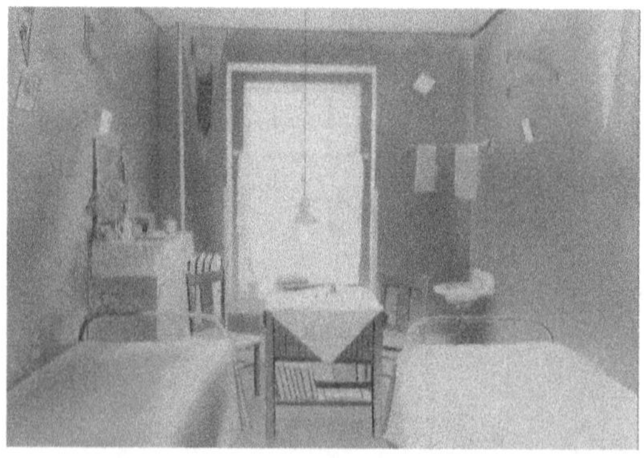

This image of a MPCI Dorm room published in the college catalogue appears to be a photo-graph. However, it is actually a stylized draw –ing. The image is based on a dorm room after 1916 when each room had electric lights, steam heat, and a lavatory.

MPCI Baseball 1870's

MPCI Baseball 1917

MPCI Baseball 1928

MPCI Football 1911

MPCI Football 1923 Roy Webster, Coach

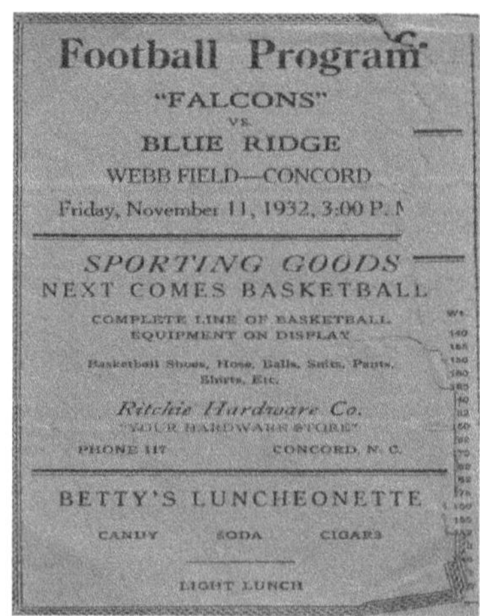

Football Program

"FALCONS"

VS.

BLUE RIDGE

WEBB FIELD—CONCORD

Friday, November 11, 1932, 3:00 P. M

SPORTING GOODS

NEXT COMES BASKETBALL

COMPLETE LINE OF BASKETBALL
EQUIPMENT ON DISPLAY

Basketball Shoes, Hose, Balls, Suits, Pants,
Shirts, Etc.

Ritchie Hardware Co.

"YOUR HARDWARE STORE"

PHONE 117 CONCORD, N. C.

BETTY'S LUNCHEONETTE

CANDY SODA CIGARS

LIGHT LUNCH

Football Program from MPCI 1932 Homecoming game. Note that the game was played in Concord and that the team had changed its mascot from "Red Devils" to "Falcons." The Falcons won 20-6

MPCI Basketball 1928

MPCI Tennis (no date)

MPCI Boxing 1932-1933

MPCI Orchestra 1928

Students in costume for a play. This undated photo could be from NC College or MPCI, both of which presented many student theatrical performances

A student? with his "special guests" on the administration building roof which was off limits but apparently visited frequently.

"PROMISES UNFULFILLED"

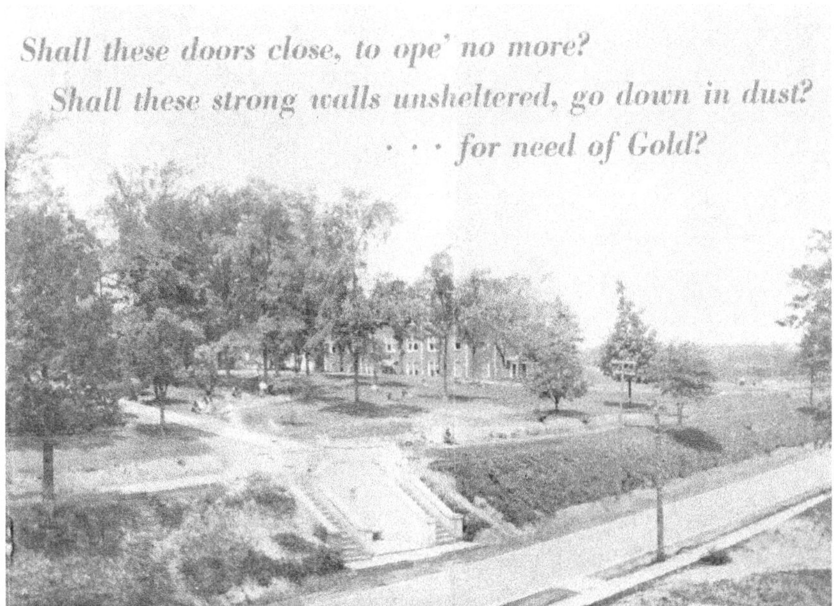

Shall these doors close, to ope' no more?
Shall these strong walls unsheltered, go down in dust?
. . . for need of Gold?

This photo was taken sometime after 1926. It shows the "entrance" to the campus which was completed in that year along N. Main St. In the background is the "new" dormitory that was completed in 1925. The caption was applied to the photo and published in the 1930 catalogue to help raise funds when the Lutheran Synod withdrew its support from MPCI.

II

ACADEMICS

Part II of this narrative describes the planning and implementation of the educational operation of the institutions which occupied the campus for seventy-eight years. It provides a session by session account of the scholastic life of these schools, their administrators, their teachers and their students. Each school based its educational program around the "classical style" academic theories of the nineteenth century. This approach to education stressed the dictum "think-reason-persuade." An institution's purpose was to develop the mental ability of the student to pass on the cultural heritage to the next generation. Classical schools placed an emphasis on western culture and tradition. Reason and moral virtue were at the core of the cirrculum. Classroom procedures were rigidly set. Students stood when called upon to recite, often verbatim, from the text. Much emphasis was placed on public speaking, debate, memorization and constant drill.[617]

THE WESTERN CAROLINA MALE ACADEMY

1855-56

Although its new facilities were not yet completed, the Academy opened for classes on 1 Mar 1855 in a "suitable building in the village [Mt. Pleasant]." In May 1854, the Board of Trustees had appointed Reverend William Gerhardt as the "first Professor" of the Academy. Reverend Gerhardt was inaugurated as Principal in May of 1855.[618] His inaugural address was initially published in local papers and the Board of Directors authorized the address printed for sale to the public. This attempt to produce funds for the school may have had some negative effects, as in

January 1856, the Board rescinded its earlier motion "in relation to selling Prof. Gerhardt's address," and instructed the professor "to distribute them gratuitously."[619]

At the 1855 NC Synod convention held at Fredericktown Church in Davidson County, Christopher Melchor, President of the Academy's Board of Directors noted:

> "We are now entering a new era in the history of our Church in North Carolina. Heretofore we have been sending our money North and South to build up institutions of learning, under the belief that we were too poor to build ourselves; - but this was all a mistake – for we have one now nearly completed and have commenced school under very flattering circumstances, and if fostered and protected by all the Churches in our Synod, will soon vie with any institution of a similar kind in the State."[620]

The exact number of students attending the first session of the Academy is not known, but records indicate that enrollment averaged between fifty and sixty students per year between 1855 and 1859. The scholastic year was forty-two weeks long and was divided into a winter session of twenty-five weeks beginning on the third Thursday in September and a Summer session of seventeen weeks beginning on the third Thursday of April.[621]

In October 1855 the students were able to move into their new building. The building was described in an early catalogue as:

> "a neat, substantial, three story brick building, 75' by 40', containing a commodious Chapel, a Preparatory Department, several Recitation Rooms, a Reading Room, two Society Halls, three Library Rooms, and a number of other rooms sufficient to accommodate about fifty students."

Room rent was $4 per month in the winter and $2 per month in the summer.[622]

The campus was further described as:

> "Contain[ing] about four acres and enclosed by a neat fence. When once properly improved, it will become a beautiful and attractive spot. A neat and commodious Professor's House has also been erected, ranging in front

of the Academy edifice. It is also contemplated to build a church close to the institution, for the convenience of the students and community."[623]

In addition to himself, Rev. Gerhardt obtained the teaching services of an instructor, Rev. John D. Scheck. Rev. Scheck was a member of the Academy Board of Directors and served on various committees appointed by the Board. He was also serving as the minister at St. John's Church, located just outside the village of Mt. Peasant. In January of 1856, Rev. Scheck was censured by the Board of Trustees for a violation of the school rules and subsequently resigned his position at the Academy and the Board of Trustees. [See Part III for details.] The new assistant professor was A. M. Byers. He remained employed for only a few months, resigning in September 1856.[624]

The Academy continued to have problems with staffing into its next session. In January 1857, Professor Gerhardt proffered his resignation citing low pay. Responding to Professor Gerhardt's action, the Board of Directors gave him a vote of confidence and resolved to raise his pay to $700. In addition, "the Professor [was] permitted to deliver a course of lectures on such subjects as he may select for the benefit of the institution and income arising therefrom [would be] added to his salary" provided that the salary did not rise beyond $800. Any amount over $800 was to be transferred to the Academy for the purchase of chemical and philosophical apparatus.[625]

Professor Gerhardt withdrew his resignation and according to the school catalogue for 1857 the Academy faculty consisted of President Gerhardt as Principal, Rev. Caleb Lentz, Assistant, and William L. Barrier, Tutor.[626]

In May of 1856, the Board of Directors established fifty limited "scholarships" of $100 each that were to be good for a term of six years and another fifty of $55 each that would have a term of three years. These scholarships were made available to those persons who contributed to the fund that established the Academy for distribution as they preferred.[627]

1856-57

The 1857 Catalogue covered the winter session of 1856 and the spring session of 1857 and cited enrollment of forty-two students. Eleven students were enrolled in the Primary Division – William L. Barrier, Paul A. Barrier, Wiley A. Barrier, and Rufus A. Barrier, all from Mt. Pleasant; James I. Honeycutt from Gold Hill; L. H. Rothrock, from Rockville (Rockwell); and M. H. Seaford from China Grove.

The first class of the Preparatory Department contained eleven students and the second class named ten members. The Junior Preparatorians class included fourteen students. [See Appendix 15 for roster.]

The school calendar published in 1857 noted that the Academy conducted a winter session of six months and a summer session of four months. There were two vacations of five weeks, each commencing on the 3rd Thursdays of April and September.[628]

By 1857 plans were underway to stock the Library with additional books. The Academy library now contained 170 volumes, the Crescent Society held 237 Volumes, and the Philalaethian Society, 230 volumes. A reading room containing "valuable Papers, Journals, Magazines, Reviews, etc.," was open to subscribers during recreation hours.[629]

President Gerhardt's wife of was directing a campaign "among the mothers and daughters of the church to raise $1,000 for the purchase of Chemical and Philosophical Apparatus, and donations have been made toward the formation of a Cabinet of Minerals, Curiosities, etc."[630]

The course of study was the typical classical cirriculum. Emphasis was on Greek and Roman Literature, Latin, and the basics in grammar, math, science, and history. The school also offered courses in book-keeping, music and agriculture. Normally students entered the Academy at about the age of fourteen, but this could vary greatly. The "level" of instruction for students was usually determined by a test or tests as to their ability in the "three r's" (reading, writing and arithmetic).

The 1857 Academy catalogue listed the following courses of study:

Preparatory classes (the first level of instruction) included Reading, Writing, Orthography and the definition of words, English, Grammar (Bullion's), Arithmetic (Emerson's), Book-keeping, Geography (Mitchel's Intermediate), History of NC (Wiley's), History of the United States (Grimshaw's), Natural Philosophy (Comstock's), Agriculture, Bullion's Latin and Greek Grammars, Latin and Greek Readers (-commenced), Davie's Elementary Algebra (commenced), Vocal Music, Composition and Declamation.

Academic (the second level of instruction) was divided into three "divisions" embracing a three-year course, almost equivalent to a regular college course.

Primary Division

1st Term – Caesar, Virgil, Greek reader (continued), Xenophon's Anabasis, Algebra (Hutton's), History, Watts on the Mind, Latin & Greek Exercises.

2nd Term – Sallust & Cicero's Orations, Anabasis continued, Classical Literature, Manual of History, Geometry (Hutton's), Algebra completed, Latin & Greek Exercises.

Progressive Division

1st Term – Livy & Odes of Horace, Gareca Majors Vol 1, Manual of History, Classical Literature continued, Blair's Rhetoric, Geometry completed, Conic Sections (Hutton's), Plane Trigonometry (Hutton's), Chemistry (Comstock's), Latin & Greek Exercises.

2nd Term – Satires, etc. of Horace, Gareca Majors continued, Rhetoric continued, History continued, Classical Literature completed, Surveying (Gummer's), Mensuration (Hutton's), Chemistry completed, Greek Testament, Latin & Greek Exercises.

Advanced Division

1st Term – Cicero de Officiis, Cicero de Oratore, Gareca Majora Vol 2, Rhetoric completed, History completed, Mental Philosophy (Upham's), Analytical, Plane and Spherical Trigonometry (Hutton's), Analytical Geometry (Hutton's), Latin & Greek Exercises.

2nd Term – Tacitus, Gareca Majora vol. 2, Logic (Hedge's), Political Economy (Waylnand's), Evidences of Christianity, Calculus & Mechanics (Hutton's), Optics (Brewster's), Astronomy (Herschel's), Latin & Greek Exercises, Forensic Disputations.

Composition and Declamation were attended to in every class. The Advanced Division deliver original declamations. Agriculture studied throughout the whole course. Daily exercises in Vocal Music.

Optional Studies with extra classes – German, French, Hebrew, Instrumental Music.[631]

1857-1858

In his report to the Synod in April 1858, Christopher Melchor, President of the Board of Trustees stated that there were "between 40 and 50 scholars" in attendance during the past year. He also noted that the two instructors at the school "had done their duty faithfully," and that the Board had found it necessary to hire the school's financial agent, Caleb Lentz, as a part-time instructor at a salary of $400 a year.[632]

1858-1859

As discussions concerning chartering the school as a College proceeded, Western Carolina Male Academy began what was to be its final session. "About forty students" were enrolled and were initially taught by Reverend Gerhardt and Reverend Caleb Lentz.

During this session, an incident (previously mentioned in Part 1) occurred that led to the loss of a faculty member. The episode involved local hotel owner William R. Scott who the Board of Trustees accused of "selling liquor and allowing men to become intoxicated in his confectionary." Apparently the Academy's rules against the sale or consumption of liquor produced some dissatisfaction among a group of local citizens, who, while "visiting" Scott's hotel, made negative comments concerning the school and/or someone connected to it. Professor Lentz was a witness to these comments, but did not report them to the Principal.

As a result of the incident, the Board of Directors requested that local authorities enforce the ban on selling liquor within two miles of the school. They passed a resolution stating:

> "[The Board] highly disapproves of any speeches or essays made in this institution against any individual personally. We consider it an honor debasing offense to be met by the faculty. We deem it unfortunate that Prof. Lentz, who was present where such a speech was made that more stringent measures were not taken against the offender."

Reverend Lentz resigned his teaching position and was replaced by Rev. Louis A. Bikle, a recent graduate of Gettysburg College.[633]

NORTH CAROLINA COLLEGE

1859-1860

Reverend Daniel H. Bittle was appointed President of North Carolina College in October 1858. In addition to Rev. Bittle, the Board of Trustees sought two additional professors. It is not clear whether the Board considered retaining Rev. Gerhardt as President of the College but according to the Board's minutes, he was offered a position as a Professor of Mathematics. He declined but was allowed to remain in the "Professor's House" until September of 1859.[634]

William Grimm became the Professor of Mathematics and the second faculty position was filled by Rev. Bikle who was already on the teaching staff. The salaries of the Professors were set at $500.[635]

The following advertisement appeared in the *Raleigh Register* on September 7, 1859.

> "North Carolina College. Mt. Pleasant, Cabarrus Co. NC. This promising institution exhibits a course of study inferior to none in the State; and the Board of Trustees feel confident that the prescribed course will be ably, strictly and satisfactorily carried out, having secured the services of men in the selection of their faculty, qualified to teach upon the most approved system. The expenses are less than those of any similar institution in the entire South. This arises in part from the endowment, and in part from its location in a healthy and productive section of the country, and in a wealthy and moral community. The exercises will open on the 28th of Sept. next, and continue for forty-two weeks without intermission except an examination and literary contest during the week, including the 22nd of February. Terms: In the Preparatory Department, which is intended to furnish young men thoroughly for the College classes, for board, tuition, room rent, washing, fuel, &c, for the year $107.00. In the Collegiate Department. do. $115.00. One-half invariably in advance. For further particulars address for circular, Colonel John Shimpoch, Secretary of the Board, Rev. D.

H. Bittle, President N. C. College Mt. Pleasant, NC July 23rd, 1859."[636]

At its opening session in September 1859, North Carolina College counted sixty-two registered students – one Sophomore, nine Freshmen, fifteen Primarians (preparing to enter the Freshman Class), and thirty-seven Junior Preps. There were forty-six students from North Carolina, fifteen from South Carolina, and one from Massachusetts.[637]

Entrance requirements for students were "good moral character and proper application of study during the first four weeks." The College determined the "year" (scholastic level) of entering students by examination. "Before being admitted to the College, candidates for Freshman Class [would] be examined on the following with which they [must] be accurately and thoroughly acquainted: English Literature and Grammar; U. S. History; Greek (through one book of Anabasis); Latin (through Virgil and Cicero); and Mathematics (through Quadratics)." The course of study was forty-two weeks long (divided into two sessions) from September through the middle of July without interruption, except for an examination in the middle of each session and a Literary Contest between the two debating societies held in February.[638]

Students received instruction in Ancient Languages (Latin and Greek); Modern Languages (German and French); Mathematics (Arithmetic, Algebra, Geometry, Trigonometry, Mensuration, Surveying and Calculus); Natural Science (Chemistry, Natural Philosophy, Astronomy, Meteorology, Botany and Geology); Moral Science (Ethics, Evidence of Christianity, Analogy of Religion, and Natural Theology), and Intellectual Science (Rhetoric, Elements of Criticism, Logic, Mental Philosophy and Rational Psychology, Geography, History, Composition, and Declamation).[639]

The College faculty, which consisted of two professors and the College President, played a pivotal role in the success of the institution. Not only was the faculty responsible for instruction in the classroom, they were also expected to maintain discipline and high moral standards among the students. Faculty and students apparently maintained a close relationship, as "a small group [of students] took special pleasure in playing every possible kind of prank on the faculty."[640]

But not every interaction between faculty and students was positive in nature. Professor William Grimm, who resigned from the faculty in

July 1860, wrote the following letter to the Board of Trustees. Grimm, a mathematics instructor, was only twenty-two years old. He and three college students, ages twenty-six and twenty-seven, resided with Mr. J. J. Misenheimer in Mt. Pleasant.

18 Jul 1860

C. Melchor Esq.

Through you, as President of the Board of Trustees of NC College, at its suggestion, I present to the Board my resignation of the department I now hold in this institution and in doing so permit me to assign several reasons for the same. From various sources, I have learned that my instructions were not giving satisfaction to those placed under my charge. This charge, to whatever magnitude it may have been swelled by "common fame" had its origin among those whom I was called to instruct – boys and young men in the Preparatory Department and Freshman Class of a new College. No comment is necessary – it is self evident to every intelligent reflective mind that if I had intellect or even duplicity enough to pass honorably through a college of standing myself, that I ought to satisfactorily instruct young men under the above mentioned circumstances. But even they do not urge the charge of incompetency (nor does this board), but vagueness and obscurity in delivering my instructions, and apparent hesitancy and slowness in giving explanations. Are those young men perfectly sure that the vagueness and obscuring are altogether with me or may they not be sometimes in their own minds? I ??? think the latter to be occasionally the case, as I think I could substantiate if I had diligently written down the instances as they did and thus let the outside world become acquainted with what should never pass beyond the walls of the lecture room. As for other faults, I claim that time and experience have not been afforded me to pass judgment upon them, but that my love of reputation and the natural ambition to excel which has a home in even generous beasts should afford

> a fair presumption that, it time, these defects would be remedied, and that that time would be shortened by ??? of friendly admonitions and warnings given. …
>
> Outside I have been individually and covertly assailed and traduced. Now I hold that in order to live happily in a community, it is necessary to enjoy the respect, confidence and sympathy of that community, and when these are lost or forfeited by any means whatsoever, it is better that a separation should take place….

I cannot but protest the proceeding had by this Board whereby I tender[ed] my resignation. I think when men, by a solemn oath find community or an institution, at the expense of doing an act of justice, it is an unenviable position in which they have placed themselves. The meanest criminal in the land, arraigned for the most heinous offense, under the most outrageous circumstances is held innocent until proved guilty by a due process of law, whilst I – but I forbear to go on. I have done. W. Grimm."[641]

1860-1861

Rev. Bittle was formally inaugurated as President of North Carolina College on July 17th, 1860 at a ceremony conducted at the nearby Methodist Church. The fall term of 1860 opened on September 26th with 100 students registered, the majority of whom were in the "lower" and college preparatory classes. Students over the age of fourteen were accepted from eight Southern states. Tuition and room and board ranged from $115 to $136 per year, depending upon the "class" of the student and his living arrangements. Most of the young men were housed on the campus, but several resided in private residences that were located near the campus.[642]

The College Catalogue listed four categories of students – College, Primarians, Junior Preparatorians and Partial (part-time). There was no distinction given in the catalogue between Junior "Preps" and Primarians except that both were part of the "Preparatory" Department and as such were enrolled in a two year course that was designed "to give pupils a thorough preparation for the College classes."[643]

The College faculty consisted of Rev. Bittle who taught Mental and Moral Science, Rev. L. A. Bikle, Professor of Mathematics, and G.

F. Schaffer who was hired in August to teach Ancient Languages. In September of 1860, the Board of Trustees approved the establishment of positions for a Professor of History and a Professor of German but these posts were to remain vacant until $10,000 cash could be raised to fund them.

A project initiated in 1857 by Mrs. Gerhardt, the wife of the former Academy Principal, was completed during the school year. The Ladies Aid Society of the NC Lutheran Synod presented the College with funds to purchase equipment for a "Chemical and Philosophical Laboratory."[644] Plans were devised to "purchase a library" for the College. In October 1859, the Board of Trustees appointed a committee of ladies in the community who would offer a $50 gold watch to the lady who, by the 4th of July 1860, provided the most money toward a library for the College.[645]

As noted in Part I, the positive atmosphere at the beginning of the 1860 Fall Term was soon overshadowed by events on the national stage. In November, Abraham Lincoln, a Republican from Illinois, was elected President of the United States from among a slate of four candidates who reflected the divided nature of the country over the issues of states' rights and slavery. South Carolina seceded from the Union on December 20th, 1860.

In his report to the Board of Trustees, Bittle stated:

> "Political troubles in our sister state were of sufficient importance on the part of parents & Guardians [for them] to withdraw their sons and wards for the present, and in nearly every instance with the assurance that so soon as the difficult be overpassed they will return."

Of the 100 students who initially registered for classes, eighty-seven enrolled, and only sixty-five remained at the end of year. One student was classified as a Senior, six were Sophomores and sixteen were Freshmen. There were fourteen students in the "Preparatory" class, and twenty-eight in the "lower" classes. Rev. Bittle stated that of the eighty-seven students "enrolled on the catalogue," forty were Lutheran, twenty-two were Methodist, fourteen were Baptist and eleven were Presbyterian. Sixty-four students listed their home state as North Carolina. Eighteen were from South Carolina, two from Mississippi, one from Maryland, one from Georgia, and one from Texas.[646]

Rev. Bittle anticipated enrollment for the upcoming session to be over 100 students and identified the need for a tutor or "some other arrangement." He also stated that the school needed a janitor "whose duty it will be to sweep the building, make the beds, etc. and at leisure hours take care of the grounds and premises of the buildings."[647]

In the shadow of the approaching conflict, NC College began its Spring term in January 1861 with only sixty-three students - seven Sophomores, thirteen Freshmen, seventeen preparatory students and twenty-five "lower" class members. The faculty consisted of Rev. Bittle, President of the College and Professor of Mental & Moral Science; Rev. L. A. Bikle, Professor of Mathematics and the Military Department; Mr. G. F. Schaffer, Professor of Latin & Greek Languages, and Mr. Robert C. Holland, Principal of the Preparatory Department.[648] The College remained open through April when Ft. Sumter was fired upon and Lincoln called for troops to put down the rebellion. It continued in session through May 20th when North Carolina seceded from the Union.

Commencement ceremonies for the academic year began on July 17th, 1861 with a Literary Address on July 18th. One Senior, Irenaeus Condor from Steven's Mill in Union County, NC, was listed in the School Catalogue. School records stated that he graduated but his biography in *Life Sketches of NC Lutheran Ministers* lists no degree.[649]

1861-1866

On August 14th, 1861, following a recruiting drive and muster on the College campus during which thirteen students enlisted in the NC State Troops, an advertisement appeared in the *Raleigh Register* announcing that North Carolina College would open for the Fall session on September 25th, 1861. The advertisement specified that the Board of Trustees had instituted military drilling as part of the school's activities.[650]

It is not clear if the College opened in September for by that time at least fifty of its students were enlisted in the army. As related in Part I, Rev. Bittle submitted his resignation on October 2nd, 1861 and in November the remaining professors resigned and the school was closed.[651] The College remained closed for the duration of the Civil War, but discussions continued regarding re-opening.

1866-1867

On the first Monday in August 1866, the College re-opened after a five year "suspension." There were thirty-three students in attendance and "the prospects for a large increase in the number of students the next scholastic year ... [were] promising. If plentiful crops are made this season, the Directors will be enabled to procure the necessary means to pay the salaries of all the Professors that may be required to carry on successfully the operations of the College."[652] The school operated with only one Professor (Rev. L. A. Bikle), through the 1866-'67 academic year. Reverend Charles F. Bansemer accepted the Presidency in September of 1867.

1867-1868

The 1867 session of the College opened in September with sixty-five students on the role but only "some forty-seven or forty-eight in regular attendance." The faculty consisted of Rev. Bansemer, Rev. L. A. Bikle and a student tutor, Benjamin F. Rogers. The 1867 College Catalogue described the following curriculum:

> "The whole course of instruction occupies four years, there being a single session of forty-two weeks in each year. The different classes attend three recitations a day."
> Freshman Class – Sallust; Cicero's Orations; Livy; Latin Prose Composition; Latin Grammar; Xenophon's Anabasis or Cyropedia; Greek Prose Composition; Greek Grammar; Algebra; Geometry; English Literature; Rhetoric; History; Composition and Declamation
> Sophomore Class – Odes of Horace; Cicero de Officis or Cicero de Oratore; Latin Exercises and Prosody; Herodotus; Xenophon's Memorabilia; Greek Exercises and Prosody; Classical Literature; Conic Sections; Plane Trigonometry; Mensuration; Surveying; Spherical and Analytical Geometry; Calculus; Mechanics; History, Rhetoric; Mental Philosophy
>
> Junior Class – Horace (Satires, Epistles, and Ars Poetica); Cicero's Tusculan Disputations or Letters to Atticus; Latin Composition; Iliad of Homer; Plato's Gorgias'; Greek Composition; Natural Philosophy;

Chemistry; Meteorology; Natural Theology; Logic; Rational Psychology; Elements of Criticism

Senior Class – Tacitus' Germania and Agricola; Juvenal; Plantus; Latin Composition; Demosthenes on the Crown; The Antigone or The Electra of Sophocles; Greek Composition; Astronomy; Geology; Keith on the Globes; Moral Philosophy; Political Economy; Evidence of Christianity; Butler's Analogy; Anatomy and Physiology; Revision of Course.

"The Preparatory Department embraces a solid and thorough English Education, whilst those who desire to prepare for business, or for college, have every advantage for the acquisition of the elements of Mathematics and of the Latin and Greek Languages.

For those who propose receiving a regular Collegiate education, the course of instruction contemplates a period of three years; but the student is taken through a longer or shorter period, according to his attainments, abilities and applications. The list of studies in this Department is the following:

Reading, Writing, Orthography and definition of words, English Grammar, Modern Geography, first lessons in Natural Philosophy, History of the United States, Book-keeping, Arithmetic, Elementary Algebra, Ancient Geography, Watts of the Mind, Latin Grammar, Latin Lessons, Latin Reader, Caesar, Virgil, Nepos, Greek Grammar, Greek Lessons, Greek Reader, Composition and Declamation.

Students sufficiently advanced in this department are permitted to attend recitations with the College classes in any of the branches they require, such as Chemistry, Geometry, Surveying, Mensuration. Rhetoric, etc."[653]

The school now consisted of two Departments – the College Department and the Preparatory Department. The Preparatory Department was a three year curriculum described as "embracing a solid and thorough English Education, whilst those who desire to prepare for business, or for college, have every advantage or the acquisition of the elements of Mathematics and of the Latin and Greek languages."[654]

In March 1868, Rev. Bansemer delivered his Inaugural Address with the following conclusion:

> "... and to you, young men, students of the College, I say, let excelsior be your motto. Be not carried away by the example and suggestions of the thoughtless and indolent, the lovers of inglorious, vulgar ease. Climb up to the highest pinnacle of Minerva's temple. ... Woman is sheltered by fond arms and loving counsel, old age is protected by its experience, and manhood by its strength. But the young man stands alone amidst the temptations of the world. The cultivation of your minds will protect you from imposition, religion will shield you from the fiery darts of the adversary. Never let it be said of you, that you helped to swell the tide of sin, by directing your influence on its channels. ... Gentlemen! To you I look for encouragement and zealous cooperation in discharging the important duties I have assumed. No effort shall be spared to secure the approbation and full confidence of our patrons. If you will stand by us, a firm support, then we shall fondly indulge the hope, that under the protection and guidance of Almighty God, our undertaking will eventually prove a complete success, beyond our sanguine expectations."[655]

Commencement exercises were held on May 27th-28th, 1868 at the Mt. Pleasant Methodist Church. There were no degrees awarded at the commencement but Capt. Robert P. Waring of Charlotte, NC was the featured speaker.[656]

1868-1869

The academic year 1868-69 began with only two students enrolled in the College Department. Sixty-three students were on the rolls in the "Preparatory" (pre-college) Department. The only two faculty members on record were President Bansemer and Rev. L. A. Bikle.[657]

An advertisement in the *North Carolina Argus,* Wadesboro, NC, dated

17 Dec 1868 stated that the cost of attending NC College (including washing, fuel, lights, etc.) for a ten-month session was about $170, "German and French extra."[658]

Classes offered in the Collegiate Department included Latin & Greek, German & French, Arithmetic, Algebra, Geometry, Trigonometry, Menstruation, Surveying & Calculus, Chemistry, Natural Philosophy, Astronomy, Meteorology, Botany & Geology, Ethics, Evidence of Christianity, Analogy of Religion & Natural Theology, Rhetoric, Elements of Criticism, Logic, Mental Philosophy & Rational Psychology, Geography & History, and Composition & Declamation. Also, according to the Catalogue, "an excellent Philosophical and Chemical Apparatus has been purchased by the College at a cost of $1000, for which amount we are indebted to the ladies of North Carolina."[659]

As discussed in Part I, Rev. Bansemer's tenure was tumultuous. He resigned in mid-term. The new faculty who finished the academic year consisted of Rev. L. A. Bikle, Philip Bikle, and tutor H. T. J. Ludwig. There is no record of commencement ceremonies for 1868-'89, but it is known that no college degrees were awarded.

1869-1870

The 1869 academic year began in September with eighty-one students but with only fifty-four in regular attendance. There were nine students in the Academic (College) Class – two Juniors and seven Freshmen. The faculty consisted of Rev. L. A. Bikle, Acting President and Professor of Mathematics; Rev. Philip M. Bikle, Professor of Latin and Greek, and H. T. J. Ludwig, Tutor.[660]

Bikle informed the Board of Trustees that the session opened favorably "as could be expected under existing circumstances," and the number of students was the largest since the end of the war.[661]

The Preparatory Department now consisted of two divisions. One division contained three classes designated Primarian, Second Class and Third Class. Students in these classes ranged in age sixteen to twenty-nine. The second division was called Junior Preparatorians and consisted of two classes designated First Class and Second Class. Students in these classes ranged in from age seven to fifteen.[662]

No further records have been found concerning the academic year of 1869-'70 or the commencement exercises. It is known that no College Degrees were awarded.

1870-1871

In August 1870, the College reported eighty-four students registered for the session beginning that month, but the term opened with only fifty students attending classes.[663]

The College Catalogue announced former President Rev. Daniel Bittle as the President-elect. However, as mentioned in Part 1, he turned down the position before the beginning of the school year. For the second year, Rev. L. A. Bikle was designated Acting President and Professor of Math, Astronomy and Physics. Other faculty included Rev. Daniel I. Dreher, Professor of History and English; Dr. Paul A. Barrier, Professor of Chemistry, Anatomy, and Physiology, and H. T. J. Ludwig, Tutor.[664]

On December 30th, 1870, a newspaper advertisement appeared in *The Old North State* stating that North Carolina College would open for its second half session on January 2nd, 1871.[665]

There are no records of the commencement ceremonies for the academic year 1870-'71, but the College awarded its first degrees since it reopened in 1866. John M. Reid and H. T. J. Ludwig received Bachelor of Arts Degrees.[666]

1871-1872

The College opened on August 7th, 1871 with 102 students enrolled. The Board of Trustees reported that the faculty consisted of Rev. L. A. Bikle, President and Professor of Mental and Moral Science, Rev. William E. Hubbert, Professor of Ancient Languages and Literature, and H. T. J. Ludwig, Professor of Mathematics and Natural Science. Professor Ludwig, formerly employed as a tutor while attending the college, was hired as a full-time faculty member immediately following his graduation in May of 1871.[667]

During the session the College added several new courses and the full-time faculty was assisted by several guest lecturers. Dr. Paul A. Barrier, MD, lectured on Chemistry, Anatomy and Physiology. Capt. Wiley A. Barrier, a student and former officer with the 1st NC Cavalry, instructed in "penmanship."[668]

In a newly formed Theological Department, Rev. L. A. Bikle taught Apologetics, Dogmatics and Greek Exercises. Rev. William E. Hubbert taught Homiletics, Hermeneutics and Hebrew. Rev. Jacob G. Neiffer, as a guest instructor, taught Symbolics and Liturgics, and Rev. Levi C. Groseclose, another guest lecturer, taught Ecclesiastical and Sacred History.

The College Catalogue stated that the college curriculum gave "pre-eminence to the study of the English language," and as a "valuable adjunct to the usual College curriculum," an English and Scientific Course was provided "for such as desire a good business education." According to the catalogue this new curriculum was created to meet the change in the "peculiar institution" of the South which "must change its old mode of farming if it was going to be profitable in the future."[669]

Commencement exercises for the year were conducted May 28th-30th, 1872, with addresses by students John M. Henderson, Jonathan C. Moser and Frank P. Cook. Wiley A. Barrier was the only person listed as receiving a BA Degree. He also presented an address on "Popular Education." Reverend Irenaeus Condor was awarded an AM Degree.

At the commencement ceremony, the College announced the creation of the Martha Pettit Hubbert Medal. The Medal was funded by faculty member, W. E. Hubbert, to be awarded annually in honor of Professor Hubbert's first wife to the "student who shall have attained the greatest proficiency in Composition and Oratory."[670]

1872-1873

The academic year began on August 5th, 1872 with 130 students registered. President Bikle reported that eighty-seven were present by Christmas with twenty-six more registering by January 8th. Full-time faculty members were Rev. Bikle, Rev. Hubbert, and H. T. J. Ludwig. Part-time instructors and lecturers included Dr. Paul A. Barrier, Capt. Wiley A. Barrier and Rev. Levi C. Groseclose, the minister at nearby Holy Trinity Lutheran Church.[671]

Commencement ceremonies occurred on May 25th, 1873. College records indicate that only two students received BA Degrees, Henry M. Brown and Jason C. Moser. The College also announced a Doctor of Divinity Degree awarded to Rev. John. B. Davis of Roanoke College and two Master of Arts Degrees awarded to James M. Henderson and to Professor H. T. J. Ludwig, "in view of his mental qualifications and devotion to science."[672]

1873-1874

The College opened the 1873-'74 session at the verge of an international depression. Very little information is available about the academic year. One hundred fifteen students registered for classes, but it is not known how many arrived to begin the session. The faculty remained the same as the previous year. In the Spring of 1874, the Board of Trustees recommended five seniors for receipt of BA Degrees.[673]

The faculty decided to award co-honors to the top two Seniors, C. W. Sifford and John F. Moser, as the difference in grade between the two was very little. Sifford was selected to present the Valedictory address and Moser the Salutatory speech.[674]

Commencement ceremonies were conducted from May 23rd-27th, 1874. Capt. Wiley A. Barrier '72 presented an address on the morning of the 27th and Walter L. Steele, a former member of the NC Legislature and a member of the University of North Carolina Board of Trustees, offered the commencement address that same evening. Prof. Benjamin Hyde Benton of New Market Polytechnic Institutional was awarded an AM Degree.[675]

It was announced that one of the five graduating seniors, J. Adolphus Linn, had accepted a position as a tutor at the College.[676]

1874-1875

Still in the grip of an economic depression, the 1874-'75 session began in August 1874 with 105 students registered - one Senior, two Juniors, two Sophomores, nine Freshmen, and ninety-one Preparatorians. This was a drop of ten students from the previous year. The full-time faculty included Rev. L. A. Bikle, Rev. W. E. Hubbert, and Prof. H. T. J. Ludwig.[677]

Academic year 1874-'75 was marked by financial problems and culminated in the resignations of Rev. Bikle and H. T. J. Ludwig.

Graduation ceremonies were conducted from May 23rd-26th, 1875. Rev. James H. Turner of Blacksburg, VA addressed the Literary Societies. Interestingly, departing faculty member H. T. J. Ludwig gave the Alumni Address. On May 26th, 1875, Frank M. Wadsworth received his BA Degree and Capt. W. A. Barrier '72, received an AM Degree.[678]

1875-1876

The 1875-'76 College session launched with an increased enrollment of 114 students. The school had a new President, Rev. John B. Davis, who also served as Professor of Mental & Moral Science. Rev. W. E. Hubbert was Professor of Ancients Languages and Literature, and Rev. James H. Turner was listed as the new Professor of Mathematics. Dr. Paul A. Barrier served as a lecturer on Anatomy and Physiology.

Apparently, there was some issue with Rev. Turner's employment after the catalogue was printed. At the beginning of the school year Professor Turner was not assigned duties in the Mathematics Department. Instead, two Senior students, Adolphus L. Yount and David L. Crouse, were hired as "interim" Math Department instructors. In October Professor Turner resigned his position and left the school "abruptly, acting in bad faith in the matter." A. L. Yount was appointed Professor of Mathematics and D. L. Crouse was listed as an Adjunct Professor of Ancient Languages and Principal of the Preparatory Department at a salary of $300. It is not clear from existing records what new position Rev. Hubbert filled. Yount and Crouse remained in their positions for the remainder of the school year, although neither graduated until May of 1876.

Graduation ceremonies for academic year 1875-'76 occurred from May 21st-25th, 1876. Rev. F. W. Conrad of Philadelphia, PA delivered the Baccalaureate Sermon on Sunday, May 21st. Rev. Thomas Dosh of Salisbury spoke to the YMCA on Sunday evening. Orations by Juniors J. W. Moore and J. D. Heilig were presented on Monday. Dr. Conrad addressed the Debating Societies and the local church congregations on Tuesday morning. Rev. J. C. Moser '71 spoke to the Alumni on Tuesday afternoon.[679]

On Wednesday, Seniors presented their orations and A. L. Yount offered the valedictory address. Bachelor of Arts Degrees were awarded to D. L. Crouse and A. L. Yount. AM Degrees were granted to Rev. Joseph A. Linn '74, Rev. Henry M. Brown '73, Rev. Franklin P. Cook '73, and John M. Henderson '73. The commencement concluded with the installation of Rev. Davis as President of the College.[680]

1876-1877

Academic year 1876-'77 began on September 6th, 1876 with a

thirty-five percent drop in enrollment and continuing financial struggles. The College Faculty consisted of President J. B. Davis, Professor of Mental & Moral Science; Rev. W. E. Hubbert, Professor of Ancient Languages & Literature; D. L. Crouse, Principal of the Preparatory Department, and newly hired R. H. Brown, Professor of Mathematics. President Davis presented "a thorough course of Agricultural Lectures" without extra charge.[681]

During the year, the Crescent and the Philalaethian Literary Societies petitioned the Board of Trustees to require all students to join one of the two groups. The Board granted the petition and directed the faculty to see that all students "united with the Literary Societies, or that they organize all such as refuse into a separate class for instruction in declamation, composition and debate."[682]

Commencement exercises for the 1876-'77 year were conducted from June 17th-21st, 1877. Rev. Thomas Dosh preached the Baccalaureate Sermon on the 17th. The debating contest took place on the 19th, and on the 20th, Senior addresses were presented. John W. Moose spoke on "The Old North State and Her Education." H. W. Betts topic was "The Poets." Robert A. Yoder delivered a speech on "The Golden Mean" as well as the valedictory address. Bachelor of Arts Degrees were awarded to Henry W. Betts, John W. Moose, and Robert A. Yoder. Rev. Samuel Rothrock received an honorary AM Degree. Rev. Calvin W. Libber and John F. Mason, received MA Degrees. Rev. G. D. Bernheim, and Rev. W. H. Bobbitt were granted DD Degrees.[683]

1877-1878

The administration of the school changed once again at the end of the 1877 school year. The Synod had voted to adopt the "farming out" plan for operation of the College whereby the Professors leased the school buildings and grounds and took their salaries from the income they generated. Seventy students were enrolled as the term commenced on Monday, August 6th, 1877. Rev. L. A. Bikle was President of the Faculty and Professor of Moral and Intellectual Philosophy. H. T. J. Ludwig resumed his former position as Professor of Mathematics, Astronomy, and Physics. Rev. S. S. Rahn served as Secretary of the Faculty and Professor of Ancient Languages and Classical Literature. Dr. Paul A. Barrier continued to serve as a lecturer on Anatomy and Physiology and Mr. S. S. Lindler, the only Senior at the College, was employed as a Tutor.[684]

Graduation ceremonies for the 1877-'78 academic year were conducted from May 19th-22nd, 1878. President Bikle preached the Baccalaureate Sermon on the 19th. On Tuesday, the 21st, Colonel Paul Barringer Means addressed the Literary Societies at the College chapel. Rev. J. T. Moser '73 addressed the Alumni Association. On the 22nd Junior orations were delivered by S. J. Welsh, C. A. Misenheimer, and L. W. Barrier. S. S. Lindler, the only Senior, received his BA Degree, and Thomas Wadsworth '75 received an AM Degree.[685]

1878-1879

The 1878-'79 session began on August 5, 1878 with the first sizable increase in enrollment in seven years. The year began with ninety-nine students enrolled including three Seniors, two Juniors, eight Freshmen and eighty-six Academics (formerly Preparatorians or Primarians). The faculty consisted of President Bikle, Professor of Moral and Intellectual Philosophy; H. T. J. Ludwig, Professor of Mathematics, Astronomy, and Physics, and Rev. S. S. Rahn, Professor of Ancient Languages and Classical Literature. Dr. Paul A. Barrier once again served as lecturer on Anatomy and Physiology.[686]

The school advertised a "course of studies, full, both in the Collegiate and Academic Department. The Corps of instructors furnishes superior advantages for obtaining a thorough Classical and business education".[687]

The winter session saw a sharp decrease in the number of students attending classes. A January 1879 article in *The Wilmington Sun* stated that the College had "upwards of sixty students" attending for the winter/spring session.[688]

Commencement exercises began on Sunday, May 18th, 1879 with the Baccalaureate Sermon preached by President Bikle. Rev. J. A. Linn '74 spoke to the Alumni Association and Rev. Braxton Craven of Trinity College delivered an address to the Literary Societies.[689] Seniors Charles A. Misenheimer and Lawson W. Barrier were awarded Bachelor of Arts Degrees.[690]

1879-1880

On August 4th, 1879, the College began its fall session with eighty-four students, a decrease of previous fall but higher than the enrollment from the previous winter session. The College Catalogue listed one Senior, no Juniors, six Sophomores, eight Freshmen, thirteen Sub-Freshmen, and fifty-six Academics. According to the catalogue, one Sophomore and two Freshmen were expelled during the academic year.[691]

Rev. L. A. Bikle and Prof. H. T. J. Ludwig continued to hold the lease for the College. Rev. Bikle served as President and took over as Professor of Ancient Languages and Classical Literature after Rev. S. S. Rahn resigned at the end of the previous session. H. T. J. Ludwig taught Mathematics, Astronomy and Physics and Dr. P. A. Barrier remained as lecturer on Anatomy and Physiology. Former President of the College Rev. J. B. Davis was hired to instruct Natural Science and Physiology coursework.[692]

Commencement ceremonies were conducted from May 23rd-26th, 1880. Charles R. Jones, Editor of the *Charlotte Observer*, delivered an address before the Literary Societies. Clarence G. Heilig presented the Senior Address entitled "The Skeptics of the Present Day." Receiving BA Degrees were Clarence G. Heilig, S. J. Welsh (already attending Medical School in New York) and Clarence A. Rose (graduated in January). AM Degrees were conferred on Dr. H. W. Betts '77, Dr. John W. Moose '77, and Rev. R. A. Yoder '77. Former Principal of Western Carolina Male Academy Rev. William Gerhardt received a DD Degree.[693]

1880-1881

Classes for the 1880-'81 scholastic year began on August 2nd, 1880. The minutes of the NC Lutheran Synod stated that there were eighty-one students enrolled in May of 1881. However, only fifty students attended classes. The faculty remained the same as the previous year but included additional classes taught by Lewis H. Rothrock, the son of Rev. Samuel Rothrock and Principal at Mont Amoena Seminary.[694] No record of the commencement ceremonies, if any were conducted, has been located to date. Based on College records there were no graduates and no honorary degrees awarded in the spring of 1881.

1881-1882

As described in Part I, the status of the College in the fall of 1881 was very unclear. It appears that at the opening of the school Rev. Bikle was listed as the President but it is not known if he was present on campus. Rev. G. D. Bernheim was appointed as the new President in January 1882, but it is also not clear if he began work immediately. Records do not list the faculty or how many total students were registered for the session. Six new student enrollments were noted in September 1881 and two students began classes during the spring '82 session. There were no graduates at the end of either the fall or spring terms.[695]

Both Rev. Bikle and Rev. Bernheim were present at a Board of Trustees meeting held on May 23rd, 1882. Rev. Bikle recommended several persons for advanced degrees. These included Rev. S. L. Harkey from Pennsylvania, DD Degree; Rev. Jacob Hawkins of South Carolina, DD Degree; Rev. C. H. Bansemer of Florida, former President of NCC, DD Degree; C. A. Misenheimer, NCC '79, AM Degree; Lawson W. Barrier, NCC '79, AM Degree, and Dr. S. J. Welsh, NCC '80, AM Degree.[696]

Commencement exercises were held on May 24th, 1882. Mr. Henry S. Puryear of Concord addressed the Literary Societies and Rev. Bernheim was formally inaugurated.[697]

1882-1883

In the face of the continuing national economic crisis, NC College managed to open on August 7th, 1882 with new President, Rev. Gotthard D. Bernheim, DD, succeeding Rev. Bikle. There is no record of the number of students attending the College, which, like the previous two years, produced no graduates. Two new members joined the faculty. Rev. Holmes Dysinger, A. M. was Professor of Ancient Languages and Classical Literature, and Clarence G. Heilig, A. B., Class of '80 was appointed Principal of the Preparatory Department. Rev. Bernheim served as Professor of Mental & Moral Sciences, History, English and German Literature. The sole returning faculty member was Professor H. T. J. Ludwig who continued to instruct Mathematics, Astronomy and Physics.[698]

During the previous summer, John D. Barrier became Steward of the College. As such, he was offering board (meals) at his home for $7 per month. Barrier attended the College in 1861, was a Civil War veteran, and in 1880 was living on N. Main St. in Mt. Pleasant about a block from the College. He was employed as a carpenter.[699]

Although the year began on a reasonably positive note, the situation deteriorated quickly. Rev. Bernheim resigned in January and the school suspended operations on April 1, 1883. There are no academic records for the school year, but student rosters list one new student enrolling in the fall session and four in the soon to be suspended spring session.[700]

1884 (Half-session)

The College did not open for a fall session in 1883. With a new President and enough funding to continue operation, NC College opened on January 1st, 1884 "despite extreme weather, for a "half-session" with sixty or more students." Rev. George Francis Schaeffer, A. M. served as President and Professor of Mental and Moral Science. At the time of his appointment as President of the College, Rev. Schaeffer was the Minister at Mt. Carmel Lutheran Church south of Mt. Pleasant and 1st Lutheran Church in nearby Albemarle, NC.

Professor H. T. J. Ludwig returned to the school and resumed his position of Instructor of Mathematics, Astronomy and Physics. Rev. J. B. Davis taught Natural Science while also serving as Minister of Holy Trinity Church in Mt. Pleasant. Three new faculty members joined the staff - Rev. F. W. E. Peschau, A.M. (who had earlier declined the Presidency of the College) was a lecturer on History, Elocution and Science. L. H. Rothrock, A. M., was Principal of the Preparatory Department, and James P. Cook, a member of the Junior Class, was an assistant in the Preparatory Department.[701]

Registration for the "half-session" listed three students in the Collegiate Department, one Junior, and two Freshmen; thirty-nine students in the Academic Department and nineteen in the Preparatory Department.

The catalogue specified that to complete the Academic course

four years were required. Each cohort attended three or more recitations or lectures a day."

The courses were listed as follows:

> Freshman Class (First Term) – Latin Grammar and Prose Composition; Virgil; Greek Grammar and Prose Composition; Xenophon's Anabasis; Ancient Geography;

English Grammar; General History; Complete Algebra, and Plane Geometry; (Second Term) – Latin and Greek Grammar; Cicero's Orations; Latin Prose Composition; Herodotus and Greek Prose Composition; Solid and Spherical Geometry; English Grammar; Physical Geography; Rhetoric; and General History.

Sophomore Class (First Term) – Odes and Epodes of Horace; Latin Prose Composition; Xenophon's Memorabilia, or Thucydides; Greek Prose Composition; Trigonometry; Surveying and Navigation; English Grammar, and Rhetoric; (Second Term) – Greek and Latin Prose Composition; Livy; Homer's Iliad; Classical Antiquities; Analytical Geometry; English Literature, and History.

Junior Class (First Term) – Satires, Epistles, and Ars Poetica of Horace; Greek and Latin Prose; Demosthenes on the Crown; Differential and Integral Calculus; Chemistry; Mental Philosophy; Logic; German Grammar and Exercises; (Second Term) – Cicero de Officiis; Greek and Latin Prose Composition; Aeschylus (Prometheus); Mechanics; Natural Philosophy; Physiology and Chemistry; Meteorology, German.

Senior Class (First Term) – Tacitus (Germania et Agricolae Vita); Greek and Latin Composition and Original Exercises; Antigone of Sophocles; Geology; Moral Philosophy; Astronomy, and German; (Second Term) – Juvenal (Satires); Plato; Original Exercise in Greek and Latin Composition; Political Economy; Natural Theology; Review of the whole Course.

Composition and Declamation [were] taught during the entire course.[702]

In April of 1884, North Carolina College was listed as one of nine male colleges in the state. Others included the University of NC at Chapel Hill, Trinity College, Davidson College, Biddle University in Charlotte, Shaw University in Raleigh, Rutherford College, Wake Forest College, and Weaverville College.[703]

The "half-session" commencement ceremonies began on May 18th, 1884 with an address by Rev. Walter S. Creasy, a Methodist Minister from Concord. Reverend Peschau spoke before the Literary Societies. College records list only one graduate, Lewis Rothrock, who received both his BA and AM Degrees. Events culminated on May 22nd with the formal inauguration of the new President, Reverend George F. Schaffer.[704]

1884-1885

Under Rev. Schaeffer, the school took on a new air of organization. On August 4th, 1884 a full session of the College commenced with ninety-four students registered and, for the first time since re-opening in 1866, a full faculty. The students included two Seniors, three Sophomores, eight Freshmen, twenty-three Sub-Freshmen and fifty-eight Academics (Preparatory) students.

Returning faculty included H. T. J. Ludwig, Professor of Mathematics; Luther H. Rothrock, Professor of History and Principal of the Preparatory Department; Rev. F. W. E. Peschau, Lecturer on History and Rev. J. B. Davis, Lecturer on Chemistry and Botany. The new member of the faculty was Rev. John C. F. Rupp, A. M., formerly of Pittsburg, PA, who taught Ancient Languages and Literature. The College listed new Officers to carry out the business tasks of the school. Jonas Cook was the School Treasurer and Rev. Schaeffer was the Financial Secretary. An Executive Committee consisted of Rev. Schaeffer, Jonas Cook, and Dr. P. A. Barrier. Professor Rothrock was the Secretary of the Faculty, and H. T. J. Ludwig was the School Librarian. Even an alumni association was organized with Rev. J. C. Moser serving as President and H. T. J. Ludwig as Secretary.[705]

The 1884-'85 School catalogue contained, for the first time, a description of Honors and Degrees available to members of graduating classes. Any Senior who achieved a general average in scholarship, conduct and attendance of 92.5 during his last two years was awarded "First Honor." Any Senior who attained an average between 85 and 92.5 was awarded "Second Honor." Seniors "in full and regular standing", were, at the recommendation of the Faculty, conferred a Bachelor of Arts (BA) degree by the Board of Trustees.

The the Degree of Master of Art (AM) had been awarded since 1875 to "Bachelors of three or more years standing, who had been regularly admitted to either of the three professions, or upon others of scholarly attainments."[706]

There is no record of the College conferring Doctor of Philosphy (PhD) Degrees, but it did grant honorary Doctor of Divinity Degrees.

A week of commencement exercises began on May 17th, 1885 with a Baccalaureate Sermon by President Schaeffer, examinations on May 18th and 19th and an Academic Exhibition on the evening of the 19th. A Literary Society Contest on the 20th was followed by a concert by the MP Female Academy, and graduation on May 21st. Two Seniors, Charles B. Miller and James P. Cook, received BA Degrees,[707]

1885-1886

The College began the Academic year of 1885-'86 on August 3rd, 1885 with Rev. Schaeffer returning for his third term as President of the College. He also continued to serve as Professor of Mental and Moral Science. All the faculty from the previous year returned except Rev. Rupp. Rupp's position as Professor of Ancient Languages and Literature was "temporarily supplied."

With no explanation or records describing the circumstances, the first term of the 1885-'86 academic year began with a loss of thirty-five students. No Seniors, four Juniors, six Sophomores, and eight Freshman were registered, There were fifteen Sub-Freshmen, and twenty-nine Academics.[708]

As usual, examinations for admission to the College level were held for several days before the opening of school. Entering Freshmen were examined on English (grammar, geography, spelling, and Elementary Natural Philosophy), Greek (White's Lessons, Goodwin's Grammar, and Anabasis), Latin (Harkness' Exercises, Caesar's Gallic War, Bucolics of Virgil and the Aeneid), and Mathematics (Arithmetic Complete, Algebra through Quadratics and Plane Geometry). Admission required "an accurate and thorough acquaintance with these subjects," … in order to receive the full benefit of the College course. If imperfectly prepared for the class they enter, students are embarrassed in their entire future progress."

The College Catalogue stated that:

> "the course of instruction, including all branches usually required for the degree of Bachelor of Arts. The Institution

> has made no provision for a philosophical or scientific course, but Faculty have the authority to make the proper substitutions in the curriculum in exceptional cases, to provide for the philosophical or scientific degree."

The College library contained more than one thousand volumes and "leading papers and magazines." The reading room was maintained by the Athenaeum.

There were two Literary Societies, the Philalaethian and the Pi Sigma Phi, that "exert a healthful and stimulating influence in the cultivation and pursuit of composition, debate and oratory."[709]

The College ended its 1885-'86 academic year during the last two weeks of May. Final examinations were conducted from May 19th through May 21st. Commencement exercises began the following week with an Academic Exhibition on May 24th followed by a contest for the Declaimer's Medal on the 25th. On the 26th of May, Mr. Zebulon A. Morris addressed the Literary Societies, and a Debating Contest by the Literary Societies was held in the evening. No Diplomas or advanced Degrees were awarded.[710]

1886-1887

The fall session of the College's 1886-'87 academic year began on August 30th with an enrollment of fifty-three students. Three Seniors were listed - Lawson E. Heilig and Henry M. Petrea of Mt. Pleasant, and Peter E. Wright of Enochville. Peter Wright completed his course at the end of the first session (Jan 1886) and was employed as an instructor for the second session and as a full Professor beginning in 1887-'88. In addition to the three Seniors, there were two Juniors, four Sophomores, fifteen Freshmen, ten Sub-Freshmen and nineteen Academics. The Academic students were divided into two classes – second year (fourteen) and first year (five).

The faculty listed at the beginning of the session was the same as the previous year with the addition of Peter Wright during the spring session.

Entrance requirements to the College and the course of study remained the same as the previous year. Sub-Freshmen were required to take courses in English Grammar, Composition and Etymology, Plane Geometry, Algebra, Watts on the Mind, Book-keeping, Business Arithmetic, and Commercial Law.

First year Academics were given instruction in reading, penmanship, spelling and defining, English Grammar, composition, dictation exercise, modern geography & map drawing, NC History, arithmetic, elementary algebra and declamation.

Second year Academics took courses in reading, spelling and defining, English Grammar and analysis, composition, declamation, penmanship, US History, English History, higher arithmetic, algebra, elementary geometry, good morals and gentle manners.

Two College Department curriculums were described in the catalogue. A "practical course" consisted of classes on the Constitution of US & NC, Theory of Teaching, Physiology & Hygiene, Principles of Agriculture, Geometry, Chemistry, Popular Geology and Declamation. A more "classical course" contained courses on Ancient Geography, Classical mythology, Caesar or Nepos, Sallust, Virgil's Bucolics, First Lessons in Greek, Goodwin's Greek Grammar and Anabasis.[711]

Commencement exercises were held jointly with the Mont Amoena Female Seminary from May 29th - June 2nd, 1887. On Sunday, May 29th, Rev. W. G. Campbell of Concord delivered the Baccalaureate Sermon. Declamations and exhibitions were conducted at the College on Monday, and on Tuesday evening, "at the Church," the Literary Societies conducted debates. On Wednesday the Rev. R. A. Yoder, '77 BA, '80 AM, delivered the Alumni Address titled "From the Human to the Divine." The Declaimer's Medal was presented to A. H. Peninger and a medal from the Phi Sigma Phi Society was presented to B. S. Nunamaker. Lawson E. Heilig and Henry M. Petrea were awarded Bachelor of Arts Degrees.[712]

1887-1888

The College opened the new academic year on August 29th, 1887 with fifty-five students and a new President. There were three Seniors, John L. Deaton and his twin brother, Willis A. Deaton, of China Grove, and John H. Ritchie of Mt. Pleasant. Other students included three Juniors, four Sophomores, eight Freshmen, six Sub-Freshmen, twenty second year Academics and eleven first year Academics.[713]

The reduction in full-time faculty represented a major change from the preceding year. To curb expenses, the College now employed only three full time Instructors and only two of these taught at the College level. President Shaidt served as Professor of Mental and Moral Science and taught German. He also served as the Minister at Holy Trinity Lutheran Church in Mt. Pleasant. H. T. J. Ludwig, the only returning faculty member, taught Mathematics, Astronomy and Physics. P. E. Wright, Class of '87, was hired as Principal of the Preparatory Department. The Deaton twins were employed as part-time instructors. John Deaton taught Geography and History and Willis Deaton, taught English Grammar.[714]

1888-1889

The 1888-'89 academic year saw few changes from the preceding year. Rev. Shaidt returned as President and Professor of Mental and Moral Science. H. T. J. Ludwig and P. E. Wright also returned to their respective positions. No part-time instructors were employed during the year but several "Lecturers to the Athenaeum" were named – Rev. J. A. Linn, Rev. G. H. Cox, Rev. A. T. Gantt and Rev. F. W. E. Peschau. There was a note on the faculty in the Catalogue stating that "the Faculty will be increased next year."[715]

Forty-nine students enrolled during the year. These included three Seniors, John A. Blackwelder of Concord, Jeremiah H. Dreher from Mt. Pleasant and Benjamin S. Nunamaker from Columbia, SC. Two Juniors, six Sophomores, and six Freshmen also attended the College. The Academic Department listed nine Sub-Freshmen, four second-year Academics, and nineteen first-year Academics.[716]

Graduation ceremonies for the NC College Class of 1889 were held jointly with the Mt. Pleasant Female Seminary. They began on Sunday, June 2nd, 1889 and continued through Thursday, June 6th. The Baccalaureate Ceremony was held at Holy Trinity Lutheran Church where College President Rev. Schaidt delivered the sermon.

On Monday evening, June 3rd, the College Preparatory classes gave a presentation consisting of a series of declamations on various subjects. On Tuesday, June 4th, six students competed in the Declaimer's Contest at the Lutheran Church. J. L. D. Barringer spoke on "Respect the Foundation of National Government." W. J. Boger addressed "America, Her Glory and Her Shame." M. A. Boger's topic was "Lost Thoughts," and C. B. Cox spoke of "David's Lament for Absalom." J. R. Faggart's topic was "Spartacus to the Envoy of Rome," and T. L. File presented "The National Flag." Following the Declaimers, two Junior Orators, John M. Cook and B. H. W. Runge, spoke for thirty minutes each. Cook's topic was "Democracy" and Runge spoke on "Discontent."

On the rainy Wednesday morning of June 5th, four contestants entered the Sophomore Class Orator's contest. H. N. Miller spoke on "True Religion;" W. N. Misenheimer on "Human Responsibilities;" R. L. Patterson on "The Curse of Ambition," and R. L. Bame on "The Reformation – A Benefit to Man."

Formal Commencement services began at 10:30AM on Thursday, June 6th. Salutatory Addresses were given by J. A. Blackwelder and B. S. Nunamaker. The Valedictory Address was presented by J. H. Dreher. Mont Amoena Seminary graduates Leah Blackwelder and Sallie E. Fisher read their graduation essays.

The winners of the Declamation and Oration contests, W. J. Boger and H. N. Miller, received medals. Diplomas were then presented by Rev. J. A. Linn, Jr., Principal of Mont Amoena and Rev. J. G. Schaidt, President of NC College.[717]

In July of 1889, Reverend Schaidt unexpectedly announced his resignation to accept a position at Concordia College in Newton. After unsuccessfully offering the position to former student and faculty member Wiley Barrier, the Synod and Board of Trustees appointed Rev. John D. Shirey, minister at Salem Lutheran Church in Rowan County, as the new President.

1889-1890

The 1889-'90 school year began on September 2nd, 1889 with ninety-seven students registered. Newly appointed President Rev. J. D. Shirey was joined by a faculty of three Professors, one instructor, and three tutors. Rev. Shirey served as Professor of Mental and Moral Science. H. T. J. Ludwig. the only returning faculty member, continued to teach Mathematics, Astronomy and Physics. Two new Professors were brothers, Rev. Charles L. T. Fisher and Rev. James H. C. Fisher from Rowan County, NC. The Fisher brothers both attended NC College, first enrolling in 1875 as Academics. They received their B.A. Degrees at Gettysburg College and both were ordained by the Maryland Synod. Charles served churches in Maryland and Nebraska before returning to North Carolina in 1889. At NC College, Charles Fisher served as Professor of Ancient Languages and Literature and James Fisher was the Principal of the Preparatory (Academic) Department and adjunct Professor of Ancient Languages.[718]

Four members faculty were students at the College. Boughart H. W. Runge was a Senior from Wilmington, NC who taught German. The other three students employed as tutors in the Preparatory Department were Junior Henderson Miller from Salisbury; Junior Henry E. H. Sloop from China Grove, and Sophomore Joseph A. Graham from China Grove.

At the beginning of the academic year, the College and the local "common schools" engaged in a program combining students in the College Preparatory department with students in the public schools. There is no information about the nature of this curriculum except that Rev. Shirey noted in his year-end report that it did not prove successful.[719] The number of students enrolled in the College Department was unchanged at seventeen. There were two Seniors, John Mathew Cook, son of College treasurer, Jonas Cook, and Boughart H. Runge. Four Juniors were enrolled along with five Sophomores and eight Freshman. The Sub-freshman class listed fourteen students, while the Preparatory (Academic) classes listed twenty-eight second year and thirty-five first year members.

The course of instruction for the new year did not change from the previous year but the requirements for "First Distinction" and "Second Distinction" awards were raised. To be awarded First Distinction a graduating Senior was now required maintain an overall average of not less than ninety-five. To be eligible for Second Distinction a Senior had to achieve an average of between ninety and ninety-five.

Other changes implemented in the new year were significant modifications in the school calendar and the tuition/fee schedule. In previous years the calendar was based on a two-term academic year of twenty weeks each where the first term began on the first week in September and the second term began on the third Monday in January. Under the new calendar, the school year was divided into three terms of fifteen, twelve and twelve weeks with the first term beginning on the second Thursday of September.

Just prior to the end of the session, a new student publication, *The Advance*, proclaimed that the future of the College looked brighter. "Under his [President Shirey] administration a new life has entered the affairs of the College, and there is every indication that the institution has entered upon a new era of prosperity."[720]

The academic year ended with graduation exercises conducted jointly with Mont Amoena Female Seminary from May 31st through June 4th, 1890. On May 31st, the declamation contest included six underclassmen vying for the Demorest Medal. Walter Cook was awarded the prize. The Baccalaureate Sermon was delivered on Sunday, June 1st, by Rev. H. C. Hathcock.

On Monday, June 2nd, J. A. Suther won the Declaimers Medal, speaking on "Greece As She Was and Is." In the afternoon, an Essay Contest and Debate proceeded on the subject "Resolved: That the character of Oliver Cromwell is more admired than that of Napoleon Bonaparte." The Mt. Pleasant Coronet Band and the Concord String Band provided music for the events. James P. Cook delivered the Alumni Address and Rev. G. W. Holland, President of Newberry College, presented the Commencement Address. Two degrees were awarded. B. H. W. Runge received a Bachelor of Arts Diploma and James M. Cook received a Bachelor of Science Diploma.

On Wednesday evening following the graduation ceremony, the students of NC College and Mont Amoena Seminary gave a play entitled "The Sparkling Cup." The newspaper described the event as amusement for the attendees and a fund-raiser for repairs to the schools. $36.05 was raised.[721]

1890-1891

The 1890-'91 Academic year began on September 11th. The College was in better condition than in the past several years, both physically and financially. Rev. Shirey returned for the second year as President of the College along with three faculty members, H. T. J. Ludwig, C. L. T. Fisher and J. H. C. Fisher. A new faculty member, Dr. J. S. Flow, was retained to teach German and French. Joseph A. Graham, now a Junior at the College, continued as a Tutor in the Preparatory Department.[722]

During the year two guest lecturers also taught classes. Rev. Wright Campbell lectured on Anatomy, Physiology, and Hygiene, and Henderson N. Miller, a Senior at the College, lectured on the Volapuk Language.[723]

The College Catalogue listed seventy-nine students, a decrease of eighteen students from the previous year. However, the Collegiate

Department increased from seventeen to twenty members. There were four Seniors, three Juniors, five Sophomores, and seven Freshman registered, plus one "non-resident" student, William T. Whitsett. The Preparatory Class contained nine "regular" Sub-freshmen, twenty-seven "elective" Sub-Freshmen, sixteen second year Academics and seven third year Academics.

As an explanation of the decrease in enrollment, the catalogue stated that

> "the attention of the friends of the college is called to the fact that the real increase in college patronage this year over last is eighteen percent, while there is an apparent decrease, having catalogued last year ninety-six. This arises from the fact that many day scholars, who were last year in the primary department, were this year transferred to the two public schools of Mt. Pleasant."

In 1890-'91 the College introduced a new "Scientific Course" which led to a Bachelor of Science Degree. This course contained the same classes as the Literary Course but omitted classes on Greek, substituting courses in Mathematics and Science.[724]

Commencement exercises for the 1890-'91school year took place from June 7th-10th, 1891. Speakers included Congressman John S. Henderson, NC Synod Vice- President, Rev. C. A. Rose, Rev. C. B. King, Secretary of the Synod, and Rev. Paul Barringer who presented a lecture on "Pluck and Luck." The Declaimers Medal was awarded to V. C. Ridenhour. Bachelor of Arts Degrees were conferred upon R. L. Bame, H. N. Miller and R. L. Patterson. Henry E. Sloop received a PhB. Notedbly, all the graduates were from Rowan County. Master's Degrees were awarded to W. T. Whitsett, Principal of Gibsonville High School; Rev. G. H. Cox; Rev. H. M. Petrea '87; Rev. J. L. Deaton '88, and Rev. W. A. Deaton '88. Rev. F. W. E. Peschau of Wilmington received a DD Degree.[725]

1891-1892

The 1891-'92 academic year began on September 17th, 1891, with the "spirit of work and success," ... "a strong and working force of managers," ... and a "confidence on the part of the church in the institution."[726]

The school year, divided into three terms of sixteen, eleven, and eleven weeks, opened with a complete faculty and seventy-six students.

Rev. Shirey returned as President and Professor of Mental & Moral Science. Other returning faculty included H. T. J. Ludwig, Professor of Mathematics, Astronomy, and Physics; Rev. C. L. T. Fisher, Professor of Ancient Languages and Literature, and Rev. J. H. C. Fisher, Principal of the Preparatory Department. The faculty no longer included the position of Instructor of German and French but these classes were "temporarily supplied" by Prof. Ludwig and Prof. J. H. C. Fisher. A newly created position, Professor of Elocution, was filled by Rev. George H. Cox. Post-graduate student H. N. Miller served as a tutor, and Joseph A. Graham, now a Senior, was listed as an assistant instructor. Lecturers included Rev. F. W. E. Peschau, Rev. W. A. Lutz, Rev. Bachman S. Brown, Mr. James M. Cook, and Rev. C. A. Marks.[727]

The seventy-six students enrolled included one "non-resident," William T. Whitsett of Gibsonville, one post-graduate, H. N. Miller of Mt. Pleasant, and two Seniors, Charles H. Barnhardt of Mt. Pleasant and Joseph A. Graham of China Grove. There were three Juniors, four Sophomores, and nine Freshmen in the College Department. The Preparatory Department included six "regular" Sub-Freshmen, and thirty-one "elective" Sub-Freshmen. There were fifteen Second year and four Preparatory students. The catalogue listed sixty-three students from North Carolina, ten from South Carolina, one from Virginia, one from Arkansas and one from Illinois.

While the core curriculum was essentially unchanged from the previous term, the College offered two "new" courses. The new Bachelor of Philosophy course was the same as that leading to a Bachelor of Arts degree except that classes in Latin & Greek were optional after the sophomore year, and included additional work in Literature, History, Mathematics and Physical Science.

The second new course was a Business Course which was "designed to prepare young men for the active affairs of life." This course, which included twenty-two of the seventy-six students enrolled in the Preparatory Department, was taught by Prof. H. T. J. Ludwig. It included instruction in single entry and double entry book-keeping, business arithmetic, commercial law, letter writing, business correspondence, and general instruction about money, currency, trade, commerce, banks, and banking. Students could take one or more classes in the other College departments but would incur a delay in completing the degree. The cost was the same as the Collegiate Department.

The 1891-'92 academic year ended during the week of May 25th – June 1st, 1892. Examinations were held on May 25th and 26th. An academic exhibition was presented on Saturday, May 28th and the Baccalaureate Sermon was given by Rev. W. S. Bowman of Charlotte on May 29th. Debate and oratory contests were held on Monday, May 30th, and George Cromer of Newberry, SC presented an address to the Literary Societies on May 31st. The Alumni address and a concert were also presented at the female seminary on May 31st, Graduation exercises were held on Wednesday, June 1st.[728]

In addition to Commencement exercises, the Board of Trustees met on May 31st to address several issues. Mr. L. H. Aull of Newberry SC offered to establish a Gold Medal for the best original essay composed by a member of the Senior Class. The Board of Trustees awarded a MA Degree to Jeremiah Dreher. Dreher graduated from the College in 1889 and in 1892 was employed as a dentist residing in Philadelphia, PA.[729]

1892-1893

Unlike the previous year, the 1892-'93 school year opened on a somber note. Only fifty-three students were enrolled, a significant drop (thirty percent) from the previous year. The College Department enrollment increased from nineteen to twenty-three but the Preparatory Department numbers decreased by twenty-six. William Whitsett was still registered as a non-resident student. There were two Seniors, brothers Martin A. Boger and William J. Boger, two Junior's, ten Sophomores and eight Freshmen. The Preparatory Department listed seventeen Sub-Freshmen and thirteen Preparatorians. The drop in enrollment was again due to public schools.

During the summer, Rev. C. L. T. Fisher resigned his teaching position at the College and accepted the Principal's position of the nearby female academy, Mont Amoena Seminary. His position was filled by E. B. Setzer, who became Professor of Ancient Languages & Literature.[730]

Rev. Shirey returned for his fourth term of President of the College but was now tasked as the school's financial agent. Despite his claim for back pay, H. T. J. Ludwig returned as Professor of Mathematics, Astronomy and Physics. Professor Ludwig was appointed Principal of the newly created

Commercial Department which was developed from the former Business Course established two years earlier. There were seven students enrolled in this "new" Department, including the two Seniors, one Sophomore and four members of the Preparatory Department.[731]

Rev. J. H. C. Fisher returned as the Principal of the Preparatory Department and Jesse L. McLendon, a member of the Sophomore class, was employed as an instructor in penmanship. Lecturers for the year included Rev. G. D. Bernheim, Rev. W. G. Campbell, Rev. Bachmann S. Brown, and Mr. J. A. Blackwelder.[732]

No information has been located concerning activities during the academic year. Commencement ceremonies for the 1892-'93 school year were conducted jointly with Mont Amoena Female Seminary during the last week in May. Rev. J. C. Moser, '73 delivered the Baccalaureate Sermon on May 28th. The Declaimer's Contest was held on Monday, May 29th. Participants included Ralph W. Barrier, W. A. Foil, Edgar E. Hendricks, J. Walter Peacock, G. M. Poole and Alexander A. Springs. A. A. Springs claimed the Medal. The Orator's competition was won by B. B. Miller, speaking on "Modern Oratory."

An address before the Literary Societies was presented by Rev. L. A. Gotwald, DD, Professor of Theology at Whittenburg Seminary, Springfield, OH, and the Alumni Address was given by Rev. S. S. Lindler, AM, class of 1878. Diplomas were presented at 10:30 AM on May 30th, 1893. Graduates were William J. Boger, Valedictorian, and his brother, M. Augustus Boger. William Whitsett, class of 1891, was awarded a PhD.[733]

1893-1894

The 1893-'94 Academic year opened on September 7th with seventy-one students registered. The Collegiate Department grew from twenty-three to twenty-nine students, its second increase in two years. There was one Senior, C. Brown Cox from Organ Church, seven Juniors, five Sophomores, and sixteen Freshmen. There were nine sub-Freshmen registered and thirty-three Preparatory Students. There were four students registered in the Commercial Class. Three terms of fifteen, twelve, and eleven weeks cost between $100.50 and $142.00 per year, depending on class status.

The College faculty remained unchanged from the previous year and ten lecturers spoke on numerous topics. Mr. R. L. Patterson lectured on "A Critical Period in American History." Prof. John McCorkle spoke on the subject of "Phrenology." Other presentations included a lesson on "Christian Character," by Rev. W. S. Bowman; a lecture on "Man" given by Rev. V. R. Stickley; a session on "Education" conducted by Rev. W. R. Brown; a message on "Conscience" given by Rev. Bachman S. Brown; an address on "Manly Purity" presented by Dr. M. L. Stevens, and a lecture on "The Demands of the Coming Generation" delivered by Rev. George W. Callahan. Staff Professors H. T. J. Ludwig and E. B. Setzer also presented special classes on "Socialism," and "The South as a Field for the Poet."

The Academic year concluded with Junior Orations on June 6th. Because the one Senior, C. Brown Cox, did not complete his examinations, he was not eligible for graduation, thus no diplomas were awarded. The College presented a Doctor of Divinity Degree to Rev. J. L. Smith of Pittsburg, PA and an AM Degree to Rev. Robert L. Patterson, '91. The Declaimer's Medal was awarded to Preparatory student P. Wilburn Tucker of Mt. Pleasant, and the Orator's Medal was presented to Freshman J. Homer Barnhardt of Mt. Pleasant.

Due to a change in requirements during the preceding year, members of all the classes were eligible for First Distinction and Second Distinction Honors. Freshman George F. McAllister and Sophomore C. E. Boger earned First Distinction honors in 1893-'94. Boger also received the Medal for the Highest Academic Average. Twenty-two students were awarded Second Distinction awards.[734]

1894-95

The 1894-'95 Academic Year began on September 2nd, 1894 with seventy students. There were seven Seniors, five Juniors, eight Sophomores, and eight freshmen in the College Department, a decrease of one from the previous year. Sixteen sub-Freshmen were registered as well as twenty-six Preparatory Department students. Of this number, eleven were enrolled in the Commercial Department.

Rev. Shirey returned for his fifth term as President of the College and Professor of Mental & Moral Science. He continued as financial agent for the school. Professors Ludwig and Setzler returned in their respective positions. In addition to his duties in the Math and Commercial Departments, Ludwig also taught French. Setzler added instruction of German to his Ancient Languages and Literature courses. Professor J. H. C. Fisher resigned his post as Principal of the Preparatory Department to accept a call as the Minister at Luther's Lutheran Church in Rowan County. His replacement was Martin A. Boger, Class of '93.

Guest lecturers during the school year included Rev. Bachman S. Brown who presented a lecture on "The Teacher." James P. Cook, '85, spoke on "The People are as Restless as the Sea." John M. Cook, '90, gave a talk on "Fanaticism," and Rev. M. D. Giles lectured on "Psychology." In addition to the guest speakers, faculty members presented lectures. Professor Ludwig spoke on two subjects, "The Student" and "The Seasons, Past and Present." Professor Setzler lectured on "Education's Importance the Consequences of Its Purpose", and Prof. Boger gave a presentation on "Know Something and Do Something."

Following the traditional week of celebration and exercises, the academic year ended with Commencement on June 5th, 1895. On June 4th former NC Governor Thomas J. Jarvis gave an address before the Literary Societies. Rev. A. L. Yount,'76 presented the Alumni Address and was awarded a Doctor of Divinity Degree. Seven Seniors received diplomas. A PhB Degree was awarded to C. D. Cobb and AM Degrees were given to Rev. D. H. Runge, '90, and Rev. H. N. Miller. First Distinction Honors were awarded for the second year to Junior Charles E. Boger and Sophomore George F. McAllister. The Declaimer's Medal was claimed by Sub-Freshman J. Walter Peacock. Winner of the Orator's Medal was Junior Herbert Barrier. A Bible History Award for the best written examination on Bible History was presented to Sophomore J. Homer Barnhardt, and the Greek Medal for the student with the best standing in examinations in Greek was given to George F. McAllister.[735]

1895-1896

The 1895-'96 College session began on September 4th with examinations and assignment of recitations for all classes. Regular classes began on September 5th. Seventy-one students were enrolled but only twenty-three were in the College program and eleven of these were classified as irregular or in a special course. The College listed four Seniors, four Juniors, three

Sophomores and twelve Freshmen. The Sub-Freshmen class consisted of eighteen members and there were fifteen pupils in the 2nd Year Preparatory Class and thirteen in the 1st Year Class. Eight students studied in the Commercial Class.

For the second time in three years, the school faculty returned intact. Special lecturers for the year included Rev. P. W. Huddler, whose subject was "Success in Life;" Rev. H. N. Miller; "The Adaptation of Christianity to the Needs of Man;" Rev. Paul Barringer, "Undercurrents which Threaten our Free Institutions;" Rev. B. S. Brown, "The Thirty Years War and its Lessons;" C. H. Barnhardt, "Public Hygiene;" Prof. J. A. Graham, "The Age & Its Demands;" Rev. P. H. E. Derrick, "Your Life, Its Responsibilities, Possibilities and its Great Design;" Prof. E. B. Setzer, "The Army of Northern Virginia," and Prof. H. T. J. Ludwig, "The Sun."

In 1895-'96 the College course consisted of three terms of fifteen, twelve and eleven weeks, respectively. Freshman classes included:

> (1st Term) Latin - Cicero's Select Orations; Allen & Greenough's Grammar; Greek - Xenophon's Anabasis; Goodwin's Grammar; Mathematics - Algebra to Theory of Equations, Plane Geometry; History - General History (Myers); English - English Grammar (Fowler); Bible History, Essays & Declamations throughout the year; (2nd Term) Latin – Livy, Book I; Grammar, continued; Prose Composition; Greek – Xenophon's Memorabilia; Grammar, continued; Prose Composition (Jones); Algebra – Algebra, completed; Introduction to Determinants; Plane and Solid Geometry; English – English Grammar (Fowler); Rhetoric (Hill); (3rd Term) Latin – Livy, Book XXI; Grammar and Prose Composition continued; Greek – Xenophon's Memorabilia; Grammar and Prose Composition continued; Mathematics – Solid and Spherical Geometry; Introduction to Modern Geometry; Application of Algebra to Geometry; English – Methods of Philological Study of the English Language; Rhetoric (Hill).
>
> The Sophomore Year courses included (1st Term) Latin – Satires, Odes, or Epistles of Horace; Prose

Composition; Greek – Lysias; Prose Composition (Jones), concluded; Mathematics – Plane and Spherical Trigonometry, Mensuration, Surveying and Navigation; Geometrical Conics; History – Medieval and Modern (Myers); English – Logic (Hill) Jevon's; Science of Rhetoric (Hill); Bible History, Essays, and Declamation throughout the year; (2nd Term) Latin – Horace, Tacitus, or Plautus, Prose Composition Greek – Lysias, Homer's Iliad, or Demosthenes; Exercises in Syntax (Boise); Mathematics – Analytical Geometry, Differential Calculus; English – Logic, English Literature, Science of Rhetoric; History – Natural History (Hooker); (3rd Term) Latin – Tacitus or Plautus; Composition; Greek – Homer or Demosthenes; Exercises in Syntax; Mathematics – Integral Calculus; Science – Physiology and Hygiene (Tracy); English – English and American Literature; Theses on assigned subjects.

The Junior Year offered (1st Term) Latin – Quintilian (De Institutione Oratoria); Greek* - The Prometheus Vinctus of Aeschylus, or the Antigone of Sophocles; Mathematics – Statics; Lessons in Kinematics; Science – Political Economy; Mental Philosophy (Haven); English – Criticism; French – Grammar and Exercises; German – Schmitz's Elements of the German Language, Conversation; Bible History throughout the year; (2nd Term) Latin – Quintilian; Juvenal (Hart); Greek*- Aeschylus or Sophocles, Euripides; Mathematics – Dynamics; Science – Natural Philosophy (Acoustics and Optics); Chemistry; Moral Philosophy (Haven); English – Criticism; French – Grammar and Exercises; German – Schmitz's Elements, continued Conversation; (3rd Term) Latin – Juvenal; Greek*- Euripides; Mathematics – Dynamics (continued); Science – Natural Philosophy (Heat and Electricity); Meteorology; Principles of Constitutional Government and Law (Young); Natural Law in the Spiritual World (Drummond), Chemical Philosophy,

Botany; English – Theses on Select Subjects; Essays; Declamations, Orations and Debates throughout the year; French – Grammar and Exercises; German – Schmitz's Elements, continued Conversation *Elective provided – German or French could be substituted.

Senior Year course consisted of (1st Term)Latin – Cicero de Natura Deorum, or Terence; Greek* - Plato's Republic or New Testament; Mathematics – Selected Subjects and Lectures; Science – Astronomy (Young); Natural Theology (Valentine); Empirical and Rational Psychology (Schuyler); Analogy of Religion (Butler); French – Grammar and Translation; German – Storm's "Immensee," Schiller's "Der Neffe als Onkel," Conversation and Translation; Bible History throughout the year; (2nd Term) Latin – Cicero de Natura Deorum, Tertullian; Greek* - Aristophanes or New Testament; Mathematics – Selected Subjects and Lectures; Science – Geology (Le Conte); History of Civilization (Guizot), Evidences of Christianity (Alexander), History of Political Economy; French – Grammar and Translation; German – Hillern's "Hoher als die Kirche," or Lessing's "Minna von Barnhelm," Grammar and Conversation; (3rd Term) Latin – Tertullian; Greek* - Aristophanes or New Testament; Mathematics – Selected Subjects and Lectures; Science – History of Philosophy; German – Goethe's "Hermann and Dorothea"; Orations and Debates; Commercial Course; *Elective provided German or French could be substituted.[736]

The academic year ended on a somber note as President Shirey died two months before the end of the term. Examinations were conducted from May 27th through the 29th. An Academic exhibition was held on Friday, May 29th. The Baccalaureate Sermon was delivered on May 31st by Rev. E. A. Wingard and the Declaimers Contest and Junior Orations took place on June 1st. The Declaimer's Medal was won by Alonzo Blackwelder a 2nd year Academic, and Benedict M. Setzler, son of Professor E. B. Setzler, claimed the Junior Orator's Medal and the Bible History Award. On Tuesday, June

2nd, former US Senator Thomas J. Jarvis delivered the Commencement Address and the Honorable Charles F. McKesson addressed the Literary Societies. Rev. C. W. Sifferd, '74, gave the Alumni Address.

Graduation ceremonies were held at 8 PM on Wednesday, June 3rd, 1896. Four Seniors received Bachelor of Arts Degrees – Herbert E. Barrier, Charles E. Boger, Caleb P. Nifong and Theodore C. Parker. Receiving Master of Arts Degrees were John M. Cook, '90; H. E. H. Sloop, '91; J. A. Graham, '92; W. J. Boger, '93, and M. A. Boger. Doctor of Divinity Degrees were awarded to Rev. Prof. J. C. Moser, '73, and Rev. C. W. Sifferd, '74.[737]

1896-1897

The 1896-'97 Academic Year began on Sept. 2nd, 1896 with thirty students registered in the College Department, nineteen in the Sub-Freshman Class and nineteen in the Preparatory Department. There were two Seniors, George F. McAllister and Benedict M. Setzler, two Juniors, nine Sophomores, and seventeen Freshmen.

Reverend G. G. Scherer began his first term as President of the College and instructor of Mental and Moral Science. H. T. J. Ludwig returned as Professor of Mathematics, Astronomy and Physics and as head of the Commercial Department. E. B. Setzler remained in his position as Professor of Ancient Languages & Literature, supplied as the Professor of German and French and served as the school Librarian. A new faculty member, Rev. P. H. E. Derrick, was hired as the Principal of the Preparatory Department. Derrick resigned after the first term and George F. McAllister, who graduated in January 1897, was hired as the temporary Principal for the remainder of the school year.

Special lecturers during the year included Rev. S. D. Steffy who spoke on "Advanced Thought;" Rev. C. C. Lyerly, "Educational Hints;" Mr. B. B. Miller, "The College Boy;" Prof. J. F. Shinn, "The Reader;" Rev. Prof. M. G. G. Sherer, "College Days and Other Days;" Prof. E. B. Setzler, "The Constitution As It Was;" Rev. A. E. Wiley, "Moral Culture & What Should Be its Ultimate Aim;" Rev. Prof. P. H. E. Derrick; "The Elements of Success," and Prof. H. T. J. Ludwig, "John Stuart Mill."

The school year ended with final examinations on May 26th - 28th, 1897. An academic exhibition was held on the evening of May 28th, and the

Declaimers Contest and Junior Orations were presented on May 31st. On June 1st, Rev. Henry A. McCullough, the minister at Mt. Hermon/Cold Water Lutheran Church near Concord, addressed the Literary Societies, and Rev. Charles B. Miller, '75, the minister at St. James, Concord, gave the Alumni address. Commencement exercises were conducted on June 2nd, 1897. The Declaimers Medal was awarded to Sub-Freshman T. Marvin Wiley and the Bible History Award was won by Junior Jacob L. Morgan. Master of Arts Degrees were presented to C. H. Barnhardt,'92; Rev. C. C. Lyerly; Rev. R. L. Bame, '91, and Dr. C. M. Poole.[738]

1897-1898

The academic year 1897-'98 began on Sept. 1st, 1897 with seventy-two students enrolled (the Trustees report to the Synod stated there were seventy-five enrolled). There were twenty-nine members of the College Department which included two Seniors, Pleasant E. Monroe and Clarence E. Moser, five Juniors, nine Sophomores and thirteen Freshmen. In the Preparatory Department there were nineteen Sub-Freshmen, eighteen 2nd year and nine 1st year pupils. There were seven students in the Commercial Class.

Reverend Scherer returned for his second year as President of the College and Professor of Mental & Moral Science. H. T. J. Ludwig continued as Professor of Mathematics, Astronomy and Physics. A new Professor, Edgar Bowers, of Gerardstown, West Virginia, replaced E. B. Setzler as head of the Ancient & Modern Languages Department. This Department acquired a new title as it no longer included "Ancient Literature." Instead, it incorporated the instruction of German in its curriculum. French was apparently not offered in the College Department. George F. McAllister, was the temporary Principal of the Preparatory Department at a salary of $350. Lecturers during the year included Prof. Holland Thompson, "The Realization of a Motto;" Prof. E. B. Lewis, "The Background of History;" L. M. Swink, Attorney, "Law and Lawyers;" Rev. J. Q. Wertz,"Character;" Mr. J. B. D. Fisher, "Literary Improvement;" T. L. Hartsell, Attorney, "What Will You Make of Life," and H. T. J. Ludwig, "Books."[739]

Commencement exercises for the 1897-'98 school year began on Friday, May 27th, 1898 with the traditional academic exhibition. A Baccalaureate sermon was delivered on Sunday, May 29th by Rev. Samuel T. Hallman of South Carolina. Rev. Hallman was a Confederate veteran and the son-in-law of th late long-time Board of Trustees member, Rev. Samuel Rothrock.[740]

The Declaimers Contest and Junior Orations were held on May 30th and the Alumni Address was presented on May 31st by Rev. Robert L. Patterson, BA '91, MA '94. On the 31st, Prof. Charles D. McIver, President of the State Normal & Industrial College located in Greensboro (now UNC-Greensboro), addressed the Literary Societies. Commencement exercises were held on June 1st. Master of Arts Degrees were awarded to Charles E. Cobb '95, Walter M. Cook '95, Bachman B. Miller '95, Luther S. Shirey '95, Rev. C. Brown Cox '95, J. Deberry Fisher '95, Rev. W. W. J. Ritchie '95, and John H. Ritchie'88. The Declaimer's Medal was awarded to Sub-Freshman Wesley W. Kennerly and Junior Edward Fulenwider claimed the Bible History Award and the Junior Orator's medal.[741]

At its meeting on May 31st, 1898, the College Board of Trustees appointed G. F. McAllister as the full-time Principal of the Preparatory Department and awarded a Doctor of Divinity Degree to Rev. Jonathan Garver of Pennsylvania. The Board also clarified the College's standard for a Master of Arts Degree. "A Master of Arts Degree may be conferred on an individual in like manner upon [holders of] Bachelor's [Degrees] who have pursued studies in a profession during a period of three years or who have successfully completed such a course of study as may be required by the faculty."[742]

1898-1899

Academic Year 1898-'99 began on September 1st. The faculty remained the same as the previous year, but student registration decreased by twenty from the previous year (28%). The fifty-two students included four Seniors, six Juniors, seven Sophomores, eight Freshmen, nine Sub-Freshmen and eighteen Preparatory students.

Special Lectures during the year were presented by three guest speakers and all members of the Faculty. Prof. Ludwig spoke on "Assassinations and Assassins" and "Annexation, Colonization, Imperialism." Prof. Bowers lectured on "Utility of College Education." Rev. Scherer presented "Dr. Samuel Johnson" and G. F. McAllister spoke on "Citizenship." Guest Lecturers were Rev. George A. Riser whose topic was "Everblooming

Laurel;" Rev. W. B. Oney, "Our Bodies and How to Care for Them," and Prof. C. S. Coler, "Four Naval Heroes."[743]

Commencement exercises began on Friday, May 26th with the Academic Exhibition followed by the Baccalaureate Sermon on May 28th delivered by Rev. R. C. Holland. The Declaimer's Contest and Junior Orations were held on May 29th. George T. Barringer was granted the Declaimer's Medal and Junior Alonzo Blackwelder won the Orator's prize. Murray Long received a Gold Eagle prize given by James P. Cook, '85 for best written examination in U. S. History. On May 30th, Theodore F. Klutts, a member of the US House of Representatives, delivered the Literary Society Address and John M. Cook, '90 presented the Alumni Address. Diplomas were presented on May 31st to four graduating Seniors, Jacob L. Morgan, Edward Fulenwider (Valedictorian), Victor C. Ridenhour and Charles A. Phillips, who also received a PhB Degree. The Board of Trustees awarded an AM Degree to T. C. Parker, '96; a PhD Degree to Rev. Shadrack Simpson, Western Maryland College, Westminster, MD, and a DD Degree to Rev. R. A. Yoder, '77, President of Lenoir College.[744]

In his closing remarks, Rev. Scherer stated, "a few have gotten the idea that the College work will cease; this is erroneous. The College work will continue indefinitely. We hope to have the pleasure of the return of all the old students and they accompanied by many new ones."[745]

1899-1900

The College began a new Academic Year on September 6th, 1899. Enrollment increased by seven students. Fifty-nine men were registered for the year, including four Seniors, four Juniors, four Sophomores, thirteen Freshmen, nine Sub-Freshmen and twenty-five Preparatorians.

Reverend Scherer had abruptly resigned in June in an apparent protest over the lack of support for the College. Due to his late departure, the Board of Trustees, for the first time in its history, selected a non-minister to head the School. Edgar Bowers, a Professor at the College since 1897, was appointed Acting President and Professor of Ancient and Modern Languages. H. T. J. Ludwig continued to serve as Professor of Mathematics, Astronomy and Physics. George F. McAllister was the Principal of the Preparatory Department. A member of the Senior Class, J. Marshall Tice, was employed as an Assistant in the Preparatory Department.

The School Catalogue described the course curriculum, the number of recitations (classes) required each week per subject and quantified that each recitation lasted forty-five minutes. Senior recitations consisted of two classes each week in Latin, two in Greek, three in either German or French, two in Mathematics, two in Natural Science, two in Political Science, five in Mental Science, one in Religious History and one in English. Juniors and Seniors received the same number of classes in languages, Religious History and English and were required to attend three recitations in Mathematics, and seven classes in Mental, Natural and Political Science. Sophomores attended three classes each week in Latin and Greek, five in Mathematics, four in History and three in English. Freshmen attended five classes in Latin and Greek, five in Mathematics, four in History and three in English.

Sub-Freshmen received five recitations per week in English, Higher Arithmetic, Algebra, Latin, and Greek, one class in Declamation and Composition and optional classes in Physiology or Natural Philosophy. In the second and third terms, Plane Geometry replaced Physiology. Preparatory students received instruction in Reading, Writing, Defining, English Grammar, State and US History, Geography, Arithmetic, Elementary Algebra, and Latin.

Students who chose to enroll in the Commercial Course attended classes in single and double entry Book-keeping, Commercial Law, Commercial Arithmetic, Business Correspondence and Commercial Forms. These students could also take "approved" classes from the regular curriculum.

The College Catalogue itemized the cost of a full year (38 weeks) of College Classes at between $99 and $105, including tuition, fees, room and board. The cost for Sub-Freshman was between $89 and $95 per year, and Preparatory Students paid between $84 and $90 per year. The school year was divided into three terms of fifteen, twelve and eleven weeks respectively. Room rent, half-tuition and incidental/contingent fees were to be paid in advance.[746]

During the year, special lectures were provided by Rev. S. D. Steffey, speaking on "Edgar Allan Poe;" M. B. Stickly, "North Carolina;" Rev. J. A. Linn – "The Ideal Student;" Prof. Ludwig, "The Downmost Man;" Rev. L. T. Cordell, "The Building of Manhood;" James P. Cook, "Murder;" Rev.

J. H. Barnhardt, "A Saner Citizenship" and Prof. Bowers, "The Origin of the English Language."[747]

The ladies of Mt. Pleasant donated four "elegant chairs for use by professors at commencement exercises that began on May 25th, 1900. The Baccalaureate Sermon was delivered by Rev. William A. Lutz on Sunday, May 27th. The Declaimers Contest and Junior Orations were held on May 28th. Zebulon Barnhardt claimed the Declaimer's Award and Edward L. Ritchie won the Orator's Contest. Diplomas were conferred on May 31st to three Seniors, Hugh A. Crigler, Clifford P. Fisher, and J. Marshall Tice.[748]

1900-1901

The College opened for classes on Sep 5th, 1900 with 102 students and a new President. The Board of Trustees hired Reverend William A. Lutz in June shortly after he spoke at the College commencement.[749] To accommodate its newly burgeoning enrollment, the College rented a portion of Cook & Foil's store for use as a boarding hall and made changes in the Philalaethian Society Hall to allow for three student rooms on the first floor.[750]

The College Department consisted of four Seniors, two Juniors, eight Sophomores, and sixteen Freshmen. There were fourteen students in the Sub-Freshman class and fifty-eight students in the Preparatory Department. Eleven students were enrolled in the Commercial Class.

Rev. Lutz served as President of the College and Professor of Mental, Moral and Political Science. Other faculty included two returning members. Edgar Bowers taught Ancient & Modern Languages and George F. McAllister continued as Principal of the Preparatory Department. New faculty included N. E. Aull, a graduate of Newberry College, Professor of Mathematics, Physics and Astronomy who replaced the late H. T. J. Ludwig. A second new faculty member, Ernest E. Johnson, a graduate of Bucknell University taught Organic Science, Chemistry and English.

Guest lecturers during the school year included M. H. Caldwell, C. S. Coler, Rev. J. A. B. Fry, Rev. Thomas W. Smith, Rev. G. H. Cornelson, Jr., Thomas P. Harrison, Colonel Paul B. Means, and Mr. M. B. Stickley.

The College Catalogue listed the requirements for BA and BS Degrees as follows:

Bachelor of Arts (48 courses)

6 Courses in Modern Languages	6 Courses in Mathematics
6 Courses in Latin	1 Course in English Literature
6 Courses in Greek	3 Courses in History
1 Course in Etymology	1 Course in Rhetori
1 Course in Biology	2 Courses in Chemistry
1 Course in Sociology	1 Course in Economics
1 Course in Psychology	1 Course in Ethics
1 Course in Theism	
10 Electives	

Bachelor of Science (48 courses)

6 Courses in Modern Languages	3 Courses in Latin
8 Courses in Pure Mathematics	1 Course in English Literature
1 Course in Astronomy	3 Courses in Physics
3 Courses in History	1 Course in Etymology
1 Course in Rhetoric	2 Courses in Biology
1 Course in Geology	1 Course in Ethics
3 Courses in Chemistry	1 Course in Sociolog
1 Course in Theism	1 Course in Psychology
1 Course in Economics	
10 Electives	

Each Course consisted of five recitations (classes) per week each term. Candidates for Degrees could take no less than four and no more than five full courses per term and no student would be allowed to pursue a fifth course unless he had attained an average of ninety or more for the preceding term.

Students who had not completed more than five of the required courses were considered Freshmen. To enter the Sophomore Class, completion of eight courses was required. Juniors must have completed at least twenty-two courses and to be considered a Senior, thirty-six courses must have been completed. A total of forty-eight courses were required for graduation.

Students entering the College or the Preparatory Department agreed to the following "Matriculation Vow:"

> "We, whose names are hereunto annexed, do severally and individually promise on our sacred truth and honor, to observe all the rules and regulations as laid down by the President of the North Carolina College pertaining to moral, mental and spiritual culture. Our private conduct, subordination to and respect for our Professors, and our conduct toward our fellow students shall be such as to cultivate virtuous principles. We will, therefore, abstain from smoking cigarettes, drinking intoxicants, and gambling, and will faithfully attend Church and the College Sunday School, unless excused by the President so long as we remain students of this institution."[751]

Reverend Lutz was formally inaugurated as President of the College on October 24th, 1900. Reverend Levi E. Busby, the Minister at St. John's Lutheran Church in Salisbury, gave the inauguration address appropriately titled "The Value of An Education and the Duty of the NC Synod to Place the Same within Easy Reach of Her Boys & Girls."[752]

Commencement exercises for the 1900-'01 academic year began on Friday, May 24th with the annual Academic Exercises. Daniel A. Thompkins, owner and publisher of *The Charlotte Observer,* delivered the address to the Literary Societies on May 27th. Diplomas were distributed on Wednesday, May 29th, 1901. One Master of Arts Degree was awarded to P. E. Monroe, '98, and three ministers received Doctor of Divinity Degrees – Rev. Clinton E. Walter of York, PA; Rev. Marion J. Kline of Harrisburg, PA, and Rev. Levi E. Busby, the speaker at President Lutz's inauguration in October 1900.[753]

This was the last class to graduate from North Carolina College.

1901-1902

North Carolina College opened the academic year of 1901-'02 on Sept. 4th, 1901, with only sixty-five students, a decrease of thirty-seven over the previous year. The faculty consisted of Rev. Lutz, President of the College and Professor of Mental, Moral and Political Science; Edgar Bowers, Professor of Ancient & Modern Languages; George F. McAllister, Principal of the Preparatory Department; Ernest E. Johnson, Professor of Organic Science, Chemistry and English, and Rev. J. L. Keller, Instructor in Mathematics. There was no catalogue published for the year. Professors McAllister, Johnson and Bowers submitted their resignations effective December 27th, 1901, but were convinced to remain for the present. In March 1902, the Board was forced to settle accounts with Professor Johnson, but at the request of the Synod, Professors Bowers and McAllister agreed to keep the school open for underclassmen until the end of the session.[754]

There is no information regarding how many students finished the session in May or if a commencement ceremony was held. The College was suspended at the end of the session. The still active Board of Trustees worked toward an agreement that would maintain some type of school on the campus.

THE CAROLINA ENGLISH AND CLASSICAL SCHOOL

1902-1903

The Carolina English and Classical School (CE&C) opened its doors on Sept. 16th, 1902. Reverend Levi E. Busby and George F. McAllister were the only faculty named. The pamphlet announcing the school assured:

> "The school enters the field of education at the solicitation of the people .... We propose to give patrons value received for all charges in careful and pains-taking instruction of their sons, and to build success upon positive merit. We feel we can guarantee this by methods and discipline which have been tried and proved successful after long years of school management."[755]

The CE&C School was organized into three departments, Primary, Academic and Collegiate. Records listed thirty-seven students enrolled, ranging in ages eleven to twenty-one. Tuition rates were $14 per term for Collegiates, $10 per term for Academics, and $7 per term for Primary students. Room rent was 50¢ per month for students boarding at the school. Laundry, fuel and lights cost $10 per session. The curriculum was described as:

> "meeting the needs of young men desiring to complete their course in College and prepares them for the advanced classes. Such branches as are required to fit young men for commercial pursuits are included during study. We aim by condensation to accomplish a large amount of work as possible in the shortest time."[756]

McAllister's December, 1902 class register listed classes in half-hour increments beginning at 9:00 AM and ending at 4:00 PM. Courses described in the register were Language; Latin; Algebra I, II, & III; NC History, US History, and General History; Geometry I; Geography I; Arithmetic III; Physics; Astronomy, and Spelling. In addition, there were classes for the Debating Society in Declamation, Essays, Debate, Reading, and Letters. There were thirty-three student members of the Society.[757]

As related in Part I, the CE&C School survived only one year because Reverend Busby died in March of 1903.

THE MT. PLEASANT COLLEGIATE INSTITUTE

1903-1904

During the Summer of 1903, G. F. McAllister and Rev. Henry A. McCullough, the new Minister at Holy Trinity Lutheran Church, formed a partnership to operate a "new" school on the College campus beginning in the Fall of 1903.

The opening ceremony of Mt. Pleasant Collegiate Institute on September 16th, 1903 was described in the *Concord Tribune* as "the largest for years." A crowd of about 300 persons heard addresses by Rev. J. England of the local Methodist Church; Rev. T. C. Parker of St. John's, NCC '96; Rev. Edward Fulenwider of Concord, NCC '99, and Rev. C. P. Fisher, NCC '00. Reformed Church Minister, Rev. Paul Barringer, also welcomed the students.[758]

The Institute opened with thirty-five students initially registered, but only twenty-eight students were listed on the class roll book during the first term. Co-Principal G. F. McAllister, NCC '97, began the session alone as Rev. McCullough was not available until Nov 1st. Former NC College graduate, Rev. J. A. Linn, '73 was employed temporarily as an instructor, and another NC College alumnus, Alonzo Blackwelder, '89 served as "head" of the Primary Department.[759]

A pamphlet advertising the school assured that "the school is manned by experienced teachers. None but those of approved competency are employed. No students are engaged to teach. Each Department has a teacher…." The pamphlet went on to say that "the curriculum is carefully and systematically arranged and is equal to that of the best schools. The course of study when complete fits young men for business or teaching and prepares them for entrance into the Junior Class of our leading Colleges."[760]

During its first year MPCI had only one debating society. The Gerhardt Literary Society was named in honor of the first Principal of Western Carolina Male Academy, Rev. William Gerhardt, and was "one of the strong features of this school in which the faculty takes especial pride and interest. It exerts a healthful and stimulating influence in the cultivation and pursuit of composition, declamation, debate and oratory."

There was no school catalogue for the first year of the school, but according to G. F. McAllister's September 1903 class register some of the classes offered included Greek I, II, & III; Geometry; Algebra I, II, & III, and Arithmetic I, II, & III. The first full session of MPCI ended on May 25, 1904.[761]

1904-1905

The 1904-'05 academic year at MPCI opened on Sept. 20th, 1904 with a student body more than double that of the previous year. Eighty-six students were registered for classes at the beginning of the session, but the faculty remained at only three teachers, G. F. McAllister, and H. A. McCullough, Co-Principals, and Alonzo Blackwelder, Preparatory Department.[762]

In October 1904, North Carolina, Governor Charles B. Aycock visited Mt. Pleasant and was honored with a large parade and rally at MPCI. Governor Aycock prepared for his speech in Principal McAllister's room at the Institute and McAllister introduced him to the crowd of over two thousand. Following the Governor's speech, the crowd was served "dinner on the grounds," but Aycock, "feeling too much exhausted," took his meal in Principal McAllister's room.[763]

During the Institute's second year, the Ludwig Literary Society was founded and named in honor of the late H. T. J. Ludwig who taught at NC College for almost 30 years.[764] The public was invited to literary society debates throughout the school year. The debates touched on timely subjects such as - “Resolved, That the South Did Wrong in Seceding,” and “Resolved, the present high Tariff is not in the interest of the American People.”[765]

The Fall term ended on December 23rd, 1904 and was described in an article in the *Concord Tribune* (perhaps with tongue in cheek) as:

> “The most successful term in the history of the Collegiate Institute.’ The members of the Gerhardt & Ludwig Literary Societies held a joint debate on the question – ‘Resolved. That North Carolina Should Have Compulsory Education.’ Music was furnished by the Glee Club aided by Misses Mabel Barrier and Maggie McAllister of the graded school. The old students will all return [after Christmas] and work will be resumed at the Institute.”[766]

The second year of the Collegiate Institute ended with commencement exercises from May 19th-May 21st, 1905. The festivities included a sermon by Rev. J. E. Schenk and an address to the Literary Societies by Prof. A. G. Voight. A “drama” was held on May 22nd and the contest for the Declaimers Medal was conducted on May 23rd. The annual debate, “Resolved, That Labor is justified in forming Unions,” preceded the awarding of diplomas. The ceremonies ended with a reception on the evening of May 23rd.[767]

1905-1906

An advertisement in *The Concord Tribune* running from June through September, 1905, read, “Course of study embraces five years’ work, giving young men thorough foundational training, and fits them the for business, teaching, or prepares them for regular entrance into the Junior Class of College. … A faculty of five College or University Men. Expenses from $80-$100.”[768]

The 1905-06 MPCI academic year began on September 12th, 1905. School records listed 107 students registered, but a newspaper article stated that “The Collegiate Institute opened with “nearly ninety students.”[769]

In 1905, the Institute described itself as “under the auspices of the

North Carolina Evangelical Lutheran Synod, a high-grade Secondary School with a definite purpose."[770]

The school faculty consisted of eight persons. G. F. McAllister and Rev. H. A. McCullough remained Associate Principals. McAllister taught Mathematics and McCullough taught English and Literature. A new faculty member, Dewayt Rahn Riser, a South Carolina native and graduate of Newberry College, was hired to teach Latin & Greek. Riser also took courses at Yale University. Alonzo Blackwelder remained as head of the Preparatory Department, where he was joined by Sidney Jacob Ludwig, a graduate of NC College and the brother of longtime NC College Professor, the late H. T. J. Ludwig. Mrs. Lilly Blackwelder McCullough, the wife of Rev. McCullough and a graduate of Mont Amoena Seminary and Southern Business College, was hired to teach stenography and typewriting. Daniel L. Ritchie, a student at the Institute, was an instructor in Penmanship.[771]

Space on the first floor of the Administration building was completely renovated. The chapel located next to the main library was furnished with opera chairs and an organ. Each day of classes began in the chapel with roll call, singing, reading of Scripture, prayer and announcements. There were also libraries in each of the Society Halls and together they contained about 4,000 volumes. In addition to the libraries, there was a reading room furnished with newspapers and magazines. A laboratory for the Physics, Chemistry and Biology Departments was located on the first floor of Ludwig Society Hall (north wing building) and furnished with several "first class compound microscopes."

The curriculum required five years to complete with at least eighteen recitations (classes) per week. Sub-Freshmen classes consisted of Spelling, English Grammar, English, English History, Latin, Greek, Arithmetic, Algebra, and Literary Society Work, which entailed instruction on debate, declamation, essays, letter-writing, criticism, and parliamentary usage. The Intermediate classes included Spelling, English Literature, English Grammar, US History, Geography, Civil Government, Latin, Arithmetic, Algebra and Society work. The Junior class continued Spelling, English Grammar, US History, Geography, Arithmetic, and Society Work, but added Reading, Physical Geography, Physiology.

The Collegiate curriculum was divided into three terms. The Freshman and Sophomore years consisted of courses in Latin, Greek, Mathematics, English, English Bible, Civil Government, and Literary Society work. History was taught in the Freshman year and Civil Government in the Sophomore year.

Certificates were granted "to students who satisfactorily completed the course of study and complied with the regulations of the Institution and young men holding certificates will be accredited to the Junior Class in leading Colleges."

The Institute Catalogue described four gold medals available to students who excelled in each of several areas. The gold medal for Scholarship was established by the late Professor H. T. J. Ludwig and was to be awarded annually at commencement to a student taking the regular course with the highest general average during the year. A gold medal in Oratory was presented annually at commencement to a member of the Sophomore class who wrote and delivered the most outstanding oration. The gold medal in Debate established by Mr. B. M. Setzler, '97 and Mr. E. E. Hendrix, NCC, was to be awarded annually at commencement for proficiency in debate as determined by a contest between Freshman and Sophomore debate teams. A gold medal in Declamation established by Mr. Claude R. Blackwelder was awarded annually at commencement for proficiency in declamation as determined by a commencement week contest among six Preparatory Department students.[772]

Commencement ceremonies were held jointly with Mont Amoena Female Seminary on May 18th - May 21st, 1906 at the town auditorium. According to the *Concord Tribune*, the "prep exhibition" scheduled for Friday, May 18th was canceled "for certain good reasons," and the Freshman debate was substituted. The "question under discussion" was "Does education have more to do with formation of character than nature?" Speaking in the Affirmative were G. O. Ritchie and O. D. Ritchie. The negative was argued by M. L. Kestler and J. M. Peck. The affirmative arguments prevailed. O. D. Ritchie won the Debaters Medal. Following the debate, C. C. Hatley delivered an oration on "The Triumphs of Right." Rev. C. E. Weltner of Columbia, SC, gave the Baccalaureate Sermon on May 20th and four graduates received diplomas - P. D. Brown, J. B. Moose, B. E. Petrea and D. B. Welsh on May 21st.[773]

1906-1907

The academic year 1906-'07 began on Sept 11th, 1906. There were 102 students registered for classes. Faculty for the year included Associate Principals McAllister and McCullough and, Alonzo Blackwelder and S. J. Ludwig who remained in the Preparatory Department. D. R. Riser began the year on the faculty but left in December. Roy Webster, a Wofford College graduate, was hired to teach Latin & Greek for one session.[774]

The Principals' Report to the Synod stated that extensive improvements had been made in the furnishings and equipment of the school; the society halls remodeled, and new roofs put on several buildings. McAllister reported that with the increased faculty, the course of study had been broadened to make it easier for graduates to enter Junior College.[775]

Final examinations occurred from May 13th through May 17th, 1907 and commencement week began on Friday, May 17th with exercises by the Preparatory Department. The Debate contest was conducted on the evening of May 18th and the Baccalaureate Sermon delivered on May 19th. On May 20th, an address was presented to the Literary Societies by H. N. Snyder, President of Wofford College, SC. Medal winners included C. B. Moore, Debater's Medal; H. S. Petrea, Declaimer's Medal; C. C. Hatley, Orator's Medal, and Scholarship Medal, O. D. Ritchie. Nine students received diplomas from the Institute on Commencement Day, May 21st, 1907.[776]

1907-1908

On September 10, 1907, MPCI opened for its fifth session. There were seventy-four students registered for classes - three Sophomores and twelve Freshmen in the Collegiate Department and fourteen Sub-Freshmen, thirty-one Intermediates, and fourteen Juniors in the Preparatory Department.[777]

The Institute faculty retained two former members. G. F. McAllister maintained his position as Co-Principal and Math Instructor and Alonzo Blackwelder remained as head of the Preparatory Department. Two new faculty members included Co-Principal Rev. Jefferson P. Miller and Latin and History Instructor, Arthur W. George.

Reverend J. P. Miller was the new minister at Holy Trinity Lutheran Church in Mt. Pleasant. He was a native of Catawba Co. NC and graduated

Concordia College in Catawba County and Chicago Seminary. He was ordained by the Tennessee Synod in 1889 and served parishes in Alexander County, Catawba County, Rowan County, Orangeburg, SC and Burke's Garden, VA before coming to Mt. Pleasant. While at MPCI, Miller also taught classes at Mont Amoena Seminary.[778] Arthur W. George taught previously at Harmony School in Iredell County and at Crescent Academy in Rowan County.[779]

The school was publicized as being the "best equipped secondary school for young men in this section of the State." The cost of attending the school was now advertised as between $100 and $130 per session.[780] MPCI and Mont Amoena Seminary held a joint Commencement program from May 17th – 19th, 1908. Reverend W. H. Greever, editor of *The Southern Visitor*, delivered the Baccalaureate Sermon on the 17th. The Literary Address was given by E. D. Sikes, PhD, of Wake Forest College. On the 18th, students from both schools presented a play entitled, "Under Two Flags."[781]

No one from MPCI graduated, however, Coram Alexander, of Concord, won the Declaimer's Medal. L. A. Thomas, of Salisbury, was awarded the Debater's Medal for his performance arguing the affirmative on the subject, "Resolved, That Naval Expansion is the best policy for our Country." The Orator's Medal was claimed by Myron C. Fisher of Salisbury and C. N. B. Williams from Mt. Pleasant was presented the Ludwig Scholarship Medal by Reverend Plato Durham.[782]

1908-1909

In August 1908, Principal G. F. McAllister sent the following letter announcing the opening of the new school year and the implementation of the "military system" he described to the Board of Trustees and Synod in April. The letter was apparently written to new and prospective students, their parents, and visitors who might wish to attend the opening.

> 'We send you greetings from the Collegiate Institute and hope you will be present for the opening, Wednesday, September 9th. There will be a reception given on the Campus, Wednesday evening, to the students and Faculty and friends of town. Do not miss this, for it is a pleasant beginning of the school year, when, amidst meetings and greetings, all are made to feel that they are among friends.

The formal opening exercises will take place in the chapel, Thursday morning, 10 o'clock, at which time approximate addresses will be made by invited speakers and members of the Faculty.

If you desire a room in the Dormitory and have not already engaged one, you should do so at once, as they will soon be all taken. The rooms in the Dormitory are all nice and fresh, that building having been recently renovated throughout. The rooms are furnished with bedstead, wardrobe, chairs, washstand, bookcase, table and heater. You should bring bedding (except mattress) with you. Mattress and other needed articles, such as bowl, pitcher, lamp, oil can, broom, etc., can be procured at very reasonable cost here. It is not necessary for any one student to bring all the bedding needed for a bed, for his roommate should supply one-half of the needed furnishings. A first-class boarding hall will be run on the school grounds, in an orderly, home-like manner, where good, wholesome board, as good as that to be had in any private homes, will be furnished at cost – not to exceed $7 per calendar month. Board at the hall will have to be paid for without exception in advance.

The Military System has received the hearty approval of our patrons – we have not yet heard a single dissenting voice. It will be very helpful in many ways to students. To gain the best results, students will all wear uniform. This will entail no extra expense, as students cannot be nicely and substantially dressed in any other style at less cost. The uniform, including cap, will cost from $12 to $15, and it will be of first-class goods and well made. We ask patrons to bear in mind the fact that students will wear uniform when they are getting their sons ready for school.

The prospect is very bright for a large attendance. Important improvements have been made on our equipment, buildings and grounds. The course of study has been broadened, and another member added to the

> Faculty – Prof. J. W. Campbell, graduate of the South Carolina Military Academy, who will be Commandant.
>
> Therefore, the Institute which has an established reputation for thorough work – a reputation which has recently been strengthened by the exceptionally fine records of her graduates – offers still better advantages to students. We welcome you to participation [sic] in these advantages. Students expecting to come by way of Concord will be met (at their expense) by conveyances at the station if they will notify the Principal. If you have not yet planned for entering, and desire to do so, please write to us without delay. Yours for Service, G. F. McAllister J. P. Miller[783]

The 1908-'09 academic year opened on September 9th, 1908 with ninety-three students registered for classes. The new military model was organized much like that of existing military academies such as West Point, The Citadel, and VMI. Students were referred to as Cadets and were separated into Companies based upon their class standing.

G. F. McAllister and Rev. J. P. Miller again served as co-principals of the Institute. McAllister, who had been awarded a Master of Arts Degree from Newberry College in the summer, assumed the rank of "Colonel" within the new military system. Arthur George returned as Professor of Latin & History. New faculty member J. W. Campbell served as "Commandant of Cadets" and oversaw the military aspects of the school. He was assigned the rank of Captain. Students took on ranks based upon their academic standing and/or other responsibilities on the campus.

Military style drills were conducted daily and rules and regulations were written and carried out in a military manner. Discipline was also applied in a military manner including receiving "additional' guard duty or "tours" for infractions.[784]

Except for the added military drills, academics at the Institute remained basically unchanged. Commencement exercises took place on May 17th-18th, 1909. In the Debate Contest on the question, "Resolved, That the signs of the times indicated universal peace," J. C. Peck won the Debater's Medal arguing for the affirmative. The Declaimer's Medal was awarded to H. A. Fisher of Salisbury and the Orator's metal was claimed by R. L. Trexler.

Henry J. Harms, President of Newberry College, presented the address to the Literary Societies and Dr. M. M. Kinard of Salisbury delivered the Baccalaureate Sermon. Eight Seniors graduated.[785]

1909-1910

MPCI's 1909-'10 academic session began on Sept 8th, 1909 with 102 students enrolled. The new classes consisted of eight Sophomores, nine Feshmen, twenty-nine Sub-freshmen, thirty-eight Intermediate (Preparatory) and eighteen Junior (Preparatory) students. The faculty consisted of five Professors. McAllister, Co-Principal Rev. J. P. Miller, and Capt. W. B. Porcher returned from the previous year. Miller taught only one course, English Bible, for one hour per week. Porcher served as the Commandant of Cadets. Two new instructors were J. B. Moose and D. B. Welsh.[786]

John B. Moose had attended MPCI in 1903-'04 and graduated from Newberry College in 1908. He taught Latin, Greek, Bible and History. Dennis B. Welsh had attended MPCI in 1903-'04 and graduated from Roanoke College in 1908. He taught English. Capt. W. B. Porcher, served as Commandant of Cadets.

To replace the facilities lost when Ludwig Hall burned, a new kitchen and dining facility was constructed just across College Street on the west side of the campus. The new facility became known as "The Boarding Hall." Two rooms in Gerhardt Society Hall previously used for dining were opened as classrooms. The Ludwig Literary Society conducted its meetings in the chapel in the main building.[787]

Valuable additions were made to the Institute's inventory during the year. Mr. Charles J. Parker donated a globe. Mrs. Mary Bangle Barrier presented several books from the library of her late husband, Dr. Paul A. Barrier. Mrs. Barrier also gave valuable anatomical specimens to the institute "in trust." During the year, the Institute entered a subscription contest conducted by the *Concord Times*, and with an expenditure of $75 for livery hire, won the first prize, a Cote Upright piano valued at $400. This piano was placed in the chapel and used during morning services.[788]

In January 1910, a smallpox scare in the surrounding area reduced attendance by more than fifty percent (only sixty-three students attended classes during January and February). According to McAllister, "precautions were taken against contagion, and there was but one mild case." There were several cases of measles in the spring.

McAllister reported that "the institute has acquired something of a reputation for excellence [in debate] and it has been our policy to maintain and strengthen the work of the department. Literary society work is required in all classes ... and three literary societies meet at regular hours, once a week under the supervision of the faculty."[789]

Commencement ceremonies were held at the Institute on May 18th, 1910 and six students graduated. J. L. Yost was awarded the Declaimer's Medal. The Debater's Medal went to H. A. Fisher and the Orator's Medal was claimed by J. C. Peck. Z. B. Trexler won the Thomas Ludwig Scholarship Medal with the highest academic average during the year. Class Distinction Awards for students with an average grade in scholarship, conduct and attendance not under ninety-three were awarded to O. L. Flowe, F. B. Lingle, J. O. Moose, W. L. Moose, J. C. Peck, D. L. Ridenhour, D. C. Trexler, Z. B. Trexler, and J. L. Yost.[790]

1910-1911

As discussions concerning its status continued within the Synod, the Collegiate Institute opened the 1910-'11 academic session in September with 114 students. Students drawn from four states included six Sophomores, eighteen Freshmen, twenty Sub-freshmen, forty-two Intermediate Preparatory, and eighteen Junior Preparatory.[791]

"Colonel" G. F. McAllister remained Principal of the school and taught Math and Physics. Other returning faculty members were D. B. Welsh, Professor of English and Rev. R. P. Miller. New faculty members included Stuart E. Brown, Commandant of Cadets and Professor of History and Physics. Brown, from Richmond, VA, was a 1908 graduate of Virginia Military Institute. Calvin V. Williams became the Instructor of Latin & Greek. Williams attended MPCI in 1908-'09 and apparently taught at MPCI without an advanced degree. He was the son of E. Garver Williams, a Lutheran minister who was the director of the Nazareth Children's Home in Rowan Co. NC.[792]

Cadet Officers were D. G. Trexler, Lieutenant and Adjutant; G. F.

Davis, Sergeant Major; H. A. Fisher and Z. B. Trexler, Captains; H. E. Cline and I. R. Crane, 1st Lieutenants; F. S. Cline and D. C. Trexler, 2nd Lieutenants. J. L. Yost and F. B. Lingle were 1st Sergeants.[793]

The Institute published its first listing of its coursework in the 1910-'11 catalogue. Sophomores (the highest class in the "Collegiate" Department) took courses for three "terms" four days a week in Latin, Greek, Math, French and German. English was taught four days a week for two terms and two days per week for one term. Classes in Physics were offered three days per week. Mythology was studied two days per week for one term. English Bible was taught one day per week for all three terms. Part of the curriculum was Literary Society Work which included Debate, Declamation, Essays, Letter-Writing, Criticism, and Parliamentary Usage, required one day a week for all three terms.

Freshmen also took courses in Latin, Greek, Math, French and German. Their schedule required classes in these subjects five days per week. English was taught four days a week for two terms and two days a week for one term. History was offered two days a week for two terms and three days a week for one term. English Bible was available one day a week for all three terms. Literary Society work was also required of Freshmen, one day a week for each term.

Sub-Freshmen (the equivalent of High School Seniors) took courses in Spelling, English Grammar, English History, Rhetoric, Latin, Greek, Arithmetic, Algebra, and Agriculture along with Literary Society work. Intermediate students received instruction in Spelling, English Literature, English Grammar, US History, Geography, Civil Government, Latin, Arithmetic, Algebra, and Agriculture. Intermediate students were not required to take Literary Society Work but were given instruction in Essays, Letters, Criticisms and Declamation.

Junior students (the youngest class) took courses in Spelling, Reading, English Grammar, US and NC History, Geography, Physiology and Arithmetic. They also received instruction in Essays, Criticisms and Declamation.[794]

Commencement exercises for the academic year were held during the week of May 15th - May 18th, 1911, with most events taking place at the Mt. Pleasant Town Auditorium. The *Concord Times* newspaper devoted most of the second page of its May 18th edition to the ceremonies.

Rev. Charles P. MacLaughlin of St. James Lutheran Church in Concord delivered the Baccalaureate Sermon and S. C. Mitchell, President of The University of South Carolina, gave the Literary Address. As the ceremonies coincided closely with Confederate Memorial Day and the 50th anniversary of the beginning of the Civil War, many of the student declamations were of a "patriotic" nature. Frank G. Davis spoke on "Lest We Forget." Frank R. Henderson's topic was "Our United Country." Fred R. Peck proclaimed "America Ideals." Hedrick M. Penninger's topic was "The Confederate Dead," and Clyde O. Ritchie memorialized "Men and Memories of the Southland." The Declaimer's Medal was awarded to Homer C. Ritchie who spoke on the subject, "Supposed Speech of Patrick Henry."[795]

Interestingly, the Commencement debate subject was described as more "timely" than patriotic. The question was, "Resolved, That the Federal Government should establish a system of parcels post with a maximum of twelve pounds." Juniors H. M. Faggart, F. B. Lingle, and L. R. Crane argued in the affirmative. The negative was presented by C. W. Misenheimer, C. H. Crane (brother to L. R. Crane), and C. E. Linker. The *Times* reported that the two sides "entrenching themselves behind a wall of facts, figures and theories, made the outcome extremely doubtful." In the end, the contest was decided in favor of the team from the affirmative, with H. M. Faggart receiving the Debater's Medal. One gentleman was heard to declare, "I've heard debates for twenty years, but I have heard nothing to surpass the efforts of the young debaters this morning."[796]

The Orators Medal was awarded to Zeb B. Trexler speaking on the topic, "Universal Peace." The Ludwig Scholastic Medal was given to the youngest student to have yet received it, Lester Johnson, a member of the Junior (Preparatory) Class.

1911-1912

The new year began on Sept. 13th, 1911 with 100 enrolled students (sixteen less than the previous session). There were five Sophomores, twelve Freshmen, thirty-nine sub-Freshmen, thirty-nine Intermediate Preparatory, and five Junior Preps.[797]

G. F. McAllister returned to the Institute as Principal and Professor of Math and Physics. After taking classes at the University of NC in the summer, McAllister listed NCC and UNC as his alma maters. Returning faculty members were D. B. Welsh, Professor of English & History, and C. V. Williams, Professor of Latin & Greek.[798]

Three new faculty members completed the staff. Rev. Reuben A. Goodman, AB, was Professor of English Bible and Ancient Languages. Goodman was a native of Iredell County and had graduated from Roanoke College in 1906 and the Southern Theological Seminary in South Carolina in 1909.

Gurley D. Moose, '01 AB, PharD, MD, was a lecturer on Physiology & Hygiene. Moose was the son of the local Pharmacist, A. W. Moose, who was, at age 17, the youngest person ever receive a Degree from NC College.[799]

The third new "faculty" member was Zebulon B. Trexler, a recent graduate of MPCI, employed as the Assistant Librarian.[800]

Cadet Officers for the academic year were H. M. Faggart, Staff Lieutenant and Adjutant and E. R. Murray, Sergeant Major. Captains were J. L. Yost and C. H. Crane; 1st Lieutenants, F. L. Harkey and G. F. Davis; 2nd Lieutenants, C. H. Ritchie and A. L. Morgan and 1st Sergeants, J. R. Cress and H. M. Penninger.

During 1911-'12 the Institute hosted several guest lecturers. These included Rev. N. R. Richardson; Rev. Paul Barringer; Rev. Stanly; Rev. A. J. Stirewalt; Rev. M. M. Kinard; Rev. W. McMaster; Dr. G. D. Moose; NC State Senator, Whitehead Kluttz; J. A. Morehead, President of Roanoke College, and W. L. Poteat, President of Wake Forest College.[801]

In 1911, as part of its "System of Government" Section, the College catalogue added the following statement which remained unchanged in all College catalogues through 1932.

> "Recognizing the thoroughness of the academic and military training received at the Institute, and the strong personnel of the student body, Congressmen have recently selected several MPCI men for appointment to the government schools at West Point and Annapolis. Splendid progress has been made by those who availed themselves of the appointment."[802]

The President's report noted that several students had been forced to leave school during the year to return home to work on their farms.

Commencement exercises were held from May 19th-22nd, 1912. Rev.

W. A. Snyder of Wilmington, NC delivered the Baccalaureate Sermon on the May 19th. The Honorable Whitehead Kluttz, former NC State Senator from Rowan County, spoke to the YMCA gathering. Dr. Walter Poteat, President of Wake Forest College, addressed the Literary Societies on the 21st. F. L. Broad won the Declaimer's Medal, speaking on "His Last Song." The subject of the annual debate was "Resolved, That the National Government should aid in the construction and maintenance of good roads." Charles B. King, arguing in the affirmative, was awarded the Debater's Medal. The Oratory Medal was presented to John L. Yost, speaking on "The Problems of Today." Five diplomas were awarded.[803]

1912-1913

The academic year 1912-'13 opened on Sep 17th, 1912 with 107 students registered at the Institute. The faculty included returning instructors G. F. McAllister, Principal and Professor of Math & Physics; C. V Williams, Professor of Latin & Greek and Rev. R. A. Goodman, AB, Professor of English Bible and Ancient Languages. Two new teachers included Mr. M. R. Adams, a native of Tennessee and graduate of Roanoke College, Professor of English & History and Mr. A. F. Littlejohn, a graduate of the Citadel, Commandant of Cadets.

McAllister reported that the "Junior" class was the largest to date at the Institute. Students were from North Carolina, South Carolina, Georgia, Virginia, Tennessee, and Illinois.[804]

The 1912-'13 academic year ended with Commencement ceremonies from May 25th-28th, 1913. In his annual report to the Board of Trustees in May 1913, McAllister acknowledged that five "Seniors" were eligible for graduation and that all planned to attend college. Several planned to prepare for the ministry.[805]

The Baccalaureate Sermon was delivered by Rev. F. B. Clausen of Wilmington, NC. Rev. V. C. Ridenhour of Albemarle addressed the YMCA. The Commencement Address was presented by Dean Edward K. Graham of the University of North Carolina.[806]

The Declaimer's Medal was awarded to W. W. Johnston. The Debate Medal went to Z. L. Edwards. G. F. Davis, speaking on "International Peace," received the Orator's Medal, and C. A. Reap claimed the Scholarship Medal. Students awarded 1st Distinction were J. G. Lyerly, C. A. Reap, G.

Kindley, E. W. Fisher, and C. O. P. Trexler. Second Distinction went to Z. L. Edwards, J. L. Cress, W. R. Lenhardt, C. D. Porter, E. L. Norman, J. D. Thomas, and K. J. Kindley.[807]

1913-1914

In the Summer of 1913, the following advertisement appeared in several North Carolina newspapers:

> "Mt. Pleasant Collegiate Institute 'Merit the Measure of Success,' A high grade Institution for young men and boys, preparing for business life, teaching, or the Junior class in college. Government that appeals to manliness and develops self-control. Accredited relations with University. Beautiful and healthful location in Piedmont Carolina. Commodious brick buildings on an elevated, shady campus. Splendid athletics grounds. Total expenses for the session under $225."[808]

The 1913-'14 school year began on September 17th, 1913 with 102 students from seven states. Because of the large enrollment, many students were forced to find housing in the town. Several local ministers gave welcoming speeches to the students gathered in the chapel.[809]

G. F. McAllister continued as Principal and Professor Math & Physics. Other faculty included Rev. Charles P. McLaughlin, Professor of English Bible. He was from Pennsylvania and was serving as the Minister at St. James Lutheran Church in Concord. McLaughlin was also a member of the College Board of Trustees. M. R. Adams, a graduate of Roanoke College, was Professor of English & History. John W. Weeks, a Citadel graduate, served as Commandant of Cadets and taught History and Science. R. L. Stanley, a graduate of Franklin & Marshall College and formerly a teacher at Mercersburg Academy in Pennsylvania, was Professor of Latin and Greek. E. W. Fisher, a recent MPCI graduate, served as Asst. Librarian. Cadet Officers were P. E. Monroe, Staff Lieutenant and Adjutant; W. R. Lenhardt, Sgt. Major; W. W. Johnson, Sgt. and Musician; S. W. Edwards, Color Sergeant. Cadet Captains were C. O. Ritchie and Z. L. Edwards. Lieutenants were F. R. Peck, C. E. Ridenhour, G. S. Bowden, and P. Barringer. V. J. Crow and E. W. Fisher served as 1st Sergeants.[810]

In March of 1914, Colonel McAllister announced two scholarships for the fall session. One scholarship would be awarded to a boy, fifteen to eighteen years old, who "shall stand the best examination in 7th grade work on all subjects" as judged by the "Superintendent and assistants." The second scholarship would be awarded to a boy, fifteen to eighteen years old, "who is prepared to do eighth grade work, [and] who shall produce the greatest yield of corn per acre, total cost taken into consideration." McAllister stated that, "We trust that this generous offer will be an incentive for better and more thorough work on the part of our students, and the means of starting two of our boys for a higher education."[811]

The newly organized MPCI Alumni Association held its first meeting in May of 1914.[812]

Commencement exercises for the 1913-1914 were held from May 24th - May 27th, 1914. Eight students graduated. Professor J. M. McConnell, Chairman of the History and Economics Department at Davidson College, delivered the address to the Literary Societies.[813]

The annual debate topic was, "Resolved, That the President of the United States should be elected to a term of six years and be ineligible for re-election." O. F. Blackwelder, arguing in the Affirmative, won the Debater's Medal. The Declaimer's Medal was awarded to C. J. M. Blume. C. E. Ridenhour claimed the Orator's Medal. The Ludwig Scholarship Medal was given to C. J. M. Blume, and a new Greek Medal was awarded to C. O. Ritchie. Claiming 1st Distinction were C. J. M. Blume and C. W. Trexler. 2nd Distinctions went to Z. L. Edwards, W. R. Lenhardt, O. F. Blackwelder, E. K. Bodie, M. D. Kluttz, P. E. Monroe, A. L. Ritchie, P. M. Price, and G. E. Kindley.[814]

1914-1915

As the academic year 1914-'15 opened on Sept. 16th, 1914, and as described in Part I, the number of students registering fell by over 25% from the previous year to 75. The Institute faculty was reduced to four due to the drop in enrollment. Principal McAllister taught Math, Physics and Bible. Professor Adams continued to teach English. Professor Stanley remained the instructor in Latin & Greek. Capt. Weeks once again taught History & Science and served as Commandant of Cadets.[815]

The school year concluded with commencement exercises from May 21st through May 25th, 1915, and with thirteen students eligible for graduation. Rev. C. A. Brown delivered the Baccalaureate Sermon and Prof. J. C. Seegers of the Lutheran Seminary in Columbia, SC spoke to the YMCA. O. D. Ritchie, '07, addressed the Alumni Association.[816]

First Distinctions were awarded to L. R. Allman, C. J. M. Blume, W. J. Edwards, W. J. Edwards, L. M. Bost, R. M. Price, and M. L. Troutman. The Debater's Award went to Burton W. Blackwelder, arguing in the Negative on the subject, *"Resolved, The Monroe Doctrine should be Discontinued as a Part of Permanent Foreign Policy of the US."* The Declaimer's Medal was awarded to C. G. Rahn whose topic was *"Plea for the Old South Church."* The Orator's Medal was won by O. F. Blackwelder, speaking on *"The Voice of Nature."* R. M. Price received the Ludwig Scholarship Medal and the Greek Medal went to J. L. Cress. O. F. Blackwelder also received a prize for Extemporaneous Debate and J. L. Cress was noted as having received no demerits during the year.[817]

1915-1916

The MPCI academic year 1915-'16 opened in September 1915 with another drop in enrollment. Only fifty-five students were registered. Colonel McAllister remained as Principal and Professor of Mathematics, Physics and Bible. Two other faculty members returned from the previous year - B. L. Stanley, Professor of Latin and Greek and J. W. Weeks, Professor of History, Science and Commandant of Cadets. New faculty member F. L. Harkey was a MPCI alumnus and recent graduate of Davidson College. He served as Professor of German and English. Dr. J. M. Earnhardt provided regular lectures on Physiology, Hygiene and Sanitation, and C. J. M. Blume, a MPCI student, worked as Assistant Librarian.[818]

Guest Lecturers during the year included Rev. C. P. McLaughlin, Rev. R. S. Dasher, Rev. G. H. C. Parks, Rev. C. R. Pless, Rev. William Lyerly, Dr. Bruce Amsbary, Rev. J. F. Crigler, Rev. C. P. Fisher and Dr. Archibald Johnson.[819]

In 1915, for the first time, the Institute advertised its "College Department" directly. As previously noted, McAllister had tried multiple strategies to obtain Junior College status for the Institute, without success. Previous catalogues listed courses in the "Collegiate Department," and stated that one of the school's missions was the preparation of students to enter the Junior Class of college, but, to date, no specific announcement clarified the intention. McAllister's 1915 announcement read:

> "This Department covers two full years of College work. A high standard is maintained, the design being to make the course equivalent to that offered by leading colleges, as far as it goes. The graduates of the Institute have demonstrated in leading colleges and universities the thoroughness of the work done in our College Department. Entering the Junior Class of leading colleges, they have not only maintained creditable records, but have been the frequent winners of scholastic honors. They are sought by other institutions, and scholarships are, as a rule, available for a graduate of the Institute. …"[820]

The academic year ended with commencement exercises from May 21st through May 24th and five students eligible for diplomas. The Baccalaureate Sermon was presented on Sunday, May 21st by Rev. J. F. Crigler, from St. Mark's Lutheran Church in Charlotte. Rev. C. P. Fisher from Immanuel Lutheran Church in Faith addressed the YMCA later in the day.

On May 22nd, Reverend L. A. Thomas, NCC '69, presented the Alumni Address and on the 23rd, Dr. Archibald Johnson, Editor of the Baptist publication, *Charity and Children*, presented the Literary Address. The Debating Contest addressed the query, "Resolved: That in the Settlement of International Disputes, Law Can and Should be Substituted for Armed Force."

On May 24th, the Oratory Contest involved five presentations – "The Future of the Republic" – D. J. Boger; "Back to Nature" – G. E. Kindley; "Peace of Nations" – K. J. Kindley; "Education for Service" – A. R. Kluttz, and "Beauty of Simplicity" – W. F. Loflin. Following the Oratory Contest, diplomas were awarded to Daniel J. Boger, Giles E. Kindley, Kenneth J. Kindley, Adam R. Kluttz, and William F. Loflin.[821]

1916-1917

The academic year of 1916-'17 opened on Sept. 13th, 1916 with eighty-five students from four states. Student enrollment dropped to seventy-eight by the end of the year. The Institute faculty remained the same except for the replacement of J. W. Weeks who was drafted into military service.

Paul E. Monroe, a MPCI alumni and graduate of Newberry College, now served as Professor of History, Science and Military and as Commandant of Cadets.[822]

Lecturers for the year included Rev. Paul Barringer, Rev. G. H. C. Park, Rev. N. D. Bodie, Rev. D. H. Banslin, Rev. E. C. Cronk, Lucian Edgar Fallansbee, Rev. C. P. Fisher, Rev. M. L. Stirewalt, Rev. I. E. Long, and J. H. Harmes, President of Newberry College.[823]

At the Board of Trustee's meeting of April 11th, 1917, Principal McAllister reported that the curriculum had been strengthened by broadening the course in History and the introduction of Chemistry. According to McAllister, this "would enable our graduates to enter the Junior Classes of 'our Lutheran Colleges' without being hampered by conditions."[824] Since the former Chemistry laboratory had been destroyed by fire in 1909, it is not known where the new classroom was located. McAllister added that the additional classes:

> "mean more work for our own teachers and students. A proper adjustment of our courses and accommodation of many who came to the Institute scarcely prepared for the Freshman class call for an additional,"Sub-Freshman," class and at least one more teacher."[825]

MPCI and Mont Amoena Seminary conducted joint commencement ceremonies on May 21st-23rd, 1917. Rev. M. L. Stirewalt of St. James Lutheran Church in Concord delivered the Baccalaureate Sermon. Rev I. E. Long of Winston-Salem addressed the YMCA. Diplomas were awarded at the Mt. Pleasant Town Auditorium.[826]

Eleven students were commended for receiving no demerits during the year – L. H. Barringer, R. M. Cline, M. A. Petrea, C. J. M. Blume, L. C. Moose, H. C. Petrea, R. W. Bost, J. H. McDaniel, W. A. Ritchie, W. N. Bost, and J. K. Peck. First Distinction Awards were given to C. J. M. Blume, J. H. McDaniel, C. J. Beaver, R. W. Bost, L. V. Schenck, Miles H. Wolff, J. L. Lucas and J. H. Coley.[827]

Miles Wolff won the Scholarship Medal. C. J. M. Blume was awarded the Oratory Medal for the subject, "Martin Luther, The Reformer," and John H. McDaniel won a Medal offered by the *Kannapolis Independent* newspaper for best essay on the American Short Story.[828]

1917-1918

MPCI opened for its fifteenth year in newly renovated space on Sept. 20th, 1917 with eighty-seven registered students. According to Principal McAllister, "the remodeled building and the installation of modern conveniences were a decided aid to the management of the school and in interesting prospective patrons" and "the enjoyment of the comforts afforded produced great satisfaction and contentment so essential to good school work."[829]

The school faculty consisted of Colonel G. F. McAllister, Principal and Professor of Mathematics and Physics, F. L. Harkey as Professor of English & German and Mr. W. J. Proctor who succeeded Major P. E. Monroe (who had been drafted into the Army) as Professor of History and Commandant of Cadets. Proctor was an MPCI alumni and graduate of Newberry College. Mr. P. S. Sykes, a graduate of Wake Forest College, was hired to replace B. L. Stanley as Professor of Latin & Greek. Sykes was drafted in April 1918. The remaining faculty assumed his duties for the last two months of the session. Dr. J. M. Earnhardt returned as a Lecturer on Physiology, Hygiene and Sanitation, and three current students, L. M. Bost, W. A. Mahler, and J. E. Schenck were employed as tutors in the Preparatory Department and in Latin.[830]

On February 23rd, 1918, The Gerhardt Literary Society conducted its Fifteenth Anniversary debate on the query, "Resolved, That the President should be elected by direct vote of the people."[831] Commencement ceremonies for the academic year were held from May 26th thru May 29th, 1918. Seven students received diplomas. The Scholarship Medal was awarded to J. E. Schenck. J. G. Park won the Declaimer's Medal. O. E. Kluttz took the Orator's Medal and H. J. Coley claimed both the Debater's Medal and the prize for Extemporaneous Debate.[832]

1918-1919

The academic year at MPCI opened on Sept. 12th, 1918 with enrollment of 103 students from five states. Except for Colonel McAllister, who remained Principal and Professor of Mathematics and Physics, the entire faculty was new. J. B. Moose, an MPCI alumni and graduate of Newberry College and the Southern Theological Seminary returned as Professor of Greek & History. Moose previously taught at the Institute in 1909-'10. T. C. Johnson, a graduate of Furman University and former Principal of Mooresville, NC High School, was Professor of English & Latin. J. E. Schenck, a 1918 "graduate" of the Institute and the Plattsburg, NY Officers Training Camp, was designated Commandant of Cadets and served as an Instructor in the Preparatory Branch.[833] C. H. Monsees, Jr., a MPCI student, was an Instructor in Penmanship, and another MPCI student, R. E. L. Landrum, Jr., was the Asst. Librarian.[834]

Commencement exercises were held from May 25th through May 28th, 1919. Nine students graduated. First Distinction awards went to Robert M. Brown, George Stelljes, R. W. Bost, J. G. Park, L. V. Schenck, P. E. Fulenwider and C. B. Morton. The Scholarship Medal and the Latin Medal were awarded to George Stelljes. John H. McDaniel won the Orator's Medal, speaking on "The New Era." L. V. Schenck claimed the Debater's Medal and R. M. Brown won the Prize for Extemporaneous Debate. The Declaimer's Medal was presented to F. L. Ritchie.[835]

1919-1920

With its expansion campaign finally showing positive results in recruiting, MPCI opened its next session on Sept. 11th, 1919 with a significant increase in enrollment. 173 students from six states were registered and Colonel McAllister reported that the school turned away many applicants due to lack of space. "For the greater part of the session, [more students] were quartered in the town than were housed on campus."[836]

The increased enrollment required an additional faculty position. The entire faculty from the previous session returned and the new position to teach French was filled by Colonel McAllister's wife, Ethelyn Crabtree McAllister. Mrs. McAllister moved to the Institute after five years as the English and French Instructor at Mont Amoena Seminary.

Claude H. Monsees, Jr., previously a student Instructor of Penmanship and 1919 graduate was designated Commandant of Cadets and Instructor in the Preparatory Branch.

Commencement exercises for the 1919-'20 session were conducted from May 16th through May 19th, 1920. The Baccalaureate Sermon was presented by Rev. John C. Seegers of Wilmington, NC on May 16th, Rev. J. L. Yost, MPCI Class of 1912, delivered the Alumni Address on May 17th and Dr. William J. McGlothlin, President of Furman College, addressed the Literary Societies on May 18th.[837]

Nineteen Seniors graduated on May 19th. First Distinctions were presented to R. W. Bost, L. E. Blackwelder, C. E. Cornelius, Martin B. Foil, R. C. Harris, L. V. Schenck, and J. G. Park. The Scholarship Medal and Latin Medal were awarded to L. E. Blackwelder. Martin B. Foil received the Orator's Medal with a presentation on "Yesterday, Today and Tomorrow." J. G. Park won the Debater's Medal. The Declaimer's Medal went to J. F. Haithcox and R. W. Bost was granted the Greek Medal. A. E. Sheppard received the award for Extemporaneous Debate. W. F. Smithdeal claimed the Military Medal. Company A, under the command of Cadet Captain W. L. Morris, won the Trophy Cup.[838]

1920-1921

The Institute opened in September 1920 with and enrollment of 165 students. There were twenty-six Seniors, thirty-six Juniors, fifty Sophomores and forty-six Freshmen from five states. The faculty consisted of Colonel G. F. McAllister, Principal and Professor of Mathematics and Science; J. B. Moose, Professor of Greek and History; W. W. Holman, Professor of English and Latin; E. E. Sechriest, Professor of French and Physics and Commandant of Cadets; John H. McDaniel, Instructor in the Preparatory Branch, and C. R. Ritchie, Asst. Librarian. Professor Holman was a graduate of Wofford College and held an MA Degree from the University of South Carolina. He previously served as the Principal of Prospect Graded School in Prospect, SC. E. E. Sechriest was a graduate of Elon College and was previously employed as a history instructor at Elon College. J. H. McDaniel was a graduate of MPCI and was Principal of the Mt. Pleasant Graded Schools for one year prior to coming to MPCI.

As the merger of the NC and Tennessee Synods proceeded, Colonel McAllister delivered his annual report to the MPCI Board of Trustees. "The deportment of students has been commendable, only one case requiring extreme discipline [expulsion]. … A representative of the Institute was the winner in both the Tri-state Declaimers' Contest and the State-wide Contest. Graduates of the Institute at college continue to be leaders in Debate and Oratory."[839]

The 1920-'21 academic year ended with joint (MPCI and Mont

Amoena) commencement exercises on May 22nd through May 25th at the Mont Amoena auditorium. Twenty-one Seniors, the largest MPCI class to date, graduated. First Distinctions were awarded to H. H. Alexander, W. B. Bost, R. C. Harris (2nd year), C. B. Morton, J. G. Park (2nd year), A. L. Patterson and E. C. Thomas. The Scholarship Medal was presented to James G. Park. The Orator's Medal was won by L. E. Mabry speaking on "The Responsibility of Christian Citizenship." R. C. Harris claimed the Declaimer's Medal. C. M. Ritchie won both the Debater's Medal and the Prize for Extemporaneous Debate. The debate topic was "Resolved, the Power to Declare War Should be Given to the People." The French Medal was awarded to A. E. Moorer. The Military Medal was presented to H. H. Alexander. The Trophy Cup for the Best Drilled Company was won by Co. A commanded by Cadet Captain C. W. Seiler.[840]

1921-1922

The academic year of 1921-'22 began on Sept. 15th, 1921 with 164 students registered for classes. Colonel McAllister returned as Principal and Professor of Mathematics and Science. Other returning faculty members included J. B. Moose, Professor of Greek and History and W. W. Holman, Professor of English and Latin. Two new members of the faculty were W. M. Albergotti, a recent graduate of the Citadel, Professor of French and Science and Commandant of Cadets, and C. J. M. Blume, a MPCI alumnus and graduate of Newberry College, Instructor in the Preparatory Branch. S. E. Griffin, a MPCI student, served as Assistant Librarian.[841]

Notably, for the first time since 1906, the Institute catalogue changed the statement regarding graduates entering Colleges at an advanced level. Prior to 1921, the catalogue stated **that "men holding certificates of graduation will be accredited to the Junior Class** [emphasis added] in leading colleges."[842] The 1921-'22 Catalogue stated **"men holding certificates of graduation will be accredited to the advanced classes [emphasis added] in the leading colleges."** This was the first, albeit, very subtle public indication that the Institute was having problems obtaining certification as an accredited Junior College.

McAllister explained the "academic standing" of the Institute.

> "We offer a five-year course-the first three covering a High School course and the last two being of College

level. The High School work was rated A1 by the State Department of Education, but our college work was not recognized, due in the main to the fact that we do not have income independent of tuition receipts amounting $5000 per year. Our graduates have been granted credit for one to two years of College work by the University of North Carolina and standard colleges in this and other states. However, there is an element of uncertainty as to the exact credits … will be given at standard higher institutions. This situation is a source of no little trouble to our representatives in the field during the summer [while recruiting] and to the authorities during the session."[843]

Commencement exercises were conducted from May 22nd-24th, 1922. At the alumni luncheon on the 23rd of May, Colonel McAllister was presented a gift in acknowledgement of his twenty-five years of service to NC College and MPCI. The Alumni Association meeting was the "most largely attended meeting ever held" and music for the alumni dance was provided by the Roanoke College orchestra.[844]

On May 24th, twenty-four Seniors, the largest class in Institute history, received diplomas. First Distinctions were awarded to R. C. Harris (3rd year), J. A. Kern, C. B. Morton (2nd year), S. R. McEachern, and E. C. Thomas (2nd year). The Scholarship and Latin Medals were claimed by C. B. Morton. C. M. Ritchie won the Orator's Medal for the 2nd year in a row arguing in the affirmative "That Capital Punishment Should be Abolished in North Carolina." Marion C. Davis was awarded the Debater's Medal and the award for Extemporaneous Debate. W. R. Quarterman received the Declaimer's Medal. R. L. Gandy won the French Medal. The Military Medal went to R. C. Harris and Trophy Cup for Best Drilled Company was claimed by Co. B, commanded by Capt. C. D. Moretz.[845]

1922-1923

MPCI's twentieth session began on Sept. 14th, 1922 with 161 students from eight states. There were thirty-one Seniors, forty-one Juniors, forty-two Sophomores, twenty-three Freshmen, and twenty-four Sub-Freshmen – from NC (136), SC (10), FL (7), VA (4), GA (2), PA (1), and WV (1).

The faculty had expanded to six members and an Asst. Librarian. Colonel McAllister remained Principal and Professor of Mathematics & Physics. Other returning faculty included Major J. B. Moose, Professor of Greek & History; Capt. W. W. Holman, Professor of English & Latin; Major W. M. Albergotti, Professor of French & Science and Commandant of Cadets, and Capt. C. J. M. Blume, Instructor in the Preparatory Branch and Asst. Commandant of Cadets. New faculty member Capt. L.E. Blackwelder was a MPCI alumni and graduate of Newberry College. He served as an Instructor in the Preparatory Branch. R. L. Fisher, a MPCI student, served as Asst. Librarian.[846]

Against the backdrop of Lenoir College's campaign and its own building promotion, the Institute held its commencement exercises from May 20th through May 23rd, 1923. Thirty Seniors constituted the largest graduating class in the history of the Institute. Eighteen graduates would be pursing post-secondary degrees from various Colleges and Universities. First Distinctions were awarded to R. C. Harris (4th year) and S. R. McEachern (2nd year). R. C. Harris won the Scholarship Medal and the Latin Medals. C. G. Smithdeal claimed the Orator's Medal, speaking on "The South's Greatest Men." The Debater's medal was awarded to H. G. Watson, and L. B. Hahn won the Declaimer's Medal. L. G. Russell received the French Medal and F. O. Conrad was named the top Cadet. Company A, commanded by Cadet Captain R. C. Harris, won the Trophy Cup.[847]

1923-24

After a strong advertising campaign in the summer of 1923, the Institute began the 1923-'24 academic year with 173 registered students. For the second time in five years, the Institute enrolled over 170 students.

The school year began on Sept. 13th, 1923 and, except for one change, the faculty remained the same as the previous year. Former faculty member Roy Webster replaced J. B. Moose as Professor of History and Greek. Webster taught at the Institute in 1907 for one semester and since that time had obtained a law degree from the University of South Carolina and a Master's Degree from Columbia University. He had also served as the Superintendent of Schools in Martinsville, VA for two years.[848]

In May 1924, Colonel McAllister reported to the Trustees that the school year had been a year "of more than ordinary success" in terms of the high enrollment, deportment, and the health of the students and faculty.[849]

Commencement ceremonies were conducted from May 18th through May 21st, 1924. Of the twenty-three students who began the year as Seniors, thirteen were recommended for graduation. First Distinctions were awarded to Ralph M. Cline, S. B. Stewart, A. L. Horne, F. A. Moser, and Carl A. Honeycutt. The Greek Medal was awarded to Ralph M. Cline. Fred O. Conrad won the Orator's Medal and Sleiman R. McEachern claimed the Debater's Medal. M. H. Smith received the French Medal and C. A. Honeycutt won the Declaimer's Medal. The Military Medal was awarded to John A. Kern, Jr. and the Trophy Cup was claimed by Co. B, commanded by Caet Captain James Harward.[850]

1924-1925

The 1924-'25 academic year was marked by a sharp decrease in enrollment from the previous year, as only 146 students were registered. Except for Colonel McAllister, there was a complete turnover of faculty. Several teachers left to seek advanced degrees. The new faculty consisted of Major R. C. Glenn, Professor of History & Greek; John H. McDaniel (MPCI '19), Professor of English and Asst. Commandant of Cadets; H. R. Middlesworth, Professor of Latin & Bible; William W. Cone, Professor of French and Science and Commandant of Cadets, and D. Jack Gore (MPCI '20), Professor of Chemistry and Instructor in the Preparatory Department. Cone and Gore became the football coaches for the 1924-'25 season. L. W. Griggs, a MPCI student, was an Asst. Librarian.

The Collegiate Institute's first yearbook was published in the Spring of 1925. Entitled *The Tour Path*, the book was published by the MPCI Senior Class and printed by the Observer Printing House, Inc. in Charlotte, NC. The book contained individual photos of the members of the Senior Class and group photos of the Junior, Sophomore, Freshman, Sub-Freshman classes. The Senior photos also listed information about each student's accomplishments along with their "nicknames." The 124-page book contained sections devoted to the Faculty, the Military, Athletics, Activities and Humor. It also included a section depicting seven female students from Mont Amoena who were sponsored by various groups on the Institute campus. The Editor-in-Chief of the yearbook was Charles

MacLaughlin from Pittsburg, PA, who did the extensive artwork contained in the volume. MacLaughlin later worked for the *Atlanta Constitution*.[851]

Commencement exercises for the 1924-'25 academic year began on May 24th, 1925 with a Baccalaureate sermon given by Rev. E. R. McCauley, DD, from Raleigh. An evening address was given by Rev. H. P. Wyrick of Burlington. On the 25th a Commencement Drama, "If I Were King, A Romantic Comedy" was presented, and on the 26th, the Alumni Address was delivered by Fred W. Morrison '07, who was currently a faculty member at NC Woman's College in Greensboro.

On May 27th, diplomas were presented to twenty-two graduates and awards were presented. The age of the graduating Seniors ranged from sixteen to twenty-two years old. First Distinctions were awarded to Archie L. Barringer, Marvin B. Dry, and Carl A. Honeycutt (2nd Year). The Senior Oratorical Contest was won by S. R. McEachern. The Scholarship Medal was awarded to Marvin B. Dry. Murray L. Penninger, Jr. claimed the Greek Medal and Arthur R. Rietzel won the French Medal. S. A. Grovenstein was awarded the Declamation Medal. C. A. Honeycutt was presented the History Medal and John D. Suther won the Military Medal. The Best Company Award went to Co. B, commanded by Cadet Capt. R. Brown McAllister.[852]

1925-1926

The academic year of 1925-26 began on Sept. 10th, 1925 with 117 registered students. There were thirteen Seniors, twenty-two Juniors, twenty-five Sophomores, thirty-nine Freshmen and eighteen Sub-Freshmen from ten states including North Carolina, South Carolina, Virginia, Georgia, Alabama, Florida, New York, Ohio, and West Virginia.[853]

The faculty consisted of six men, two of whom were new. Colonel McAllister continued his service as Principal of the Institute and taught Mathematics and Physics. Other returning faculty were Capt. H. R. Middlesworth, Professor of Latin and Bible; Capt. John H. McDaniel, Professor of English, and Major R. C. Glenn, Professor of Greek and History. Major H. M. Carley, a graduate of The Citadel, was the new Commandant of Cadets. He taught Science and was Asst. Professor of Mathematics. The second new faculty member was Capt. H. C. Hainer, a Massachusetts native and graduate of Elon College. Hainer served as

Professor of French and the Director of Athletics. MPCI Senior, A. Y. Davis was the Assistant Librarian.[854]

Commencement activities occurred from May 23rd – May 26th, 1926. First Distinctions were awarded to Archie L. Barringer (2nd Year), B. L. Allen, C. A. Honeycutt (3rd Year), Marvin B. Dry (2nd Year), Lloyd B. Hahn, Harvey C. McAllister, H. A. McCullough, Jr., and H. H. Sloop.

The Orator's Medal was awarded to P. G. Stoner. P. H. Lipe won the Declaimer's Medal and Lloyd B. Hahn claimed the Debater's Medal. The History Medal was won by H. H. Sloop and the French Medal went to B. L. Allen. W. L. Ezzell was awarded the Science Medal.[855]

1926-27

Academic year 1926-'27 began on Sept. 9th, 1926 with 106 registered students. There were ten Seniors, twenty Juniors, twenty-nine Sophomores, thirty Freshmen, and seventeen Sub-Freshmen from eight states.[856] Colonel McAllister was Principal and Professor of Mathematics and Physics. Two other faculty members returned from the previous session, Major R. C. Glenn, Professor of Latin and Greek and Capt. John H. McDaniel, Professor of English. Major Roy Webster returned to the faculty after a two-year absence while attending Columbia University. Maj. Webster was Professor of History and Bible. New faculty members included Major R. B. Still, a graduate of the Citadel, as Professor of French, Asst. Professor of Mathematics and Commandant of Cadets. Capt. R. L. Abstance, a graduate of Furman University, served as Professor of Science and Director of Athletics.

The 1926 Collegiate Institute catalogue listed the school as "A Preparatory and Junior College," even though it had not received Junior College certification from the State Board of Education. No Junior College Diplomas were awarded and students attending College after graduation from the Institute were never accepted as having a previous Junior College degree.[857]

The 1926-'27 academic year closed with commencement exercises during the week of May 22nd through May 26th, 1927. McAllister stated to the Board of Trustees that the year had been "a very satisfactory one" with a "splendid, capable and faithful faculty." The school had displayed the "best spirit in years."[858]

Students awarded 1st Distinction were H. E. Barrier, C. A. Honeycutt (4th year), and H. A. McCullough, Jr. (2nd year). The Declaimer's Medal was won by G. D. Bellis. C. A. Honeycutt claimed the Debater's Medal. H. A. McCullough, Jr. won the Scholarship Medal and the Science Medal. The Orator's Medal was awarded to James H. Taylor and the French Medal was given to J. D. Suther. The Military Medal was presented to J. A. Fowler and the Best Company Trophy Cup was claimed by Co. B, commanded by Cadet Capt. H. H. Sloop.[859]

1927-1928

The Institute opened for its 1927-'28 Fall Session in on Sept. 14th, 1927. One hundred-four students were listed in the school catalogue, but the yearbook listed only eighty-seven. At the time the yearbook was published there were nineteen Seniors, twenty-one Juniors, twenty-one Sophomores, nineteen Freshmen, and seven Sub-freshmen. Two "firsts" were recorded as the year began. For the first time a Jewish student attended the Institute and nine students were female. The women, all of whom had previously attended Mont Amoena Seminary, did not reside on campus but boarded in the Town of Mt. Pleasant. Students Alma Irene Tucker, Ruth B. Barrier, Verna M. Hahn, Martha Shirey, Julia Shirey, Frances McAllister and Virginia McAllister were from Mt. Pleasant. Margaret Shulenberger was from Charlotte and Blanche McCullen was from Clearwater, Florida.[860]

Noting the presence of the female students, *The Institute News* alumni newspaper, stated:

> "... of course, it is understood that the Collegiate Institute is a Boy's School and that the military feature has become definitely established. The idea of co-education, therefore, is incongruous. However, under the circumstances there would seem to be no insurmountable difficulties in the way of admitting local girls. A Study Hall removed from the dormitories has been provided for them."[861]

Principal McAllister commented:

> "An added touch toward the refinement of the finished product – a 100 percent successful school year – will be realized, let us believe, in the presence of a limited number

of sisters counted for the first time in our student body. Just enough to give color to a handsome picture, and to set the pace, maybe in scholastic achievements."[862]

The returning faculty included G. F. McAllister, Principal and Professor of Mathematics; Major Roy Webster, Professor of History and Bible; R. C. Glenn, Professor of Latin and Greek; John H. McDaniel, Professor of English, and R. B. Still, Commandant, Professor of French and Asst. Prof of Mathematics.

The new faculty member was Daniel Linder Rhoad, Jr., Professor of Sciences & Director of Athletics. D. L. Rhoad was born in Branchville, South Carolina and graduated from Wofford College in 1926. He attended the UNC Coaching School in 1926 and served as the Director of Athletics and Professor of Science at South Georgia College.[863] In June of 1927 he wrote Colonel McAllister applying for a position at the Institute. Colonel McAllister replied:

> "Having examined your credentials and found same favorable and having had a satisfactory personal interview with you, I have recommended your election. Accordingly, you have been elected to the position and on acceptance, will be expected to report here Sept. 5th to the 8th of Sept (exact date to be agreed upon later). You are to receive a salary of $1500.00 and your board and room. Salary is to be paid in ten monthly payments.
>
> You will be expected to live in one of the dormitories (as do other faculty members) and take your meals at our Boarding Hall. You will, of course, be expected to cooperate with and assist the other faculty members in work that is done jointly and assume your reasonable share of responsibility in the maintenance of good order and discipline. You will have about five 45 minute recitations per day and have charge of coaching the athletics teams."[864]

McAllister also reported that the Institute was "making full use of Laboratory equipment (funds for which were provided by John S. Efird in 1926) now and our students will be spared the task of making up Laboratory work when they enter higher institution."[865]

During the school year, the Institute began "supervised evening study," proctored by Professor Roy Webster. McAllister described the new program:

> "The entire roll of students is canvassed every two weeks. Those who show unsatisfactory progress in as many as two studies are assigned to the evening Study Hall for a period of two weeks. Faculty members take turn supervision the Study Hall. A lamentable fact is that so many young people enter Secondary Schools (and doubtless College, too) and have not learned how to study."[866]

Tragedy struck the Institute on Feb 28th, 1928. Euclid Liston Miller, a Senior from Manassas, VA, suffered an attack of acute gastroenteritis and died two days later in Concord, NC. Miller was a student at MPCI since 1925 and was a member of the Ludwig Literary Society. He held the student rank of 1st Lieutenant and Adjutant of Cadets. In a Memoriam printed in the Institute Yearbook, Prof. Roy Webster stated that [Miller] "was an unusually quiet young man, but beneath that calm exterior beat a heart of gold. ... He was strict, but absolutely fair, and gained and held [the] confidence and respect of his fellow students."[867]

In the Spring of 1928, the Senior Class published the Institute's second yearbook. *The Sabre*, a 107-page volume containing individual photos of the Faculty, Senior Class and Junior Class, group photos of the lower classes, and many photos of clubs, athletic teams, buildings, and various campus activities. The book was dedicated to Professor Roy Webster and contained sections on Organizations, Military, Athletics, Jokes and Advertisements. The Editor-in-Chief was Carl A. Honeycutt from Gold Hill, NC and the book was printed by the Queen City Printing Co., Charlotte, NC.[868]

The yearbook also commented on the "Girls at MPCI" stating:

> "The girls who were enrolled have fulfilled the 'prophecy.' The cut of the 'Specials' is evidence of the enhancement of the 'color' and 'refinement' of the student body; and, those who have access to the record can testify that the girls suffer not in comparison in the matter of scholastic achievement."[869]

Graduation exercises for 1927-28 took place during the week of May

27th-30th, 1928. The Baccalaureate Sermon was delivered on May 27th by Rev. Edwin F. Keever of St. Paul's Lutheran Church, Wilmington, NC. Rev. Charles A. Phillips (NCC '99) of St. Mark's in Mooresville, NC delivered an address on Sunday evening. On Tuesday, May 29th, Rev. Henry G. Hardin of Main St. Methodist Church in Gastonia spoke to the Literary Societies. Along with debates, declamations, and social events, fourteen Seniors graduated, and awards were presented. Carl A. Honeycutt (Sr.), Virginia S. McAllister (Sub-Freshman), R. J. Piland, Jr. (Jr.), Paul H. Rhodes (Sr.), and Margaret Shulenberger (Jr.) were awarded First Distinction (above a 93 avg.) and Second Distinction (bet 90-93 avg.) went to John William Link (Sub-Freshman) and F. T. Teague (Soph.). Medals awarded included Declamation – to J. C. Keiffer; Debate – M. D. Norris; Oratory – C. R. Huffman; Military (individual excellence in drill) – F. T. Teague; French – George L. Barrier; Scholarship (highest academic avg.) – Carl A. Honeycutt; Greek - Carl A. Honeycutt; Science – Paul H. Rhodes, and Trophy Cup (best drilled Company) – Co. B, Cadet Capt. H. H. Sloop.[870]

1928-1929

In July 1928, the following article appeared in *The Twin-City Sentinel*, Winston-Salem, NC.

> "The Collegiate Institute at Mt. Pleasant continues to use a military training system after giving the method a test of two decades. Many other institutions, including our own Oak Ridge Institute, have had the same satisfactory experience with military training ... the Collegiate Institute's new catalogue sets forth excellent reasons for using the military system and without effort silences opposition to its use. ...
>
> Col. G. F. McAllister states, 'the object of the military system was the proper regulation and control of the school, and to furnish students needed physical exercise and development. ... The system has abundantly justified itself.' Those acquainted with the work of the Institute for the past several decades bear willing testimony that it is one of the best regulated schools in the country. There

> is, of course, no purpose to foster the spirit of militarism. As an incident, however, the military training proved of invaluable worth to the hundreds of Institute men who were in service in the recent war. Their rise in training camp and actual service was marked and rapid. As far as records show, there was not one but that ranked above private.
>
> Military training does vastly more for a boy or a young man. President McAllister writes and affirms that it 'makes him quick of perception and accurate in execution; it teaches him to be prompt, regular, and systematic in the performance of his duty. It gives him a stronger physique and an erect carriage.'
>
> The educator of many years' experience thus sets forth the merits of the military training system as used in one of the State's high rating junior colleges and if others who sometimes criticize the ROTC would study the matter as thoroughly as has Dr. McAllister, they would arrive at the same conclusion."[871]

The 26th year of the Mount Pleasant Collegiate Institute opened on Sept. 13th, 1928. Enrollment dropped from the previous year. Only 95 students were registered. Fourteen Seniors and fourteen Juniors began the year. There were again nine females attending as day students. Only eleven of the students were from Mt. Pleasant.[872]

With one exception, the faculty from the previous year returned. The new faculty member was James C. Hair who replaced D. L. Rhoad as Professor of Sciences and Director of Athletics. Prof. Hair was a native of South Carolina. He attended Blacksville High School in Barnwell Co. SC and graduated from Clemson College in 1928 with a BS Degree in Chemistry. Hair played football at Clemson for three years and the position at MPCI was his first job after graduation.[873]

In February of 1929 the Seniors at MPCI completed the State High School Senior Examination administered by the North Carolina Department of Public Instruction. Colonel McAllister compared MPCI's sixteen students to the 12,803 student State Median - Reading and Study Habits (MPCI-15.5, State-15.3); Reading/Literary (MPCI-12, State-14.2);

Reading/Historical (MPCI-12, State-13.2); English Forms (MPCI-7.4, State-8.5); Mathematics (MPCI-9, State-6.7); General Science (MPCI-13.5, State-12.1); American History (MPCI-13.8, State-12.1); Latin (MPCI-19, State-9); French (MPCI-12, State-10.7), Agriculture (MPCI-14, State-11.3).[874]

Graduation exercises for the year 1928-'29 were held from May 19th-22nd, 1929. There is no record of the number of Seniors who graduated or any details about the activities which took place during the ceremonies. Awards included First Distinction to Virginia S. McAllister (Fr), daughter of Colonel McAllister. Second Distinctions went to E. T. Bost, Jr., G. F. Hart, Jr., A.W. Kornahrens, J. Lester Link, J. W. Link, Jr., H. N. McCall, I. S. Preston, J. L. Shirey, and B. A. Chaney, Jr. Medals were awarded to I. S. Preston, Declamation; E. T. Bost, Jr., Debate; J. Lester Link, Oratory & Science; Charles Gibbons, Military (Drill); W. M. Freed, French; and J. L. Shirey, Latin. The Trophy Cup for best Drill went to Co. A commanded by Cadet Captain H. W. Czarnitski.[875]

1929-1930

The academic year 1929-'30 began on Sept 18th, 1929. Again, there was drop in attendance as only eighty-nine students registered for classes. Less than fifty percent of the students (forty-four) were from North Carolina and only seven of these were from Mt. Pleasant. There were students from eleven other states, Cuba (three), Panama (two), and Costa Rica (one). Five of the students were female and one-third were Lutheran. There were fourteen Seniors.[876]

The faculty for the new year saw G. F. McAllister return as Principal and Professor of Mathematics. Other returning teachers were Roy Webster, History & Bible; J. H. McDaniel, English, and R. B. Still, Commandant and Professor of French. Two new faculty members included Theodore Patton, Professor of Latin & Greek and W. Frank Shealy, Professor of Sciences and Director of Athletics.[877]

Theodore Patton was born in Grundy Co., TN in 1907. He attended the McAllie Military School in Chattanooga and Sewanee Military Academy in Sewanee, TN. He received an AB Degree from The University of The South, Sewanee, TN, in 1929. After one year at MPCI, Patton was ordained as an Episcopal Minister and served as a Navy Chaplain in WWII.[878]

W. Frank Shealey was born in Little Mountain, Newberry Co. SC. He was a graduate of Newberry College (1922) where he played football, baseball and basketball and became a member of the Newberry College Sports Hall of Fame. He coached Freshman football at Newberry in 1923. He served as Principal and Football Coach/Athletic Director at Kershaw (SC) High School (1923-'24) and Spencer (NC) High School (1924-'29). He attended summer school at Catawba College in 1929.[879]

Commencement exercises for the year 1929-'30 were held from May 25th-28th. Rev. Alfred. R. Beck, DD, Editor of the *NC Lutheran* and the former President of the Tennessee Synod, delivered the Baccalaureate Address on May 25th. Rev. Pleasant E. Monroe, DD (NC College '98, MA '01), the minister at St. James in Concord, delivered the address to the religious organizations of the school on May 25th. The Honorable Alfred L. Bulwinkle of Gastonia, a member of the US House of Representatives representing the 9th District, delivered the Literary Address on May 27th.[880]

The Declaimer's Contest was held on May 26th. Speakers included R. H. Brown of Baltimore, MD presenting "Regulus to the Carthaginians"; H. N. McCall of New Bern presenting "The March of the Flag"; C. E. Ledingham of Salem, VA – "The Cross of Gold"; J. L. Shirey of Mt. Pleasant – "The Farmer's Home"; J. W. Link, Jr. of Mt. Pleasant – "The Farmer's Home" and R. L. Smith of Charlotte, NC – "Capitals of the Spirit."[881]

The Junior Class Debates were held on the afternoon of May 27th. The topic of the Debate was "Resolved: That Socialism Would be the Best Remedy for the Evils of American Society." Speaking in the affirmative were Ludwig Literary Society members A. L. Mattes (Scranton, PA), I. R. Preston (NY) and C. J. Sanders (Rock Hill, SC). The negative was argued by members of the Gerhardt Society H. W. Czarnitski (Columbia, SC), W. D. Dubois (Wilson, NC) and J. W. Moran (N. Platte, NE).[882]

On the morning of May 28th the Orator's contest was conducted with the following speeches: E. B. Bolick, Blowing Rock, "Glorified Peace"; E. T. Bost, Jr., Bost Mill, "Law and Order"; G. F. Hart, Jr., Savannah, GA, "The South's Greatest Gift to America"; E. B. Heidt, Marlowe, GA, "The Spirit of Modern Youth"; F. H. Lentz, Hendersonville, "The United States and the World Court"; C. G. Rudisill, Jr., Lincolnton, "The Changing South"; F. W. Seegers, Columbia, SC, "The Menace"; F. K. Shealy, Columbia, SC, "Fighter or Thinker –Which?"; Jose Antonio Tarte, Panama City, RP, "The Latin-American Countries."[883]

Diplomas and medals were presented in the chapel of the old Mont Amoena Seminary. Thirteen Seniors (eleven men and two women) graduated. Medals were awarded to R. H. Brown – Declaimers; A. L. Mattes – Debate; E. B. Bolick – Orator; E. A. Tarte – Military; F. K. Shealy – French; Virginia S. McAllister – Science and I. S. Preston – Latin. The Trophy Cup for Best Drill was won by Co. A, H. W. Czarnitzki, Cadet Captain.[884]

1930-1931

The new academic year began on September 17th, 1930. Eighty-three students were registered, a drop of six students from the previous year. Just over fifty percent (forty-two) students were from North Carolina, but only five were from Mt. Pleasant. Twelve other states were represented as well as two foreign countries, Cuba (three) and Panama (three). It appears that there were only three females registered. After four years advertising itself as a "Preparatory School and Junior College," the Institute now presented itself as "A High-Grade School, Offering Standard High School Courses and Two Years of Advanced Work."[885]

The faculty for the '30-'31 school year had three new members. Colonel McAllister remained Principal and Professor of Mathematics. Other remaining teachers were Roy Webster, Professor of Government & History; John H. McDaniel, Professor of English, and W. F. Shealy, Professor of Sciences and Director of Athletics. New faculty were William S. Gerhardt, Professor of Latin & Bible; Edward L. Black, Professor of French, Asst. Professor of Mathematics and Commandant, and Hubert H. Sloop, Instructor in the Preparatory Branch and Asst. Commandant. Current students, I. S. Preston and R. H. Brown, served as Tutors in Spanish and Asst. Librarian, respectively.[886]

Professor William Seibert Gerhardt was born in Lancaster Co., PA in 1892. He graduated from Franklin & Marshall College in Lancaster in 1903 and the Eastern Theological Seminary in Lynchburg, VA in 1909. He served as a teacher and Principal at several schools in Pennsylvania through 1923 and as a minister for several churches before coming to MPCI.

Professor Edward L. Black was born in York Co. SC in 1907. He graduated from the Citadel in Charleston, SC in 1928. He served as Principal of a school in St. Matthew's, SC and attended the University of Virginia in 1929 before coming to MPCI. He was also a Lieutenant in the US Army Reserves.

Hubert Harvey Sloop was born in China Grove in 1904. In 1920, at age sixteen, he served in the United States Navy, listing his age as 18. He entered MPCI in 1923 and graduated in 1928. He received an AB Degree from Roanoke College, VA in 1930. Following his employment at MPCI, Sloop re-entered the Navy, attained the rank of Lieutenant and saw duty in WWII.[887]

Graduation ceremonies took place in from May 24th through May 27th, 1931. The Baccalaureate Sermon was delivered by Rev. E. C. Cooper of Kannapolis. Rev. I. Harding Hughes, an Episcopal Minister, also spoke. Rev. L. E. Blackwelder (MPCI '20) gave the Alumni Address. The Debating Contest was held on May 25 on the query: "Resolved, That Congress May, By Two-Thirds Vote of Each House, Set Aside Decisions of the Supreme Court, Declaring National Laws Unconstitutional."

Awards for First Distinction (GPA not under 93) were received by Virginia S. McAllister from Mt. Pleasant and J. A. Pless of Monroe. J. A. Pless also won the Declaimer's Medal and the Latin Medal. R. H. Brown from Baltimore was awarded the Debater's Medal. The Orator's Medal went to I. S. Preston of New York, speaking on the topic, "Why I Believe in God." The Military Medal was claimed by A. E. Stewart, Jr. of Wilson, NC, and the Science Medal was awarded to Lloyd F. Hancock of High Point. The Best Drilled Company "Trophy Cup" was won by Co. B, Commanded by Cadet Captain W. A. Pritchett, 1st Lt. J. W. Moran, and 2nd Lt. T. D. Cloninger.[888]

1931-1932

For the first time in its history, MPCI began 1931–'32 year operating as an "independent" institution with no financial support from the Lutheran Synod. The school opened on September 16th, 1931 with eighty-nine students from eleven states, Panama (three), and Cuba (three). Sixty-six students were from North Carolina, and eleven were from Mt. Pleasant. Two females, Virginia S. McAllister and Dorothy L. Johnston, were enrolled.[889]

The College Catalogue opened with the statement, "Merit, the Measure of Success", The Collegiate Institute, A High-Grade School offering standard High School Courses and two years of Advanced Work."[890]

The faculty for the year was G. F. McAllister, AB, MA – President and Prof of Mathematics; Roy Webster, Prof. of Government and History; William S. Gerhardt, AB, Prof of Latin and Bible; J. H. McDaniel, AB, Prof of English; Edward L. Black, AB, Commandant, Prof of French and Asst. Prof of Mathematics; W. F. Shealy, AB, Prof of Sciences and Athletic Coach, and J. E. Magner, Director of Athletics. H. L. Cento, a Senior from Cuba was a Tutor in Spanish.[891]

The 1931-'32 catalogue listed the following classes:

Classical Course - Sub Freshman:

English-Emerson & Bender, Book II; Spelling-Webster; Literature and Life, Book I; Math-Arithmetic, Milne, Book III; Algebra-1st Year, Wells & Hart; Latin-Elementary Latin, Smith; Civics-Textbook in Citizenship, Hughes. Scientific Course: Substitute for Latin-Geography by Stull & Hatch, and New Agriculture by Waters.

Classical Course - Freshman:

English-Advanced Grammar, Kittredge and Farley; Spelling-Sandwick & Bacon; Literature & Life, Book III; Math-Commercial Arithmetic, Robinson; Algebra-High School, Milne; Latin-Caesar, Kelsey, Grammar-Bennett; History-Ancient, Robinson and Breasted. Scientific Course: Substitute for Latin-General Science by Caldwell and Eikenberry.

Classical Course - Sophomore:

English, English & American Literature by Long; Rhetoric & Composition by D. J. Hill; Math-Advanced Algebra, Milne; Plane Geometry, Phillips & Fisher; Latin-Cicero's Select Orations, Grammar & Composition, Bennett; History-Medieval and Modern, Robinson &

Beard; General Science, Caldwell & Eikenberry. Scientific Course: Substitute Biology for Latin.

Classical Course -Junior:

English-Poetry and Prose by Newcomer-Andrews-Hall; Composition, Woolley; Theme work; Math-Solid Geometry, Phillips & Fisher; College Algebra, Milner; Latin-Vergil's Aenid, Grammar & Composition, Bennett; History-Political History of the US, Hockett (1492-1828); Schlesinger (1829-1925); Bible-History, Blaikie; Modern Language-French, Fraser and Squair or Spanish, L. Sinagnan. Scientific Course: Substitute for Latin-Physics by Mann & Twiss for Latin.

Classical Course - Senior:

English-American Poetry & Prose, Newcomer-Andrews-Hall; College Composition, Shepherd; Literary Criticism, Painter, and Theme work; Math-Plane & Spherical Trigonometry, Phillips & Strong; Plane Surveying, Barton; Latin-Livy, Books XXI & XXII or Horace, Odes and Epodes, Grammar & Composition; History-American Government and Politics, Beard; Bible-Teaching, Stump; Study of Sheatsley; Modern Language-French second year or Spanish second year; Physics-Mann & Twiss. Scientific Course: Substitute Chemistry by Godfrey for Latin.[892]

Commencement ceremonies were conducted from May 22nd-24th, 1932. Rev J. H. Henderlite of Gastonia delivered the Baccalaureate Sermon on May 22nd. Dr. G. T. Rowe, Chairman of the Religion Department at Duke University, addressed the school's religious organizations. These programs were conducted at Holy Trinity Church in Mt. Pleasant. On May 23rd, Professor Hilbert A. Fisher of North Carolina State University[893] delivered the alumni address. The Declaimers and the Debate Contest were also held on the 23rd. The query of the debate was "Resolved, The United States Government should grant independence to the people of the Philippines."

The winners of Medals included: W. B. Woollen, Charlotte, NC, Latin Medal; Virginia S. McAllister, Mt. Pleasant, Orator's Medal; H. G. Warlick, Mt. Pleasant, Debater's Medal; H. R. Knebel, Salisbury, NC,

Declaimer's Medal; M. G. "Mac" Ewer, Jr., Birmingham, MI, Science Medal and Jerry Morgan, Havana, Cuba, Military Medal. Fifteen Seniors, including two females, graduated. First distinctions were achieved by Virginia B. McAllister, F. B. Sloop, and M. G. Ewer.[894]

At the May Board of Directors meeting, McAllister discussed how the Institute's courses would, in the future, be applied to college work. Based on a report from the NC Department of Education, he advised that the school was officially credited with approximately 45 semester hours of college work, the equivalent of almost one and one-half years of college credit. Prerequisites for attaining two full years of college credit, or unqualified Junior College rating, were also specified. They were: (1) additional income independent of receipts from students; (2) the addition of more modern books to the Library and improvement of Library facilities; and (3) a further broadening of the curriculum, providing for wider latitude in elective course.[895]

1932-1933

In August 1932 Colonel McAllister wrote to his incoming students.

> "Dear Cadet: You will be interested in some news items from MPCI. The summer has found us busy planning and working for a bigger and better Institute. There have been obstacles and discouragements, yes. But if we would succeed in this world, we must learn to fight all the harder when obstacles beset us. ... Coach Magner writes confidently concerning his football line-up. A good schedule has been arranged with strong teams in the Carolinas and Virginia. Undoubtedly our athletic program should place us more prominently on the map. Some new courses will be offered next session, giving those who carry them additional college credits, 3rd year French, 3rd year Spanish ... and probably a course in Economics and an additional course in History.
>
> With the upturn in business within the next 30 days, there will be more boys arranging to go to school. We want our share of them. Your cooperation will mean much. Remember, in union there is strength. Let's administer a

> knockout blow to 'Old Man Depression' and show him where he gets off."[896]

The MPCI academic year 1932-1933 opened on September 13th, 1932. The school catalogue stated that "the Collegiate Institute [is] a high school offering standard High School courses and two years of advanced work." Eighty-one students from nine states were enrolled, however, only fifty-nine were "in attendance". Forty-seven were registered in the "College Program," and thirty-five in the High School Program. There were seventeen Seniors, fifteen Juniors, seventeen Sophomores and ten Freshmen/Sub-freshmen.[897]

The faculty consisted of eight instructors, four of whom were new. Colonel McAllister returned as President and Professor of Mathematics. Roy Webster was Professor of Government & History. W. F. Shealy remained as Professor of Sciences and Athletic Coach, and J. E. Manger was the Director of Athletics. The new instructors were Paul B. Fry, a graduate of Davidson College, Professor of English and Latin and Director of Music; William A. McKnight, BS, Davidson College, Professor of Modern Languages and Biology; D. K. Barrington, Jr., BS, The Citadel, Asst. Professor of Mathematics, Science and Bible and Commandant of Cadets, and Hubert Sloop, MPCI '28, AB, Roanoke College, Instructor of Preparatory Branches and Registrar.[898]

The school catalogue further declared that MPCI offered:

> "1. A five-years course embracing a High School course and forty-five semester hours of college work, fully accredited by the State Department of Education and accepted by leading colleges and universities. 2. Thorough instruction by highly trained, experienced teachers. 3. Large ratio of teachers to number of students, insuring individual attention and instruction. 4. Wholesome discipline of body and mind in an environment which is conducive to sustained application. 5. Close association of teachers and students, contributing to pleasant relationship and character building. 6. Military system for making men, not soldiers. 7. Training for every student in public speaking in four Literary Societies supervised by faculty members. 8. A program designed to educate the whole

man, hence including the leading sports. 9. An education which stresses character as much as knowledge. 10. The commendation of three generations of satisfied persons. 11. A continuous policy under the same management for thirty-six years. 12. All the forgoing at moderate costs."[899]

Commencement ceremonies for the 1932-'33 academic year began on May 21st, 1933 with the Baccalaureate Sermon delivered at Holy Trinity Lutheran Church by Rev. Joel S. Snyder of Fayetteville. Later in the day, Rev. Tom A. Sykes of High Point gave a religious address. The remaining events were held in the Mont Amoena Seminary auditorium. The Latin Medal was awarded to W. M. Fain, Jr. R. C. Lyerly claimed the Science Medal. The Debater's medal was won by J. W. Jelks, and F. B. Sloop took the Orator's Medal. The only female member of the Senior class, Daphne Bunn, placed first in the Declaimer's contest with her topic, "Lest We Forget." The Trophy Cup for outstanding Cadet was awarded to F. D. Younce.[900]

At 10 AM on Tuesday, May 23rd, 1933, diplomas were awarded to seventeen seniors. No one among the hundreds attending the event could have known that this would be the last graduation ceremony at MPCI.[901]

III

CAMPUS LIFE

Central to the soul of any educational institution is the social fabric that surrounds the people who are a part of it. Just as business and academics were important elements of North Carolina College and MPCI, so too were the rules of behavior, personal and group activities, and community interaction that defined the life of the schools.

As noted in the introduction, religion played a large role in the formation of the first academy and in the "rules" governing the behavior of the faculty, students and staff on a day to day basis. It also affected how the school and the surrounding community related to each other. It is clear from the NC Lutheran Synod's resolution of 1852 that one of the primary purposes for establishing a school within the bounds of the Synod was "for the proper training of her youth, and a more general diffusion of knowledge among the people at large."[902] There was also no doubt that the community that sought to have the school located in its midst had an interest beyond business and academics.

RULES & REGULATIONS

The first advertisements for the school, then the Western Carolina Male Academy, stated, "The strictest attention will be paid to the academic and moral development of the Pupils. The government will be mild and parental, yet firm and decided."[903]

After six weeks of matriculation at the academy, students over the age of fifteen were required to sign a pledge of behavior which read:

> "I, _________, declare it to be my serious intention to devote myself, as I have talent, to the acquisition of useful knowledge: and solemnly promise that, so long as I remain a member of this Institution, I will faithfully and diligently attend on all the instructions of this Institution; that I will conscientiously and vigilantly observe all the regulations of the constitution and by-laws of the same; and that I will pay due respect and obedience to my Professors, treat my fellow students as brethren, and all other men with the utmost respect and decorum. I further solemnly promise that I will abstain from the profanation of the Lord's day, from the use of profane language, from drunkenness, * from licentiousness or lewdness; from all kinds of gambling, disorderly behavior, and from disrespectful conduct towards any man."[904]

Students under fifteen years of age were placed under the immediate supervision of one or more of the Instructors during both study and recreation hours.

All students were required to adhere to the following set of rules of behavior.

> "Every student shall be diligent and industrious in all his studies.
>
> Every student shall treat his Teachers with the greatest deference and respect, and all persons with civility, and shall yield a prompt and ready obedience to all the lawful requisitions of the Professors and Directors.
>
> No student shall violate the Sabbath day, by engaging in worldly employments or recreation.
>
> No student shall go visiting or encourage persons from the vicinity to visit students' rooms on the Sabbath day.
>
> No student shall engage in any merriment, music, or noise of any kind during study hours.
>
> No student shall pass through the building faster than a walk.

No student shall injure, deface, or pollute books, benches, desks, chairs, walls, etc., and every student will be held responsible for such damages.

No student shall leave the college ground to visit home, or any other place whatever, or go beyond the limits of an ordinary walk for recreation, without express permission.

No student shall play at cards, dice, or any immoral games.

All students, whether lodging in the Academy or elsewhere, shall be in their respective rooms during study hours; and no student shall be absent from recitation or lecture, without permission from the officiating professor.

Students shall appear cleanly in dress and keep their rooms in becoming order. All sweeping must be done during recreation. No water or any refuse shall be thrown out of the windows. Spittoons must be kept clean. No tobacco chewing allowed in the Chapel and Recitation rooms. Spitting on the floor, anywhere in the building, expressly prohibited. Chewers will take notice of this.

No more than one hour is allotted to students to go to and return from their boarding houses at mealtimes.

No loitering about the stores, shops, or any public place permitted.

No spirituous liquors on any kind shall be kept in the Academy building, or elsewhere, as a common drink. When required for medicinal purposes, it shall be given to the Principal, to be kept in his house.

No firearms, or other deadly weapons of any description whatever, shall be allowed in the building or kept concealed about the person of any student.

The violation of any law of the State shall be regarded as a violation of a law of the Institution.

No student shall use profane language at any time.

No student shall be guilty of excessive expenses in dress, unnecessary book, or sweet meats.

Night suppers, being regarded as injurious to health and a hindrance to study, are not allowed.

> The penalties shall be private and public admonition and reproof, suspension and expulsion.
>
> A record is kept by each Professor of the deportment, scholarship, etc. of each student, and a report of same given to the parents, or guardians, at the close of each session."[905]

Students were required to be in their rooms at 8 o'clock PM in the summer and 7 PM in the winter and it was "the duty of one of the Tutors to visit the rooms at that hour and at all times deemed necessary." No running about from room to room was allowed during study and school hours.

Weekly prayer meeting was held in the Chapel every Friday. Students were required to attend public worship on Sundays wherever directed by the Faculty, parents or guardians. A member of the faculty conducted Bible recitation on Sunday afternoons. Literary Societies held their meetings on Wednesday afternoons.[906]

As the WCMA transitioned to North Carolina College, few of the basic rules changed, but experience dictated certain adjustments. Most of the new rules dealt with student conduct.

The 1860-61 catalogue stated:

> "The Government of the College is parental and free, yet firm and decided. The strictest attention will be paid … to the moral education of the student. Efforts will be made to win the judgment and heart to what is right, and to invigorate character by treating it with proper confidence, thus appealing to the honor and moral sense of the pupil, rather than immediately resorting to stringent measures."[907]

In 1867, upon reopening following the Civil War, a paragraph was added to the earlier statement.

> "The President, under whose immediate supervision the building is placed, with the other officers, exercises a constant guardianship over the whole establishment so that parents at a distance have all the security they may desire for the proper government of their sons."[908]

In 1873, rules were instituted prohibiting "unbecoming language [with]in the hearing of or addressed to persons passing by the College;

ringing of the bell at uncalled for hours, and throwing slop or wastewater from the room windows. Hollowing and whistling at passersby from buildings on campus [was also] forbidden."

The punishment for violating these "new" regulations was a reprimand for the first offense and suspension for the second. Also, students were not allowed to discontinue study (during study hours) without permission from the faculty.[909]

In 1874 the Faculty instituted a system of demerits related to student behavior.

> "Resolved that demerits shall be given for every offense which in the estimation of the faculty may be worthy of it, especially profanity, drunkenness, use of obscene language, absence from class or from college, and bad recitations.
>
> Resolved that any student receiving 50 demerits shall be immediately expelled from the college.
>
> Resolved that all demerits given during the week shall be announced to the students on the morning following the regular meeting of the faculty."[910]

In 1875 the Faculty voted that no student pursuing a regular course with a view toward graduation shall be allowed to preach unless given permission by the faculty.[911]

In 1878 the College catalogue repeated the 1860-61 statement on the Government of the College and added, "Card playing, drinking, swearing, and use of indecent language are strictly forbidden. Daily religious exercises in the Chapel [are conducted]. Service on Lord's day in one of the churches in the village is required."[912]

In 1886 the College Catalogue mandated that "Disorder, confusion, and loafing in others' rooms during study hours will not be tolerated. The faculty and students cooperate in rendering the building quiet and orderly. Hours for study and recitation begin at 6 AM ending at 12 Mid; at 2 PM ending at 5 PM; at 8 PM ending at 10 PM."

The Catalogue also contained an updated list of Rules & Regulations:

> "The hours of study, recitation, and recreation will be indicated by the ringing of the bell, according to appointment from time to time by the faculty.

1. The students occupying rooms in the College building must have the same set in order before 7 o'clock each morning.

2. The use of tobacco and congregating in rooms during school or study hours, and the making of unnecessary noise at any time in the College building is strictly forbidden. The occupants of rooms will be held responsible for the order therein.

3. Playing at cards or dice, night suppers, the use of obscene or profane language will not be tolerated.

4. No student shall use or have in his possession intoxicating liquor, firearms, or other deadly weapon, under penalty of expulsion.

5. Students must not leave the College building during school or study hour, nor at any time are they allowed to go beyond the corporate limits without permission of the President.

6. Students are required to have at least sixteen recitations per week unless otherwise directed by the Faculty.

7. Students whose average grade shall fall below 7 for three consecutive months, and students having five unexcused absences against them during that time will be dismissed.

8. Cleanliness of dress and person and gentlemanly behavior at all places and under any circumstances are required of all students so long as they relate to the College.

9. Students are not allowed to visit other's rooms during school or study hours, and students residing in the town are not allowed to visit the College grounds or building on Saturday's and Sundays except by permission of the President.

10. Students must not at any time receive visitors not connected with the College, except by permission of the President.

> 11. Improper treatment of fellow students, damage to property, and disrespect towards strangers will not be tolerated.
>
> 12. The bell will be rung at 10 p. m. at which time students are expected to retire, otherwise no disturbing noise of any kind must be made in the building.
>
> 13. Students are reminded of their matriculation obligation, and as honorable persons are expected to fulfill the same.
>
> 14. Omitted
>
> 15. The penalties for violating any of the rules, both written, and those communicated orally, are penal marks, suspension, dismission or expulsion, at the discretion of the Faculty. Provided, that forty penal marks, during a term of twenty weeks, shall subject the student receiving them to dismission or expulsion."[913]

By 1901 the pledge signed by students entering the College had been revised to read:

> "We whose names appear are hereunto annexed do solemnly promise on our truth and honor to observe all the rules & regulations of Mt. Pleasant Collegiate Institute pertaining to the acquisition of knowledge, to public and private conduct, to subordination and respect due our professors, to proper deportment toward our fellow students to the cultivation of virtuous principles and to the abstinence from all vicious habits, so long as we remain connected as students with this institution."[914]

At the opening of Mt. Pleasant Collegiate Institute in 1903, student behavior appears to have been a significant issue. In May 1905 Co-Principal McAllister prefaced his report to the Board of Trustees with a statement about behavior.

> "Hazing and Rowdyism are not practiced [at the school] and many of the objectionable features incident to student life have been banished. A sense of honor is consequently fostered which proves invaluable in the proper regulation of the school."[915]

There is no doubt that one of the major reasons that McAllister decided to adopt a "military style system" in 1908, was to deal more effectively with behavior and discipline. It is not known when the first formal "military regulations" were put into place at the Institute. The earliest document located appears to have been printed in 1909 in a small pamphlet entitled "Regulations of Mount Pleasant Collegiate Institute."[916]

While there is no date on the pamphlet, the regulations were authorized by the now sole Principal, Colonel McAllister, and the Commandant of Cadets, Capt. W. B. Porcher. Porcher held his position for only one academic year (1909-1910), but was directly responsible for formulating the rules to be followed by cadets. These regulations, written in military terms, described such areas as arrests, confinement and tours, delinquencies, formations, furlough and leave, guard, officer of day, orderly, inspection, inter-police of barracks, liberty, military courtesy, drill, rifles, uniform, visiting, and telephone use.[917]

In 1914 the rules were expanded and further codified into what became known as "The Blue Book." This document was updated in 1927 and 1930, and generally remained the final word on the military system and behavior at the Institute. [See Appendix 8 & 11]

The Institute was never reluctant to express its view toward discipline. Beginning in 1916, the catalogue contained a full-page declaration with artwork that clarified the school's attitude toward the type of students it encouraged. Under the heading, "Some young men not desired," the catalogue read:

> "The Collegiate Institute is giving its time and its life to the endowment of manhood, and herein it seeks its chief reward. There are some habits which, if long indulged in, unfit young men for education or life. Cigarette smoking stupefies the brain, unsettles the nerves, lessens the energy, and lowers the ambition, hence militates against those ennobling principles for which Christian education stands. The Collegiate Institute feels that it is not its mission to waste time on young men who persist in habits that defeat mental discipline and development. Therefore, the use of cigarettes and intoxicants will not be tolerated. This is no compromise on this point. A student who indulges

> in these things thereby severs his connection with the Institute. Young men who come to college to 'have a good time' are not wanted at the Institute. We seek only those whom we can benefit."

Under the heading, "Not a Reformatory," the catalogue continued:

> "Because the Institute insists upon and maintains sound discipline it is not to be considered a reformatory. Boys who have done no good in the home school and who are unmanageable at home are not wanted here. Parents of such boys will spare us from an embarrassing duty, the son from a lasting stigma, and themselves regret by keeping them away from the Institute."[918]

In 1930, Colonel McAllister found it necessary to send a letter to the parents of incoming students to clarify the school rules.

> "To accomplish the best results in training youth, you will agree that cooperation of patrons and school authorities is highly essential. I am sure you want to give the cooperation necessary. To this end, I want to mention some particulars in which it is important that you work in harmony with the policies of the school.
>
> First – Insist that your son abide by the regulations of the school, as he promised on his truth and honor to do when he matriculated.
>
> Second – Do not ask for him to have leave away from the school or consent for him to have leave over week-ends oftener than once in four or six weeks; and not that often, of course, if he lives at a great distance from the Institute. Experience abundantly proves that the fewer trips a student makes away from the school, the better progress he makes in school.
>
> Third – When the son has a leave to go home, see to it that he does not overstay his leave. This is essential to the maintenance of our system which is administered in the interest of the cadets and the school. Not infrequently parents think that overstaying a half day or a day does not make so much difference. It does. Besides time lost from

classes, the effect of such practices mars the morale of the school management.

Fourth – Impress upon the son the seriousness of running away from school without permission either alone or in the company of any number of other cadets. On the 11th of November a large number of students petitioned for a holiday. Inasmuch as Thanksgiving comes in November and we give a holiday then, and since we have missed some classes this fall on account of football, I did not think it best to grant a holiday on the 11th. A goodly number ran off. Several times on April 1st the cadet corps has taken French leave. This sort of thing has to stop. I made it very clear to the entire school, following the incident on Nov. 11th, that if at any time in the future cadets ran off from the school, they had just as well go on home, for they would thereby cut themselves off from the school. I want to make it very clear to you that such will be the result. Therefore, if you do not want your son to meet this fate, warn him against running off from the school under any circumstances. Your son was not one of these who ran off Nov. 11th.

Fifth – Encourage your son to exhibit a friendly attitude. I cannot stress this point too much. Teachers are human beings. It is altogether to the interest of the student to manifest a friendly attitude. He will accomplish vastly more by so doing. The right or wrong attitude of the student often means the difference between contented school life and splendid progress on the one hand, or dissatisfaction and failure in his studies on the other.

Sixth – If at any time anything goes wrong with your son in school, if he writes a blue or critical letter home, do not hastily conclude that he has been wrongfully treated. He may be homesick, and I have known young persons suffering from temporary homesickness to do the greatest violence to the truth. On account of violation of rules, he may have received considerable punishment and concluded that it was too severe. Remember always that there are two sides to every question and please believe that the school authorities are exercising their best efforts and best judgment in the all-important business of training and developing the your sons under their care.

Seventh – Missing Classes. Too many classes are missed by some cadets on the ground[s] of 'sickness.' Very many students fail to put the proper emphasis on the importance of not missing classes. We are finding it necessary to lay down stricter regulations regarding class attendance. Unexcused absences mean zero grades on these recitations. An outside limit is going to be fixed to the number of recitations a cadet may miss for whatever reason and still pass that subject. So, if you are concerned about your son passing his work, impress upon him the necessity of meeting classes. The Report we send you each Term shows the number of classes missed, both the excused absences and the unexcused absences.

Eighth – Wearing Uniforms. The Catalog states that uniforms will be worn exclusively throughout the school year, including Commencement. This is of more importance that patrons might suspect. It identifies a cadet as a student of the Institute. It is less expensive for the patron. We expect cooperation of parents and guardians in this. Sometimes civilian clothes are sent from home to the cadet at Christmas, Easter or Commencement. This is not cooperating with the school, and we ask you not to do it.

Ninth – Sending eatables to students. Excepting fruits, it is best that you do not send the son boxes of "eats." We furnish good, wholesome food and plenty of it. Boxes from home all too often mean overeating, temporary sickness and missing classes. We ask you not to send them.

Tenth – Give us your cooperation, please, in reasonably prompt attention to bills rendered. It is absolutely necessary that the school collect its bills in order that it may provide good, wholesome food in liberal quantity, furnish comfortable quarters, and support competent, faithful teachers. You contribute more than you might think to your son's success in school by meeting on time your financial obligations to the school.

I want to ask you to file this letter for reference. It will help if you will read it at least once every term.

Thanking you for your cooperation, I am. Yours Sincerely, G. F. McAllister, Principal"[919]

INCIDENTS AND DISCIPLINE

If rules are made to be broken, those of the College and Institute were no exception. The following section describes some related "incidents" of transgression.

One of the earliest documented breaches occurred at the Western Carolina Male Academy in January of 1856. The incident involved a teacher rather than a student. Instructor and Board Member Rev. John D. Scheck,was disciplined by the Board of Directors for conduct involving unauthorized "visiting [of] the rooms of some of the students during study hours."

The specific charges read:

"Rev. J. D. Scheck ... has been in the habit at sundry times and without permission from the Professor of visiting the rooms of some of the students of this institution during study hours. Therefore – 1. Resolved that the conduct of Rev. J. D. Scheck in this particular is highly culpable and reprehensible. 2. Because his conduct is a direct violation of the rules of the school. 3. Because due courtesy and respect for the Professor as well as due regard for the interests of the School require that permission from the Professor be first obtained by any person and especially a member of this Board wishing to call upon any student in his room during study hours. 1. In the interest of the maintenance of sound discipline and wholesome government in the School – 2. Therefore, resolved that Rev. J. D. Scheck ought to be and hereby is censured and reprimanded by this Board for his conduct in the matter referred to. 3. Resolved that taking his general course in relation to this institution as the standard by which to form an opinion – Rev. J. D. Scheck gives room to doubt the sincerity of his friendship for the institution over the interests of which he as a member of this Board is called to preside – and therefore room to doubt his fidelity to the obligations assumed in the formula of induction to office as prescribe by the constitution."[920]

As a result of the disciplinary action, Scheck resigned from the Board of Directors and apparently left the Academy since the Board resolved to seek a new assistant professor in March of 1856.[921]

In 1856, the Principal reported "difficulties between faculty and students due to excessive absences where students refused to provide explanations." Those who refused were suspended.[922]

Reverend Bittle, President of two-year-old NC College, reported in 1861 that:

> "In regard to general deportment and observance of rules, I am happy to say that the number of whom I cannot testify favorably is comparatively small. At the beginning of the half-session, I found some trouble, and the Faculty were under the necessity of expelling two [students] and privately discharging three others who seemed disposed to be refractory…, [however] since the 1st of January, matters seem to have glided along more smoothly. There seems to be an almost unanimous satisfaction on the part of students now present and favorable representations made by them to their friends abroad."[923]

Curiously, when Christopher Melchor, President of the Board of Trustees, paraphrased Rev. Bittle's remarks to the Synod, he omitted the information about the expulsions and stated that "The President of the Board of Trustees expresses himself highly pleased with the Professors connected with our College, and that harmony and good feeling subsist between them and the students committed to their care."[924]

College faculty minutes from the mid-1870's record an eventful period of disciplinary actions. It is not clear if these issues were unique to the time period or if they were typical of ongoing behaviors. These documents are the only existing record of faculty meetings. Similar incidents are not recorded in Board of Trustee minutes or other documents.

In March 1873, "Mr. Lowery, was cited to appear before Faculty to account for the throwing of water from his room. Having made a satisfactory explanation, he was exonerated." (Lowery had been a student for only two months.)[925]

In February 1875, R. E. Blakeney, James A. Comer, E. L. Lybrand, Benjamin F. Welsh, and Henry D. Petrea were called to account for "singing on the roof of the college, etc." The parties claimed that it was "thoughtlessness and not intended as insult or defiance to the law." Their punishment was to have their names called at morning exercises and other students were warned to not repeat the action.[926]

In March 1876, William Howie received forty demerits and was suspended for swearing and cursing at Prof. Crouse.[927] In April of the same year, Solomon A. Henkel was charged with using objectionable words.[928]

In September 1875, Benjamin Welsh was placed on probation for having a knife in his hand during an argument.[929] Welsh appeared before the Faculty again in October when he was accused of "idleness" and the "passing of words" between him and another student, D. B. Tucker.[930] A year later, Welsh was expelled for "repeated violations and having a pistol on campus and firing it."[931]

Incidents of "offensive or threating language" eventually resulted in a Faculty resolution prohibiting "writing, making or securing a challenge implicated in a duel".[932]

Despite rules prohibiting the possession of "deadly weapons" on campus, the College experienced a series of incidents involving firearms and knives.

In March 1874, students John Burkhead and John Stevens engaged in a fight in which Burkhead received two knife wounds. Following a "trial", the faculty resolved to make the penalty as severe as possible short of expulsion. Both students received thirty demerits but were allowed to remain in school provided they "comply strictly with regulations during the remainder of the session by gentlemanly deportment, regular attendance [in class], diligent application of study and ready compliance with the wishes of the faculty." If either student failed in the performance of these rules they would be suspended indefinitely.[933]

The faculty also resolved that demerits would be given for every offense which, "in the estimation of the faculty may be worthy of it, especially profanity, drunkenness, use of obscene language, absence from class or from college, and bad recitations." Lastly, they resolved that any student receiving fifty demerits would be suspended from attendance of the school.[934]

One of the most troublesome problems on and near the College campus involved "intoxicating liquors."

The College charter forbade the sale of liquor within a three-mile radius of the campus. This was, of course, an unrealistic prohibition. Notably, the Lentz Hotel in Mt. Pleasant, a half-mile from the school and a center of community social activity, served liquor routinely. As early as 1858, Principal Gerhardt reported "problems with alcohol" on the campus[935] and there was an incident (described in Part II) involving "selling liquor and allowing men to become intoxicated" at the local Hotel. The incident led to the resignation of an instructor and further resolutions by the faculty.

Faculty minutes from the 1870's record several instances of "alcohol violations." Student W. T. Timmons was charged with bringing liquor onto campus. He admitted the offense and agreed that he had done so several times but claimed that he did not know it was a violation of the regulations. He was given ten demerits.[936]

In 1874, Timmons, Julius Crowell, J. D. Horne, and Samuel P. Barrett were charged with intoxication and having left campus without permission. Timmons, Horne and Barrett were suspended indefinitely and Crowell's case was deferred until he returned from a leave of absence. Upon his return he was given five demerits (he had not left campus without permission.)[937]

In 1876 the Board of Trustees resolved that the faculty disallow students to board at hotels or with private families where intoxicating liquors were habitually used. The Board specified that "the sale of Brandy Peaches does not conform with the College spirit" and instructed the

President of the College to prosecute sellers of wines and liquors within the corporate limits of the College.[938]

In 1901 the Board of Trustees appealed to the Mt. Pleasant Town Board to address the issue of liquor sales near the College. The Mayor of Mt. Pleasant, A. W. Moose, replied:

> "… now all that is necessary to have the above laws enforced is proof that someone sold, gave away, or conveyed whiskey or wine to some person or persons. Inasmuch as there is no officer who is paid to look after violators, and for the good of the Town, Schools and Mills, it becomes the duty of each citizen to report to an officer all violations that he has personal knowledge of or when he knows of one or more persons as eye witnesses to a violation of any of the above laws. Then it becomes that officer's duty to enforce the law"[939]

Principal G. F. McAllister's papers list numerous disciplinary actions concerning liquor on and around the campus. Some of the incidents involving alcohol resulted in responses from students.

In 1915, two Seniors, J. C. Friemuth and G. E. Worsley, were charged with alcohol violations and expelled. In defense of their classmates, several Seniors filed a petition with Principal McAllister and the Faculty.

> "Whereas, the regulations regarding the use of intoxicants in the Collegiate Institute has been violated by Messrs. J. C. Freimuth and G. E. Worsley, and, Whereas, they have by thus indulging severed themselves from the institution and its privileges as students, and, Whereas, there are the following extenuating circumstances which affect the case: First, that the said Freimuth is nearing the completion of his work in this institution; second, that prayerful intercession has been made in his behalf by his parents; third, that he is physically afflicted; fourth, that the said Worsley's previous record has been on the whole exemplary; fifth, that he was prevailed upon to indulge in this practice by his companions; sixth, that both are thoroughly penitent and have suffered the full punishment of conscience for their misconduct in view of

the consequent tragedy; Therefore, we the undersigned, with full knowledge of the gravity of the situation hereby petition the faculty to reinstate the said Freimuth and Worsley, pledging ourselves on our truth and sacred honor so to act that the school shall never have occasion so as long as we are students to enforce the violated regulation.
W. W. Johnson, Pres. Senior Class
Jay L. Cress, Earl A. Bodie, Oscar F. Blackwelder,
Peter J. Coon, Ralph M. Bodie, Earl A. Bodie,
E. T. W. Cronk"[940]

It is not known if this petition led to any change the expulsion of the offending students.

An even more interesting example of "student involvement" occurred in 1926- '27. In December 1926, several MPCI students were apparently charged with a violation of school rules by purchasing a half-gallon of liquor from two Mt. Pleasant citizens. One of the students was Jesse Finna, a Cuban national and President of the Senior Class. A series of letters and statements contained in the McAllister Papers documents the incident.

"We, the undersigned, being questioned on our truth and honor, state to the Faculty of the Collegiate Institute that on the morning of Dec 18th, 1926, between 1:30 and 2 o'clock, we purchased a half gallon of liquor contained in a glass jar from Horace Barringer and Jack Faggart. Horace Barringer brought the liquor from a Ford Roadster which he left standing by the curbing at the North East Corner of the public square in Mt. Pleasant, and delivered it, the liquor, into the hands of Jesse Finna. Then said Barringer and Jack Faggart got into the Ford Roadster and drove off East toward Albemarle.

There were eight of us students present when this transaction took place, J. H. Bennett, Jesse Finna, C. R. Huffman, C. E. Lytle, E. L. Miller, S. E. Parker, R. E. Sawyer, and R. M. Wilson. Messers. Finna, Huffman, Lytle, Parker, Sawyer, and Wilson each paid a dollar into the hands of said Horace Barringer, making $6.00 for one half gallon of liquor. Signed, Jesse Finna &. M. Wilson."[941]

A petition from members of the Senior Class accompanied the statement.

> "As regards the "shipping" case of Cadet Jesse Finna, the Senior Class of MPCI Class of 1927 goes on record as being resolved that: Whereas Cadet Finna is of different race, different environment, from the faculty and students and whereas the thing he is guilty of is not considered wrong where he comes from, and Whereas he has benefited the school in many ways, and Whereas he has been guilty of this offense but this one time, and Whereas he is our Class President and active in school activities and is really a conscientious boy, Be it resolved by the Senior Class requests that Cadet Finna be given a second chance, and that he be put on the campus indefinitely and be put on strict probation. Signed Senior Class. H. A. McCullough, C. R. Little, J. D. Suther, H. L. Coughman, J. H. Taylor, B. Davis, Fred A. Moser, W. J. Prevo."[942]

Again, the petition's effect on the disciplinary action is unknown.

It appears that at least one student involved in this incident was not expelled (yet), but he continued to have some disciplinary problems. In March 1928, R. M. Wilson was found guilty of "having cigarettes, a whiskey bottle, knucks and other unallowable [sic] articles in his room, with the evidence pointing to his use of these things." Wilson also had two footballs belonging to the Institute in his room. For these offenses, Wilson was expelled by unanimous vote of the faculty and was ordered to leave campus with his belongings by midnight.[943]

In addition to the incidents involving weapons and alcohol, numerous "lesser" violations, including smoking, were noted in school records. Cadet Wayne Stiles received twenty-five demerits and walked twenty-five tours for smoking cigarettes. Cadet Stiles was disciplined a second time for overstaying leave thirteen hours and smoking cigarettes. He and Cadet Frank Jarret, who was also guilty of smoking cigarettes, were required to walk two tours per day until released by the Faculty. Any further offenses were to result in automatic dismissal.

Cadet Van Mechelin received twenty-five demerits and walked

twenty-five tours for smoking. His tours would be walked during vacant periods until the punishment was served.

Cadet J. C. Robbins received the same punishment as Van Mechelin for the same offense.

Cadet W. D. Dubois received fifty demerits and fifty tours for his second offense of smoking cigarettes.

Cadet A. E. Wescott received fifty demerits and fifty tours for his second offense of smoking and was placed on probation.

Another recurrent violation was the unauthorized absence from campus. This offense was a very common violation among Cadets and often resulted in harsh discipline.

Cadet Dickerson was given 20 demerits and required to walk fifteen tours for leaving campus without permission.

Cadets Alexander, Lohr & Hall each received twenty demerits and were confined to campus indefinitely for leaving campus.

Cadet Berry was confined to campus for going downtown without permission.

Cadet J. A. Fowler, Jr. was confined to campus and required to walk two tours for overstaying leave four hours, loitering around filling station within a half mile of town for one and a half hours, and making unnecessary remarks to correcting officer.

Cadet Gibbons was disciplined for going to a place other than that specified in his application and overstaying his leave two hours. He was confined to the campus required to walk two tours on Saturdays while confined.

In one of the only references to corporal punishment, Cadet F. B. Meyer received "ten licks," was confined to campus, and required to walk two tours on Saturdays for running away from the Institute for a week.

Cadet W. M. Brazelton was confined to campus and required to walk three tours on Saturdays for going to Concord in a different way than that specified and making a false statement about it.

Cadet E. N. Kjellsvig was required to walk two tours until released by the Faculty for cooking in his room and going off campus to Concord after an application for leave was disapproved.

Cadet Betancourt was expelled for defiance of faculty member and running away from school.

Cadet R. E. Hinson was "dishonorably discharged" for leaving school while under punishment.

Cadet T. S. Irwin was dismissed for "desertion."

Cadets M. D. Love and A. B. Betancourt were expelled for defiance of a faculty member and for running away from school.

Cadet Paul Goodnight was expelled for repeatedly running away from school without permission.[944]

Other less serious offenses included:

Cadets M. S. Berry and O. L. Plaster were confined to campus for a week for misconduct in Church.

Cadets Robert Harkey and Walter Yount were confined to campus and given fifteen demerits each for mis- treating a fellow cadet. Cadet A. Stork was confined to campus and given five demerits for complicity in said mistreatment.

Cadet R. G. Tate was confined to campus, given thirty demerits and placed on probation for thirty days for disorderly conduct on the streets.[945]

A rule violation that appears to have been quite troubling to Principal McAllister was addressed in a "Faculty Order" issued on May 3rd, 1930.

> "A situation has developed which it is necessary for the faculty to take cognizance of in order to safeguard students and protect the honor and good name of the Collegiate Institute. Girls and women have been visiting the campus in daytime and at night unaccompanied by male attendants. They have attracted cadets from their rooms during study hours and have carried cadets to ride beyond the corporate limits of the town, when said cadets did not want to leave.
>
> Regardless of who these girls or women are, this is a practice that cannot be reconciled with the proprieties and a well-ordered school. The law offers protection against such invasion of the campus of a chartered institution and holds it to be trespass. Therefore, those who persist in such practice lay themselves liable to arrest for trespass. Nor is the use of a street or highway adjoining our campus

> permissible for the purpose of attracting or getting with students at unauthorized hours. Now, let it be understood that this order is not directed against the mothers, sisters or legitimate lady callers who may, rightfully visit the Institute for the purpose of seeing and talking with cadets. But these visits are expected to be made and end before the hour for retreat. In the event that circumstances render it impracticable for mothers, sisters or legitimate lady visitors to conclude their visits before retreat, then in each and every instance it will be expected that the cadet or cadets whom these visitors call to see will communicate the names, relationships and addresses of such visitors to the Commandant, Principal or other member of the faculty. Let it be understood further that this order is issued in the interest of the safety of cadets and the good name and honor of the Collegiate Institute. The Faculty means to protect its students and the good name and honor of the Collegiate Institute. For the sake of the reputation of all concerned, the Faculty bespeaks the cooperation of students in carrying out of this Order. If those who have no legitimate business on the campus of the Collegiate Institute and disregard the hours for legitimate visits and thus show that they are not intending to cooperate with the Faculty in upholding the proprieties and maintaining the good order will subject themselves to the Law against trespassers."[946]

FACILITIES, TUITION, ROOM & BOARD

Records provide significant information regarding the cost of attending NC College and MPCI. There is less detail describing the living quarters, room furnishings and elements involved in daily campus life.

From the early days of the Academy, students were housed both on campus and in the community. On-campus housing was basic with no running water in the dorm. Students were charged a "fuel fee", but It is not known if each room had a wood stove or if there was some type of "central" heating. Lighting was by oil lamps or candles. Meals were provided off campus as was laundry service. Room furniture could be furnished by the student or rented. Later, meals were provided on campus, rooms were furnished, and plumbing, electricity and steam heating were added.

The charge for room rent was determined by location, either on-campus or off-campus. Room rent on-campus was very inexpensive, while off-campus rates were determined by the community. Board (meals) cost varied greatly over the course time depending upon location, availability and housing status. Tuition and fees were kept relatively low, often the point of non-sustainability. These costs were typically modified based on the national economic situation, or to encourage enrollment, satisfy a Synod priority, afford higher faculty salaries, or simply to provide an income stream.

In 1855-1856, tuition at the Western Carolina Academy was based on the entry level of each student. The Preparatory Department provided the "Common English Branches" and included Reading, Writing, Orthography, Arithmetic and Geography at a cost of $12 for the winter session and $8 for the summer session. If the student chose the courses of English Grammar, History of North Carolina, History of the United States, and Latin & Greek Grammar, the cost rose to $14 and $10 respectively.

The Academic Department provided the above courses plus Mathematics, Natural Sciences and Classics. The cost of these additional courses raised tuition to $17 for the winter session and $13 for the summer session. Instruction in German, French or Hebrew added further additional fees.[947]

In 1857 expenses were described as about $67 for the six-month winter session. Tuition was $14 and room rent on campus was $2. Lights (candles or oil lamps) were provided at about $2 per session. The school provided no dining or laundry facilities on site. Students "boarded" with local families who furnished meals and laundry services for $8 per session. The cost of the Summer session of four months was $44, with tuition of only $10 and room rent, and lights reduced to $1. Students could reside in a private home or boarding house "in the country" for $60 p/mth. Students living "off campus" paid a session tax of $1 for the winter and 50¢ for summer.[948]

Tuition and room rent were due in advance and no deduction could be made for absence except in case of protracted illness.

Students with a scholarship (usually relatives of original donors) received "reduced" tuition of $18 per year (two sessions) upon presentation of a certificate from the owner of the scholarship.[949]

The early Administration building contained "a number of other rooms, sufficient to accommodate about fifty students. The original "rooms" had no closets and the central "hallway" was wider than the current layout.[950]

During the summer of 1860, the Board of Trustees recommended that to accommodate more students "the walls of the little rooms should be removed" so that four students could occupy the space. It was also recommended that "in the event it is necessary to house students in the Professor's house," each student in a four-person room would pay a fee of $6.25 and those in two person rooms, $12.50.[951]

According to an early school catalogue, off–campus housing included several boarding houses which "all convenient and have generally given entire satisfaction. All things considered; this institution is one of the cheapest in the state."[952]

In 1859, the first year of NC College, the total cost of a ten month (42-week session) was between $115 and $136 (there was no explanation for the range in cost). Tuition was $32 for College Classes. On campus room rent and fees ranged from $5 to $6.25, and the cost for washing and meals (provided off campus), fuel, lights, etc. was $15. Room furniture was not included in the rent. Minors under 14 years of age could be boarded with private families, as recommended by the Faculty. These rates remained constant during the two years prior to the school closure due to the Civil War.[953]

With the reopening of the College in 1866, expenses increased to $167 for 40 weeks. In 1867-'68, tuition for the College Department was $40 and $30 for the Preparatory Department. These Departments, as described in Part II, were basically equivalent to College, High School, and Junior High School. On campus room rent was $5 per month. Board (meals provided off campus) was listed at $105 for forty-two weeks. The cost of washing, fuel, lights, etc., increased to $20. Room Furniture was not included in the above estimate.[954]

When the school reopened after the war, The Board of Trustees instituted a new provision stating that "indigent young men maimed in the late war and incapacitated for severe physical exertion will be charged but one-half of the above rates of tuition."[955]

Between 1870 and 1885 the cost of attending the College Department changed only slightly. In 1870, tuition was $40 for each of two twenty-week terms. Board and room rent totaled $97. Washing, fuel, lights cost $20 per year.[956]

In 1871 the cost of board (meals) ranged from $75-$90, but no explanation was given for the change. Other costs, including room rent, remained the same. In 1871 the catalogue stated that sons of ministers and indigent/disabled Civil War veterans would be charged only half tuition ($20). A further provision declared that "indigent young men with the ministry in view" would be given free tuition provided they signed a promissory note that the money would be repaid if they did not, in fact, become ministers.[957]

In 1872 the fee schedule described in the catalogue was divided into two Departments, reflecting the school's organization since 1867. The Preparatory Department was further divided into Academic and Primary Division. Board costs for each section was $80-$100 for two twenty-week terms. Room rent was $12, and washing, lights and fuel still cost $20. Tuition in the College Department was $50; $25 to $40 in the Academic Division, and ranged from $15 to $25 in the Primary Division. The variance in Tuition in the Preparatory Divisions was dependent upon what foreign language classes were taken.[958]

The 1871-'72 Catalogue is the first to mention a "mess club" as a way for students to reduce boarding costs, but evidently meals were still not provided on campus. This announcement was repeated in subsequent catalogues. Beginning in 1874, an additional statement indicated that the Board of Trustees was considering building a dining facility. This announcement was repeated through 1879.

Building a dining facility was not mentioned in 1880-'81 but in 1884, the half-session catalogue stated that "board convenient to the College can be had in private homes in the village at any time." Simultaneously, the catalogue said that "students can materially reduce the expense by boarding in the College Boarding house, the cost of board during the present term has been less than $5." There was no information in the catalogue or elsewhere regarding when or where the "College boarding house" was built.[959]

The 1885 Catalogue stated further that "Board may be procured at private houses convenient to the College from $6.50 to $8.00 per month," and repeated the announcement of the College boarding house.[960]

In 1889 the catalogue again changed the status of "board," stating that "board may be procured at private houses convenient to the College for $6 to $8 per month. Boarding and lodging, $10, Boarding in a club, if the students desire to form a club – a room and cooking utensils are at hand."[961]

The 1890 catalogue contained the following – "there is an excellent boarding club under the direction of the faculty and conducted by a leading and responsible citizen of Mt. Pleasant, of which good substantial board can be had at $5 per month."[962]

After 1891, the options of a campus boarding club or the private boarding club were no longer mentioned in the college catalogue, but the 1900-'01 Catalogue contained a photograph of students in the dining hall which is clearly located in one of the two Literary Society buildings.[963]

In 1885-'86, the College provided furnished rooms for an extra charge. The fee schedule was divided into sub-categories by class and term. The College year consisted of two terms of twenty weeks each. Tuition (per term) for the 1st year of the Academic Class was $10; 2nd year - $15; 3rd year - $20. Sub-Freshman and College Department tuition for one term was $20. The rental cost per term of an unfurnished room was $3.75 and a furnished room $5.75. Contingent and Library fees were $1.25 per term. Washing, fuel and lights were $10 per term, and Boarding fees were between $25 - $40 per term.

Students were required to room in the College buildings unless all the rooms were occupied, and there was no remission of room rent except to students whose parents resided in the village (Mt. Pleasant). The furnished rooms were provided by different Lutheran congregations within the state.[964]

In 1889-'90 the College reduced the academic year from forty weeks to thirty-nine weeks, divided into three terms of fifteen weeks, twelve weeks and twelve weeks. Yearly cost, however, remained the same as the forty-week session, but it was charged on a per term basis. Below is the fee schedule as presented in the College Catalogue.

Tuition for 1st Year Academics

1st Term - $7.50	2nd Term - $6.25	3rd Term - $6.25

Tuition for 2nd Year Academics

1st Term - $12.00	2nd Term - $9.00	3rd Term - $9.00

Tuition for Sub-Freshman Year

1st Term - $15.50	2nd Term - $12.25	3rd Term - $12.25

Tuition for College Department

1st Term - $15.50	2nd Term - $12.25	3rd Term - $12.25

Rent for unfurnished room

1st Term - $2.80	2nd Term - $2.30	3rd Term - $2.30

Rent for a furnished room

1st Term - $4.00	2nd Term - $3.00	3rd Term - $3.00

Contingent & Library Fees

1st Term - $1.00	2nd Term - $.75	3rd Term - $.75

Washing, fuel, and lights (appx)

1st Term - $8.00	2nd Term - $6.00	3rd Term - $6.00

Board (meals)

1st Term - $22 to $27	2nd Term - $18 to $23	3rd Term - $18 to $23

The total costs of three terms based on the costs outlined ranged from $105.90 to $145.50.[965]

In 1890-'91 the academic year still consisted of three terms but the reduction of the first term to fourteen weeks decreased the total year to thirty-eight weeks. Tuition for the year remained unchanged. Room rent for a furnished room remained the same, but the cost of an unfurnished room increased by 10¢. Boarding costs reflected the reduction of the length of the first term. Board for the 1st term now ranged from $17.50 to $27; 2nd term - $15 to $24, and 3rd term $15 to $24. Total costs were advertised as ranging from $92.65 to $147.50.

The College catalogue listed the items included in a "furnished room." These included a bedstead, a stove, two chairs, a table, a washstand, and a bookcase. The source is not clear if each resident received two chairs, a table, a washstand and a bookcase, but it is assumed that each student did have his own bed, and there was only one stove per room.[966]

During the 1890's student expenses varied based on the length of the terms. In 1894-'95 there was a sharp decrease in tuition and board. The "reduced" fees held for three years and rose again in 1897-'98.[967]

The last catalogue published by NC College included a list of "Wants and Needs". Among these were a larger chapel, a well-equipped gymnasium, recitation (class) rooms apart from the dormitory, a more adequate library and a reading room away from the noise of the dormitory.[968]

As NC College transitioned into the Mt. Pleasant College Institute in 1903, daily activities of the school continued much as before. The Institute retained the three-term academic year with thirty-seven weeks of classes. Tuition for the 1903-'04 session was $7.50 per term for the Primary Department with a 50¢ discount if one attended all three terms. Academic Department tuition was $10.50 per term or $30 for three terms. The Collegiate Department, which was a post high-school or "prep" school department, cost $15 per term or $42 for the entire year. No extra fees were charged. Boarding cost for the year for students living on the campus was $64 a year, included washing, fuel, and lights, but still involved taking meals in private homes. Furniture in the rooms was an extra charge of 50¢ per month.[969]

In 1904-'05 MPCI modified its class organization to one like the NC College model which contained three sections in its Primary (renamed Preparatory) Department. First year Preps paid $6 per term or $16 for the entire session. Second year Preps paid $7.50 per term, $20 per session. Third year Preps were charged $9 per term, $24 per session. Members of the Academic Department paid $10 per term, $28 per session. Collegiates paid $14 per term, $38 per session. A ten percent discount was applied to tuition if two or more students came from the same family. Sons of ministers were charged one-half tuition. Washing, fuel and lights were estimated at $6 per month and room rent on campus was 50¢, with an additional 50¢ per month for a bed, table, chair and washstand. Books were furnished at cost. The Institute pamphlet stated that "no annoying fees are charged at this institution. Incidental and other fees in many schools raise the expenses far above parents' expectations."[970]

In 1905-'06, the Institute reorganized the Preparatory and Academic Departments. The Preparatory Department had three groups of students - Sub-Freshmen, Intermediates and Juniors. Sub-Freshmen (1st Year) paid $8.00 per term, Intermediate (2nd Year) students paid $9.00 per term, and Juniors (3rd Year) paid $10.00 per term.

The "Collegiate" Department, which now consisted of Freshman and Sophomore classes, each cost $13.50 per term. There was also a Society and Library fee of 50¢ per term. Laundry, fuel and lights were $10 per session for a two-person room. Room rent rates were not stated in the catalogue, but an additional 60¢ per month was charged for a room furnished with a bed, table, chair and washstand. Books were furnished at cost. A summary of expenses stated that the total cost of the Preparatory Department was between $95 and $105 per session and the cost of the Collegiate Department ranged between $110 and $125 per session."[971]

All boarding students were required to live in the dormitory on the 2nd and 3rd floors of the Administration building. According to the school catalogue, there were accommodations for seventy-five students in the dormitory.[972]

Sometime between 1904 and 1909, a portion of the lower floor of the Philalaethian/Gerhardt Debating Hall was converted into a dining area. It is not known if the meals were prepared on campus or were brought in by private individuals. Meals were still available in private homes.

With the beginning of the 1908-'09 school year, the Collegiate Institute instituted its "military system" for incoming students. In addition to the usual school expenses, the cost of uniforms and other related items was added to the students' accounts.

The estimated costs of a session (three terms) for the Collegiate Department was between $130-$140 and $115-$125 for the Preparatory Department, not including uniforms. Uniforms consisted of a fatigue uniform (blouse, trousers, cap, and gloves) and a dress uniform, at a cost of $16.00.[973]

During the summer of 1909, the Pi Sigma Phi/Ludwig Literary Society Hall burned. To accommodate the lost space, a new building was constructed on the west side of the campus and the dining hall was moved from Gerhardt hall to this building in 1911.

Tuition to attend the Institute in 1910-1911 was $13.50 per term (three terms) for Sophomores and Freshmen, $12.00 per term for Sub-freshman (designated Senior in the Catalogue), $10.00 per term for Intermediates, and $9.00 per term for Juniors. In addition to tuition, students paid $1.00 per month room rent. Collegiate students paid $1.00 per month Society, Library and Reading Room fees. Preparatory students paid 50¢ per month. Use of a gun or sword was $1.00 with 50¢ refunded at the end of the year. There was a $5.00 charge if a gun or sword was lost or broken. Meals for students living on campus cost $9.00 per month, and laundry, fuel and lights cost between $10.00 and $12.50 per year.[974]

In 1916 and 1917 the main administration building and dormitory were extensively renovated to install heating and plumbing. Dorm room size was standardized and each had a lavatory (sink), and radiator for heat. Closets were installed in the rooms. Furnishings in the rooms were standardized to include "two single iron beds with springs and mattresses, a table with book-cases built in, a chiffonier (nightstand), chairs, a lavatory and set fixtures."[975]

During 1917-'18, tuition and expenses for students increased by over twenty percent over the previous year. Seniors and Juniors paid $15.00 per term and Sophomores and Freshmen were charged $14.00 per term. Room rent increased from $1.50 per month to $2.50 per month and electric lights, steam heat and running water were included. Board, which included meals and laundry, increased from $10.00 to $12.00 per month. Overall, the cost of a two-term session increased from $145-$160 to $175-$200 during 1917-'18.[976]

In 1918-'19, tuition, fees and expenses for the new year increased again. Tuition for Seniors and Juniors was now $16.00 per term and $15.00 per term for Sophomores and Freshmen. Room rent did not increase but boarding fees rose to $13.50 from $12.00 per month. Overall expense for two terms increased by $25 to $200-$225 per session.[977]

In 1918, the Institute implemented a room reservation policy whereby a returning cadet had the option of retaining his same room for the next year (session). Room assignments were held until July 10th of the preceding year and could be retained for a $5 fee (credited to the room rent account) deposited with the Principal. If a student did not return to school after posting a deposit, he could request a refund before September 1st of the new academic year. If two or more students wanted a new room the decision would be decided by lot, but new students would receive first choice of an unoccupied room. Students were not allowed to switch rooms without permission of the Principal.[978]

In 1919-'20, the cost of attending the Institute rose for the third straight year. Tuition increased by 50¢ per term. Seniors and Juniors now paid $16.50 per term, while Sophomores and Freshmen paid $15.50 a term. "Regular" rooms now cost $3.00 per month (previously $2.50) and "corner" rooms on the third floor (with windows on two sides) were priced at $3.50 per month (also previously $2.50). Board increased by ten percent to $15.00 per month. Overall expenses now stood at $207.50-$220 a session.[979]

In 1920-'21, student expenses increased by twenty-five percent to $250-$275 per year. Tuition rose from $16.50 to $20.00 per term for Seniors and Juniors and from $15.50 to $18.00 per term for Sophomores and Freshmen.[980]

In 1924-'25, although the number of students decreased from the previous year, the cost of attending the Institute increased by seven percent from $335.50 to $358.50 ($381 if residing in a "corner room). Tuition rose from $20 per term ($60 per three term session) to $75 per session. Room rent for standard rooms remained at $4 per month, but corner room rent rose from $4.50 to $6.50 a month. Board rose from $153 per session to $170 per session. Library and military fees remained unchanged at $4.50 and $2 per session. The athletic fee that was instituted during the previous year rose from $6 to $7.50 per year. The cost of uniforms rose from $63.75 to $66.50.[981]

In the fall of 1925, the new dormitory was opened and fifty-four more of the 117 cadets were now able to reside on campus. While the total number of cadets decreased (by twenty-nine) from the previous year, "the new living quarters were enthusiastically received by students, faculty and staff."[982]

By 1926-'27 the cost of attending the Institute had increased to $383.50 per session for the Preparatory Department and $397.00 for the College Department.[983]

The costs of attending the Institute in 1927-28 were calculated differently from previous years. Expenses, which included tuition, board, room rent, and fees such as a season Lyceum ticket and a subscription to the Institute News, were all listed in a "lump sum" total of $400.00 per session for boarding students in all Classes, and $100 per session for day students. As in the past, the cost of books was not included in the itemized expenses, but they could be purchased at the bookstore "for a reasonable price."

Parents and students were reminded that "sufficient funds must be provided upon entering to pay for text-books" and could be deposited with Treasurer of the Institute. Uniforms and equipment, which included a dress uniform, service uniform, and an extra shirt cost $72.50. A "regulation" overcoat was also available for $27.50. The cost of laundry was no longer included in the catalogue as this service "will be done by a number of parties in the vicinity of the Institute, or agencies of the steam laundries ..."[984]

The 1928 Catalogue advised incoming students that:

> "Each cadet should bring with him one pillow, two pillow cases, four sheets, one blanket, one quilt, one counterpane (all for single bed, if assigned a room in one of the dormitories; otherwise inquire before packing trunk), one small rug, brush and comb, tooth brush, and paste, clothes bag, towels, and knife, fork and spoon for his use, in case he has to be served meals in his room."

Patrons were advised that:

> "Students do not need automobiles at the school, since we have an excellent schedule for jitneys and public buses. Private automobiles militate against steady application on the part of students. Therefore, boarding students will not bring automobiles to the school, except under special arrangement with the Principal."[985]

In 1929-'30, the cost of attending the Institute rose to $450 for boarding students. Uniform costs increased by $10 to $82.50 and included three additional shirts. The $27.50 overcoat was no longer optional. Book costs were not itemized, but "local" laundry expenses were listed at 10¢ apiece for shirts, long underwear, and pajamas, and 5¢ apiece for pillowcases, sheets, towels, three handkerchiefs, and three pairs of socks.[986]

In 1931-'32, boarding students were accommodated in the dormitories as space was available. Rooms off campus were subject to approval by the Principal. Students personally provided a Bible, a Dictionary, sheets, blankets, counterpanes, towels, pajamas, bath robe, pillow and pillow cases, a rug, table napkins, clothes brush, shoe brush, hair brush and comb, tooth brush, drinking cup, eating utensils, and a bag for soiled clothes. Except under special circumstances, boarding students were not allowed to have a car or motorcycle at the school. Expenses for room and board were $450 per session for boarding students and $100 for day students.

The cost of a dress uniform was $44.50 and included a cap, cap device, collar devices, wide belt, black tie, white gloves, and two white shirts. Service uniforms cost $37.50 and included a cap, cap device, two flannel shirts, two Irish Poplin shirts, a sweater, black tie, and belt. A regulation overcoat priced at $25 was also required.

The Mt. Pleasant Collegiate Institute schedule for 1931-'32 was:

6:40 AM Reveille

6:50 AM Assembly, Roll Call & Calisthenics

7:20 AM Fatigue Call & Inspection

7:25 AM Meal Call

7:30 AM Assembly –Breakfast

8:00 AM First Bell for Chapel Exercises

8:30 AM Chapel Exercises

9:00 AM -12 Noon – Recitations & Study

12:00 Noon – Meal Call

12:10 PM Assembly – Dinner

12:30-1:00 PM Recreation

1:00 PM to 4:00 PM – Recitations & Study

4:00 PM Drill Call

4:10 PM Assembly

In the fall and spring, drill period was in the morning, between breakfast and chapel services. This afforded time for athletic practice in the afternoon.

5:00 PM Recall; Street Privilege until supper

6:00 PM Bell for Supper

6:05 PM Call for Supper

6:10 PM Supper (variable depending upon the season)

7:00 PM Call for Quarters

7:10 PM Inspection

10:00 PM Tattoo

10:30 PM Tabs. Lights out

8:30 AM – 8:30 PM on Saturdays – Cadets not having restrictions are allowed street privileges. Special permission was necessary if out past 8:30 PM.

1:30-2:30 PM on Sundays - Quite hour.

Seniors had certain special privileges: They could wear white duck or white flannel trousers instead of dress uniform trousers. They were not required to attend retreat on Saturdays. They could also walk to and from church out of ranks and they were allowed weekend leave upon approval. "Fatigue Call and Inspection," required that every cadet to be dressed, have his room well swept, bedding and furniture neatly arranged, books in book-case, hair brushed, shoes shined, and coat buttoned throughout. Cadets were required to be in their rooms and standing at attention while inspection was conducted.[987]

LITERARY SOCIETIES

At the opening of Western Carolina Male Academy in 1855, one of Principal Gerhardt's first actions was to organize the Crescent Literary Society "the object of which was the discussion of such subjects as tend to mental improvement."[988]

By 1857 the Academy had formed a second Literary Society. On September 16th, 1857, the "Crescent" and "Philalaethian" Societies were opened with a lecture by Dr. Lewis Eichelberger on "The Worth of Life Illustrated and How to be Useful and Succeed in Life."[989]

Society Constitutions stated that the purpose of the organizations was, "for our improvement in Literature, Science and Eloquence …" Literary Society exercises included Declamation (public speaking), Composition, and Forensic Disputation (debate). The Societies were open to all students and virtually everyone participated. The Societies served both an academic and a social purpose and were an important part of the Academy and later the College and Institute curriculums. Their activities were major social events on the campus and in the town. [See Appendix 5 for the entire Constitution and By-laws of the Societies.][990]

The importance of the Literary Societies was most vividly expressed by the fact that when the Male Academy was chartered as a College, one of the Board of Trustees first actions was to authorize construction of two buildings on the campus dedicated to the sole use of the organizations. The Pi Sigma Phi (formerly Crescent) Society and Philalaethian Society buildings each contained a "debating hall," a library, and a reading room.

The 1899-1900 College Catalogue affirmed that: "the two Literary Societies ... exert a healthful and stimulating influence in the cultivation ... They have large and well-furnished halls and libraries of well-selected books. ... All students over fourteen years of age are required to join one of the societies."[991]

The MPCI catalogues of the twentieth century elaborated further on the Societies.

> "The Gerhardt and Ludwig Literary Societies are one of the strong features of this school in which the faculty takes special pride and interest. ... Weekly exercises are held in each (Society Hall) under the supervision of a member of the faculty.
>
> Several public exercises and entertainments are also given by the Societies during the session, which afford the young men special opportunities for self-improvement. By the practice afforded in these exercises, the young men become more self-confident, learn to think on their feet, and improve greatly in public speaking. Realizing the importance of such training, they eagerly grasp the opportunities offered, and the Societies have established an enviable reputation for the excellence of their work in declamation, oratory, and debate."[992]

In the 1920's, the growing number of students at the Collegiate Institute led to the creation two additional literary societies. The Preparatory Literary Society was formed in the lower grades of the school, and the Calhoun Debating Club was created in 1922 for members from the Junior and Senior Classes who exhibited "a good record in application, deportment and Literary Society work."[993]

While the principal function of the Literary Societies was academic in nature, they also provided much of the "social" activity of the College and the Institute. Various programs were conducted throughout the school year and included Declaimer's Contests, Orations, and the highlight of most events, the Debates. Many of the contests were announced in local newspapers, in notices posted around the town, and with formal "invitations" distributed by mail and throughout the community.

Most of these events were "elimination" competitions intended to select the participants for the "final" contests which took place during Commencement week. Medals in all Society categories were awarded during Commencement. Without a doubt, one of the most interesting debates occurred on February 20th, 1925 when the Gerhardt Society debate addressed the question, "That the Ku Klux Klan as an organization is more detrimental than beneficial to the Country." M. B. Dry and Bernard W. Cruse argued the affirmative, while S. R. McEachern and W. C. Thomas maintained the negative.[994]

An image of the Gerhardt Society's 25th Anniversary Exercise (1927) is presented below.

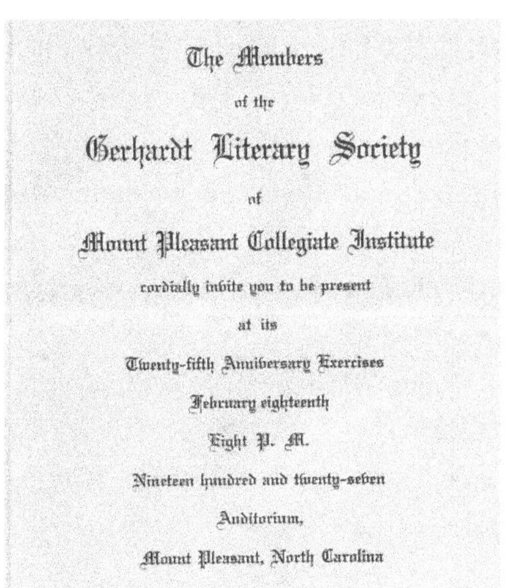

The Members
of the
Gerhardt Literary Society
of
Mount Pleasant Collegiate Institute
cordially invite you to be present
at its
Twenty-fifth Anniversary Exercises
February eighteenth
Eight P. M.
Nineteen hundred and twenty-seven
Auditorium,
Mount Pleasant, North Carolina

The Declaimers Contest for the 1933 Gold Medal was held in the Mont Amoena Seminary Chapel at 10:30 AM on May 22nd. The event began with an invocation and music, followed by the first two declamations (essays). Daphne Bunn's topic was "Lest We Forget" and R. L. Green wrote on "The Honor of Labor." Following a musical selection, the third and fourth essays, "Men and Memories of the Southland" and "The South-of What She May be Proud," were delivered by C. W. Miller and M. M. Rose, respectively. After another musical interlude, B. B. Russell and W.

B. Woollen read the final two selections, "Planning a Career," and "One Niche Higher." The Judges deliberated during a final musical interval and finally presented the 1933 Gold Medal for Declamation to Miss Daphne Bunn. The program was closed with a benediction.[995]

In addition to conducting local events, the Societies were heavily involved in Literary Contests throughout the state. These competitions were usually between High Schools, Colleges and other academic Literary Societies and were conducted on various College campuses or at the civic auditoriums of a local city or town.

North Carolina College, and later, the MPCI Debate Teams, developed a high reputation throughout the state for their skills at these events. In 1911 MPCI sent a representative to the Inter-collegiate Orator's Contest in Durham, NC.[996]

In 1915, Declaimers from the Institute competing against Trinity College and Elon College placed in the final contests. Also, in 1915 representatives from MPCI participated in the third annual statewide triangular debates sponsored by the University of North Carolina. The triangular debates involved over 1000 students from 250 high schools in ninety counties of North Carolina.[997] Both teams from MPCI won their competitions and were entitled to participate in the contest for the Aycock Memorial Award at Chapel Hill. For unknown reasons, the MPCI team chose "not to avail themselves of the privilege."[998]

Cadet Captain Carl W. Seiler of MPCI won the 1921 Tri-state Declaimer's Contest held at Trinity College and the state-wide contest held at Wake Forest University. Seiler attended the Virginia Military Institute after graduation from MPCI.[999]

The Collegiate Institute had at least one "authorized" fraternity. The Beta Chapter of Beta Mu was formed on the campus on February 19th, 1922, with the permission of the Alpha chapter of the Beta Mu Fraternity located at Duke University. The minutes of the first meeting named ten members and outlined the rules and regulations, the materials to be obtained for initiation, assigned "nicknames" to the members, and generally outlined the group's social calendar for the coming months. [See End Note for a complete transcript of the minutes.][1000]

THE ARTS – MUSIC AND DRAMA

One of earliest existing documents from the Western Carolina Male Academy (circa 1857) is a "playbill" announcing a student sponsored "Programme" including declamations and dialogue accompanied by music and vocals. At the time, the exhibition was probably considered more academic than entertainment in nature, but it was open to the public. It appears to have been one of the first of what were to become regular presentations conducted by the school.[1001]

Although early WCMA and North Carolina College catalogues of do not specifically mention organized music or other artistic events, such activities no doubt occurred and often in conjunction with nearby Mont Amoena Female Seminary. Independence Day, Thanksgiving, and Washington's Birthday were celebrated, but by far the most important celebration was College Commencement with its public examinations, orations, graduation dances and the final graduation ceremony.[1002]

In 1890, a group of College and Seminary students combined efforts to buy an organ for the College Chapel. The group produced and presented a "farcical drama" entitled "Not Such a Fool He Looks," to raise funds for the organ. The play was performed at the Mont Amoena Seminary and was accompanied by the Mt. Pleasant String Band.[1003]

The arts became more prominent on the campus during the MPCI years. The first "official" cultural organization was formed prior to 1908. The Glee Club was organized "to add to the innocent amusements of student life and to stimulate the cultivation of musical talent." Membership was based upon "compliance with certain definite conditions prescribed by the faculty," and all public entertainments given were to be supervised by a teacher. The Glee Club became an umbrella for the Institute Quartette and the Institute Orchestra. The Quartette not only sang at Institute and Seminary events but participated in musical contests and was featured at many social and religious occasions throughout the state.[1004]

In 1923 the Institute student handbook stated that "the Glee Club was not very active, due mostly to the lack of a leader. They presented a negro minstrel and operetta in conjunction with the Seminary. A quartette was also organized which sang at functions in various parts of the state." A "start was made" to re-organize a school orchestra.[1005]

In 1924 and 1925, the Quartette was extraordinary successful. The MPCI Quartette won consecutive silver cups for the best group in its category among thirty-eight schools at the statewide Musical Contest held in Greensboro. In 1925 and again in 1928, the group's Bass Soloist won the silver cup.[1006]

In 1928 a seven-piece orchestra was organized and a Drum & Bugle Corps was formed. The Drum and Bugle Corps accompanied the entire Corps in several local parades.[1007]

MPCI had several different school songs in the 1920's. "Alma Mater" appeared in the 1923 Student handbook:

Alma Mater (Old College Tune)
1. There's a school we love to think of
In the old North State
Whose name we ought to raise above
Ere it be too late
Hail to C. I. Keep it Ringing
Through the hard fought game
Old man time will then be bringing
Fame to thy dear name.
2. Hastening through thy halls of learning
Which we've learned to love
Ever will thy name be burning in the sky above.
3. When we're far away from C. I.
WE shall ne'er forget
To sing thy praises till we die
And pay to thee our debt.[1008]

The 1925 College Yearbook, *The Tour Path*, included the current school song.

There's a Place we all love, with affection true,
And we'll tell you of it now.
Why it holds our love, why we'd fight for it,
To have it win somehow.
It stands on a hill high o'er a town
Midst trees majestic all around.
It's our Alma Mater of which we sing,
Let us make her praises ring.

Then up with MPCI down with all mighty foes,
We know it can be done and do it – sure we will!
And when at last we win, all her sons we'll gather in
And cheer and shout day in and out
For old MPCI
We love it deeper as each year rolls by,
Time endears it more and more.
It's because of the spirit that lives on "The Hill,"
The spirit of "the boys" of yore.
Travel where we may, travel where we will,
The CI spirit follows us still.
It moulds our lives from day to day,
And helps us on our way.[1009]

A program from a 1978 MPCI Reunion recounted yet a third "MPCI School Song" as:

College ties can ne'er be broken
Formed at old MP
For Surpassing wealth unspoken
They'll forever be.
When our College days are over
And our ways shall part
Still to thee we'll be united
Still be one in heart.
MPCI Hail to thee!
Thou hast been kind to us.
Ever shall we cherish for thee
Thoughts of love and praise.[1010]

By 1933 "Musical Organizations" were proudly described on a full page in the College Catalogue. "Realizing the importance of musical training in the education of youth, it is the aim of the Collegiate Institute to encourage the cultivation of musical talent of students to afford each one, should he so desire, the opportunity of developing such talents."[1011]

The Glee Club was composed of twenty members and rehearsals were held regularly under direction of the faculty. A hall was at the "disposal" of the organization for practices, and the "best in classics" were attempted.[1012] The Orchestra also held regular rehearsals and performed both classical and popular music. Special attention was given to students interested in a particular instrument.[1013]

Probably the most popular of the cultural arts at MPCI was drama. The production and/or presentation of plays and skits, often in partnership with Mont Amoena Seminary, was considered the highlight of the "social season" for the schools and the community. Performances were conducted at either MPCI or Mont Amoena until 1904, when a Town Auditorium was constructed on the second floor of the Cook & Foil Merchantile on West Franklin St. Between 1904 and 1928 most of the student productions were held in the Mt. Pleasant Auditorium.

Among the plays presented were:

May 15th, 1911 – Commencement Drama – "Ingomar" – a play in four acts adapted from Friedrich Halms, "Der Sohn Der Wildniss," written by Maria Lovell.[1014]

May 22nd, 1922 – Commencement Drama - "Esther Wake or the Spirit of the Regulators" – A play in four acts created by the UNC Dramatic Club.[1015]

November 4th, 1927 – "Much Ado About Betty," a comedy in three acts by Walter Ben Hare – MPCI Athletic Association Fund Raiser.[1016]

May 28th, 1828 - Commencement Drama - "Romeo & Jane" – A Comedy in Four Acts by Edward Childs Carpenter. Presented by the MPCI English Department at the Mt. Pleasant Town Auditorium.[1017]

"The Lyceum" was another of the MPCI's "cultural" endeavors. This program was a partnership among the Institute, Mont Amoena Seminary and the citizens of Mt. Pleasant. The Lyceum created a local association to provide theater, lectures, music, and other entertainment for the community.

Organized about 1910, the Lyceum was described in the College catalogue as "entertainment, wholesome & refined and of real educational value." The cost of a season ticket in 1911 was $2.50 and consisted of "a half-dozen or more," events. Initially, MPCI students were not required to become members of the association but were "advised to avail themselves of the inspiring examples of high-class song, comedy, drama and lectures."[1018] In 1910 the season opened with the "The Scottish Singers."[1019] In 1911 the

Lyceum presented three attractions in one week – "Rip Van Winkle," "As You Like It," and "Othello." Additionally, MPCI Professor D. B. Welsh was preparing to present a melodrama by local talent at an early date.[1020] In 1917, Dr. Lucian Edgar Follonsbee, a noted lecturer, provided an address on various subjects.[1021]

The arts thus served not only the College and the Seminary but created a significant bond between the schools and the community.

ATHLETICS

Athletics and physical activity were apparently not of major concern during the early years of the College. But from 1871 through 1884 the College catalogues contained a paragraph stating that "as health is the greatest of earthly blessings, so that which contributes to it is to be highly appreciated. No place in the State surpasses Mt. Pleasant in point of health. … Good health is necessary to successful study, and the situation and regulations of the College properly promote it."[1022]

In his history of the College, Rev. Michael C. D. McDaniel stated that "in the absence of any organized system of athletics, students found the most attractive sports in hunting and in a game called 'bandy.'"[1023]

The first reference in College records concerning organized school sports was an 1874 petition from the "baseball club". The baseball club asked to "travel to Monroe to play a match game." The Faculty granted the request but stated that this was "not to be regarded as a precedent to be repeated," and that "the party leave after 12 Noon on Friday and return by Sat. night the 24th."[1024]

In October 1875, another reference to baseball was mentioned in the minutes of the Board of Trustees. The Trustees admonished that "present finances preclude furnishing of a baseball outfit at this time."[1025]

An early but undated photo at the Eastern Cabarrus Historical Society Library is labeled "the NC College baseball team". Based on the style of the "uniforms", which included "stovepipe hats", white shirts and dark pants, this team was active in the late 1870's or early 1880's.

The College had an active baseball team by 1893. An article in the *Daily Concord Standard* stated that in preparing for commencement, "the boys play ball, and the young ladies, don't."[1026] In 1893, the students requested "a better ball ground." College Treasurer, Jonas Cook, provided a "ball ground" on his property about 200 yards east of the school across North Main Street. It is not clear if this was the old "ball ground" or the "better" one requested by the students. An 1896 photo at the Eastern Cabarrus Historical Society Library displays a twelve-member NCC baseball team.[1027] *The Concord Standard* published an article in 1897 describing a "match game" between the College and the Town team that would be played in a few days."

In 1899 another article was published in the Standard about a baseball game between Concord High School and North Carolina College.

> "On last Saturday, the Concord High School boys went over to Mt. Pleasant and crossed bats with the North Carolina College boys. ... Mr. Alonzo Blackwelder, of the college, acted as umpire and no 'kicks' worth mentioning were offered. The game resulted in a victory for the college boys in a score of 25 to 6."[1028]

In 1900 the "College nine" met the "second nine" from Concord on the College field in Mt. Pleasant. The College won by a score of 10 to 5.[1029]

Organized athletics was a highly integrated part of student life at MPCI. A baseball team and a tennis team were both formed by 1904. Tennis courts were located on the north end of the campus. Tennis teams existed until the school closed in 1933 but no information beyond photographs has been located. Baseball, however, was well documented.

The school created an Athletic Association Pass in 1907 "good for all Games on Athletic Association Grounds for the Season of 1907."[1030] An article in the *Concord Times* in February 1907 stated that the Institute Athletic Association "has perfected a schedule for a series of games with other schools of the state." In March and April, the baseball team, managed by Professor of Greek and Latin Roy Webster, played games against Davidson College, Lenoir College, St. Mary's College and Roanoke College.[1031] The 1909 baseball team played teams from Concord, Salisbury, Charlotte, Davidson College, Belmont Abbey College, and Lenoir College in Hickory.

By 1911 the MPCI catalogue contained a full paragraph on "Athletics."

> "The faculty, while never sacrificing scholarship, emphasizes the importance of physical culture, and recommends open-air exercise. The large and beautiful

grounds of the Collegiate Institute afford ample opportunity for out-door sports."[1032]

The Collegiate Institute fielded a baseball team throughout its existence. Local newspapers and the School yearbooks recorded their schedules, box scores and rosters. The teams played a varied group of opponents including Colleges, Junior Colleges, Prep Schools, High Schools and Town teams.

In 1923 the team won six games and lost eight. Opponents included Kannapolis, Shelby, Lenoir College, Lock Mill, St. John's, Weaver College, Mars Hill College, Trinity College freshmen, and Davidson freshmen. The coach was Commandant of Cadets C. J. M. Blume and the team Captain was Cadet Marvin Watts. Marvin Watts and his brother, Herman "Ginger" Watts, Cabarrus County natives, both played several seasons for the Institute and went on to notable careers in Minor Leagues, Textile League and Outlaw League baseball.[1033]

In 1926 the team posted nine wins and five losses. The Cadets defeated Catawba College twice and did well against opponents Belmont Abby, Rutherford College, Oak Ridge Institute and Wingate College. The coach was H. C. Hainer, Professor of French and Director of Athletics. Marvin Watts was again team Captain.

The 1930 Institute baseball team shared the League Championship with Rutherford College. The star pitcher of the team was Frank Shealy. Records show that Shealy graduated from MPCI in 1929 and was employed as a Science Professor and Athletic Director in 1929-'30.[1034]

The Watts brothers mentioned above went on to careers in the Minor Leagues as did another student, Frank Hopkins. The Institute's one Major League baseball player, Herman Fink, a Concord native, was on the baseball roster in 1932. Fink played Major League baseball from 1935-1937 with Connie Mack's Philadelphia Athletics. His "best" season was in 1936 when he pitched in 34 games and had a record of ten wins and twenty losses.[1035]

On September 21, 1911, the *Concord Daily Tribune* wrote, "football will be introduced at the Collegiate Institute this season for the first time, so far as we have been able to learn, in [the] history of the institutions here."[1036] Coached by Professor of English Dennis B. Welch and Captained by Cadet Captain Benjamin Cripps, the team's first tryout involved many volunteers and Professor Welsh commented that the "boys seemed pretty well prepared."[1037]

The 1911 team's first game was against the Baird School of Charlotte and resulted in a 0-10 loss. Other opponents included Bingham School from Asheville, Catawba College and Lenoir College from Hickory.[1038]

Early optimism in 1912 turned sour quickly. *The Charlotte Observer* reported in October, "the students of Mt. Pleasant Collegiate Institute and inhabitants of the town are congratulating themselves on the splendid way in which the football team is rounding into form."[1039] Games were again scheduled against the Baird School, Bingham School, and Catawba College. New opponents, High Point High School and Davidson College were added. The team, coached by Cadet Leland F. Valley, won its first game of the season against the Baird School, 16-6, but from that point on the season took a serious nose-dive. On October 19th, the Institute lost to Davidson College 125-0, and eight days later they suffered a defeat of 110-0 at the hands of the Bingham School in Asheville.[1040]

Following the 1912 season, even though the team finished with a "break-even" record, it was apparently decided to discontinue the football program for the foreseeable future.

It was not until 1923 that football returned to the Institute. The "MPCI Red Devils" coached by Professor of History & Greek Roy Webster won four games and lost three in 1923.

MPCI	12	Landis	0
MPCI	12	Charlotte	9
MPCI	44	Albemarle	0
MPCI	46	Belmont Abbey	0
MPCI	6	Concord	7
MPCI	6	Statesville	7

School spirit ran high as cadets adopted several "yells" in support of the team. Some of the "yells" were featured in the 1923-1924 Student Handbook:

(1) Alla-gnee-gnack-gnack

(4) To the Tune "Annie Laurie"

Alla-gnee-gnack-gnack
Woo-Rah! Woo-Rah!
Mt. Pleasant

(2) One-A-Zip-Two-A-Zip
Three-A-Zipa-Zam-Four
A-Zipa-Five-A-Zipa-Don't
Give-A-Hobble-Gobble
Razzel, Dazzel-Sis
Boom-Bah

(3) Boom-A-Laka
Boom-A-Laka
Boom-A Laka Bine
and the band played
Annie Laurie -----
Boom! Rah!
Mt. Pleasant

(5) He's A Peach
He's A Dream
He's The Captain of our Team
(Supply Name 3 Times)

(6) M.P. M. P. C. I. C. I. M. P. C. I. C. I
Rah! Rah! Rah!
Mt. Pleasant! Mt. Pleasant
Hold That Line[1041]

A somewhat nostalgic article in the *Institute News* in 1927, described "The Great Team of 1923."

"With practically no general equipment, with each student furnishing his playing outfit and with only one football which was used throughout the season, they vanquished enemy after enemy usually rolling up an overwhelming score. The team was composed of men, in every sense of the word, men of strength, of stamina, of courage and of manhood." … Major Webster coached the team which ran practically all of its plays from the jump formation."[1042]

In 1924 the "Red Devils" opened the season with NC State High School Champions, Rockingham High School. The MPCI team, together for only one week, lost the game "on a very muddy field" by a score of 12-0. The second game was with Oak Ridge Institute, State Prep School Champions. This contest also ended in a loss, 24-0. The team got no relief as its third game was against a strong Davidson Athletic Club "featuring a galaxy of former college stars." The Red Devils showed great determination and were able to hold on for a 0-0 tie. The team won its next four games to finish with a 4-2-1 record.[1043]

In October 1928, the Institute elected Bryson C. Renno and Julia

Shirey as cheerleaders. They held their first "pep meeting" on October 11th.[1044]

In 1929 the Institute lost to Weaver College 0-13 in a game to decide the NC State Junior College championship.[1045]

In 1932 the Red Devils, coached by Athletic Director J. E. Magner, won their first eight games before losing to Oak Ridge Institute.

MPCI – 38	Leaksville HS	- 0
MPCI - 7	Kannapolis HS	- 0
MPCI – 33	Presbyterian Jr College	- 8
MPCI – 14	Massanutten Military Academy	- 0
MPCI - 12	Weaver Jr College	- 2
MPCI - 36	Carlisle School	- 6
MPCI - 13	Hargrave Military Academy	- 7
MPCI - 20	Blue Ridge	- 6
MPCI - 0	Oak Ridge Military Institute	- 38[1046]

The first basketball team at the Institute was organized by Cadets in September 1916.[1047] The "home court" was a dirt surface located on the north side of the campus near the tennis courts. The team was led by brothers Jay and Luther Schenck. Most of the early games were played against local High School teams.

The cadets had a successful first season. A *Concord Times* article in March 1917 recorded that the school concluded its season with a 5 and 2 record, however, other articles list the team playing at least nine games. (If the games were played outside, they could have been "rained out.")[1048]

In January 1917, the cadets won three games in two days, defeating Winecoff High school by a score of 48 to 10 on the afternoon of January 26th, and then winning over Concord High School 41 to 20 in the evening. On the 27th of January the team beat Howell High School 42 to 4.[1049]

The team lost at least one game in their first season, falling to Kannapolis High School 35 to 20 on February 21st.

The 1917 schedule as recorded from various newspapers.

December 9, 1916	MPCI – 16	China Grove HS – 7[1050]
December 16, 1916	MPCI vs	Lowell HS (no report)[1051]
January 26, 1917	MPCI – 48	Winecoff HS – 10[1052]

January 26, 1917	MPCI - 41	Concord HS – 20[1053]
January 28, 1917	MPCI – 42	Howell HS – 4[1054]
February 21, 1917	MPCI – 20	Kannapolis HS – 35[1055]
February 23, 1917	MPCI vs	Winecoff HS (no report)[1056]
March 9, 1917	MPCI – 25	Howell HS - 15[1057]
March 16, 1917	MPCI vs	Fairview HS (no report)[1058]

The 1924 basketball team was coached by Professor of Chemistry and Commandant of Cadets A.M. Albergotti. The team compiled a record of seven wins and three losses. Games were played against Concord YMCA, Concord High School, Lenoir College, Hickory (City), Polarine (Charlotte), Southmont (played on a muddy court), Cornelius High School, and Highland Park (in a congested room with no room to pass the ball).[1059]

The 1925 team was coached by Professor of French and new Commandant of Cadets William W. Cone who coached all Institute sports except tennis that year. According to the Institute yearbook, the *Tour Path*, after the preceding year's successful season, much was expected of the "Varsity Squad" which returned all but three players.

> "But as fate would have it, it seemed that every material force worked against us. ... We were handicapped by the lack of a suitable indoor court and two of the last year 'stars' were ruled off the team on account of certain handicaps. The schedule consisted of seven games, although losing most of these, a hard fight was put up at all times."[1060]

One of the most memorable games of the 1925 season was played against the University of North Carolina freshman team. The *Tour Path* described the game played on the University campus as "very close," but according to the UNC *Daily Tar Heel*, the Carolina freshmen "swamped" the Institute team by a score of 38 to 14.[1061]

As mentioned previously, the Institute offered tennis as a sport as early as 1904, but it is uncertain if a team was organized to complete against other schools until 1925. According to a page in the 1925 *Tour Path* yearbook, "in response to the call for tennis candidates, a goodly number of budding 'Tildens' presented themselves. The schedule played, while not imposing, has started a sport which should create a great of interest in the years to come." The 1925 team was coached by Professor of Latin and Bible

A. M. Middlesworth, and listed four players – Richard B. Giles (Captain), Paul B. Cline, Claiborne N. Alexander and?? Wiley.[1062]

In 1928, Major Still, Commandant of Cadets, was converting the old tennis courts into a drill field and ordered the courts moved to a new site which had yet been determined. The *Institute News* declared, "tennis friends do not give up hope."[1063]

The Institute offered one other sport in its last year of operation. The 1933 yearbook, *The Falcon*, contained a page with a photograph and team member names for "Boxing." The team "Instructor" was a Cadet, Brown "Pee Wee' Russell, and the faculty advisor was Professor D. K. Barsington, Commandant of Cadets. It is unknown if the team competed outside of the school.[1064]

THE MILITARY SYSTEM

The "Military System" instituted by Principal McAllister in 1907 involved many changes to the structure of the academic and social organization of the school.

One of the first modifications was the use of military rank. Principal McAllister appears to have assigned himself the rank of Colonel and Instructors were awarded the ranks of Major or Captain according to their responsibilities and seniority. Cadet ranks were assigned based upon attaining certain scholastic and leadership accomplishments. Cadet ranks included Cadet Captain, 1st & 2nd Lieutenant, 1st Sergeant, Sergeant, Corporal and Adjutant. Cadet Officers wore insignias or patches to designate their status and were delegated specified responsibilities and accorded privileges accordingly.[1065]

The uniform style worn by Instructors and Cadets evolved over the years and generally reflected the US Military style of the time. The first uniforms were of simple design with a high collar tunic, rounded cap and matching pants. The 1909-1910 catalogue described the uniform as "made of the most durable material" and "with good care it will be serviceable for two sessions." Every "suit" was made to order, and the uniform was:

> "... a necessity in the Military System, therefore, all cadets at the Institute will wear uniforms. The uniform consists

> of a blouse, trousers, military cap and gloves. Besides being necessary to a military school, the uniform has merits to commend it. It does away with distinctions of dress, gives a handsome appearance … and is more economical than citizens clothes."

The cost of the uniform was $16.00.[1066]

By 1916, a khaki uniform with duck trousers and leggings were worn in the fall and spring. The cost of a fatigue uniform and cap was $18. A dress uniform was $16 and a khaki uniform with cap and leggings was $7.50. Duck trousers were $1.65 a pair, and gloves were 25¢.[1067]

In 1920, the uniform was re-designed to "aid in improving the physique" and consisted of a khaki uniform for drill and a dress uniform of a blue blouse, gray trousers, blue cap and white gloves. The dress uniform cost $35-$40 and the khaki uniform was $17.50-$22.50.[1068]

In 1924 the dress uniform included a cap, cap device, and gloves priced at $36. The service uniform included breeches, flannel shirt, campaign hat, hat cord, hat strap, leggings, and web belt for $16.50. The price of the uniform increased steadily. By 1927 a dress uniforms cost $42.50 and the service uniform cost $25.00.[1069]

In 1927 the uniform style changed from the closed front tunic design to the more popular "open jacket" style with accompanying dress shirt, tie, and "wide belt." With the change in uniform style, the school required that uniforms be worn at all times. Upon arrival on opening day of the session, all civilian clothes were to be sent back home.[1070]

Like the uniform, insignias and patches evolved. Early photographs show the "MPCI" sown on the collar of the tunic. Later images show pins on collars. The uniform hat changed from a rounded style to the more familiar "service cap" style of the 1930's. Photos taken shortly before and following World War I show a "campaign hat" worn during drills and exercises.

Dress uniforms for Instructors and Cadet Officers included a sword with accompanying belt. Following World War I, Instructors wore calf high boots. There is no information or images which show leggings, but it is probable that they were available.

The basic piece of military equipment issued to cadets was a rifle. There is no information in the Institute records about what type of rifles were used by the early cadets, but based on existing photographs they appear to have been Springfield Model 1873-1892 surplus. Again, based upon existing information, it is probable that these weapons could not be fired and that, at least in the early years of MPCI, the cadets kept their rifles in their rooms.

The rifles were acquired by Colonel McAllister, most probably as military surplus. Cadets were charged a fee of $1 when they were issued a rifle, and refunded 50¢ when the gun was returned at the end of the academic session or when the student left the school. There are no records of any misuse or other disruptive behavior involving rifles and it appears that they were closely monitored by the faculty.[1071]

At some point, probably when the administration building was remodeled in 1916-'17, two rooms on the second floor were converted into an armory and weapons and related equipment were stored there. By 1919, rifles issued by the Institute appear to have been fully operational. Photographs show "target practice" conducted on the fields east of the school (the same location as the athletic fields).

In 1929, Colonel McAllister acquired eighty "new" rifles, either to replace or supplement the existing weapons. These weapons, .30 caliber M1917 rifles, were fully functional. Cadets were required to familiarize themselves with the operation of the rifle, including firing it at "target practice" three times a year.[1072]

Cadets at the Institute participated in military drills and other Military Exercises four times a week as prescribed by the US Army Infantry Drill Regulations. During the first twenty-five years of the Institute, drills lasted forty minutes and were conducted the end of classroom sessions, at 4PM. After 1929 drills were extended to fifty minutes. At commencement ceremonies each spring an individual cadet was awarded a medal for "best in drill". The two cadet companies competed for the "Trophy Cup" which was awarded to the Company judged most exceptional in Drill.[1073]

During its thirty years of operation, the Institute maintained several types of living quarters for cadets. The top two floors of the Administration building were the main "dormitory." In 1920, Colonel McAllister acquired the "Blackwelder house" on the corner of North Main and Walnut St. and established his residence there. He converted several of the rooms into quarters for MPCI cadets. The house was designated Barracks No. 2.

The "Weiser house," originally the home of the first NC College President, Rev. D. H. Bittle, was obtained in 1921 and designated Barracks No. 3. The "President's House" was also used to house students and faculty. A "new dormitory" on the north side of the campus was opened in 1925.

Cadets were required to live in a barracks unless authorized otherwise by the Principal. The Commandant of Cadets was also required to reside in a barracks unless he was married, and faculty took their meals in the boarding hall.

Cadets were required to attend Sunday School at one of the nearby churches. The Institute rules stated that:

> "[Cadets] Must go and come in an orderly manner. Cadets will go in a body to church accompanied by a member of the faculty or a cadet officer. Quite hours on Sunday and devote time to study of Sunday School lesson and read Bible. Privileges allowed after quite hours until Supper."[1074]

In September 1918, at the height of World War I, the Institute initiated what it termed an "encampment." It was described in the catalogue as:

> "... several days including a Saturday in early May, spent by the cadets in camp. The object is to give them the advantage of a hike, to acquaint them with the camp life and various duties pertaining thereto, and to afford a brief recreation period just before Final Examinations. The Commandant and other officers of the faculty accompany the cadets, of course, [and] aid [the cadets] in their preparations for examinations and Commencement Exercises and supervise them in their military duties and in their sports."[1075]

The encampment site was near Bost's Mill on Rocky River about eight miles south of Mt. Pleasant. According to the catalogue, the site had been a "popular resort" along the river for many years. Activities included hiking, athletics, bathing, boating, fishing and seining, and "lessons," and it was "eagerly looked forward to by the whole school."[1076]

Although the "military system" was initially incorporated into the Institute to improve discipline and encourage enrollment, it also produced young men who would be prepared for the two world wars which were to come. Ten years after the Institute became a military school, the United States entered World War I. Former students entered the military with at least some experience in the military arts.

Research done by Nick McEntire, History Professor at Rowan-Cabarrus Community College, identified 171 MPCI students who served in World War I. Four of those students died during the war. One notable death was that of Corporal Everette McAllister, a student at MPCI from 1912-1914 and the nephew of Principal G. F. McAllister. Cpl. McAllister, a "lineman" serving with US Army 6th Engineers was the first soldier from Cabarrus County, NC to die "in action" in WWI. He was electrocuted while stringing wire near enemy lines in France on July 15, 1918.[1077]

Fourteen MPCI alumni served as Officers in World War I. The highest rank attained by a MPCI alumnus was Captain, achieved by Edward Murray of Charlotte, 43rd US Infantry. Another former student, Dr. William H. Kern of Salisbury, a Veterinarian serving with the 6th US Artillery, received the French Legion of Honor for his care of military horses during the war.[1078]

TOWN, GOWN & SOCIAL LIFE

Western Carolina Male Academy/NC College/MPCI and the town of Mt. Pleasant demonstrated a symbiotic relationship for many years. While the small village existed before the school, it predictably and undoubtedly owed its continued growth and prosperity to the educational institutions located there. The community's "bid" for the right to host the school was almost $2,000 more than the next contender. Over ninety-eight locals contributed to the original endowment and 450 gave to the initial building fund. 174 local donors contributed to the second building campaign in 1859.[1079]

These numbers demonstrated the high level of support for the Academy/College and there is also no doubt that the residents realized early on that having the school in their community would be of great cultural and financial benefit. This support brought with it a high degree of expectation that they, the contributors, would have an active role in the life of the school.

In 1858, the news that the town was selected for the site of the College precipitated processions, flaming tar-barrels, fireworks, music and the ringing of bells all through Mt. Pleasant. The citizens resolved "to cordially co-operate with the N. C. Synod in building up and sustaining the college as now located."

A Town Ordinance enacted on February 5th, 1894 provides an indication of the partnership between the school(s) and the town, and the effort to incorporate the schools into the governing process.

> "It is enacted that any person who shall willfully interrupt, or disturb any public or private school, college or Seminary in the town of Mount Pleasant, or who shall in any way interfere with the pupils of said schools, or who shall unlawfully assemble on the grounds or in the buildings, or who shall assemble on any street near said school for the said purpose, or who shall injure or deface any of the said school buildings shall be guilty of a misdemeanor and fined the sum of $25."[1080]

The ledgers of local general stores and the financial records of the College list multiple purchases and other transactions by the College and later the Institute. It is clear from one College record that the school attempted to "spread the wealth" by making separate purchases at each of the village's general stores and by hiring many local citizens to perform various services for the institutions.[1081]

The school catalogues recommended that students have their clothes cleaned by a local laundress or one of the cleaning businesses in town. Old photographs also show local women setting up "wash days" on the campus.

Several local businesses catered directly to students. A. W. Moose Drug Company had a "crew of drugstore cowboys" who frequented the soda fountain in that establishment. Moose also built a "miniature golf course" behind his building on West Franklin St. to attract students.[1082]

One of most often mentioned enterprises frequented by MPCI and Mont Amoena students was Chulie's Goodie Garden. This business, operated by Charles G. "Chulie" Lentz, was initially located on North Main Street in the Lentz Building next to the Lentz Hotel. It later moved to West Franklin Street where it occupied a space that was once a blacksmith shop. Ice cream and sodas were favorite items consumed and the store advertised in the College Catalogue, "school supplies a specialty, MAS & MPCI Headquarters."

Before the advent of automobiles, the local livery stable on West Franklin Street was often visited. NC College students, and later, MPCI Cadets could rent a horse and buggy in which to take their friends, male and female, for "Sunday rides." One of the stable owners stated that it was a most common occurrence to have a horse and buggy returned very late at night as some students seemed to have gotten lost during their forays.

The stable also operated a passenger service to and from the train station in Concord, and by 1917, the White Car Service of Concord made daily trips between Concord, Mt. Pleasant and Albemarle.

As expected from church supported schools, NC College, MPCI and Mont Amoena played an active part in the life of the local religious institutions. In addition to the services held in the school chapel, most students attended one of the local churches. From the 1850's through the mid-1870's, the only church located in the town was the Mt. Pleasant Methodist Church. Lutheran services were held at St. John's Church, located about three miles west of the town, and at Mt. Carmel and Lutheran Union churches (later consolidated into Mt. Gilead) located southeast of the town. Rev. William Gerhardt served Mt. Carmel and Lutheran Union during his tenure as Principal at The Western Carolina Male Academy. Some College students studying to be Ministers also taught Sunday School at these churches and, on occasion, delivered sermons. "The Lutherans of the Hahn Church [Mt. Gilead] neighborhood held a very successful supper not long ago. Many Eds and co-eds ate to their pocketbooks' content."[1083]

A local congregation of Lutherans held worship services in the College Chapel in 1871 until the Lutheran Church of the Holy Trinity constructed its own building on South Main Street in 1874. Holy Trinity church played a prominent role in the religious and social lives of NC College, MPCI and Mont Amoena. After 1874, several of the ministers from Holy Trinity served as Presidents/Principals and instructors at NC College and Mont Amoena. Many College, Institute and Seminary Baccalaureate sermons and other school related events were held in the Holy Trinity sanctuary.

In 1896, a German Reformed congregation erected a building on

College Street directly across from the college campus, and in 1911, a Baptist Church was built on the south side of town.

Several accounts by local citizens recount how the MPCI Cadets would march in formation to and from these local churches on Sundays. One account relates a march in formation to St. John's Church.

The town and gown relationship was not always positive. As early 1858, an Academy instructor was disciplined for not reporting a conversation that took place in the local hotel, apparently disparaging Academy Principal, Rev. Gerhardt.

The Town of Mt. Pleasant was incorporated in the same month that North Carolina College was opened. The town adopted several ordinances which seem to have been aimed at the school and its students.

Ordinance No. 22 Prohibited the Blowing of horns, beating of drums, etc.

> "Any person who shall blow any horn, beat a drum, or with any implement make any unnecessary noise on the streets at any time, shall be deemed guilty of a misdemeanor and upon conviction thereof shall be fined Two dollars for each and every offense. Bands playing in concert or any musical concert is not a violation of this ordinance."

Ordinance No. 23 stated that "Any person who shall engage in hollowing [sic], singing or making any unnecessary noise at night after business hours shall be guilty of a misdemeanor and upon conviction shall be fined not less than one dollar."

In 1899 Town Commissioners found it necessary to consider increasing the police force during the Christmas holidays due to the probability of large crowds, fireworks and celebrations involving both town citizens and students.[1084]

Students occasionally found themselves disciplined for "unauthorized" activities with town citizens. The most frequent of these incidents involved the consumption and/or purchase of alcohol. While technically prohibited within a three-mile radius of the school, alcohol was amply available and readily consumed.

Although seldom recorded, there were undoubtedly "disagreements" and other conflicts between students and townspeople. One such incident was reported in *The Charlotte Observer* in 1921.

> "Sheriff Spears and Deputy Sheriff Propst were called to Mt. Pleasant Tuesday evening to take into custody several negroes who had been arrested there following a disturbance at the Mt. Pleasant Collegiate Institute. The trouble started when a negro, Vanderbilt Motley, pushed a student from the institute off the sidewalk near the college about 6 o'clock. Several other negroes were nearby when the trouble started but they made no move to help Motley. Students from the college soon came to their friend's assistance and Motley started to run, after having shot twice at the student. The crowd chased Motley across the creek near Tuscarora mill where he escaped. The negroes who had been with Motley at first were joined by the cook of one of the college professors and when the crowd started back to Mt. Pleasant it noticed that this negro had a shotgun in his hand. The crowd then decided to arrest and search all the negroes. This was done and three pistols and the shotgun were found."[1085]

RELATIONSHIPS AND CONNECTIONS

The most frequent interaction among students and townspeople was the obvious social contact between men and women. The College/Institute and Mont Amoena Seminary had strict rules concerning the association of their students with members of the opposite sex but they encouraged "proper" academic and social contacts.

Church activities, the Lyceum program, athletic events, debates, plays, music performances and graduation ceremonies provided frequent occasions for "mixers" among men and women from the schools and the town and were deemed totally appropriate.

Other "approved" events included holiday parties and dances following football games. The 1917 College catalogue described a "Halloween Social" held at the Institute Chapel where "locust beer and pumpkin pie were served in Major Glenn's classroom."[1086]

In 1922 the MPCI "B.M. Club" hosted a dinner party at the Myers Park Country Club in Charlotte, NC. The guest list included club members Charles Moretz, Curtis Smithfield, H. M. O'Brien, J. S. Crouse, W. T. Miller, C. B. Griffin and Hoy A. Moose who were accompanied by Misses Katherine Hargrave, Martha Smith, Thelma Fassous, Jean Crowell, Edwina Moretz, Louise Moretz and Zan Link.[1087]

The 1924 College catalogue described a Committee appointed to arrange a social evening for the students shortly after the opening of the school year.[1088]

In 1932, the "after game" dance following the MPCI vs Blue Ridge football game was held at the Cannon Ball Room in the Concord Hotel. It began at 9:30 PM and lasted until 2:00 AM.[1089]

There were also, no doubt, occasional "unauthorized" activities. Future Lutheran minister, Reverend Walter Yount, a student at MPCI from 1923-1926, recounted the following anecdote about an "unapproved social interaction" between the men and women of the Institute, Seminary and Town.

> "One of the infrequent 'social events' was a chicken stew, to which some of us [MPCI students] would invite some girls to join us at the home of a friendly resident of Mt. Pleasant. Oh, yes, we got caught once and we were confined to campus for 30 days, and the girls were equally disciplined, but it was worth it."[1090]

The proximity of an all-male school and a female seminary in a very small town, would, inevitability, lead to more "serious" relationships. The number of marriages between students and teachers at the educational institutions and between students, teachers and town residents over the span of seventy-eight years are too numerous to list, but a few notable "matches" deserve mention.

A most important local marriage did not actually involve a student at the College or the Institute but it greatly impacted the institutions. In 1861, Harvey C. McAllister, a brick mason from Gaston County, NC who helped build the Academy buildings, married his cousin and Mt. Pleasant resident Francis Christine Cook, the daughter of local merchant, Mathew Cook and Mary Costner Cook. The McAllister-Cook marriage was significant not only as an example of a town and gown union, but also as a foundation for the lasting bond that developed between a community and its school. Not only did H. C. McAllister literally help to construct the first NC College buildings, his father-in-law was a major financial supporter of the school and all four of McAllister's sons attended NC College. He and his brother-in-law Jonas Cook, formed a personal relationship that facilitated their joint guidance of the school through its most difficult times. McAllister was the Secretary and President of the College Board of Trustees for over twenty years and Cook served as the College Treasurer for more than ten years. Both men were on the Board at the closing of the College and at the beginning of the Collegiate Institute.

H. C. McAllister's three sons, his three sons-in-law and one grandson all attended NC College. Eleven grand-sons and two grand-daughters attended MPCI. His son, George, taught at NC College and was the Principal of MPCI throughout its existence. Jonas Cook's three sons and four sons-in-law attended NC College and five grand-sons and two grand-daughters were students at MPCI. One grand-daughter, Mildred J. Barrier, married John H. McDaniel, a MPCI student and Teacher. John and Mildred McDaniel's son, Michael C. D. McDaniel, became a Lutheran Minister and served as Bishop of the North Carolina Lutheran Synod from 1982-1991. This work is dedicated to Bishop McDaniel.

Another marriage of note was that of Rev. Josephus A. Linn and Mary Cordelia Miller in 1888. Linn attended NC College and served as a Tutor and later became the Principal of Mont Amoena Seminary. Reverend Josephus A. Linn's father was Rev. Joseph A. Linn, who first proposed the creation of a "high school of collegiate character." Mary C. Miller, from Rowan County, attended Mont Amoena Seminary. The couple married in 1888.

In 1897 James H. C. Fisher, a student and Instructor at NC College and later Principal of Mont Amoena Seminary, married Leah Blackwelder, a Mont Amoena student and Mt. Pleasant resident.

In 1913 George F. McAllister, President of Mt. Pleasant Collegiate Institute and son of H. C. McAllister, married Ethelyn Crabtree, a resident of Virginia and teacher at Mont Amoena Seminary.

After a six year courtship which began when he first taught at MPCI, Professor Roy Webster returned to the school in 1913 and married Elma R. Welch. The bride was the daughter of a College/Town marriage as well. Her father was NC College alumnus, Benjamin F. Welch, and her mother, Mary Ella Barrier, was a town resident. Both Elma and her mother attended Mont Amoena Seminary.

Along with the McAllister and Cook legacies, no other family better represents the bond formed by NC College/MPCI and the local community than the Shirey family. John D. Shirey was the President of NC College from 1889-1896. He was the only College President to die while serving the College. Rev. Shirey was a native of Virginia, but after his death his family remained in Mt. Pleasant.

Rev. Shirey's son, Luther, a MPCI student, married Ruth Winona Cook, daughter of Jonas Cook. Winona, a local resident, attended Mont Amoena. Rev. Shirey's daughter and a Mont Amoena student, Alma, married Matthew John Cook, son of Jonas Cook. Margaret Salome Shirey, daughter of Luther Shirey and Winona Cook, married MPCI student Olmedo A. DeDiego, a MPCI student from Cuba. Rev. Shirey's daughter, Mary Julia, attended Mont Amoena and became an Instructor there in 1888. Mary was stricken ill with typhoid and died on July 29, 1892.

Julia Catherine Shirey and Martha Cook Shirey, daughters of Luther Shirey, were two of the nine women who transferred from Mont Amoena to MPCI when the Seminary closed in 1927. Another daughter, Miriam, never married but served as a long time missionary and "Deaconess" with the North Carolina Lutheran Synod. Her home congregation was Holy Trinity Church in Mt. Pleasant.[1091]

These family legacies and the countless other students and townspeople who came together to form lasting bonds that are clearly present today. The NC College and MPCI buildings serve the Mt. Pleasant community as the site of the Eastern Cabarrus Historical Sociey museum which houses the tangible history of the surrounding area and contributes heavily to "Preserving the past for the future" for North Carolina. Several of the homes used as school dormitories/barracks or the site of many student meals stand as cherished private homes today. Although many of the promises from the past were "unfulfilled," the impact of the educational institution and its dedicated individuals remain the essence of the Mt. Pleasant community 150 years later.

APPENDICES

APPENDIX 1

List of Pledges for Western Carolina Male Academy

The list of pledges below was found in the records of North Carolina College dated August 2nd, 1852. The pledges appear to have been collected as part of Mt. Pleasant's bid to host the new school, but the amount exceeds the total reported in December 1852. There were, however, other references in Synod records concerning the amount of funds on hand after Mt. Pleasant was selected as the site of the academy which more closely reflect these pledges.

North Carolina Mount Pleasant
Cabarrus County August 2nd 1852

We the undersigned bind ourselves Execs and Adms to pay the sums annexed to our respective nams for the purpose of erecting suitable buildings for a collegiate school within the bounds of the Evangelical Lutheran Synod of N. C, provided the school shall be located at Mt. Pleasant Cabarrus County.
Otherwise to be null and void.

Moses Barrier	300.00	Absalom Hahn	2.50
John Shimpock	200.00	Abram Dry	5.00
Daniel Barrier	300.00	Solomon Dry	5.00
Jacob Ludwick	75.00	Michael Isenhour	0.50
W. R. Kindley	50.00	Elias Cress	10.00
M. Melchor	50.00	Moses Shimpock	20.00
M. A. Ury	50.00	John Troutman	5.00
Matthew Cook	100.00	Alex. Misenheimer	5.00

Wm. A. Coleman	5.00	Geo. Misenheimer	20.00
Lawson Ury?	5.00	Franklin Ridenhour	1.50
M. A. Barringer	25.00	Alen Blackwelder	5.00
Matthew Petre	50.00	Jacob Barrier, Sr.	3.00
Isaac Moose	100.00	Fed? Barrier	1.00
M. H. Carter	5.00	Peter Troutman, Sr.	1.00
Simeon Cauble	10.00	E. B. Barrier	1.00
Jacob Costner	5.00	Paul M. Barringer	3.00
Thomas Goodman	3.00	Jacob W. Udy	1.00
N. Lefler	25.00	Caleb Barrier	1.00
Jhn M. Harkey	15.00	John Barrier	1.00
John L. Henderson	15.00	David Melchor	2.50
Paul B. C. Smith	50.00	Mathew Barringer	10.00
George Ritchy	100.00	H. T. Pentergrass	2.50
J. W. House	10.00	Jacob Lyerly	5.00
George Ury	30.00	Clab. Misenheimer	5.00
Charles Ludewick	40.00	Daniel Plyler	1.00
P. J. A. Haines	10.00	Christopher Lyerly	1.00
David Harkey, Sr.	10.00	Nelson Lefler	1.00
J. W. Scott	20.00	David D. Lentz	2.00
Mathias Barrier	300.00	Eldridge Sides	1.00
David Barrier	200.00	John Lentz	1.00
John Ritchy, Sr.	75.00	Peter J. Lentz	2.50
Henry Walker	25.00	Wesley T. Miller	5.00
John Faggart	50.00	William Lefler	1.00
Jacob Misenheimer	100.00	Henry B. Barrier	2.00
George Cline	10.00	Andrew Barrier	1.00
Isaac Beaver	50.00	Wilson Huneycutt	2.50
J. J. Misenheimer	25.00	Henry Beaver	2.50
John A. Troutman	25.00	Mathias Miller	25.00
Archibald Cline	5.00	J. ? Faggart	10.00
Daniel Bost	3.00	D. M. Lefler	5.00
Nicholas idenhour,	25.00	George Lefler	5.00

Adam Barnhardt	5.00	W. C. Lentz	5.00
Peter Blackwelder	5.00	David Lyerly	2.00
P. A. Barrier	12.00	Solomon Nussman	5.00
D. M. Barrier	15.00	John Ridenhour, Sr.	1.00
Martin A. Ritchey	10.00	D. H. Rendleman	1.00
Eli Harkey	3.00	Daniel Sides	1.00
Jacob Peacock	2.50	Caleb Lefler	2.00
John H. Miller	300.00	J. W. Scott	20.00
Julius A. Lefler	5.00	M. M. Plunket	35.00
Robert E. Love	25.00	Kiah P. Harris	25.00
Nicholas Lefler	15.00	Abner Krimminger	2.00
Jacob Ludwick	25.00	Wilis Elkings	3.00
George Ury	10.00	Polly Walter	10.00
Mathew Cook	50.00	Reuben Blackwelder	25.00
P. B. C. Smith	25.00	Daniel Lefler, Sr.	15.00
Abram Dry	5.00	Thomas Rowland	5.00
Henry D. Smith	2.00	J. C. Williams	5.00
Benjamin Rogers	3.00	C. P. Cox	10.00
M. H. Carter	5.00	Riley Kindley	25.00
Simeon Cauble	5.00	John Williams	10.00
Maths Faggert	10.00	Isaac Moose	50.00
Dr. P. J. A. Haines	10.00	Monroe Wilhelm	2.00
J. J. Misenheimer	50.00	Monroe Shoe	2.00
john Ritchey, Sr.	15.00	K. M. Cox	5.00
John Eagle	10.00	Wm. R. Lefler	2.00
Moses Lipe	10.00	N. N. Mitchell	25.00
D. Morgan	10.00		

State of North Carolina
Cabarrus County August 2nd, 1852

We the undersigned bine [sic] ourselves Execs and Adms. to pay Moses Barrier the sums annexed to our respective names for the purpose of erecting a suitable Building for a collegiate school within the bounds of the

Evangelical Lutheran Synod of N. C. provide the School shall be located at Mt. Pleasant Cabarrus County otherwise to be null and void.

J. M. Harkey	5.00	John Eagle	10.00
Levi Moose	15.00	Moses Lipe	10.00
Jacob Moose	2.50	J. W. Scott	20.00
John H. Miller	300.00	M. M. Plunkett	35.00
Julus Lefler	5.00	Kiah P. Harris	25.00
Robert E. Love	25.00	Abner Krimminger	2.00
Nicholas Lefler	15.00	Milas Elkins?	3.00
J. Ludwick	25.00	Polly Watter?	10.00
George Ury	10.00	Reuben Blackwelder	25.00
Mathew Cook	15.00	Daniel Lefler	15.00
P. B. C. Smith	15.00	Thos Rowland	5.00
Abram Dry	5.00	Jacob C. Williams	5.00
Henry D. Smith	2.00	C. P. Cox	10.00
Benjamin Rogers	3.00	Riley Kindley	5.00
M. H. Carter	5.00	John Williams	10.00
Simeon Cauble	5.00	Isaac Moose	25.00
Maths Faggart	10.00	Monore Wilhelm	2.00
P.J. A. Haines	10.00	Monroe Shoe	2.00
J. J. Misenheimer	25.00	K. M. Cox	5.00
John Misenheimer	5.00	William R. Lefler	2.00
John Ritchey	15.00	Harris Biles	2.00

APPENDIX 2

Western Carolina Male Academy Deed

State of North Carolina

Cabarrus County

This Indenture made this the 30th day of June AD 1853 between Matthias Barrier of said State and County of the first part: and Christopher Melchor, President of the Board of Directors of the Western North Carolina Academy and Joseph A. Linn, Simeon Scherer, L. C. Groseclose; William G. Harter, Samuel Rothrock, John D. Scheck, Charles L. Parter, Caleb Heilig, Daniel Barrier and John Shimpock of the Western North Carolina Academy of the second part, witnessed that the said party of the first part for and in consideration_of the sum of eighty one dollars and twenty five cents to him in hand paid, the receipt whereof is hereby acknowledged doth this day bargained, sold and conveyed, aliened, confirmed and enfeoffed, and doth hereby bargain, sell, convey, alien, confirm and enfeoff to the said parties of the second part and their successors in office all that tract or parcel of land located in the village of Mount Pleasant in the County aforesaid and adjoining the lands of the said party of the first part, William R. Kinley and others, containing sixteen and a quarter acres be the same more or less and bounded as follows to wit:

Beginning at a stone on the said W. R. Kinley's line thence

West 23 poles and 4 links to a stake, thence N 2 poles 15 links to an elm, N70 1/2W 9 poles to a dogwood, thence N85E 16 1/2 poles to a stake in the Salisbury Road near a poplar and sugarberry pointers, thence South 2 1/2 E 44 poles and 10 links to a hickory, Hurlocker and said Kinley's corner, thence S2W, 7 poles and 13 links to the beginning:

To have and to hold the same to them and their successors in office, together with all the appurtenances thereunto belonging forever, and in further consideration of the said sum of Eighty One Dollars and twenty five cents the said party of the first part doth hereby give, grant, bargain, sell and convey to the said parties of the second part, and their successors in office the right of way, on lands adjoining the above described premises and owned by the said party of the first part, the usual width of all public highways, commencing on the Salisbury Road next to the beginning corner of the lands hereinafter conveyed, running with the line first called for in this deed to the top of the hill, and thence along the curve of said hill, or as nearly so as convenient, in the direction of the Concord Road to the Southern Boundary of the lands belonging to the said party of the first part, and the right of way is hereby made one appurtenance forever to the said parties of the second part and their successors in office to the lands hereinbefore described, and by this indenture conveyed by the said party of the first part to the said parties of the second part and their successors in office. And the said party of the first part doth hereby covenant for himself and his heirs to and with the said parties of the second part and their successors in office to defend and warrant the premises herein before described, together with said right of way hereinbefore conveyed, against the claim or claims of all persons whatsoever either in law or equity, and the said party of the first part doth further covenant for himself and his heirs to and with the said parties of the second part and their successors in office, that he the said party of the first part is seized in fee simple of the premises hereinbefore and hereby conveyed, and of the premises over which as an appurtenance thereunto the said right of way in hereinbefore conveyed, and that he hath a right to convey and doth hereby convey title in fee to said parties of the second part and their successors in office forever, a certain Religious Society, known as the North Carolina Evangelical Lutheran Synod, to locate thereon a certain institution of learning for the promotion of morals and religion and the general diffusion of knowledge and education, to erect thereon all buildings necessary and proper to promote the successful operation and the general prosperity of said Institution, and to secure the ends and purposes fairly fully and truly for which said Institution was projected as set forth in the Constitution accepted and published by said Religious Society. And in further trust to the said parties of the second part to convey the sum that is to say the lands herein upon described and the right of way hereinbefore conveyed by such title and with such obligations as said lands together with said right of way have been and are hereby conveyed, to any heirs, or persons or corporation that may at any time here after be designated by said North Carolina Evangelical Lutheran Synod either by a committee appointed for that purpose or by any other means of signifying their wishes said Religious Society may ask of it. The testimony whereof the said party of first part hath this day herewith signed his name and affixed his seal.

Signed sealed and delivered in the presence of

Mathias Barrier

John L. Henderson

Robt. Edom

State of North Carolina Court of Pleas and Quarter Sessions Cabarrus County April Term 1860.

I Nelson Stough Clerk of the Court of Pleas and Quarter Sessions of the County and State aforesaid do hereby certify that the execution of the written and foregoing deed was duly acknowledged before me in open Court by the grantor let it be registered together with this certificate.

Nelson Stough Clerk

North Carolina

Cabarrus County

J. R. Winecoff, Registrar do hereby certify that the foregoing deed came to hand for Registry May 5th, 1860 and was also duly Registered in [this] office. Book No 21 and Page 38.

R. Winecoff,

APPENDIX 3

Constitution of Western Carolina Male Academy

Article I

Design of This Institution

In order that the public may become fully apprised of the designs of this Institution, it is proper to make a summary statement of the objects aimed at by its founders, and of the benefits to be expected from it by its patrons. It is designed:

Section 1. To provide a large portion of North Carolina's citizens with more immediate facilities for the proper training of her youth, and a more general diffusion of knowledge among her people at large; by elevating the standard of education among our teachers of Common Schools, and multiplying the number of men qualified for any of the business departments of life.

Sec. 2. Being under the control of the Evan. Luth. Synod of North Carolina, it is designed to provide that branch of the Christian Church with an increased number of Ministers, so as to meet her demand, by affording those young me in her bosom, who are seeking the Ministry, an opportunity of preparing themselves at least in the first stage, for that sacred office.

Sec. 3. It is designed to add to the list of studies usually taught in Colleges, on of recent date, and as yet admitted into but few schools in this country: It is the Science of Agriculture – in importance, second to none that are taught. Surely! if as God had declared, "the profit of the earth is for all; the king himself is served by the field," that science which tends to its profit should be cultivated not merely by the practical farmer, but theoretically by every student. It was the first science to encourage the study of man and should not now be the last. For while in the sinless perfection of his original nature, "the Lord God put him into the Garden Eden, to dress it and to keep it." – It has been well said, "That to Agriculture, under the influence of a sound morality, must we look for the permanent strength, the glory, and happiness of our great Republic."

Article II

Of the Board of Directors

Sec. 1. This Board shall be known as the Board of Directors of Western Carolina Male Academy, located at Mount Pleasant, Cabarrus county; and under the control of the Evan. Lutheran Synod of North Carolina, as provided for in the Statutes or plan of said Institution.

Sec. 2. Every Director, before he takes his seat as a member of this Board, shall solemnly subscribe the following formula, viz: Sincerely approving the design of this Institution of the Evangelical Lutheran Synod of N. C., as detailed in its statutes, and of the provisions of this Constitution and other statutes for the regulation of this Institution hereafter to be created; I do solemnly declare and promise in the presence of God and this Board, that I will faithfully endeavor to carry into effect all of the provisions of said Constitution and statutes, and thus promote the design of said Institution.

Sec. 3. The Board shall annually choose out of their own number, a President, Vice President, and Secretary, who shall always be re-eligible. In the absence of the President, the Vice President shall preside, and in his absence the Board shall elect a President, pro. tem.

Sec. 4. The Board of Directors shall elect some suitable person as the Treasurer of the Board, who may be selected out of their own number, or the Laity of the church, whose duty it shall be to fulfill the objects specified in the statutes of this Institution. He shall in no case, whatever, pay out any money, except when ordered by a vote of the Board, and shall render to them at every semi-annual meeting, a faithful statement of this account, and shall hold his office, together with the funds of this Institution, subject to the exclusive direction of the Board.

Sec. 5. Every meeting of the Board Shall be opened and closed with prayer. And at every stated meeting in the Spring, the whole of the regulations and Constitution of said Institution [shall] be read before the Directors, in order that they distinctly keep in mind the design of the Institution and the duties incumbent upon them.

Sec. 6. All special meetings of the Board Shall be called by the President, or in case of his absence or death, by the Vice President, whenever a written request for such a meeting is presented to him, signed by at least five Directors. The mode of calling such a meeting, when thus lawfully requested, shall be by a circular or letter addressed to each Director, specifying the time of meeting, and the business to be transacted. This letter shall be addressed at least ten days before the time of said meeting, and no business can be transacted except that specified in the notice.

Sec. 7. The Board shall inaugurate the Professors and give direction what exercises shall be performed on such occasions. They shall, in the main, prescribe the course of instruction to be pursued by the Professors: and any Professor wishing to introduce any important change in his department of the course, shall first submit it to the Board for their approbation.

Sec. 8. The Board of Directors shall inspect the fidelity of the Professors, as well regarding the tendency of the branches taught, as to the manner of teaching them. In any just reason be given them to suspect either the morality, or habitual indulgence in immoral habits, or capacity of a Professor or his devotedness to the interests of this Institution, it shall be their sacred duty to institute an investigation at the next regular meeting, or by calling a special meeting for the purpose. If, after candid and deliberate examination, they shall judge any Professor guilty of either of the above charges alledged [sic] against him, it shall be their duty to depose him from office, and to take the earliest constitutional measures to elect a new Professor.

Sec. 9. It shall be the duty of the Board of Directors to keep a watch over the conduct and interests of the students; to redress their grievances, to review and sanction, or reverse the decision of the Faculty.

Sect. 10. At every stated meeting of the Evangelical Luth. Synod of N. C., the Board shall forward to said body in writing, a detailed and faithful account of the state of this Institution. Said Synod may recommend to the Board any measures they may deem conducive to the welfare of the Institution; and every such recommendation shall be considered at the next regular meeting of the Board, and may be accepted or rejected, as the majority of the Directors shall see fit.

Sec. 11. All matters requiring the sense of this Board, shall be viewed as final, whenever voted for by the majority of the same; and in all cases those who are necessarily absent may vote by proxy or letter.

Sec. 12. In their efforts to promote the grand designs of this Institution, and in all their official acts, the Directors shall conform to its Constitution, and the statutes on which it is founded: and if at any time they should act contrary thereto or transcend the powers therein granted them, the party deeming itself aggrieved, shall first submit the case to the Evangelical Lutheran Synod of N. C. for arbitration; and if still aggrieved, may have redress by appeal to the judges of the Supreme Court of the State of North Carolina, who are hereby constituted and authorized to judge in such cases, a majority of whom may declare null and void any decision of this Board, from which an appeal is made to them, and which after mature deliberation, they believe to be contrary to the design of this Institution, or the statutes on which it is founded.

Article III

Of the Professors

Sec. 1. No person shall be eligible to the office of Professor, who is not a regular member of some orthodox Christian denomination, and of high repute for his piety and talents. And no person shall be eligible to the Presidency, or principal Professorship of this Institution, who has not in addition to the above qualifications, officiated as Teacher or Professor, to have acquired a enough experience.

Sec. 2. Every Professor elect of this Institution shall, on the day of his inauguration, or before he assumes the duties of his office as Teacher, publicly pronounce and subscribe the following oath of office.

I solemnly declare in the presence of God and the Directors of this Institution, that I do *ex animo*, believe the Scriptures of the Old and New Testament to be the inspired Word of God, and the only perfect rule of faith and practice. I declare that I approve of the general principles of basis of this Institution, and the rules and regulations adopted by the Board for its government. And I do solemnly promise that I will use every laudable means to elevate the Literary, Scientific, and Moral character of said Institution. I do further promise not to teach anything, either directly or by insinuation which shall appear to me to contradict or to be in any degree remote, inconsistent with the wishes or principles avowed by the Board of this Institution. On the contrary, I promise by the aid of God, to vindicate and inculcate the doctrines and principles of orthodox Christianity in opposition to the views of Atheists, Deists, Jews, Socinians, Unitarians, Arians, Universalists, Pelagians, Antinominas and all other errorsts, while I remain a Professor in this Institution.

Sec. 3. The preceding declaration shall be repeated by each Professor at the expiration of every term of *three years*, in the presence of the Directors: and at any intermediate time, if required to do so by a vote of the Board of Directors. And no man shall be retained as Professor who shall refuse to make and repeat this declaration, in the manner and at the times above specified.

Sec. 4. Each Professor shall, if practicable, have at least ten lectures or recitations in a week.

Sec. 5. The Salary of the Professors shall be fixed by the Board and shall be equal to a comfortable support and provision for a family.

Sec. 6. Should any Professor wish to resign his office, he shall give the Directors six months previous notice of his intention.

Sec. 7. The Professors of this Institution shall constitute a Faculty, of which each member shall have an equal vote, and of which the President or principal Professor shall, when present, be *ex officio* chairman. The Faculty shall convene at the request of any one of its members. They may call in any one or more of the members of the Board as advisory members but in no case shall they be allowed to vote. They shall keep a record of their proceedings, which shall be laid before the Directors at every regular meeting.

Sec. 8. The faculty shall have power to determine the hours of recitation; to examine and decide on all cases of discipline and questions of order; to admit students; to determine the rules of decorum and duty, not herein prescribed, which the students are to observe, which rules shall be publicly read to the students ant the commencement of each session; to admonish and dismiss any student, who shall prove immoral, or disobedient; or whom they shall judge on any account a dangerous or unprofitable member of the Institution.

Sec. 9. The Professors, together with the students, shall attend Divine Services at such time and place as the Board hereafter may be able to make arrangement for.

Article IV
Of Students

Sec. 1. This Institution shall be open for the reception of all male students, who have secured their right of Tuition by the purchase of a Scholarship, or half Scholarship; and also to all others who shall pay in advance the rates of Tuition established by the Board of Directors.

Sec. 2. Patrons of this Institution who are in the receipt of whole Scholarships, shall be permitted to send one pupil at a time during all the sessions of school, and in case of death or expulsion for misconduct of any such student, his place may be supplied by another at any time. Persons holding half Scholarships may be permitted to send one pupil at a time continuously for a period not exceeding three years, after which they shall not be permitted to send for a corresponding period.

Sec. 3. Every applicant for admission into this Institution, not having secured the right of Tuition by the purchase of a Scholarship, and having arrived at the age of *Fifteen* years, shall produce satisfactory testimonials that he possesses good natural talents, is of prudent and discreet deportment, and good moral habits. And any student coming from another Institution must bring a certificate of regular and honorable dismissal.

Sec. 4. No student whatever shall be matriculated until he is fifteen years of age and has been six weeks in the Institution; until this, he is merely a probationer, and will not be admitted unless his moral conduct and habits of study are satisfactory.

Sec. 5. Every student before he enters into regular connection with this Institution, and at the same time of his matriculation, shall solemnly make and subscribe the following declaration: I, ABC, declare it to be my serious intention to devote myself, according as I have talent, to the acquisition of all useful knowledge: and I solemnly promise that, so long as I remain a member of this Institution, I will faithfully and diligently attend on all the instructions of this Institution; that I will conscientiously and vigilantly observe all the regulation of the Constitution and By-Laws of the same; and that I will pay due respect and obedience to the Professors; treat my fellow students as brethren, and all other men with the utmost respect and decorum. I further solemnly promise that I will abstain from the profanation of the Lord's day: from the use of profane language, from drunkenness, from licentiousness or lewdness; from all kinds of gambling, from all indecent, disorderly behavior, and from disrespectful conduct toward any man.

Sec. 6. All pupils under fifteen years of age shall be placed under the immediate supervision of one or more of the Teachers during the hours both of study and recreation.

Sec. 7. Habitual diligence and industry in study shall be required of all the students, unless the want of health prevent, for which the Professors shall make do allowance.

Sec. 8. Every student shall be expected to treat his Teachers with the greatest deference and respect, and all persons with civility; and all students shall yield a prompt and ready obedience to all the lawful requisitions of the Professors and Directors.

Sec. 9. Cleanliness in dress and habit shall be observed by every student; but all excessive expense in clothing is strictly forbidden.

Article V

Course of Study, Examinations, and Vacations

Sec. 1. This Institution contemplates a course of study both primary and Academic in its character.

I. - Preparatory Department

The course of instruction in this department shall embrace a solid and thorough English education, whilst those who desire to prepare for business or for Academy, may have every advantage for the elements of Mathematics and the Latin, Greek, etc. The following includes in the main, the list of studies: Reading, Writing, Orthography, and the definition of words; English Grammar, Arithmetic, Book Keeping, Geography, (Modern,) History of North Carolina, and the United States; Composition, Natural Philosophy, Agriculture, Latin and Greek Grammar, Latin and Greek Reader, commenced; Algebra, commenced. – Throughout the whole Course the student will be required to attend to English Grammar, Composition and Declamation.

II.- Academic Department

In this Department it is designed, that all the branches usually taught in Academies shall be attended to; and should the interests of the Institution demand it, suitable provision will be made whereby students may receive Graduating Diplomas, as in any other graduating college. In this event, the whole course of instruction in this Department, will occupy *four years*, each being divided into two sessions.

Sec. 2. At the close of each session, there shall be a regular examination of all the classes in both Departments on the studies of that session, conducted by the Professors, in the presence of such of the Directors, patrons and other literary gentlemen as may be present. And at the close of their coursed, the Senior Class shall in like manner be examined on all the studies in the whole course. The Thesis of the Senior Class shall be assigned them by the Faculty, three months before the time, when they are to be publicly defended. Provision may also be made by the Faculty for suitable and profitable contests and public exhibitions.

Sec. 3. There shall be two vacations in each year, of five weeks continuance each, to commence on the third Thursday of April and September.

Sec. 4. All students, whether boarding in the Academy edifice or elsewhere, shall be in their respective rooms during study hours, and no students shall be absent for recitation or lecture except for sickness or with the permission of the officiating Professor.

Article VI

Of the Library

Sec.1. The acquisition of a select and comprehensive Classical, Literary and Scientific Library, shall be considered as an object of the highest importance to this Institution.

Sec. 2. The Directors shall, therefore, from time to time, make such arrangements as they shall deem best calculated to attain the object in view, and so soon as funds are secured for that purpose, purchase the most necessary works.

Sec. 3. A Librarian shall keep a correct catalogue of all the books belonging to the Library, and of all the donors who have made contributions to it.

Sec. 4. A suitable room shall be appropriated for the Library; and shelves shall be erected and divided into alcoves. If any Synod or individual shall fill one of the compartments, the name of the donor shall be conspicuously place over it.

Sec. 5. The Librarian shall keep a correct catalogue of all the books belonging to the Library, and of all the donors who have made contributions to it.

Sec. 6. No person shall have a right to borrow books, except the Professors and Students of the Institution.

Sec. 7. The Librarian shall form a detailed system of regulations, embracing the leading features specified in this Constitution for the management of the Library; which, after having been sanctioned by the Directors, shall remain in force, subject to the amendment or revisal of the Board.

Sec. 8. The stated time for loaning and returning books, shall be from one to three o'clock of every Saturday afternoon in term time. Nor shall the Library be opened in the intermediate time, excepting by the Professors, to whom the key of the Library shall at any time be given.

Sec. 9. A list of the most necessary books shall be presented to the Directors by the Professors, in order that those which are most needed, may be purchased first.

Sec. 10. Books which are of such size and nature, that they ought rarely to be taken from the Library, shall be used in it, during Library hours; *Provided always,* that they may be taken out by the Professors, or by a student, who shall have obtained a written order from a Professor. The Faculty shall give the Librarian a list of the books referred to in this section.

Article VII

Of the Steward and Commons

Sec. 1. In the event this Institution shall demand the services of a Steward, he shall be employed by the Directors, and shall hold his station under such stipulations as may be agreed upon by them.

Sec. 2. It is desirable that all students should board in Commons, and will be required so to do, excepting residents, and persons having near relatives in the vicinity of the Institution, who are at liberty to board with them.

Article VIII

Of the Funds

Sec. 1. The funds of this Institution shall at all times be kept entirely separate and distinct from all other funds or monies whatever; and the

Directors shall deposite [sic] them in the hands of such corporation, or dispose of them in such other manner for safe keeping and improvement as they may see proper.

Sec. 2. The Directors shall endeavor from time to time to devise means for the gradual enlargement of the funds, until they become adequate to the necessities of the Institution.

Sec. 3. It shall be the duty of the Directors sacredly to execute the intention and directions of Testators or donors, in regard to monies, or other property, left or given to this Institution.

Sec. 4. All monies collected for funds obtained, shall be paid into the general fund, until provision is made for the support of the Professors, and the erection of all the necessary buildings.

Article IV

Sec. 1. No alteration or amendment of this constitution shall be made except at a regular meeting of the Board, and every alteration or amendment proposed shall be submitted in writing at one regular meeting and lie over to the next regular meeting of the Board for the adoption or rejection.

APPENDIX 4

Charter of North Carolina College

AN ACT to incorporate the Trustees of North Carolina College.

Section1. Be it enacted by the General Assembly of the State of North Carolina and it is hereby enacted by the authority of the same, That Christopher Melchor, Matthias Barrier, Samuel Rothrock, Daniel I. Dreher, Daniel Barrier, Jacob Crim, Levi C. Groseclose, Paul A. Siffert, Joseph A. Linn, Godhard D. Bernheim, Caleb A. Heilig, John Shimpoch, and Daniel H. Bittle, and their successors duly elected, be and they are hereby made, constituted and declared a body corporate in the name of the "Trustees of North Carolina College" for the instruction of youths, in the various branches of science, literature, and art, with perpetual succession, with all the immunities and privileges and subject to all the restrictions prescribed in chapter 26 of the Revised Code entitled "Corporations."

Sec. 2. Be it further enacted That the President and Professors of said College, by and with the consent of the Trustees, shall have the power of conferring all such degrees or marks of literary distinction as are usually conferred in Colleges and Universities.

Sec. 3. Be it further enacted, That it shall not be lawful for any person or persons to set up or continue any gaming billiard table, or any device whatever for playing at any game of chance or hazard, or to exhibit any sleight of hand, theatrical or equestrian performance, dramatic recitation, rope or wire dancing, or other itinerant, natural or artificial curiosities; nor shall it be lawful for any person to sell any wines, spirituous or malt liquors to any person within three miles of said North Carolina College, except for medical purposes, nor give and convey to the students of said College any intoxicating liquors without the special permission in writing of the Faculty of said College; any person or persons violating any of the provisions of this Act shall be considered guilty of a misdemeanor, and be prosecuted in any Court having cognizance thereof; and moreover, subject to a penalty of fifty dollars, to be recovered on a warrant before any Justice of the Peace, one half to the person, warranting for the same, and the other half to the use of said College.

Sec. 4. Be it further enacted, That the Trustees of said College shall at no time exceed eighteen in number; and when vacancies occur in the Board of Trustees, they shall be filled by the Evangelical Lutheran Synod of North Carolina, and such other Synods of the Lutheran Church as may hereafter become associated with it in patronizing said College; and in case such Synod or Synods fails to fill such vacancies, then the Trustees shall have power to fill vacancies in their body.

Sec. 5. Be it further enacted, that said College shall be situated at Mt. Pleasant, in the County of Cabarrus.

Sec. 6. Be it further enacted, That said corporation may take, hold, bargain, and sell, such real estate, moneys, stocks, and other personal chattels, as may be necessary for the transactions of its business, and the carrying out of the purposes of its creation, not exceeding in value four hundred thousand dollars.

Sec. 7. Be it further enacted, that this act shall be in force from and after its ratification.

Read three times and ratified in General Assembly, this 21st day of January 1859.

Thos. Settle, Jr., SHC
Henry T. Clark, SS

APPENDIX 5

Constitution & By Laws of the Pi Sigma Phi and Philalaethian Literary Societies of NC College

Preamble

Whereas it has become the unanimous wish of the members of this society known as the Crescent Society of NC College to revise the constitution and bylaws of the same. We in full meeting assembled still cherishing the object of the Society have in view by its founders the social intellectual and moral improvements of its members do adopt the following Constitution and by Laws

Constitution

This society shall be known as the Pi Sigma Phi Society of NC College

The object of the society shall be the acquisition of knowledge, the cultivation of eloquence and refinement and the general improvement of all the members.

Membership

Any matriculated student may become a member of this society

Any gentleman may be elected to honorary membership in this body who will exert his influence to promote its prosperity and may be present at its meetings and permitted to speak on all questions pertaining to this society, but not allowed to vote.

Officers

The officers of this society shall consist of a President, VP, Rec. Sec, [???] Sec, Treasurer, Librarian and Asst. Librarian, Marshall and Chaplain[1]

[1]"Papers of Charles P. Bansemer," contained in *NC College/MPCI Papers*, Southern Historical Collection, Wilson Library, University of North Carolina, Chapel Hill, NC.

The Constitution and By-Laws of the Philalaethian Literary Society for 1857

"For our improvement in Literature, Science and Eloquence, we form ourselves into an Association to be known as the Philalaethian Literary Society

Article XII The exercises shall consist of Declamation, Composition, and Forensic Disputation and in these exercises all the members shall participate, except the President.

Article XIII The initiation fee of this society shall be ($5.00) dollars, payable in installments of twenty-five cents, (25c) per month.

Article XIV The ordinary members of this society shall consist of students connected with this institution; and the honorary members shall be persons of good moral character and of distinguished literary ability, who shall be elected by a vote of two thirds of the society.

By Laws

No. 1 It shall the duty of the custodians to keep fires, attend to the lamps, keep hall in the proper condition and keep water on the rostrum during the meeting of the society. …

No. 11 No composition shall be less than twenty-five lines of "Legal Cap" paper, nor written with a lead pencil, everyone shall be original. Fine 25c.

No. 12 Any member reading the same essay in the hall more than once, shall be fined 25c.

No. 15 The doorkeeper shall sit by the door and shall not permit more than three members to go out of the hall at the same time.

No. 16 Any member going out of the hall with out the door-keeper's permission, and not having a valid excuse, shall be fined 23c.

No. 22 Coming into the hall or being in the hall with hat on … shall be considered disrespect.

No. 23 Any member leaning against the wall, romping on the carpet, putting his foot, on a chair or round a chair, putting his leg over the arm of a chair shall be fined 25c.

No. 24 Any member spitting on the floor, furniture, or out of the window … shall be fined 25c.

No. 42 Any member coming into the hall intoxicated, shall be fined $5.00.

No. 43 Any member playing cards in the hall shall be fined $5.00.

No. 44 Any member sleeping in the hall shall be fined 50 cents.

No. 56 Any member using low or vulgar slang shall be fined 50 cents.

No. 59 Any member using profane language in the hall shall be fined $5.00.

No. 60 Any member using obscene language in the hall shall be fined 50 cents.[2]

[2] "The Constitution and By-Laws of the Philalaethian Literary Society, 1857," unpublished manuscript, Eastern Cabarrus Historical Society Library, Mt. Pleasant, NC.

APPENDIX 6

Revised Charter of North Carolina College - 1909

Private Laws of the State of North Carolina – 1909 Chapter 357, p. 792

An Act to Revise the Charter of the Trustees of North Carolina College, Mount Pleasant, North Carolina

The General Assembly of North Carolina do enact:

Section 1. That H. C. McAllister, Jonas Cook, G. L. Barrier, C. D. Barringer and W. H. Fisher of Mount Pleasant, North Carolina; J. E. Shenk, J. A. Cline, George E. Ritchie, V. Y. Boozer and M. B. Stickley of Concord, North Carolina; C. M. Pool, H. A. Trexler, and C. P. Fisher of Salisbury, North Carolina; W. A. Dutton of Richfield, North Carolina; G. W. Dry of Gold Hill, North Carolina; J. S. Efird and H. A. McCullough of Albemarle, North Carolina, and J. M. Brown of Efird's Mill, North Carolina, and their successors be and they are hereby created a corporation for the promotion of religion, morality, and learning, under the name of Trustees of North Carolina College, and in such name shall contract and be contracted with, sue and be sued, plead and be impleaded, and the persons so mentioned shall constitute the board of trustees of said corporation until their successors shall be elected and qualified.

Sec. 2. That it shall be the duty of the Evangelical Lutheran Synod and Ministerium of North Carolina to elect eighteen trustees of said corporation who shall hold office for a period of three years from the date of election, in the following manner: one-third of the said board of trustees shall be elected at the regular meeting of the Synod in May, one thousand nine hundred and nine, to take the places of J. E. Shenk, H. M. Brown, J. A. Cline, G. L. Barrier, C. M. Pool and C. D. Barringer, and one-third shall be elected at the regular meeting of said synod in one thousand nine hundred and ten, to take the place of W. H. Fisher, George E. Ritchie, H. A. McCullough, G. W. Dry, M. B. Stickley and V. Y. Boozer, and the remaining one-third shall be elected at the regular meeting of said synod in one thousand nine hundred and eleven to take the places of H. C. McAllister, Jonas Cook, H. A. Trexler, J. S. Efird, W. A. Dutton, and C. P. Fisher; and every year there-after six trustees shall be elected at the regular meeting of said synod. One-third of said trustees shall be clergymen who are members of the North Carolina Synod, and two-thirds laymen, four of whom shall be eligible for re-election. Any vacancies occurring among said trustees by death, resignation, or otherwise, or by failure of election by said synod shall be filled by the said board of trustees.

Sec. 3. That it shall be unlawful for any person or persons to set up or continue any gaming billiard table, or any device whatever for playing at any game of chance or hazard, or to exhibit any sleight of hand, theatrical or equestrian performance, dramatic recitation, rope or wire dancing, or other itinerant, natural or artificial curiosities; nor shall it be lawful for any person to sell any wines, spirituous or malt liquors to any person within three miles of said North Carolina College, except for medical purposes, nor give and convey to the students of said College any intoxicating liquors without the special permission in writing of the Faculty of said College; any person or persons violating any of the provisions of this Act shall be considered guilty of a misdemeanor.

Sec. 4. That the said trustees shall meet annually in the town of Mount Pleasant, North Carolina, and at such other times and places as may be deemed expedient for the good of the college. They shall at the first meeting elect from their number a chairman, secretary and treasurer and an executive committee of five, the chairman of the board of trustees o be a member of the committee to carry out all the rules, regulations and orders of the said board of trustees which said board is authorized and empowered to make.

Sec. 5. That said corporation shall adopt a common seal, and may take, hold, demand, receive and possess all lands, tenements, moneys, goods and chattels which have been given to the Trustees of North Carolina College, and shall succeed to all rights, privileges and property, both real and personal, owned and possessed by said Trustees of North Carolina College, and shall be the lawful successors thereto, and it shall have the right accept and receive all property given it or its predecessors (the Trustees of North Carolina College). and it shall have the right to loan and invest all funds that the said Trustees of North Carolina College now have on hand or may hereafter collect. If at any time the object of property for which any funds, donations or gifts were acquired shall fail, the said corporation is hereby authorized to transfer said property to the Evangelical Lutheran Synod and Ministerium of North Carolina and its successors to office, to be invested and used by said synod to such manner as will carry out the intention of the grantor or donor, in so far as the circumstances and conditions will warrant.

Sec. 6. That the said corporation shall use all moneys, funds and gifs of every kind and description for the use and benefit of said college. It shall be its duty to maintain a Mount Pleasant, North Carolina, a school for promotion of religion, morality, and learning, and teaching the various branches of science, literature and art, under such name as the board of trustees may adopt; and upon the recommendation of the faculty of said college, the said board of trustees shall have the power of conferring all such degrees or marks of literary distinction as are conferred in colleges and universities.

Sec. 7. The said board of trustees shall have the right to elect and employ a president of said college and professors to teach in the institution, and to remove them for sufficient cause: or if it deemed advisable, said board of trustees shall have the right to lease, for the purposes and objects above set out, said college grounds, buildings, libraries and all other property belonging thereto, for a term of years, and appropriated and use the income of said college to further and carry on the objects of said lease.

Sec. 8. That the Evangelical Lutheran Synod and Ministerium of North Carolina and is successors in office may make such loans and donations to said college as may be deemed advisable, and it shall have the right to indicate the policies that the board of trustees of said college may adopt in carrying out and furthering the purposes of its creation. The said board of trustees shall have to make such conveyances to said synod to secure loans and donations as may be mutually agreed upon by the executive committees of the respective bodies.

Sec. 9. That the said college shall be in Mount Pleasant, county of Cabarrus, State of North Carolina.

Sec. 10. That the board of trustees shall have the power to adopt such by-laws as may be necessary for their government to the transaction of business and determine the number to constitute a quorum.

Sec. 11. That all laws and clauses of laws in conflict with this act are hereby repealed.

Sec. 12. That this act shall be in full force and effect from and after its ratification.

Ratified this 8th day of March, A. D. 1909.

APPENDIX 7

Regulations of Mount Pleasant Collegiate Institute

All rules and regulations for the government of the Institute are subject to amendment when deemed necessary by the faculty.

Arrest – No cadet in arrest shall be allowed to perform guard duty but shall confine himself to his room except when necessary to attend recitations, meals, formations and other necessary occasions to be stipulated by announcement. He shall repot his departure and return therefrom to the officer of the day. No cadet in arrest will make a visit to a superior officer without the permission of the Commandant of Cadets, and in case of business, he shall make known his object in writing.

Bulletin Board – Cadets shall inform themselves of all official matter published on the Bulletin Board. Nothing but official matter will be displayed on the Bulletin Board unless permission is granted by a member of the Faculty.

Campus – Cadets will not be allowed to leave the Campus except at times hereinafter designated and at other times when deemed necessary by a member of the faculty. Cadets will not be allowed to congregate, play or loiter on the Campus during recitation or study hours. Members of the sub-Freshman, Freshman, and Sophomore classes not residing in Barracks may occupy the chapel when not on recitation, or they may study with a classmate rooming in the Barracks upon special written permission from a member of the Faculty. They will be required to preserve good order when availing themselves of these privileges. A cadet confined to the Campus will not go off the Campus until released by Commandant of Cadets or some other member of the Faculty. Cadets who reside in town are under the control of their parents but must always observe the regulations. Cadets rooming in town will remain within the yard at all times when the cadets rooming in Barracks are required to be on Campus.

Call To Quarters – At Call to Quarters or signal for same a cadet will proceed to his room unless he has duty elsewhere to perform

Chapel Services – All cadets are required to attend devotional exercises in Chapel every school day.

Church and Divine Services – All cadets will be required to attend Sunday school and Divine services every Sunday morning. Cadets will attend the Sunday school of their church, if represented; otherwise, the one selected. A cadet excused for any reason from attending Sunday school and Divine service will be required to remain in his room until the Company to which he belongs had returned therefrom. He will also remain on the Campus the remainder of the day. Cadets rooming in Barracks will attend Church with their regular Company organization. Talking or sitting with arms on back of pews during service is prohibited.

Confinements and Tours – Regulations for Confinement and Tours will be published in orders.

Delinquencies – All delinquencies reported will be published to the Chapel on the day the report is submitted to the Commandant. No cadet will address another cadet who has reported him for a delinquency, on the subject of such of a report unless permission is first given. The reporting officer will be under the same restrictions. A cadet receiving 100 demerits will be dismissed.

Dining Hall – At meal call the cadets boarding in the Dining Hall will be formed and marched to the Dining Hall. The cadet in charge of the Company will, before marching the Company into the Dining Hall, divide the Company into squads, corresponding to the number of tables for the cadets. Cadet offices will act as Carvers, and they are required to see that good behavior is observed. All loud talking or boisterous conduct in the Dining Hall is prohibited. The Carvers only shall call or speak to the waiters.

Wasting provisions, or taking them from the Dining Hall, or damaging or abstracting furniture of any kind is prohibited. The Carvers will report all acts inconsistent with the proper deportment of a gentleman at table. Cadets are not allowed to leave their seats until the command to rise is given by the Carver.

Explanations – A cadet reported for an offense may submit an explanation of the circumstances of the report. Explanations shall include only such statements of facts and of the conduct or intentions of the cadet as may be necessary for a full and correct understanding of the case: they shall not be made in the medium of complaint or criticism. Explanations shall be in writing and on form and blanks furnished by school. Explanations will be submitted between 8 and 9 o'clock AM, the day following the publication of the report on the Bulletin Board. In case a cade claims the responsibility rests upon another cadet the name of the latter will be stated, to whom the explanation will be referred for remarks and explanation, if necessary. In case a cadet is reported for absence he will submit an explanation, stating his whereabouts at the time of absence.

Formations – Formations at the Institute shall be according to the "Bell Ringer's" time. At all formations cadets commanding shall take post in front of and facing their entire commands when the assembly ceases and supervise the formation. Lieutenants shall be in the immediate vicinity of their post at the assembly and in their places, standing at attention with swords drawn, if under arms, when the Captain assumes command of the Company. Cadets shall be reported absent from any formation when not in ranks before the cadet calling the roll makes his report. This report will be made immediately upon the completion of the roll call. Cadets shall be reported late at any formation if not in their respective places when the assembly ceases. A cadet officer excused from any formation shall notify his Company Commander. A cadet non-commissioned officer or private shall notify his First Sergeant. A cadet leaving drill, or any other duty shall report his leaving to the officer of the day and his return also in case of return. The cadet in charge of the organization will enter a report through the officer of the day against a cadet who leaves the organization before the duty upon which he is engaged has been completed.

Furlough and Leaves – Leaves will be granted to the cadets as follows: Every afternoon from after drill until supper formation. Every Saturday from after inspection of Barracks by the Commandant in the morning until 10:30 PM. From after church until supper on Sundays. Taps will be sounded at 11:00 PM on Saturday nights. Cadets having confinements or tours to serve will serve them during leave hours. The uniform will be worn when leave is granted. Furloughs will be granted to cadets to go home on Saturdays and Sundays, upon the request of the parent or guardian of cadet. Cadets will not be allowed to depart on Friday afternoon until they have performed all their duties in the classrooms and in society. A cadet going on furlough will report his departure and return to the officer of the day. Cadets will be required to have the article s and furniture in their rooms arranged in perfect order when they depart for furlough. A cadet will immediately report his return if he returns to tow before the completion of the time granted in the furlough. Cadets cannot take advantage of the furlough to be out of town at times other than leave hours.

Guard – Guard duty shall be performed in such manner as herein prescribed, with alternatives if deemed necessary, by the Faculty. No changing of tours or reliefs will be permitted except on written application approved by the Commandant of Cadets or any other member of the Faculty. No cadet will interfere with or interrupt any member of the guard in any way whatever.

Officer of the Day – He shall report for orders to the Commandant of Cadets and will also carry into effect any orders that may be given him by any member of the Faculty. He shall take prompt and effectual measures for suppressing all irregularities and disturbances that may occur in or near Barracks at any time. He shall be present at all formations. He shall receive all reports of Company or detachment roll calls promptly, reporting all who may be late or absent. He shall immediately seek all cadets reported to him as absent without authority from any formation and order them to repair forthwith to their respective places of duty. He shall report immediately to Commandant all whom he does not find, and such as fail to obey his orders. In case of absences at taps he shall in addition to the report prescribed above inspect the rooms of the absent cadets at intervals of fifteen minutes until their return. He will inspect the rooms of cadets at irregular intervals during study hours. He will also inspect Barracks at fatigue call, at call to quarters, and at taps. Cadets will be required to be in their rooms at these inspections. He will make out in person his own delinquency list. Visiting by the officer of the day unofficially will be regarded as inconsistent with his duty.

Orderly – When detailed for Orderly a cadet will gather the mail to be taken to the Post Office and mail same. He will also go to the Post Office for the mail in the morning and afternoon and deliver it to the cadets on the Campus. He will be at the command of the officer of the day and Faculty to perform other duties of like nature. There will be no interference with the Orderly in the performance of these duties.

Inspection – At police inspection every cadet will be required to be in his room, have the room well swept, beds neatly made up, and everything in perfect order. Cadets will be required to be dressed, have their hair brushed, shoes polished, and waste bucket emptied at this inspection. A cadet will stand at attention and uncover when his room is inspected. At taps every cadet will be required to have his light out, be undressed and in bed at the inspection. The officer of the day will have a lantern and ascertain that the above is observed. The officer of the day and musician will be allowed a light for a period of one half an hour after taps.

Inter-Police of Barracks – Cadets shall not throw water, trash, stones or any other article from their windows or in or about their rooms. No cadet will post any placard in or about the building, nor shall he cut, deface, mark or damage the school property whatsoever. The use of cigarettes and intoxicants will not be tolerated. Cadets shall walk the halls and stairways with as little noise as possible at all times; running, loud talking or scuffling in Barracks is forbidden. Loitering or idling about the Barracks or on Campus is forbidden during study or recitation periods. Civilians are requested not to enter the Barracks without permission. Cadets are forbidden to invite civilians into the Barracks without first obtaining permission from some member of the Faculty. The employment of cadets of the servants of the Institute to execute errands in prohibited. When a First Sergeant is to be absent from any formation, he will notify the next ranking man and turn over to him a roll of the Company.

Library – No person not a student of the Institute shall be allowed to draw books from the Library except on special permission from a member of the Faculty. No book, magazine, or paper shall be taken from the Library without the knowledge and presence of the Librarian. Every book drawn from the Library shall be recorded by the Librarian. No cadet will be allowed to have out more than one volume except by permission from Faculty Librarian. No person shall lend any book drawn from the Library. No cadet shall be allowed to keep any book more than one month without special permission. All persons drawing books from the Library shall be responsible for any damage done to them.

Lights – Whenever the occupants of a room are to be absent for more than ten minutes the light shall be extinguished. No cadet shall keep a light after taps except when specially authorized to do so.

Limits – The limits of the Campus are defined as follows: The road to the North, West and South and the street on the East. Cadets are not allowed to exceed the limits of the town at any time without permission. Cadets will be allowed the limits of the Campus at all hours, other than study and recitation periods.

Military Courtesy – Cadets are required to salute each other in a military fashion when they meet outside the Campus. (See U. S. A. Regulations) Cadets will salute when approaching or passing member of the Faculty. All officers will acknowledge the salutations of cadets. Whenever an officer enters a room in the academic building where there are cadets, all cadets will rise and remain standing at attention until the officer leaves the room. Cadets at meals do not rise. Cadets shall make use of the word "Sir" in answering official questions asked by commissioned officers or cadets as such. In official communications between cadets the last name shall be used, and the communication shall be made in a dignified manner. Cadets escorting ladies, or when not on duty with troops, meeting officers escorting ladies may salute by raising the cap.

Drill Exercises – There shall be drill on Mondays, Tuesdays, Wednesdays and Thursdays when the weather is favorable. There shall be inspection on the arms as often as the Commandant of Cadets may direct. All drills and ceremonies will be conducted in accordance with the provisions of the U. S. Army Drill regulations.

Official Communications – All official communications from cadets shall be addressed to Commandant of Cadets. In official communications the term "Cadet" and not "Mr." shall be used. Forms will be furnished.

Rifles – The rifles to the cadets are school property and must be taken care of. When a rifle is broken the price, $5.00, will be charged to the cadet to whom the rifle was issued. No portion of the rifle except the ramrod will be removed. The ramrod may be temporarily removed for the purpose of cleaning the barrel. Snapping the piece is prohibited. Rifles will be kept in places provided for them when not in use.

Room – Cadets will be assigned to rooms by the Faculty and in no case will a cadet change rooms o boarding places without first conferring with the Faculty. Rooms will be kept neat and clean at all times. Cooking in rooms will not be allowed. The wardrobe shall be open for inspection on Saturday. Everything shall have a regular place and shall be kept in its place. The inmates of a room are responsible for the conduct therein, and for the condition, order and arrangement of property in their charge. Each cadet shall immediately after reveille arrange his bedding, clothing, arms, accoutrements, and personal effects in order. The floors and walls of the room must be kept clean and free from stains. All windows and mirrors must be thoroughly cleaned for the regular Saturday inspection. Books shall be kept on the bookshelf and be neatly arranged.

Classrooms – Cadets absent from recitations will be reported. In absence of an instructor the senior cadet present will see that order is preserved in classroom.

Telephone – The telephone in the Principal's residence may be used by cadets in answering calls, but at the following hours only: 7:30 to 8:30 AM and 5 to 7 PM. (The supper period exclusive.)

Uniform – The uniform will be worn by all cadets except such as excused by reason of age. A cadet going beyond the limits of the Campus will wear the uniform prescribed. The blouse will be buttoned throughout when worn outside of the room. Badges of the literary societies and badges presented for forms of schoolwork may be worn by cadets, but no other badge, pin or anything of the like shall be affixed to the uniform coat. Caps shall be worn square on the head.

Visiting – Visiting in Barracks during study hours is forbidden. Permission may be given by the members of the Faculty rooming in the building.

By order of Colonel G. F. McAllister, Prin., Capt. W. B. Porcher, Commandant of Cadets.

APPENDIX 8

MPCI Blue Book 1914

1 This Book is to be known officially as the Blue Book

2 Each room shall be provided with a copy of the Blue Book, for which the inmates of the room shall be responsible

3 …

4 …

Arrest

5 Cadets will be placed in arrest only upon order of the Principal or Commandant of Cadets.

6 No Cadet shall be allowed to exercise command or perform general duty, but shall confine himself to his quarters until released, except when required to be absent therefrom for the performance of his academic or military duties, and except on a necessary occasion, and to march to and from meals. Cadets in arrest shall attend all drills and academic exercises and religious exercises unless otherwise directed.

7 Cadets visiting in a room where another Cadet is in arrest shall be placed in arrest for a period equal to that which is being served by the Cadet whose room is visited.

8 No Cadet in arrest shall make a visit to a superior officer unless sent for by him. In case of business he will submit an application for permission to make the desired visit.

9 Cadets in arrest will sit at a separate table during meals if possible. They will serve confinement in their quarters at all release from quarters, and during vacant study periods and walk extra tours during the punishment period each day.

10 Cadets in arrest will march to meals in rear of the battalion.

Section marchers in arrest take their places in ranks; the Cadet who stands next in military rank will march the section. At drill, officers and non-commissioned officers take their place in line of file closers.

11 Cadets in arrest are authorized to place their official communications in the box at the Principal's office, and to visit the bulletin board at the proper time and for the proper purpose only.

12 Cadets in arrest leaving their room will report their departure and return to the Officer of the Day.

13 No Cadet will be released from arrest except by authority of the Principal or Commandant.

14 Breach of arrest will subject a Cadet to dismissal

Battalion Staff

15 The members of the staff shall be in the vicinity of the grounds upon which the companies form at all roll calls. They will report to the Adjutant, and he will report all absences to the Officer of the Day.

16 They are not required to march to the dining hall with the battalion but must enter and leave the hall before the battalion.

17 They shall remain in the vicinity where the battalion is formed and preserve silence during the publication of orders or other matters at formation.

Bulletin Boards

18 Cadets are required to inform themselves in regard to all matters published on the bulletin board.

19 No one except those having authority to do so, will place anything on, or remove anything from the bulletin board.

Call to Quarters

20 At assembly for class formations and evening call to quarters, each Cadet shall proceed immediately to his room unless required for duty elsewhere.

21 The time between reveille and first call for breakfast is study hours, and visiting in the barracks is prohibited.

22 Visiting in barracks during any study period is prohibited. Visiting

in these Regulations is defined to be any communication whatever during call to quarters by a Cadet with the occupant or occupants of another room except when on duty. It matters not for what purpose the communication may be, whether to obtain or return an article or to give or receive any information.

Church

23 All Cadets except the Officer of the Day and the sick are required to attend, both morning and evening services.

24 All Cadets are required to attend morning services in the Chapel, except those who are sick

25 Cadets excused from attending divine service for any cause, except those on duty, will remain in their rooms until the company to which they belong has returned from Church, and will remain on the campus until retreat.

Confinement and Punishment Tours

26 Confinement means confinement to the Cadet's room and the Cadet will conduct himself as if in arrest for the time being, and will comply with all the requirements of a Cadet in arrest ...

27 A Cadet serving confinement will be reported by the Officer of the Day whenever he leaves his room and if he should be absent for more than ten minutes he will not be credited with confinement.

28 A breach of confinement will be equivalent to a breach of arrest ...

29 Officers and non-commissioned officers of the guard and officer of the day cannot served confinements while on duty.

30 Cadets who have both tours and confinements will serve the tours first except on Sundays when only confinements will be served

31 Cadets who have confinements will serve them under the direction of the Officer of the Day, according to published orders.

32 The punishment squad will be formed and posted in the same manner as a relief of the guard. . . . Cadets walking punishment tours shall wear the service uniform and be equipped with the rifle. They shall

walk their post in a military manner, taking the regular duty step. Any infraction of this regulation will be severely punished.

33 A Cadet walking a tour, if relieved for any purpose, will not be credited with the tour.

34 Any Cadet in the Institute, town Cadets, as well as those in barracks, who have punishments to serve, will remain on the campus in the afternoon to serve them. **No excuses will be accepted.** This rule will be strictly adhered to, and any infractions will be punishable by not less than ten demerits, and punishments as deemed wise by the Principal and Commandant.

35 On Saturdays, tours will be walked from 9 AM until retreat, according to published orders. Friday afternoon will be an "off afternoon" in which all Cadets, excepting those confined the campus by special orders may have leave from after society until retreat. This does not include the Officer of the Day. He must get permission from the Commandant before going on leave.

Delinquencies

36 All delinquencies for which the Cadets have been reported will be published at retreat, on the day that reports are submitted.

37 No Cadet shall address a Cadet who has reported him on the subject of a report unless permitted to do so by the Principal or Commandant of Cadets . . .

38 Cursing or maltreating a Cadet in any way on account of a report will subject the offender to expulsion.

Explanations

39 Any Cadet reported for an offense may submit a written explanation of the circumstances of the report. Such explanations shall contain only such statements of facts, and of the conduct and intentions of Cadets as may be necessary to a full and correct understanding of the case; they shall not be made a medium of complaint or criticism.

40 Explanations must be submitted in writing on the official blank form, before 8:30 AM on the second day following the publication of the report.

41 If necessary, the Commandant may refer the explanation to the reporting officer for remarks. He shall indorse [sic] thereon the facts of the case and return at once to the Commandant of Cadets.

42 Each explanation shall bear the date of the "report of delinquencies" on which the report appears.

43 Explanations MUST be made for absences from any duty, or formation, or from quarters. They must also be made for the damage of any property in the Institute.

44 In an explanation for being absent if the absence was unintentional the Cadets shall expressly so state. He must also state where he was at the time of the report.

45 In an explanation for neglect of studies, the Cadet shall state how long he studied the lesson, and also whether more time was available.

46 When the claim is made that the responsibility for an offense rests with another Cadet, the name of the latter shall be stated.

Formations

47 All formations shall be according to the "Bell Ringer's" time.

48 At all formations, Cadets commanding shall be at their post at attention, in front of, and facing the center of their respective commands when the assembly ceases and supervise the formation.

49 Cadet Lieutenants shall be in the vicinity of their posts at assembly, and in their places with sabres drawn, when the captain takes charge of the company.

50 Cadets shall be reported absent from any formation when not in ranks before the Cadet who calls the roll makes his report. ...

51 Cadets shall be reported late at any formation, if not in ranks, and at attention, when the assembly ceases.

52 A Cadet Officer, excused from any formation, shall notify his company commander before said rollcall.

53 A Cadet, non-commissioned Officer, or private excused from any formation shall notify his First Sergeant before said rollcall.

54 When general leave is granted to the corps, the rolls will not be called at formations for meals. ...

55 Cadets on leaving any duty will report their departure and return

to the Officer of the Day. The Cadet in charge of the organization from which the Cadet leaves will report said Cadet through the Officer of the Day. In like manner, a section marcher will report all Cadets who are excused from a section room.

56 Sections will be dismissed by instructors immediately upon the ringing of the first bell, no Cadet will remain but will march out in a military way. The section marcher, or the file closer, will report any misconduct or loud noise while leaving a section room.

57 Sections will be allowed three minutes after dismissal from a section room before returning for the next recitation.

58 Every Cadet, unless excused by the Commandant will march with his section. Cadets who are excused will report to the Officer of the Day before coming to class and will enter the section room with his class.

59 At class formation the Officer of the Day will take his post where the center of the sections will rest; at the prescribed signal the sections will form in regular order, the senior class on the right. When the sections are formed the Officer of the Day will command "call your rolls," at which command rolls will be called in succession from right to left; each section marcher facing the front when he has completed calling his roll. When all section marchers have faced the front the Officer of the Day will command "Report," then the section marchers will report in succession from right to left. The Officer of the Day will then command "Rear ranks, close up; right face; march off our sections."

60 The file closer of a section is charged with the duty of maintaining order in his section, and he must report any unmilitary conduct. Any misconduct on the part of the file closer, or any breach in the performance of his duty will be severely punished. The section marcher will be dealt with likewise.

61 Cadets who are not required to be in ranks at the publication of orders must remain in the immediate vicinity during such publication.

Guard

62 [Skipped]

63 When deemed necessary guard duty shall be performed as prescribed in the "Manual of Guard Duty, US Army."

64 No changing of tour, reliefs, or posts will be permitted except on written application approved by the Commandant of Cadets.

65 Every person in the Institute must show the greatest respect toward the sentinels and shall not interrupt or interfere with any member of the guard in any way.

Officer in Charge

66 (a) Each officer of the faculty shall in turn be detailed as Officer in Charge. His tour of duty shall begin at guard mounting, or at the time when the Officer of the Day is relieved, when he will relieve the old Officer in Charge.

(b) He shall remain in or near barracks, and at no time during his tour shall he absent himself therefrom, except when called away on some urgent duty. During evening study hours, he will remain in the Principal's office.

(c) He shall conduct the exercises in the chapel

(d) He shall be present at every formation during his tour and shall see that all duties are performed in a military manner, according to regulations.

(e) He shall visit the quarters of the cadets at irregular times, both during the day and during the evening study hours.

(f) He shall report any individuals that may come within his knowledge and especially shall it be his duty to see that the Cadets who are on duty report all violations.

(g) On being relieved, he shall make such suggestions as may be of service to the Commandant in discharging his duty.

Officer of the Day

67 (a) He shall be known as "Mr. Officer of the Day."

(b) He will remain constantly at the guard room from reveille until taps, except when preparing for and going to meals, and when making required inspections, and performing other necessary duties.

(c) He shall cause all necessary signals to be sounded at the proper time.

(d) He shall take prompt and effectual measures for the suppression of all irregularities.

(e) He shall be held responsible for all property left in the guard room

(f) He shall be present at all formations.

(g) He shall receive the reports of all rollcalls promptly reporting all company commanders or section marchers who may be late or absent

(h) He shall seek immediately all Cadets reported absent from any formation and order them to repair forthwith to their respective places of duty. He shall report to the Commandant immediately those whom he cannot find or those who refuse to obey his orders.

(i) In case of absence at taps he shall visit the room of the Cadet who was reported absent, at intervals of fifteen minutes until the Cadet returns.

(j) He shall be present at the return and dismissal of all organizations.

(k) He shall inspect for Cadets in confinement at least once each hour and verify their presence by seeing them in rooms.

(l) If sentinels are on post, he shall inspect each relief at irregular intervals.

(m) He shall make out his own delinquency list in person.

(n) He shall not on his report the time of his inspections.

(o) Visiting the Officer of the Day unofficially will be regarded as inconsistent with the certificate required of him. He may visit his own room, however, when necessary.

(p) On being relieved he shall turn over to the Commandant the punishment list, and his report of delinquencies. The report of the delinquencies of the Officer of the Day shall contain all violations of orders or regulations coming within his knowledge, and a **certificate to that effect shall be signed.**

(q) The Officer of the Day must at all times be dressed in the uniform prescribed for the battalion and shall wear his sabre and white gloves.

Sergeants & Corporals of the Guard

68 (a) Sergeants and Corporals of the guard, or non-commissioned officers of the guard shall not at any time take advantage of their position to visit in barracks.

(b) They shall inspect sentinels while on post, and instruct them concerning their duties, and see that they perform their duties properly.

(c) They shall be excused from reciting the first recitation period the day they march off.

(d) They shall execute orders received from the Officer of the Day, and shall assist him in maintaining order in barracks.

(e) Each non-commissioned officer will be assigned to a relief while sentinels are walking post, and he shall remain at his post of duty until his relief has marched off and is relieved by the succeeding non-commissioned officer.

(f) He shall raise the flag at reveille each morning and shall lower it at retreat.

(g) The period that the punishment squad is posted on Saturday shall be divided between three watches, which shall be kept by the non-commissioned officers on duty successively beginning with the senior.

(h) They will form the punishment squad, call the roll, post them, and report all absences to the Officer of the Day.

(i) When violations of the regulations are reported to the corporal, or when such comes within his knowledge, he shall report same to the Officer of the Day immediately.

Orderly

69 (a) The orderly will be detailed by the Cadet Adjutant and will report to the Commandant of Cadets when he comes on duty.

(b) Immediately after breakfast he will carry the Institute mail to the post office and return with morning mail. He carries the song books from the office to the chapel each morning and carry them back to the office after chapel. He will close and fasten the windows of the chapel after chapel service and lock the door. He will turn the library mail over to the librarian and will deliver the mail for the faculty and students.

(c) He will be excused from the 9 o'clock recitation period and drill

Sentinels

70 (a) Sentinels shall be excused from reciting the first period of the day they march off.

(b) They shall perform their duties in accordance with the U. S. drill regulations.

(c) Any breach in the performance of their will be dealt with severely. Sitting down on post, loitering on post, or allowing any misconduct on post shall be punished by not less than seven demerits and ten tours.

Sub-division Inspectors

71 There shall be two sub-divisions in each barracks, one on the upper hallway, which shall be inspected by the Senior Captain, and one on the second hallway, including the rooms on the bottom floor, which shall be inspected by the Second Captain. The officers shall be responsible for the preservation of good order, and the police of the barracks.

72 At police call every morning he shall visit and thoroughly inspect every room in his sub-division.

73 He shall inspect at taps and positively assure himself that all Cadets are in bed properly, or present as required.

74 In case of any noise, or improper conduct of any kind, in his sub-division, the inspector will repair instantly to the spot, suppress the disorder and report the Cadets who are responsible. If the irregularity be of sufficient importance, he will report the matter to the Officer in Charge immediately if in barracks, otherwise to the Commandant of

75 The Officer of the Day will receive the inspectors' reports at taps

76 In case an inspector is to be absent at taps, he will notify the next Cadet in rank, before he absents himself from the barracks, and he will make the required inspection.

77 The Commandant will inspect each subdivision at least once every week at the regular police inspection, and at taps, and at other times when deemed necessary.

Police of Barracks

78 Cadets shall not throw stone, water, or any other article from or to any windows or in or about the barracks

79 No Cadet shall place placards anywhere on the school buildings or grounds, neither shall he deface any property.

80 Singing, whistling, loud talking, running, dancing or any boisterous conduct is prohibited.

81 Calling to Cadets from one room to another, from a window to the ground or the reverse is prohibited

82 Loitering about the barracks, or at any other place is prohibited during study hours.

83 No Cadets shall introduce a civilian into barracks at any time, without permission.

84 No Cadet shall introduce any animals or anything into barracks to create a nuisance.

85 No Cadet shall play any musical instrument in the barracks during study hours.

Leaves

86 For all leaves, except general leave, a Cadet will submit a special application, stating why he wants leave, the time he desires his leave to begin, and when he shall return.

87 When a First Sergeant is to be absent from his company, he shall prepare a list of all the Cadets who are required to be at formation during his absence, and turn it over to the senior member of the company who is required to attend formation.

88 No Cadet shall use any leave, except to go home, who has been on the sick list during the past twenty-four hours.

89 No Cadet shall use any leave who received over ten confinements and tours during any one week. In this case the Cadet must remain on the campus from Monday when his punishment begins, until the following Monday.

90 To all Cadets not disqualified, leave will be granted as follows: Sunday, from after Quite Hour until retreat. Every afternoon from after drill until retreat, and on Saturday from after all inspections until 9:30 PM. However, all Cadets must attend retreat on Saturday.

91 Cadets who go on leave, when they are disqualified will lay themselves liable to expulsion.

92 Every Cadet shall wear his uniform on leave, and any Cadet found on the street wearing civilian clothes, or wearing a uniform and a citizen's hat, shall be confined to the campus for not less than one week, and shall receive not less than ten tours, and ten demerits. Cadets who have damaged uniforms or who lose their uniforms will remain on campus.

Library

93 No book or magazine shall be taken from the library without the permission of the librarian.

94 No person shall keep any book more than two weeks without special permission.

95 All persons drawing books from the library shall be responsible for damage done to them.

Lights

96 Whenever any occupant of a room is present, during evening study hours, he shall have his light burning.

97 No Cadet shall keep a light after taps, unless authorized to do so.

98 Inspectors and the Officer of the Day must keep their light burning for fifteen minutes after taps.

99 Cadets returning from leave after taps may have ten minutes to keep their lights.

100 The Officer of the Day will see that all lights except those authorized, are extinguished at taps.

Limits

101 The limits of the campus are defined as follows: The road on the north, west and south and the street on the east. Cadets are not allowed to exceed the limits of the town at any time without permission. Cadets not disqualified will be allowed the limits of the campus at all times, other than study or recitation periods.

Dining Hall

102 The senior Cadet officer present shall be commandant at the dining hall. It shall be his duty, aided by the carvers, to enforce the dining hall regulations.

103 The battalion will be formed at the proper time and marched to the dining hall. The Commandant of the dining hall shall divide the corps

into two squads, corresponding with the number of tables and shall assign two carvers to each table.

104 Before putting the battalion in motion to march to the dining hall he shall see that all tables are properly formed, and that the battalion is closed up properly

105 All loud talking, or speaking from one table to another is prohibited. Only carvers will speak to the waiters.

106 Wasting provisions or taking them from the hall is prohibited. Nor shall any food be introduced by Cadets into the dining hall

107 Cadets entering the dining hall after battalion, or leaving before the battalion, shall report to the Commandant of the hall, and he shall report the Cadet for the offense.

108 The Commandant of Cadets will make a careful inspection of the dining hall after each meal and will report carvers, providing they fail to report to him those who soiled the table cloth, or otherwise broke the dining hall regulations.

Military Courtesy

109 It is enjoined upon Cadets to salute each other in a military way when they meet outside the school grounds.

110 All officers shall duly acknowledge the salute of Cadets in the form and manner prescribed in the regulation aforesaid.

111 Officers and Cadets shall render the salute prescribed in the army regulations to the colors when "The Star-Spangled Banner" or "To the Colors" is sounded.

112 Whenever an officer of the faculty enters a room in the building where there are Cadets all Cadets will rise and remain standing in the position of a soldier until the officer leaves the room or directs the Cadets to resume their seats or to continue the occupation upon which they are engaged. Cadets at meals or those engaged in examinations do not rise.

113 At all inspections of barracks by the Officer of the Day or subdivision inspectors, between reveille and taps, cadets will, irrespective of rank, rise and remain standing in the position of a solder until the inspector leaves the room. At police inspection, caps must be removed, and blouses be on and buttoned throughout.

114 Cadets shall make use of the ford "Sir" in answering official questions asked by the commissioned officers or Cadets acting as such.

115 In official communications between Cadets, the last name shall be used, and the communication shall be made in a dignified manner.

116 Cadets shall salute with the hand prescribed for officers in the Infantry Drill Regulations, U. S. Army.

117 Cadets escorting ladies or, when not escorting ladies, meeting Cadets escorting ladies, may salute by raising the cap.

118 In private houses, Cadets will extend to each other the courtesy due from one gentleman to another.

Military Exercises

119 There shall be infantry drill every day when the weather is favorable except on Friday, Saturday and Sunday.

120 Each drill will continue for forty minutes, at least beginning at 4:10 PM.

Regulations

121 Every Cadet must acquaint himself with the provisions of the Blue Book.

122 Every Cadet shall be required to read carefully every paragraph of the Blue Book and sign a statement to that effect between the first and seventh day of school. They will submit these statements to the Commandant of Cadets.

Rooms

123 Cadets will be assigned to rooms by the Principal and in no case will a Cadet change rooms or boarding places without first conferring with the Principal. Rooms will be kept neat and clean at all times. Cooking in rooms will not be allowed. The wardrobe shall be open for inspection on Saturdays and Sundays. Everything shall have a regular place and shall be kept in its place. Bed linen must be changed weekly and must be clean and turned back at Sunday morning inspection.

124 The inmates of a room are responsible for the conduct therein, and for the condition, order and arrangements of property in their charge.

125 Each Cadet, immediately after reveille, shall arrange his bedding, clothe, arms, accoutrements and personal effects in order.

126 The floor and walls of the room must be kept clean and free from stains.

127 All windows and mirrors must be thoroughly cleaned for the regular Saturday inspection.

128 Books shall be kept on the bookshelf, neatly arranged.

Section Room [Classrooms]

129 Section marchers shall preserve order in the section room during the absence of the instructor.

130 On entering a section room, the file closer shall enter the room first and the section marcher shall follow the section. The file closer shall remain near the door until the section marcher enters, when he will take his proper place in the section. As soon as he enters the room each member of the section will take his place by the seat assigned to him and face to the front. The marcher will then give the order, "seats," and report the absentees to the Instructor. When dismissed by the instructor, at the close of a recitation, the marcher will take his post near the door and give the order, "Rise, march out," and will remain in the room until all the other members of the section have passed out.

131 Cadets reciting will assume the position of a soldier standing at attention unless the instructor prefers that he remain seated.

132 Every Cadet permitted to leave the section room, shall return as soon as possible. Should any Cadet remain out more than ten minutes, the instructor will send the section marcher to report the fact to the Officer of the Day, who will look for the absent Cadet and require him to report forthwith to his section, and in every case enter a report against the Cadet.

133 In case an instructor is absent from the section room on the arrival of the section, the section marcher will send the next ranking Cadet to report the fact to the Officer of the Day, who will at once notify the instructor. In case the instructor does not arrive within ten minutes, after the section reaches the section room, the section will be dismissed, the section marcher reporting the fact to the Officer of the Day, who will make note of the fact in his report.

134 Under no conditions shall an instructor detain his section after the signal to dismiss had been sounded.

Visiting

135 Visiting in barracks is authorized when leave is granted to the corps, and during release from quarters, except by Cadets serving confinements or in arrests.

136 No Cadet shall visit in a room at any time when any of the occupants are in arrest or serving confinements.

137 Visiting in barracks, except as above stated is prohibited. However, members of the Junior and Senior classes, who take Greek, Latin or Mathematics, may, upon special permission, confer with each other concerning their work during evening hours.

138 There shall never be more than five Cadets in a Cadet room at one time, without special permission from the Commandant. Should more than this number be found in any room, all Cadets therein shall be reported.

139 Visiting during evening study hours shall be punishable by not less than five demerits and seven tours.

Fire Escape – Use of

140 Cadets are not to go on the fire escape at the north end of the barracks except in the case of fire or fire-drill. Any Cadet violating this regulation will be severely punished.

Fire-Drill

141 From time to time, under the direction of the Commandant of Cadets, there will be fire-drills to teach Cadets to vacate the barracks with dispatch [sic].

(a) A definite fire signal will be adopted, and under no circumstances will this signal be sounded, except in case of a fire or fire drill.

(b) Only those Cadets rooming on second and third floors or barracks (or who may be on one or the other of these floors when the fire-signal is sounded) and instructors on these floors are to use the fire-escape.

(c) When the fire-signal sounds, all persons on the second and third floors of the barracks, will immediately hold themselves in readiness to obey orders.

(d) The instructor rooming on a given floor will be in command of Cadets rooming on that floor, and in case he be absent the ranking Cadet officer.

(e) As soon as fire-signal is sounded it shall be the duty of those in command of the Cadets on the different floors to ascertain, if possible, in what part of the building the fire is. If it is on the first or second floor, the Cadets will be moved from the second floor (via the fire-escape) first' then those on the third floor.

(f) The order in which rooms are to be vacated is as follows: Second floor, 7, 17, 8, 16, 9, 15, 10, 14, 11, 13, 12. Third floor, 18, 29, 19, 28, 20, 27, 21, 26, 22, 25, 23, 24.

(g) Safety is the all-important thing in the presence of danger, and cool heads are the surest safeguards. When the fire-signal sounds keep perfectly cool and quiet; nothing can possibly be gained by getting excited and boisterous; much may be lost.

(h) When the order is given for occupants of a room to move, absolute obedience is required. There must be no loitering behind to try to save belongings.

(i) Cadets ordered to move from their rooms will move at once and with dispatch (but not run) to the north window and proceed down the fire-escape, taking care not to injure someone ahead.

Appendix "A"

Special attention is called to the following, owing to the penalty affixed for such offenses.

1 Any Cadet who shall disobey a command of any member of the faculty, or any Cadet officer on duty, or conduct himself in a refractory manner, shall be dismissed or otherwise less severely punished according to the nature of the case.

2 Any Cadet found guilty of drinking intoxicating liquor, or anyone found with such in his possession shall be dismissed.

3 No Cadet shall play any game of cards or any game of chance,

neither shall any Cadet have in his possession materials used in games of chance.

4 Any Cadet who shall absent himself from his room between evening call to quarters and reveille, or any Cadet who shall exceed the limits at any time without permission shall render himself liable to expulsion.

5 Any Cadet who shall knowingly make a false statement, or any Cadet who shall utter a falsehood by answering for another at rollcall shall be severely punished, and a repetition of such offenses will result in expulsion.

6 Any Cadet who shall call to personal account (either by word of mouth or by laying hand upon said Cadet) another Cadet for having, whilst in the execution of his duty, corrected or reported said Cadet shall be punished accordingly.

7 Any Cadet who shall wantonly damage any school property, or who shall remove same from its proper place shall be severely punished.

8 Cadets found guilty of smoking cigarettes shall be expelled.

9 Cadets guilty of unmilitary or boisterous conduct while marching to or from Church shall be dealt with severely.

10 Any Cadet found guilty of introducing or exploding any explosives in or around barracks shall be dismissed.

11 No wood or other material shall be thrown in or around barracks, neither shall any water be thrown from the windows. The punishment for such offenses shall be severe.

12 A cadet found guilty of stealing shall suffer the pain of expulsion.

13 Any member of the Senior Class or any member of the Junior Class who shall receive 175 demerits, or any member of the Sophomore or Freshman Class, who shall receive 200 demerits, shall be dismissed from the Institute.

14 All breaches of the Regulations, though not herein expressly mentioned, shall be punished according to the nature and degree of the offense.

15 Cadets who are found guilty of absenting themselves from their room during evening study hours for a period of time greater than 20 minutes shall be severely punished.

APPENDIX 9

Resolutions Concerning North Carolina College

The following resolutions were passed:

a) Whereas action has been taken by Synod that will undoubtedly mean the closing of the Collegiate Institute as a Synodical Institution at the close of the present school year; And, as Synod has agreed to take over and pay off the indebtedness of $20,000.00 now standing against the Institution:

And, whereas, the Synod is the one to benefit from the sale of the Property, or the preservation of same until such sale can be made;

Therefore, Be it Resolved by the Executive Committee of the United Evangelical Lutheran Synod of North Carolina, that the Board of Trustees of North Carolina College and the Board of Trustees for Educational Institutions be and are hereby requested to convey the title to all of said property to the United Evangelical Lutheran Synod of North Carolina as consideration for the payment of said debit; subject to such indebtedness as may legally exist against the same.

b) Whereas the title of the property of North Carolina College will probably be conveyed to the Synod in consideration of the payment by Synod of the $20,000.00 debit against said College; And in the event of such conveyance, it is the sense of this committee that overtures should be made to Prof. G. F. McAllister with the view to leasing the property to him for school purposes.

Therefore, Be It Resolved, That a committee of three be appointed with power to act to endeavor to lease said property to Prof. G. F. McAllister for school purposes for a period not to exceed ten years, and upon condition that said lessee shall carry and pay the premium on $20,000.00

fire insurance on said property during the term of said lease; and shall maintain the property in as good condition as it now is, ordinary wear and tear excepted; and that said lease shall contain a cancellation clause satisfactory to both parties.

c) Whereas the United Evangelical Lutheran Synod of North Carolina, in convention at Newton, NC, February 9th to the 12th, 1931, voted to assume, as a direct obligation, the $20,000.00 indebtedness of the Board of Trustees of North Carolina College, as evidenced by certain notes held by Cabarrus Bank and Trust Company, at Concord.

Therefore, Be It Resolved, That the President of the Synod and the Secretary of Synod be and are hereby instructed, authorized and directed to execute upon behalf of Synod such note or notes as may be required by said bank in connection with said loan and successive renewals thereof until such time as the loan can be paid in full.[1]

[1] *Minutes of the One Hundred and Twenty-eighth Convention of the United Evangelical Lutheran Synod of North Carolina*, First Lutheran Church, Albemarle, NC, Feb 9-12, 1932, [np, npp], p. 41-42.

APPENDIX 10

Amended Charter of North Carolina College - 1921

Private Laws of the State of North Carolina – Extra Session 1921
Chapter 1

An Act To Amend Chapter 357 of Private Laws of 1909, Raleigh 8th Day of March 1909. Amending the Charter of North Carolina College, Mt. Pleasant, NC.

The General Assembly of North Carolina do enact:

Section 1. That the act revising the charter of the trustees of North Carolina College, ratified eight day of March, one thousand nine hundred and nine, chapter three hundred and fifty-seven. Private Laws of one thousand nine hundred and nine be amended by striking out all of section two of said ac and inserting in lieu thereof the following:

"Section 1. That it shall be the duty of the United Evangelical Lutheran Synod of North Carolina to nominate and elect a board of trustees for educational institutions at its annual convention in November, one thousand nine hundred and twenty-two, twenty-one members in groups of seven, for one two, and three years respectively, and thereafter seven members annually, and such others as may be required to fill vacancies, who, together with the president of the Synod and president of the college, who are hereby made *ex officio* advisory members without a vote, shall constitute the board of trustees of this corporation. That the board of North Carolina College shall always be composed of the same individuals as those of the board of Trustees for educational institutions of the United Evangelical Lutheran Synod of North Carolina, and that the board of trustees for educational institutions of the United Evangelical Lutheran Synod of North Carolina is hereby authorized and empowered to act for and in behalf of the board of Trustees of North Carolina College. Any vacancies occurring among said trustees by death, resignation or otherwise, or by failure of election by said Synod, shall be filled by the said board or trustees, and such persons so elected shall only hold office until the following meeting of Synod subsequent to their election.[1]

[1] "An Act To Amend Chapter 357 of Private Laws of 1909, Raleigh 8th Day of March 1909. Amending the Charter of North Carolina College, Mt. Pleasant, NC," *State of North Carolina Private Laws of the State of North Carolina Enacted by the General Assembly at its Extra of 1921 Session begun on December 6, 1921, Raleigh, NC,* Chapter 1, p. 1, Mitchell Printing Co., State Printers, Raleigh, NC, 1922.

APPENDIX 11

MPCI Blue Book 1930

Regulations for the Discipline & Police of Cadets Mt. Pleasant Collegiate Institute 1930.

Cadets will be placed under arrest only upon the order of the Principal or Commandant of Cadets.

Arrest

5 No Cadet under arrest shall be allowed to exercise command or perform general duty.

6 ... He shall confine himself to his quarters until released ...

When a Cadet under arrest must visit the toilet, he shall report his departure and return to an officer or a non-commissioned officer of the Guar.

7 Cadets visiting in a room where another Cadet is in arrest shall be placed in arrest for a period equal to that which is being served by the Cadet whose room is visited.

9 Cadets in arrest will sit at a separate table during meals if possible.

10 Cadets in arrest will march to meals in rear of the battalion.

12 Breach of arrest will subject a Cadet to dismissal

Battalion Staff

13 The members of the staff shall be in the vicinity of the grounds upon which the companies form at all roll calls. They will report to the Adjutant, and he will report all absences to the Officer of the Day.

Bulletin Boards

16 Cadets are required to inform themselves in regard to all matters published on the bulletin board.

Call to Quarters

19 Visiting in barracks in prohibited between reveille and first call for breakfast

20 Visiting in barracks during any study period is prohibited.

Church

21 All Cadets except the Officer of the Day and the sick are required to attend morning Church services and also evening services as prescribed in General Order.

22 All Cadets are required to attend morning services in the Chapel, except the O. D. of the guard and those who are sick

Confinement and Punishment Tours

24 Confinement means confinement to the Cadet's room and the Cadet will conduct himself as if in arrest for the time being, and will comply with all the requirements of a Cadet in arrest ...

25 A Cadet serving confinement will be reported by the Officer of the Day whenever he leaves his room and if he should be absent for more than ten minutes he will not be credited with confinement.

26 A breach of confinement will be equivalent to a breach of arrest 27 Officers and non-commissioned officers of the guard and officer of the day cannot serve confinements while on duty.

28 Cadets who have both tours and confinements will serve the tours first except on Sundays when only confinements will be served

30 The punishment squad will be formed and posted in the same manner as a relief of the guard. ... Cadets walking punishment tours shall wear the service uniform and be equipped with the rifle. They shall walk their post in a military manner, taking the regular duty step. Any infraction of this regulation will be severely punished.

31 A Cadet walking a tour, if relieved for any purpose, will not be credited with the tour.

32 Any Cadet in the Institute, town Cadets, as well as those in barracks, who have punishments to serve, will remain on the campus in the afternoon to serve them. No excuses will be accepted.

33 On Saturdays, tours will be walked from 9 AM until retreat, according to published orders. Friday afternoon will be an "off afternoon" in which all Cadets, excepting those confined the campus by special orders may have leave from after society (but not before 4 PM) until retreat.

Delinquencies

34 All delinquencies for which the Cadets have been reported will be published at retreat, on the day that reports are submitted.

35 No Cadet shall address a Cadet who has reported him on the subject of a report unless permitted to do so by the Principal or Commandant of Cadets ...

36 Any Cadet who shall call to personal account (either by word of mouth or by laying hand upon said Cadet) another Cadet for having whilst in the execution of his duty, corrected or reported said Cadet shall be punished accordingly.

37 Cursing or maltreating a Cadet in any way on account of a report will subject the offender to expulsion.

Explanations

38 Any Cadet reported for an offense may submit a written explanation of the circumstances of the report. Such explanations shall contain only such statements of facts, and of the conduct and intentions of Cadets as may be necessary to a full and correct understanding of the case; they shall not be made a medium of complaint or criticism.

39 Explanations must be submitted in writing on the official blank form, before 8:30 AM on the second day following the publication of the report.

42 Explanations MUST be made for absences from any duty, or formation, or from quarters. They must also be made for the damage of any property in the Institute.

43 In an explanation for being absent if the absence was unintentional the Cadets shall expressly so state. He must also state where he was at the time of the report.

44 In an explanation for neglect of studies, the Cadet shall state how long he studied the lesson, and whether more time was available.

45 When the claim is made that the responsibility for an offense rests with another Cadet, the name of the latter shall be stated.

Formations

46 All formations shall be according to the "Bell Ringer's" time.

47 At all formations, Cadets commanding shall be at their post at attention, in front of, and facing the center of their respective commands when the assembly ceases and supervise the formation.

48 Cadet Lieutenants shall be in the vicinity of their posts at assembly, and in their places with sabres drawn, when the captain takes charge of the company.

49 Cadets shall be reported absent from any formation when not in ranks before the Cadet who calls the roll makes his report.

50 Cadets shall be reported late at any formation, if not in ranks, and at attention, when the assembly ceases.

51 …

52 A Cadet, non-commissioned Officer, or private excused from any formation shall notify his First Sergeant before said rollcall.

53 When general leave is granted to the corps, the rolls will not be called at formations for meals.

54 Cadets on leaving any duty will report their departure and return to the Officer of the Day.

56 Sections will be allowed three minutes after dismissal from a section room before returning for the next recitation.

Guard

61 When deemed necessary, guard duty shall be performed as prescribed in the "Manual of Guard Duty, US Army."

62 No changing of tour, reliefs, or posts will be permitted except on written application approved by the Commandant of Cadets.

63 Every person in the Institute must show the greatest respect toward the sentinels and shall not interrupt or interfere with any member of the guard in any way.

Officer of the Day

64 (a) He shall be known as "Mr. Officer of the Day."

(b) He will remain constantly at the guard room from reveille until taps, except when preparing for and going to meals, and when making required inspections, and performing other necessary duties.

(c) He shall cause all necessary signals to be sounded at the proper time.

(d) He shall take prompt and effectual measures for the suppression of all irregularities.

(e) He shall be held responsible for all property left in the guard room

(f) He shall be present at all formations.

(g) He shall receive the reports of all rollcalls promptly reporting all company commanders or section marchers who may be late or absent

(h) He shall seek immediately all Cadets reported absent … and order them to repair forthwith to their respective places of duty.

(i) In case of absence at taps he shall visit the room of the Cadet who was reported absent, at intervals of fifteen minutes until the Cadet returns.

(j) …

(k) He shall inspect for Cadets in confinement at least once each hour . . .

(l) If sentinels are on post, he shall inspect each relief at irregular intervals.

(m) …

(n) …

(o) Visiting the Officer of the Day unofficially will be regarded as inconsistent with the certificate required of him. He may visit his own room, however, when necessary.

(p) …

(q) The Officer of the Day must at all times be dressed in the uniform prescribed for the battalion and shall wear his sabre.

Sergeants & Corporals of the Guard

65 (a) Sergeants and Corporals of the guard, or non-commissioned officers of the guard shall not at any time take advantage of their position to visit the barracks.

(b) ...

(c) They shall be excused from reciting the first recitation period the day they march off.

(d) ...

(e) ...

(f) He shall raise the flag at reveille each morning and shall lower it at retreat.

(g) The period that the punishment squad is posted on Saturday shall be divided between three watches, which shall be kept by the non-commissioned officers on duty successively beginning with the senior.

Orderly

66 (a) The orderly will be detailed by the Cadet Adjutant and will report to the Commandant of Cadets when he comes on duty.

(b) Immediately after breakfast he will carry the Institute mail to the post office and return with morning mail. He will distribute and collect the song books at chapel each morning. He will close the windows of the chapel after service. He will turn the library mail over to the librarian and will deliver the mail for the faculty and students.

(c) He will be excused from the 9 o'clock recitation period and drill.

Sentinels

67 (a) Sentinels shall be excused from reciting the first period of the day they march off

(b) They shall perform their duties in accordance with the U. S. drill regulations.

(c) Any breach in the performance of their will be dealt with severely. Sitting down on post, loitering on post, or allowing any misconduct on post shall be punished by not less than seven demerits and ten tours.

Sub-division Inspectors

68 There shall be two sub-divisions in each barracks, one on the upper hallway, which shall be inspected by the ranking Cadet in the building; and one on the second hallway, including rooms on the bottom floor, which shall be inspected by the next Cadet in rank.

69 At police call every morning he shall visit and thoroughly inspect every room in his sub-division.

70 He shall inspect at taps and positively assure himself that all Cadets are in bed properly, or present as required.

71 In case of any noise, or improper conduct of any kind, in his sub-division, the inspector will repair instantly to the spot, suppress the disorder and report the Cadets who are responsible. If the irregularity be of sufficient importance, he will report the matter to the Commandant of Cadets.

Police of Barracks

75 Cadets shall not throw stone, water, or any other article from or to any windows or in or about the barracks

76 No Cadet shall place placards anywhere on the school buildings or grounds, neither shall he deface any property.

77 Singing, whistling, loud talking, running, dancing or any boisterous conduct is prohibited.

78 Calling to Cadets from one room to another, from a window to the ground or the reverse is prohibited

79 Loitering about the barracks, or at any other place is prohibited during study hours.

80 No Cadets shall introduce a civilian into barracks at any time, without permission.

81 No Cadet shall introduce any animals or anything into barracks to create a nuisance.

82 No Cadet shall play any musical instrument in the barracks during study hours.

Leaves

83 For all leaves, except general leave, a Cadet will submit a special application, stating why he wants leave, the time he desires his leave to begin, and when he shall return.

84 …

85 No Cadet shall use any leave, except to go home, who has been on the sick list during the past twenty-four hours

86 No Cadet shall use any leave who received over ten confinements and tours during any one week. In this case the Cadet must remain on the campus from Monday when his punishment begins, until the following Monday.

87 To all Cadets not disqualified, leave will be granted as follows: Sunday, from after Quite Hour until retreat. Every afternoon from after drill until retreat, and on Saturday from after all inspections until 8:30 PM. However, all Cadets must attend retreat on Saturday.

88 Cadets who go on leave, when they are disqualified will lay themselves liable to expulsion.

89 Every Cadet shall wear his uniform on leave, and any Cadet found on the street wearing civilian clothes, or wearing a broken uniform, shall be confined to the campus for not less than one week, and shall receive not less than ten tours, and ten demerits. …

(a) Any Cadet returning to Mt. Pleasant from a leave must report to the Institute for duty immediately whether his leave has expired or not.

Library

90 No book or magazine shall be taken from the library without the permission of the librarian.

91 No person shall keep any book more than two weeks without special permission.

Lights

93 Whenever any occupant of a room is present, during evening study hours, he shall have his light burning.

94 No Cadet shall keep a light after taps, unless authorized to do so.

(a) A light burning in a room when the occupant is on leave will subject the occupant to report.

95 Inspectors and the Officer of the Day must keep their lights burning for fifteen minutes after taps.

96 Cadets returning from leave after taps may have ten minutes to keep their lights.

Limits

98 The limits of the campus are defined as follows: The road on the north, 100 feet below the road to the west, the road on the south and the street to the east. Cadets are not allowed to exceed the limits of the town at any time without permission. Cadets not disqualified will be allowed the limits of the campus at all times, other than study or recitation periods.

Dining Hall

99 The senior Cadet officer present shall be commandant at the dining hall. . . .

100 The battalion will be formed at the proper time and marched to the dining hall. The Commandant of the dining hall shall divide the corps into two squads, corresponding with the number of tables and shall assign two carvers to each table.

101 Before putting the battalion in motion to march to the dining hall he shall see that all tables are properly formed, and that the battalion is closed up properly

102 All loud talking or speaking from one table to another is prohibited. Only carvers will speak to the waiters.

103 Wasting provisions or taking them from the hall is prohibited. Nor shall any food be introduced by Cadets into the dining hall

104 …

105 The Commandant of Cadets will make a careful inspection of the dining hall after each meal and will report carvers, providing they fail to report to him those who soiled the tablecloth, or otherwise broke the dining hall regulations.

Military Courtesy

106 It is enjoined upon Cadets to salute each other in a military way when they meet outside the school grounds.

107 ...

108 ...

109 Whenever an officer of the faculty enters a room in the building where there are Cadets all Cadets will rise and remain standing in the position of a soldier until the officer leaves the room or directs the Cadets to resume their seats ... Cadets at meals or those engaged in examinations do not rise.

110 ...

111 Cadets shall make use of the ford "Sir" in answering official questions asked by the commissioned officers or Cadets acting as such.

112 In official communications between Cadets, the last name shall be used, and the communication shall be made in a dignified manner.

113 Cadets shall salute with the hand prescribed for officers in the Infantry Drill Regulations, U. S. Army.

114 Cadets escorting ladies or, when not escorting ladies, meeting Cadets escorting ladies, may salute by raising the cap.

115 In private houses, Cadets will extend to each other the courtesy due from one gentleman to another.

Military Exercises

116 There shall be infantry drill every day when the weather is favorable except on Friday, Saturday and Sunday.

117 Each drill will continue for forty minutes at least.

Regulations

118 ...

119 ...

Rooms

120 Cadets will be assigned to rooms by the Principal and in no case will a Cadet change rooms without first conferring with the Principal.

Section Room (Classrooms)

127 Section marchers shall preserve order in the section room during the absence of the instructor.

128 On entering a section room, the file closer shall enter the room first and the section marcher shall follow the section. The file closer shall remain near the door until the section marcher enters, when he will take his proper place in the section. As soon as he enters the room each member of the section will take his place by the seat assigned to him and face to the front. The marcher will then give the order, "seats," and report the absentees to the Instructor. When dismissed by the instructor, at the close of a recitation, the marcher will take his post near the door and give the order, "Rise, march out," and will remain in the room until all the other members of the section have passed out.

129 Cadets reciting will assume the position of a soldier standing at attention unless the instructor prefers that he remain seated.

131 …

132 Under no conditions shall an instructor detain his section after the signal to dismiss had been sounded.

Visiting

133 Visiting in barracks is authorized when leave is granted to the corps, and during release from quarters, except by Cadets serving confinements or in arrest, and except at time designated for setting rooms in order.

134 No Cadet shall visit in a room at any time when any of the occupants are in arrest or serving confinements.

135 Visiting in barracks, except in the above stated is prohibited. However, members of the Junior and Senior classes, who take Greek, Latin or Mathematics, may, upon special permission, confer with each other concerning their work during evening hours.

136 There shall never be more than five Cadets in a Cadet room at one time, without special permission from the Commandant. …

137 Visiting during evening study hours shall be punishable by not less than five demerits and seven tours.

Fire Escape – Use of

138 Cadets are not to go on the fire escape at the north end of the barracks except in the case of fire or fire-drill. Appendix “A”

1 Any Cadet who shall disobey a command of any member of the faculty, or any Cadet officer on duty, or conduct himself in a refractory manner, shall be dismissed or otherwise less severely punished according to the nature of the case.

2 Any Cadet found guilty of drinking intoxicating liquor, or anyone found with such in his possession will subject himself to expulsion.

3 No Cadet shall play any game of cards or any game of chance, neither shall any Cadet have in his possession materials used in games of chance.

7 Cadets found guilty of smoking cigarettes will be subject to expulsion

9 Any Cadet found guilty of introducing or exploding any explosives in or around barracks will be dismissed.

12 Any member of the Senior Class or any member of the Junior Class who shall receive 175 demerits, or any member of the Sophomore or Freshman Class, who shall receive 200 demerits, shall be dismissed from the Institute.

List of Common Offenses and Penalties Attached

	Demerits	Confinements	Tours
Absent from any formation	4	0	4
Answering for another at roll call	4	0	4
Asleep on bed during study hours	2	2	0
Assuming duties of an officer	2	0	3
Bed not properly made	2	2	0
Being on street without permission	Arrest		
Books not properly arranged	1	0	0
Books grossly disarranged	2	2	0
Clothes not in proper place	1	0	0
Clothes grossly disarranged	2	2	0
Chewing in ranks	3	0	3

	Demerits	Confinements	Tours
Cooking in barracks	5	0	7
Dirty bed clothes	2	2	0
Door locked while in room	5	0	5
Door locked at taps	1	2	0
Dust on furniture or woodwork at inspection	2	2	0
Dirt, oil, or rust on gun at inspection	2	0	2
Rifle not prepared for inspection	4	0	4
Expectorating in ranks	2	0	2
Entering store or any place of business on Sunday	2	3	5
Entering Guard Room without permission	2	2	0
Entering Principal's or Commandants office without permission of OD	2	2	0
In wrong part of hallway during study hours	2	0	2
Improperly dressed at any inspection or formation	2	2	0
Improperly dressed in hallways	2	2	0
Loud talking or unnecessary noise in or around buildings	2	0	2
Light burning while out of room	2	2	0
Light burning after taps	2	2	0
Late for any formation	2	0	2
Leaving room before recall	2	0	2
Leaving room within 30 minutes after taps	2	3	5
Leaving books out of room overnight	2	2	0
Making False official statement	Arrest – Faculty Action		
Misconduct on drill	4	0	4
Misconduct on class	2	5	7
Misconduct in dining hall	3	0	3
Misusing leave	4	0	10
More than (5) in room at one time	1	3	5
Making unnecessary noise after taps	3	0	4
Not performing academic or military duties assigned	2	2	0
Not leaving key with Commandant when occupants of room are on leave	2	2	0
Not showing proper respect to national colors	3	5	10
Not standing at attention properly	2	0	2
Not submitting explanation to E. R. report	2	2	0
Not ringing bell or blowing bugle on time	3	5	10
Demerits Confinements Tours			
Not reporting to the proper authorities when sick, excused from any military duties or when going on leave	2	3	4
Not reporting Cadets absent from formation	2	3	5
Not properly approaching an officer concerning a report	2	3	5
Not obeying a superior officer	2	3	4
Not carrying piece properly	2	0	2
Not serving punishments	5	5	7
Not saluting faculty officer properly	2	0	4
Not saluting other Cadets on street	2	0	4
Not showing proper respect for Cadet Officers	1	2	3
Not undressed or not in bed at taps	2	2	0

	Demerits	Confinements	Tours
Not answering to name properly	1	0	1
Overstaying Leave – for each minute up to four	1	0	1
For each ten minutes thereafter	1	1	0
Out of room undue length of time during evening study hours	5	0	7
On bed during study hours	1	0	1
On street within 24 hours after expiration of sickness	3	0	3
Out of room at taps	2	3	5
Using electrical apparatus in barracks	5	0	5
Confiscation of apparatus			
Room not properly swept for inspection	2	2	0
Room not prepared for inspection	4	0	4
Running in barracks	2	0	2
Scuffling in room or hallway	5	0	5
Smoking at unauthorized time	2	0	4
Shoes not properly shined	2	0	2
Submitting application or communication late	2	2	0
Sweeping during or after inspection	2	2	0
Talking or yelling from ground to window or reverse	3	3	0
Trifling at any time	4	0	4
Talking back to officer	3	4	5
Throwing water, paper, cans or refuse, or any kind of object out of window, in building or on campus	3	0	4
Talking in ranks	2	0	2
Using tobacco in building	Faculty Action		
Using profanity	3	5	7
Visiting during evening study hours	5	10	0
Visiting during day study hours, drill hours, quiet hours or between reveille and police inspection	3	5	0
Wasting food on table	2	0	2
Wearing broken uniform	2	3	4
DIRECT INSUBORINATION – That is, refusing to obey an officer in the performance of his duties	Arrest		
LEAVING TOWN WITHOUT PROPER AUTHORITY	Arrest		
Making incorrect report for company – unintentionally	2	2	0

APPENDIX 12

Sale of North Carolina College Property

December 21, 1941

Mr. H. E. Isenhour reported on the sale of North Carolina College Property as follows:

Purchaser						
Kindley Cotton Mill	$	180.00	$	180.00		
C. H. Barringer	$	953.00	$	953.00		
Town of Mt. Pleasant	$	50.00	$	50.00		
A. W. Fisher	$	186.00	$	186.00		
S. J. Linker	$	100.00	$	30.48	$	69.52
Furr & Widenhouse	$	3,860.00	$	3,860.00		
Lee McAllister	$	734.00	$	734.00		
Dr. L. L. Ezell	$	390.00	$	130.00		
R. Moose	$	114.00	$	75.00	$	39.00
A. L. Barringer	$	510.00	$	170.00	$	340.00
Hoy Moose	$	900.00	$	900.00		
Totals	$	7, 977.00	$	7, 268.48	$	708.52
Received from H. E. Cline out of rents for Expense					$	200.00
Total received, Cash					$	7,468.48
Disbursements:						
Recording Plat			$	1.00		
Town of MP Balance in full. St. paving			$	156.63		
Revenue Stamps			$	12.10		
Seal			$	5.59		
Probate fee, Plat			$	.25		
Deed forms			$	.50		
Typing			$	5.00		
Walter Gurley Auction Co.			$	997.70		
Total			$	1,178.77		
Balance on deposit, Wachovia Bank & Trust Co.					$	6,289.71

Note: The above unpaid balance represents the purchases who took advantage of the terms offered at the sale. It is due as follows:

	Due: 6-16-42	Due: 12-17-42	Total
Dr. L. L. Ezell	$ 130.00	$ 130.00	$ 260.00
Robert A. Moose	$ 7.00	$ 32.00	$ 39.00
S. J. Linker	$ 34.76	$ 34.76	$ 69.52
A. L. Barringer	$ 170.00	$ 170.00	$ 340.00
	$ 341.76	$ 341.76	$ 708.52

Deeds for purchase not fully paid are held in escrow by H. E. Isenhour.
Respectfully submitted,
H. E. Isenhour, Agent for the Board

The report was approved, and Mr. Isenhour was authorized to pay the net proceeds of the sale $6,289.71, with other funds received, to Carl V. Cline, Treasurer of North Carolina College.

By motion duly passed, Mr. C. V. Cline was authorized to pay Mr. H. E. Isenhour $50.00 for his services and expenses in connection with the sale and the balance to the Treasurer of the North Carolina Synod.

Plat Plan of NC College with lots divided for sale – December 21, 1941.

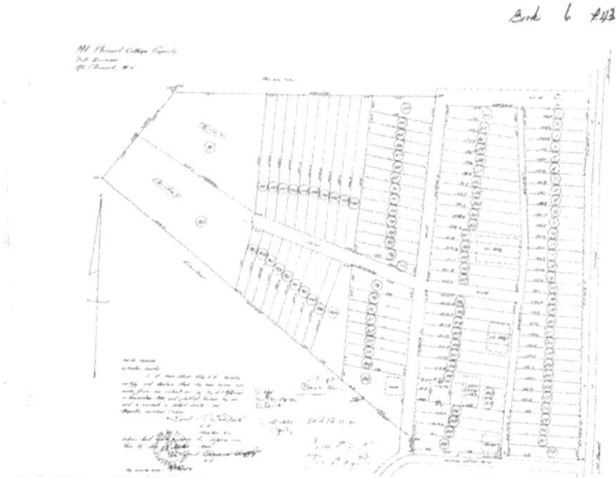

Lots 1-10 A. L. Barringer
Lots 11-14 Robert M. Moose
Lots 15-26 Dr. L. L. Ezzell
Lots 27-35 A. L. Barringer
Lots 36-40 Hoy A. Moose
Lots 41-52 A. P. Furr, A. C. & W. J. Widenhouse
Lots 63-77 A. W. Fisher
Lots 78-86 Lee McAllister
Lots 87-97 No Record
Lots 97-98 Kindley Mill (A. N. James)
2 Lots un-numbered (Town of MP)
Unknown Lots S. J. Linker

APPENDIX 13

Boards of Directors/Trustees

Board of Directors Western Carolina Male Academy
Appointed 22 Jul 1852

Rev. William Artz
Rev. John D. Scheck
Rev. Samuel Rothrock
Rev. William G. Harter
Rev. B. Arey
Rev. Jacob A. Linn

Mr. Matthias Barrier
Mr. Paul A. Seaford
Mr. William C. Means
Mr. Caleb A. Heilig
Mr. Martin L. Brown
Mr. Christopher Melchor

Board Directors of Western Carolina Male Academy
Elected 29 Apr 1853

Rev. Samuel Rothrock
Rev. John D. Scheck
Rev. W. G. Harter
Rev. Simeon Scherer
Rev. Levi C. Groseclose
Rev. Joseph A. Linn

Mr. Christopher Melchor
Mr. John Shimpock
Mr. Caleb A. Heilig
Mr. Matthias Barrier
Mr. C. L. Partee
Mr. Daniel Barrier

Board of Directors Western Carolina Male Academy
1857 Catalogue

Mr. Christopher Melchor, President
Mr. Caleb A. Heilig, VP
Colonel John Shimpoch, Secretary
Mr. Mathias Barrier, Treasurer
Mr. Daniel Barrier
Dr. Paul A. Seaford

Rev. Samuel Rothrock
Rev. Joseph A. Linn
Rev. Levi. C. Groseclose
Rev. John S. Heilig
Rev. D. I. Dreher
Rev. J. Crim

Board of Trustees North Carolina College
1859 Synod Records

Rev. John S. Heilig
Mr. Ludwig Summers
Rev. Joseph A. Linn
Mr. Christopher Melchor
Colonel John Shimpoch
Rev. William Artz
Rev. Levi C. Groseclose
Mr. P. N. Heilig
Rev. Daniel I. Dreher

Rev. Samuel Rothrock
Hon. Thomas Bragg
Mr. Alexander Brown
President of NC College
Hon. Burton Craige
Hon. Daniel M. Barringer
Mr. H. B. Eilers
Gen.William C. Means

Board of Trustees North Carolina College
1859 Catalogue

Mr. Christopher Melchor, President
Colonel John Shimpoch, Secretary
Mr. Mathias Barrier, Treasurer
Mr. Daniel Barrier
Dr. P. A. Seaford
Mr. Paul N Heilig
Mr. H. B. Eilers
Dr. James E. McEachern
Gen. William C. Means
Hon. Burton Craige
Rev. Samuel Rothrock
Rev. Levi. C. Groseclose
Rev. J. B. Anthony
Rev. Daniel I. Dreher
Rev. Joseph A. Linn
Rev. William Artz
Hon. D. M. Barringer
Hon. Thomas Bragg
Prof. Daniel H. Bittle

Board of Trustees NC College
1860-61 Catalogue

Mr. Christopher Melchor, President
Colonel John Shimpoch, Secretary
Mr. Mathias Barrier, Treasurer
Mr. L. G. Heilig
Maj. Paul N Heilig
Mr. H. B. Eilers
Dr. James E. McEachern
Gen. William C. Means
Rev. Samuel Rothrock
Rev. Levi. C. Groseclose
Rev. J. B. Anthony
Rev. Daniel I. Dreher
Rev. William Artz
Hon. D. M. Barringer
Hon. Thomas Bragg
Prof. Daniel H. Bittle

Board of Trustees NC College
1861-62 Catalogue

Mr. Christopher Melchor, President
Colonel John Shimpoch, Secretary
Mr. Mathias Barrier, Treasurer
Mr. L. G. Heilig
Maj. Paul N Heilig
Mr. H. B. Eilers
Dr. James E. McEachern
Gen. William C. Means
Rev. J. A. Linn
Hon. Burton Craige
Rev. Samuel Rothrock
Rev. Levi. C. Groseclose
Rev. J. B. Anthony
Rev. Daniel I. Dreher
Rev. William Artz
Hon. D. M. Barringer
Hon. Thomas Bragg
Prof. Daniel H. Bittle
Rev. Samuel Rothrock

Board of Trustees NC College
1867 Synod Records

Mr. Christopher Melchor, President
Mr. John Shimpoch, Secretary
Mr. Matthias Barrier, Treasurer
Rev. G. D. Bernheim
Rev. L. C. Groseclose
Rev. Samuel Rothrock
Rev. D. I. Dreher
Rev. W. H. Cone
Rev. Simeon Scherer
Maj. L. G. Heilig
Colonel P. N. Heilig
Mr. Daniel Barrier
Rev. Nicodemus Aldrich
Rev. W. Artz
Mr. Alexander Brown
Mr. W. A. Walton
Capt. J. A. Fisher
Mr. Peter Fogleman

Board of Trustees NC College
1868-'69 Catalogue

Mr. Christopher Melchor, President
Colonel P. N. Heilig

Mr. John Shimpoch, Secretary
Mr. Matthias Barrier, Treasurer
Rev. G. D. Bernheim
Rev. L. C. Groseclose
Rev. Samuel Rothrock
Rev. D. I. Dreher
Rev. Simeon Scherer
Mr. Daniel Barrier
Rev. Nicodemus Aldrich
Rev. W. Artz
Mr. W. A. Walton
Capt. J. A. Fisher
Mr. Peter Fogleman
Maj. L. G. Heilig

Board of Trustees NC College
1871-'72 Catalogue
Mr. L. G. Heilig, President
Colonel John Shimpoch, Secretary
Capt. Alexander Foil, Treasurer
Rev. Samuel Rothrock
Rev. G. D. Bernheim
Rev. L. C. Groseclose
Rev. Nicodemus Aldrich
Rev. W. H. Cone
Rev. Whitson Kimball
Mr. Monroe Melchor
Colonel P. N. Heilig
Mr. J. L. Graber (NCC)
Mr. Daniel Barrier
Rev. William Artz
Mr. William A. Walton
Dr. P. A. Sifferd
Capt. Jacob A. Fisher
Mr. John Sloop

Board of Trustees NC College
1873 Minutes of NC Lutheran Synod
Rev. William Artz
Alexander Foil
Dr. P. A. Sifferd
Rev. Nicodemus Aldrich
Rev. J. D. Bowles
Colonel Paul N. Heilig
Rev. Samuel Rothrock
Rev. W. H. Cone
Mr. Monroe Melchor
Daniel Barrier
Rev. G. D. Bernheim
John Shimpock
Caleb T. Bernhardt
Rev. D. M. Henkel
Rev. Whitson Kimball
Mr. J. L. Graber (NCC)
Maj. L. G. Heilig

Board of Trustees NC College
1874-'75-'76 Catalogue
Maj. L. G. Heilig, President
Colonel John Shimpock, Secretary
Capt. Jonas Cook, Treasurer (NCC)
Rev. Samuel Rothrock
Rev. W. H. Cone
Rev. Whitson Kimball
Mr. Caleb T. Bernhardt (WCMA)
Mr. J. L. Graeber (NCC)
Mr. Daniel Barrier
Rev. Timothy Moser (Tennessee Synod)
Dr. P. A. Sifferd
Capt. Alexander Foil
Rev. D. M. Henkel
Colonel Paul N. Heilig
Rev. Thomas Dosh
Rev. W. A. Julian (WCMA)
Capt. Jacob A. Fisher
Mr. John M. Harkey (NCC)

Board of Trustees NC College
1875 Minutes of NC Lutheran Synod
Maj. L. G. Heilig
Colonel John Shimpock
Jacob A. Fisher
Rev. Samuel Rothrock
Dr. P. A. Sifford
Capt. Alexander Foil
Rev. D. M. Henkel
Colonel Paul N. Heilig

Rev. W. H. Cone
Rev. Whitson Kimball
Mr. Caleb T. Bernhardt (WCMA)
Mr. J. L. Graeber (NCC)
Mr. Daniel Barrier
Rev. Timothy Moser (Tennessee Synod)
Rev. Philip A. Strobel
Rev. J. G. Neifer
Rev. W. A. Julian (WCMA)
Mr. John M. Harkey (NCC)

Board of Trustees NC College
1877-'78 Catalogue
Colonel John Shimpock, President
Capt. Alexander Foil, Secretary
Capt. Jonas Cook, Treasurer (NCC)
Maj. L. G. Heilig
Rev. Samuel Rothrock
Rev. W. H. Cone
Rev. Whitson Kimball
Mr. Caleb T. Bernhardt (WCMA)
Mr. Daniel Barrier
Rev. L. A. Bikle
Rev. W. A. Julian (WCMA)
Rev. Timothy Moser
Mr. D. R. Hoover
Capt. Jacob A. Fisher
Mr. John M. Harkey (NCC)
Rev. C. H. Bernheim
Mr. H. C. McAllister
Mr. J. L. Graeber (NCC)

Board of Trustees NC College
1878-'79 Catalogue
Colonel John Shimpock, President
Mr. H. C. McAllister, Secretary
Rev. Samuel Rothrock
Rev. L. A. Bikle
Rev. W. H. Cone
Rev. Whitson Kimball
Rev. R. W. Petrea
Rev. J. A. Linn '74
Maj. L. G. Heilig
Capt. Alexander Foil
Rev. G. D. Bernheim
Mr. Daniel Barrier
Mr. John M. Harkey (NCC)
Mr. J. W. Miller (NCC)
Mr. George E. Ritchie (NCC)
Rev. J. C. Moser '74

Board of Trustees NC College
1879-'80 Catalogue
Colonel John Shimpock, President
Mr. H. C. McAllister, Secretary
Rev. Samuel Rothrock
Rev. L. A. Bikle
Rev. W. H. Cone
Rev. Whitson Kimball
Rev. R. W. Petrea
Rev. J. A. Linn '74
Mr. Caleb T. Bernhardt (WCMA)
Maj. L. G. Heilig
Capt. Alexander Foil
Rev. J. C. Moser '74
Mr. Daniel Barrier
Mr. John M. Harkey (NCC)
Mr. Jesse W. Miller (NCC)
Mr. George E. Ritchie (NCC)
Mr. D. R. Hoover
Rev. G. D. Bernheim

Board of Trustees NC College
1881 Minutes of NC Lutheran Synod Convention
Colonel John Shimpock, President
Mr. H. C. McAllister, Secretary
Rev. Samuel Rothrock
Mr. Daniel Barrier
Rev. W. H. Cone
Mr. Jesse W. Miller (NCC)
Rev. R. W. Petrea
Maj. L. G. Heilig
Capt. Alexander Foil
Rev. L. A. Bikle
Mr. S. R. Hearne
Rev. Whitson Kimball
Rev. G. D. Bernheim
Mr. George E. Ritchie (NCC)

Rev. J. A. Linn '74
Rev. S. T. Hallman
Mr. Caleb T. Bernhardt (WCMA)
Mr. D. R. Hoover
Mr. S. R. Hearne

Board of Trustees NC College
From the Minutes of the NC College Board of Trustees May 23, 1882 (partial list)
Rev. Samuel Rothrock, President
L. G. Heilig, Vice-President
H. C. McAllister, Secretary
Rev. G. D. Bernheim
Rev. S. T. Hallman
Rev. L. A. Bikle
D. Barrier
P. N. Heilig
George E. Ritchie (NCC)
R. W. Petrea
Rev. T. H. Strohecker

Board of Trustees NC College
1883 Minutes of the NC Lutheran Synod
Rev. Samuel Rothrock, President
L. G. Heilig, Vice-President
H. C. McAllister, Secretary
R. W. Petrea
Rev. S. T. Hallman
Rev. L. A. Bikle
Rev. J. A. Linn '74
Mr. S. R. Hearne
Mr. D. R. Hoover
Daniel Barrier
P. N. Heilig
George E. Ritchie (NCC)
Rev. Whitson Kimball
Rev. T. H. Strohecker
Rev. F. W. Peschau
Mr. C. T. Bernhardt
Mr. Jesse W. Miller (NCC)
Mr. Alexander Foil

Board of Trustees NC College
1886-'87 Catalogue
Rev. Samuel Rothrock, President
Mr. H. C. McAllister, Secretary
Capt. Jonas Cook, Treasurer (NCC)
Rev. W. G. Campbell
Rev. F. W. E. Peschau
Rev. J. A. Linn '73
Rev. R. W. Petrea
Dr. P. A. Barrier (WCMA)
Mr. George E. Ritchie (NCC)
Dr. R. A. Shimpock
Mr. J. W. Miller (NCC)
Capt. W. A. Barrier '72
Rev. J. W. Strickler
Rev. C. A. Rose (NCC)
Mr. Marvel Ritchie
Mr. R. A. Brown
Rev. H. M. Brown '73
Mr. H. A. Blackwelder (WCMA)

Board of Trustees NC College
1889-'90 Catalogue
Rev. Samuel Rothrock, President
Rev. George H. Cox, VP
Rev. J. A. Linn '73
Mr. H. C. McAllister, Secretary
Capt. Jonas Cook, Treasurer (NCC)
Rev. W. G. Campbell
Rev. C. A. Rose (NCC)
Rev. R. W. Petrea
Dr. P. A. Barrier (WCMA)
Mr. George E. Ritchie (NCC)
Dr. R. A. Shimpock
Rev. S. L. Keller
Rev. F. W. E. Peschau
Mr. J. W. Miller (NCC)
Capt. W. A. Barrier '72
Rev. J. W. Strickler
Mr. Marvel Ritchie
Mr. R. A. Brown
Rev. H. M. Brown '73
Mr. H. A. Blackwelder (WCMA) (dec)

Board of Trustees NC College
1890-'91 Catalogue

Rev. George H. Cox, President
Rev. J. A. Linn, VP '73
Mr. H. C. McAllister, Secretary
Capt. Jonas Cook, Treasurer (NCC)
Rev. Samuel Rothrock
Rev. F. W. E. Peschau
Mr. George E. Ritchie (NCC)
Rev. W. R. Brown (NCC)
Mr. Jesse W. Miller
Rev. C. A. Rose (NCC)
Mr. Marvel Ritchie
Mr. R. A. Brown
Rev. H. M. Brown '73
Mr. Daniel D. Barrier (NCC)
Dr. R. A. Shimpock
~~Rev. J. M. Hedrick~~

Board of Trustees NC College
1892-'93 Catalogue

Rev. J. A. Linn, President '73
Rev. W. R. Brown, VP (NCC)
Mr. C. G. Heilig, Secretary '80
Capt. Jonas Cook, Treasurer (NCC)
Rev. Samuel Rothrock
Rev. George H. Cox
Rev. F. W. E. Peschau
Dr. P. A. Barrier (WCMA)
Mr. H. C. McAllister
Mr. George E. Ritchie (NCC)
Rev. C. A. Rose (NCC)
Mr. Marvel Ritchie
Mr. R. A. Brown
Rev. H. M. Brown '73
Mr. Daniel D. Barrier (NCC)
Rev. Peter Miller (NCC)
Rev. J. D. Shirey
Mr. Jesse Miller

Board of Trustees NC College
1893-'94 Catalogue

Mr. H. C. McAllister, President
Rev. C. A. Rose, VP (NCC)
Mr. C. G. Heilig, Secretary '80
Capt. Jonas Cook, Treasurer (NCC)
Rev. Samuel Rothrock
Rev. F. W. E. Peschau
Dr. P. A. Barrier (WCMA)
Mr. Marvel Ritchie
Mr. Daniel D. Barrier (NCC)
Rev. J. D. Shirey
Mr. I. F. Patterson (NCC)
Rev. C. B. King
Mr. George E. Ritchie (NCC)
Mr. Jesse Miller

Board of Trustees NC College
1894-'95 Catalogue

Mr. H. C. McAllister, President
Rev. J. Q. Wertz, VP
Mr. C. G. Heilig, Secretary '80
Capt. Jonas Cook, Treasurer (NCC)
Rev. Charles B. King
Rev. F. W. E. Peschau
Dr. R. A. Shimpock
Dr. P. A. Barrier (WCMA)
Mr. George E. Ritchie (NCC)
Mr. Marvel Ritchie
Rev. C. A. Rose (NCC)
Rev. J. D. Shirey
Mr. I. F. Patterson (NCC)
Mr. John K. Patterson (NCC)
Mr. Daniel D. Barrier (NCC)
Rev. Gideon G. Sherer
Rev. Vastine R. Stickley
Mr. Jesse W. Miller

Board of Trustees NC College
1896-'97 Catalogue

Mr. H. C. McAllister, President
Rev. J. Q. Wertz, VP
Mr. C. G. Heilig, Secretary '80
Mr. Marvel Ritchie
Dr. M. L. Stevens (NCC)
Rev. J. D. Shirey

Capt. Jonas Cook, Treasurer (NCC)
Rev. Charles B. King
Rev. W. P. Huddle
Dr. R. A. Shimpock
Dr. P. A. Barrier (WCMA)
Mr. George E. Ritchie (NCC)
Rev. Henderson N. Miller
Mr. John K. Patterson (NCC)
Mr. Daniel D. Barrier (NCC)
Rev. Gideon G. Sherer
Rev. Vastine R. Stickley
Mr. Jesse Miller

Board of Trustees NC College
1897-'98 Catalogue
Mr. H. C. McAllister, President
Rev. Vastine R. Stickley, VP
Mr. C. G. Heilig, Secretary '80
Capt. Jonas Cook, Treasurer (NCC)
Rev. Sidney D. Steffey
Rev. Charles B. Miller '85
Dr. Paul A. Barrier (WCMA)
Mr. George E. Ritchie (NCC)
Rev. Charles B. King
Dr. C. M. Poole (NCC)
Mr. Marvel Ritchie
Rev. W. B. Oney
Mr. John K. Patterson (NCC)
Dr. R. A. Shimpock
Rev. C. A. Rose (NCC)
Dr. M. L. Stevens (NCC)
Mr. Daniel D. Barrier (NCC)
Rev. G. G. Scherer

Board of Trustees NC College
1898-'99 Catalogue
Mr. H. C. McAllister, President
Rev. Vastine R. Stickley, VP
Mr. C. G. Heilig, Secretary '80
Capt. Jonas Cook, Treasurer (NCC)
Rev. Sidney D. Steffey
Rev. Charles B. Miller '85
Dr. Paul A. Barrier (WCMA)
Mr. George E. Ritchie (NCC)
Rev. Charles B. King
James D. Heilig (NCC)
Mr. Marvel Ritchie
Rev. W. B. Oney
Mr. John K. Patterson (NCC)
Dr. R. A. Shimpock
Rev. C. A. Rose (NCC)
Dr. M. L. Stevens (NCC)
Mr. Daniel D. Barrier (NCC)
Rev. G. G. Scherer

Board of Trustees NC College
1899-'00 Catalogue
Mr. H. C. McAllister, President
Rev. Vastine R. Stickley, VP
Mr. C. G. Heilig, Secretary '80
Capt. Jonas Cook, Treasurer (NCC)
Rev. Sidney D. Steffey
Rev. Charles B. Miller '85
Dr. Paul A. Barrier (WCMA)
Mr. George E. Ritchie (NCC)
Rev. Charles B. King
Rev. V. Y. Boozer
Mr. Marvel Ritchie
Mr. W. N. Misenheimer (NCC)
Mr. John K. Patterson (NCC)
Dr. R. A. Shimpock
Rev. Charles A. Brown (NCC)
Dr. M. L. Stevens (NCC)
Mr. Daniel D. Barrier (NCC)
Mr. James D. Heilig (NCC)

Board of Trustees NC College
1900-'01 Catalogue
Mr. H. C. McAllister, President
Rev. Vastine R. Stickley, VP
Mr. C. G. Heilig, Secretary '80
Capt. Jonas Cook, Treasurer (NCC)
Rev. Sidney D. Steffey
Rev. Charles B. Miller '85
Rev. Chrisenberry A. Brown
Dr. M. L. Stevens (NCC)
Rev. Charles B. King
Mr. John K. Patterson (NCC)
Dr. R. A. Shimpock
Mr. W. N. Misenheimer (NCC)

Dr. Paul A. Barrier (WCMA)
Mr. George E. Ritchie (NCC)
Rev. Virgil Y. Boozer
Mr. Daniel D. Barrier (NCC)

Board of Trustees NC College
1902 Synod Records

H. C. McAllister
Capt. Jonas Cook (NCC)
Rev. H. A. Trexler (NCC)
Rev. Robert C. Holland
Rev. William A. Dutton
D. R. Hoover
P. A. Sloop
George E. Ritchie (NCC)
W. N. Misenheimer (NCC)
William H. Fisher
Marvel Ritchie
M. B. Stickley
Rev. W. H. Hiller
S. H. Hearne
Rev. C. B. King
John K. Patterson (NCC)
Dr. R. A. Shimpock
Rev. George H. Cox

Board of Trustees NC College
1905 Synod Minutes

Rev. T. C. Parker
Rev. H. M. Brown (NCC)
J. A. Cline
J. C. Lingle
Dr. C. M. Poole (NCC)
Jonas Cook (NCC)
P. A. Sloop
George W. Dry
M. B. Stickley
D. R. Hoover
Rev. W.A. Dutton
Rev. Robert C. Holland
Rev. H. A. Trexler (NCC)
Cager D. Barringer
George E. Ritchie (NCC)
William H. Fisher
H. C. McAllister
Rev. W. H. Hiller

Board of Trustees NC College
1906 Catalogue

P. A. Sloop
William H. Fisher
M. B. Stickley
H. C. McAllister
Rev. H. A. Trexler (NCC)
Rev. W.A. Dutton
Rev. J. E. Shenk
J. A. Cline
Dr. C. M. Poole (NCC)
George E. Ritchie (NCC)
George W. Dry
Rev. W. H. Hiller
Jonas Cook (NCC)
Rev. Robert C. Holland
Rev. C. P. Fisher
Rev. H. M. Brown (NCC)
George L. Barrier (NCC)
Cager D. Barringer

Board of Trustees NC College
1908 Synod Minutes

H. C. McAllister
Rev. H. A. Trexler (NCC)
Rev. William A. Dutton
Rev. Clifford P. Fisher '00
John A. Cline
Cager D. Barringer
Bachman B. Miller (NCC)
George W. Dry
Rev. H. A. McCullough
Jonas Cook (NCC)
Rev. Robert C. Holland
D. R. Hoover
Rev. Jacob E. Shenk
George L. Barrier (NCC)
Dr. C. M. Poole (NCC)
George E. Ritchie (NCC)
M. B. Strickley
Rev. V. Y. Boozer

Board of Trustees NC College
1909 Board of Trustees Minutes

H. C. McAllister
Rev. H. A. Trexler (NCC)
Rev. William A. Dutton
Rev. Clifford P. Fisher '00
John A. Cline
Cager D. Barringer
George E. Ritchie (NCC)
M. B. Strickley
Rev. H. A. McCullough
Rev. H. M. Brown (NCC)
Jonas Cook (NCC)
Rev. Robert C. Holland
D. R. Hoover
Rev. Jacob E. Shenk
George L. Barrier (NCC)
Dr. C. M. Poole (NCC)
George W. Dry
J. S. M. Efird
Rev. V. Y. Boozer
W. H. Fisher (NCC)

Board of Trustees NC College
1910-1911 MPCI Catalogue

Rev. Jacob E. Shenk
Rev. H. M. Brown (NCC)
John A. Cline
George L. Barrier (NCC)
Dr. C. M. Poole (NCC)
Cager D. Barringer
W. H. Fisher (NCC)
George E. Ritchie (NCC)
Rev. H. A. McCullough
George W. Dry
M. B. Stickley
Rev. V. Y. Boozer
H. C. McAllister
Jonas Cook (NCC)
Rev. H. A. Trexler (NCC)
A. H. Litaker (NCC)
Rev. G. H. L. Lingle '01
Rev. John J. Long

Board of Trustees NC College
1911-1912 MPCI Catalogue

W. H. Fisher (NCC)
George E. Ritchie (NCC)
Rev. R. A. Goodman
George W. Dry
M. B. Stickley
Rev. V. Y. Boozer
H. C. McAllister
John M. Cook '90
Rev. H. A. Trexler (NCC)
A. H. Litaker (NCC)
Rev. G. H. L. Lingle '01
Rev. John J. Long
Rev. C. P. McLaughlin
Rev. H. M. Brown (NCC)
John A. Cline
George L. Barrier (NCC)
L. R. Lingle
Walter B. Fisher (NCC)

Board of Trustees
1913-1914 MPCI Catalogue

Rev. C. P. McLaughlin
Rev. H. M. Brown (NCC) (dec)
John A. Cline
L. R. Lingle
Walter B. Fisher (NCC)
George E. Ritchie (NCC)
Rev. R. A. Goodman
W. H. Fisher
John W. Cress (NCC)
George W. Dry
Paul A. Barger
Rev. Victor C. Ridenhour '99
H. C. McAllister
John M. Cook '90
Rev. H. A. Trexler (NCC)
A. H. Litaker (NCC)
Rev. G. H. L. Lingle '01
Rev. John J. Long

Board of Trustees
1914-1915 Board of Trustee Minutes

Rev. C. P. McLaughlin
Paul A. Barger
John A. Cline
L. R. Lingle
Walter B. Fisher (NCC)
George E. Ritchie (NCC)
A. H. Litaker (NCC)
W. H. Fisher
John W. Cress (NCC)
Rev. R. A. Goodman (resigned)
George W. Dry
Rev. Charles R. (NCC)
Rev. Victor C. Ridenhour '99
H. C. McAllister (dec)
John M. Cook '90
Rev. H. A. Trexler (NCC)
Rev. Nathan D. Bodie
Rev. G. H. L. Lingle '01
Rev. John J. Long
Rev. Charles R. Pless '00

Board of Trustees
1915 MPCI Letterhead

Rev. N. D. Bodie, Pres
Hon. J. P. Cook, VP '85
Rev. V. C. Ridenhour, Sec '99
Jno M. Cook, Treas '90
W. H. Fisher
Geo. E. Ritchie (NCC)
Rev. C. R. Pless '00
L. R. Lingle
Paul M. Barger
J. M. Earnhardt, MD
Rev. H. A. Trexler (NCC)
A. H. Litaker (NCC)
Rev. G. H. L. Lingle '01
Rev. C. P. McLaughlin, DD
Rev. I. E. Long
Jno. W. Cress (NCC)
Walter B. Fisher (NCC)
Geo. W. Dry

Board of Trustees
1915-'16 MPCI Catalogue

Rev. N. D. Bodie, President
Hon. James P. Cook, VP '85
A. H. Litaker (NCC)
Jno M. Cook, Treas '90
W. H. Fisher
Rev. I. E. Long
Jno. W. Cress (NCC)
L. R. Lingle
Paul M. Barger
J. M. Earnhardt, MD
Rev. H. A. Trexler (NCC)
Rev. F. B. Clausen
Rev. G. H. L. Lingle '01
Geo. E. Ritchie (NCC)
Rev. C. R. Pless '00
Rev. P. D. Brown
Walter B. Fisher (NCC)
Geo. W. Dry

Board of Trustees
1916-'17 MPCI Catalogue

Rev. N. D. Bodie, President
Hon. John M. Cook, Treas '90
Rev. F. B. Clausen
Rev. G. H. L. Lingle '01
W. H. Fisher
Rev. I. E. Long
Rev. C. R. Pless '00
L. R. Lingle
Paul M. Barger
J. M. Earnhardt, MD
D. W. Moose (NCC)
C. E. Reitzel, MD
Hon. James P. Cook, VP '85
W. F. Aberly
Rev. Pleasant D. Brown (MPCI)
Jno. W. Cress (NCC)
Walter B. Fisher (NCC)
Geo. W. Dry

Board of Trustees
1919-'20 MPCI Catalogue

Rev. Nathan D. Bodie, President
Hon. John M. Cook, Treas '90
C. E. Reitzel, MD
Hon. James P. Cook, VP '85
Rev. Irving E. Long
Rev. C. R. Pless '00
Paul M. Barger
Geo. W. Dry
Rev. Pleasant D. Brown
J. M. Earnhardt, MD
D. W. Moose (NCC)
J. A. Kellenberger
John W. Cress (NCC)
W. B. Fisher (MPCI)
Edward Ahrens
J. H. Rheder (resigned)
Rev. Martin L. Stirewalt (MPCI)

Board of Trustees
1920-'21 MPCI Catalogue

Rev. Nathan D. Bodie, President
Gilbert Hendrix, Treas (MPCI)
C. E. Reitzel, MD
Hon. James P. Cook, '85
A. W. Fisher (MPCI)
Rev. Irving E. Long
Dr. C. A. Misenheimer (NCC)
H. E. Bonitz
W. T. Busby
J. M. Earnhardt, MD
Rev. Pleasant D. Brown (MPCI)
J. A. Kellenberger
Rev. G. H. L. Lingle '01
John W. Cress (NCC)
W. B. Fisher (MPCI)
Paul M. Barger
O. D. Ritchie (MPCI)
Rev. Martin L. Stirewalt, VP

Board of Trustees
1921-'22 MPCI Catalogue

D. W. Aderholdt, Chairman
W. L. Dixon, Treasurer
J. H. C. Huitt
C. E. Reitzel, MD
Rev. Edward Fulenwider (NCC)
J. A. Moretz
J. B. Robertson
L. M. Swink
Rev. Nathan D. Bodie, Vice-Chairman
Rev. Martin L. Stirewalt
C. A. Rudisill
Rev. Luther A. Thomas, Sec (MPCI)
H. B. Wilkinson
Rev. Willis A. Deaton '88
J. J. George
Roland W. Leiby

Board of Trustees
1923-'24 MPCI Catalogue

D. W. Aderholdt, Chairman
Rev. William J. Boger (NCC '93)
J. H. C. Huitt
C. E. Reitzel, MD
Rev. John F. Crigler
J. A. Moretz
J. S. Mauney
J. B. Robertson
L. M. Swink
Rev. Alfred R. Beck, Sec
J. V. Sutton
Rev. Nathan D. Bodie
Rev. Francis K. Roof
C. A. Rudisill
Rev. Luther A. Thomas (MPCI)
H. B. Wilkinson
Rev. John C. Dietz
Rev. Willis A. Deaton '88
J. J. George
Roland W. Leiby
Rev. G. H. L. Lingle '01
W. L. Dixon, Treasurer (not on Board of Trustees)

Board of Trustees
1924-'25 MPCI Catalogue
D. W. Aderholdt, Chairman
Rev. William J. Boger (NCC '93)
J. H. C. Huitt
C. E. Reitzel, MD
Rev. John F. Crigler
J. A. Moretz
W. K. Mauney
J. J. George
L. M. Swink
Rev. G. H. L. Lingle '01
J. V. Sutton
Rev. Nathan D. Bodie (Newberry '93)
A. C. Kellenberger, Jr.
C. A. Rudisill
Rev. Luther A. Thomas (MPCI)
H. B. Wilkinson, Treas
Rev. John C. Dietz
Rev. Willis A. Deaton '88
Rev. Paul J. Bame
Rev. Alfred R. Beck, Secretary
A. C. Lineberger, Jr.

Board of Trustees
1925-'26 MPCI Catalogue
Rev. William J. Boger (NCC '93), Pres
C. A. Rudisill
Rev. Luther A. Thomas (MPCI)
Rev. John F. Crigler
J. A. Moretz
W. K. Mauney
W. B. Rhyne
L. M. Swink
A. C. Lineberger, Jr.
V. Sutton
Rev. Rubertus M. Carpenter
J. H. C. Huitt
J. A. Kellenberger
Jerome J. Efird (MPCI)
H. B. Wilkinson, Treas
Rev. John C. Dietz, Sec
Rev. Edwin F. Keever
A. L. Bulwinkle
Rev. G. H. L. Lingle (NCC '01)
Rev. James D. Kinard
Rev. Nathan D. Bodie

Board of Trustees
1926-'27 Catalogue
Rev. William J. Boger (NCC '93), Pres
C. A. Rudisill
Rev. Luther A. Thomas (MPCI)
Rev. John F. Crigler
J. A. Moretz
W. K. Mauney
A. L. Bulwinkle
L. M. Swink
A. C. Lineberger, Jr.
J. V. Sutton
W. B. Rhyne
J. H. C. Huitt
J. A. Kellenberger
Jerome J. Efird (MPCI)
H. B. Wilkinson, Treas
Rev. John C. Dietz, Sec
Rev. Flavius L. Conrad
Rev. Charles E. Ridenhour (MPCI)
Rev. G. H. L. Lingle (NCC '01)
Rev. James D. Kinard
Rev. Rubertus M. Carpenter

Board of Trustees
Collegiate Institute (1927-'28)
A. L. Bulwinkle
Rev. J. D. Kinard
Rev. J. F. Crigler
Rev. F. L. Conrad
W. B. Rhyne
J. J. Efird (MPCI)
D. P. Rhoads
J. V. Sutton (NCC)
Rev. L. A. Thomas (MPCI)
H. B. Wilkinson
Rev. L. D. Miller
Rev. C. E. Ridenhour (MPCI)
H. E. Isenhour (MPCI)
Rev. V. C. Ridenhour (NCC '99)

Rev. W. J. Boger '93
J. H. C. Huitt
Rev. G. H. L. Lingle (NCC '01)
C. A. Rudisill
Prof. G. F. McAllister, Ex-Offico (NCC '97)
A. C. Lineberger, Jr.
W. K. Mauney
J. A. Moretz
Rev. J. L. Morgan, Ex-Offico

Board of Trustees
Collegiate Institute (1928-'29)
Rev. W. J. Boger '93, President
J. V. Sutton (NCC)
Rev. L. A. Thomas (MPCI)
Rev. J. F. Crigler
Rev. F. L. Conrad
W. B. Rhyne
J. J. Efird (MPCI)
Rev. V. C. Ridenhour '99
J. H. C. Huitt
Rev. G. H. L. Lingle (NCC '01)
C. A. Rudisill
Prof. G. F. McAllister, Ex-Offico '97
A. L. Starr
A. C. Lineberger, Jr.
Rev. Edward Fulenwider '99
H. B. Wilkinson
Rev. L. D. Miller
Rev. C. E. Ridenhour (MPCI)
D. P. Rhoads
H. E. Isenhour (MPCI)
W. K. Mauney
J. A. Moretz
Rev. J. L. Morgan, Ex-Offico

Board of Trustees
Collegiate Institute (1929-'30)
Rev. W. J. Boger '93), President
J. V. Sutton (NCC)
Rev. C. P. Fisher '00
Rev. J. F. Crigler
Rev. F. L. Conrad
W. B. Rhyne
J. J. Efird (MPCI)
Rev. V. C. Ridenhour '99
Rev. Bachman S. Brown
Rev. G. H. L. Lingle '01
C. A. Rudisill
Rev. J. L. Morgan, Ex-Offico
A. L. Starr
H. L Arndt
Rev. Edward Fulenwider '99
H. B. Wilkinson
Arthur W. Fisher (MPCI)
Rev. C. E. Ridenhour (MPCI)
D. P. Rhoads
H. E. Isenhour (MPCI)
W. K. Mauney
J. A. Moretz
Prof. G. F. McAllister, Ex-Offico '97

Board of Trustees for North Carolina College (1930-'31)
Rev. W. J. Boger '93, President
Rev. L. D. Miller
Rev. C. E. Ridenhour (MPCI)
A. C. Lineberger, Jr.
W. K. Mauney
J. A. Moretz
Hon. A. L. Starr
Rev. J. F. Crigler
Rev. F. L. Conrad
W. B. Rhyne
Rev. J. L. Morgan, Ex-Offico
Rev. Edward Fulenwider '99
J. J. Efird (MPCI)
D. P. Rhoads
Rev. C. P. Fisher '00
Rev. Bachman S. Brown
C. A. Rudisill
J. V. Sutton (NCC)
H. L. Arndt
Arthur W. Fisher (NCC/MPCI)
Prof. G. F. McAllister, Ex-Officio '97

* The Board of Directors for the Mt. Pleasant Collegiate Institute was created by MPCI Principal, G. F. McAllister in 1931 after the NC Lutheran Synod withdrew its support and G.

F. McAllister "leased" the buildings for his own school. At the same time, the Synod retained its own Board of Trustees of North Carolina College, thus creating two Boards who oversaw different parts of the operation of the school.

Board of Directors Collegiate Institute (1931-32)*

Arthur W. Fisher (NCC/MPCI)
H. L. Beckerdite
Hon. R. L. Doughton
Harry E. Isenhour (MPCI)
Adolphus N. James
Dr. Hoy A. Moose (MPCI)
Dr. R. Matt Patterson
Rev. George S. Bowden (MPCI)
Dr. Zeno L. Edwards (MPCI)
Barron R. Hinson (MPCI)
A. C. Lineberger, Jr.
William M. Sherrill, Chairman
Carl M. Cook (NCC)
Mrs. J. S. (Bertha) Efird
J. L. Fisher
D. F. Giles
Dr. Joe F. Hartsell
Clarence G. Heilig, Jr. (MPCI)
A. R. Hoover
Dr. F. W. Morrison (MPCI)
Colonel G. F. McAllister, Ex-Officio (NCC '97)

Board of Directors Collegiate Institute (1932-33)*

Arthur W. Fisher (NCC) (Chairman)
H. L. Beckerdite
Hon. R. L. Doughton
Harry E. Isenhour (MPCI)
Adolphus N. James
Dr. Hoy A. Moose (MPCI)
Dr. R. Matt Patterson
Rev. George S. Bowden (MPCI)
Dr. Zeno L. Edwards (MPCI)
Dr. F. W. Morrison (MPCI)
A. C. Lineberger, Jr.
C. G. Heilig, Jr. (MPCI)
George H. Faggart (MPCI)
William M. Sherrill
Carl M. Cook (NCC)
Mrs. J. S. (Bertha) Efird
J. L. Fisher
D. F. Giles
Dr. Joe F. Hartsell
Clarence G. Heilig, Jr. (MPCI)
A. R. Hoover
W. L. Burns
Barron R. Hinson (MPCI)
F. L. Harkey (MPCI)
Colonel G. F. McAllister, Ex-Officio '97

NC Synod Board of Trustees for North Carolina College
(Synod Minutes 10 Oct 1933)

Rev. F. L. Conrad, Chairman
Rev. Bachman S. Brown, Jr.
Charles A. Graeber
J. A. Moretz
Rev. C. P. Fisher '00
Rev. Lester D. Miller
Rev. Jefferson L. Norris
Mr. Futchs
C. A. Rudisill
Rev. Pleasant E. Monroe, Ex-Officio
Rev. Martin L. Stirewalt
C. L. Miller
Rev. J. F. Crigler
Rev. Jacob L. Morgan, '99
H. E. Isenhour (MPCI)
H. L. Arndt
Hon. A. L. Starr
W. B. Rhyne
W. K. Mauney

APPENDIX 14

Faculty of WCMA, NC College, CE&CS, & MPCI

Western Carolina Male Academy

1855 –'56– WCMA
Rev. William Gerhardt, Principal
Rev. John D. Scheck, Asst. Professor (resigned Jan 1856)
A. M. Byers, Asst. Professor (hired Mar 1856, resigned Sep 1856)

1856 – '57 – WCMA
Rev. William Gerhardt, Principal
Rev. Caleb Lentz, Asst. Professor
William L. Barrier, Tutor

1857-'58 – WCMA
Rev. William Gerhardt, Principal
Rev. Caleb Lentz, Asst. Professor (resigned)
Rev. Louis A. Bikle, Asst. Professor (replaced Lentz)

North Carolina College

1859 –'60 NCC
Rev. Daniel H. Bittle, President & Professor of Mental/Moral Science
Rev. Louis A. Bikle, Professor of Ancient Languages
William Grimm, Professor of Mathematics (resigned Jul 1860)

1860-'61 NCC
Rev. Daniel H. Bittle, President & Professor of Mental/Moral Science

Rev. Louis A. Bikle, Professor of Mathematics
George F. Schaffer, Professor of Ancient Languages
R. C. Holland, Principal of the Preparatory Department
1861 NCC (Suspended operations in Nov 1861)
Rev. Daniel H. Bittle, President & Professor of Mental/Moral Science (resigned Oct 1861)
Other faculty unknown.
1862-1866 College closed
1866-'67 NCC
Rev. Louis A. Bikle, President

1867-'68 NCC
Rev. Charles H. Bansemer, President & Professor of Mental/Moral Science (hired Sep 1867)
Rev. Louis A. Bikle, Asst. Professor
B. F. Rogers, Tutor

1868-'69 NCC
Rev. Charles H. Bansemer, President & Professor of Mental/Moral Science (resigned Dec 1868)
Rev. Louis A. Bikle, Asst. Professor (Acting President Jan 1869)
Rev. Philip M. Bikle, Professor of Latin & Greek (hired in Jan 1869)
Henry T. J. Ludwig, Tutor (student at the College, hired in Jan 1869)

1869-'70 NCC
Rev. Louis A. Bikle, Acting President
Henry T. J. Ludwig, Tutor (still a student)

1870-'71 NCC
Rev. Louis A. Bikle, Acting President (Appointed President Jan 1871)
Henry T. J. Ludwig, Tutor (graduated May 1871)

1871-'72 NCC
Rev. Louis A. Bikle, President & Professor of Mental/Moral Science
Henry T. J. Ludwig, Professor of Mathematics & Natural Science
Rev. W. E. Hubbert, Professor of Ancient Languages & Literature

1872-'73 NCC

Rev. Louis A. Bikle, President & Professor of Mental/Moral Science. Also instructed in the newly formed Theological Dept., teaching Apologetics, Dogmatics and Greek Exercises.

Henry T. J. Ludwig, Professor of Mathematics & Natural Science

Rev. W. E. Hubbert, Professor of Ancient Languages & Literature. Also instructed in the newly formed Theological Dept. instructing in omiletics, Hermeneutics and Hebrew

Guest instructors/lecturers included:

Dr. Paul A. Barrier, WCMA '56, lectured on Chemistry, Anatomy and Physiology

Capt. Wiley A. Barrier, NCC '72 instructed in "penmanship"

Rev. L. C. Groseclose, lectured on Ecclesiastical & Sacred History

1873-'74 NCC

Rev. Louis A. Bikle, President & Professor of Mental/Moral Science

Henry T. J. Ludwig, Professor of Mathematics & Natural Science

Rev. W. E. Hubbert, Professor of Ancient Languages & Literature

1874-'75 NCC

Rev. Louis A. Bikle, President & Professor of Mental/Moral Science (resigned Oct 1874, effective Apr 1875)

Henry T. J. Ludwig, Professor of Mathematics & Natural Science (resigned Nov 1874, effective Apr 1875)

Rev. W. E. Hubbert, Professor of Ancient Languages & Literature

Joseph A. Linn, (NCC Student), Tutor

1875-76 NCC

Rev. John B. Davis, (DD '1873 NCC), President & Professor of Mental/Moral Science

Rev. W. E. Hubbert, Professor of Ancient Languages & Literature

Rev. J. H. Turner, Hired as Professor of Mathematics but listed in Catalogue as Adjunct Professor of Ancient Languages and Principal of the Preparatory Department (resigned Oct 1875)

Rev. Adolphus L. Yount, listed as Professor of Mathematics (NCC Student)

Dr. Paul A. Barrier, lectured on Anatomy and Physiology

David L. Crouse, (NCC Student), Adjunct Professor of Ancient Languages and Principal of the Preparatory Department

1876-'77 NCC

Rev. John B. Davis, (DD '1873 NCC), President & Professor of Mental/ Moral Science

R. H. Brown, Professor of Mathematics

Rev. W. E. Hubbert, Professor of Ancient Languages & Literature

David L. Crouse, Principal of the Preparatory Department

1877-'78 NCC

Rev. Louis A. Bikle, President & Professor Mental/Moral Science

Rev. S. S. Rahn, Professor of Ancient Languages and Classical Literature

Henry T. J. Ludwig, Professor of Mathematics, Astronomy and Physics

S. S. Lindler, Tutor (student)

Dr. Paul A. Barrier, lectured on Anatomy and Physiology

1878-'79 NCC

Rev. Louis A. Bikle, President & Professor Mental/Moral Science

Henry T. J. Ludwig, Professor of Mathematics, Astronomy and Physics

Rev. S. S. Rahn, Professor of Ancient Languages and Classical Literature

Dr. Paul A. Barrier, lectured on Anatomy and Physiology

1879-'80 NCC

Rev. Louis A. Bikle, President & Professor of Ancient Languages & Classical Literature

Henry T. J. Ludwig, Professor of Mathematics, Astronomy and Physics

Rev. John B. Davis, Professor of Natural Science & Mental Philosophy

Dr. Paul A. Barrier, lectured on Anatomy and Physiology

1880-'81 NCC

No official information is available, however, it appears from several contemporary newspaper articles that the faculty for 1880-'81 consisted of Rev. L. A. Bikle, H. T. J. Ludwig, and Rev. J. B. Davis.

1881-'82 NCC

Rev. L. A. Bikle (There was no College catalogue produced for the 1881-82 session of the College "due to the new arrangement [which] was entered into by the Board of Trustees with the College faculty [which made] a reorganization of the college necessary" However, several Newspaper articles from 1882, list Bikle as the "President of NC College.")

Rev. Gotthard D. Bernheim was elected President of the College in January 1882 and inaugurated May. It is not clear if he began his duties in January or after May 1882.

1882-'83 NCC

Rev. Gotthard D. Bernheim, President & Professor of Moral/Mental Science, History, English and German Literature

Henry T. J. Ludwig, Professor of Mathematics, Astronomy and Physics

Rev. Holmes Dysinger, Professor of Ancient Languages and Classical Literature

Clarence G. Heilig, '80, Principal of Preparatory Department.

1883 NCC

The College was closed during the fall of 1883 but reopened for a "half-session" in Jan 1884.

1884 (half-session) NCC

Rev. George F. Schaeffer, President & Professor of Moral/Mental Science

Henry T. J. Ludwig, Professor of Mathematics, Astronomy and Physics

Rev. J. B. Davis, Professor of Natural Science

Luther H. Rothrock, '84, Principal of the Preparatory Department

John P. Cook, Asst. Principal of the Preparatory Department (student)

Rev. F. W. E. Peschau, Lecturer on History, Elocution and Science

1884-'85 NCC

Rev. George F. Schaeffer, President & Professor of Moral/Mental Science

Henry T. J. Ludwig, Professor of Mathematics, Astronomy and Physics

Lewis H. Rothrock, Professor of History & Principal of the Preparatory Department

John C. F. Rupp, Professor of Ancient Languages and Literature

Rev. J. B. Davis, Lecturer on Chemistry and Botany
Rev. F. W. E. Peschau, Lecturer on History

1885-'86 NCC
Rev. George F. Schaeffer, President & Professor of Moral/Mental Science
Henry T. J. Ludwig, Professor of Mathematics, Astronomy and Physics
Lewis H. Rothrock, Professor of History & Principal of the Preparatory Department
Rev. J. B. Davis, Lecturer on Chemistry and Botany
Rev. F. W. E. Peschau, Lecturer on History

1886-'87 NCC
Rev. George F. Schaeffer, President & Professor of Moral/Mental Science
Henry T. J. Ludwig, Professor of Mathematics, Astronomy and Physics
Lewis H. Rothrock, Professor of History & Principal of the Preparatory Department
Peter E. Wright, Instructor (graduated in Dec 1886 and was employed part-time during spring of 1887)
Rev. J. B. Davis, Lecturer on Chemistry and Botany
Rev. F. W. E. Peschau, Lecturer on History

1887-'88 NCC
Rev. John G. Schaidt, President & Professor of Moral/Mental Science
Henry T. J. Ludwig, Professor of Mathematics, Astronomy and Physics
Peter E. Wright, Instructor, Principal of the Preparatory Department
John Deaton, Instructor in Geography & History (student)
Willis A. Deaton, Instructor in English Grammar (student)

1888-'89 NCC
Rev. John G. Schaidt, President & Professor of Moral/Mental Science
Henry T. J. Ludwig, Professor of Mathematics, Astronomy and Physics
Peter E. Wright, Instructor, Principal of the Preparatory Department
Rev. J. A. Linn, '73, Lecturer to the Athenaeum
Rev. A. T. Gantt, Lecturer to the Athenaeum
Rev. F. W. E. Peschau, Lecturer to the Antenaeum

1889-'90 NCC

Rev. John D. Shirey, President & Professor of Moral/Mental Science
Henry T. J. Ludwig, Professor of Mathematics, Astronomy and Physics
Rev. Charles L. T. Fisher, Professor of Ancient Languages & Literature
Rev. James H. C. Fisher, Principal of the Preparatory Department & Adjunct Professor of Ancient Languages
Boughart H. W. Runge, Instructor in German (student)
Henderson Miller, Tutor in Preparatory Dept. (student)
Henry Sloop, Tutor in Preparatory Dept. (student)
Joseph A. Graham, Tutor in Preparatory Dept. (student)

1890-'91 NCC

Rev. John D. Shirey, President & Professor of Moral/Mental Science
Henry T. J. Ludwig, Professor of Mathematics, Astronomy and Physics
Rev. Charles L. T. Fisher, Professor of Ancient Languages & Literature
Rev. James H. C. Fisher, Principal of the Preparatory Department & Adjunct Professor of Ancient Languages
Dr. J. S. Flow, Professor of German & French
Joseph A. Graham, Tutor in Preparatory Dept. (student)
Rev. Wright Campbell, Lecturer on Anatomy, Physiology, and Hygiene
Henderson N. Miller, Lecturer on the Volapuk Language (Dec '90).

1891-'92 NCC

Rev. John D. Shirey, President & Professor of Moral/Mental Science
Henry T. J. Ludwig, Professor of Mathematics, Astronomy and Physics, Temporary Instructor of German
Rev. Charles L. T. Fisher, Professor of Ancient Languages & Literature
Rev. James H. C. Fisher, Principal of the Preparatory Department & Adjunct Professor of Ancient Languages, Temporary instructor of French
Rev. George H. Cox, Professor of Elocution
H. N. Miller, Tutor (Post-graduate student)
Joseph A. Graham, Asst. Instructor (student)
Rev. F. W. E. Peschau, Lecturer
Rev. W. A. Lutz, Lecturer
Rev. Bachman S. Brown, Lecturer

Mr. James M. Cook, Lecturer
Rev. C. A. Marks, Lecturer

1892-'93 NCC
Rev. John D. Shirey, President & Professor of Moral/Mental Science
Henry T. J. Ludwig, Professor of Mathematics, Astronomy and Physics, Principal Commercial Dept.
Edwin B. Setzler, Professor of Ancient Languages & Literature
Rev. James H. C. Fisher, Principal of the Preparatory Department
Jesse L. McLendon, Instructor in Penmanship (student)
Rev. G. D. Bernheim, Lecturer
Rev. W. G. Campbell, Lecturer
Rev. Bachman S. Brown, Lecturer
J. A. Blackwelder, '89, Lecturer

1893-'94 NCC
Rev. John D. Shirey, President & Professor of Moral/Mental Science
Henry T. J. Ludwig, Professor of Mathematics, Astronomy and Physics, Principal Commercial Dept., Lecturer
Edwin B. Setzler, Professor of Ancient Languages & Literature, Lecturer
Rev. James H. C. Fisher, Principal of the Preparatory Department
John McCorkle, Lecturer
R. L. Patterson, Lecturer
Rev. W. S. Bowman, Lecturer
Rev. V. R. Stickley, Lecturer
Rev. W. R. Brown, Lecturer
Rev. Bachman S. Brown, Lecturer
Dr. M. L. Stevens, Lecturer
Rev. George W. Callahan, Lecturer

1894-'95 NCC
Rev. John D. Shirey, President & Professor of Moral/Mental Science
Henry T. J. Ludwig, Professor of Mathematics, Astronomy and
Physics, Principal Commercial Dept., Instructor– French, Lecturer
Edwin B. Setzler, Professor of Ancient Languages & Literature, Instructor in German, Lecturer

Martin A. Boger, '93, Principal of the Preparatory Department, Lecturer
Rev. Bachman S. Brown, Lecturer
James P. Cook, Lecturer
Rev. M. D. Giles, Lecturer
John M. Cook, Lecturer

1895-'96 NCC
Rev. John D. Shirey, President & Professor of Moral/Mental Science (died Apr 1896)
Henry T. J. Ludwig, Professor of Mathematics, Astronomy and Physics, Principal Commercial Dept., Instructor - French, Lecturer
Edwin B. Setzler, Professor of Ancient Languages & Literature, Instructor in German, Lecturer
Martin A. Boger, Principal of the Preparatory Department
Rev. Bachman S. Brown, Lecturer
Rev. Paul Barringer, Lecturer
Rev. H. N. Miller, Lecturer
C. H. Barnhardt, '92, Lecturer
Prof. J. A. Graham, Lecturer
Rev. P.W. Huddler, Lecturer
Rev. P. H. E. Derrick, Lecturer

1896-'97 NCC
Rev. Melanchthon G. G. Scherer, President & Professor of Moral/Mental Science, Lecturer
Henry T. J. Ludwig, Professor of Mathematics, Astronomy and Physics, Principal Commercial Dept., Lecturer
Edwin B. Setzler, Professor of Ancient Languages & Literature, Professor of German & French, Lecturer
Rev. P. H. E. Derrick, Principal of Preparatory Department, Lecturer (resigned Jan 1897)
George F. McAllister, Temporary Principal of Preparatory Department (graduated and hired in January 1897)
Rev. S. D. Steffy,
Rev. C. C. Lyerly,
B. B. Miller, Lecturer

Prof. J. F. Shinn, Lecturer
Rev. A. E. Wiley, Lectuer

1897-'98 NCC
Rev. Melanchthon G. G. Scherer, President and Professor of Moral/Mental Science
Henry T. J. Ludwig, Professor of Mathematics, Astronomy and Physics, Principal Commercial Dept., Lecturer
Edgar Bowers, Professor of Ancient Languages and Literature
George F. McAllister, '97, Temporary Principal of Preparatory Department
Prof. Holland Thompson, Lecturer
Prof. E. B. Lewis, Lecturer
L. M. Swink, Lecturer
Rev. J. Q. Wertz, Lecturer
Mr. J. B. D. Fisher, Lecturer
T. L. Hartsell, Lecturer

1898-'99 NCC
Rev. Melanchthon G. G. Scherer, President & Professor of Moral/Mental Science, Lecturer
Henry T. J. Ludwig, Professor of Mathematics, Astronomy and Physics, Principal Commercial Dept., Lecturer
Edgar Bowers, Professor of Ancient Languages and Literature, Lecturer
George F. McAllister, Principal of the Preparatory Department, Lecturer
Rev. George A. Riser, Lecturer
Rev. W. B. Oney, Lecturer
Prof. C. S. Coler, Lecturer

1899-'00 NCC
Edgar Bowers, Acting President, Professor of Ancient Languages and Literature, Lecturer
Henry T. J. Ludwig, Professor of Mathematics, Astronomy and Physics, Principal Commercial Dept., Lecturer (died Jul 1900)
George F. McAllister, Principal of the Preparatory Department
J. Marshall Tice, Assistant in the Preparatory Department (student)
Rev. S. D. Steffey, Lecturer

M. B. Stickley, Lecturer
Rev. J. A. Linn, Lecturer
Rev. L. T. Cordell, Lecturer
James P. Cook, Lecturer
Rev. J. H. Barnhardt, Lecturer

1900-'01 NCC
Rev. William A. Lutz, President, Professor of Mental/Moral/Political Science
Edgar Bowers, Professor of Ancient & Modern Languages
N. E. Aull, Professor of Mathematics, Physics and Astronomy, Principal of Commercial Dept.
Ernest F. Johnson, Professor of Organic Science and Chemistry, Instructor in English
George F. McAllister, Principal of Preparatory Department
M. H. Caldwell, Lecturer
Prof. C. S. Coler, Lecturer
Rev. J. A. B. Fry, Lecturer
Rev. Thomas W. Smith, Lecturer
Rev. G. H. Cornelson, Jr., Lecturer
Prof. Thomas P. Harrison, Lecturer
Colonel Paul B. Means, Lecturer
M. B. Stickley, Lecturer
1901-'02 NCC (classes suspended May 1902; the College did not reopen)
Rev. William A. Lutz, President, Professor of Mental/Moral/Political Science (resigned Mar 1902)
Edgar Bowers, Professor of Ancient & Modern Languages (resigned Nov 1901 effective May 1902)
Ernest F. Johnson, Professor of Organic Science and Chemistry, Instructor in English (resigned Nov 1901, effective, Mar 1902)
Rev. J. L. Keller, Instructor in Mathematics
George F. McAllister, Principal of Preparatory Department (resigned Nov 1901, effective, May 1902)

The Carolina English & Classical School

1902-'03 CE&CS
G. F. McAllister, Co-Principal
Rev. Levi E. Busby, Co-Principal (died Mar 1903)

Mt. Pleasant Collegiate Institute

1903-'04 MPCI
George F. McAllister, Associate Principal
Rev. Henry A. McCullough, Associate Principal (took position Nov 1903)
Alonzo Blackwelder, Director of in the Preparatory Department
Rev. J. A. Linn, Temporary Instructor until Nov 1903

1904-'05 MPCI
George F. McAllister, Associate Principal
Rev. Henry A. McCullough, Associate Principal
Alonzo Blackwelder, Director of in the Preparatory Department

1905-'06 MPCI
George F. McAllister, Associate Principal
Rev. Henry A. McCullough, Associate Principal
D. R. Riser, Professor of Latin & Greek
Alonzo Blackwelder, Director of in the Preparatory Department
Rev. Edward Fulenwider, NCC' 99, Lecturer
Rev. H. M. Brown, NCC '73, Lecturer
Prof. N. W. Walker, Lecturer
Rev. J. A. B. Shearer, Lecturer
Sidney J. Ludwig, Instructor in the Preparatory Department

1906-'07 MPCI
George F. McAllister, Co-Principal
Rev. Henry A. McCullough, Co-Principal (resigned May 1907)
D. R. Riser, Professor of Latin & Greek (resigned 1907)
Alonzo Blackwelder, Director of the Preparatory Department

Mrs. Lillian Blackwelder McCullough, Instructor of Stenography & Typewriting (wife of Rev. H. A. McCullough)
Sidney J. Ludwig, Instructor in the Preparatory Department
Roy Webster, Professor of Latin & Greek (hired in 1907 for one term to replace D. R. Riser)
D. L. Ritchie, Instructor in Penmanship

1907-'08 MPCI
George F. McAllister, Co-Principal, Professor of Mathematics & Physics
Rev. Jefferson P. Miller, Co-Principal, Professor of Greek & English
Roy Webster, Professor of Latin & Greek (resigned in 1908)
Arthur W. George, Professor of Latin & History (hired to replace Roy Webster)
Alonzo Blackwelder, Director of the Preparatory Department
Sidney J. Ludwig, Instructor in the Preparatory Department, Baseball Manager

1908-'09 MPCI (Military Model adopted)
George F. McAllister, Co-Principal, Professor of Mathematics & Physics
J. P. Miller, Co-Principal (resigned in May 1909)
Arthur W. George, Latin & History
J. W. Campbell, Commandant of Cadets
Alonzo Blackwelder, Director of the Preparatory Department

1909-'10 MPCI
George F. McAllister, Principal
Alonzo Blackwelder, Director of the Preparatory Department
J. W. Campbell, Commandant of Cadets
John B. Moose (MPCI) Bible, Latin, Greek, History
Dennis B. Welsh (MPCI) English
W. P. Porcher, Commandant of Cadets
J. P. Miller, English Bible

1910-'11 MPCI
George F. McAllister, Principal
Calvin V. Williams (MPCI), Latin & Greek

Dennis B. Welsh, English
Stuart E. Brown, Commandant of Cadets, History & Physics
J. P. Miller, English Bible

1911-'12 MPCI
George F. McAllister, Principal, Math & Physics
Dennis B. Welsh, English
C. V. Williams (MPCI), Latin & Greek
Rev. Reuben A. Goodman, English Bible and Ancient Languages
Dr. Gurley B. Moose, AB (NCC '01), PharmD, MD, Lecturer in Physiology & Hygiene
Zebulon B. Trexler (MPCI), Asst. Librarian

1912-'13 MPCI
George F. McAllister, Principal and Professor of Math & Physics
C. V. Williams (MPCI), Latin & Greek
Rev. Reuben A. Goodman, English Bible and Ancient Languages
M. R. Adams, English & History
A. F. Littlejohn, Commandant of Cadets

1913-'14 MPCI
George F. McAllister, Principal and Professor of Math & Physics
Charles P. McLaughlin, English Bible
M. R. Adams, English & History
J. W. Weeks, Commandant of Cadets, History, Science
B. L. Stanley, Latin & Greek
E. W. Fisher (MPCI), Asst. Librarian

1914-'15 MPCI
George F. McAllister, Principal and Professor of Math & Physics
M. R. Adams, English & History
J. W. Weeks, Commandant of Cadets, History, Science
B. L. Stanley, Latin & Greek

1915-'16 MPCI
George F. McAllister, Principal and Professor of Math & Physics
J. W. Weeks, Commandant of Cadets, History, Science

B. L. Stanley, Latin & Greek
F. L. Harkey (MPCI), English & German
Dr. J. M. Earnhardt, Lecturer on Physiology, Hygiene, and Sanitation
C. J. M. Blume (MPCI), Asst. Librarian

1916-'17 MPCI
George F. McAllister, Principal and Professor of Math & Physics
P. E. Monroe (MPCI), Commandant of Cadets, History, Science
B. L. Stanley, Latin & Greek
F. L. Harkey (MPCI), English & German
Dr. J. M. Earnhardt, Lecturer on Physiology, Hygiene, and Sanitation
C. J. M. Blume (MPCI), Asst. Librarian

1917-'18 MCPI
George F. McAllister, Principal and Professor of Math & Physics
W. J. Proctor (MPCI), Commandant of Cadets, History
P. S. Sykes, Latin & Greek
F. L. Harkey (MPCI), English & German
Dr. J. M. Earnhardt, Lecturer on Physiology, Hygiene, and Sanitation
L. M. Bost (MPCI Student) Tutor in Preparatory Dept. & Asst. Librarian
W. A. Mahler (MPCI Student) Tutor in Preparatory Dept.
J. E. Schenck, (MPCI Student) Tutor in Latin

1918-'19 MPCI
George F. McAllister, Principal and Professor of Math & Physics
J. B. Moose (MPCI), Greek and History
Talmadge Casey Johnson, English & Latin
J. E. Schenck (MPCI '18), Commandant of Cadets, Preparatory Instructor
C. H. Monsees, Jr. (MPCI Student), Instructor in Penmanship

1919-'20 MPCI
George F. McAllister, Principal and Professor of Math & Physics
J. B. Moose (MPCI '06), Greek and History
Talmadge Casey Johnson, English & Latin
J. E. Schenck (MPCI '18), Commandant of Cadets, Preparatory Instructor
C. H. Monsees, Jr. (MPCI Student), Instructor in Penmanship

Mrs. Ethelyn C. McAllister, Teacher of French
J. B. Cassell (MPCI Student), Asst. Librarian

1920-'21 MPCI
George F. McAllister, Principal and Professor of Math & Physics
J. B. Moose (MPCI '06), Greek and History
W. W. Holman, English & Latin
E. E. Sechriest, French & Physics, Commandant of Cadets
John H. McDaniel (MPCI '19), Instructor in Preparatory Dept.
C. R. Ritchie (MPCI Student), Asst. Librarian

1921-'22 MPCI
George F. McAllister, Principal and Professor of Math & Physics
J. B. Moose (MPCI '06), Greek and History
W. W. Holman, English & Latin
W. M. Albergotti, French & Science, Commandant of Cadets
C. J. M. Blume (MPCI '17), Instructor in Preparatory Dept.
S. E. Griffin (MPCI), Asst. Librarian

1922-'23 MPCI
George F. McAllister, Principal and Professor of Math & Physics
J. B. Moose (MPCI '06), Greek and History
W. W. Holman, English & Latin
W. M. Albergotti, French & Science, Commandant of Cadets
C. J. M. Blume (MPCI '17), Instructor in Preparatory Dept., Asst. Commandant of Cadets
L. E. Blackwelder (MPCI '20), Instructor in Preparatory Dept.
R. L. Fisher (MPCI) Asst. Librarian

1923-'24 MPCI
George F. McAllister, Principal and Professor of Math & Physics
Roy Webster, History and Greek
W. W. Holman, English & Latin
W. M. Albergotti, French & Science, Commandant of Cadets
C. J. M. Blume (MPCI '17), Instructor in Preparatory Dept., Asst. Commandant of Cadets

L. E. Blackwelder (MPCI '20), Instructor in Preparatory Dept.
D. L. Heglar (MPCI), Asst. Librarian

1924 –'25 MPCI
George F. McAllister, Principal and Professor of Math & Physics
R. C. Glenn, History & Greek
J. H. McDaniel (MPCI '19), English, Asst. Commandant of Cadets
H. R. Middlesworth, Latin & Bible
William W. Cone, French & Science, Commandant of Cadets
D. J. Gore, Chemistry, Instructor in Preparatory Dept.
L. W. Griggs (MPCI), Asst. Librarian

1925-'26 MPCI
George F. McAllister, Principal and Professor of Math & Physics
R. C. Glenn, Professor of History & Greek
John H. McDaniel (MPCI '19), Professor of English
H. R. Middlesworth, Professor of Latin & Bible
H. M. Carley, Professor of Science and Asst. Professor of Mathematics
A. Y. Davis (MPCI), Asst. Librarian
H. C. Hainer, Professor of French and Director of Athletics

1926-'27 MPCI
George F. McAllister, .Principal and Professor of Math & Physics
R. C. Glenn, Professor of Latin & Greek
John H. McDaniel (MPCI '19), Professor of English
Roy Webster, Professor of History & Latin
R. B. Still, Professor of French, Commandant of Cadets
R. L. Abstance, Professor of Science, Director of Athletics

1927-'28 MPCI
G. F. McAllister, Principal and Professor of Mathematics
Roy Webster, Professor of History and Bible
R. C. Glenn, Professor of Latin and Greek
John H. McDaniel, (MPCI '19), Professor of English
R. B. Still, Commandant, Professor of French and Asst. Prof of Mathematics
Daniel Linder Rhoad, Jr, Professor of Sciences & Director of Athletics

1828-'29 MCPI
G. F. McAllister, Principal and Professor of Mathematics
Roy Webster, Professor of History and Bible
R. C. Glenn, Professor of Latin and Greek
John H. McDaniel, (MPCI '19), Professor of English
R. B. Still, Commandant, Professor of French and Asst. Prof of Mathematics
James C. Hair, Professor of Sciences & Director of Athletics
R. A. Cheney, (MPCI) Tutor in Spanish
E. B. Bolick, (MPCI) Asst. Librarian

1929-'30 MPCI
G. F. McAllister, Principal and Professor of Mathematics
Roy Webster, Professor of History and Bible
Theodore Patton, Professor of Latin and Greek
John H. McDaniel, (MPCI '19), Professor of English
R. B. Still, Commandant, Professor of French and Asst. Prof of Mathematics
W. F. Shealy, Professor of Sciences and Director of Athletics
I. S. Preston, (MPCI), Tutor in Spanish
E. B. Bolick, (MPCI), Asst. Librarian

1930-'31 MPCI
G. F. McAllister, Principal and Professor of Mathematics
Roy Webster, Professor of Government & History
William S. Gerhardt, Professor of Latin & Bible
John H. McDaniel, (MPCI '19), Professor of English
Edward L. Black, Professor of French and Asst. Prof of Mathematics, Commandant
W. F. Shealy, Professor of Sciences and Director of Athletics
Hubert H. Sloop, (MPCI '28), Asst. Commandant and Instructor in Preparatory Branch
I. S. Preston (MPCI), Tutor in Spanish
R. H. Brown (MPCI), Asst. Librarian

1931-'32 MPCI
G. F. McAllister, Principal and Professor of Mathematics
Roy Webster, Professor of Government & History

William S. Gerhardt, Professor of Latin & Bible

John H. McDaniel, (MPCI '19), Professor of English

Edward L. Black, Professor of French and Asst. Prof of Mathematics, Commandant

W. F. Shealy, Professor of Sciences and Athletics Coach

Hubert H. Sloop, (MPCI '28), Asst. Commandant and Instructor in Preparatory Branch

J. E. Magner, Director of Athletics

H. L. Cento (MPCI) Tutor in Spanish

1932-'33 MPCI

G. F. McAllister, President & Professor of Mathematics

Roy Webster, Professor of Government & History, Instructor in Government, Bible Teachings, & Economics

Daulton K. Brasington, Commandant of Cadets, Instructor in Science, Math & Bible History

Hubert H. Sloop, Registrar, Instructor in Preparatory Branches

W. F. Shealy, Instructor of Chemistry, Social Science & Math and Athletic Coach

J. E. Magner, Director of Athletics

P. B. Fry, Director of Music, Instructor of English & Latin

W. A. McKnight, Librarian, Director of Dramatics, Instructor of Spanish & French

Brown B. Russell, (MPCI), Instructor of Boxing

APPENDIX 15

Index of All Known Students of WCMA, NC College, CECS & MPCI

WCMA – Western Carolina Male Academy
NCC – North Carolina College
CECS – Carolina English & Classical School
MPCI – Mt. Pleasant Collegiate Institute

The Western Carolina Male Academy

The Western Carolina Male Academy existed from 1 Mar 1855 through May 1859. No roster has been found for the 1st year of its operation and the roster for the 2nd year is incomplete. Some of the names were taken from an undated playbill entitled "Exhibition by Students of the Western Carolina Male Academy."

Name	Date of Registration or Attendance	Degrees/Other
Barnhardt, Caleb T.	1856-57	Co. F, 1st NC Cavalry
Barrier, Augustus C.	1856-57	Co. H, 8th NC Regt.
Barrier, Caleb C.	1856-57	Co. F, 1st NC Cavalry
Barrier, Jacob W. †	1856-57	Co. F, 1st NC Cavalry
Barrier, Paul Alexander	1856-57	Co. H, 8th NC & 34th VA Regt., Asst. Surgeon
Barrier, Rufus Alexander	1856-57	Co. H, 8th NC Regt., Lt. Colonel
Barrier, Wiley Alexander	1856-57	Co. G, 1st NC Cavalry, Captain (see NCC)
Barrier, William L.	1856-57	Co. F, 1st NC Cavalry
Barringer, John P. M.	****	Co. G, 6th NC Regt.
Bangle, Rufus W.	1856-57	Co. F, 1st NC Cavalry
Bangle, William H. H.	1856-57	Co. H, 7th NC Regt.
Blackwelder, Henry Allison	1856-57	Co. F, 1st NC Cavalry
Bost, Caleb I.	1856-57	Co. E, 4th NC Cavalry
Bost, Henry C.	1856-57	Co. F, 1st NC Cavalry

Name	Date of Registration or Attendance	Degrees/Other
Bost, James K. P.	1856-57	Co. G, 6th NC Regt.
Bost, Martin	1856-57	Co. F, 1st NC Cavalry
Brown, G. Henry	1856-57	Co. G, 6th NC Regt.
Brown, Nathan	1857-58	Co. H, 7th NC Regt.
Brown, Stephen A.	1856-57	Co. F, 57th NC Regt.
Carter, John M.	1856-57	Co. B, 20th NC Regt.
Cress, Henry	1856-57	Co. F, 57th NC Regt.
Eagle, Daniel M.	1856-57	Co. H, 20th NC Regt.
Eddleman, Jerimiah Anderson	****	Co. K, 4th NC Regt.
Faggart, George H.	1856-57	Co. B, 20th NC Regt.
Fisher, Charles Henry	1856-57	Co. H, 8th NC Regt.
Goodman, Michael M.	1856-57	Co. H, 14th NC Regt.
Harkey, Adam E.	1856-57	Co. H, 8th NC Regt.
Hearne, William H.	1856-57	Co. H, 14th NC Regt., 1st Lieutenant
Honeycutt, James A.	1856-57	
Huffman, Joseph	1856-57	Co. H, 3rd SC Regt., 2nd Lieutenant
Isenhour, H. F.	1856-57	
Julian, William Alexander †	1855-1857	
Kestler, T. J. H.	1856-1857	Co. D, 34th NC Regt.
Kluttz, G. A.	1856-1857	
Lefler, Peter A.	1856-1857	Co. F, 1st NC Cavalry
Miller, Henry Graeber	1856-1857	Co. F, 1st NC Cavalry
Miller, Martin Monroe †	1856-1857	Co. G, 6th NC Regt.
Moose, John Fritch	****	
Peeler, Tobias	****	
Rendleman, G. R.	****	
Ridenhour, Charles T.	1856-1857	
Ritchey, Henry A.	1856-1857	Co. B, 20th NC Regt.
Rodgers, Benjamin F.	1856-1857	Co. A, 17th NC Regt.
Rothrock, Luther H.	1856-1857	Co. B, 33rd NC Regt., 1st Lieutenant
† denotes Minister		
Seaford, M. K.	1856-1857	Co. K, 8th NC Regt.
Shimpoch, John L.	****	Co. C, 33rd NC Regt.
Shimpoch, Rufus A.	1856-1857	
Schuler, P. L.	****	
† denotes Minister		

North Carolina College

North Carolina College was in operation from September 1859 through May 1902 with several suspensions of classes due to the Civil War and lack of funding. The roster of students is taken from various sources including actual registration records, College catalogues, and from an index compiled by an unknown person.

NCC awarded advanced degrees for work completed outside of the school which was approved by the Faculty and Board of Trustees. These were usually in the form of AM (Master of Arts), PhB (Advanced degrees in Business) or DD (Doctor of Divinity).

Most of the persons listed as NCC students attended only the Preparatory (non-College) program and never continued to the post –secondary program. The only "official" listing of graduates of the College is a list of alumni contained in some College catalogues. Some of the advanced degrees were awarded as "honorary" degrees to out of state ministers and others never actually attended the College.

Name	Date of Registration or Attendance	Degrees/Other
Abernathy, Charles W.	31 Oct 1879	
Agner, H. M. L.	25 Jan 1884	
Albright, George	15 Aug 1884	
Aldrich, Alfred T.	21 Feb 1868	
Anderson, Clarence	20 Oct 1893	
Anthony, Jacob Bachman	1861	
Anthony, William Dawson	29 Mar 1861	Co. F, 1st NC Cavalry
Arey, James	1869	
Arey, Moses	1869	
Atwell, M. E.	15 Aug 1884	
Bailey, T. C.	30 Aug 1878	
Bame, Richard Louis †	****	'91 BA/'97 AM
Bangle, Henry G.	2 Sep 1897	
Bangle, T. M. M.	26 Aug 1875	
Bansemer, Charles H. †	****	'82 DD
Barger, P	29 Jan 1861	
Barnhardt, Caleb T.	6 Nov 1859	Co. F, 1st NC Cavalry
Barnhardt, Charles H.	9 Sep 1887	'92 BA/'97 AM
Barnhardt, Frank B.	9 Oct 1891	
Barnhardt, George F.	9 Sep 1885	
Barnhardt, George H.	17 Sep 1886	
Barnhardt, H. S.	6 Feb 1891	
Barnhardt, J. A.	21 Feb 1868	
Barnhardt, J. E.	2 Sep 1897	
Barnhardt, James Edney H.	20 Jun 1860	
Barnhardt, James Henderson †	6 Mar 1891	
Barnhardt, Thomas	27 Jan 1876	
Barnhardt, Worth P.	30 Jan 1891	
Barnhardt, Zebulon Elonzo †	1899-1901	
Barnhart, A. E.	15 Aug 1884	
Barrett, J. H.	1869	
Barrett, Samuel P.	6 Mar 1874	

Name	Date of Registration or Attendance	Degrees/Other
Barrier, Moses Adolphus	25 Aug 1874	
Barrier, Albert Lafayette	25 Aug 1874	
Barrier, Augustus Cicero	9 Nov 1859	Co. H, 8th NC Regt.
Barrier, Daniel Dixon	22 Feb 1878	
Barrier, Ernest Edgar	16 Sep 1887	
Barrier, George Louis	16 Sep 1887	
Barrier, Herbert E.	30 Jan 1885	'96 BA
Barrier, Hope Mitchell	16 Oct 1889	
Barrier, Horace B.	10 Oct 1890	
Barrier, Howard Miller	1900-1901	
Barrier, Hugh Winfred	7 Oct 1892	
Barrier, J. E.	1869	
Barrier, Jacob W.	9 Nov 1859	Co. F, 1st NC Cavalry
Barrier, Jesse M. DeWitt	7 Sep 1881	
Barrier, John C.	27 Jan 1876	
Barrier, John Daniel Scheck	29 Jan 1861	Co. F, 57th NC Regt.
Barrier, John Daniel Scheck	21 Feb 1868	
Barrier, Lawson Whitfield	1 Mar 1872	'79 BA/'82 AM
Barrier, Levi C.	9 Nov 1859	Co. E, 20th NC Regt.
Barrier, Luther Melanchthon	8 Sep 1871	
Barrier, Martin Franklin	31 Jan 1873	
Barrier, Ralph Waldo	7 Oct 1892	
Barrier, Robert Lee	1900-1901	
Barrier, Victor Francis	1869	
Barrier, Wade A.	7 Oct 1892	
Barrier, Walter Guy	5 Oct 1894	
Barrier, Wiley Alexander	21 Mar 1860	Co. F & Co. I, 1st NC Cavalry, Captain; '72 BA/'75 AM
Barrier, William Walton	5 Dec 1884	
Barrier, Willie M.	18 Jan 1878	
Barringer, Andrew Layfette	1869	8th Battalion, NC Jr. Reserves
Barringer, Daniel L.	20 Oct 1893	
Barringer, Daniel Monroe	8 Sep 1871	
Barringer, David M.	9 Nov 1859	Co. K, 8th NC Regt.
Barringer, Edward Spencer	1900-1901	
Barringer, George Richter	1899-1901	
Barringer, George T.	22 Oct 1891	
Barringer, Paul Daniel	23 May 1860	Co K., 5th NC Regt.
Barringer, John Daniel	8 Sep 1871	
Barringer, John Henry	8 Sep 1882	
Barringer, John Lawson D.	15 Feb 1884	
Barringer, John N.	11 Mar 1885	
Barringer, John T.	3 Oct 1884	
Barringer, Marshall Otho	8 Feb 1884	
Barringer, Martin Henry	1899-1901	
Barringer, Martin L.	1896	
Barringer, Martin Luther	1870	

Name	Date of Registration or Attendance	Degrees/Other
Barringer, Monroe	1869	
Barringer, Otha Alvin	1900-1901	
Barringer, Paul	1869	
Barringer, Paul †	16 Aug 1872	
Barringer, Willie Adolphus	30 Sep 1887	
Barringer, W. D.	24 Jan 1879	
Bauer, Edward	4 Apr 1884	
Beatty, Harold E. †	2 Sep 1897	
Beaver, L. W.	30 Jan 1880	
Beaver, William Neary	8 Feb 1877	
Bennett, C. F.	29 Aug 1879	
Bennett, L. P.	30 Jan 1880	
Bennett, R. R.	21 Feb 1868	
Bennett, Samuel P.	15 Feb 1860	Co. B, 31st NC Regt.
Bennett, W. N.	7 Mar 1879	
Benton, Benjamin Hyde	****	'74 AM
Benton, J. W.	21 Feb 1879	
Bernhardt, Clarence T.	1900-1901	
Bernhardt, Harvey A.	25 Aug 1874	
Bernhardt, James Leak	1900-1901	
Bernhardt, Paul H.	14 Feb 1890	
Bernheim, E. Clayton	2 Sep 1881	
Bernheim, Gottlieb D. †	****	'77 DD
Bethune, A. J.	9 Feb 1860	Co. D, 2nd NC Cavalry
Betts, Clarence T.	14 Sep 1896	
Betts, Henry Watson	27 Jan 1876	'77 BA/'80 AM
Betts, James Russell	8 Feb 1877	
Betts, Paul G.	13 Sep 1895	
Betts, Willie A.	21 Oct 1875/27 Jan 1876	
Bikle, Louis Albert	30 Jan 1880	
Bikle, Philip M.	10 Jul 1860	
Black, James Cyrus	23 Aug 1878	
Blackwelder, Alonzo	1899-1900	
Blackwelder, Asa Isaiah	7 Jan 1881	'89 AM
Blackwelder, Augustus P.	7 Jan 1881	
Blackwelder, G. W.	29 Jan 1874	
Blackwelder, Henry Hampton	17 Sep 1880	
Blackwelder, J. H.	29 Aug 1879	
Blackwelder, John Wilson	21 Feb 1868	
Blackwelder, James Marcellus	7 Oct 1892	
Blackwelder, John Alonzo	1900-1901	
Blackwelder, M. S.	29 Aug 1879	
Blackwelder, John A.	30 Jan 1885	
Blackwelder, Pinkney D.	7 Oct 1892	
Blackwell, John F.	10 Oct 1890	
Blackwell, William A.	20 Oct 1893	
Blakeney. Rochelle E.	29 Jan 1875	
Blakeney, Preston B.	13 Feb 1874	

Name	Date of Registration or Attendance	Degrees/Other
Blakeney, W. S.	30 Aug 1878	
Blume, Martin B.	10 Oct 1890	
Blume, Martin Luther	9 Sep 1887	
Bobbitt, W. H. †	****	'77 DD
Boger, Charles Edgar	19 Feb 1892	'96 BA
Boger, John L.	24 Jan 1879	
Boger, M. Augustus	8 Feb 1889	'93 BA/'96 AM
Boger, William Jennings †	8 Feb 1889	'93 BA/'96 AM
Bost, D. L.	5 Feb 1878	
Bost, J. F.	24 Oct 1878	
Bost, J. F. C.	11 Sep 1896	
Bost, J. Howard	1899-1900	
Bost, J. L.	1869	
Bost, James Knox Polk	1861	Co. E, 4th NC Cavalry
Bost, James W.	21 Nov 1893	
Bost, John D.	18 Feb 1885	
Bost, John Howard	1900-1901	
Bost, John Rowan	1900-1901	
Bost, Joseph H.	1899-1900	
Bost, L. Cecil	1900-1901	
Bost, Luther H.	6 Oct 1893	
Bost, Paul	7 Oct 1892	
Bost, R. P.	9 Feb 1860	
Bost, Tinsley L.	1869	
Bost, William Arthur	1900-1901	
Bowers, Charles	10 Oct 1873	
Bowers, Edgar Fox	1900-1901	
Bowers, John Gordon	1900-1901	
Boyete, A. W.	24 Jan 1879	
Boyete, J. H.	10 Sep 1880	
Boyete, Josiah M.	30 Aug 1872	
Boyete, William A.	23 Aug 1872	
Branch, John G.	2 Oct 1891	
Brasington, E. C.	30 Aug 1878	
Bremer, John M.	21 Oct 1875	
Bremer, Matthias	21 Oct 1875	
Bingle, G. W.	24 Mar 1881	
Brown, Luther H.	1898	
Brown, Bachman Samuel †	1870	Honorary
Brown, C. A.	25 Jan 1878	
Brown, Charlie A.	10 Oct 1890	
Brown, Henry Maxwell †	8 Sep 1871	'73 AM
Brown, J. A.	6 Feb 1861	
Brown, John Leonard	1900-1901	
Brown, J. M.	1869	
Brown, P. A.	1869	
Brown, Richard L. †	1870	
Brown, Robert Luther	1870	

Name	Date of Registration or Attendance	Degrees/Other
Brown, Stephen A.	9 Nov 1859	Co. K, 4th NC Regt.
Brown, William A.	9 Nov 1859	Co. H, 8th NC Regt.
Buchanan, E. G.	13 Mar 1888	
Buchanan, E. J.	11 Feb 1884	
Burleyson, J. V.	6 Oct 1893	
Burkhead, John	6 Sep 1872	
Burleyson, Robert R.	1900 –1901	
Busby, John Carroll	****	
Busby, Levi E. †	****	'01 DD
Busby, Willie Thomas	1900-1901	
Campbell, C. A.	14 Mar 1884	
Cannon, John Theophilus	****	
Canup, Martin Luther †	1900-1901	
Canup, Samuel L.	5 Sep 1873	
Carter, E. A.	1871	
Castor, L. I. B.	19 Feb 1892	
Cauble, J. A.	29 Aug 1873	
Cauble, W. A.	24 Oct 1860	Co. K, 43rd NC Regt.
Clemmer, Cephus M.	29 Mar 1861	Co. H, 37th NC Regt.
Clemmer, John L.	1861	Co. B, 28th NC Regt.
Cline, Berry R.	2 Sep 1897	
Cline, L. A. D.	19 Feb 1892	
Cline, M. L.	30 Jan 1880	
Cloninger, Edward L.	1871	
Clyburn, W. W.	25 Aug 1874	
Cobb, Charles D.	2 Oct 1891	'95 PhB/'98 AM
Colley, Martin Samuel	11 Apr 1890	
Condor, Irenaeus †	23 May 1860	'72 AM
Cook, Carl Matthew	1899-1901	
Cook, Franklin Pierce †	21 Feb 1868	'74 BA
Cook, H. A.	18 Oct 1895	
Cook, J. Frank	1899-1900	
Cook, James P.	27 Jan 1876	'85 BA
Cook, John Mathew	2 Mar 1868	71st NC Regt. (2nd Jr. Reserves)
Cook, Jonas	9 Nov 1859	Co. H, 8th NC Regt., Captain
Cook, Mathew John	11 Feb 1885	'90 BS/'96 AM
Cook, Michael	1861	Co. H, 8th NC Regt.
Cook, Walter Miller	1887	'95 BA/'98 AM
Cope, George C.	26 Aug 1875	
Cope, Victor Fleming	1900-1901	
Cordell, Arthur Walton	1900-1901	
Corl, Buford Dove	1900-1901	
Correll, Noah A.	1900-1901	
Corriher, Calvin Washington	8 Sep 1871	
Corriher, John F.	8 Sep 1871	
Corzine, Luther H.	14 Sep 1896	
Corzine, Robert C.	18 Jan 1895	
Costner, Hiram J.	29 Mar 1861	Co. B, 28th NC Regt.

Name	Date of Registration or Attendance	Degrees/Other
Costner, Jacob	1871	
Cox, A. C.	18 Feb 1881	
Cox, A. McDonald	d	19 Jan 1875
Cox, Clarence Brown †	19 Oct 1888	'93 BA/'98 AM
Cox, Elbert William	16 Oct 1889	
Cox, George H. †	****	'91 AM
Cox, William Franklin	23 Feb 1872	
Crawford, E. G.	1869	
Cress, Elias	23 May 1860	
Cress, J. W.	30 Jan 1880	
Cress, Joseph T.	9 Oct 1891	
Cress, S. M.	19 Aug 1885	
Cress, Valentine	9 Nov 1859	Co. B, 20th NC Regt.
Cress, William M.	30 Jan 1891	
Crigler, Hugh A.	2 Sep 1897	'00 BA
Cromer, James Albert †	29 Jan 1875	
Croswell, L. M.	7 Mar 1860	
Crouch, Amos Comenius	1900-1901	
Crouse, D. L.	30 Aug 1872	'76 BA
Crowell, Addison	6 Feb 1874	
Crowell, Buckner K.	28 Mar 1860	Co. I, 52nd NC Regt.
Crowell, G. Edward	1899-1900	
Crowell, Giles T.	31 Jan 1873	
Crowell, J. A.	31 Jan 1873	
Crowell, John Ivy	1900-1901	
Crowell, Thomas O.	5 Oct 1894	
Crowell, W. M.	31 Jan 1893	
Crump, James F.	9 Nov 1859	Co. A, 23rd NC Regt.
Cruse, George Lewis	1900-1901	
Cruse, John R.	24 Jan 1879	
Cruse, Orlin	4 Oct 1889	
Culp, Charles Howard	13 Jan 1888	
Culp, John Ripley, Jr.	16 Jan 1885	
Davis, George W.	9 Nov 1859	Co. D, 37th NC Regt., 2nd Lieutenant
Davis, James Locke	1900-1901	
Davis, Jeff	27 Jan 1876	
Davis, John Barton †	****	'73 DD
Davis, John Barton, Jr.	21 Oct 1875	
Dayvault, W. A.	6 Oct 1893	
Daywalt, G. W.	24 Jan 1879	
Daywalt, Robert A.	18 Apr 1879	
Deal, Caleb Pinkney	1899-1901	
Deal, Carl Hosea †	1900-1901	
Deaton, John Leroy †	4 Apr 1884	'88 BA/'91 AM
Deaton, Willis Alexander †	1 Feb 1884	'88 BA/'91 AM
Deberry, E. P.	21 Feb 1868	

Name	Date of Registration or Attendance	Degrees/Other
Dixon, Albert O.	7 Mar 1860	Co. F, 9th SC Regt.
Dixon, Rivers L.	21 Mar 1860	Co. E, 6th SC Regt.
Doscher, J. D., Jr.	20 Sep 1895	
Drafts, J. C.	27 Jan 1876	
Drake, Preston C.	24 Oct 1860	Co. E, 19th SC Calvary Battalion
Drake, Zachariah J.	24 Oct 1860	
Dreher, Augustus	1 Oct 1880	
Dreher, Daniel Isaiah †	****	'DD
Dreher, Jeremiah H.	14 Jan 1881	'89 BA/'92 AM
Dry, Eustis M.	1899-1900	
Dry, Finley Otis	19 Oct 1888	
Dry. H. W.	21 Feb 1868	
Dry, J. A.	25 Aug 1874	
Dry, John A.	1871	
Dry, Maxwell D.	22 Mar 1897	
Dry, Paul	18 Apr 1879	
Dry, Washington Whitfield	25 Jan 1878	
Dumas, J. P.	9 Nov 1859	
Durant, James A.	24 Oct 1860	2nd SC Regt. (Palmetto Guards)
Eargle, Joseph W.	1871	
Earnhardt, Daniel Luther	3 Sep 1873	
Earnhardt, Turner	1869	
Eddleman, H. A.	19 Aug 1885	
Eddleman, Henry A.	2 Oct 1891	
Eddleman, J. A.	15 Aug 1884	
Eddleman, John M.	20 Jun 1860	Co. C, 57th NC Regt.
Eddleman, Jeremiah Anderson	9 Nov 1859	Co. K, 4th NC Regt.
Eddleman, Samuel Oscar	1900-1901	
Edwards, Simon J.	9 Nov 1859	Co. C, 14th NC Regt.
Efird, Jason	26 Aug 1875	
Efird, Lee	1900-1901	
Efird, William Titus	1900-1901	
Efird, F. B.	30 Jan 1880	
Efird, Jacob Killian †	29 Aug 1873	
Erwin, William F.	18 Oct 1872	
Eudy, J. A.	20 Aug 1875	
Eudy, Jacob H. W.	1872	
Eury, A. P.	18 Apr 1873	
Eury, Joshua	1872	
Evans, George M.	5 Sep 1873	
Evans, John S.	28 Feb 1873	
Evans, T. P.	1869	
Faggart, James R.	5 Jan 1888	
Faggart, John B.	29 Jan 1875	
Faggart, Preston M.	15 Aug 1884	
Fesperman, Eugene	17 Feb 1893	

Name	Date of Registration or Attendance	Degrees/Other
File, Jacob N.	15 Feb 1860	Co. H, 8th NC Regt., 1st Lieutenant; Co. C, 30th NC Regt.
File, T. L.	13 Mar 1888	
Finger, James Avery	1869-1870	
Finger, Robert	3 Sep 1885	
Fink, Adam F.	8 Sep 1881	
Fink, W. E.	7 Jan 1881	
Fisher, Albert Luther V.	1900-1901	
Fisher, Arthur Willie	1899-1901	
Fisher, Charles Henry	25 Apr 1860	Co. F, 1st NC Cavalry
Fisher, Charles L. T. †	26 Aug 1875	
Fisher, Clifford Paul †	20 Sep 1895	'00 BA
Fisher, G. H.	24 Oct 1860	
Fisher, George L.	22 Oct 1880	
Fisher, Henry Junius	2 Sep 1897	
Fisher, J. W.	15 Jan 1892	
Fisher, James Henry Charles †	1870	
Fisher, John Deberry	10 Oct 1890	'95 BA/'98 AM
Fisher, Michael G. M.	26 Aug 1875	
Fisher, R. M.	18 Apr 1873	
Fisher, W. B.	16 Jan 1889	
Fisher, William T.	9 Sep 1885	
Fitzgerald, J. Y.	17 Sep 1880	
Fleming, W. J.	30 Jan 1885	
Fletcher, W. R.	26 Aug 1875	
Flow, David Clark	21 Feb 1868	
Flow, D. C.	18 Jan 1878	
Flow, Marshall Decastro	1870	
Foil, Warren Deberry	11 Mar 1885	
Foil, Ernest Linwood	1900-1901	
Foil, Fred Wadsworth	14 Sep 1896	
Foil, George Webster	1884	
Foil, Harry Edmond	1899-1901	
Foil, John Henderson	30 Aug 1878	
Foil, John Moses	13 Sep 1895	
Foil, Lawson Jeremiah	6 Sep 1873	
Foil, Lee Evans	1900-1901	
Foil, Moses Alexander	19 Jan 1883	
Foil, William A.	7 Oct 1892	
Fox, James P.	6 Sep 1877	
Fox, Luther Augustine †	6 Nov 1859	
Frick, David A.	17 Feb 1893	
Fulenwider, Edward †	20 Oct 1893	'99 BA
Fulenwider, John Osborne	5 Oct 1894	
Funderburk, B. G.	9 Oct 1891	
Funderburk, Eugene T.	7 Oct 1896	
Furr, M. Franklin	1 Oct 1886	

Name	Date of Registration or Attendance	Degrees/Other
Furr, Franklin H.	9 Nov 1859	Co. B, 7th NC Regt.
Furr, H. M.	27 Aug 1880	
Furr, Henry	13 Jan 1897	
Gaither, W. Edgar	5 Oct 1894	
Garver, Jonathan †	****	'99 DD
Gathings, John	30 Aug 1872	
Gerhardt, William †	****	'80 DD
Giles, Marvin S.	18 Jan 1895	
Gillespie, C.	9 Nov 1859	
Glover, John Franklin	31 Jan 1890	
Goode, Robert John	****	
Goodman, D. L.	8 Jan 1896	
Goodman, J. Paul	1900-1901	
Goodman, Mack	1900-1901	
Gouger, Willie L	28 Feb 1873	
Graeber, Charles H.	11 Jan 1895	
Graeber, H. T.	8 Sep 1871	
Graeber, John L.	11 Jan 1895	
Graham, C. W. M.	15 Aug 1873	
Graham, James L.	27 Sep 1889	
Graham, Joseph A. †	7 Sep 1888	'92 BA/'96AM
Graham, M. B.	18 Jan 1872	
Greening, Phillip †	21 Feb 1868	
Gregory, A. C.	30 Aug 1874	
Gregory, George W.	25 Aug 1874	
Gregory, H. Jackson	25 Aug 1874	
Gregory, J. Owen	25 Aug 1874	
Gregory, Rochelle E.	27 Jan 1876	
Gregory, Thomas S.	25 Aug 1874	
Gregory, W. Thurlow	25 Aug 1874	
Groner, C. L.	6 Feb 1880	
Groseclose, George W. Bittle	1 Mar 1872	
Groseclose, J. Jacob Hawkins	21 Feb 1868	
Gulledge, W. D.	1869	
Haar, William	16 Sep 1887	
Haas, John	9 Oct 1891	
Hager, H. C. D.	5 Dec1873	
Hahn, Adam R.	10 Jan 1896	
Hahn, Atlas Eugene	5 Oct 1894	
Hahn, Clifford H.	1898	
Hahn, Hubert L.	2 Oct 1891	
Hahn, James A.	2 Oct 1891	
Hahn, Julius Alexander	1870	
Hahn, Justus N.	1899-1900	
Hahn, Luther Erastus	1899-1900	
Hahn, Matthew Deberry	13 Sep 1895	
Hahn, Paul Alexander	9 Oct 1891	
Hahn, Richard Whitefield	2 Sep 1897	

Name	Date of Registration or Attendance	Degrees/Other
Haines, John Sydenham	12 Oct 1871	
Hall, A. G.	23 May 1860	
Hamilton, M. W.	7 Feb 1873	
Hamilton, William A.	31 Jan 1873	
Haring, Louis A.	21 Feb 1868	
Harkey, Adolphus	2 Sep 1897	
Harkey, J. B.	10 Oct 188	
Harkey, John M.	28 Mar 1860	Co. H, 8th NC Regt.
Harkey, Sidney Levi †	****	'82 DD
Harkey, Thomas	2 Sep 1881	
Harkey, Victor Harrison	1869	
Harkey, Victor Harris	26 Aug 1875	
Harkey, Walter	5 Oct 894	
Harkey, William L.	16Aug 1872	
Harking, Simeon	21 Feb 1868	
Harrell, S. D. M.	21 Mar 1860	Co. B, 21st SC Regt.
Harrell, W. R.	23 Feb 1872	
Harris, B. Lawton	30 Jan 1891	
Harris C. W.	30 Jan 1891	
Harrison, George Alexander	1869-1870	
Hartman, Henry L.	2 Sep 1897	
Hartsell, A. F.	11 Nov 1887	
Hartsell, Atlas Monroe	2 Mar 1868	
Hartsell, Lewis H.	1899-1901	
Harvin, Septimus Arthur	21 Mar 1860	Co. C, Hampton's Legion (SC)
Harwood, H. D.	9 Oct 1887	
Hatley, Charles Cleveland	1900-1901	
Hawkins, Jacob A. †	****	'82 DD; Co. G, 13th SC Volunteers
Hearne, Thomas C.	18 Apr 1873	
Hedrick, D. C.	30 Aug 1878	
Heglar, G. C.	29 Aug 1873	
Heilig, Augustus Franklin	2 Mar 1868	
Heilig, Caleb Augustus	1900-1901	
Heilig, Clarence G.	18 Sep 1873	'80 BA
Heilig, E. L.	14 Jan 1881	
Heilig, Edwin L.	19 Jan 1872	
Heilig, George Augustus	21 Feb 1868	
Heilig, George John	17 Sep 1886	
Heilig, George Phifer	1900-1901	
Heilig, James D.	11 Feb 1876	
Heilig, John Gilbert	2 Mar 1868	
Heilig, Lawson Edwin	30 Jan 1880	'87 BA
Heilig, Lewis H.	26 Feb 1884	
Heilig, Luther F.	19 Jan 1872	
Heilig, Orlando Lillington	1880	

Name	Date of Registration or Attendance	Degrees/Other
Henderson, James McConnaughy	2 Mar 1878	'73 AM
Hendley, Charles James	1900-1901	
Hendrix, Edgar Emanuel	15 Sep 1893	
Hendrix, Harry Mathews	10 Jan 1896	
Hendrix, John Maxey	26 Aug 1875	
Henkel, Socrates †	****	'77 DD
Henkel, Solon A.	17 Jan 1873	
Henkel, Luther S.	1874	
Henley, R. B.	31 Jan 1873	
Henley, William D.	29 Aug 1873	
Henning, Frank W.	1873	
Henning, Luther S.	1873	
Henning, Joseph B.	1872	
Henning, Joseph H.	11 Apr 1883	
Henning, ? N	18 Apr 1883	
Hilton, Thomas L.	7 Nov 1890	
Hinson, F. M.	29 Aug 1873	
Hoffner, J. G.	24 Apr 1884	
Hoffner, William H.	21 Mar 1860	Co. D, 1st NC Artillery
Holleyman, William H.	15 Feb 1860	Co. B, 3rd SC Regt.
Holman, M. S.	24 Sep 1880	
Holmes, Reuben	20 Feb 1891	
Holshouser, H. A.	7 Jan 1881	
Home, J. D.	21 Feb 1868	
Honeycutt, Edward Deberry	14 Sep 1896	
Horne, Henry H.	6 Mar 1874	
Houston, J. W.	30 Aug 1872	
Howie, W. L.	29 Aug 1873	
Hoyle, Thomas C.	8 Feb 1884	
Hubbert, C. B.	21 Oct 1875	
Hudson, Michael A.	31 Jan 1873	
Hudson, Richard A.	1872	
Hudson, W. F.	24 Jan 1879	
Huss, J. F.	25 Aug 1874	
Huztin, J. Kinsley	5 Oct 1894	
Ingle, G. F.	30 Aug 1878	
Ingram, Eben Presley	9 Nov 1859	
Ingram, William S.	15 Feb 1860	Co. K, 26th NC Regt., 2nd Lieutenant
Isenhour, William Nelson	13 Jan 1897	
James, H. S.	26 Jan 1883	
James, H. A.	21 Mar 1860	
James, Herbert H.	14 Sep 1896	
Jeffcoat, Willie Cecil	1900-1901	
Johnson, James T.	5 Dec 1879	
Johnson, William Preston	1900-1901	

Name	Date of Registration or Attendance	Degrees/Other
Johnston, Luke	23 Jan 1896	
Johnston, Samuel Clyde	****	
Johnston, William Howard	1900-1901	
Julian, A. J. P.	26 Aug 1875	
Julian, Charles A.	12 Sep 1884	
Julian, H. M.	24 Oct 1878	
Kaminer, J. J.	31 Jan 1873	
Karriker, Edward Lock	1900-1901	
Keith, W. L.	19 Jan 1883	
Kenerly, Wesley Whitefield †	2 Sep 1897	
Kerns, Thomas Cleveland	1900-1901	
Kesler, James H.	9 Nov 1859	Co. K, 8th NC Regt.
Kesler, W. W.	31 Mar 1882	
Kesler, William A.	9 Nov 1859	Co. K, 8th NC Regt.
Ketchie, Ernest, Lee	1900-01	
Ketchie, Gustavus A.	2 Oct 1891	
Ketchie, Jno. D.	9 Sep 1887	
Ketchie, L. J.	31 Jan 1873	
Ketchie, Pleasant Liddell	1900-01	
Ketchie, W. F. Hubert	2 Oct 1891	
Ketchie, William Rufus †	1861	
Ketner, Monroe N.	29 Jan 1875	
Killian, Lee	11 Feb 1891	
Kimball, C. M.	27 Jan 1876	
Kimball, Charles J.	27 Sep 1889	
Kimball, H?. B.	8 Feb 1877	
Kimball, William Luther M.	9 Sep 1887	
Kindley, Adam	1869	
Kindley, John S.	2 Sep 1881	
Kindley, Samuel Ernest	****	
Kindley, William Adam	24 Jan 1879	
Kistler, T. J. H.	24 Oct 1860	Co. D, 34th NC Regt.
Kitchie, M. L.	27 Jan 1876	
Kline, Marion †	****	'01 DD
Klutts, E. E.	11 Apr 1873	
Klutts, L.	15 Aug 1884	
Kluttz, Albert J.	6 Oct 1893	
Kluttz, G. O.	6 Feb 1891	
Kluttz, J. K?.	11 Oct 1876	
Kluttz, J. M.	11 Oct 1876	
Kluttz, L. M.	8 Apr 1885	
Kluttz, P. W. L.	19 Oct 1888	
Kyles, R. S.	7 Oct 1892	
Leach, A. McN.	6 Feb 1861	Co. E, 28th NC Regt.
Liard, Trezevant R. †	1872	
Ledbetter, Clarence	1899	
Lefler, C.	21 Feb 1868	
Lefler, Charles F.	1900-1901	

Name	Date of Registration or Attendance	Degrees/Other
Lefler, James L.	8 Sep 1871	
Lefler, John D.	30 Aug 1878	
Lefler, L. T.	1869	
Lefler, Robert L.	30 Aug 1878	
LeGrand, J. E.	28 Mar 1860	Co. E, 38th NC Regt.
Lemmond, A. W.	31 Jan 1873	
Lentz, A. D.	21 Feb 1868	
Lentz, Albert Percy	8 Sep 1871	
Lentz, C. G.	16 Oct 1889	
Lentz, Charles G.	6 Oct 1893	
Lentz, Fred Heilig	1900-1901	
Lentz, Frederick Heilig	1900-1901	
Lentz, L. K.	16 Oct 1889	
Lentz, Lawson H.	15 Aug 1873	
Lentz, P. E.	26 Aug 1875	
Lentz, Paul Augustus	1900-1901	
Lentz, Paul Erastus	1900-1901	
Libber, Calvin †	****	'77 AM
Lilly, James Nathaniel	1900-1901	
Lindler, S. S.	26 Aug 1875	'78 BA
Lineberger, A. C.	7 Feb 1873	
Lingle, George Henry Louis †	2 Sep 1897	'01 BA
Linhardt, R. L.	30 Aug 1872	
Linn, John Kenneth †	1899-1901	
Linn, Josephus Adolphus	21 Feb 1868	'74 BA
Linn, Myron Oscar	1899-1901	
Linn, Pleasant David	11 Oct 1876	
Linton, S. E., Jr.	5 Oct 1894	
Linuous, T. Y.	30 Jan 1874	
Lipe, Deberry	20 Oct 1893	
Lipe, Howard	6 Jan 1898	
Lipe, L. A.	30 Sep 1887	
Lipe, Martin M.	9 Oct 1891	
Lippard, J. H.	30 Aug 1878	
Lisk, J. W.	8 Sep 1871	
Litaker, A. H.	30 Jan 1880	
Litaker, Cephas Ray	2 Sep 1897	
Litaker, Charles Luther	1899-1901	
Litaker, E. A.	25 Aug 1874	
Litaker, W. F.	2 Dec 1887	
Little, George T.	9 Nov 1859	Co. C, 14th NC Regt.
Livengood, D. C.	24 Oct 1860	Co. D, 42nd NC Regt.
Livengood, Henderson E.	24 Oct 1860	Co. E, 2nd NC Regt.
Lmyse?, E. E.	29 Mar 1861	
Lockhart, J. A.	1869	
Long, A. M.	8 Sep 1871	
Long, Edward	9 Oct 1896	
Long, H. C.	24 Jan 1879	

Name	Date of Registration or Attendance	Degrees/Other
Long, H. L.	29 Jan 1861	
Long, Murray C.	1899-1901	
Long, Reece Ira	1900-1901	
Long, Seberrne Hoyle †	2 Sep 1897	
Low, Wm. G.	30 Aug 1878	
Lowder,	1898	
Lowder, Daniel M.	2 Mar 1868	
Lowe, Haywood	8 Sep 1871	
Lowery, ?. E.	31 Jan 1873	
Lowrie?, H. W.	8 Feb 1877	
Ludewick, H. A.	29 Feb 1884	
Ludwick, J. F.	6 Jan 1888	
Ludwick, James M.	8 Sep 1871	
Ludwick, Sidney J. T.	13 Sep 1877	
Ludwig, Henry T. J.	9 Nov 1859	Co. H, 8th NC Regt.; '71 AB/'72 AM
Lybrand, E. L. †	29 Jan 1875	
Lyerly, Amos E.	30 Jan 1891	
Lyerly, Calvin C. †	****	'97 AM
Lyerly, George L.	9 Nov 1859	
Lyerly, Henderson P.	10 Oct 1890	
Lyerly, Isaac A.	20 Jan 1882	
Lyerly, J. H. A.	14 Sep 1894	
Lyerly, Sidney A.	1900-1901	
Lyles, William K.	2 Oct 1891	
Mahoney. ?. D.	21 Mar 1860	
Mann, Samuel Deberry	1870	
Manous, Darling	6 Mar 1874	
Marsh, J. M.	9 Nov 1859	
Mason, John F.	****	'77 AM
Mauney, A. C.	7 Feb 1873	
McAllister, George Franklin	7 Oct 1892	'97 BA
McAllister, Harvey J.	1899-1901	
McAllister, John B.	10 Oct 1890	
McAllister, Lee Edmond	1899-1901	
McAllister, Robert L.	6 Sep 1877	
McAlwain, W. B.	30 Aug 1878	
McAnulty, J. D.	24 Sep 1880	
McBride, J. W.	21 Mar 1860	
McCain, J. T.	19 Jan 1872	
McCauley, Victor C. †	2 Oct 1891	
McEachern, David Hall	****	
McEachern, H. C.	13 Jan 1897	
McEachern, J. L.	****	
McKenzie, M. S.	24 Oct 1860	Co. B, 4th NC Regt.
McKenzie, W. M. M.	6 Feb 1891	
McLendon, Jesse	2 Oct 1891	

Name	Date of Registration or Attendance	Degrees/Other
McLucas, R. S. M.	9 Nov 1859	
McMillian, J. A.	5 Sep 1873	
McNair, A. J.	20 Feb 1861	Co. E, 3rd NC Art.
McNamar, G. E.	25 Jan 1884	
McNeill, A. A.	6 Feb 1861	Co. B, 2nd NC Art.
McSwain, L. A.	27 Jan 1876	
McWhirter, Frank Victor	1900-1901	
Meacham, W. M.	14 Sep 1894	
Meares, Gaston	24 Oct 1878	
Michael, ?. ?.	6 Sep 1877	
Michael, J.	30 Aug 1878	
Miller, ?. ?.	25 Aug 1874	
Miller, ?. F.	11 Oct 1876	
Miller, A. E.	25 Aug 1874	
Miller, Albert S.	11 Mar 1885	
Miller, Bachman Brown	10 Oct 1890	'95 BA/'98 AM
Miller, Calvin Milas J.	2 Sep 1881	
Miller, Charles Beauregard †	17 Sep 1880	'85 BA
Miller, D. A.	21 Feb 1868	
Miller, D. G.	29 Aug 1879	
Miller, G. H.	8 Feb 1877	
Miller, H.	30 Aug 1878	
Miller, H. C.	6 Feb 1861	Co. B, 4th NC Regt.
Miller, H. E.	20 Oct 1893	
Miller, H. W. A.	9 Nov 1859	
Miller, Henderson Neifer †	5 Jan 1888	'91 BA/'95 AM
Miller, J. L.	19 Oct 1888	
Miller, J. W.	17 Feb 1893	
Miller, John A.	2 Oct 1872	
Miller, John Carl	****	
Miller, Lewis Henderson	9 Apr 1897	
Miller, Louis Ray	1900-1901	
Miller, M. E.	24 Oct 1878	
Miller, P. B.	29 Aug 1879	
Miller, P. E.	28 Feb 1879	
Miller, P. M.	9 Nov 1859	
Miller, Paul R.	1899-1900	
Miller, R. L.	25 Jan 1884	
Miller, V. B.	11 Sep 1896	
Miller, W. ?.	26 Aug 1875	
Miller, William M.	1869-1870	
Miller, William Clyde	****	
Misenheimer, John H.	27 Jan 1876	
Misenhimer, C. A.	16 Sep 1886	
Misenhimer, C. J.	30 Jan 1880	
Misenhimer, Charles Augustus	8 Sep 1871	'79 BA/'82 AM
Misenhimer, D. B.	21 Jan 1881	
Misenheimer, Jacob. W	1861	Co. F, 1st NC Cavalry

Name	Date of Registration or Attendance	Degrees/Other
Misenhimer, James F.	2 Sep 1881	
Misenheimer, Theodore Frank	1869-1870	
Misenheimer, Marion Harrison	1869	
Misenhimer, W. N.	1 Feb 1884	
Monroe, Pleasant Edgar †	11 Jan 1895	'98 BA/'01 MA
Moose, Archibald W.	6 Sep 1877	
Moose, Dewey Whitfield	14 Dec 1896	
Moose, G. D.	10 Jan 1896	
Moose, Geo. H.	13 Sep 1895	
Moose, George	15 Aug 1884	
Moose, Gurley Davis	1899-1901	'01 BA
Moose, H. L.	7 Jan 1881	
Moose, J. O.	13 Sep 1895	
Moose, John Baxter †		
Moose, John Wesley	8 Sep 1871	'77 BA/'80 AM
Moose, Paul Alexander	1900-1901	
Moose, Paul Richter		
Moose, William Jennings	19 Sep 1890	
Moose. Luther Hazelous	8 Sep 1871	
Morgan, J. F.	21 Mar 1884	
Morgan, Jacob Levi †	14 Sep 1894	'99 BA
Morris, W. W.	17 Oct 1884	
Morrison, H. N.	25 Aug 1874	
Morrison, S. E.	21 Feb 1868	
Moser, Clarence E.	7 Oct 1892	'98 BA
Moser, Jason Chrysostom †	12 Oct 1871	'73 BA/'96 DD
Moser, John Franklin	12 Oct 1871	'74 BA
Moser, Walter Frederick	1899-1901	
Motley, George Henry	****	
Motley, P. R.	27 Jan 1876	
Mozingo, Joseph F.	18 Feb 1876	
Munday, J. D.	6 Feb 1861	Co. G, 52nd NC Regt.
Musselwhite, Cleveland	1899-1900	
Neal, Jas. W.	6 Nov 1891	
Neal. L?	2 Oct 1891	
Nelson, W. T.	31 Jan 1873	
Newell, W. A.	7 Sep 1894	
Nifong, C. Peeler	7 Oct 1892	'96 BA
Nunamaker, B. S.	15 Aug 1884	'89 BA
Nussman, Lewis	13 Sep 1895	
O' Dell, Harry Milton	14 Sep 1896	
Odell, J. T.	31 Jan 1873	
Overcash, H. J.	15 Aug 1884	
Palmer, R. C.	30 Aug 1878	
Parker, H. A.	29 Mar 1861	
Parker, Theodore Calvin †	21 Oct 1892	'96 BA/'99 AM
Patterson, Arthur L.	8 Jan 1896	
Patterson, Frank G.	2 Sep 1897	

Name	Date of Registration or Attendance	Degrees/Other
Patterson, J. K.	20 Sep 1872	
Patterson, Karl Bachman	1900-1901	
Patterson, J. F.	24 Oct 1860	
Patterson, Robert	15 Aug 1884	
Patterson, Robert H.	2 Oct 1891	
Patterson, Robert Leonidas †	9 Sep 1887	'91 BA/'94 AM
Peacock, J. W.	16 Oct 1889	
Peck, J. L.	5 Feb 1878	
Peebles, A. G.	20 Feb 1861	
Peeler, Arthur	14 Sep 1896	
Peeler, J. M.	6 Feb 1891	
Peeler, Jenkins A.	1 Feb 1893	
Peeler, P. A. D.	25 Jan 1884	
Peeler, S. D.	13 Jan 1888	
Pemberton, W. D.	31 Jan 1873	
Peninger, A. H.	17 Sep 1886	
Peninger, T. R.	4 Oct 1889	
Peninger, Wm. Martin	17 Jan 1879	
Peschau, Ferdinand W. E. †	****	'91 DD
Petrea, Abner Wilson	8 Sep 1871	
Petrea, Bruner Eugene †	1903-1904	
Petrea, Delma M.	1900-1901	
Petrea, G. C.	8 Feb 1877	
Petrea, Hazelious S.	****	
Petrea, Henry L.	29 Jan 1875	
Petrea, Henry Mathew†	30 Jan 1880	'87 BA/'91 AM
Petrea, J. D.	13 Sep 1895	
Petrea, M. W.	25 Oct 1895	
Petrea, R. H.	21 Feb 1868	
Petrea, Robert William †	1869	
Pharr, Y. F.	21 Feb 1868	
Phillips, Charles Arthur †	13 Sep 1895	'99 AB, PhB
Pickett, J. J.	25 Aug 1874	
Pickler, D	29 Mar 1861	
Pless, Charles Rahn †	11 Sep 1896	'00 AB
Plott, George	18 Apr 1879	
Plott, H. Anis	29 Aug 1873	
Pool, F. W.	30 Aug 1878	
Poole, C. M.	21 Oct 1875	'97 AM
Poole, G?. A.	25 Mar 1887	
Pope, F. Kirby	2 Oct 1891	
Powlas, A. L.	17 Aug 1885	
Presler, Hanan	8 Sep 1871	
Propst, John W.	16 Sep 1881	
Pyron, T. P.	30 Jan 1874	
Quantz, A. E.	21 Feb 1868	
Redwine, N.	31 Jan 1873	
Reed, C. H.	1861	

Name	Date of Registration or Attendance	Degrees/Other
Reid, James C.	6 Sep 1877	
Reid, John Monroe	21 Feb 1868	'71 BA
Reid, Milus J.	10 Oct 1890	
Reid, Robert E.	18 Apr 1879	
Rendleman, John L.	7 Sep 1888	
Rendleman, Lawrence Tobias	1861	Co. G, 6th NC Regt.
Rhyne, Daniel Efird	May 1872	
Rhyne, J. L.	30 Jan 1874	
Rhyne, L. J.	30 Jan 1874	
Ribble, H. D.	31 Jan 1873	
Richie, L. M.	8 Sep 1871	
Richie, W. W. J.	27 Sep 1889	'95 BA
Ridenhour, Ernest Winfred	1899-1901	
Ridenhour, Frederick O.	1899-1900	
Ridenhour, H. C.	20 Oct 1893	
Ridenhour, Joseph Bittle	1899-1901	
Ridenhour, L. A.	25 Aug 1874	
Ridenhour, Martin Luther †	1900-1901	
Ridenhour, Robert E.	2 Sep 1881	
Ridenhour, Rufus C.	1870	
Ridenhour, T?. H.	5 Jan 1888	
Ridenhour, Victor Clarence †	11 Feb 1891	'99 BA
Rimer John N.	9 Oct 1891	
Rindleman, ?. S.	14 Dec 1859	
Rinehart, John M.	26 Sep 1884	
Ritchey, George E.	9 Nov 1859	Co. H, 8th NC Regt., 1st Lieutenant
Ritchey, Henry A.	9 Nov 1859	Co. B, 20th NC Regt.
Ritchey, John D.	9 Nov 1859	Co. B, 20th NC Regt.
Ritchie, Berry L.	1900-1901	
Ritchie, Edward Lee †	1898-1901	'01 BA
Ritchie, George Turner	31 Jan 1890	
Ritchie, H. J.	17 Sep 1886	
Ritchie, John H.	19 Dec 1879	'88 BA/'98 AM
Ritchie, John L.	24 Jan 1894	
Ritchie, L.	25 Aug 1874	
Ritchie, L. C.	24 Jan 1879	
Ritchie, Mc. L.	27 Mar 1896	
Ritchie, Orion Delma	1900-1901	
Ritchie, R. F.	19 Oct 1888	
Ritchie, Robert Matthew	1900-1901	
Ritchie, W. D.	25 Jan 1884	
Ritchie, W. Fair	1899-1900	
Ritchie, W. L.	13 Sep 1895	
Ritchie, Wiley Washington J. †	****	'96 BA/'98 AM
Ritchie, Wm. R	25 Apr 1860	
Rodgers, Benjamin F.	9 Nov 1859	Co. A, 17th NC Regt.

Name	Date of Registration or Attendance	Degrees/Other
Rose, B. M.	19 Jan 1872	
Rose, Charles Alexander †	8 Feb 1877	'80 BA, 'AM
Rose, Junius Alexander	1900-1901	
Rose, W. R.	19 Jan 1872	
Ross, C. M.	16 Oct 1889	Co. G, 6th NC Regt., Lieutenant
Ross, L. G.	11 Sep 1896	
Rothrock, Luther Hazelous	15 Aug 1884	'84 BA, 'AM
Rothrock, Samuel †	****	'77 AM Honorary
Rumple, John W.	9 Nov 1859	Co. G, 42nd NC Regt.
Runge, B. Henry W. †	9 Sep 1887	'90 BA/'95 AM
Rushing, C. A.	19 Jan 1872	
Safrit, D. Monroe	1899-1900	
Safrit, Dock M.	2 Sep 1897	
Sayerly, A. S.	7 Jan 1881	
Scarborough, Robert H.	7 Mar 1860	Co. F, 9th SC Regt.
Scarborough, Wilson D.	21 Mar 1860	Co. F, 9th SC Regt.
Schaeffer, George Francis †	8 Aug 1884	
Scott, ?. L.	25 Aug 1874	
Scott, A. Biklia	21 Nov 1893	
Scott, Geo. R.	8 Sep 1871	
Scott, L. F.	22 Feb 1878	
Seaford, P?. K.	14 Dec 1859	
Sease, J. L.	26 Aug 1875	
Setzler, Ben M.	5 Oct 1894	'97 BA
Shankle, Henry	16 Sep 1885	
Shaver, Sidney	2 Sep 1897	
Shemwell, Baxter	6 Sep 1872	
Sherrill, A. E.	8 Sep 1871	
Sherrill, Albert	7 Sep 1888	
Sherrill, Thomas F.	23 Apr 1875	
Shimpock, Lewis William	1900-1901	
Shimpock, P. S.	27 Jan 1876	
Shinn, Geo. C.	26 Aug 1875	
Shinn, John W.	21 Oct 1875	
Shirey, Luther Shaver	14 Feb 1890	'95 BA/'98 AM
Shoemaker, John	1869	
Shoup, H. B.	18 Oct 1895	
Shuping, J. M.	21 Mar 1884	
Shuping, James M.	20 Oct 1893	
Shuping, Oscar Deberry	1900-1901	
Sibley, H. C.	28 Mar 1860	Co. C, 14th NC Regt.
Sifferd, Calvin Wright †	8 Sep 1871	'74 BA/'96 DD
Sifferd, Jeremiah Luther	1870	
Simpson, Charley N.	15 Dec 1893	
Simpson, Charlie W.	8 Sep 1871	
Simpson, M. B.	9 Nov 1859	Co. D, 37th NC Regt.
Simpson, Oscar Romulus	1899-1901	
Simpson, Shadrack	****	'99 PhD

Name	Date of Registration or Attendance	Degrees/Other
Simpson, W. B.	13 Sep 1895	
Skeen, M. T.	6 Feb 1891	
Skinner, J. D.	21 Mar 1860	
Skinner, J. E.	6 Feb 1891	
Skinner, J. M.	9 Nov 1859	
Skinner, W. C.	21 Mar 1860	
Sloop, Abraham Washington	6 Sep 1872	
Sloop, Henry Eli Hall †	17 Aug 1885	'91 PhB/'96 AM
Sloop, John A.	2 Oct 1891	
Sloop, Martin Luther Scheck	1870	
Sloop, N. J. J.	24 Oct 1860	Co. B, 4th NC Regt.
Smith, C. F.	7 Mar 1860	
Smith, F. T.	8 Sep 1871	
Smith, George Allen	1900-1901	
Smith, Green E.	7 Mar 1860	Co. I, 52nd NC Regt.
Smith, J. L.	9 Nov 1859	
Smith, J. M.	9 Nov 1859	
Smith, John Lewis †	1899-1901	
Smith, Julian L. †	****	'94 DD
Smith, R. H.	8 Sep 1871	
Smith, W. A.	15 Aug 1884	
Smyre, E. E. †	3 Feb 1901	
Snider, Arnold Holmes	1900-19901	
Sox, David Adam †		
Spears, J. H.	25 Aug 1874	
Spicer?, Chas. E.	20 Feb 1874	
Springs, Alex A.	17 Feb 1893	
Stafford, Harold Lucius	1900-1901	
Starns, R. L.	16 Mar 1888	
Staton, B. F.	9 Nov 1859	Co. F, 2nd NC Jr. Reserves
Staton, Jesse B.	29 Jan 1861	Co. B, 31st NC Regt.
Stevens, J. H.	8 Sep 1871	
Stevens, M. L.	8 Sep 1871	
Stewart, S. E.	29 Aug 1873	
Stoner, Wm.	21 Mar 1860	
Stowe, J. H.	8 Sep 1871	
Stricker, T. C.	9 Nov 1859	
Stuckey, R. F.	7 Mar 1860	Co. F, 9th SC Regt.
Sturdivant. J. W.	31 Jan 1873	
Summers, R. A.	30 Aug 1878	
Suther, J. A.	16 Jan 1889	
Sutton, J. V.	10 Jan 1896	
Swink, Louis M.	27 Sep 1889	
Teter, James M.	18 Apr 1879	
Thayer, Charles Holmes	1900-1901	
Thies, Adolph C.	19 Jan 1883	
Thies, Ernst A.	19 Jan 1883	
Thies, Gustav O.	10 Oct 1890	

Name	Date of Registration or Attendance	Degrees/Other
Thomas, Samuel L.	1900-1901	
Thompson, C. M	20 Feb 1861	Co. I, 14th NC
Thompson, Emmette Grey	1900-1901	
Thompson, Francis Marion	1869-1870	
Thompson, G. M.	11 Oct 1876	
Thompson, J. H.	7 Oct 1892	
Thompson, P. H.	8 Sep 1871	
Thompson, R. B.	8 Sep 1871	
Thompson, R. F.	11 Oct 1876	
Thompson, Wm. L	20 Feb 1861	Co. I, 14th NC
Timmons, ?. C.	8 Sep 1871	
Timmons, W. F.	30 Jan 1874	
Tise, David L.	1899-19	
Tise, J. Marshall	11 Sep 1896	'00 BA
Travis, Bernie Cornelius	1900-1901	
Trexler, Allen	21 Mar 1860	Co. D, 1st NC Artillery
Trexler, G. A.	14 Mar 1884	
Trexler, Henry Alexander †	6 Sep 1878	
Trexler, John	21 Mar 1860	Co. K, 57th NC Regt
Troutman, L. C.	9 Apr 1897	
Tucker, D. Clifford	1899-1900	
Tucker, Daniel B.	26 Aug 1875	
Tucker, George N.	20 Jan 1882	
Tucker, M. M.	2 Sep 1897	
Tucker, M. Willis	1899-1901	
Tucker, P. Wilburn	24 Jan 1894	
Tucker, T. E.?	27 Sep 1889	
Upchurch, George R.	27 Mar 1897	
Ury, G. S.	16 Jan 1889	
Van Poole, G. M.	7 Oct 1892	
Voils, W. M.	4 Feb 1887	
Wadsworth, D. H.	4 Apr 1879	
Wadsworth, Thomas M.	8 Sep 1871	'75 BA/'78 AM
Wagoner, C. T.	6 Nov 1891	
Wagoner, Jacob L.	16 Sep 1881	
Walker, Clinton E. †	****	'01 DD
Walker, J. H.	10 Jan 1881	
Walter, M. V.	24 Oct 1860	Co. F, 57th NC Regt.
Walter, Zeb C.	2 Sep 1897	
Warren, William	1890	
Watts, John A.	14 Sep 1896	
Weddington, J. F.	21 Feb 1868	
Wells, J. E.	9 Nov 1859	
Welsh, Benj. F.	29 Jan 1875	
Welsh, Daniel Barrier	1900-1901	
Welsh, Jas. W.	2 Oct 1891	
Wells, J. E.	9 Nov 1859	
Welsh, John A.	2 Oct 1891	

Name	Date of Registration or Attendance	Degrees/Other
Welsh, Benj. F.	29 Jan 1875	
Welsh, Daniel Barrier	1900-1901	
Welsh, Jas. W.	2 Oct 1891	
Welsh, John A.	2 Oct 1891	
Welsh, S. J.	25 Aug 1874	'80 BA '82 AM
Welsh, W. B.	30 Aug 1878	
Werts, Joseph Quincy	1900-01	
Wessell, Emil A.	2 Oct 1891	
West, James H.	19 Mar 1874	
White, S. M.	5 Oct 1894	
Whitsett, William T.	1891-1893	'91 AM '93 PhD
Widenhouse, J. Adam	1899-'00	
Wilhelm, Adam A.	23 Mar 1895	
Wilhelm, J. E.	18 Feb 1881	
Wilhelm, W. L.	19 Aug 1885	
Williams, W. C.	4 Feb 1885	
Wilson, J. S.	3 Mar 1881	
Wood, C. H.	21 Mar 1860	
Woodham, C. W.	11 Oct 1876	
Woods, P. P.	25 Aug 1874	
Wright, Gaston A.	1900-01	
Wright, Peter E. †	11 Feb 1885	'86 BA
Yoder, Robert Anderson †	6 Sep 1872	'77 BA '80 AM '99 DD
Yost, James Ogatha	1900-01	
Yount, Adolphus Leroy †	11 Apr 1873	'76 BA '95 DD

The Carolina English and Classical School

The CECS existed from September 1902 through May 1903. It was a private academy operated by a former instructor at NC College, George F. McAllister, and Rev. Levi E. Busby, the minister at Holy Trinity Lutheran Church in Mt. Pleasant. Rev. Busby died in March 1903 and the school ceased operation in May 1903. The list of names of the CECS is very incomplete.

Name	Date of Registration or Attendance	Degrees/Other
Shimpock. Lewis William	1902	
Wagoner, Chris Columbus	1902	
Welsh, Dennis Barrier	1902	See NC College & MPCI
Winecoff, Cress Alexander	1902	

the roster below were taken from school records, year books, alumni records, and other proven sources. Although many graduates of MPCI were able to enter various Colleges with advanced standing, the school itself never achieved status as a Junior College. A diploma from MPCI was the equivalent of a present-day High School Diploma.

Name	Date of Registration or Attendance	Degrees/Other
Abernathy, Tom Wade	1925-1926	
Abernathy, William Sidney, Jr.	1922-1924	
Adams, Steve	1927-1928	
Adams, Walter Clarence	1912-1913	WWI
Agee, William Spencer	1924-1928	
Agner, E. L.	1904-1906	
Agner, R. L.	1904-1906	
Aiken, Keever	1925-1926	
Albright, M. F. †	Sep 1904	
Alexander, Charles David	1932-1933	
Alexander, Claibourne Neal	1924-1928	
Alexander, Corum Dewitt	1906-1909	
Alexander, Hugh Harris	1920-1923	
Alexander, Richard Clinton	1929-1930	
Allen, Bransford Lake	1922-1926	
Alligood, Ceyrel Ruskin	1927-1928	
Alligood, L. C.	1919-1920	
Allman, Clifford Dutton	1924-1925	
Allman, Homer Mack	1915-1917	WWI
Allman, J. M.	1920-1921	
Allmond, Lemuel R.	1914-1917	
Allred, Joseph Franklin	1922-1924	
Allred, Roger P.	1910-1911	WWI
Almond, Lemuel Ransome	1915-1916	
Almquist, Irving E.	1932-1933	
Ameglio, Louis Alberto	1931-1932	
Amick, Leroy Phelan	1919-1924	
Anderson, Benjamin Mason	1928-1929	
Anderson, Irvin Dale	1932-1933	
Anderson, James	1906-1909	
Antley, Thomas Boger	1928-1929	
Archer, Cyrus Nathaniel	1919-1920	
Archer, James Ralph	1923-1924	
Arey, Bruce Deal	1923-1925	
Arias, Olmedo Ernesto	1930-1932	
Armfield, Mead Kemp	1917-1918	
Armfield, Stuart McGuire	1924-1925	

Name	Date of Registration or Attendance	Degrees/Other
Armstrong, Rapley Cleon	1922-1923	
Arrington, Richard Addler, Jr.	1926-1927	
Artz, James Leroy	1917-1918	
Asendorf, Adolph John	1920-1921	
Atwell, Floyd Elmer	1918-1920	
Atwell, John Cline	1919-1920	
Auten, Frank Jordan	1910-1913	WWI
Auten, Graham	1910-1911	
Auten, J. N.	Sep 1909	WWI
Babington, Richard T.	1925-1926	
Bailes, Alva Boyce	1923-1926	
Bailes, Leonard Brevard	1923-1926	
Bailey, George Lee	1913-1915	
Bailey, James S.	1917-1918	
Bailey, Nathan Thomas	1931-1932	
Bailey, Robert Henry	1920-1923	
Bain, J. M.	1910-1911	WWI
Baker, Paul Wellington	1932-1933	
Baldwin, William Ingraham	1926-1927	
Ballard, William Thomas	1923-1925	
Barger, C. E.	Sep 1904	
Barnes, Henry Eugene	1925-1926	
Barnhardt, George O.	Sep 1904	
Barnhardt, John Jacob	1906-1909	WWI
Barnhardt, Oscar Leon	1913-1914	
Barnhardt, Paul Archie	1916-1918	
Barnhardt, Robert Lee	1915-1917	WWI
Barnhardt, W. W.	Sep 1909	WWI
Barrett, B. E.	Sep 1909	
Barrier, Charles Sherril	1931-1932	
Barrier, Clarence Young	1920-1922	
Barrier, Cleveland Ralen	1906-1909	
Barrier, Clyde Monroe	1919-1921	
Barrier, Ed Moore	1916-1918/1922-1923	
Barrier, Elmore	1915-1916	
Barrier, Ferdinand Louis	1922-1923	
Barrier, George Louis, II	1923-1924/1925-1928	
Barrier, George William	1910-1911	WWI
Barrier, Harry Eugene	1925-1927	
Barrier, Henry Webster	1910-1914	WWI
Barrier, John Daniel	1920-1924	
Barrier, Luther Benjamin	1926-1927	
Barrier, Luther Bowman	1913-1915/1916-1917	
Barrier, Oscar Luther	1904-1906	
Barrier, Paul Alexander	Sep 1904	
Barrier, Robert Lee	1903-1904	
Barrier, Ruth Boger	1927-1928	
Barrier, Shuford Clyde	1910-1914	

Name	Date of Registration or Attendance	Degrees/Other
Barrier, W. A.	Sep 1904	
Barrier, Zeb Alonzo	1926-1927	
Barringer, Archibald Lipe	1924-1926	
Barringer, Benjamin Alfred †	1906-1911	WWI
Barringer, Bevan Kyle	1918-1919	
Barringer, Cager Parks	1906-1909/1910-1911	
Barringer, Calvin Ray	1921-1925	
Barringer, Cecil Culp	1926-1927/1930-1932	
Barringer, Charlie L.	Sep 1904	
Barringer, Emmett T.	1918-1920	
Barringer, George Lewis	1924-1925	
Barringer, H. Price	1910-1911/1912-1913	
Barringer, Harry Otis	1925-1926	
Barringer, Hilbert W.	1924-1928	
Barringer, Hiller Davis	1922-1925	
Barringer, Homer Monroe	1916-1917	
Barringer, James Richard Monroe	1906-1909	
Barringer, Lawson Herman	1915-1918	
Barringer, Martin Henry	1903	
Barringer, Otha Alvin	1903-1904	
Barringer, Phillip Monroe	1909-1914	WWI
Barringer, Thomas Avery	1906-1909	
Barringer, William Hoy	1922-1924	
Basinger, W. A.	1919	
Baugh, Al	1904	
Baugh, Arthur Lee	1913-1914	
Baxley, Craig Thompson	1928-1929	
Beard, Wilbur Jackson	1926-1927	
Beaver, Carl Jennings	1916-1920	
Beaver, Coy Douglas	1921-1924	
Beaver, Edwin Heller	1903	
Beaver, Ernest Leroy	1930-1931	
Beaver, Ervin Taylor	1931-1933	
Beaver, George Augustus	1922-1924	
Beaver, Guy Moody	1910-1911/1912-1913	WWI
Beaver, J. H.	Sep 1904	
Beaver, Jesse Leander	1914-1916/1917-1918	WWI
Beaver, M. L.	Sep 1909	
Beaver, Myron Holmes	1913-1914	
Beaver, Roy William	1920-1922/1923-1924	
Beaver, William Berley	1909/1911-1913	WWI
Beeker, James Elmore	1913-1914	
Beeker, William Sparks	1913-1914	
Bell, John William	1928-1932	
Bellis, George David	1925-1928	
Bennett, John Henry	1923-1924/1925-1927	
Bennett, Richard Bowie	1921-1925	
Berry, Malcolm Sterling	1928-1931	

Name	Date of Registration or Attendance	Degrees/Other
Berryhill, Joe Caldwell	1913-1914	
Betancourt, Allen Beauregard	1927-1928	
Bigger, Ernest W.	1906-1909	
Biggers, Lacy Cleo	1922-1924	
Biles, W. H.	1903	
Bishop, Onias Blumer, Jr.	1925-1926	
Bivens, S. B.	1910-1911	
Black, Fred	Sep 1904	
Blackwelder, Buford W.	1914-1915	WWI
Blackwelder, Charles Reuben	1919-1920	
Blackwelder, Clyde A.	1909	WWI
Blackwelder, Leroy	1906-1909	
Blackwelder, Leroy Emerson †	1917-1920	
Blackwelder, Oscar Fisher †	1913-1915	
Blackwelder, Ralph Eugene	1920-1923	
Blackwelder, Sidney Hoyle	1918-1920	
Blume, Clarence Jno. Martin	1913-1917	WWI
Bodie, Earl Kennan †	1913-1915	
Bodie, Henry Cromer	1921-1924	
Bodie, Ralph Gilbert	1913-1915	
Boger, Bonnen	1920-1921	
Boger, Charles	1914-1915	
Boger, Daniel Jennings	1915-1916	
Boger, Marvin Adam	1921-1925	
Boger, Will	1910-1911	
Boldt, Karl Lewis John	1918-1922	
Bolick, Ernest Bernard	1925-1929	
Bolick, J. Glenn	1925-1926	
Bolton, Jesse Herman	1923-1925	
Bond, Charles Kenneth	1922-1924	
Bonds, H. E.	Sep 1909	
Bonham, William Lee	1923-1924	
Boozer, Virgil, Young	1925-1926	
Bost, C. W.	Sep 1909	
Bost, Caleb Watson	1928-1929	
Bost, Charles W.	1914-1915	
Bost, Eugene Thompson	1922-1924/1927-1929	
Bost, G. R.	Sep 1909	
Bost, J. B.	Sep 1909	
Bost, James Aaron	1928-1929	
Bost, John Beard	1912-1913	
Bost, John Henry	1906-1909	
Bost, John Lafayette	1928-1929/1930-1931	
Bost, Lewis Monroe	1914-1918	
Bost, M. L.	1932-1933	
Bost, Morris Ardelle	1923-1924	
Bost, Peter Boger	1919-1923	
Bost, Ralph Walter	1916-1920	

Name	Date of Registration or Attendance	Degrees/Other
Bost, Walter Brown	1919-1923	
Bost, William Charles	1915-1916	
Bost, William Jackson	1919-1922	
Bost, William Nelson	1914-1917	
Bost, Wilson Bailey	1916-1918	WWI
Bostian, Basil J.	1906-1909	
Bostian, W. H.	1904-1906	
Bowden, George Stewart †	1910-1911/1912-1914	
Bowen, George Harveston	1927-1929	
Bowers, James Rufus	1928-1929	
Boyd, N. B.	Sep 1909	
Boyles, Alva Paul	1918-1919	
Boylin, David Franklin	1925-1926	
Braswell, C. C.	1920-1922	
Brawley, J. G.	Sep 1904	
Brazelton, Walter Harr	1928-1929	
Breuggeman, Chas. A.	1915-1916	
Britt, Stacy Herrin	1932-1933	
Broad, Frederick Lee.	1910-1911/1912-1913	
Brooks, Robert Rhodes	1926-1927	
Broome, L. C.	1904-1906	WWI
Broughton, John, Jr.	1931-1933	
Brown, Andrew J.	1906-1909	
Brown, Bruce Oswald	1920-1922	
Brown, C. F.	1919	
Brown, Charles Alexander, Jr.	1923-1924	
Brown, Charles Alfred	1918-1919	
Brown, Herman	1914-1915	
Brown, Hiram Berlin	1920-1921	
Brown, Jesse Oscar	1912-1913	WWI
Brown, John Albert	1919-1920	
Brown, Marion Kirk	1920-1922	
Brown, N. M.	Sep 1904	
Brown, Pleasant David †	1904-1906	
Brown, Richard Halley	1928-1932	
Brown, Robert Marshall	1917-1919	
Bruggeman, Charles Augustus.	1916-1919	
Brumley, F. E.	Sep 1909	
Bruton, D.	1919-1920	
Bruton, James Ralph	1918-1919	
Bryan, C. E.	Sep 1909	
Bryan, Joseph William	1919-1920	
Buchanan, James Graham	1921-1923	
Buck, B. C.	1904-1906	
Buck, B. F.	1910-1911	
Buck, William Guy	1911-1913	
Buck, William McGilvery	1932-1933	
Bunn, Daphne Rose	1932-1933	

Name	Date of Registration or Attendance	Degrees/Other
Bunts, Alton Albert	1930-1933	
Burleson, Max Dry	1927-1928	
Burris, J. A.	Sep 1904	
Burwell, Clyde Morton	1924-1925	
Bussey, John Hubert	1927-1928	
Butler, Edward Nelson	1919-1920	
Calloway, Arthur Willie	1906-1909	
Calloway, F. E.	Sep 1909	WWI
Cameron, Lauchlin	1921-1923	
Campbell, James J. W.	1932-1933	
Campbell, James Owen	1921-1923	
Cannon, W. F.	1904-1906	
Carpenter, Paul	1923-1924	
Carpenter, William Plato	1919-1920	
Carrigan, Bruce Reid	1918-1919	
Carson, Louis Ashton	1914-1916	
Carson, William Guerin	1930-1932	
Carter, Robert Love	1918-1919	
Case, Lloyd G.	1932-1933	
Casper, Burley Lee	1915-1916	
Casper, Gurley Morrison	1931-1933	
Cassell, Joseph Buchanan †	1918-1921	
Castor, Bradshaw Dekime †	1917-1918	WWI
Castor, Henry Carmon	1920-1922	
Cates, Ralph Edward	1924-1925	
Cauble, Albert	1906-1909	
Cauble, Charlie Lynn	1918-1919	
Cauble, J. A.	1910-1911	
Cauble, Junius Elwood	1923-1924	
Cauble, M. E.	Sep 1909	
Caudill, Clinton Rupert	1928-1929	
Caughman, Arthur Walton	1926-1927	
Caughman, Frank Leon	1924-1927	
Caughman, Nesbit Harper	1921-1923	
Cento, S. Henry Luis	1928-1932	
Chappell, James Alton	1922-1923	
Cheney, Benjamin Arnold	1928-1929	
Christenbury, Plase Maxwell	1924-1926	
Christenbury, Silas Woodly	1924-1925	
Christmus, William Elmore	1927-1929	
Clark, Edmund B.	1914-1915	WWI
Clinard, Charles Brown	1918-1919	
Cline, Frank S.	Sep 1909	WWI
Cline, George Fred	1920-1921	
Cline, H. E.	1906-1909	
Cline, Howard Bostian	1922-1924	
Cline, J. A.	Sep 1909	
Cline, John Ivy	1906-1909	

Name	Date of Registration or Attendance	Degrees/Other
Cline, John Stricter	1918-1920	
Cline, Paul Burgess	1923-1925	
Cline, Ralph Murray	1915-1917/1922-1924	
Cline, William Harvey	1920-1921	
Cloninger, Thomas Dewitt	1928-1931	
Cobb, Eugene Boyd	1921-1923	
Cobb, James Virgil	1916-1917	
Cobb, Robert Lingle	1921-1923	
Cobb, Voight Wagoner	1920-1923	
Cobb, William Clayton	1918-1919	
Cobble, Ernest Alvin	1913-1914	
Cochran, Parks	1924-1925	
Cole, William Bouden	1922-1923	
Coleman, George	1915-1916	WWI
Coley, Henderson Jonah	1915-1919	
Collier, Sterling Kenneth	1923-1924	
Conrad, Fred Oscar	1922-1924	
Conrad, G. F.	1910-1911	
Conrad, James Bradford	1927-1929	
Conrad, Kenneth Fritz	1925-1928	
Conrad, Ralph	1920-1922	
Cook, Horace Edward	1912-1914	
Cook, Robert Monroe, Jr.	1931-1933	
Copeland, Marshall Wesley	1924-1926	
Copeland, Robert Royal, Jr.	1932-1933	
Coppage, Dinkins Ocpaque	1923-1925	
Cornelius, Chalmers E.	1919-1920	
Corriher, H. D.	Sep 1904	
Corriher, W. S.	Sep 1909	
Coughenour, Charlie P.	1906-1909	
Coughenour, Thomas A.	1906-1909	
Counts, Frank Alfred	1924-1925	
Cousins, Luther Edwin	1920-1922	
Cox, Heathman Gurley	1924-1927	
Cox, Howard Wesley	1926-1927	
Cox, William Fred	1913-1914/1917-1918	
Coxe, Felix Glenn	1924-1925	
Crabtree, Charles Alfred	1917-1918	
Crane, C. H.	1910-1911	
Crane, J. R.	Sep 1909	
Cranford, Phillip D.	1919-1920	
Cress, David Steffey	1915-1916	
Cress, E. M.	1910-1911	
Cress, Frank Pierce	1912-1914	
Cress, J. L.	1910-1911	
Cress, Jay Lewis	1912-1915	WWI
Cress, Jno. Ross	Sep 1909	
Cress, John Calvin	1922-1924	

Name	Date of Registration or Attendance	Degrees/Other
Cress, Kirby Lee	1906-1909	
Cress, Lester Barrier	1914-1917	
Cripps, Benjamin T.	1911	WWI
Cress, Wesley Earl	1913-1914	
Cress, Wiley Earle	1912-1913/1916-1917	
Cronenburg, Henry M	1915-1916	WWI
Cronk, Earl T. W.	1913-1915	
Crouse, Jacob Franklin	1920-1922	
Crow, Vester Jesse	1910-1915	WWI
Crowell, Alexander M.	1919-1920	
Crowell, Andrew M	1913-1914	WWI
Crowell, Boone Lafayette	1906-1909	
Crowell, G. Edward.	Dec 1903	
Crowell, Lee Smith	1912-1913	
Crowell, Verden Clifford	1917-1922	
Crowell, Walter Lee	1921-1922	
Cruse, Bernard William	1922-1925	
Cruse, C. A.	Sep 1909	
Cruse, Zeb Paul	1916-1917	
Culpepper, Harry Lee	1922-1923	
Currie, Gordon	1924-1925	
Curry, James Clayton	1926-1928	
Curtis, Melvin George	1918-1919	
Curtis, Walter Louis, Jr.	1932-1933	
Czarnitski, Herbert Walter	1926-1931	
Dalton,	1920-1921	
Dasher, H. L.	1919	
Dasher, John Benjamin	1918-1920	
Daves, Kenneth William	1928-1929	
Davies, Robert Allen	1927-1929	
Davis, Allen Yerby	1925-1926	
Davis, Clyde Ray	1920-1921	
Davis, Dewey Lee	1926-1927	
Davis, George Franklin	1910-1911/1912-1913	
Davis, James Samuel	1926-1928	
Davis, John Williamson	1920-1922	
Davis, Lewis Bates	1925-1927	
Davis, Marion Cecil	1921-1922	
Davis, Martin Van	1923-1924	
Davis, Robert Edward	1923-1927	
Davis, Roy Wilson	1920-1921	
Davis, Steve	1926-1927	
Davis, Victor Eugene	1931-1933	
Deal, John Obadiah	1920-1921/1923-1924	
DeAmond, William Orr	1916-1917	WWI
Decker, Darrell	1932-1933	
deDiego, Olmedo Aurelio	1930-1932	
Denaro, Louis Francis	1919-1921	

Name	Date of Registration or Attendance	Degrees/Other
Dennis, L. L.	Sep 1909	
Derrick, Zeddie Guy	1922-1923	
Dickerson, Charles Crowder	1928-1929	
Dickson, Louis James	1923-1925	
Dorton, Teddy Richardson	1923-1924	
Dove, Harry	1906-1909	
Dry, Benton Haskell	1918-1919/1920-1922	
Dry, C. M.	Sep 1904	
Dry, Clarence D.	1916-1918	
Dry, Marvin Banks	1922-1925	
Dry, Vern Edwards	1923-1926	
Dry, Wade Edgar	1917-1918	
Drye, Neva Maree	1910-1911	
Dubois, Willard Daniel	1928-1929	
Duke, Jordan Pinkney	1925-1927	
Dulin, Grady Nicholson	1920-1921	
Dulin, Martin Odell	1919-1921	
Duncan, Isaac Dewey	1923-1924	
Duncan, James Meek	1921-1923	
Dunlap, Dewey L.	1920-1921	
Dunn, John Leith	1909/1912-1913	
Durham, Henry Oscar, Jr.	1921-1922	
Dutton, Vance O.	1904-1906	
Dutton, Wade Hampton †	1904-1906	
Dysard, Thomas Lee	1927-1928	
Eargle, Dalton O'Farrow	1921-1923	
Eargle, George Milton	1928-1929/1930-1931	
Earle, H. J.	Sep 1904	
Early, Horace Hobson	1916-1917	
Early, Hoyle Alexander	1918-1919	
Early, James Clarence	1921-1923	
Early, N. C.	1903-1904	
Earnhardt, Charlie C.	1903-1904	
Earnhardt, Houston Harold	1925-1927	
Earnhardt, Reid Stephen	1918-1920	
Edwards, Earl Lee	1926-1927	
Edwards, J. Lester	1910-1911	
Edwards, John Jackson	1930-1931	
Edwards, Snowdie McGovern	1910-1911/1912-1914	
Edwards, William Jasper	1914-1915	
Edwards, William Zeno	1915-1916	WWI
Edwards, Wm. Jasper	1915-1916	
Edwards, Zeno Lester	1912-1914	
Efird, Abner Bahnson	1919-1920	
Efird, C. L.	Sep 1904	
Efird, Craig C.	1915-1916	
Efird, Fred Carl	1913-1914	WWI
Efird, Ira P.	1915-1916	

Name	Date of Registration or Attendance	Degrees/Other
Efird, Jerome Jasper	1904-1906	WWI
Efird, John Joshua	1917-1918	
Efird, John Snuggs	1927-1928	
Efird, T. C.	1910-1911	
Efird, William Titus	1904-1906	
Efird, Willie A.	1906-1909	
Elks, Charlie O.	1910-1911	
Eller, J. W.	1910-1911	
Eller, Lonnie R.	1913-1914	WWI
Ellington, Melvin Cornelius	1928-1929/1931-1933	
Elliott, John Gary	1910-1911/1912-1913	
Ellsworth, Henry Kirkwood	1918-1920	
Elms, Henry Stroud	1920-1921	
Ervin, Hubert Cline	1926-1928	
Eubanks, H. B.	1909	
Eubanks, P. H.	1909	
Eudy, Arthur Thaddeus	1913-1914	WWI
Eudy, Etta Christine	1930-1931	
Eudy, Jay Theodore	1915-1917	
Eudy, John Clinton	1918-1920	
Eudy, Mebben Matthew	1916-1918	
Eudy, Z. J.	Sep 1904	
Ewer, Malcolm Graham, Jr.	1931-1933	
Exley, Sled Heywood	1918-1919	
Ezzell, Wendell Linn	1924-1926	
Faggart, George Henry	1906-1909	
Faggart, Harold Lee	1924-1926	
Faggart, Hedrick Miller	1906-1909	WWI
Fain, William Mercer, Jr.	1932-1933	
Farmer, Charles Glenn	1922-1925	
Farrell, Leo James	1919-1920	
Feldman, Lewis	1910-1911	
Fennell, Alva Beckham	1920-1921	
Fesperman, James Floyd	1914-1915	WWI
Fesperman, L.A.	1906-1909	
Finch, Harry Brown	1926-1927	
Fink, Carl Dutton	1920-1924	
Fink, Daniel Hallman	1931-1932	
Fink, Frank Reuben	1915-1916	
Fink, H. A.	1932	
Fink, Homer Lee	1921-1922	
Fink, John Ralph	1914-1915	WWI
Fink, L. Bradley	Sep 1904	
Finna, Jesse	1924-1927	
Fishburne, Edward Stokes	1927-1929	
Fisher, Archie Baxter	1924-1926	
Fisher, Arthur W.	1903-1904	WWI
Fisher, C. E. G.	Sep 1904	

Name	Date of Registration or Attendance	Degrees/Other
Fisher, Edgar Walter Eugene	1912-1915	
Fisher, Guy Earl	1913-1916	WWI
Fisher, Henry Lee	1924-1929	
Fisher, Hilbert A. H.	1906-1911	WWI
Fisher, James Crowell	1931-1932	
Fisher, L. A.	Sep 1904	
Fisher, Luther Lee	1921-1922	
Fisher, Myron	1904-1906	
Fisher, Ramon Leroy	1912-1913	
Fisher, Roy Linn †	1920-1923	
Fisher, Van Grady	1918-1919	
Fleming, Clifton Earl	1930-1931	
Fleming, John Joseph	1932-1933	
Flow, James Alexander	1919-1920	
Flow, O. L.	Sep 1909	WWI
Flow, William Harry	1916-1917/1918-1919	
Flowe,	1920-1921	
Flowe, Edgar A.	1932-1933	
Fogleman, Paul Foust	1925-1927	
Foil, Frank Wadsworth	1931-1933	
Foil, Harry E.	1903-1904	
Foil, Henry Harbough	1923-1926	
Foil, Homer	1904-1906	
Foil, Horace Elwood	1916-1918	WWI
Foil, J. L. C.	1904-1906	
Foil, Joe Orchard	1922-1924	
Foil, Lee Evans	1903-1904	
Foil, Martin Boger	1918-1920	
Foil, Oliver Spencer	1920-1924	
Foil, Paul Baxter	1910-1911/1912-1914	WWI
Foil, Robert Edmond	1917-1918	WWI
Foil, S.	1919-1920	
Forsyth, William Frank	1931-1932	
Fowler, J. Stacey	1903-1904	
Fowler, John Anderson	1924-1929	
Fowler, P. V.	1912-1913	WWI
Foy, E. R.	1919-1920	
Foy, Henry Joshua	1921-1923	
Franklin, Robert	1906-1909	
Franks, Richard Furman	1915-1916	
Freed, William Miller	1926-1929	
Freesmith, John Christopher	1913-1915	
Frick, Jos. Gideon	1912-1913	
Friedman, David	1927-1928	
Frix, Walter Brinson	1914-1916	
Frolin, Teddy Nathan	1923-1924	
Fryar, C. F.	Sep 1909	
Frye, Leon Frank	1919-1920	

Name	Date of Registration or Attendance	Degrees/Other
Fryling, Lawrence	1906-1909	WWI
Fuetz, James Clarence	1922-1924	
Fuetz, Thomas Oscar	1922-1924	
Fulenwider, George Osborne	1921-1922	
Fulenwider, Joe	1904-1906	
Fulenwider, Paul Edward	1918-1920	
Fulenwider, Phifer	1904-1906	
Funderburk, Thomas Lee	1917-1918	
Furpless, James Palmer	1920-1922	
Furr, Jacob Ely	1919-1920	
Furr, John Lewis	1923-1924	
Gaddy, Thomas Earl	1924-1925	
Galloway, Thomas Ervin	1924-1926	
Galloway, Willie Frank	1914-1915	
Gammage, Elton Ashley	1924-1927	
Gantt, Edward Lee	1924-1928	
Gardner, James Linnell	1920-1923	
Garibaldi, William Thomas	1923-1925	
Garmon, Hal Peryere	1906-1909	
Garren, Nelson Merrell	1925-1927	
Garrett, George Washington	1925-1929	
Garrison, W. M.	1906-1909	
Gay, Stanley Johnson	1919-1920	
Gibbons, Charles	1927-1929/1930-1931	
Gibbons, Stephen Wallace	1927-1929/1930-1931	
Gibbs, John Blackwelder	1922-1924	
Giles, Richard Bynum	1921-1925	
Gilland, Kenneth Ensor	1926-1927	
Glenn, Couler Edwin, Jr.	1928-1929/1930-1932	
Glenn, Emanuel Gerst	1919-1920	
Glover, William Elton	1928-1929/1930-1932	
Gluyas, J. O.	Sep 1909	
Gnann, Alvin Holland	1919-1920	
Godfrey,	1924-1925	
Gooding, George R.	1910-1911	
Gooding, Robert P.	1910-1911	
Goodman, F. S.	Sep 1909	
Goodman, John	1921-1927	
Goodman, Mason	Sep 1904	
Goodman, Myron	1924-1925	
Goodman, Ree Velt	1923-1925	
Goodnight, Paul B.	1928-1929	
Gore, Calvin Ward	1919-1920	
Gore, Daniel Jackson	1919-1920	
Graham, Carlton Warren	1921-1923	
Grandy, Clifton Glenwood	1918-1922	
Grandy, Joseph Dutf, Jr.	1921-1922	
Grandy, Randy Leon	1919-1922	

Name	Date of Registration or Attendance	Degrees/Other
Green, Abraham B.	1913-1914	
Green, Joe Marven	1906-1909	
Green, Robert Eugene	1922-1925	
Green, Robert Lee	1932-1933	
Greever, Theodore	1930-1931/1932-1933	
Greever, William Otis, Jr.	1930-1932	
Gregory, George Winfield, Jr.	1920-1921	
Gregory, Robert Thornwell	1928-1929	
Gregory, Thomas Twitty	1922-1924	
Gregory, Warren Carey	1920-1921	
Grier, Thomas P.	1913-1914	WWI
Griffin, Charlie Brady	1921-1922	
Griffin, Clyde Riddick	1921-1925	
Griffin, David H.	1932-1933	
Griffin, Stephen Earle	1919-1923	
Griffin, William Henry	1925-1928	
Griggs, Louis Wharton	1924-1925	
Groover, Charles Alexander	1923-1925	
Groover, George W.	1914-1915	
Groover, Joseph W.	1913-1914	WWI
Groseclose, James Benton	1919-1920	
Groseclose, P. B.	1917-1918	
Grovenstein, Sidney Angus	1924-1926	
Guann, Alvin H.	1918-1919	
Guann, Herman Cletus	1917-1919	
Hafer, Berlie Lemuel	1921-1926	
Hafer, Robert Glenn	1924-1926	
Hager, Wylvie	1927-1928	
Hagood, Monts	1916-1917	
Hahn, Arlie Alexander	1931-1933	
Hahn, Arthur Leroy †	1920-1924	
Hahn, Charles Glenn	1923-1928	
Hahn, Charlie Pryce	1906-1909	
Hahn, Gilbert Whitfield	1932-1933	
Hahn, John Marvin	1921-1925	
Hahn, Lloyd Baxter	1922-1926	
Hahn, Robert Young	1926-1929	
Hahn, Verna Mae	1927-1929	
Hahn, Willis Edward	1906-1909	
Haithcock, Ralph	1916-1917	
Haithcox, James Fox, Jr.	1921-1922	
Haithcox, James Frank	1919-1921	
Haley, Ralph Henry	1910-1911/1912-1913	WWI
Hallman, Felix H.	1906-1909	WWI
Hallman, Lem Walter	1906-1909	
Hallman, Will Lee	1913-1914	WWI
Haltiwanger, James Herman, Jr.	1922-1923	
Halton, Jack Anthony Cummings	1921-1923	

Name	Date of Registration or Attendance	Degrees/Other
Hammill, Roy Davis	1924-1925	
Hampton, Mark Watson	1912-1913	
Hamrick, Fred Garland	1913-1915	WWI
Hancock, Lloyd Franklin	1928-1929/1930-1932	
Hankla, James Wadsworth	1930-1931	
Hansen, Geo. Cress	1912-1913	
Harden, Pat Law	1919-1920	
Hardester, E. A.	1920-1921	
Hardesty, John S.	1910-1911/1912-1913	WWI
Hardesty, Wm. J.	1912-1913	WWI
Hardy, Harmon Sidney	1920-1921	
Harkey, Fred L.	1910-1911	
Harkey, George Lawson	1922-1923	
Harkey, Jesse G.	1910-1911	
Harkey, John Baim	1906-1909	
Harkey, Martin Luther	1916-1918	WWI
Harkey, Ralph Lee	1925-1928	
Harkey, Robert Miller	1923-1924	
Harmon, Julian Pope	1916-1920	
Harms, Alfred Precht	1930-1932	
Harms, Ernest Henry	1928-1931	
Harms, Herman	Sep 1909	
Harris, Clifton Gray	1918-1921	
Harris, James Wiley	1916-1917	
Harris, Robert Chalmers	1919-1923	
Harris, Robert Wells	1928-1929/1930-1931	
Harris, Royal Thomas	1927-1928	
Harrison, Charles Franklin, Jr.	1922-1924	
Harry, John McKamie	1920-1923	
Hart, E. T.	1904-1906	
Hart, George Franklin, Jr.	1928-1929	
Hart, George Frederick, Jr.	1928-1929	
Hart, S. B.	1906-1909	
Harton, James Harold	1924-1925	
Hartsell, Franck Seneca	1920-1921	
Hartsell, John Sharp Williams	1923-1925	
Hartsell, L. E.	1910-1911	
Hartsell, Miller, Jr.	1923-1924	
Hartsell, Robert Alton Parker	1923-1925	
Harvell, C. W.	1910-1911	
Harward, James	1921-1924	
Harwood, Edward Graham	1928-1929	
Hasty, Hoyle Fisher	1913-1915	
Hatbry, J. C.	Sep 1909	
Hatley, Charles Cleveland	1903-1904	
Hatley, Homer McGhee	1913-1915	WWI
Hatley, J. F.	1904-1906	
Hawthorne, Clarence E.	1915-1916	WWI

Name	Date of Registration or Attendance	Degrees/Other
Hayes, Norris A.	1906-1909	
Haynes, Junius Lawrence	1915-1916	WWI
Hayward, Charles Webster	1930-1932	
Heglar, Dewey Lee †	1922-1924	
Heglar, G. H.	Sep 1904	
Heidt, Emory Bartow	1928-1929	
Heilig, Clarence Gilbert, Jr.	1919-1923	
Heilig, Lawson Linn	1912-1913	
Heilig, Ralph Eugene	1910-1911/1912-1913	
Heins, Max Thomas	1906-1909	WWI
Heintz, Carl Monroe	1910-1911/1912-1913	WWI
Heintz, Fred L.	1910-1911/912-1913	
Heintz, John Harmon	1916-1918	
Heintz, Z. V.	Sep 1904	
Heinze, Lewis Robert	1906-1909	
Heishman, Hugh McIver	1919-1920	
Heitman, John Adolphus H.	1917-1919	
Helms, Robert Olden	1922-1923/1924-1925	
Henderson, Frank R.	1910-1911	
Henderson, John E.	1919-1920	
Hendley, Albert Eugene, Jr.	1923-1925	
Hendrix, George	1922-1923	
Hendrix, Gilbert	1910-1911	
Hendrix, Harry M.	1903-1904	
Hendrix, Walter Fred	1925-1926	
Herrin, Albert Franklin	1919-1920	
Herrin, Carl Wilson	1923-1925	
Herrin, Fred	1910-1911	
Herrin, Fred	1926-1927	
Herrin, George Lester	1920-1923	
Herrin, John Ray	1917-1922	
Herrin, Luther Lee	1919-1921	
Herrin, Marshall Deway	1917-1923	
Herring, Robert Barney	1926-1928	
Hester, Mark Evans	1914-1917	WWI
Hester, Otto Fulton	1914-1917	
Hester, Walter Lafayette	1915-1917	
Hicks, Patrick Henry	1919-1920	
Higgins, Harry	1924-1925	
Hileman, Conley Dewey	1914-1915	
Hill, Lawson Powell	1925-1926	
Hill, Nall Link	1924-1926	
Hiller, Robert Kendall	1925-1926	
Hiller, William Haskell, Jr.	1925-1926	
Hine, Norman Bernard	1932-1933	
Hinnant, William Lourue	1920-1921	
Hinson, Barron Renfrow	1919-1922	
Hinson, George Dewey	1916-1917	WWI

Name	Date of Registration or Attendance	Degrees/Other
Hinson, Henry Ross, Jr.	1928-1929	
Hinson, R. V.	1904-1906	
Hinson, Riley Edwin	1927-1929	
Hinson, Ted Eli	1923-1928	
Hipp, Lee Columbus	1923-1927	
Hix, M. R.	Sep 1909	
Hodge, Frank Morgan	1921-1922	
Hoffner, Ivey L.	1904-1906	
Hoge, William Harvey	1915-1916	
Holler, Carl Kenneth	1924-1925	
Holler, Vernon McKinley	1928-1929	
Holliday, Thomas Eugene	1925-1927	
Holloway, Harold Coy	1914-1915	WWI
Holloway, Joseph Clark	1919-1921	
Holmes, Eugene	1918-1921	
Holmes, Moses	1921-1923	
Holmes, V. D.	1910-1911	
Holt, Fred Lawrence	1928-1929/1930-1931	
Holt, Judge Thurman, Jr.	1930-1933	
Honeycutt, Alfred Benjamin	1920-1922	
Honeycutt, Carl Adams †	1923-1928	
Honeycutt, John Dixie	1925-1927	
Honeycutt, Keith Leonard	1925-1927	
Honeycutt, Lewis D.	1904-1906	
Honeycutt, William Reid	1910-1911/1912-1913	
Hooper, Henry T.	1919-1920	
Hopkins	1919-1922	
Hopkins, Frank H.	1931-1932	
Hopkins, H.	1932	
Horne, Alard Lewis	1923-1925	
Hotinger, Robert William	1925-1928	
House, John Williamson	1930-1931	
Houser, Blair Falls	1931-1933	
Houston, Ben Stewart	1913-1914	WWI
Houston, Mark Watson	1910-1911/1914-1915/1916-1917	WWI
Howard, James	1920-1921	
Howell, Billy S.	1912-1913	WWI
Howell, Henry Raymond	1913-1915	WWI
Howell, J. E.	1906-1909	
Howie, Robert Cochran	1921-1923	
Hubble, Henry Hobart	1913-1914/1915-1916	
Hubble, Joseph Bryce	1919-1920	
Huddle, Glenn Roy	1931-1932	
Huffman, Clifford Russell	1925-1928	
Hughes, Francis Edward	1928-1929	
Hughey, John Frank	1927-1928	
Hunter, B. McBryce	1910-1911/1912-1913	
Hurlocker, Albern Walter	1915-1917	

Name	Date of Registration or Attendance	Degrees/Other
Hurlocker, Charles Whitman	1923-1925	
Hurlocker, Paul A.	1920-1921	
Hurt, Walter Spears, Jr.	1923-1924	
Hutchinson, Bagley H.	1923-1924	
Hutto, Tom Lewis	1915-1916	WWI
Iley, Harry Bernhardt	1912-1913	
Ingram, Francis Welch	1920-1922	
Ingram, William Arthur	1919-1921	
Ingram, William Ensley	1924-1925	
Irwin, Thomas Shaw	1926-1929	
Isenhour, Harry Edward	1910-1911	
Isenhour, Robert Rufus	1919-1921	
Isenhour, Roy Elmer	1921-1923	
Isenhour, William Guy	1918-1920	
Jackson, Hazel Edward	1923-1924	
Jackson, Robert Lee	1923-1924	
James, Crawford Frank	1920-1925	
James, Voyle Emanuel	1926-1927	
James, William Howard	1925-1927	
Jarrett, Frank Thomas	1928-1929	
Jarvis, Homer Lee	1925-1926	
Jeffcoat, G. H.	1904-1906	
Jelks, Joseph William, Jr.	1932-1933	
Jenkins, Burt Carr	1910-1911/1912-1913	
John, Kelly, Jr.	1930-1931	
Johnson, Charles Lester	1910-1911/1913-1914	
Johnson, Kelly, Jr.	1931-1933	
Johnson, Marion T.	1920-1921	
Johnson, Paul	1910-1911	
Johnson, Williamson W.	1913-1915	
Johnston, Andrew Hall, Jr.	1925-1927	
Johnston, Dorothy Lee	1928-1929/1930-1932	
Johnston, George Bencini	1919-1923	
Johnston, Henry Gustave	1912-1913	
Johnston, Howard W.	1919-1921	
Johnston, Mark Caldwell	1910-1911/1912-1913	WWI
Johnston, Martha Wilhelmina	1928-1929/1930-1931	
Johnston, Robert H.	1918-1919	
Johnston, S. C.	Sep 1903	
Johnston, Williamston Wilson	1912-1913	WWI
Jolley, James Floyd	1913-1914	
Jones, C. G.	1910-1911	
Jones, Cornelius Garver	1912-1915	
Jones, Hiram Denette	1912-1913	WWI
Jones, Miles Caston	1922-1924	
Jones, Willie Frank	1914-1915	
Jowdy, Albert	1928-1932	
Joyner, Elmer Sylvester	1923-1924	

Name	Date of Registration or Attendance	Degrees/Other
Karriker, Erwin Alexander	1919-1920	
Keightley, Frederick Lockling	1931-1933	
Keller, John Henry	1922-1923	
Kennedy, Angus James	1925-1926	
Kennedy, Kenneth Newton	1925-1926	
Kennerly, Charles Frank	1927-1928	
Kennett, Sam Boaz	1906-1909	WWI
Kennington, George Winifred	1912-1913	
Kephart, Grady Anderson	1924-1928	
Kern, John Augustus	1921-1924	
Kern, W. H.	1904-1906	WWI
Kester, G. C.	1904-1906	
Kester, Moses Lee †	Sep 1904	
Ketchie, Robert Lee †	1928-1929	
Ketner, Geo. R.	1904-1906	
Ketner, John C.	1906-1909	
Kieffer, Jay Constantine	1927-1929	
Killinger, James Fred	1923-1925	
Kimball, Arthur Hugo	1918-1921	
Kimball, Ashbel Brown	1925-1927	
Kimball, Ralph Linn	1925-1928	
Kindley, Giles Edgar	1912-1916	WWI/Died
Kindley, John Kenneth	1912-1916	WWI
Kindley, R. Frank	1904-1906	
Kindley, Samuel Ernest	Sep 1904	WWI
Kindley, William Adam, Jr.	1915-1916	
King, Charles B., Jr.	1910-1911/1912-1913	WWI
King, Dallas Marvin	1919-1923	
King, Henry Mitchell	1928-1929	
Kippatuck, S. H.	1910-1911	
Kjellesvig, Erik Norman	1928-1929	
Kluttz, Adam Ross	1912-1916	
Kluttz, Calvin	1910-1911	WWI
Kluttz, Clarence V.	1906-1909	
Kluttz, Frank Martin	1914-1915	
Kluttz, Glenn R.	1918-1920	
Kluttz, Keller Spencer	1922-1925	
Kluttz, Miles Joseph †	1910-1911	
Kluttz, Moses Dwight	1913-1915/1917-1921	
Kluttz, Oren Everette	1914-1918	WWI
Kluttz, R. G.	Sep 1904	
Kluttz, Walter Herman	1924-1927	
Kluttz, William Cletus	1922-1924	
Knebel, Herman Rozzelle	1926-1928/1931-1932	
Knotts, Joseph Evander	1928-1929	
Koch, John Henry, Jr.	1932-1933	
Kohm, George Ehrhardt	1922-1924	
Kornahrens, Arnold W.	1928-1929	

Name	Date of Registration or Attendance	Degrees/Other
Kramer, Richard Louis	1926-1927	
Krider, R. L.	Sep 1909	
Krimminger, Nathan Bost	1912-1915	WWI
Kuck, Jno. Clayton	1912-1913	WWI
Kurfees, Herbert L.	1913-1914	WWI
Kurfees, John Wesley, Jr.	1922-1924	
Kurfees, Marshall Clement	1921-1922	
La Motte, Henry Thomas	1923-1926	
Lambeth, Alfred Thomas	1928-1929	
Landrum, Robert E. Lee, Jr.	1918-1919	
Lanhan, Edward J.	1916-1918	
Latham, Leonard S.	1919-1920	
Lathem, Jas. Garrison	1912-1913	WWI
Lathern, Otis	1913-1914	
Laughlin, James Eugene	1923-1924	
Lawrence, Francis J.	1919-1920	
Lawrence, Gailor Bowie	1925-1928	
Lawrence, Leo Oscar	1919-1920	
Ledingham, Albert	Sep 1904	
Ledingham, Charles Ernest Lee	1928-1929	
Lee, Homer Brown	1906-1909	
Lee, Joe Rhea	1913-1914	
Lee, Louis Wilson	1921-1922	
Lee, Luther Keller	1906-1909	
Lee, Robert Eugene	1913-1914	WWI
Lee, Robt. Edward	1912-1913	WWI
Lefler, C. F.	1904-1906	
Legler, August S.	1910-1911	
Leinster, Robert Osborne	1928-1929	
Leland, K. W.	1910-1911	WWI
Lenhardt, Wm. Richard	1912-1914	WWI
Lentz, A. D.	Sep 1909	
Lentz, A. N.	Sep 1909	
Lentz, Cecil Brown	1906-1909	
Lentz, Fred Henry	1928-1929	
Lentz, Paul Augustus	1903-1904	
Lentz, Roy Edward	1917-1921	
Lentz, Russell Barrier	1912-1914	WWI
Lentz, Samuel Cecil	1923-1924	
Lentz, Stephen C.	1916-1917	
Lenzi, Anthony T.	1932-1933	
Leonard, Eli Jennings	1921-1922	
Lester, Carl Eugene	1914-1915	
Liks, R. E.	Sep 1909	
Lilly, Henry Marvin, Jr.	1926-1929	
Lingle, Floyd Bost †	1909/1912-1913	
Lingle, William Rudolph	1923-1925	
Link, James Lester	1928-1929	

Name	Date of Registration or Attendance	Degrees/Other
Link, John William, Jr.	1927-1929	
Linker, Chas. Edgar	1906-1909	WWI
Linker, S. J.	Sep 1904	
Linn, Charles A. †	1906-1909	
Linn, John Kenneth †	Sep 1903	
Lipe, Carl Cornelius	1920-1922/1923-1924	
Lipe, Clarence Houston	1910-1914/1915-1916	WWI
Lipe, Guy Wilburn	1915-1918	
Lipe, Harvey Lester	1925-1928	
Lipe, Henry Martin	1924-1925/1926-1927	
Lipe, Herbert	Sep 1909	
Lipe, Paul Henry	1923-1929	
Lipe, William Guy	1917-1919	
Lippard, Clyde Roy	1920-1923	
Lippard, David Smith	1906-1909	
Lippard, Walter Archie	1923-1926	
Litaker, Adam Pearlie	1915-1918	
Litaker, Charles Luther	Sep 1904	
Litaker, Richard Vernon	1922-1923	
Little, Clarence Rhyne	1924-1927	
Little, Donald Jovan	1924-1926	
Little, Edward Robert	1917-1918	
Little, G. K.	1910-1911	
Little, John Richard	1921-1924	
Littlejohn, Harry Francis, Jr.	1925-1929	
Loflin, Curtis West	1919-1920	
Loflin, Wm. Franklin	1912-1913/1915-1916	
Loftise, W. F.	1910-1911	
Lohr, Thurmond Carl	1928-1932	
Long, Merl Maltby	1923-1924	
Long, Reece Ira	1903-1904	
Love, William Duncan	1927-1929	
Lovejoy, Percy Francis	1930-1931	
Lovingood, Jack Ben	1932-1933	
Lowder, C. L.	Sep 1909	
Lowder, C. O.	Sep 1904	
Lowder, D. V.	Sep 1909	
Lowder, F. J.	Sep 1909	
Lowder, Fred	1920-1924	
Lowder, Harmon Newell	1931-1933	
Lowder, Hugh Ira	1917-1918/1919-1920	
Lowder, Jay Franklin, Jr.	1926-1927	
Lowder, Fred	1919-1920	
Lowder, W. M.	Sep 1904	
Lucas, James Lynn	1916-1917	
Ludwick, T. B. S.	1906-1909	
Ludwig, J. A.	1904-1906	
Lyerly, Burley Franklin	1918-1919	

Name	Date of Registration or Attendance	Degrees/Other
Lyerly, Henry Brown	1919-1920	
Lyerly, James Gilbert	1910-1911/1912-1913	WWI
Lyerly, Paul Jacob	1910-1915	
Lyerly, R. L.	1910-1911	
Lyerly, Robert Cecil	1932-1933	
Lynch, Donald Elwood	1928-1929	
Lytle, Charles Edgar	1926-1928	
Mabrey, Crowell Benton	1931-1932	
Mabry, Lewis Edward	1917-1921	
Mabry, Robert Cline	1927-1928	
MacAnulty, John Howard	1923-1924	
Mahler, Carl Von K.	1916-1918	
Mahler, Henry George	1922-1923	
Mahler, William August	1916-1918	
Mangum, P. H.	Sep 1909	WWI
Manning, J. Frank	1928-1929	
Martin, Jno. Chandler	1906-1909	
Mattes, Alfred Luke	1928-1929/1930-1931	
Matthews, W. D.	1906-1909	
Mauney, Joseph Stanhope	1926-1928	
May, James Darnell, Jr.	1922-1924	
May, Julian Glenn	1924-1925	
Mayer, Luther Voight	1918-1919	
McAllister, Ben	Sep 1904	WWI
McAllister, Everette	1912-1914	WWI-KIA
McAllister, Frances Foil	1927-1929	
McAllister, George W.	1920-1926	
McAllister, Harmon Carlisle	1923-1928	
McAllister, Harvey J.	1903-1904	
McAllister, John Myles	1917-1918	
McAllister, Joseph Banks	1918-1922	
McAllister, Lee Edmond	Sep 1904	WWI
McAllister, Robert Brown	1921-1926	
McAllister, Virginia Shirey	1927-1931	
McBride, Carl Eugene	1931-1932	
McCall, Horace Nathan	1928-1929	
McCann, James Joseph	1932-1933	
McCarn, Lester W.	1932-1933	
McCarty, James Lindsay	1926-1927	
McCauley, William Ford	1916-1917	
McCormick, Norris Bruce	1928-1932	
McCoy, Jas. B.	1906-1909	
McCoy, L. A.	Sep 1909	
McCoy, R. O.	Sep 1909	WWI
McCullough, Henry Antine, Jr. †	1925-1927	
McCullough, Paul Gerhending †	1919-1922	
McDaniel, John Henry	1916-1919	
McEachern, David Ray		

Name	Date of Registration or Attendance	Degrees/Other
McEachern, Jesse Y.	Sep 1904	
McEachern, Luther Edward	1919-1922	
McEachern, R. L.	1910-1911	
McEachern, Roy David	1906-1909	
McEachern, Sleiman Rutledge	1921-1925	
McEwen, Walter Harold	1921-1922	
McGlohon, Solomon A.	1917-1918	
McKeown, Maxwell Burtell	1928-1929	
McKinley, Kenneth Wright	1921-1922	
McKinley, Reynold A.	1906-1909	
McKnight, George G.	1918-1919	
McLaughlin, Alexander Henry	1923-1925	
McLaughlin, Charles Phillip	1923-1925	
McLaughlin, D. William	1916-1917	
McLaughlin, Thomas Gillespie	1923-1924	
McLendon, Walter Jones	1931-1932	
McManus, Bernard Augustus	1925-1926	
McManus, Curtis Heywood	1919-1921	
McManus, Donovan	1919-1921	
McMullen, Blanche Elizabeth	1927-1928	
McNair, J. P., Jr.	1910-1911	
McNeely, Grady Polk	1913-1914	WWI
McNeely, Jacob B.	1918-1919	
McPherson, Robert Edward	1919-1920	
McSwain, Wyatt	1923-1925	
Medlin, Charles Gustave	1/2/1919	
Medlin, William Wager	1928-1929	
Melchor, A. O.	1919	
Melchor, Hoy Ivey	1917-1918	
Melchor, Lex Dry	1926-1931	
Mendenhall, Delk Fremont	1925-1929	
Metzger, George Snooks	1920-1922	
Meyer, Francis Burns	1928-1929	
Miler, Euclid Liston	1925-1926	
Miller, Albert M.	Sep 1904	
Miller, Arthur Deberry	1913-1914	
Miller, Arthur Willliam	1917-1918	
Miller, Carl J.	1903-1904	
Miller, Charles, E.	1910-1911	
Miller, Claude Wilson	1932-1933	
Miller, Clyde W.	1903-1904	
Miller, Euclid Leston	1926-1928	
Miller, George Hooper	1931-1932	
Miller, J. E.	1906-1909	
Miller, John Ellison	1931-1932	
Miller, Louis Ray	1903-1904	
Miller, Marvin George	1922-1924	
Miller, Robert Centclair	1920-1922	

Name	Date of Registration or Attendance	Degrees/Other
Miller, Robert Leroy	1906-1909	
Miller, Walter Timothy	1919-1922	
Miller, William Adam L.	1906-1909	
Miller, William Albert	1926-1928	
Mills, Harris D.	1920-1921	
Mills, John Pinkney	1913-1914	WWI
Minges, Richard Beryl	1931-1933	
Misamor, R. A.	1904-1906	
Misenheimer, C. W.	1906-1909	WWI
Misenheimer, Ernest L.	Sep 1904	
Misenheimer, G. R.	Sep 1909	
Misenheimer, J. C.	1910-1911	
Misenheimer, Jas. Caswell	1912-1914/1917-1918	
Misenheimer, Mack Holland	1918-1919	
Misenheimer, Rufus S.	1903-1904	
Misenheimer, Whitson K.	1906-1909	
Mock, William Thomas, Jr.	1921-1925	
Monore, R. C.	1904-1906	
Monroe, Paul Eugene †	1910-1914	WWI
Monsees, Carl Henry †	1917-1919	
Moody, J. H.	1910-1911	WWI
Moore, E. R.	1910-1911	
Moore, Thomas Gibbs, Jr.	1928-1929	
Moore, William Archibald	1925-1927/1932-1933	
Moorer, Alfred Edward	1919-1921	
Moose, A. B.	1910-1911	
Moose, Bernard Lee	1926-1927	
Moose, Cromer Banks	1912-1913/1915-1916	WWI
Moose, Frank Raymond	1920-1924	
Moose, Hoy Archibald	1918-1922	
Moose, Hugh Monroe	1919-1921	
Moose, J. D.	1910-1911	
Moose, J. O.	Sep 1909	
Moose, Jacob O.	1914-1915	WWI
Moose, John B.	1903-1904	
Moose, John S.	1920-1921	
Moose, Lewis Cager	1916-1920	
Moose, M. Earl	Sep 1904	
Moose, Paul Alexander	1903-1904	
Moose, Paul Rictor	1911	
Moose, Perry Earl	1921-1924	
Moose, Walter Lee	1909/1912-1914	WWI
Moose, William Jennings, Jr.	1921-1923	
Moose, Wyatt Hileman	1915-1917	
Moran, John William	1928-1931	
Morath, Randolph John	1928-1929	
Morath, Roland Henry	1928-1929	
Moretz, Alfred Dale	1925-1927	

Name	Date of Registration or Attendance	Degrees/Other
Moretz, Charles Deaton	1919-1922	
Moretz, Herbert Leon	1924-1925	
Morgan, Allen Duke	1920-1921	
Morgan, Arthur Lee	1910-1911	
Morgan, J. M.	1904-1906	
Morgan, Jerry	1930-1932	
Morgan, M. W.	1919	
Morgan, Shelby Val	1913-1914	WWI
Morgan, Solomon Rether	1906-1909	
Morris, Edwin Alexander	1917-1919	
Morris, Harry Banks	1921-1922	
Morris, William Lee Meek	1917-1920	
Morrison, Fred	1904-1906	
Morrison, James Wilson	1921-1924	
Morrison, W. S.	1906-1909	
Morton, Claude Bryan	1918-1922	
Morton, Daniel Boone	1930-1932	
Morton, Marvin Hugh	1928-1931	
Moser, Fred Alexander	1922-1925/1926-1927	
Motley, E. P. F.	1904-1906	
Mowrer, Doy Chasion	1919-1921	
Mowrer, Harry	1920-1921	
Moyer, L.	1919-1920	
Murray, E. T.	Sep 1909	WWI
Murray, Edward	1910-1911	WWI
Murray, Jno. Wallen	1912-1913	
Murray, John Asbury	1932-1933	
Murray, Johnnie	1910-1911	
Myles, Lewis Edward	1930-1931	
Nachman, Louis Isadore	1931-1932	
Napier, Will	1910-1911	
Neas, Marcus R.	1913-1914	
Nebel, Arthur Ernest John	1925-1928	
Newell, William Clifford	1910-1913	WWI
Newsome, George Edwin	1931-1933	
Nicholson, J. T.	1924-1925	
Noland, Melvin Knight	1918-1919	
Norman, Ernest C.	1912-1913	
Norman, James Harrison	1917-1918	
Norris, Kenneth McCoy	1920-1922	
Norris, Millard Dean	1926-1928	
Nungezer, William Herman	1917-1920	
Nussman, George Henry Cox	1909/1912-1913	
Nussman, Love	1910-1914	WWI
O'Brien, Euclid Harvey	1924-1925	
O'Brien, Hal Miller	1919-1923	
O'Brien, William Lee	1918-1920	
Oglesby, William Wirt	1906-1909	

Name	Date of Registration or Attendance	Degrees/Other
Olsson, Oscar Helmer	1926-1927	
Orr, James Latta	1913-1914	
Owen, Horage G., Jr.	1932-1933	
Owens, Jonas	1917-1918	
Palmer, Charles Gordon	1919-1920	
Palmer, Henry	1932-1933	
Palmer, Lucius Wilber	1906-1909	
Park, Henry C.	1904-1906	
Park, James Gilbert	1917-1921	
Parker, J. T.	1910-1911	
Parker, James Alfred	1932-1933	
Parker, Lawson DeBerry	1919-1921	
Parker, Stephen Emanuel	1926-1928	
Pate, William Andrew, Jr.	1930-1931	
Patterson, Alexander McLeod	1919-1922	
Patterson, Frank	1910-1911	
Patterson, George R.	1914-1915	
Patterson, Luther Weidner	1921-1923	
Patterson, R. L.	1910-1911	WWI
Patton, Joseph Collis	1930-1931	
Paxton, Andrew Jackson	1926-1927	
Payne, Richard Johnson	1928-1929/1930-1931	
Payne, Samuel Hogan	1924-1926	
Peace, Thomas Arthur	1927-1929	
Peacock, Thomas Ludwig	1932-1933	
Peck, D.	1920-1921	
Peck, Frederick Roy	1910-1914	WWI
Peck, J. C.	1904-1906	
Peck, J. M. †	1903-1904	
Peck, James Keller	1915-1920	
Peck, John Murphy	1906-1909	
Peeler, G. Carl	1906-1909	
Peeler, Wilburn Leon	1918-1920	
Peninger, George Hoyle	1922-1924	
Peninger, H. M.	Sep 1909	
Penney, Charles Brantley	1932-1933	
Penney, Jennings Bryan	1932-1933	
Penninger, C. M.	1904-1906	
Penninger, F. H.	Sep 1904	
Penninger, Homer Clifford	1921-1922	
Penninger, Murray Leonard, Jr.	1921-1925	
Penninger, Ralph Lester	1919-1921	
Perkins, Sam Y.	1920-1921	
Petel, Garah McCullough	1916-1917	
Pethel, Carl Bryan	1916-1918	WWI
Pethel, Garah McC.	1917-1918	
Petrea, Brunner Eugene †		
Petrea, George Washington	1921-1922	

Name	Date of Registration or Attendance	Degrees/Other
Petrea, Gurley Ray	1924-1926	
Petrea, Hugh Columbus	1912-1917	WWI
Petrea, Luther Parker	1920-1924	
Petrea, M. Depna	Sep 1904	
Petrea, M. W.	1910-1911	
Petrea, Marvin Allen	1914-1915/1916-1917	
Petrea, O. A.	Sep 1904	
Petrea, Paul Otis	1917-1921	
Petrea, Smith Henry †	1906-1909	
Petrea, Victor Leslie	1919-1922	
Petrea, Vyron Lyerly	1924-1927	
Petrea, William Price	1917-1919	
Petree, Samuel Lindsay	1922-1925	
Phelgar, Donald Reene	1928-1929	
Phillips, John Christopher †	1926-1929	
Piland, Raphael Julian	1927-1928	
Plaster, Osborne Louis	1928-1929	
Pless, Charles Miller	1931-1932	
Pless, John Albert †	1930-1933	
Plott, E. A.	Sep 1904	
Plott, Fred Arney	1916-1917	
Plott, Glenn Cardell	1925-1926	
Plott, Hugh Franklin	1921-1922	
Plott, J. G.	1920-1921	
Plott, L. J.	1903-1904	
Plyler, Ardrey Jones	1919-1920	
Poole, C. A.	1904-1906	
Poole, Orpheus Williams	1917-1920	
Poole, Ray Irvin	1930-1931	
Poole, Robert Linn	1906-1909	
Porter, Charles Davis	1912-1913	WWI
Praether, George Wilson	1921-1924	
Preston, Irving Sherwood	1928-1929/1930-1931	
Prevo, Willard Jackson	1924-1927	
Price, James Avery	1931-1932	
Price, Robert McCollum †	1913-1915	WWI
Priddy, Henry Washington	1925-1926	
Pritchard, James Tennyson	1921-1922	
Pritchett, William Albert, Jr.	1927-1931	
Proctor, Jasper	1912-1913	
Proctor, William Con, Jr.	1910-1911/1913-1915	
Proctor, William Jasper	1913-1915	WWI
Propst, J.	1919-1920	
Puckett, Lester Alexander	1919-1920	
Pusser, Theodore Roosevelt	1925-1926	
Quante, Fred Henry, Jr.	1920-1923	
Quarterman, William Ruddell	1921-1924	
Quickel, John Cephus	1923-1924	

Name	Date of Registration or Attendance	Degrees/Other
Rahn, Charles G.	1914-1916	WWI
Ramsey, James Franklin	1927-1929	
Rawls, Edward Montrose	1919-1920	
Rayney, James Walter	1915-1916	
Reap, Charles Augustus	1912-1913	WWI
Reeves, Rufus Edgar	1919-1920	
Reeves, Willis Welch	1919-1920	
Reiff, John Donald	1932-1933	
Reiner, Charles Lyman	1928-1929/1930-1931	
Reitzel, Arthur Raymond	1921-1925	
Renno, Bryson Carl	1927-1929	
Respess, Samuel Richard	1926-1927	
Rheinhardt, Robert August	1923-1925	
Rhodes, Paul Heilig	1927-1928	
Rhyne, J. D.	1924-1926	
Rhyne, Paul C.	1903-1904	
Richardson, Frank R.	Sep 1909	
Riddle, D. M.	1910-1911	WWI
Riddle, Jno. Albert	1912-1913	
Riddle, Wilber Lentz	1926-1927	
Ridenhour, Carl Barringer	1919-1922/1923-1924	
Ridenhour, Charles Elmore †	1910-1914	
Ridenhour, Derring Lee	1904-1096	
Ridenhour, Edgar Wertz	1913-1914	
Ridenhour, Homer Lee	1913-1917	WWI
Ridenhour, James	1906-1909	
Ridenhour, L. W.	1904-1906	
Ridenhour, Martin Luther †	1903-1904	
Ridenhour, Paul F.	1912-1913	
Ridenhour, Ralph Lynn	1/2/1919	
Ridenhour, Roy Tiber	1914-1915	WWI
Ridenhour, William Archie	1919-1920	
Rinehardt, A. L.	Sep 1904	
Rinehardt, F. M.	Sep 1904	
Riser, Rupert Sumner	1920-1923	
Ritchie, Adwin LeRoy	1913-1914	
Ritchie, Albert Lee	1922-1924	
Ritchie, C. W.	Sep 1909	
Ritchie, Charles Matthias	1920-1922	
Ritchie, Clarence Homer	1910-1914	WWI
Ritchie, Clarence Ross †	1919-1922	
Ritchie, Clyde Otto	1910-1914	
Ritchie, Crowell Preston	1919-1921	
Ritchie, David L.	1904-1906	WWI
Ritchie, Frank Lutz	1916-1920	
Ritchie, G. Clarence	Sep 1904	
Ritchie, Grover Oscar †	1903-1904	
Ritchie, H.T.	1904-1906	

Name	Date of Registration or Attendance	Degrees/Other
Ritchie, Howard Carr	1917-1918	
Ritchie, Hugh Steffey	1912-1917	WWI
Ritchie, J. T.	1904-1906	
Ritchie, Jesse David	1916-1917	
Ritchie, L. R.	1910-1911	
Ritchie, Malvin	1904-1906	
Ritchie, Orion Delma	Sep 1904	
Ritchie, R. H.	1910-1911	
Ritchie, Ralph Lee	1912-1914	WWI
Ritchie, Ray M.	Sep 1909	WWI
Ritchie, Roy Homer	1912-1913	WWI
Ritchie, Wade Hampton	1916-1918	WWI
Ritchie, Walter Arthur	1915-1918	
Ritchie, William Guy	1922-1924	
Ritz, Daniel	1912-1913	
Robbins, John Cornell	1928-1932	
Roberts, John B.	Sep 1904	
Roberts, Ray Robert	1919-1923	
Robinson, Wideman Christopher	1928-1929	
Rodeffer, John Marshall	1928-1929	
Rodriquez, Orlando Ernesto	1930-1932	
Rogers, Ed. Steward	1906-1909	
Rogers, H. B.	1904-1906	
Rogers, Howard Russell	1928-1929	
Rohr, Ernest Adams	1932-1933	
Rose, Joe Oliver	1928-1929/1930-1931	
Rose, Merrell Mitchell	1932-1933	
Rose, William Andrew	1928-1931	
Rosen, Stanley Jerome	1928-1929	
Rothrock, M. V.	1910-1911	WWI
Roundtree, James Braswell	1919-1920	
Rouse, Eugene D.	1910-1911	WWI
Rowe, C. C.	Sep 1909	
Rowe, J.	Sep 1909	
Royal, Arthur Douglas	1924-1928	
Rubaiz, Cornelius Washington	1920-1923	
Rudisill, Clarence Guy	1927-1929	
Ruffin, David Winston	1921-1923	
Russell, Brown B.	1932-1933	
Russell, Lewis Glenn	1921-1923	
Russell, R. W.	1904-1906	
Rutledge, Ralph Casper	1922-1923	
Safriet, A. A.	1904-1906	
Safrit, C. H.	1910-1911	
Safrit, Harry Lee	1922-1924	
Safrit, Roy Daniel Alexander	1919-1920	
Sanders, Carl Julian	1928-1931	
Sanders, Henry Hannibal	1921-1922	

Name	Date of Registration or Attendance	Degrees/Other
Sappenfield, R. M.	1910-1911	
Saunders, Weldon Washington	1926-1927	
Sauva, George	1932-1933	
Sawyer, Rupert Edgar	1926-1928	
Schenck, Gordon Harry	1916-1918	WWI
Schenck, Jay Ernest	1916-1918	
Schenck, Luther Virgil	1916-1920	
Schnibben, Martin George	1916-1918	
Scott, George Rider	1924-1925	
Scott, J. N., Jr.	1910-1911	
Seaford, Henry Wade	1918-1920	
Sechler, Ernest William	1919-1923	
Seegers, Frank William, Jr.	1927-1929	
Sehorn, Robert Edwin	1920-1923	
Seiler, Carl Wilfred	1918-1921	
Seilter, C. F.	Sep 1909	
Severs, John W.	1920-1921	
Shank, Charles Martin Luther	1927-1928	
Shankle, C. R.	1904-1906	
Shaver, Train Everit	1906-1909	
Shaw, Daniel Alexander	1923-1924/1925-1926	
Shealy, Franklin Carl	1927-1929	
Shepherd, John Dillon †	1921-1923	
Sheppard, Albert Edward	1919-1920	
Sherrill, Charles Marvin	1912-1914	
Shimpock, Lewis William	Sep 1904	WWI
Shinnick, W. B.	1922-1923	
Shirey, John Luther	1927-1932	
Shirey, Julia Katherine	1927-1929	
Shirey, Martha Cook	1927-1929	
Shirley, James Fletcher	1932-1933	
Shoaf, Harry Burton	1926-1927	
Shoe, Arthur Hardy	1906-1909	
Shoe, Berley Davis	1910-1913	WWI
Shoe, Irwin Monroe	1912-1915	WWI
Shoe, J. C.	1904-1906	
Shoe, J. J.	Sep 1909	
Shoe, Oscar Deberry	1906-1909	
Shoe, Robert Lee	1918-1920	
Short, Paul G.	1920-1921	
Shuford, Robert Thomas	1924-1926	
Shulenberger, Margaret S.	1927-1928	
Shulenberger, William Arthur	1923-1927	
Shuping, Oscar Deberry	1903-1904	WWI
Sides, James Fetzer	1906-1909	
Sides, John Adams	1913-1914	
Sides, Ogden Oglesby	1914-1916	WWI
Siegling, Rudolph	1921-1923	

Name	Date of Registration or Attendance	Degrees/Other
Sifford, Harvey Lee	1914-1915	WWI
Sifford, John Craig	1919-1920/1922-1924	
Sifford, Robert Clayborne	1928-1929	
Sifford, W. J.	1910-1911	
Silliman, Robert B.	1914-1916	
Singleton, D. T.	1910-1911	WWI
Sink, Robert Wade	1918-1919	
Sligh, Wilmot H.	1920-1921	
Sloan, David Luther, Jr.	1923-1924	
Sloan, John Gaither	1915-1916	WWI
Sloop, B. C.	Sep 1904	
Sloop, Carl Valentine	1913-1916	
Sloop, Frank Brown	1931-1933	
Sloop, Hubert Harvey	1923-1928	
Sloop, Jas. Francis	1906-1909	
Smith, Daniel L.	1920-1921	
Smith, Earl Basil	1930-1932	
Smith, Edgar Neal, Jr.	1927-1928	
Smith, H. R.	Sep 1904	
Smith, Howard Raymond	1925-1926	
Smith, J. W.	Sep 1909	
Smith, Jacob Archie	1931-1933	
Smith, James G.	1920-1921	
Smith, James N.	1920-1921	
Smith, John Elmer	1921-1922	
Smith, Joseph Newton	1919-1925	
Smith, Martin Luther	1913-1914	WWI
Smith, Milton Monroe	1922-1924	
Smith, Paul Barringer Charles	1924-1927	
Smith, Reginald Lowell	1928-1929	
Smith, Roland Fisher	1922-1923	
Smith, Samuel Bernard	1931-1932	
Smith, Thomas Julian	1919-1920	
Smith, Walter DeWitt	1915-1916	
Smith, Wilkie McKinney	1931-1932	
Smith, William Curtis	1924-1926	
Smithdeal, Clifton Broadnax	1919-1923	
Smithdeal, George Curtis	1919-1923	
Smithdeal, Henry Vestal	1919-1920	
Smithdeal, William Franklin	1919-1923	
Smoak, Charles Robert	1928-1929	
Smyre, Ernest Earl		
Snyder, William Frederick	1927-1928	
Sockwell, George Robert	1913-1915	
Somers, Earnest	1906-1909	
Sorrick, David Cromer	1922-1923	
Sparrow, Thomas, Jr.	1922-1923	
Spears, Davis Heisia	1906-1909	

Name	Date of Registration or Attendance	Degrees/Other
Spradley, H. H.	1919	
Springs, James Columbus	1926-1927	
Stallings, Ernest	1910-1911	
Stallings, Paul Ernest	1912-1913	
Stamper, Clarence A.	1917-1918	
Stark, Abram	1923-1924	
Stark, Fred Rudolph	1923-1924	
Starnes, Ernest Edward	1910-1914	WWI
Steele, George Grisham	1919-1920	
Stellges, George, Jr.	1917-1919	
Stern, Edwin Leopold	1932-1933	
Stevens, Albert	Sep 1904	
Stevens, J. F.	Sep 1904	
Stewart, Arthur Emerson	1928-1929/1930-1931	
Stewart, Samuel Besley	1922-1925	
Stickley, Robert Palmer	Sep 1909	WWI
Stiles, John Wayne	1928-1929/1930-1931	
Stilwell, Meredith Hoil	1921-1922	
Stinson, F.	1931-1932	
Stirewalt, C. H.	1904-1906	
Stirewalt, Clifford Paul	1926-1927	
Stirewalt, Craig	1906-1909	
Stirewalt, H. A.	1904-1906	WWI
Stirewalt, Shirley Monroe	1924-1926	
Stone, Paul Glenn	1923-1926	
Stowe, Roby Conrad	1932-1933	
Streetman, Fred Wimberly	1918-1920	
Stricklin, J. N.	1920-1921	
Stringer, Orum Krehl	1926-1927	
Stroupe, Preston Faison	1921-1924	
Sullivan, Rufus Blair	1923-1925	
Summers, Everett Rivers	1906-1909	WWI
Summerville, Leighton Sloan	1923-1924/1925-1926	
Sumrow, Carl Melvin	1918-1919	
Suther, John Daniel	1922-1927	
Swicegood, Paul Alexander	1930-1931	
Swicegood, Walter James	1924-1925	
Swindell, Roy Carl	1928-1929	
Tarleton, Alonzo Leroy	1926-1927	
Tarte, Enrique Alberto	1928-1929/1930-1931	
Tarte, Jose Antonio	1928-1929	
Tate, Robah Gray	1922-1924	
Taylor, Ernest Brown	1932-1933	
Taylor, G. N.	1910-1911	WWI
Taylor, H. M.	Sep 1909	
Taylor, James Hunter	1924-1927	
Taylor, John Hugh	1917-1918	
Taylor, Otho Allynn	1918-1920	

Name	Date of Registration or Attendance	Degrees/Other
Taylor, Ralph Henderson	1924-1926	
Taylor, Ralph Walter	1924-1926	
Taylor, W. F.	1920-1921	
Teachey, Joseph Daniel	1920-1922	
Teague, Floyd Theodore	1926-1928	
Teeter, H. B.	Sep 1909	
Teeter, M. F.	1910-1911	
Teeter, Mark Harris	1916-1917	
Teeter, Thera Alonzo	1917-1918	
Teeter, William W.	1920-1921	
Teeter, Zebulon †	1913-1914	
Templeton, James Edward	1919-1920	
Thomas, Adam Ray	1918-1921	
Thomas, Arthur J. L.	1904-1906	
Thomas, Elijah Clyde	1919-1922	
Thomas, Irvin Morris	1915-1916	WWI
Thomas, Junius Daniel	1910-1911/1912-1913	
Thomas, Luther Alexander †	1906-1909	
Thomas, Walter Carr	1921-1925	
Thomason, Carl Gradon	1923-1924	
Thomason, Claude Fisher	1921-1926	
Thomason, Harold Elwood	1917-1921	
Thompson, Benjamin Jackson	1923-1926	
Thompson, Coyet A.	1918-1919	
Thompson, E. E.	1920-1921	
Thompson, Frank R.	1917-1918	
Thompson, John Thomas	1925-1927	
Thompson, John Willard	1930-1932	
Thompson, Percy Maron	1919-1920	
Thorpe, Carl Barnwell	1919-1920	
Threat, Ward Beecher	1912-1913	WWI
Timnes, Edgar Briscoe	1916-1918	
Tobiassen, Thoralph Johann	1918-1921	
Towe, Lloyd Everett	1926-1927	
Townsend, Henry Clay	1931-1932	
Traiano, Anthony Michael	1928-1932	
Trammell, Earl William	1927-1928	
Tranum, Howard Broadway	1928-1929	
Trevey, John Lockridge	1931-1932	
Trexler, Caleb Lee	1922-1925	
Trexler, Charles Otho P.	1910-1915	
Trexler, Clarence William	1913-1917	WWI
Trexler, Duke Caleb	1906-1909	
Trexler, E. B. C.	1910-1911	
Trexler, Edgar Calvin Ray †	1917-1918/1919-1922	
Trexler, Harvey L.	1906-1909	WWI
Trexler, J. F.	1910-1911	
Trexler, Richard Floyd	1912-1913	

Name	Date of Registration or Attendance	Degrees/Other
Trexler, Robert Lee	1906-1909	
Trexler, Wm. R.	1912-1913	
Trexler, Zebulon Baxter	1906-1909	
Trimpey, John S.	1932-1933	
Trioiano, A. M.	1932	
Troutman, Hawley Buford	1913-1915	
Troutman, Martin Luther	1914-1916	WWI
Tucker, Alma Irene	1927-1928	
Tucker, C. H.	Sep 1904	
Tucker, Herman	1915-1916	
Tucker, Milton Lee	1913-1914	WWI
Tucker, W. S.	1925-1926	
Turner, Augustus Harris	1928-1931	
Turner, Curtis Wertz	1927-1929	
Turner, H. D.	Sep 1904	
Turner, James Harold	1922-1923	
Tysinger, Jno. Lloyd	1916-1917	
Umana, C. Humberto Julio	1928-1929	
Ury, Arthur Giles	1912-1915	WWI
Ury, John H.	1919-1920	
Valley, Leland F.	1912-1913	
Van Mechelen, Carl Victor L.	1928-1929/1930-1931	
Van Poole, Glen Martin	1921-1923	
Van Poole, Otho Lee	1913-1914/1915-1916	
Vandewater, Harman	1928-1929	
Vaughan, Russell James	1924-1925	
Verica, John E.	1932-1933	
Vestal, Albert Cecil	1920-1923	
Vickers, John Soule	1928-1929/1930-1931	
Vogler, C. F.	Sep 1909	
Vreeland, Donald G.	1912-1913	
Wade, Torrance M	1916-1918	
Wagg, W. H.	Sep 1904	
Wagoner, George Andy	1913-1914	WWI
Wagoner, Hubert Edward	1930-1932	
Walker, Donald Aaron J.	1906-1909	
Walker, I. M.	1904-1906	
Walker, J. H.	1906-1909	
Walker, James Ernest †	1919-1923	
Walker, Oscar T.	1906-1909	
Walker, Paul Alexander	1913-1914	
Walker, R. H.	1906-1909	WWI
Walker, R. L.	1906-1909	
Walker, Sidney Franklin	1917-1918/1919-1920	
Wall, Turner Samuel Pinkney	1924-1925	
Walters, Charles Keueppelberg	1922-1925	
Walters, James Penn	1922-1923	
Walton, Thomas Myron	1931-1933	

Name	Date of Registration or Attendance	Degrees/Other
Ward, Lester Ellsworth	1931-1932	
Waring, F. G.	1910-1911	
Warlick, Charles Wharton, Jr.	1922-1925	
Warlick, Hal Gerhardt	1931-1933	
Warlick, Maxwell	1922-1923	
Warren, Clarence Allen	1921-1922	
Waters, Gordon McDavid	1931-1932	
Waters, James Howell	1930-1933	
Watkins, Charles Duard	1906-1909	WWI
Watkins, James Arthur	1931-1932	
Watson, Henry Gilbert	1922-1924	
Watson, John Allison	1928-1929/1930-1931	
Watts, Herman Hugh	1923-1927	
Watts, Marvin Craig	1922-1927	
Watts, William Allen	1918-1922	
Weant, Will W.	1906-1909	
Weatherman, Robert Preston	1919-1920	
Webster, Frederick Lee	1931-1932	
Weir, W. H.	1920-1921	
Weiser, Charles Henry	1921-1926	
Weisner, Albert Kenneth	1922-1925	
Wells, Robert Russell	1932-1933	
Welsh, Dennis Barrier	1903-1904	WWI (See NC College & CECS)
Welsh, Jno. Calvin	1912-1913	
Welsh, Steve	1904-1906	WWI
West, Arthur	1904-1906	
West, Clarence Milton	1920-1922	
West, George Elvester	1916-1917	WWI
Westcott, Arthur Edward	1928-1929/1930-1931	
Wharton, Donald Lincoln Lee	1931-1933	
Wheless, Glenn	1923-1924	
Wheless, Richard D.	1923-1924	
Wheless, Richard Vann	1924-1925	
White, Archie Horatio, Jr.	1923-1926	
White, Carey Culp	1932-1933	
White, Howard Osborne	1915-1916	
White, Ralph Hall	1918-1919	
Whitesides, John Edward, Jr.	1919-1922	
Whitley, Ayer Crouch	1924-1926	
Whitley, C. A.	1904-1906	
Whitley, D. P.	Sep 1909	WWI
Whitley, Henry Ward B.	1906-1909	
Whitley, Lawrence B.	1906-1909	
Whitley, Roscoe Bruner	1922-1923	
Whitley, William Grier	1906-1909	
Widenhouse Ernest C. †	1906-1909	
Widenhouse, D. T.	1910-1911	

Name	Date of Registration or Attendance	Degrees/Other
Widenhouse, Donald F.	1912-1913	
Widenhouse, J. C.	1903	
Widenhouse, Lloyd	1927-1928	
Widenhouse, Marvin Gibson	1923-1924	
Wilhelm, Jas. W.	1906-1909	
Wilhelm, Robert Forest	1912-1913	WWI
Wilhite, Julius Arnold	1918-1920	
Wilkerson, James Heilig	1923-1924	
Williams, Calvin V. B.	1906-1909	
Williams, George Austin	1921-1922	
Williams, John Thomas	1931-1932	
Williams, M. W.	1904-1906	
Willis, Bert Capehart	1928-1922	
Willis, Charlie McDonald	1918-1919	
Willis, M.	1919-1920	
Wills, Leonard	1931-1932	
Wilson, Brice Beverly	1919-1920/1921-1922	
Wilson, Britton Ezell	1912-1913	
Wilson, Geo. Wm.	1910-1913	WWI
Wilson, Rupert Marley	1925-1928	
Winecoff, Cress Alexander	1903-1904	
Winecoff, E. J.	Sep 1909	
Winecoff, Wm. Harley	1914-1915	WWI/KIA
Wingard, John Ralph	1914-1915/1916-1917	WWI
Winslow, Thomas Russell	1932-1933	
Winstead, James Edwin	1930-1932	
Wise, W. C.	Sep 1909	
Wolff, Miles Hoffman	1915-1917	WWI
Wollen, Warren Boyd	1931-1932	
Woodall, Leigh Cedrick	1930-1933	
Woods, John P.	1932-1933	
Woolard, Beverly Thomas	1927-1929	
Woolard, Justin	1927-1929	
Woollen, Warren Boyd	1932-1933	
Worsley, Gaston E.	1914-1915	WWI
Writhcett, William Albert, Jr.	1928-1929	
Wyche, Norman Hunter	1928-1929	
Wylie, Lathan Brown	1924-1925	
Yarborough, Edgar Calvin, Jr.	1923-1924	
Yonce, Frank David	1930-1933	
Yorke, Claude Elwood	1924-1926	
Yost, John Lewis †	1906-1909	
Yost, Lonnie Mitchell	1916-1917	WWI
Yost, O. H.	Sep 1904	
Younce, Charles Kepley	1913-1914	
Yount, Walter Nicholas †	1923-1926	

ENDNOTES

The Beginning

1 Arthur Dobbs, "Letter to Board of Trade of Great Britain, Aug 1755," *The Colonial Records of North Carolina, Vol. 5*, p. 356, William L. Saunders (ed.), Secretary of State, (Raleigh: Josephus Daniels, Printer for the State, 1887), http://docsouth.unc.edu, CSR Documents in Vol. 5, #112.

2 Ben F. Callahan, *The Founders & Associated Families of St. Stephen's Lutheran Church,* Unpublished manuscript, 2011.

3 Bernard W. Cruse, Jr., *Union Churches in North Carolina During the Eighteenth & Nineteenth Century*, (Published by Bernard W. Cruse, Jr. 2001,) vii.

4 William K Boyd and Charles A. Krummel (eds.), "German Tracts Concerning the Lutheran Church in North Carolina During the Eighteenth Century," *North Carolina Historical Review*, Vol. VII, No. (Jan 1930), pp. & 89.

5 Jacob L. Morgan, DD; Bachman S. Brown, Jr., DD, and John D.Hall, (eds.), *History of the Lutheran Church in North Carolina, 1803-1853,* (United Evangelical Lutheran Church of North Carolina, 1953), p. 23.

6 Ibid.

7 John A. Suther, *History of St. John's,* https://www.stjhonslutheran church.net/our-history.

8 Gotthardt D. Bernheim, DD and George H. Cox, *The History of The Evangelical Lutheran Synod and Ministerium of North Carolina,* (Lutheran Publication Society, Philadelphia, PA,1902), p.25.

9 Ibid., p. 178.

10 "Lutheran Theological Seminary," Wikipedia contributors, https://en.wikipedia.org.

11 *History of the Evangelical Lutheran Synod*, p. 180.

12 Jacob A. Linn, "President's Address," *Minutes of The Forty-ninth Meeting of Evangelical Lutheran Synod of North Carolina, convened at Frieden's Church, Guilford Co. NC on Apr 1852,* (J. J. Bruner, Book, Salisbury, NC, 1852), p. 5.

"... we have but one subject that we would recommend to your wisdom and discretion, one which we conceive of vital importance to the interests of our Church in North Carolina, and one amply precedented. The educational wants of that portion of our beloved Zion, embraced within the limits of our Synod, has long been a desideratum. Believing with many others that the resources necessary to the establishment of a High School of a collegiate character, are amply sufficient, and adding to this the general wish of our laity, and their expressed willingness to support such an Institution, the time, we believe, has come when we should nobly act on this subject. ... And shall we fail to develop the talent and intellect within our own church, by neglecting to secure the means through which such desirable object be effected? ...

That the German mind, comprising the great majority of our Laity, is susceptible of the most profound, as well as useful thought and investigation, is evidenced in all the different departments of literature, science, and theology of Germany – our ancestral land. Shall be bury that mind, committed to our care and tuition, for want of action in supplying the means necessary to its improvement? Nay, verily, brethren. But our object was merely to present this subject to your prayerful and prudent consideration. We have no plan or basis of an institution to present – no suggestion to make relative to a place of location. These considerations should be the result of the united deliberations of this body..."

13 Ibid., p. 16.

14 "Proceedings of NC Synod Appointed Convention at Concord, NC, July 22, 1852," *Records of the North Carolina Synod Evangelical Lutheran Church in America, 1852.* Carl L. Rudisill, Lenoir-Rhyne University, Hickory, NC.

15 Ibid.

"Whereas, The Evangelical Lutheran Synod of North Carolina, having deemed it not only expedient and essentially necessary, but a solemn duty imposed on her Ministry and Membership, to establish an Institution of high Literary and Scientific character within her bounds for the proper training of her youth, and a more general diffusion of knowledge among the people at large; and to effect said desirable object, has created this Convention by a resolution at its last session,

Therefore, Resolved, I. That this Convention, in the name of the Triune God, and in humble reliance on His aid, and the efficient co-operation of all concerned; proceed to mature a plan for the establishment of an Institution (hereafter to be named and located) to be exclusively devoted to the classical education, literacy training, and moral improvement of all who may come under its tuitionary and fostering care.

II. Resolved, That we will, in reliance upon the charity of the people at large, and "according as God has prospered us" raise the sum of $20,000 as a perpetual investment of the endowment of Professorships; and that we regard the Scholarship plan, as possessing man peculiar advantages, and as the one best calculated to promote the success of said Institution, and to secure the amount above specified.

III. Resolved, That this Convention adopt some method to procure the above named sum by the sale of one hundred Scholarships at two hundred dollars each, said Scholarships to be perpetual and transferable as any other invested capital.

IV. Resolved, That it be left to the option of the purchaser to pay the Two Hundred Dollars at the time of purchasing, into the hands of the Treasurer, or to secure the same by giving bond with approved securities, and the payment of lawful semi-annually: but that said Two Hundred Dollars be required to be paid into the hands of the Treasurer of said Institution, within ten years from the time of purchase.

V. Resolved, That the regular Tuition of all patrons of said Institution, not possessing Scholarships, shall be double the amount of the above rates.

VI. Resolved, That this Institution shall be under the government of a Board of Directors, to meet semi-annually, and as often at intermediate times as they may think expedient – Said Board to be subject to the advice and control of the Evangelical Lutheran Synod of North Carolina, and to which they shall present a written report at each of her annual meetings, concerning the fiscal state and prosperity of said Institution, and such recommendations as may be deemed advisable.

VII. Resolved, That this Board consist of Twelve Directors, six of whom shall be chosen from among the Ordained Ministers in connection with the Ev. Luth. Synod of NC and six laymen, who may be chosen from among the Lutheran membership, or from any other Christian denomination.

VIII. Resolved, That this Convention elect a temporary Board of Directors, agreeably to the provisions in the preceding resolution, to remain in office until the next annual meeting of Synod, when a new Board shall be created by Synod, and their respective terms of office defined; and that said Synod ever after have the exclusive right of electing the Board of Directors.

IX. Resolved, That after the aggregate sum of ten thousand dollars has been secured, the Evan. Luth. Synod of NC either at its regular annual meeting or a called session, shall proceed to elect and call a Professor to said Institution, after which the Board of Directors shall forever have the exclusive authority of electing additional Professors and filling up all vacancies.

X. Resolved, That in the event any sister Synod shall contribute to the funds of this institution to the amount of $1,000 in actual cash; or shall send up to the Treasurer of this Institution lawful annual interest of the above amount, shall be entitled to a Directorship, and for every additional $1,000 an additional Director in said Institution.

XI. Resolved, That the Board of Directors be responsible to the Synod of North Carolina and may be removed from office by the same for such causes and in such manner as said Synod shall specify.

XII. Resolved, That the Board of Directors frame a Constitution in consonance with the principles embodied in the foregoing resolutions, for the government and regulation of said Institution.

XIII. Resolved, That this Convention, forthwith, or through its Board of Directors within thirty days from this date select and put in nomination two or more sites as suitable places of location for said Institution and that a Committee of three be appointed at each place by the same, whose duty it shall be to open books for subscription in their respective localities, to raise funds wherewith to purchase suitable College grounds and to erect suitable buildings thereon; and that said books remain open until 12 o'clock, M., of the first day of December, 1852, at which time, on comparing said subscriptions, all shall be annulled excepting the highest, at which place said Institution shall be located.

XIV. Resolved, That five suitable individuals be appointed by the Board of Directors, a Building Committee, whose duty it shall be so soon as the locality is determined, and the ten thousand dollars of perpetual investment aforesaid secured, to make the necessary arrangements and superintend the construction of a suitable building or buildings for said Institution, and that the dimensions and style of said building or buildings, be so regulated as to correspond in some degree to the amount of the funds raised: Provided, however, that said building or buildings be neither too ordinary to command respect, nor too expensive to involve us in unnecessary cost.

XV. Resolved, That it be recommended to every Minister connected with the Evan. Luth. Synod of NC to present the claims of this Institution to the people of his charge.

XVI. Resolved, That the Board of Directors elect a Treasurer, whose duty shall be to take charge of all monies belonging to said Institution, and shall keep them subject to the order of said Board: Said Treasurer to give bond with approved security in such sum as the Board may direct, and present at each annual meeting of Synod a detailed and faithful account of the state of the Treasury. Respectfully submitted Joseph A. Linn, Chairman"

16 Ibid.

17 *Records of the North Carolina Synod Evangelical Lutheran Church in America, 1853.*

The Mt. Pleasant proposal consisted of pledges from over 200 individuals and an offer of sixteen acres of land from Mathias Barrier, Secretary of the Board of Directors.

18 Ibid.

19 Minutes of the Board of Directors of Western Carolina Male Academy, (MS), Carl A. Rudisill Library, Lenoir-Rhyne University, Hickory, NC, (herein after cited as Minutes WCMA).

20 Ibid.

21 *Minutes of the Fiftieth Meeting of Evangelical Lutheran Synod of North Carolina, convened at Newton, Catawba Co. on Apr 1853,* (The Carolina Watchman Office, Salisbury, NC, 1853), p. 9.

The Tennessee Synod – in 1819 there developed in the North Carolina Lutheran Synod a disagreement over the ordination of a Pastoral candidate, David Henkel. At the time Henkel was a "Catechist" within the Synod, being allowed to preach and baptize. He was serving as the Minister at several congregations in Lincoln County, NC. At the Convention held at St. John's Lutheran Church in Cabarrus County in 1819, the Synod, after learning of some "complaints" against Henkel (there were also several disputes between members of the Synod and Henkel over interpretation of church doctrine) the voted not to grant him ordination. A week after the Synod Convention ended, Henkel's father, Rev. David Henkel, a well-known Lutheran Minister, held an unauthorized meeting, again at St. John's, and proceeded in defiance of the Synod, to ordain his son. At the next convention in 1820, held in a church served by David Henkel, the Synod refused to recognize "the unlawful ordination." As a result of the Synod's decision, Henkel's supporters held a meeting in Sullivan County, TN in July 1820 and formed what was to be called The Evangelical Lutheran Tennessee Synod. Following the creation of the Tennessee Synod, several congregations in North Carolina, mainly in the western portion of the state, left the NC Synod or formed new churches under the Tennessee Synod.[1] By 1853, the Tennessee Synod reported 75 congregations in four states, with at least 50 in North Carolina.[2] The Tennessee remained a strong presence in western NC and established its own school in Newton, NC in 1880. This school became Concordia College in 1881 and remained affiliated with the Tennessee Synod until 1892. In 1895, the Tennessee Synod affiliated itself with Lenoir College in Hickory, NC. In 1920, the Tennessee Lutheran Synod and the North Carolina Lutheran Synod reunited to form the United Evangelical Lutheran Synod of North Carolina and Lenoir College was established as the new Synod's institution of higher learning. Lenoir College was renamed Lenoir-Rhyne College in 1924.[3]

[1] *The History of The Evangelical Lutheran Synod,* pp. 44-49.

[2] Socrates Henkel, DD, *History of the Evangelical Tennessee Lutheran Synod,* (Henkel & Co., New Market, VA, 1890), pp, 137 & 270.

[3] https://en.wikipedia.org/wiki/Concordia_College_and_University and Morris, Jeff L. and Ellis G. Boatmon, *A Centennial History of Lenoir Rhyne College,* (Downing and Company, Virginia Beach, VA), p. 12.

22 *Minutes of the Fiftieth Meeting of Evangelical Lutheran Synod,* p. 9.

"That as the cause of education is all-important in promoting an enlightened Christianity and the advancement of the best interests of the

Redeemer's kingdom, and never more so than at the present time; your committee have learned with lively satisfaction that their brethren of the NC Synod feel encouraged to engage in the establishment of an Institution, which may secure to this church within the bounds of said Synod, the advantage it is intended to confer. Whilst your committee are aware of the general difficulties connected with the establishment of an Institution of learning, however much needed, they hope that in the present case, these difficulties will not be such to discourage them in the enterprise in which they are about to engage. They are pleased to learn that the circumstances in the present case are such as to give the hope of encouraging success, therefore:

Resolved, That in the establishment of a Classical Institution by the Synod of NC that body has the best wishes of this Synod for its success.

Resolved, That in view of the obligations resting on this body, in sustaining the institution already depending on its support, this Synod regrets its inability to do more than express the Christian sympathy and good wishes of this body on its behalf.

Resolved, That should such an Institution be established, we hope it may tend to preserve and strengthen the bond of union which should characterize the relation existing between us."

23 Ibid., p. 9.

24 Ibid., p. 11.

25 Ibid., p. 13.

26 Ibid., pp. 20-21.

Part I-Business

27 *Minutes WCMA*, June 13, 1853.

28 Ibid.

29 *Minutes of the Fiftieth Meeting of Evangelical Lutheran Synod*, p. 21.

30 *Minutes of the Evangelical Lutheran Synod and Ministerium of North Carolina, Bethel Lutheran Church, Stanly Co. NC, May 1854,* n.p., n.p.p, p. 37.

William Gerhardt, b. 28 Oct 1817 in Hesse, Demstadt, Germany, the son of Baltzer Gerhardt and Anna Maria Henz. He received his BA degree in 1841 from Gettysburg College, PA and taught school in Maryland and Ohio for the next several years. He attended the Lutheran Seminary in Gettysburg, PA and was ordained in 1847. From 1847 until 1855, he served in various education positions in Pennsylvania. He was appointed Principal of Western Carolina Male Academy in 1855 and served in that position until 1859. During this time he also served as Minister to Mt. Carmel Lutheran Church, located near the village of Mt. Pleasant. He served as President of the NC Lutheran Synod in 1856-57. In 1859, Rev. Gerhardt became the Principal of Franklin Academy in Concord, NC. Later in 1859, he returned to Pennsylvania where he served as a minister in several churches. In 1860, he moved to Lebanon Co. PA and in 1867 he became the minister in Martinsburg, WV, where he remained for several years as a minister and Principal of several schools. Rev. Gerhardt retired in 1890 at the age of 73. He died on 6 Dec 1917 at the age of 100 and is buried in Martinsburg, WVA.[1]

[1] "Gerhardt, William," *Life Sketches of Lutheran Ministers: North Carolina & Tennessee Synods – 1773-1965.* Bachman S. Brown, DD, et al. (eds), (North Carolina Synod of the Lutheran Church in America, The State Printing Co., Columbia, SC, 1966.), p. 74.

31 Papers of Charles P. Bansemer, June 13, 1853, C. F. Bansemer Papers #3688, The Southern Historical Collection, Wilson Library, University of North Carolina at Chapel Hill, Chapel Hill, NC, (hereafter cited as Bansemer Papers.)

"One day after date Jacob Ludwick as principal and J. J. Misenheimer, C. P. Cox, John L. Henderson, and P. J. A. Haines as securities promise to pay to Christopher Melchor, President of the Board of Directors and Joseph Linn, — Thesis, L. C. Groseclose, William G. Harter, Samuel Rothrock, John D. Scheck, Matthias Barrier, Charles L. Partee, Caleb Heilig, Daniel Barrier and John Shimpock, Directors of the Western North Carolina Academy and their successors in office as trustees of the Evangelical Lutheran Synod of North Carolina the sum of twelve thousand dollars for the faithful and true payment when we find ourselves our Heirs? Administrators Executors and Assignees. In testimony whereof we have herewith signed our names and affixed our seals this 13th day of June 1853.

The conditions of the above obligation are such that whereas at a Meeting of the aforesaid Directors of the aforesaid Western Carolina Academy in Mount Pleasant on the 8th day of June 1853, according to adjournment the said Jacob Ludwick was duly elected Treas of the Building Fund of said Literary Institution; now in the event the said Jacob Ludwick shall faithfully collect and pay on the above mentioned fund according to the order of the aforesaid President and Directors of said Western North Carolina Academy Trustees as aforesaid and in all other respects faithfully discharge the trust and consideration reposed in him as Treasurer of said fund then the above obligation to be null and void but otherwise to remain in full force and effect.

Teste Robt. E. Love, Jacob Ludwick, John L. Henderson, J. J. Misenheimer, C. P. Cox, P. J. A. Haines."

32 *Minutes WCMA,* June 13, 1853."

William Addison Weddington was born in Cabarrus Co. NC on 8 Sep 1808, the son of John and Mary Goodman Weddington. He died in Cabarrus Co. NC on 29 November 1876. Weddington was orphaned at age 14 and was adopted by Richard Martin, under whom he served his apprenticeship as a carpenter and builder. He became a well known builder of several local churches including Bethpage Methodist, Poplar Tent Presbyterian, Prospect Presbyterian, and Central Methodist.[1]

[1] "The Weddington Webpage," http://Millenium.Fortunecity.com [This webpage is no longer active.]

33 Ibid.

34 "North Carolina College–Origins and Some Facts of Its History," *NC College Advance*, Mt. Pleasant, NC, June 1890, p. 136.

35 Ibid.

Daniel Moreau Barringer was the son of "General" Paul M. Barringer of Mecklenburg/Cabarrus Co. NC. Daniel Barringer's grandfather, John Paul Barringer, a German immigrant to the US in the 1740's, moved to North Carolina from Pennsylvania in the 1740's and settled along Dutch Buffalo Creek about two miles from what later became the village of Mt. Pleasant. John Paul Barringer was a member of Dutch Buffalo Church, one the first Lutheran Congregations in the state of North Carolina and he was a founding member and major benefactor of St. John's Lutheran Church built in the early 1770's in what was then Mecklenburg Co. NC. John Paul Barringer also introduced the bill in the NC Legislature to create Cabarrus Co. NC from Mecklenburg County in 1792. Daniel Barringer was a member of the NC State Legislature in 1829-34, 1840-42, and 1854. He was a member of the US House of Representatives from the 2nd District of NC 1843-47 & 3rd District 1847-49. He served as the US Minister to Spain from 1849-1853.[1]

[1] Carolyn A. Wallace, "Daniel Moreau Barringer," www.ncpedia. org/biography/barringer-daniel-moreau.

36 Minutes WCMA.

37 *Minutes of the Evangelical Lutheran Synod and Ministerium of North Carolina, convened at Bethel Lutheran Church, Stanly Co. NC on May 1854,* (Miller & James, Salisbury, NC, 1854), p. 19.

38 *Minutes WCMA*, December, 1854.

39 *Minutes WCMA*, January, 1855.

40 "Papers of George Franklin McAllister", Eastern Cabarrus Historical Society Library, Mt. Pleasant, NC. (hereafter cited as McAllister Papers, ECHS).

One of the brickmasons from Gaston County was Harvey Caswell McAllister, an 18 year old of Scots-Irish descent, whose cousin, Mary Costner, was married to a Mt. Pleasant merchant, Matthew Cook. While working on the Academy building, McAllister resided with his cousin's family. After his work was finished on the Academy, McAllister returned home to Gaston County and in 1861, with the outbreak of the Civil War, he enlisted in the 20th NC Regiment. He served with the 20th Regiment only a short time, however, when he transferred to Co. H of the 8th NC Regiment, a unit organized in Mt. Pleasant by his cousin, Jonas Cook, son of Mathew Cook. McAllister was elected 3rd Lieutenant in Co. H. in August 1861 and in 1862, he and his fellow soldiers were stationed on Roanoke Island on the coast of North Carolina. In January of 1862, Roanoke Island was attacked by Federal soldiers and McAllister, along with virtually all of the 8th Regiment were captured and placed on parole. While on parole and awaiting "exchange" the soldiers were allowed to return to their homes. McAllister, however, chose not to return to his native Gaston County, but instead moved back to Mt. Pleasant where he again resided with his cousin's family. This second stay in Mt. Pleasant apparently rekindled some old relationships as McAllister and his 17 year old cousin, Francis Cook, daughter of Mathew Cook, began courting, and eventually McAllister asked for Francis' hand in marriage. Since Francis was a minor, permission for her to marry had to be given by her father, who, when asked, refused to give his consent. As a result, on the evening of June 19th, 1962, H. C. and Francis "eloped" to the "other side of Mt. Pleasant," where, with Francis' brother, Jonas, acting as a witness, H. C. and Francis were married by a local minister.

H. C. and Francis had little time to celebrate their wedding, for in August, the members of Co. H were officially "exchanged" and the 8th Regiment was reorganized. H. C. and his new brother-in-law, Jonas Cook, reported for duty and continued in service for the next three years. H. C. was wounded twice and achieved the rank of 1st Lieutenant before the end of the war.

When H. C. returned home at the end of the war, he proceeded to move his wife and two children to Gaston County where he returned to his work as a brickmason. Sometime after 1870, however, H. C. moved his family back to Cabarrus County and purchased a farm just west of Mt. Pleasant. In 1880, McAllister moved his family into the Town of Mt. Pleasant and constructed a home across the street from his father-in-law and a short distance from NC College. In 1877 H. C. was appointed to the Board of Directors of NC College. He served on the Board for over 30 years with several terms as Treasurer, Secretary and President. During the later years of his life, McAllister was one of the foremost advocates for NC College and for education in general in Cabarrus County. He served on the Cabarrus County School Board and was quite active in organizing the local County Agriculture Fair, an event which came to be conducted in almost every county in the state in the early 1900's. McAllister died in 1914 and is buried at the Holy Trinity Lutheran Cemetery in Mt. Pleasant, NC.[1]

[1] "McAllister Family Papers," Eastern Cabarrus Historical Society, Mt. Pleasant, NC.

41 *Minutes of the Evangelical Lutheran Synod and Ministerium of North Carolina, Bethel Lutheran Church,* p. 20.

42 Ibid.

43 *Minutes of the Evangelical Lutheran Synod and Ministerium of North Carolina, convened at Frederick Town, Davidson Co. NC, convened on May 1855,(*Miller & James, Salisbury, NC), p. 17.

44 Ibid.

45 *Minutes WCMA,* April, 1855.

46 Ibid.

47 *Minutes of the 53rd Annual Meeting of The Evangelical Lutheran Synod and Ministerium of North Carolina, convened at St. Paul's Lutheran Church, Iredell Co. NC. on April 1857,* (J. J. Bruner, Book and Job Printer, Salisbury, NC, 1857), pp. 26-27.

48 *Minutes WCMA*, April, 1856.

49 Cabarrus County Deed Book 20, pp. 383-384, Mar 1858. Cabarrus County Register of Deeds, Concord, NC.

In 1858 William A. Weddington declared debts totaling $1,516 owed to fourteen individual or businesses. Several of these debts were to persons or businesses in Mt. Pleasant. Weddington employed William R. Scott, owner of the Mt. Pleasant Hotel, as his trustee in settling these debts. It is not clear if the debts were paid but Weddington declared bankruptcy in 1873.

50 *Minutes of the 53rd Annual Meeting of The Evangelical Lutheran Synod and Ministerium of North Carolina, convened at St. Paul's Lutheran Church, Iredell Co. NC. on April 1857,* (J. J. Bruner, Book and Job Printer, Salisbury, NC, 1857), pp. 8-9.

51 Ibid. pp. 26-27.

52 *Minutes of the Fiftieth Meeting of Evangelical Lutheran Synod of North Carolina*, 1853, p.11.

53 *Minutes of the 54th Annual Meeting of the Evangelical Lutheran Synod and Ministerium of North Carolina convened at St. Paul's Lutheran Church, Alamance County, NC on April 29, 1858,* n.p., n.p.p, p. 9.

54 Ibid., pp. 10-11.

55 Ibid., p. 20.

56 *Minutes of Special Session of Synod of Synod convened on August 27, at Lutheran Chapel, Stanly County, NC. Contained in Minutes of the 54th Annual Meeting of the Evangelical Lutheran Synod and Ministerium of North Carolina, 1858,* p. 4.

57 *Minutes of Special Session of Synod of Synod convened on August 27, at Lutheran Chapel, Stanly County, NC. Contained in Minutes of the 54th Annual Meeting of the Evangelical Lutheran Synod*, p. 4.

58 A Joyous Occasion-The Illumination of Mt. Pleasant, Unattributed manuscript, Eastern Cabarrus Historical Society, Mt. Pleasant, NC.

59 McAllister Papers, ECHS.

60 *Minutes of the Evangelical Lutheran Synod and Ministerium of North Carolina, convened at St. James Lutheran Church, Concord, NC, April 28, 1859,* (North Carolina Watchman Office, Salisbury, NC. 1859), p. 19.

61 *Minutes WCMA, 1858.*

Rev. Daniel Howard Bittle was born near Middletown, MD on June 6, 1819. He attended Gettysburg College in Pennsylvania graduating in 1843. He attended Lane Seminary in Cincinnati, OH, graduating in 1849. He was ordained by the Miami (OH) Synod in 1849. He served congregations in Ohio, IN, MD, PA, and VA. He also assisted his brother, Rev. David F. Bittle, in the building up Roanoke College, VA. He was elected the first President of North Carolina College in Mt. Pleasant NC in 1859. He served there until 1861 before moving to Austin, TX where he served as President of a female seminary. After the Civil War he taught at Roanoke College and served as minister to the Lutheran of Ascension in Savannah, GA from 1871 until his death in 1874. Rev. Bittle was married to Susan E. Bigelow, who served as the first Principal of the Mont Amoena Female Academy in Mt. Pleasant, NC. Rev. Bittle died in Savannah, GA on January 14, 1874 and is buried at Laurel Grove Cemetery in Savannah, GA.[1]

[1] "Bittle, Daniel Howard, Dd," John H. Mc'Clintock, DD and James Strong, James, STD,(eds), *Cyclopedia of Biblical, Theological and EcclesiasticalLterature,*https://www.biblicalcyclopedia.com/B/ bittle-daniel-howard-dd.html.

62 Minutes WCMA, 1858.

On the same day that North Carolina College was chartered by the State, the Town of Mt. Pleasant was officially incorporated and became the second such town in Cabarrus County.

63 Ibid.

64 "Notice to Builders," *The Western Democrat*, Charlotte, NC, April 5, 1859, p. 3, www.newspapers.com.

65 Ibid.

66 Minutes of Board of Trustees of North Carolina College, February, 1861, (MS), Carl A. Rudisill Memorial Library, Lenoir-Rhyne University, Hickory, NC, (hereafter cited as Minutes NCC).

67 *Minutes of the Fifty-Eighth Annual Meeting of the Evangelical Lutheran Synod & Ministerium of North Carolina, convened at Wilmington, NC on May 2, 1861,* (J. J. Bruner, Printer, Salisbury, NC.), p. 15.

68 Ibid.

69 Ibid.

70 Minutes NCC, May 29, 1861.

71 Ibid.

72 Ibid.

73 *Piedmont Neighbors,* Clarence E. Horton, Jr. and Kathryn L. Bridges, (eds), (Historic Cabarrus, Inc., Concord, NC, 1999), pp. 407-408.

74 *North Carolina State Troops, 1861-1865, A Roster*, Vol. IV, (North Carolina State Archives & History, Raleigh, NC, 1973).

75 Historical Data Systems, American Civil War Research Database, civilwardata.com.

76 "Account Books of North Carolina College, Jonas Cook, Treasurer," Minutes NCC.

77 Minutes NCC.

78 Ibid.

79 Ibid.

80 *Minutes of the Fifty-Ninth Annual Meeting of the Evangelical Lutheran Synod & Ministerium of North Carolina, convened at Organ Lutheran Church, Rowan County, NC on May 1, 1862,* (J. J. Bruner, Printer, Salisbury, NC), p. 18.

81 Minutes NCC.

82 Ibid.

83 Ibid.

84 *Minutes of the Fifty-Ninth Evangelical Lutheran Synod, 1862.*

85 Civil War Poster (MSS), Eastern Cabarrus Historical Society Museum, Mt. Pleasant, NC.

Recruiting Poster announcing "Men Wanted for Cavalry, $100 Bounty. Volunteers will for the present address me at the Recruiting Camp of the 1st NC Cavalry at the Old College, Mt. Pleasant, Jun 21, 22, 1863."

86 *Minutes of the Sixtieth Annual Meeting of the Evangelical Lutheran Synod & Ministerium of North Carolina, convened at St. Mark's Lutheran Church, Charlotte, NC on April 30, 1863,* (J. J. Bruner, Printer, Salisbury, NC), p. 16.

87 Minutes NCC.

88 *Minutes of the Sixty-First Annual Meeting of the Evangelical Lutheran Synod & Ministerium of North Carolina,* (J. J. Bruner, Printer, Salisbury, NC., 1864), p 16.

89 Ibid.

90 Ibid.

"That the reunion entered into between the Synod and the Synod of South Carolina in reference to her Seminary Fund, be and is hereby dissolved." ... inasmuch as the original agreement between the Synod of South Carolina and the Synod of North Carolina does not fully indicate that the Seminary Fund was created to impart only a Theological Education in the Theological Seminary of the South Carolina Synod, that we have the right to apply it at any institution of learning for the benefit of indigent young men having the ministry in view. [And] that as an institution of learning has been established by us in the bounds of which this fund was created, that we deposit that Fund in the Endowment of North Carolina College, reserving the right to recall the deposit of the same at any time that this Synod may deem advisable."

91 Ibid., pp. 16-17.

92 *Minutes of the Sixty-Second and Sixty-third Annual Convention of the Evangelical Lutheran Synod and Ministerium of North Carolina*, (J. J. Bruner, Printer, Salisbury, NC, 1866), p. 5.

93 Ibid.

94 Minutes NCC.

95 Bansemer Papers, 1830-1866.

Bikle's reply to the letter from Dreher referenced in his letter to Rev Cone, stated, "I wish that in your letter containing the announcement of my election to the chair of Ancient Languages in NC College, you had stated the probable income of the Institution, judging from the past year and the character or those $600 which the Board propose dividing between their Professors. On the supposition, however, that you would not have elected me, after the correspondence that passed between Bro. Anthony and myself, unless those $600 were equivalent to that amount in "green-backs or National Currency and that there was every reason to believe that the attendance of young men next year will be large enough to justify the expectation of an additional amount over and above expenses of the Institution that will prove a fair compensation for services. I promise to hold myself in readiness to return to Mt. Pleasant whenever the Board desire me to commence operations."[1]

[1] Letter from Bikle to Dreher, dated Winchester, VA 12 May 1866, contained in "Bansemer Papers."

96 "Minutes of the Sixty-Second and Sixty-Third Synod," p. 20.

General James H. Lane was born in Virginia in 1833. He attended the University of Virginia and taught at the Virginia Military Institute with Thomas J. "Stonewall" Jackson. He also taught at the State Seminary in Tallahassee, Florida (later Florida State University) and at the North Carolina Military Institute in Charlotte, NC. At the outbreak of the Civil War Lane was again on the faculty of VMI when he volunteered for service in the Confederate Army where he was appointed to the rank Colonel in command of the 28th VA Regiment, CSA. In November, 1862, he became the youngest General in the Confederate Army when he was promoted to command the Brigade formerly commanded by General L. O. Branch. Lane was wounded three times during the war and commanded troops at every battle of the Army of Northern Virginia. After the war, in which he lost two sons, Lane returned to his former profession in education. He opened two private schools for boys in Richmond, VA and Concord, NC. Neither school was successful. While Lane did accept a position at NC College in April of 1866, when the school opened in August he was not on the faculty. He taught briefly in Wilmington, NC, and in 1872 he was a Professor at Virginia Agricultural and Mechanical College (later Virginia Tech). He taught at the Alabama Polytechnic Institute (later Auburn University) for twenty-five years before retiring in 1907. He died in 1907 in Auburn, Alabama.[1]

[1] Kenneth E. Phillips, "James Henry Lane and the War for Southern Independence," Master's Thesis, Auburn University, 982, Wallace Community College, www.encyclopediaofalabama.org.

97 Minutes NCC, July 25, 1866.

98 Minutes of the Evangelical Lutheran Synod & Ministerium of North Carolina, convened at St. John's, Salisbury, NC, May 2, 1867. (Printed at the "Evangelical Lutheran Office," Charlotte, NC. 1867), p. 22.

Rev. D. M. Gilbert of Savannah, GA, had declined the position in August.

99 Ibid.

100 Bansemer Papers.

Charles F. Bansemer was a native of Prussia who migrated to the United States sometime before 1839. He attended the Lutheran Seminary in Lexington, SC, 1839-1841, he served as a licentiate in McPersonville and Brailsfordville, SC, 1841-1842, and entered the ministry, February 1842. He served congregations in the Beaufort and Colleton districts of South Carolina, and acted as the Principal of an academy in Beaufort for two years. He was later the Superintendent of the Chesterville Male Academy, Chester, SC, and administrator at Mount Zion Collegiate Institute, Winnesboro, SC.[1]

[1] Bansemer Papers," UNC-Chapel Hill, NC.

101 "Treasurer's Report, Oct 1867,." Bansemer Papers.

102 *Minutes of the Sixty-fifth Convention of the Evangelical Lutheran Synod & Ministerium of North Carolina, convened at Lau's Church, Guilford County, NC, April 30,* (Independent Press Office, Concord, NC, 1868), p. 18.

103 Ibid., pp. 18-19

104 "President's Report, October 15, 1868," Bransemer Papers.

105 Bransemer Papers.

106 Ibid.

107 Ibid.

108 *Catalogue of North Carolina College for Third Collegiate Year ending May 1869*(n.p.,. n.p.p.), Eastern Cabarrus Historical Society Library, Mt. Pleasant, NC, (hereafter cited as NCC Catalogue).

Henry Thomas Jefferson Ludwig, was the son of one of the founders of NC College and Board of Trustee member, Jacob Ludwig He was a native of Mt. Pleasant and entered NC College in 1859, but left in 1861 to in the Civil War as a musician with Co. H, 8th NC Regiment. He returned home from the war and re-entered NC College in 1867. Ludwig graduated in the first group of men to receive diplomas from the College in 1871, and he was immediately employed as a full-time member of the faculty. He served as Professor of Mathematics, Astronomy and Physics and was also chairman of the Commercial Department which was formed in 1892. Professor Ludwig received his AM Degree from NCC in 1872. In 1894 he was given an honorary PhD from Newberry College. He was considered one of the foremost mathematicians in the state. He wrote numerous articles concerning mathematics and other subjects and was well known for his ability to solve complicated mathematical problems known today as "brain teasers." Professor "Tom" died in 1900 while still a member of the NC College faculty. In 1903, Professor Ludwig was posthumously honored by the students and faculty of the Mt. Pleasant Collegiate Institute with the renaming of one of the school's debating halls and societies for him.

109 *Minutes of the Sixty-Sixth Convention of the Evangelical Lutheran Synod & Ministerium of North Carolina, convened at Frieden's Lutheran Church, Alamance Co. NC, May 2, 1869,* (Printed at the "Independent Press" Office, Concord, NC, 1868), p. 14.

110 Ibid.

111 *The Western Democrat,* Charlotte, NC, May 1869, p. 2,. www.newspapers.com.

112 Bansemer Papers.

113 *Minutes of the Sixty-Seventh Convention of the Evangelical Lutheran Synod & Ministerium of North Carolina, convened at Lutheran Chapel, Rowan Co. NC, Aug 25, 1870,* p. 15.

114 Ibid.

115 Ibid.

116 Ibid.

117 Ibid. p. 18.

118 Ibid. p. 19.

119 Minutes NCC, May 1871.

120 *Minutes of the Sixty-Eighth Convention of the Evangelical Lutheran Synod & Ministerium of North Carolina, convened at Pilgrim Lutheran, Davidson Co. NC, August, 1871,* p. 6.

121 Ibid., p. 13.

122 Ibid. Minutes of the Sixty-Eighth Convention of the Evangelical Lutheran Synod & Ministerium of North Carolina, convened at Pilgrim Lutheran, Davidson Co. NC, August, 1871, p. 6.

123 Minutes NCC, November 11, 1871.

124 *Minutes of the Sixty-Ninth Convention of the Evangelical Lutheran Synod & Ministerium of North Carolina, convened at Organ Church, Rowan Co. NC, August, 1872,* pp. & 15.

125 Ibid., p. 21.

126 Ibid., p. 15.

127 "Panic of 1873", *St. James Encyclopedia of Labor History Worldwide: Major Events in Labor History and Their Impact,* The Gale Group Inc., www.Encyclopedia.com.

The "Panic" lasted until 1879 and continued to impact the College during the next several years.

128 *Minutes of the Seventy-First Convention of the Evangelical Lutheran Synod & Ministerium of North Carolina, convened at St. Paul's Lutheran Church, Wilmington, NC, May 1, 1874*, pp. 22-23.

129 Ibid., p. 23.

130 Bransemer Papers.

131 Ibid., October 7, 1874.

132 Ibid.

133 Ibid., November & 4, 1874.

134 Ibid., December 10, and Minutes, NCC.

John Barton Davis was born in Winchester, VA in 1808. He graduated from Gettysburg College in 1835 and received his AM Degree in 1853. He was ordained by the Virginia Synod and served as President of the Synod for three terms. He was a Professor of Natural Science at Roanoke College, 1865-75. He transferred to the NC Synod in 1875 upon accepting the position of President of NC College. While at NC College he served as the minister at Holy Trinity in Mt. Pleasant, and Mt. Olive in Cabarrus County. Rev. Davis was the author of several books and papers on scientific and religious subjects He died in Virginia in 1895.[1]

[1] "Davis, John B.," *Life Sketches of Lutheran Minsters, North Carolina & Tennessee Synods, 1773-1965*, (North Carolina Evangelical Lutheran Synod, The State Printing Co., Columbia, SC, 1966), p. 52.

135 *Minutes of the Seventy-Second Convention of the Evangelical Lutheran Synod & Ministerium of North Carolina, convened at St. John's Lutheran Church, Cabarrus Co. NC, April 28,1875*. (Henkel & Co. Printers, New Market, VA, 1875)

James H. Turner was born in Franklin, VA. He graduated from Roanoke College in 1867. Before accepting the position at NC College he was serving a congregation in Montgomery Co. VA.

136 Ibid., p. 12-13.

137 Ibid., p. 20.

138 Jonas Cook Ledger, Minutes NCC, May 25, 1875.

139 Jonas Cook Ledger, Minutes NCC, May 25, 1875.

The detailed expense account, below is an example of the typical monthly expenses of the College.

Mar-Apr-May, 1875

By cash pd for repairs caused by storm, shingles, lumber, & work $ 176.20

June 12	By cash pd Albert Heilig note	$ 155.80
June 30	By cash pd C. G. Heilig hauling lime & sand	$ 9.00
	By cash pd RR. freight	$ 2.15
July 5	By cash pd for white lead	$ 92.23
	By cash pd for expenses on money	$ .75
July 8	By cash pd RR Freight	$ 6.70
	By cash pd for 1 box glass	$ 4.10
	By cash pd C. G. Heilig, hauling paint & oil	$ 1.90
July 12	By cash pd for lime	$ 18.50
	By cash pd Jno D. Barringer inst on note	$ 24.00
July	By cash pd for labor on College buildings	$ 158.73
June	By cash pd for advertising College	$ 15.70
May 10	By cash pd for printing catalogues 73 or 74	$ 13.00
June 1	By cash pd L. G. Heilig store acct.	$ 3.05
	By cash pd Wm. Reid 6 loads wood	$ 9.00
June 11	By cash pd Laban Petrea sweeping? college	$ 65.00
	By cash pd Rev. Rothrock for circulars	$ 2.00
	By cash pd Dr. Bikle Incidental expenses	$ 45.26
June 7	By cash pd Prof. Bikle his salary in full	$ 599.30
	By cash pd Prof. Hubbert his salary in full	$ 220.46
	By cash pd Prof. Ludwig his salary in full	$ 477.85
		$ 2100.68

140 Minutes of the NC College Faculty, Nov 1875, MS, Eastern Cabarrus Historical Society Library, Mt. Pleasant, NC, p. 74.

141 *Minutes of the Seventy-third Annual Convention of the NC Lutheran Synod and Ministerium, convened at St. Enoch's Lutheran Church, Rowan Co. NC, May 2, 1876*. (New Jobs Office & Book Bindery, Raleigh, NC), pp. & 16.

142 Ibid. p. 16.

143 *The Charlotte Democrat,* Charlotte, NC, August 7, 1876, p. 4, www.newspapers.com.

144 *Minutes of the Seventy-Fourth Annual Convention of the NC Lutheran Synod and Ministerium, convened St. Peter's Lutheran Church, Rowan Co. NC, May 2, 1877.* (Henkle & Co., Printers, New Market, VA), p. 21.

145 *The Concord Register,* Concord, NC, October 7, 1876, p. 4, www.newspapers.com.

146 Ibid., p. 1.

147 *Minutes of the Seventy-Fourth Lutheran Synod*, p. 21.

148 Ibid.

149 Bransemer Papers.

150 *Minutes of the Seventy-Fourth Lutheran Synod*, p. 21.

151 Rev. Sheppard Seneca Rahn was born in Effingham Co. GA in 1845. He graduated from Newberry College and received a Doctor of Divinity Degree fromSouthern Seminary and was ordained by the Georgia Synod in 1874. He served congregations in South Carolina and Georgia before transferring

to North Carolina where he became a professor at NC College in 1877. He remained at NC College for only two years, while also serving as the minister at Ebenezer Lutheran Church in Rowan County. He moved back to South Carolina in and was Professor at Newberry College for five years. He transferred to the Tennessee Synod in and served several congregations in western NC. Rev. Rahn was married three times and had four children, two of whom died as infants. Rev. Rahn died in Columbia, SC on Jul 1911.[1]

[1] "Rahn, Sheppard Seneca," *Life Sketches of Lutheran Minsters, North Carolina & Tennessee Synods, 1773-1965,* (North Carolina Evangelical Lutheran Synod,The State Printing Co., Columbia, SC, 1966), p. 165.

152 *Minutes of the Seventy-Fifth Annual Convention of the NC Lutheran Synod and Ministerium, held in Frieden's Church, Guilford Co. NC, May 1-May 6, 1878.* (Henkle & Co., Printers, New Market, VA), p. 15.

153 Jonas Cook Account Books. 1877, Minutes NCC.

J. M. Worth of the NC Treasury Department charged Jonas Cook $6.75 to certify 9 bonds. This was half-price.

154 NCC Catalogue, 1878-1879.

155 *Minutes of the Seventy-Eighth Annual Convention of the NC Lutheran Synod and Ministerium, held in Sandy Creek Church, Tryo, Davidson Co. NC, beginning April 27, 1881.* (Henkle & Co., Printers, New Market, VA).

156 Jonas Cook Account Books, 1877.

157 Ibid.

158 "Board of Trustees Report to Synod," *Minutes of the Seventy-Sixth Annual Convention of the NC Lutheran Synod and Ministerium, held in Bethel Church, Stanly Co. NC, April 30-May 3, 1879.* (J. J. Bruner, Printer, Salisbury, NC), pp. 8-9.

The Fire Insurance Policy was with Saint Paul Fire & Marine, St. Paul, MN for $25.00. Insurance on Roofs and shingles of buildings by Seaboard Insurance Co., Norfolk VA - $2500 for $25.00. Insurance on Buildings 6 Dec 1878-6 Dec 1879 Insurance Co. of North America, Philadelphia - $2500 for $25.00.

159 Minutes of the Seventy-Eighth Synod, 1881, p. 17. "Board of Trustees Report to Synod," Minutes of the Seventy-Sixth Annual Convention of the NC Lutheran Synod and Ministerium, held in Bethel Church, Stanly Co. NC, April 30-May 3, 1879. (J. J. Bruner, Printer, Salisbury, NC), pp. 8-9.

160 *NCC Catalogue, 1880-1881.*

161 *The Concord Register*, July 15, 1881, p. 3, www. Newspapers.com.

162 *The Wilmington Post*, Wilmington, NC, August 21, 1881, p. 1, www. newspapers.com.

163 *NCC Catalogue, 1881-1882.*

164 *Concord Register*, Jan 20, 1882, p. and an article in the *Wilmington Morning Star*, Wilmington, NC, May 1882, p. 1. Listed the President of NC College as Rev. L. A. Bikle. A *Charlotte Observer* Article, May 1882, stated that the new President of NC College was Rev. G. D. Berheim. www.newspapers.com.

Gotthard Dellman Bernheim was born in Westphalia, Prussia on November 8, 1827. His father was a Lutheran minister who migrated to America in 1832. Bernheim attended the Theological Seminary at Lexington, SC, graduating in 1849. He was licensed in South Carolina 1843 and ordained in 1853. He was the minister at St. Andrews (Wentworth St.) in Charleston, SC before moved to North Carolina in 1858. In NC he served St. John's, Cabarrus Co., New Bethel, Stanly Co.; St. Mark's, Charlotte; St. Michael's, Troutman; and Ebenezer, Rowan Co., and St. Paul in Wilmington. He was a financial agent for NC College in 1858 and built a residence in Mt. Pleasant in that year.[1] He was Principal and owner of Mont Amonea Female Seminary from 1868-1870 and at his departure, conveyed the property to the NC Lutheran Synod.[2] He was on the Board of Trustees of NC College from 1869 through 1873. He was appointed President of NC College in 1882 and served in that capacity until May 1883. He was President of the NC Lutheran Synod for two terms. In 1883, he transferred to the Pennsylvania Synod but returned to NC in 1892. He was the minister at St. Mathews in Wilmington from 1892-1901 and after "retirement" he served as a "supply pastor" at St. Luke/Morning Star in Monroe, NC. He was Professor and Bible at Elizabeth College in Charlotte in 1906. Rev. Berheim died on October 25, 1916 in Charlotte and is buried at Magnolia Cemetery, Charleston, SC.[3]

[1] "Bernheim, Gotthard Dellman.," *Life Sketches of Lutheran Minsters, North Carolina & Tennessee Synods, 1773-1965,* (North Carolina Evangelical Lutheran Synod, The State Printing Co., Columbia, SC, 1966), p. 21.

[2] Denise M. McLain, *Memories of Mont Amonea Female Seminary: An Island of Culture in the Difficult Years, 1859-1927,* (Master's Thesis), UNC-Charlotte, Charlotte, NC, 2017.

[3] www.findagrave.com/ memorial/22426183/g-d-bernheim

165 "North Carolina College," *The Daily Charlotte Observer*, Charlotte, NC May 30, 1882, p. 3, https: www. newspapers. com.

166 *Minutes of the Seventy-Ninth Annual Meeting of the NC Lutheran Synod, held in St. James Church, Concord,. NC, beginning May 3, 1882,* (Henkle & Co., Printers, New Market, VA), p. 9.

167 *Abstracts of the Lutheran Visitor, 1866-and 1870-1888*, Abstracted and contributed by Edith Greisser, South Carolina Genealogy Trails at www. genealogytrails.com/scar/Lutheranvisitor and *The Eightieth Annual Meeting of the North Carolina Lutheran Synod & Ministerium, St. Stephen's Lutheran*

Church, Cabarrus Co. NC, May - 5, 1883. (Office of the Lutheran Visitor, Newberry, SC), p. 6.

168 *Minutes of Eightieth Lutheran Synod*, p.6.

169 Ibid., pp. 44-45.

The following pledges were made toward liquidating the debt of the College, Rev. J. A. Davis-$32, Rev. L. A. Bikle-$10, Rev. F. W. E. Peschau-$80, Rev. R. W. Petrea-$80, Rev. J. A. Linn-$10, Rev. T. H. Strohecker-$80, and Rev. G. F. Schaeffer-$20. Minutes of Eightieth Synod, 1883.

170 Ibid.

171 Ibid.

172 Ibid., p. 35.

173 Ibid.

174 Ibid.

A notice at the end of the NC Synod Minutes did list Rev. Peschau as President of the College.

175 *Minutes of the Eighty-first Annual Meeting of the Evangelical Lutheran Synod and Ministerium of North Carolina. Ebenezer Lutheran Church, Rowan Co. NC, April 30-May 2, 1884,* (Charlotte Observer Steam Print, Charlotte, NC), p. 21.

Under Cook's plan, those students who declared "for the ministry," signed the following pledge. "I declare it to be my serious purpose to devote my life to the Ministry of the Gospel in the Evangelical Lutheran Church and being entitled according to the Constitution of North Carolina College Benefit Association to free tuition in said College as a student from Organ Church. I obligate myself to prosecute my studies with diligence and in the event that I should at anytime abandon my studies for the Ministry, then and in that case, I promise to pay to Jonas Cook, Treasurer of said College or his successors in office, full tuition from the first Monday in August 1884 for the time of my connection with said College as a student. As witness my hand and seal, this 11 Day of October 1884."[1]

[1] Bansemer Papers.

176 *Minutes of the Eighty-first Synod,* p. 21.

The College Benefit Association - In the hour of its sore distress the friends of the College rallied to its relief by a simple but effective remedy suggested by Jonas Cook, Esq. Membership is secured in this association, and the solicitation of the College Financial Secretary, by the payment of five dollars semi-annually. When two hundred members are secured it will over a very substantial relief. The payments are due on the first of September and January of each College year. The following are present holders of scholarships.

Rev. J. A. Linn 2	Mr. W. L. Daniel	Mrs. M. A. Dreher
Mr. Elias Cress	Rev. S. Rothrock 2	Dr. J. W. Moose
Mr. H.T. J. Ludwig 2	Mr. L. H. Rothrock 2	Rev. R. W. Petrea

Mr. A. C. Barrier
Mr. T. H. Strohecker
Mr. J. H. D. Walker
Mr. G. E. Ritchie 2
Mr. E. D. Lentz 2
Mr. Jesse W. Miller 2
Mr. M. E. Miller
Mr. A. Cline
Mr. J. H. Thayer
Mr. A. Misenheimer
Mr. H. W. Overcash
Mrs. Christina Misenheimer
Mr. G. W. Blackwelder
Mr. John W. Bostian
Dr. L. A. Bikle
Mr. Aaron Ritchie
Mr. W. R. Reed
Dr. Paul A. Barrier 2
Mr. C. H. Duls
Mr. A. M. Blackwelder
Mr. D. D. Barrier
Mr. H. A. Kluppenburg
Mr. Paul Peeler
Mr. M. A. Heilig
Mr. J. M. Faggart
Rev. G. F. Schaeffer
Mr. W. A. Lentz
Ebenezer Church
St. John's Church
St. Enoch's Church
Mr. William Probat
Mr. James L. Lefler
Mr. Daniel Barrier 2
Mr. Harris Crowell
Mr. D. H. Ridenhour
Mr. John M. Harkey
Mr. C. A. Misenheimer
Mr. H. A. Holshouser
Mr. William Barringer
Mr. W. H. Fisher
Mr. M. Ritchie
Mr. J. L. Sifferd
Mr. J. H. Misenheimer
Mr. D. A. Sides
Mr. Jonas Cook 2
Capt. W. A. Barrier
Mr. J. M. Ridenhour
Mr. C. G. Heilig
Col. J. Shimpock 2
Mr. G. W. Bringle
Mr. Henry Walker
Mr. Moses Peeler
Mrs. M. A. Lentz
Mr. G. R. P. Miller
Mr. Luther Barrier
Rev. F. W. E. Peschau
Mr. S. F. Ludwig
St. Stephen's Church
St. Mark's Church
Holy Trinity Church 2
Mr. L. A. Lentz
Mr. J. L. Ritchie
Mr. A. W. Moose
Mr. L. G. Heilig 2
Mr. J. J. Newman
Mr. H. C. McAllister 2
Mr. Edmond Foil
Dr. R. A. Shimpock 2
Mr. J. E. Deaton
Mr. R. W. Misenheimer
Mr. C. H. Fisher
Mr. S. H. Hearne
Mr. J. A. Eddleman
Mr. C. D. Barringer
Mr. H. McNamar
Mr. L. J. Foil
Mr. S. E. Linton
Mr. H. A. Blackwelder
Mr. J. A. Hahn
Mr. W. R. Kindley
Mr. J. G. Hoffner
Mr. James P. Cook
Mr. William Heilig
Mrs. M. M. Fisher
Mrs. M. Roxie Barrier
Mr. M. L. Blackwelder
Organ Church
St. Peter's Church
Frieden's Church

177 *Minutes of the Eighty-First Synod, 1884, p. 21. Minutes of the Eighty-first Annual Meeting of the Evangelical Lutheran Synod and Ministerium of North Carolina. Ebenezer Lutheran Church, Rowan Co. NC, April 30-May 2, 1884*, (Charlotte Observer Steam Print, Charlotte, NC), p. 21.

Reverend George Francis Schaeffer was born in Preston Co. VA (now WVA) in 1830. He entered Gettysburg College as a Preparatory Student in 1851 and graduated in 1856. He was the Principal of an Academy in Somerset, PA from 1857-1860. He moved to North Carolina in 1860 and taught at Mont Amoena Seminary and NC College. He was licensed as a minister in 1861 and supposedly returned north at the beginning of the Civil War. One source lists him as a minister in Mt. Pleasant NC in 1865. At the outbreak of the Civil War he returned north and was licensed as a minister in 1861 and ordained by the Allegheny Synod in 1865. He was back in Somerset, PA by 1866 and served several congregations in PA through 1873. In 1873 he was vice-principal at a Female Academy in Lutherville, MD. He also served as a minister in several churches in Pennsylvania before returning to North Carolina in 1882 where he served as Principal at Mont Amoena Seminary for two years before becoming President of NC College on January 1st, 1884. He was also the minister at St. James Lutheran Church in Concord from 1884- 1886. He remained at NC College until 1887 when he "retired" to Monroe, GA. He later moved to Spartanburg Co. SC where he died on 27 Sep 1916. Rev. Schaeffer was married three times and had two children, both of whom died in 1884.[1]

[1] "George Schaeffer," *Life Sketches of Lutheran Minsters, North Carolina & Tennessee Synods, 1773-1965,* North Carolina Evangelical Lutheran Synod, (The State Printing Co., Columbia, SC, 1966), p. 180, and Edward S. Breidenbaugh, (ed), *The Pennsylvania College Book, 1832-1882,* Gettysburg College Alumni Association, (Lutheran Publication Society, Philadelphia, PA), 1882, p. 236, and "George Francis Schaeffer," books.google.com, and findagrave.com.

178 Ibid., p. 17. *Minutes of the Eighty-first Lutheran Synod*, p. 21.

179 Ibid., p. 30.

180 *NCC Catalogue, 1884-1885.*

181 Ibid.

182 Jonas Cook Account Book, Minutes NCC.

183 Ibid.

184 *NCC Catalogue, 1885-1886.*

185 Ibid.

186 Minutes NCC, October, 1885.

187 *Minutes of the Eighty-third Meeting of the Evangelical Lutheran Synod & Ministerium of North Carolina, Union Lutheran Church, Rowan Co. NC, April 30-May 5, 1886.* (Henkel & Co. Printers, New Market, VA), p. 7.

188 "The Endowment of North Carolina College," *The Concord Times*, Concord, NC, February 11, 1886, p. 1, https: www. newspapers.com.

189 "North Carolina College," *The Carolina Watchman*, Salisbury, NC, August 6, 1885, p. 3, https:www. newspapers.com.

190 *Minutes of the Eighty-third Meeting of the Evangelical Lutheran Synod & Ministerium of North Carolina, Union Lutheran Church, Rowan Co. NC, April 30-May 5, 1886,* (Henkel & Co. Printers, New Market, VA), p. 14.

Jonas Cook reported in his ledger that revenues from for 1885-86 were $2,381, while salaries of faculty totaled $2,129.

191 Ibid., pp. 14-15.

From the third session of the Synod, May 3rd, 1886 – "Resolved that the committee find it impracticable to carry out the plan of raising said endowment, and recommend that a new committee be appointed to suggest some feasible plan for raising said fund." The new committee returned with the following recommendations. "1. That the limited time of 5 years for raising the endowment be changed to 2 years. 2) That persons having scholarships [pledges] in the college be allowed to convert the sam with as much more as they may be willing to give in the "Storch Endowment Fund." 3) That instead of bond binding the heirs, executors, etc., a good note be required of subscribers. 4) That the committee be allowed to make any verbal changes not in conflict with the spirit of the plan as amened. 5) That this plan be endorsed by at least a four-fifth vote of this Synod. J. A. Linn, B. S. Brown, C. A. Kimball, W. Kimball, H. C. McAllister. Adopted."

192 Ibid., p. 19.

193 Ibid.

194 *NCC Catalogue, 1886-1887.*

195 Jonas Cook Account Book, Minutes NCC, 1887.

196 *Carolina Watchman*, Salisbury, NC, August 19, 1886, p. 4, https:www.newspapers.com.

197 *Minutes of the Eighty-Fourth Meeting of the Evangelical Lutheran Synod & Ministerium of North Carolina, St. Michael's Lutheran Church, Iredell Co. NC, April 29-May 4, 1887,* (Henkel & Co. Printers, New Market, VA), p. 12.

198 Ibid., p. 19.

Apparently, Rev. Kimball reconsidered his resignation and continued to act as financial agent as the minutes of the Eighty-Fifth Synod stated that he had raised over $15,000 in pledges to the endowment and according to one source he had preached in every NC Synod congregation in the state during the past two years.[1]

[1] *Minutes of the Eighty-Fifth Meeting of the Evangelical Lutheran & Ministerium of North Carolina convening at St. James Lutheran Church, Concord, NC, on May 4, 1888,* (The Lutheran Publication Co., Wilmington, NC), p. 13.

199 Ibid., p. 41.

200 *NCC Catalogue, 1886-1887.*

Rev. John George Schaidt was born in Cumberland Co. MD in 1846. He received his AB Degree from Muhlenburg College in Allentown, PA in 1872 and a DD Degree from Philadelphia Theological Seminary in 1875. He was ordained by the PA Synod in 1875 but transferred to the Holston, TN Synod where he served a bilingual (German-English) in Knoxville, TN. He transferred to the NC Synod when he accepted the position of President of NC College. After leaving NC College in 1889, he transferred to the Tennessee Synod and taught at Concordia College in Newton, NC. He transferred to the SC Synod in 1895 and continued his ministry in the PA and Holston Synods until his death in 1909. He died on 6 Aug 1909 and is buried in New Haven, WV.[1]

[1] "Schaidt (Schaid), John George." *Life Sketches of Lutheran Minsters, North Carolina & Tennessee Synods, 1773-1965.* (North Carolina Evangelical Lutheran Synod, The State Printing Co., Columbia, SC, 1966), p. 182.

201 Jonas Cook Account Book, Minutes NCC, May 1888.

202 *Minutes of the Eighty-Sixth Meeting of Evangelical Lutheran Synod and Ministerium of North Carolina, convened at St. John's Lutheran Church, Cabarrus Co. NC, May 3, 1889,* (Lutheran Publication Company, Newberry, SC), p. 13.

203 "Minutes NCC, June and Jonas Cook Account Book, June 1890.

204 Jonas Cook Account Book, Minutes NCC, January 1890.

"Mr. Kistler" appears to have beenWellington L. Kistler of the Bear Poplar community in Rowan County. Kistler's nephew, T.J.H. Kistler/Kestler, had attended NC College in 1860 and had died in the Civil War. W. L. Kistler was very active in local politics serving as Chairman of the Mt. Ulla Prohibition Society in 1881 and Secretary of the Alliance Fair Association of Rowan County in 1890. In 1895, his mother's estate was the subject of a law suit which involved NC College.[1]

[1] *The Carolina Watchman*, Salisbury, NC, 9 Jun 1881, pp. 3 & 22 May 1890, p. 3, newspapers.com.

205 Jonas Cook Account Book, Minutes NCC, July 1889.

206 *The Carolina Watchman,* Salisbury, NC, Jul 1889, p. 2, www.newspapers.com.

207 Minutes NCC, July 1889.

208 Ibid.

209 *NCC Catalogue, 1889-1890.*

210 Wiley Alexander Barrier was born in Cabarrus County in 1836, the son of Daniel Barrier and Nancy Matheson. He attended the Western Carolina Male Academy in and NC College in 1860. In he enlisted in the 9th NC State Troops as a Lieutenant in Co. F. The 9th State Troops were later designated the 1st NC Cavalry and Barrier was promoted to 1st Lieutenant of Co. I in and Captain in 1863. Following the war, Barrier traveled to Tennessee and then to Texas where he taught school. He returned to North Carolina in and served as Principal of Mont Amoena Seminary in Mt. Pleasant and a student NC College. While at the College he served as an instructor in penmanship. He graduated from NCC in and remained on the faculty as a part-time instructor. In he moved to Charlotte and with Rev. Nichodemus Aldridge opened an academy called Macon School. He was awarded a Master of Arts Degree from NC College in 1875. He was the Mecklenburg County Examiner for Public Instruction in 1880. Barrier was a member of the NC College Board of Trustees from 1886-(replacing his father). In May of 1890, Barrier was offered the Presidency of NC College but declined, and unfortunately died in October, 1890.[1]

[1] Ben F. Callahan, "Barrier Family Genealogy," unpublished research manuscript, Gold Hill, NC.

211 Minutes NCC, August, 1889.

212 *Minutes of Called Session Evangelical Lutheran Synod and Ministerium of North Carolina, convened at St. John's Lutheran Church, Salisbury, NC, Aug 27, 1889,* (Henkel and Company Steam Printing House, New Market, VA), p. 65.

Rev. John Daniel Shirey was born near Staunton, VA in 1836. He received a BA Degree from Roanoke College in 1857 and Gettysburg Seminary, 1860. He was ordained by the Virginia Synod in 1861 and served in that state until 1867. He moved to South Carolina and where he remained until 1882. He was President of the SC Synod in 1878. He moved to North Carolina in 1882 and served parishes in Rowan until 1889 when he was appointed President of NC College. He died on 5 Apr 1896 while serving as President of NC College. He is buried at Holy Trinity Cemetery, Mt. Pleasant, NC.[1]

[1] "Shirey, John Daniel," *Life Sketches of Lutheran Minsters, North Carolina & Tennessee Synods, 1773- 1965,* (North Carolina Evangelical Lutheran Synod, The State Printing Co., Columbia, SC, 1966), p. 193.

213 *Minutes of the Eighty-Seventh Evangelical Lutheran Synod and Ministerium of North Carolina," convened at St. Luke's Lutheran Church, Davidson Co. NC, May 2, 1890,* (Henkel and Company Printers, New Market, VA), p. 19.

214 Jonas Cook Account Book, Minutes NCC,1890.

215 *Minutes of the Eighty-Eighth Annual Convention of The Evangelical Lutheran Synod and Ministerium of North Carolina, convened at St. Enoch's Lutheran Church, Enochsville, NC, May 1, 1891,* (Henkel and Company Steam Printing House, New Market, VA), p. 24.

216 *NC College Advance.* Mt. Pleasant, NC, Vol. 1, #8, June 1890, ECHS Library, Mt. Pleasant, NC.

The North Carolina College *Advance* was a "school newspaper" initially written and published by two students, H. N. Miller and R. L. Patterson. It was advertised as "A monthly magazine devoted to the interests of North Carolina College." In their first issue in October, 1889 the editors stated, "We two students at this institution (H. N. Miller & R. L. Patterson) have for a long time seen the need of a college journal in this school."

217 "The Lutheran Synod," *Wilmington Messenger*, Wilmington, NC, May 13, 1890, p.2, www. newspapers.com.

218 *Minutes of the Eighty-Eighth Lutheran Synod,* p. 23.

219 Minutes NCC, January 1891.

220 *Minutes of the Eighty-Eighth Lutheran Synod*, p. 24.

221 Ibid.

The entire report read: "The Board of Trustees of North Carolina College is able to present to Synod, this year, the most gratifying report that has been made for years ... Last year we felt ourselves under the necessity of uniting the common school with our Preparatory Department in order that we might increase our income, but the experiment was not at all satisfactory. We therefore, this year, have none but regular students of the institution. The wisdom of the change is seen in the fact that we are able to report 79 [students] upon on the roll, a larger number than has been enrolled for eleven years, last year excepted. Of these 79, Less than one fifth are of local patronage, or in other words, four-fifths of our students are from abroad."

The finances of the institution are in a much healthier condition than they have been for years. Of the principal Endowment Fund there has been collected $2087.10. Of this amount, $2000.10 has been loaned out, secured by interest bearing mortgage notes on real estate, leaving a balance of $87 in the hands of the Treasurer... which will also soon be invested. Of the interest of the Endowment Fund there has been collected $846.77 which has been paid on the salary of the faculty. At least $100 is due and will be paid in June, 1891. The income from tuition, room rent, and incidental fees has been up to this time about $1,425.

Thus it will be seen that the income of the institution for all purposes during the year has been $4,721.06. In addition to this, the Treasurer of the Board has been duly notified of a legacy of $1,000 given to the College by Capt. W. A. Barrier, deceased, with the information from the executor of the estate, M. C. Dulls, of Charlotte that he expects and desires to pay same sometime during the coming summer. ...

We have been able to make some needed and decided improvements. During last summer's vacation, the inside of the main building (halls, chapels, and dormitories), and the Preparatory Department were completely overhauled – ceiled and painted at the cost of $250. This amount was paid for by the faculty out of their own individual funds, for which they deserve the praise and thanks of the whole Synod. The building is now in prime order, neat, comfortable, and attractive. ... The Campus has been very much improved, and when completed according to the plans adopted, will add very much to the beauty and comfort of the institution. ...

First. We need that the debts hanging over the institution should be canceled. They are not many, nor large; not near so large as may similar institutions carry, but they are a great hindrance to the advancement and success of the institution; crippling us more, perhaps, than may have supposed. ... Our second need is another building. Already all of our dormitories are full; and with the prospects before us that we now have, we expect to be still more crowded next year. Now, we are under the necessity of holding all of our commencement exercises in the church. [Holy Trinity Lutheran Church in Mt. Pleasant] The chapel is too small, and there is no other room in town large enough. What we need, pressingly need, is a new building with a hall suitable for all of our public exercises. … Brethren of the grand old North Carolina Synod, can it not be built?

Our third need is legacies and gifts. Are there not men and women, who love their church and her institutions, and who will remember it in dispensing their gifts and legacies? During the past year, one dear brother, Capt. W. A. Barrier, an alumnus, class of '72, a member of the Board, and a life-long friend of the institution, has left us a legacy of $1000. One thousand dollars! Brethren; think on these things, and may God our Heavenly Father stir up many hearts to go and do likewise. George H. Cox, President of the Board of Trustees of North Carolina College."

222 *Minutes of the Eighty-Ninth Annual Convention of The Evangelical Lutheran Synod and Ministerium of North Carolina, Convened at St. Paul's Lutheran Church, Rowan Co., NC, April 29, 1892,* (Henkel and Company Steam Printing House, New Market, VA), p. 19.

223 Ibid., pp. 19-20.

224 Minutes, NCC, May 1892.

This issue would not be resolved before Professor Ludwig died in 1900.

225 Ibid, May 1892.

226 *Minutes of Eighty-Ninth Lutheran Synod*, p. 20.

227 Minutes NCC, October 1892.

228 Ibid., March 1893.

229 Ibid., May 1893.

230 Ibid.

231 *Minutes of the Ninetieth Annual Convention of The Evangelical Lutheran Synod and Ministerium of North Carolina, convened at Lutheran Chapel Church, China Grove, NC, May 4, 1893,* (Henkel and Company Steam Printing House, New Market, VA), p. 27.

232 Ibid., pp. 59-60.

233 Minutes NCC, October 1893.

234 Minutes NCC, Nov 1893.

235 *Minutes of the Ninety-First Annual Convention of The Evangelical Lutheran Synod and Ministerium of North Carolina, convened at Organ Church, Rowan Co., NC, May 3, 1894,* (Henkel and Company Steam Printing House, New Market, VA), p. 39.

Contributions were received from:

Lows Grove	$	3.35	St. John's, Cabarrus	$	10.05
Holy Trinity (thus far)	$	5.00	Ebenezer	$	5.00
St. Mathew's, Rowan	$	3.50	Luther Chapel	$	11.27
Union	$	5.00	Concordia	$	1.83
St. Peter's	$	3.50	Grace	$	3.75
St. Paul's, Wilmington	$	20.00	Rev. C. Rose	$	6.37
Albemarle	$	2.00	Salem & St.Luke's	$	11.00

Christiana	$ 2.30	Center Grove	$ 8.40
From friends in Baltimore, Philadelphia, and NY	$ 40.00		
Rev. Peter Miller	$ 5.00		

236 Ibid., p. 40.

237 Minutes NCC, May 1894.

238 Ibid., May 1894.

239 *Minutes of Ninety-Second Annual Meeting of the Evangelical Lutheran Synod and Ministerium of North Carolina, convened at St. Michael's, Iredell Co., NC, May 2, 1895,* (Henkel and Company Steam Printing House, New Market, VA), p. 20.

240 Ibid., pp. 20-21.

241 *Minutes of Ninety-Third Annual Meeting of the Evangelical Lutheran Synod and Ministerium of North Carolina, convened at St. James Church, Concord, NC, April 30, 1896,* (Henkel and Company Steam Printing House, New Market, VA), pp.22-23.

242 *The Concord Times*, Concord, NC, April 9, 1896, p. 3, www. newspapers.com.

243 *Minutes of Ninety-Third Annual Meeting of the Evangelical Lutheran Synod and Ministerium of North Carolina, convened at St. James Church, Concord, NC, April 30, 1896,* (Henkel and Company Steam Printing House, New Market, VA), p. 42.

244 Ibid., p. 46.

245 Minutes NCC, January & May 1896.

246 Minutes NCC,June, 1896.

Rev. Melanchthon Gideon Groseclose Scherer was born in Catawba County, NC on March 16th, 1861. He was the son of Rev. Simeon Scherer, a member of the second Board of Directors of the Western Carolina Male Academy. Rev. Scherer attended Roanoke College and Southern Seminary in Salem, VA. He was ordained in 1883 by the Virginia Synod. Prior to being selected as the President of NC College, he had served congregations in West Virginia, Pennsylvania, and Concord, NC. At the time of his appointment he was serving as the Pastor at St. James Lutheran Church in Concord and Mt. Hermon in Cabarrus County.[1]

[1] "Scherer, Melanchton Gideon Groseclose," *Life Sketches of Lutheran Minsters, North Carolina & Tennessee Synods, 1773- 1965, (*North Carolina Evangelical Lutheran Synod, The State Printing Co., Columbia, SC, 1966), p. 183.

247 Minutes NCC, June, 1896.

In 1895, the Board of Trustees had entered an Iredell County probate proceeding of Catherine Barringer Kestler, widow of Henry Kestler, claiming to be a party to the estate. This probate proceeding involved the contested estate of Catherine Kestler (dec'd May 4, 1894) in which there was a dispute over the authenticity of two purported wills, one filed in Iredell County and one purportedly filed in Rowan County. The will filed in Rowan County was written on August 5, 1893 and stated that "after the death of her son during his life, it being one half of my personal property shall be paid to the trustees at North Carolina College at Mt. Pleasant to be used for the education of young men studying for the ministry in the Lutheran Church." The will filed in Iredell County, supposedly written on October 20, 1894, left nothing to NC College. The only connection that Catherine Kestler appears to have had with NC College was through her deceased son, T. J. H. Kestler, who had attended the Western Carolina Male Academy from 1855-1857. [See Student Roster in Appendix] The end result of the probate dispute was that NC College was awarded a portion of $1,000 which was given to estate of Catherine's son, Wellington Kestler. After all fees were paid to attorneys and others involved the College received $287.78.[1]

[1] Wills, 1757-1959, North Carolina Superior Court, Rowan County, NC, ancestry.com. *North Carolina, Wills and Probate Records, 1665-1998* [database on-line]. Provo, UT, USA: Ancestry.com Operations, Inc., 2015, (hereafter cited as NC Wills, ancestry.com)

248 Minutes NCC, October, 1896.

249 *Minutes of The Ninety-Fourth Annual Meeting of Evangelical Lutheran Synod & Ministerium of North Carolina, convened at St. John's Lutheran Church, Cabarrus Co., NC on April 1897.* (Henkel and Company Steam Printing House, New Market, VA.), p. 18.

250 *Minutes of The Ninety-Fifth Annual Meeting of Evangelical Lutheran Synod & Ministerium of North Carolina, convened at Macadonia Lutheran Church, Burlington., NC on April 1898.* (Henkel and Company Steam Printing House, New Market, VA.), p. 16.

251 Records of Mont Amoena Seminary, MS, The Eastern Cabarrus Historical Society Library, Mt. Pleasant, NC.

Payments of $88.40 per year were made to the College Board of Trustees through 1912 at which time the loan was repaid. The loan had remained in place for ten years after MP College closed and one year after Mont Amoena burned.

252 Minutes of the Ninety-Fifth Lutheran Synod, pp. 26-27.

253 Minutes NCC, March, 1898.

254 Jonas Cook Ledger, McAllister Papers, ECHS.

255 Ibid.

256 Minutes NCC, April, 1899.

257 *Minutes of Ninety-Sixth Meeting of the Evangelical Lutheran Synod and Ministerium, St. John's Lutheran Church, Salisbury, NC, May 4-6, 1899.* (Lutheran Publication Board, Newberry, SC.), p. 26.

258 Ibid., pp. & 26-27.

259 Ibid., p. 27.

260 Ibid., pp. 26-27.

261 Ibid., p. 26.

262 *Minutes of Called Session of the North Carolina Lutheran Synod & Ministerium, Organ Lutheran Church, Rowan Co. NC, July 6, 1898.* Printed in the *Minutes of the Ninety-Sixth Synod*, pp. 67-68.

263 *The Daily Standard*, Concord, NC, June 10, 1899, p. 5, www.newspapers.com.

264 NCC Catalogue, 1900-1901.

Edgar Bowers was born in West Virginia. He attended Roanoke College, graduating in 1888. From 1888-1891 he taught Modern Languages at Roanoke.[1] He was hired by North Carolina College in 1897 as Professor of Ancient and Modern Languages. Following his short tenure as Acting President of NC College, Bowers continued to teach at the school until it closed in the Spring of 1902.[2] In 1910 Bowers was living in Roanoke, VA where he was listed as the Steward of the College.[3] Although no dates are listed, Bowers also served as the Principal at Wartburg Seminary in Graham (Bluefield, VA) and at High Schools in Middleton, WV and Hodgesville, WV. He died in Clarksburg, WV on 14 Oct 1920.[4]

[1] *Catalogue of the Officers & Students of Roanoke College, Salem, VA. Thirty-Seventh Session. 1888-1889.* (Henkel & Company, Steam Printing, New Market, VA, 1888). [np]

[2] NCC Catalogues, 1898-1902.

[3] 1910 Census, www.ancestry.com/search/collections /1910us cenindex.

[4] https://www.findagrave.com/memorial/7739173/edgar- bowers.

265 *Minutes of the Ninety-Seventh Annual Meeting of the Evangelical Lutheran Synod and Ministerium, held at Albemarle Church, Albemarle, NC, May 3-7, 1900*, (Lutheran Publication Board, Newberry, SC), pp. 67-68.

266 *Minutes of the Called Session of the North Carolina Lutheran Synod, held at St. John's Church, Salisbury, NC, February 20, 1900,* printed in the *Minutes of the Ninety-Seventh Lutheran Synod,* pp. 68-69.

267 Ibid.

The Tennessee Synod proposal read: "Owing to the recent location of Lenoir at Hickory, and its prosperous condition we could entertain no proposition for its removal elsewhere. That we are unwilling and do not make any bid for the NC College unless your committee has thoroughly and permanently decided the question of its removal from Mt. Pleasant, NC. We do not desire to be party to any unpleasantness. In case of you have so decided we offer a gift of $10,000 the same being a half interest in Lenoir College buildings, and campus and avenue, containing twenty three acres, six hundred dollars in twelve building lots now selling for $100 each, the same being half their value. Equal representation on the Board of Trustees, etc. All of our moral support and whatever advantage there may be in uniting with a school in successful operation and in a live and growing town. Our school now has enrolled 103, eighty-five of whom are in the College classes. Of course the offer is conditional upon the adoption of articles of cooperation in case you should decide to accept it."

268 Ibid., p. 33.

269 *Minutes of Called Session of the Lutheran Synod, Organ Lutheran Church, 1898.*, p. 68.

270 *Minutes of the Called Session of Lutheran Synod, February 20, 1900*, pp. 68-69.

271 Ibid., p. 32.

272 *Minutes of the Called Session of the North Carolina Lutheran Synod, held at St. John's Church, Salisbury, NC, December 19, 1899*, printed in the Minutes of the *Ninety-Seventh Synod, 1900*, pp. 33-34.

273 *The Concord Times*, Concord, NC, May 10, 1900, p. 3, www.newspapers.com.

In response to the Synod's vote to ask for the bid to be held open, the "citizens of Salisbury" reacted quickly as described in the *Concord Times* on May 10th, 1900. "The action of the Lutheran Synod … requesting Salisbury to keep in force its bid for North Carolina College for a year, was to request an impracticable thing. New subscriptions would have to be solicited with increased difficulty at the end of the year and Hon. Jno. S. Henderson withdraws his offer of the site at the end of Fulton Street, as he does not care to have a valuable piece of property tied up for a year."

274 *Minutes of the Called Session of the North Carolina Lutheran Synod, held at St. John's Church, Salisbury, NC, December 19, 1899*, printed in the Minutes of the *Ninety-Seventh Synod, 1900*, pp. 33-34.

275 *Minutes of the Ninety-Seventh Lutheran Synod, p. 21.*

276 *NCC Catalogue, 1900-1901.*

William Alonzo Lutz was born on June 10th, 1850 in Newton, Catawba Co. NC. He graduated from Catawba College in Newton in 1874 and from the Philadelphia Seminary in 1877. He was ordained by the NC Synod in 1877 and received an AM Degree from Gaston College in 1882. From 1877 through 1892 he served congregations in Forsyth, Davidson and Rowan. He served as President of the NC Synod in 1885-86 and he helped to organize Concordia Lutheran Church in Rowan County in 1882 and Augsburg Lutheran Church in Winston-Salem, NC in 1891. He was serving as the minister at Grace Lutheran Church in Prosperity, SC when he was appointed President of NC College. Following his tenure at NC College, Rev. Lutz served parishes in

Statesville, NC; Hickory, NC; Charlotte, NC, and Brunswick Co., GA. He retired in 1926 and died on July 12th, 1941.[1]

[1] "Lutz, William Alonzo," *Life Sketches of Lutheran Minsters, North Carolina & Tennessee Synods, 1773- 1965,* (North Carolina Evangelical Lutheran Synod, The State Printing Co., Columbia, SC, 1966), p. 125.

277 Minutes NCC, August, 1900.

278 Minutes NCC, October, 1900.

279 Minutes NCC, November, 1900.

280 Minutes NCC, April, 1901.

281 Jonas Cook Account Book, McAllister Papers, ECHS.

282 *Minutes of the Ninety-Eighth Annual Meeting of the Evangelical Lutheran Synod & Ministerium of North Carolina, held at Frieden's Church, Gibsonville, NC, May 2-6, 1901,* (Henkel & Co.'s Steam Printing House, New Market, VA). pp.16-17.

283 Ibid., p. 40.

284 Ibid., pp.16-17.

285 Ibid., pp. 52-53.

286 Ibid., pp. 42-43.

287 Minutes NCC, March, 1902.

288 *Minutes of the Ninety-Ninth Annual Meeting of the Evangelical Lutheran Synod & Ministerium of North Carolina, held in St. James Church, Concord, NC, beginning April 30, 1902,* (Henkel & Co.'s Steam Printing House, Office of Our Church Paper, New Market, VA). p. 42-43.

289 Ibid.

290 Ibid., p. 11.

291 Ibid., p. 42.

292 Ibid., pp. 42-43.

"1. The committee has investigated the conditions of the College as carefully as the data at hand will allow, and find nothing to encourage Synod in it. The vitality of the institution seems to be exhausted. It is with the saddest feelings and with painful remembrance of the labors and prayers of the fathers in behalf of NC College, that we make this acknowledgment. But we deem it our duty to you to inform you of what we regard as the truth, however, unwelcome it may be.

2. Passing from general to particular statements, we remark that at present the College has almost no students and scarcely any faculty. The income of the endowment fund does not more than meet the interest on the indebtedness, so that virtually nothing of that income is directly available for payment of professor's salaries. The institution is sinking deeper and deeper into debt, until at present the indebtedness exceeds the total amount of available endowment, as the financial statement of the treasurer of the BoT shows.

3. In view of these discouraging conditions, having insufficient money, inadequate resources, no encouraging prospects, and no cheering hopes, we recommend –

a. That the BofT be instructed to suspend the operations of the College for one year.

b. That the BoT be instructed to use the interest of the endowment fund to pay back salaries of professors, and all income from other sources, after payment of necessary expenses for insurance and repair of the buildings, to liquidate the other indebtedness of the College.

4. We recommend that that part of standing resolution of Synod 23, which requires our beneficiaries to attend NC College be hereby rescinded. A. G. Voight, V. R. Stickley, C. B. Miller, B. S. Brown, John Wagener, J. A. Thom, D. J. Goodman, Committee."

293 *Minutes of Called Session of the Evangelical Lutheran Synod & Ministerium of North Carolina,. held at St. Marks Lutheran Church, China Grove, NC, June 24-25, 1902.* Printed in Minutes of the Ninety-Ninth Synod, 1902., pp. 71-72.

294 "Minutes NCC, October, 1903.

295 *The Concord Times*, Concord, NC, May 8, 1902, p. 3, www. newspapers.com.

296 George Franklin McAllister was born in Cabarrus County, North Carolina on February 18, 1874, the son of Harvey C. McAllister and Francis C. Cook McAllister. McAllister entered North Carolina College as a Preparatory student in the late 1880's. He enrolled in the College Department in and graduated in being immediately hired as the temporary Principal of the Preparatory Department at his alma mater Carolina College. He served in this capacity for one year before being appointed the full-time Principal.

After NC College closed, McAllister served as co-principal of The Carolina English and Classical School for one year and as co-principal of Mt. Pleasant Collegiate Institute for five years before becoming the sole Principal in 1909. He also taught Mathematics and Science at MPCI. McAllister remained the Principal at MPCI until it closed in 1933.

On October 18, 1937, George F. McAllister suffered a fatal heart attack at his home in Mt. Pleasant, He was buried at Holy Trinity Lutheran Cemetery, Mt. Pleasant, NC.

In 1938, the citizens of Mt. Pleasant received permission from the Cabarrus County Board of Education to have the elementary school built in their community named in honor of George F. McAllister. McAllister School remained open until 1970 and currently serves as the Municipal Offices of the Town of Mt. Pleasant.[1]

Rev. Levi E. Busby was born in Lexington District, South Carolina on September 5, 1859, the son of Benjamin C. Busby and Eva Folk Busby. Busby attended Newberry College in South Carolina, graduating in 1875. He attended the Lutheran Theological Seminary in Salem VA graduating in 1878. He was licensed in 1877 by the Southwest Virginia Synod and ordained in 1878 by the South Carolina Synod.

Rev. Busby served congregations in VA and SC from 1875-1896. He was Secretary of the South Carolina Lutheran Synod in 1881 and President from 1892-1893.

In 1896, Rev. Busby moved to North Carolina and engaged in mission work in Asheville, NC. He served St. John's, Salisbury, NC from 1996-1902. He was Secretary of the North Carolina Lutheran Synod from 1898-1900. He received a Doctor of Divinity Degree from North Carolina College in 1901.

In 1902 Rev. Busby moved to Mt. Pleasant, Cabarrus Co. NC where he served as pastor at Holy Trinity Lutheran Church and as co-principal of the "Carolina English & Classical School" on the campus of the former North Carolina College.

On March 14, 1903, Rev. Busby suffered an attack of appendicitis and died in Mt. Pleasant. He was buried at the Folk-Cannon-Busby Cemetery in Pomaria, Newberry Co. SC.[2]

[1] McCallister Family Papers, MS, Eastern Cabarrus Historical Society Museum, Mt. Pleasant, NC.

[2] "Busby, Levi E.," *Life Sketches of Lutheran Minsters, North Carolina & Tennessee Synods, 1773- 1965,* (North Carolina Evangelical Lutheran Synod, The State Printing Co., Columbia, SC, 1966), p. 35.

297 *Minutes of the One Hundredth Annual Meeting of the Evangelical Lutheran Synod & Ministerium of North Carolina, St. John's Church, Salisbury, NC, beginning on April 28, 1903.* (Henkel & Co.'s Steam Printing House, Office of Our Church Paper, New Market, VA), p. 53.

298 *The Concord Times*, Concord, NC, August 14, 1902, p. 3, www. newspapers.com.

299 Jonas Cook Account Book, 1902, McAllister Papers, ECHS.

300 "Report of Joint Special Committee Composed of a Special Committee of the Synod, and a Committee of the Board of Trustees of North Carolina College," printed in *Minutes of the One Hundredth Evangelical Lutheran Synod*, pp. 31.

301 Ibid.

302 Ibid.

303 Ibid.

304 Ibid., p. 32.

305 Ibid., pp. 36-37.

The Joint Special Committee Composed submitted as part of its report to the Synod "the status of the financial obligations in connection with notes given by the students." The Committee sent out statements to all parties indebted to the College. These included $804.89 in canceled notes, $507.01 in notes "barred by the statute of limitations," and $137.22 in legally collectible funds. The report listed all of the known indebtedness to the school. The report also contained a list of the liabilities still owed by the school as reported by the College Treasurer, Jonas Cook. These included:

Feb. 8, 1886	To Cook & Foil (note)	$	146.16
	To Cook & Foil (acct)	$	260.85
Jul 13, 1897	To Cook & Foil (note)	$	42.00
Sep 8, 1891	To Julia A. Wheeler (secured by mortgage)	$	1,000.00
Nov 28, 1893	To A. C. Barrier (secured by mortgage)	$	900.00
July 1, 1888	To Prof Ludwig (note)	$	150.00
July 1, 1889	To Prof Ludwig (note)	$	248.23
July 1, 1899	To Prof Ludwig (acct)	$	207.60
July 1, 1899	To Prof Scherer (acct)	$	174.09
July 1, 1899	To Prof E. B. Setzler (acct)	$	31.50
July 1, 1899	To Prof. G. F. McAllister	$	110.00
1900	To Henkel & Co. (acct) about	$	320.00
	To deficit in Rev. Lutz administration	$	660.00
Jun 1, 1900	To Jonas Cook, for salary as Treasurer	$	600.00
1903	To Jonas Cook, for salary as Treasurer	$	325.00
	To Appx interest in different Accts.	$	500.00
		$	5,675.43

306 Minutes NCC, May 25, 1903.

307 McAllister Papers, ECHS.

Rev. Henry Antine McCullough, Sr. was born in Newberry, South Carolina on December 18, 1849, the son of John McCullough and Margaret McNeill McCullough. McCullough graduated from Newberry College in 1893 and the Lutheran Theological Seminary, Newberry, SC. He was ordained by the South Carolina Synod in 1895. From 1895-1903 Rev. McCullough served the congregations in North & South Carolinaat St. Andrews, Mt. Hermon and Cold Water Lutheran in Cabarrus Co. NC. In 1899 he married Lilly Amelia Blackwelder, a resident of Mt. Pleasant and graduate of Mont Amonea Female Seminary. In 1903, Rev. McCullough became the minister at Holy Trinity Lutheran Church in Mt. Pleasant, NC, and he joined G. F. McAllister as Associate Principal of the newly created Mt. Pleasant Collegiate Institute. In 1907, McCullough resigned his position at MPCI and became the Minister at First Albemarle Lutheran Church in Albemarle, Stanly Co. NC. He was the Secretary of the North Carolina Synod from 1908-1911. Rev. McCullough remained at First Albemarle until moving to South Carolina in 1911where he served as the pastor at St. Paul's Lutheran Church in Columbia, South Carolina, until he retired in 1945. Rev. McCullough died on May 8, 1958. He is buried at Elmwood Cemetery, Columbia, South Carolina.[1]

[1] "McCullough, Henry Anine." *Life Sketches of Lutheran Minsters, North Carolina & Tennessee Synods, 1773- 1965,* North Carolina Evangelical Lutheran Synod. (The State Printing Co., Columbia, SC, 1966), p. 131.

308 Ibid.

309 Ibid.

310 "Principal's Report to Board of Trustees," Minutes NCC, April, 1904.

311 Minutes NCC, April, 1904.

312 "Report of The Principals of The Collegiate Institute to the Board of Trustees of North Carolina College," *Minutes of the One Hundred-First Annual Meeting of the Evangelical Lutheran Synod & Ministerium of North Carolina, Christiana, Rowan Co., NC beginning on May 11, 1904,* (Henkel & Co.'s Steam Printing House, Office of Our Church Paper, New Market, VA), pp. 24-25.

313 Jonas Cook Account Book, McAllister Papers, October, 1904.

314 *Minutes of the One Hundred-First Annual Meeting of the Evangelical Lutheran Synod & Ministerium of North Carolina, Christiana, Rowan Co., NC beginning on May 11, 1904,* (Henkel & Co.'s Steam Printing House, Office of Our Church Paper, New Market, VA),. p. 46.

315 *Minutes of the One Hundred-Second Annual Meeting of the Evangelical Lutheran Synod & Ministerium of North Carolina, held in Pilgrim Church, Davidson Co. NC beginning on May 17, 1905,* (Henkel & Co. Lutheran Publication Establishment, New Market, VA), p. 27.

316 Ibid., pp. 28-29.

317 Ibid., p. 37.

318 *Minutes of the One Hundred-Third Annual Meeting of the Evangelical Lutheran Synod & Ministerium of North Carolina, held in St. John's Church, Cabarrus Co. NC beginning on May 2, 1906,* (Henkel & Company's Lutheran Publication Establishment, New Market, VA), pp.28-29.

319 Minutes NCC, November, 1906.

320 Minutes NCC, May, 1907.

321 *Minutes of the One Hundred-Fourth Annual Meeting of the Evangelical Lutheran Synod & Ministerium of North Carolina, held in Salem Church, Rowan Co. NC beginning on May 1, 1907,* (Henkel & Co. Lutheran Publication Establishment, New Market, VA), p. 37.

322 Ibid., pp. 37-38.

323 Minutes NCC, May, 1907.

324 McAllister Papers, ECHS, Apr 1908.

325 *Minutes of the One Hundred-Fifth Annual Meeting of the Evangelical Lutheran Synod & Ministerium of North Carolina, held in Lutheran Chapel Church, China Grove, NC beginning on April 29, 1908,* (Henkel & Co. Lutheran Publication Establishment, New Market, VA). pp. 44-45. & Jonas Cook Ledger, McAllister Papers, ECHS.

326 McAllister Papers, ECHS, Apr 1908.

327 *Minutes of the One Hundred-Fifth Lutheran Synod*, p. 9.

328 Ibid., p. 48.

329 Minutes of the One Hundred-Fifth Lutheran Synod, pp. 44-and Jonas Cook Ledger, McAllister Papers, ECHS.
330 *Minutes of the One Hundred-Sixth Annual Meeting of the Evangelical Lutheran Synod & Ministerium of North Carolina, held in Faith Lutheran Church, Faith, NC beginning on April 28, 1909,* (Henkel & Co. Lutheran Publication Establishment, New Market, VA), p. 12.
331 Ibid., p. 11.
332 Minutes NCC, February 22, 1909.
333 "An Act to Revise the Charter of the Trustees of North Carolina College, Mt. Pleasant, NC," *Private Laws of the State of North Carolina Passed by the General Assembly at its Session begun on January 6, 1909, Raleigh, NC,* Chapter 357, (E. M. Uzzell & Co., Printer & Binders, Raleigh, NC), p. 792.
334 Minutes NCC, April 22, 1909.

"An institution which does the work of a college up to within two years of graduation is sadly handicapped if dependent almost entirely upon tuition receipts for maintenance. And it is this very fact that constitutes the greatest drawback to the continuance and progress of the Collegiate Institute. There is the barest support in it for the Principals who answer all financial obligations. Anything like permanent support is out of the question and that is quite a handicap to an institution that would keep abreast of the times. We would therefore ask the Board to lay this matter before the Synod and secure, if possible, the needed assistance for the Institute, or commit the matter of educational work into the hands of Synod for her disposition."

335 *Minutes of One Hundred-Sixth Lutheran Synod,* p. 45.
336 Ibid., p. 41.
337 Ibid., p. 44. *Minutes of the One Hundred-Sixth Annual Meeting of the Evangelical Lutheran Synod & Ministerium of North Carolina, held in Faith Lutheran Church, Faith, NC beginning on April 28, 1909,* (Henkel & Co. Lutheran Publication Establishment, New Market, VA), p. 11.
338 Minutes NCC, May, 1909.
339 McAllister Papers, ECHS.
340 Minutes NCC, June 17, 1909.
341 McAllister Papers, ECHS.
342 Ibid.
343 Ibid.
344 Ibid.

"Jul 9, 1909, I have given careful attention to your letter of June 24th upon which I congratulate you. If you write such letters as that to the men who are favorably disposed toward secondary Christian education, it will surprise me if you do not get what you are looking for. Permit me to say in the first place, since my advice has been asked, that I believe your best course is to go on with the development of a high grade secondary school. I do not say this because I was formerly connected with Newberry College or for any other reason except that I sincerely believe it. …

We are top-heavy with middle grade colleges, and this is especially true in the scheme of Christian education. I think that the recognition you have received from the University of North Carolina points the way to your future course, that if you persist earnestly in your effort to build up a great secondary school, you will, before many years have passed, attract a very large patronage from all parts of the country. Only yesterday a man from Los Angeles was in my office asking me to recommend a high grade preparatory school in the Southern States and I found it impossible to give him the satisfaction he desired. This plan would be of great service not only to the Lutheran Church but to Southern education. It would also be a good policy with Dr. Pearsons … He and Carnegie and Rockefeller, with the General Education Board, are vigorously opposed to the erection of new colleges and will lend their enormous influence in opposition. Since you have been out of the college field for a number of years, you would be looked upon as essentially trying to found a new college if you abandoned your present scheme of things."

345 Ibid.

346 Ibid.

347 Ibid.

"It seems unnecessary to tell any Southerner the reasons and principles for which the "United Daughters of the Confederacy" was organized. … The earlier efforts of our order were directed chiefly toward all kinds of betterment for the Confederate Soldier and preservation of our sectional History; but as the ranks of the soldiers became thinner and thinner and our membership more numerous, we find ourselves able to broaden our scope of usefulness, and are now entering on an educational campaign on behalf of worth descendants of Confederate men and women. Most of our larger chapters have a yearly scholarship in a local college or seminary that is awarded to some resident. The state body has four scholarships at the State Normal College, but we want at least one scholarship in the representative schools of the State. By our manner of award, we expect to make it a distinction and an honor to hold on of these scholarships which will redound to the good fame of the institution giving it, and we want to know if your institution cannot put such a scholarship at our disposal? Do you not know some friend of your institution who would be glad to establish a Confederate Scholarship? We shall be glad to hear from you on the subject, as we hope to have beneficiaries enjoy the advantages next session."

348 Ibid.

349 *Minutes of the One Hundred-Seventh Annual Meeting of the Evangelical Lutheran Synod & Ministerium of North Carolina, held in First Church, Albemarle, NC*

beginning on May 4, 1910, (Henkel & Co. Lutheran Publication Establishment, New Market, VA), pp. 13-14.

350 "The Collegiate Institute to be Moved." *The Concord Daily Tribune*, Concord NC, May 7, 1910, p. 1, www.newspapers. com.

Lenoir College was a Tennessee Synod school which opened in 1891 as a one room "academy" in Hickory, Catawba County, NC operated by four Lutheran ministers. The first class consisted of twelve students. After the donation of 56 acres of land by Wilkes County lawyer, Walter W. Lenoir, a new school was constructed and opened as Highland College soon changed its name to Lenoir College. Lenoir College operated as the Tennessee Synod College from 1891. Ironically, the first President of the College was Rev. Y. A. Yoder, a graduate of North Carolina College.[1]

Even though the Lutheran Church in NC split in 1821 into two different governing bodies, the NC Synod and the Tennessee Synod, there was always a group within the two organizations that worked for reconciliation. Several attempts were made over the years to bring the two Synods back together, but for various reasons, including the issue of the location and operation of a Church College, these attempts were unsuccessful. When NC College closed in 1902, many church leaders foresaw an opportunity for compromise. While neither Synod publicly acknowledged their efforts, there were those who worked behind the scenes to use the "situation" to their advantage. For its part, the NC Synod simply left the future status of North Carolina College in limbo, while parsimoniously supporting the operation of the Collegiate Institute. The Tennessee Synod, meanwhile, continued to build and develop its school into a stronger institution.

[1] "History and Traditions," Lenoir Rhyne University, https:// www.lr.edu.

351 "The Collegiate Institute to be Moved," *The Concord Daily Tribune*, p. 1.

352 Ibid.

353 "Final Plan Submitted." *The Concord Daily Tribune*, Concord, NC, May 25, 1910, p. 1, www.newspapers.com.

354 "Consolidation of Lenoir and Mt. Pleasant Seems Certainty." *Charlotte Daily Observer*, May 26, 1910, p. 1, www. newspapers.com.

355 Minutes NCC, May 17, 1910.

356 Ibid.

357 "Plan of Synod for Union College, Abandoned," *The Concord Daily Tribune*, Concord, NC, November 12, 1910, p. 1, www. newspapers.com.

358 "The Matter Solved." *The Concord Daily Tribune*, Concord, NC, November 17, 1910, p.1, www.newspapers.com.

359 "At Mt. Pleasant to Stay." *The Concord Times*, April 17, 1911, p. 3, www. newspapers.com.

360 Letter from Henry L. Smith, President of Davidson College, Apr 1911. McAllister Papers, ECHS.

361 Letter from Frank P. Venable, President of the University of North Carolina, McAllister Papers, ECHS.

362 *Minutes of the One Hundred-Eighth Annual Meeting of the Evangelical Lutheran Synod & Ministerium of North Carolina, held in St. Paul's Church, Wilmington, NC, beginning on May 10, 1911,* (Lutheran Board of Publication, Columbia, SC), p. 40.

363 Letter from Rev. J. E. Shenk, September 3, 1911, McAllister Papers, ECHS.

364 McLain, *Memories of Mont Amonea Female Seminary*, pp. 59-63.

365 Jonas Cook was born in Gaston County, NC in 1842. His father, Mathew Cook, a German immigrant, moved to Mt. Pleasant about 1845. Mathew Cook and Jacob Ludwig owned a general store in Mt. Pleasant, and Cook was a strong financial supporter of the Western Carolina Male Academy and NC College. Jonas Cook most likely attended the Western Carolina Male Academy and was a student in the first class of NC College in 1859. By 1861, Cook, while still a year old student, became one of the organizers of a local group of military volunteers that later became Co. H, 8th NC Regiment, CSA. Cook rose to the rank of Captain in Co. H and returned home in after being wounded. Following the war, Cook took a leading role in his community and at NC College. In addition to his positions with North Carolina College and MPCI, Cook served as a local magistrate, Justice of the Peace, Postmaster, Town Board member and Town Mayor. He took over ownership of his father's mercantile business and with partner, Lawson J. Foil, built "Cook & Foil" into one of the most successful business enterprises in eastern Cabarrus County. His dedication and contributions to NC College and MPCI were instrumental in keeping both schools afloat during hard financial times.[1]

[1] Ben F. Callahan, Ben, *Mt. Pleasant by the Minutes, (*Published by Ben F. Callahan, 2016).

366 Principal's Report to Synod, Apr 1912, McAllister Papers, ECHS.

367 Minutes NCC, May 21, 1912.

368 "Commission to Meet." *The Concord Daily Tribune*,. January 2, 1912, p. 1, www. newspapers. com.

369 Ibid.

370 McAllister Papers, ECHS.

371 Minutes NCC, May, 1913.

372 Ibid.

373 Ibid.

374 Minutes NCC, April, 1914.

375 *Annual Catalogue of the Trustees, Faculty and Students of the Collegiate Institute, Mt. Pleasant, NC*, MS, Eastern Cabarrus Historical Society Library, Mt. Pleasant, NC, 1914-1915, (hereafter cited as MPCI Catalogue).

376 Ibid., p. 51.

377 Ibid., p. 50.

378 Letter from Charles B. King, President of Elizabeth College, Charlotte, NC, April 8, 1914, McAllister Papers, ECHS.

379 Minutes NCC, May 4, 1914.

380 "Principal's Report to Board of Trustees," April 20, 1914, McAllister Papers, ECHS.

381 Minutes NCC, October 20, 1914.

382 Ibid.

383 Ibid., October 20, 1914.

384 Letter from Robert Wright, President of East Carolina College, January 5, 1915, McAllister Papers, ECHS.

385 Letter from Robert Wright, February 9, 1915, McAllister Papers, ECHS.

386 Letter from Senator Dennison Giles, Chairman of NC State Senate Committee on Education, February 8, 1915, McAllister Papers, ECHS.

387 "Principal's Report to Board of Trustees," April 25, 1915, McAllister Papers, ECHS.

388 Ibid.

389 Minutes NCC, April 25, 1915.

"Whereas since 1902 and 1903 according to action of the Synod of North Carolina of those years, the work of North Carolina College has been suspended. Whereas during the years intervening a Collegiate Institute providing two years of college work has been most successfully maintained. Whereas this Institute has been maintained through personal and individual supervision entailing no financial obligation upon the Board nor upon Synod. Whereas, this work has become burdensome upon those shouldering all responsibility. Therefore, be it resolved, that, in order to provide adequate equipment for the perpetuation of such an institution, the Board of Trustees of North Carolina College most respectfully request the Synod of North Carolina to authorize the raising of a fund of $40,000, one fifth of all monies thus raised to be used in payment of the amount borrowed from the endowment fund until that fund reaches $5,000 in actual cash or its full equivalent; the balance of the amount raised to be used in placing a new dormitory on the campus, in remodeling the present buildings, and in making such other necessary improvements so as to provide a modern and comfortable plant. Resolved that the Board of Trustees be empowered to take the supervision of this work and be authorized to devise ways and means so as to prosecute the work with energy and dispatch."

390 Minutes NCC, May 25, 1915.

391 Minutes NCC, July 15, 1915.

392 Letter to Henry Ford, January 7, 1916, McAllister Papers, ECHS.

"The American people honor a man who has made a success in business. You have unquestionably and fairly won the title of "Captain of Industry." There are those in our country who honor a man even more for the good he does and endeavors to do through the means he has acquired by his success in business. It is a pleasure to note that you have manifested so great an interest in the uplift of your fellow man. Your efforts in behalf of the men who work in your factories is an example of enlightened justice which, if the business world will heed, will go far toward ameliorating the condition of the working man and greatly lessen the trouble labor and capital. The pamphlet which you recently got out on the subject of the cigarette, I would like to see in the hands of every man or woman in the country who is dealing with the boys of our country. Supt. Webb of Concord, NC to whom you sent several of these pamphlets kindly handed me one. I read it with much interest and profit. It may interest you to known that cigarettes have always been under the ban at the Collegiate Institute. I am sending you a marked copy of our catalogue showing our position in regard to cigarette smoking. [Cigarette smoking stupefies the brain, unsettles the nerves, lessens the energy, and lowers the ambition, hence militates against those ennobling principles for which Christian education stands.] Greater than either of the aforementioned wise efforts of yours is the activity you are manifesting toward bringing to a close the terrible carnage in Europe. I hope and believe that such agitation as you are producing will ultimately cause the thoughtful of the world to stop and consider; and if that is done, the way will be opened for Peace. May the day be hastened when this is consummated.

Mr. Ford, the benevolent activities alluded to mark you as a man who is broad of sympathy and desirous of doing good. This being the case, I have faith to believe that you will be interested in a cause which is set forth in the accompanying folder. You are a busy man, I well know, yet I do earnestly ask you to read this folder. Having done so, I am confident that you will be interested in the cause. We should certainly be happy to number you among our friends. Won't you help our cause? Trusting that your benevolent disposition and our generous spirit may prompt you to lend a helping hand to a most worth cause, and wishing you continued business success and a happy issue for the noble enterprise upon which you have lately entered. I beg to subscribe myself your very truly."

393 Letter from G. S. Anderson, Secretary to Henry Ford, January 14, 1916, McAllister Papers, ECHS.

394 "Principle's Report to Board of Trustees, April, 1916," McAllister Papers, ECHS.

395 Ibid.

396 Minutes NCC, April 24, 1916.

397 Ibid.

398 Minutes NCC, May 16, 1916.

399 *Annual Catalogue of the Trustees, Faculty and Students of the Collegiate Institute, Mt. Pleasant, NC,* 1916-1917, (hereafter cited as *MPCI Catalogue).*

400 Minutes NCC, October 17, 1916.

401 McAllister Papers, ECHS.

402 Minutes NCC, April 17, 1917.

403 McAllister Papers, ECHS.

404 Minutes NCC, April 17, 1917.

405 Minutes NCC, May 22, 1917.

406 Minutes NCC, May 22, and Alumni Association Minutes, MS, ECHL Library.

407 Minutes NCC, May 22, 1917.

408 Letter to Lutheran Ministers, July 10, 1917, McAllister Papers, ECHS.

409 Ibid.

410 McAllister Papers, ECHS.

411 *Salisbury Evening Post*, Salisbury, NC,. July 9, 1918, p. 5, www. newspapers.com.

412 McAllister Papers, ECHS.

413 Minutes NCC, April 9, 1918.

414 Letter to J. Henry Harmes from H. C. McAllister, May 24, 1918, McAllister Papers, ECHS.

"I have your communication of the 24th and feel flattered by the same. While at our recent Synodical meeting, several persons made mention to me of a possible call to Newberry. … I did say to the member of the Board that I had always had a kindly feeling toward Newberry, would consider a call to the presidency an honor, and in the event it should come to me I would feel constrained to give it serious consideration. … I could not now give a categorical answer to the question as to what I would do if tendered the presidency of Newberry. Before I would feel justified in giving such an answer, I would want to come into possession of information, official information, on several points. … Just now we are in the midst of Commencement exercises. You see the impracticability of giving much thought to any other matter. If, based upon information you had at the time you wrote and possible later developments, there still seems to be reason for my being prepared to give an answer to the question you put in your letter, I would like to have the advantage of a conference with you. …"

415 "Locals and Otherwise," *The Concord Times*, Concord, NC, Jun 10, 1918, p. 3, www. newspapers.com.

416 "The Collegiate Institute, Mt. Pleasant," *The Concord Times*, Concord, NC, July 25, 1918, p. 4, www. newspapers.com.

417 Telegram from "Committee on Education," Washington, DC, September, 21, 1918, McAllister Papers, ECHS.

418 Telegram from Senator Lee Overman, October 2, 1918, McAllister Papers, ECHS.

419 Letter from Edward Graham, US War Department Committee on Education & Special Training, Washington, DC, October 1, 1918, McAllister Papers, ECHS.

"I am glad to answer your inquiry concerning Bailey Military Institute. Application for the admission of this school was made while I was away from my office in Washington, DC. I saw Colonel Bailey at the office of the Committee and told him that I could make no report on the school because I did not know its standards. He was insistent and I told him and the Committee that I should have to wait until I could back home. He [Co. Bailey] reported to the Committee that he would certify to the fact that the school was a full junior college, requiring 14 units for admission to its collegiate classes and giving two full years of college work. I told the Committee that if it were willing to accept Colonel Bailey's statement that I had no reason to doubt it. I had no information but that if it were satisfactory to the Committee to accept his word, that I should make no objection. On my return South, I investigated the standards of the Academy and wired the Committee that Bailey does not satisfy requirements. The Committee wired me that the unit was already granted. I do not know what action will be taken in the matter. The situation was created through no fault of mine; it is difficult to correct just now. I make this statement for your own information and will ask you to regard it as confidential. The question of whether an institution fulfills the requirement as to number is not within my jurisdiction."

420 Letter from Albert A. Meras, US War Department Committee on Education & Special Training, Washington, DC, October 7, 1918, McAllister Papers, ECHS.

421 Letter from Senator Lee Overman, October 8, 1918, McAllister Papers, ECHS.

422 Letter from Senator Lee Overman, October, 1918, McAllister Papers, ECHS.

423 Minutes NCC, October 3, 1918.

424 Ibid.

425 Minutes NCC, March 11, 1919.

426 *Minutes of the One Hundred-Sixteenth Annual Meeting of the Evangelical Lutheran Synod & Ministerium of North Carolina, held in Union Evangelical Lutheran Church, near Salisbury, NC, beginning on May 14, 1919*, (Henkel & Co., Lutheran Publication Establishment, New Market, VA), p. 57.

427 Ibid., p. 60.

428 Ibid., pp. 72-74.

429 Minutes NCC, May 27, 1919.

430 Ibid.

431 "Rhyne Gives $2,to Mt. Pleasant Institute," *The Charlotte Observer*, June 19, 1919, p. 2, www.newspapers.com.Daniel Efrid Rhyne was born in Gaston Co. NC. He attended North College in but did not graduate. He and his brother, Abel P. Rhyne erected a cotton mill in Gaston Co. NC in 1873. Rhyne, his brother and several other partners built several textile mills in Gaston & Lincoln Counties. He also had a substantial interest in many other textile mills including the Stowe-Lineberger Mills in Belmont and the Burlington Mill Corporation in Burlington, N. C. He owned 15,acres in five NC counties and was the President of several banks. He donated to the building of many Lutheran Churches and educational institutions including N. C. College, MPCI and Mont Amoena Seminary. He was a major benefactor to Lenoir College in Hickory, NC, which later added his name to become Lenoir-Rhyne College.[1]

[1] "Daniel Efird Rhyne," William S.Powell, (ed.), *Dictionary of North Carolina Biography.* (University of North Carolina Press, Chapel Hill, NC, 1994), Vol. 5, p. 210.

432 *The Concord Times*, Concord, NC, Jul 1919, p. 6, www.newspapers.com.

433 "Another Important Contribution Received," *The Concord Daily Tribune*, Concord, NC, July 4, 1919, p. 1, www. newspapers.com.

John S. Efird was born in Stanly Co. NC. In 1896, with his father, I. P. Efird, and J. W. Cannon of Concord, NC, Efird built the Efird Manufacturing Company, a textile mill Albemarle, NC. He was also the President of two banks in Albemarle and on the Board of Directors of several other textile mills. Three of his sons, and several nephews attended MPCI, and one son, Jerome J. Efird, was on the MPCI Board of Trustees. J. S. Efird was a NC State Senator in 1907 and 1915. He served on the North Carolina College Board of Trustees, the Board of Directors of Stonewall Jackson Training School in Concord, NC and was a Trustee of Lenoir-Rhyne College.[1]

[1] "John Solomon Melanchthon Efird," *Dictionary of North Carolina Biography*, Vol. 2, p. 142.

434 *The Concord Daily Tribune*, Concord, NC,. November 22, 1919, p. 3, www. newspapers.com.

435 "Launching Campaign for $150,Fund," *The Concord Daily Tribune*, Concord, NC, January 21, 1920, p. 1, www. newspapers.com.

436 "Literature Prepared for Lutheran Campaign," *The Concord Daily Tribune*, Concord, NC, February 9, 1920, p. 1, www. newspapers.com.

437 "Lutheran Campaign Heartly Endorsed," *The Dispatch*, Lexington, NC, February 10, 1920, p. 8, www.newspapers.com.

438 Ibid.

439 "The Campaign," *The Concord Daily Tribune*, Concord, NC, March 17, 1920, p. 3, www. newspapers.com.

440 *The Concord Times*, Concord, NC, April 19, 1920, p. 6, www. newspapers.com.

441 "Lenoir College Raises Its Endowment Fund," *The Hickory Record*, Hickory, NC, January 1, 1920, p. 1, www. newspapers.com.

442 "Principal's Report to Board of Trustees," April 6, 1920, McAllister Papers, ECHS.

443 Ibid.

444 Ibid.

445 "Minutes NCC, May 18, 1920.

446 Cabarrus County Deeds, Book 66, p. and Book 95, p. 196, Cabarrus County Register of Deeds, Concord, NC.

Sarah J. "Sallie" Weiser was the widow of Charles H. Weiser and the daughter of Charles Henry Fisher & Mollie Ketchie.

C. H. Fisher attended NC College in 1860 and Mollie Ketchie's brother, William Rufus Ketchie, also attended the school.[1]

[1] NC College Records, ECHS and North Carolina Death Certificates and ancestry.com.

447 Minutes NCC, January 11, 1921.

448 "Tennessee and North Carolina Synods of Lutherans to Unite," *Wilmington Morning Star*, Wilmington, NC, February 26, 1921, p. 3, www.newspapers.com.

449 Michael C. D. McDaniel, *George Franklin McAllister, 1874-1938, Lutheran Educator*. Unpublished manuscript written as partial fulfillment of the requirements of the course in American Christianity, Hamma Divinity School, Jan, 1954,. p. 22.

450 "Principal's Report to Board of Trustees," April 1921, McAllister Papers, ECHS.

451 Minutes NCC, May 24, 1921.

452 Minutes NCC, October, 1921.

453 Amendments to NC College Charter, NC College Papers, MS, Carl A. Rudisill Library, Lenoir-Rhyne University, Hickory, NC and "An Act To Amend Chapter of *Private Laws of 1909*, Raleigh, March 8,1909, 'Amending the Charter of North Carolina College, Mt. Pleasant, NC.'" *State of North Carolina Private Laws of the State of North Carolina Enacted by the General Assembly at its Extra of Session begun on December 6, 1921*, Raleigh, NC, Chapter 1, p. 1, (Mitchell Printing Co., State Printers, Raleigh, NC), 1922.

454 *The Concord Daily Tribune*, Concord, NC, November 10, 1921. p. 4, www. newspapers.com.

455 "Mt. Pleasant Collegiate Institute," *The Concord Daily Tribune*, Concord, NC, May 24, 1922. p. 4, www. newspapers.com.

456 Ibid.

457 "The Collegiate Institute," *The Progressive Farmer*, Raleigh, NC, Jul 1922, p. 12, www.newspapers.com.

458 *MPCI Catalogue, 1923-'24.*

459 "To Build New Dormitory at Mt. Pleasant School," *The Charlotte Observer*, Charlotte, NC, Dec 1922. p. 21, www. newspapers.com.

460 *MPCI Catalogue*, 1923-24, p. 29.

461 "Rhyne's Gift to Lenoir College," *Hickory Daily Record*, Hickory, NC, November 17, 1922. p. 2, www. newspapers.com.

462 "Believe $850,Campaign Certain to Be Successful," *The Concord Daily Tribune*, Concord, NC, March 8, 1923, p. 1, www. newspapers.com.

The history of Lenoir-Rhyne University states only that the College name was changed from Lenoir College to Lenoir-Rhyne in 1923 in honor of Mr. Rhyne. It does not mention that it was ever known as Daniel E. Rhyne College, however, as late as March, 1923, the press still referred to the school as "Daniel E. Rhyne College." On November 22 1922, The Herald & News, Newberry, SC stated that "the Board of Directors of the college recommended the name of the institution be changed to Daniel E. Rhyne College."1

[1] "Change Name to Daniel E. Rhyne College," The Herald & News,Newberry, SC, November 22, 1922, p. 1, www.newspapers.com.

463 "Synod Backs Appeal for College Funds," The Albemarle Press, Albemarle, NC, February 15, 1923, p. 1, www. newspapers.com.

464 Minutes NCC, May 22, 1922.

465 Ibid.

466 Letter from R. W. Leiby, Apr 1923, McAllister Papers, ECHS.

467 "This Preparatory School a Leader," *The Morning Newbernian*, New Bern, NC, June 8, 1923, p. 1, www. newspapers. com.

468 Minutes NCC, October 18, & January 2, 1924.

469 "Collegiate Institute Appeal– A Handbook, of Facts and Plans" [Pamphlet]. Apr 1924, North Carolina College Papers. *North Carolina Collection*, University of North Carolina, Chapel Hill, NC.

470 "A Worthy Cause,." *The Salisbury Post*, Salisbury, NC, [nd]. McAllister Papers, ECHS.

471 McAllister Papers, ECHS, 1924.

472 Ibid.

473 Letter from W. L. Dixon to G. F. McAllister, July 31, 1924, McAllister Papers. ECHS,

474 McAllister Papers, ECHS, July, 1924.

475 *The Institute News*, MPCI Alumni Association Newsletter, Volume II, No. 4,. p. 2, MS, ECHS Library.

476 *MPCI Catalogue, 1924-'25,* p. 11.

477 "Report to Board of Trustees," March, 1925. McAllister Papers, ECHS.

478 *The Albemarle Press*, Albemarle, NC, March 26, 1925, p. 1, www.newspapers.com.

479 Letter from W. L. Dixon to G. F. McAllister, March 27, 1925. McAllister Papers, ECHS.

480 McAllister Papers. 1925. ECHS.

481 Minutes NCC, May 26, 1925.

482 *The Institute News*, Volume IV, No. 1. November 1925, p. 1. & McAllister Papers, ECHS.

483 Ibid. The Institute News. Volume IV, No. 1. November 1925, p. 1. & McAllister Papers, ECHS.

484 "Report to Board of Trustees." May 1926. McAllister Papers, ECHS.

485 Letter from J. S. Efird to Board of Trustees of NC College, June 8, 1926. McAllister Papers, ECHS.

486 "Report to Board of Trustees, November 1, 1926." McAllister Papers, ECHS.

487 McAllister Papers, ECHS.

488 Ibid.

489 Ibid.

490 Letter from G. F. McAllister to Mrs. John M. Cook, October 16, 1926, McAllister Papers, ECHS.

491 Letter from Mrs. J. M. Cook to G. F. McAllister, October 29, 1926, McAllister Papers, ECHS.

492 Minutes NCC, February 21, 1927.

493 Minutes NCC, November 9, 1926.

494 Letter from W. J. Boger, January 27, 1927, McAllister Papers, ECHS.

495 *Minutes of The One Hundred Twenty-third Convention of the United Evangelical Lutheran Synod of North Carolina, St. John's Lutheran Church, Salisbury, NC. February 21-24, 1927*, (n.p., n.p.p), pp. 113-114.

496 Minutes, NCC, April 26, 1927.

497 *The Institute News*, September, 1927. Volume V, No.1, p. 1, ECHS Library.

498 McAllister Papers, ECHS, July 14, 1927.

499 *The Institute News*, November, 1927. Vol. V, No. 3, p. 2, ECHS Library.

500 Minutes NCC, December 8, 1927, McAllister Papers, ECHS.

501 Report to Board of Trustees, December 8, 1927. McAllister Papers, ECHS.

502 Minutes NCC, May 1928.

503 Letter from H. E. Isenhour to G. F. McAllister, June 20, 1928, McAllister Papers, ECHS.

504 Letter from H. E. Isenhour to Lawson E. Foil of Mt. Pleasant, NC June 22, 1928, McAllister Papers, ECHS.

505 Letter from H. E. Isenhour to G. F. McAllister, June 20, 1928, McAllister Papers, ECHS.

506 Letter from H. E. Isenhour to G. F. McAllister, June 22, 1928, McAllister Papers, ECHS.

507 Letter from H. E. Isenhour to G. F. McAllister, June 27, 1928, McAllister Papers, ECHS.

508 *The Institute News*, November, 1928. Vol. VI, No. 1, p. 1, ECHS Library.

509 Ibid.

510 McAllister Papers, ECHS, November, 1928.

511 Letter from US War Department dated November 9, 1928, McAllister Papers, ECHS.

512 Letter to W. J. Boger from G. F. McAllister, November 17, 1928, McAllister Papers, ECHS.

513 Letter from W. J. Boger to G. F. McAllister, November 20, 1928, McAllister Papers, ECHS.

514 McAllister Papers, ECHS.

515 Letter from H. B. Wilkinson, Board of Trustees Treasurer, to G. F. McAllister, December 17, 1928, McAllister Papers, ECHS.

516 Minutes NCC, February 4, 1929.

517 Minutes NCC, March, 1929.

518 McAllister Papers, ECHS.

519 Minutes NCC, October 4, 1929.

520 Letter from J. H. Highsmith, NC Board of Public Instruction, July 19, 1919, McAllister Papers, ECHS.

521 Minutes NCC, October 17, 1929.

522 *Minutes of The One Hundred Twenty-Seventh Convention of the United Evangelical Lutheran Synod of North Carolina. Beth Eden Evangelical Lutheran Church, Newton, NC. February 9-12, 1931*, (n.p., n.p.p.), pp. 86-87.

523 McAllister Papers, ECHS.

524 *The Institute News*, April, 1930, Special Issue, p.1, ECHS Library.

525 Carl Monsees, a native of Savannah, Georgia, had graduated from MPCI in and from Roanoke College in 1922. In 1918, while at MPCI he had served as an Officer with the Student Army Training Corps (SATC) in Plattsburg, NY. Following college, Monsees had established a Public Relations business in Maryland. Monsees later worked for several government agencies including the War Production Board, National Association of Housing, and the Office of Price Stablization.[1]

[1] McAllister Papers, ECHS and www.newspapers.com.

526 McAllister Papers, ECHS.

527 Ibid.

528 Ibid.

529 *The Concord Daily Tribune*, Concord, NC. May 27th, 1930,

530 McAllister Papers, ECHS.

531 Ibid.

532 *The Minutes of the 127th Lutheran Synod, p. 89.*

533 McAllister Papers, ECHS.

534 Letter from H. E. Isenhour to G. F. McAllister, June 4, 1930, McAllister Papers, ECHS.

535 Letter to Rev. Wickey from Col. McAllister, Jun 1930, McAllister Papers, ECHS. Reverend Norman J. G. Wickey, Chairman of the National Lutheran Church of America.

"At the time of your visit in the early spring [1929?] to the Institute I undertook to convey to you, Doctor Wickey, the situation at the Institute and the absolute need of help from the Board of Education of the United Lutheran Church. I had proceeded in preparations for the school year 1929-30 on the assumption that at least the same amount would be forthcoming from your Board, if not more, than we had been receiving. Our Board had taken action and named a committee to seek a hearing from the U.L.C. Board in reference to an increase in the appropriation to the College and the Collegiate Institute. I did not learn officially what had been the action of your Board until after the contracts had been entered into with teachers and obligations assumed from expenses in connection with printing catalogues and canvassing.

In truth, Dr. Wickey, it was the cutting down of the appropriation of the Board of Education of the United Lutheran Church that proved "the straw that broke the camel's back" in the finances of the Collegiate Institute and precipitated a crisis that necessitated the Executive Committee of the Collegiate Institute to put an agent in the field in May to endeavor to raise an emergency fund, or else face the necessity of closing the Institute. I have had the financial burden of running the Institute to carry on with meager assistance from outside, with practically no income other than that from tuition receipts. No institution doing the work of the Collegiate Institute is self-sustaining. In March, I reported to my Executive Committee that I had paid myself $400 on salary. Since that time, I have received $125. This, despite the fact that there have been those who seemed to believe that I was a well-paid school administrator. How they could figure that out, is more than I can understand. The reason I have not hitherto emphasized the meager support I have received is that the fact would have operated to the disadvantage of the Institute and it was the Institute and what it stands for that I was serving.

The North Carolina Synod has projected a campaign for this fall when it is proposed to raise for the Collegiate Institute $100,000 with which to pay an indebtedness of $20,000 and increase (or rather start) the endowment.

It was especially desirable to be able to carry on until this campaign could be put on. Yet I faced the possibility of losing all I had in an effort to tide over a very hard year (due to the depression that was so wide spread). So, I informed the Executive Committee that it was more than I felt I should do, in fairness to myself and family. I have given 33 years of my life to this work. With what fidelity, zeal, earnestness, and results educational, I leave it to those who know best the work of the Institute to say. At any rate, the Board, the Synod and the friends of this cause do not want to see it abandoned. The Collegiate Institute is standard so far as its High School course is concerned. Its college work is recognized by the State University and other high-grade colleges, though not fully accredited, because we lack endowment and fail to meet certain other requirements. However, all requirements can be met when the minimum endowment specified is secured.

In the emergency appeal now in process, local friends are manifesting real interest. Just yesterday, a millionaire of Concord, not of our church, indicated interest and said he was going to help. The Pres of the National Bank did the same thing. A visit to a very wealthy man of our church ten days ago elicited the promise to help. The Collegiate Institute is the only Preparatory School and Junior College with Military feature in the United Lutheran Church. It has a place in our system, the Church South believes. The attitude of the Board of Education of the United Lutheran Church is of vital significance, to be sure. Just now, especially, when the institution is in a veritable struggle for existence, when the North Carolina Synod is about to go in the field for $100,000 for the Institute, when friends outside of our Church indicate a willingness to assist in not only keeping it alive but raising it to the unqualified standard of an accredited Junior College, surely the Board of Education of the United Lutheran Church will not fail to lend encouragement and increased support

536 Letter to Rev. N. J. G. Wickey from J. L. Morgan, Jun 1930. McAllister Papers, ECHS.

On the same date as Colonel McAllister's letter to Rev. Wickey, Rev. Jacob L. Morgan, the first President of the merged Lutheran Synod of North Carolina and an Ex Officio member of the Board of Trustees, wrote Wickey. In this letter, Rev. Morgan reflected his true feelings about MPCI, but went on to ask Rev. Wickey to ask his Board to reconsider their decision cutting funding for the school.

"A few days ago Prof. G. F. McAllister left a letter at my office for me to read, which you had written him, in which you say that no communication had come to your office in regard to the cut in your Board's appropriation to the Collegiate Institute for the year just closed.

Permit me to say that I regard that a matter which properly should be handled through our Board of Educational Institutions, and therefore I have advised Dr. W. J. Boger of Newton, NC, Chairman of the Board, who will communicate with you as to same.

My interest and the interest of our Synod in this school, however, prompt me to say that we hope your Board will give prayerful and sympathetic consideration to the pressing needs of the Institute at this time. I am afraid a mistaken notion has gotten into the minds of some of our good brethren regarding the finances of this school. When Dr. H. B. Schaeffer and myself met with a Committee from your Board to consider the needs of the Institute and of Lenoir Rhyne College last year, some of the Board members advanced the opinion that the Institute was a splendidly paying business and that Prof. McAllister was making good money out of it. I tried then to disabuse the minds of the brethren of such a notion, for I could not see how more than a living could be made out of the school as operated [emphasis added]. A good while after that meeting I learned indirectly that an emergency grant [from the LCA] had been voted in favor or Lenoir Rhyne, which I greatly appreciated. But at the same time and in the same way I learned furthermore that a fifty percent cut had been made in the appropriation to the Institute. I regretted this cut very much, for I knew the money was needed.

It has not come to our knowledge that Prof. McAllister has lost money in his efforts to operate the school during the past year. We are advised that he has paid himself only $525 salary for his year's work and that he owes bills and accounts amounting to two thousand or twenty-five hundred dollars for the year's operations. Moreover funds are needed with which to get out catalogues and make preparations for reopening next fall. In view of these conditions, I want to urge your Board to do all it can to come to the rescue of the Institute at this time, and restore if possible at least the amount of last year's cut. In fact, more than that is needed for prior to last year another large cut had been made which effected seriously the operations of the school."

537 McAllister Papers, ECHS.

"The Collegiate Institute – Is A Business and Cultural Asset to Concord & Cabarrus – Will You Help It Continue and Expand? The Collegiate Institute's appeal to Concord & Cabarrus County citizens is a business proposition with an element of sentiment. On this basis Concord will or will not do its part in the present appeal for help and program of expansion; on this basis the Institute will secure or will not secure the amount it is asking. Whatever the result, it will be Cabarrus' and Concord's answer as to whether or not it is good business to have this institution operating in Mt. Pleasant.

The Institute charges each student four hundred ($400.00) dollars for tuition, board and room. Each student spends a minimum of two hundred ($200.00) dollars more in nine months for sundry expenses. Thus, this county receives a minimum of six hundred ($600.00) from each student in attendance. There are around one hundred boys in school; there have been more. Multiply: Six hundred ($600.00) by one hundred and you get sixty thousand ($60,000) dollars – sixty thousand dollars every year. Does it, or will it, make any difference whether this Institution operates or not? Other cities are paying big prices for Institutions of learning, because it is good business to have new money coming in every … ."

538 Ibid.

539 Letter from W. L. Morris to Rev. L. D. Miller, June 14, 1930, McAllister Papers, ECHS.

540 McAllister Papers, ECHS.

541 Letter to Rev. L. D. Miller from Carl Monsees, June 14, 1930, McAllister Papers, ECHS.

542 Ibid.

543 Ibid.

544 Letter from Rev. J. L. Morgan to G. F. McAllister, June 6, 1930, McAllister Papers, ECHS.

545 Letter from A. B. Lovett to G. F. McAllister, June 19, 1930, McAllister Papers, ECHS.

546 Letter from Thomas M. Hoynes to G. F. McAllister, June 21,1930, McAllister Papers, ECHS.

547 Minutes, NCC, June 19, 1930.

On June 25, 1930 The Executive Committee of the UEL Synod of NC voted to approve the Board of Trustees Action.

548 McAllister Papers, ECHS.

549 Letter from Carl Monsees to G. F. McAllister, July 6, 1930, McAllister Papers, ECHS.

550 Letter from Carl Monsees to G. F. McAllister, July 16, 1930, McAllister Papers, ECHS.

551 Letter to Alumni from G. F. McAllister, September 16, 1930, McAllister Papers, ECHS.

552 McAllister Papers, ECHS.

553 Letter to Chairman of the Board of Trustees of NC College (MPCI) from the Secretary of the Board of the ULCA, August 7, from the *Minutes of the 127th Lutheran Synod,* p. 90.

554 McAllister Papers, Jul 1930, ECHS Library.

555 *Minutes of 127th Lutheran Synod*, pp. & 90.

556 Ibid. pp. 105-106.

557 *The Concord Daily Tribune*, Concord, NC. February 12, 1931, p. 1.

558 Ibid.

559 *The Concord Daily Tribune*, Concord, NC. February 13, 1931, p. 6.

560 Letters from Z. L. Edwards, DDS, Washington, NC to Rev. George S. Bowden, Gastonia, NC, February 26, 1931. McAllister Papers, ECHS.

Reference decision of Synod to cancel contract of MPCI.

561 *Minutes of The One Hundred Twenty-Eighth Convention of the United Evangelical Lutheran Synod of North Carolina. 1st Albemarle Church, Albemarle, NC. February 9-12, 1932,*(n.p., n.p.p.), pp. 40-41.

562 *The Concord Tribune*, May 18, 1931.

563 *The Concord Tribune*, May 18, 1931.

564 *Minutes of the One Hundred Twenty-ninth Convention of The United Evangelical Lutheran Synod of North Carolina, Mt. Moriah Lutheran Church, China Grove, NC, Feb 7-10, 1933*, (n.p, n.p.p.), p. 77.

565 Letter from H. E. Isenhour to Col. McAllister, Nov 1931, McAllister Papers, ECHS.

566 Letter from H. E. Isenhour to Col. McAllister, Dec 1931, McAllister Papers, ECHS.

567 McAllister Papers, ECHS.

568 McAllister Papers, ECHS.

569 McAllister Papers, ECHS.

570 Ibid.

571 Letter from Joseph F Cannon to G. F. McAllister, December 31, 1932, McAllister Papers, ECHS.

Note at the bottom of the letter states that McAllister "saw him and he promised that about Feb. 10-15 he would make a donation to the Inst of $250.00."

572 Letter from G. F. McAllister to Mrs. Cameron Morrison, McAllister Papers, ECHS.

573 Letter from O. A. Glover, Sheriff of Wilson Co. NC, McAllister Papers, ECHS.

574 Ibid.

575 Report to Board of Trustees, May 18, 1933, McAllister Papers, ECHS.

576 Report to the MPCI Board of Trustees, May 18, 1933, McAllister Papers, ECHS.

"The problem of finances has been the most difficult with which we have had to deal. A year ago, I reported to you that if all tuition accounts were collected there would be a small balance in the treasury for the session 1931-32. Unfortunately, we were unable to collect all too many of these accounts. The same difficulty of collecting has been experienced this session. ... With a broader curriculum, our operating expenses have been increased. The consequence is that we close the school year with a considerable deficit.

We appealed to a limited number of friends for financial aid. Under normal conditions, it is practically certain that all would have responded favorably. But all businesses have been affected by the depression. ... Two donations were received - one for twenty-five dollars and one for two-hundred and fifty dollars. The latter was a god send in that it enabled us to save our school bus in which we had invested a considerable sum but which we were about to lose because we could meet the payments as they became due. As another oasis in this desert of apparent hopelessness, was the attitude of the larger creditors of the Institute – the firm which furnishes our uniforms and the one which supplies in large part our foodstuff. Both were candidly informed of our financial status ... But both were surprisingly considerate and advised carrying on.

I have advised my colleagues on the faculty that there is only one way in which the Collegiate Institute can continue, and that is by improving its financial status. This can be done by reducing our operating expenses and increasing our income. Those who remain at the Institute accept this plan. It is planned to solicit aid from persons interested in the program of the Collegiate Institute. Already we have promise of financial assistance from some, as soon as business recovery will make it possible. In this connection, reference should be made to the Plan of using a financial Secretary, which I proposed a year ago. ... The Plan was submitted in detail. In practically every case, the principle was approved.

However, some of the members whose judgment is respected advised that the time was inopportune. Consequently the Plan was abandoned for the time being. ...

Present needs are urgent. ... It is apparent to the Board that to keep the Collegiate going has been a real task. All enterprises have had a struggle. It seems to me that there never was a time when there was more need for institutions to do the kind of work to which the Collegiate Institute is dedicated. It is our purpose to carry on; and in our efforts for strengthening and development of MPCI, we are counting on your continued interest and cooperation."

577 *The Concord Tribune*, Concord, NC, May 23, 1933. p. 1.

578 McAllister Papers, ECHS.

579 Letter to US Representative R. L. Doughton, August, 17, 1933, McAllister Papers, ECHS.

"You have your quota and more of problems of state and I am loathe to bring to you any of my problems. But I am facing a crisis and I am writing as friend, Board Member and Congressman. It has been very difficult to get prospects to make definite decisions. That is always the case, but more especially so this year. There are plenty of youth who would enroll with us, if we could take them for $150 to $200 and let them work out the balance of the cost, but we cannot operate on such a basis. ...

Added to this is the fact that one of our larger creditors, J. W. Ayer & Son, Advertising Agency, notwithstanding a promise "to go along with us," is suing us for an account which we have been unable to pay.

Under existing circumstances, it appears with insured present enrollment, we would operate another year at a loss again. You see the crisis that faces me. It may be that within the next four weeks a considerable number of additional enrollments could be made, though as full pay students this is doubtful.

Now to the point. Is there any Federal aid available for private institutions? If so, can it be had promptly enough and under such terms as to make it advisable for the Collegiate Institute to seek it and to accept it, if available? You know how it pulls at my heart strings to even think of giving up on the work here where I have spent most days of my life. However, I also dare not allow sentiment to direct me into a course which would inevitably mean increased indebtedness. So, unless there is speed and unexpected betterment of the outlook, either through increased enrollment or outside aid, it seems to me there is no other course to pursue than to announce soon the suspension of the Collegiate Institute.

There are those who have said they were going to help the Institute but promised aid avails nothing to a drowning man unless it is rendered in time.

I crave your advice, as I said, in the capacity of friend, Board member and Congressman.

If the worst should come and we are forced to suspend, I have nothing in sight. When I was considering the matter of running the Institute independently, tentative offers were made me to teach at several institutions out of the state. I didn't like the idea of readjustment, and besides, I wanted above all to see the Collegiate Institute go on. So, if there should be a position in some Dept. of Government for which I might be fitted and which you might be able to help me secure, it goes without saying that I would be grateful for your assistance.

If you will find time in the midst of your multifarious duties to give consideration to this communication and let me hear from you, I will be grateful. G. F. McAllister."

580 McAllister Papers, ECHS.

581 Letter from G. F. McAllister to former students, August 31, 1933, McAllister Papers, ECHS.

582 *Concord Daily Tribune,* Concord, NC, September 2, 1933, p. 1.

583 Letter to Creditors of the Collegiate Institute from G. F. McAllister. September 20, 1933, McAllister Papers, ECHS.

"Gentlemen: On September 2nd, announcement was officially made that the Collegiate Institute would not open in September. This decision was reached after careful and deliberate consideration. Losses sustained in the last two years of operation and the evident fact, based on careful survey of the prospects for the coming year, made this step imperative. If we had undertaken to run on, it would have meant incurring additional indebtedness, and we didn't consider that an honest procedure.

The Collegiate Institute closed last session with a considerable amount due it on tuition accounts, but collections during the summer have been negligible. The school has no assets of any consequence. The Plant and much of the furnishings belong to the United E. L. Synod of North Carolina. Comparatively little can be realized from the property owned by the Collegiate Institute. Under the circumstances, I as Pres. and Treasurer of the Institute, am at a loss to know what can be done. I want to do the right thing, the honest thing. Since 1931, I have been continuing the Collegiate Institute under an arrangement with the Board of Trustees which holds the plant for the Synod which created the Board. I have a Board (different from the Board created by Synod) but it assumed no financial obligations.

"I have spent thirty-six years of my life with the institution and have never accumulated very much, for the school was run to make money. Considerable of what I have saved was lost several years ago in a bad investment.

I do own some shares of Cannon Mill Stock. This is now quoted at less than I paid for it, although the market quotation is rising. This stock is up for collateral at the Cabarrus Bank and Trust, Co. of Concord, NC for a loan I effected with the Bank for $8500. With a market improvement in the stock market (which may come under the N. R. A., especially if currency is inflated), this stock could be sold for an amt. sufficient to pay off the loan at the Bank and pay a fair percentage of the indebtedness of the Institute. While I do not consider myself technically responsible for the debts of the Institute, yet I recognize a moral element involved and, as I said, I want to do the honorable thing and am willing for my Cannon Mill holdings to go toward paying off the Institute's indebtedness, after the loan at the bank is taken care of. . . . ."

584 Minutes NCC, October 10, 1933, McAllister Papers, ECHS.

585 Ibid.

586 Letter from A. Jacobs & Sons, Tailors, Uniforms & Equipment, W. Fayette St., Baltimore, MD, April 5, 1934, McAllister Papers, ECHS.

587 McAllister Papers, ECHS, February 13, 1932.

588 Letter to Representative H. L. Doughton from Capt. G. F. Herbert, US Army, dated May 1934, McAllister Papers, ECHS.

589 Letter from H. L. Doughton to G. F. McAllister, May 16, 1934, McAllister Papers, ECHS.

590 Minutes of the Board of Directors of the Collegiate Institute, January 8, 1935, MS, McAllister Papers, ECHS.

591 McAllister Papers, ECHS.

592 Letter to the Secretary of the NC Synod Board of Education, from the NC College Board of Trustees, January 8, 1935, McAllister Papers, ECHS.

593 McAllister Papers, ECHS.

The items sold included 66 beds at $5 each, 29 mattresses at $5 each, 37 mattresses a $4.50 each, 18 bureaus at $4.50 each, and 17 bureaus at $7 each.

594 Letter written to the Secretary of the NC Synod Board of Education, January 8, 1935, McAllister Papers, ECHS.

595 Minutes NCC, September 8, 1936, McAllister Papers, ECHS.

596 Letter from McAllister to Dr. W. D. James of Hamlet, NC, June 1, 1935, McAllister Papers, ECHS.

Rev. F. M. Osborne was interested in establishing a "Boys School with special features." He stated that Dr. James was interested in the project. James replied on June 4, 1935 that he would have Mr. Osborne inspect the property. According to an article in the *Burlington, NC Daily Times* dated March 16, 1935, Rev. Francis M. Osborne, a former Captain of the UNC Football team (1900) and Coach at Sewanee College in Tennessee, was representing a group of "interested North Carolinians from Washington, DC," who were exploring the possibility of opening a Boys Preparatory School in North Carolina. The "special feature" was to be a state of the art athletic facility which would serve to keep young athletes from North Carolina from going out of state.[1]

[1] *Burlington Daily Times-News*, Burlington, NC, March 16, 1935, p. 4, www. newspapers.com.

597 Letter from Walter P. Steinhauser, Atlanta, GA, to G. F. McAllister, September 17, 1936, McAllister Papers, ECHS.

598 "Resolution of Board of Trustees of NC College," March 1937, Minutes, NCC, McAllister Papers, ECHS.

599 McAllister Papers, ECHS, March 27, 1937.

A document in the McAllister papers refers to "Sale Conducted by Col. McAllister 3/27/1937" and lists various lots purchased by individuals.

The auction was conducted by Penny Brothers, Auctioneers, Charlotte, NC.

Lots 24-25-26 L. H. Barringer
Lots 27-28 L. H. Barringer
Lots 1-2-3-4 L. H. Barringer $252
Lot 5 UCA L. H. Barringer
Lot 1-2 Block A George McAllister $78
Lot 10-11 Block A George McAllister $40 $115.65cash
Lot 12 Block A ???
Lots 11-16 Block C W. S. Stallings $190 $99cash
Lots 15-19 Block B Roger Stallings $112.50
Lots 3-4-5 Block A Mrs. M. A. Ritchie $90 $30cash
Lots 6-7 Block A Homer Allman $50 $20cash
Lots 5-12 Block B M. D. Kluttz $97.50 $97.50cash
Lots 13-15 Block B Lee McAllister $37.50 $37.50cash

Lots 7-9 Block C Paul A. Moose $124 $41.50cash
Lot 10 Block C Paul A. Moose ???
Lots 20-23 Block A C. J. Flowe? $100 $50cash
Lots 13-14 Block A Hoy A. Moose $70
Lots 1-4 Block B Hoy A. Moose $54 $41.50cash
Lots 9-10 Block A Marion Cline $60 $20cash

Total $13,550.50 $799.65cash
Commission $135.55
Expenses $250
Cash $185.55 Check $200

600 Letter from Roscoe Slack to G. F. McAllister, March, 1941, McAllister Papers, ECHS.

601 McAllister Papers, ECHS and *Cabarrus County Death Records*, Cabarrus County Register of Deeds, Concord, NC.

602 The editor of the *Concord Tribune* wrote these words on the day after Col. McAllister's death:

"All Cabarrus County and the State of North Carolina, as a whole, today mourns the passing of Colonel George F. McAllister, who died at home in Mount Pleasant, early Monday morning.

Colonel McAllister's life was one of service to his church and to Christian education. It was in the leading of youth that he found his greatest happiness. Throughout the land are scattered his former students of old North Carolina College and MPCI, and their success in the ministry and various other walks of life attest to the firm foundation on which he guided them.

Colonel McAllister was the kind of man who built a better world, and this world can ill afford to lose men of his type in these turbulent times. His was a steadying influence, a leader who encouraged, a man who never lost his personal sense of direction – duty to church and Christian education.

Standing as a monument to his life are the fine ideals and Christian principles he included in the lives of those men and women who were fortunate enough to share his knowledge and wisdom in the classroom. These principles will live on, serving mankind in good stead long after the walls of the Institute have crumbled to dust.

It is part of the record that he understood youth and youth's problems. He seemed to sense their hopes and aspirations, their disappointments and problems, and he was ever alert to their cause with a listening ear and wise counsel.

Colonel McAllister had a keen zest for life, possessed a radiant personality, was highly esteemed in Mt. Pleasant and far beyond the boundaries of the state.

Truly Cabarrus County has lost a distinguished son, and education and religious ranks will be deprived of a courageous leader."[1]

[1] McDaniel, *George Franklin McAllister, 1874-1938, Lutheran Educator.*

603 Minutes NCC, November 5, 1937.

604 Minutes NCC, January 14, 1938.

It is unclear what "rents" Cline collected, but apparently some of the buildings on the Institute site were rented as residences or for storage. In November 1938, Cline submitted his financial statement for the property. It included receipts for a payment of $13 by Mrs McAllister, house rents from unnamed individuals of $106.70, and rent of the water tank site by the Town of Mt. Pleasant of $85.00. He also reported repairs to the various buildings totaling $65.10. He was instructed by the Board of Trustees to retain the funds for additional repairs and expenses as necessary.[1]

[1] "Minutes NCC, November 25, 1938.

605 ""Minutes NCC, January 14, 1938.

"The Mount Pleasant Collegiate Institute was closed at the end of 1931-32 session. Unoccupied except for caretaker living in some rooms in one dormitory." The enumerator, Verna Mae Hahn, did not name the caretaker.[1]

[1] 1940 U.S. Census, Cabarrus County, North Carolina, *Population Schedule #430, Mt. Pleasant, ED 13-21, Sheet # 61A). Digital image,* www.ancestry.com.

606 *Rocky Mount Telegram*, Rocky Mount, NC, March 22, 1941, p. 12, www. newspapers. com.

607 Letter to Mr. H. E. Isenhour, c/o Isenhour Insurance & Realty Co., Salisbury, NC from E. T. Bost, Jr., Attn at Law, Concord NC, Apr 1941, MS, North Carolina Evangelical Lutheran Synod Archives, Columbia, SC.

608 "Minutes NCC, May 2, 1941.

609 *Kannapolis* Daily Independent, Kannapolis, NC, July 9, 1941, p. 1.

610 *The Statesville Record & Landmark*, Statesville, NC,. March 31, and July 21, 1941.

611 https://libguides.lr.edu/rudisilllibrary/facts and *NC College Board of Trustee's Records*, 1941, MS, Carl A. Rudisill Library, Lenoir-Rhyne University, Hickory, NC.

In 1943, Rudisill's gift of $50,000 to Lenoir-Rhyne College, resulted in the construction of the Carl Augustus Rudisill Library on the L-R Campus. Again, ironically, most of the records of NC College and MPCI are housed at this facility.

612 "Minutes NCC, November 21, 1941.

613 Ibid., November 21, 1941.

614 Ibid., March 27, 1942.

615 Letter from P. E. Monroe to H. E. Isenhour, December 26, 1941, McAllister Papers, ECHS.
616 *Kannapolis Daily Independent*, Kannapolis, NC, January, 18, 1942, p. 2.

Part II - Academics

617 "Cirriculum," Indiana University Bloomington, www.Collections. libraries. indiana.edu.
618 McDaniel, *Brief History of North Carolina College, Mt. Pleasant, NC 1859-1901.*
619 Minutes WCMA, January, 1856.
620 *Minutes of the Evangelical Lutheran Synod*, May 1855, p. 18.
621 "The Western Carolina Male Academy," *The Concord Weekly Gazette,* Concord, NC, October 13, 1855, p. 3.

The first portion of this advertisement stated that the Winter Session would begin on the third Thursday of September. The second section announced that the "Winter Session will commence on Thursday, the 25th of October next."

622 *Catalogue of the Officers and Students of Western Carolina Academy at Mt. Pleasant, Cabarrus County, NC,* (J. J. Bruner, Book and Job Printer, Salisbury, NC, 1857), p. 11, (hereafter cited as WCMA Catalogue).
623 Ibid.
624 September, 1856.
625 Ibid., March, 1856.
626 *WCMA Catalogue,* 1857, p. 3.
627 Minutes WCMA, May, 1856.
628 Ibid., May 1856, pp. 5-& 16.
629 Ibid., p. 14.
630 Ibid.
631 Ibid., pp. 9-10.
632 *Minutes of the 54th Annual Meeting of the Evangelical Lutheran Synod and Ministerium of North Carolina convened at St. Paul's Lutheran Church, Alamance County, NC on April 29, 1858*, (n.p.), (n.p.p.), p. 9.
633 Minutes WCMA,1857.

Caleb Lentz was a Rowan County, NC native. He was "licensed" by the NC Synod and ordained 1859. After resigning his teaching position, he served at Beth Eden Lutheran Church in Newton, NC. He died in Davie County, NC in 1863 at the age of 38.[1]

[1] "Lentz, Caleb." *Life Sketches of Lutheran Ministers*, p. 113.

634 Minutes WCMA,1858.
635 Minutes WCMA,1859.

Rev. Louis Albert Bikle was born Nov. 6, 1834 in Mechanicstown, MD. He graduated from Gettysburg College, in 1857 and the Gettysburg Seminary in 1859 and ordained by the North Carolina Lutheran Synod in 1862. He was hired an instructor at the Western Carolina Male Academy in Mt. Pleasant in 1858 and was appointed Professor of Latin and Greek at NC College in 1859. He remained at the College until it closed in 1861. In 1862, he enlisted into the Confederate Army and was appointed Chaplain of the 20th NC Infantry Regt. After the war he returned to NC College where he was the only faculty member at the reopening of the school in 1866. He was elected as President of the College in 1868 and served in this capacity until 1874. Also in 1874 he received his Doctor of Divinity Degree from Franklin &Marshall College in Pennsylvania. He left the NC College in 1874 but returned in 1878 and served as President again until 1881. After 1881, he served as a Professor at Gaston Female College in Dallas, NC and as the Principal of Kings Mountain High School for five years. He served four terms as the Secretary and four terms as President of the NC Lutheran Synod. He retired from the ministry in 1904 but continued to teach school for ten more years. Rev. Bikle was married to Sara Ann Chriztman and had three children. He died in Concord, NC on June 29, 1931 and is buried at Oakwood Cemetery, Concord, NC.[1]

[1] "Bikle, Louis Albert," *Life Sketches of Lutheran Minsters, North Carolina & Tennessee Synods, 1773-1965*, (North Carolina Evangelical Lutheran Synod, The State Printing Co., Columbia, SC, 1966), p. 22.

636 "North Carolina College," *Weekly Raleigh Register*, Raleigh, NC, September 7, 1859, p. 1, www. newspapers. com.

637 Bansemer Papers, 1830-1866.

638 Ibid.

639 Ibid.

640 McDaniel, *A Brief History of North Carolina College, Mt. Pleasant, NC*, p. 8.

641 Minutes NCC, July 18, 1860.

642 Bansemer Papers.

643 *North Carolina College, 1861,* pp. 10-11, hptts://archive.org.

644 "Minutes NCC, September, 1860.

645 "Minutes NCC, October, 1859.

646 "President's Report to the Board of Trustees," Bansemer Papers.

647 Ibid.

648 Ibid.

Robert Christian Holland was a native of Virginia. He graduated from Roanoke College in 1860 and took a position on the faculty of NC College in 1861. However, shortly after taking his postion as the College, he resigned and enlisted in Co. A, Salem Light Flying Artillery (9th VA Regt, CSA). He later transferred Co. I, 28th VA Infantry which became part of General

George Pickett's Division. Holland was wounded at Darbytown, VA (Battle of 2nd Manassas) in June 1862 but returned to service. On July 3rd, 1863, he participated in Pickett's Charge at the Battle of Gettysburg where he was once again wounded and captured. Following a short stay in a Federal Hospital in New York, he was exchanged and admitted to Wayside Hospital in Richmond, VA. He remained in the hospital until transferred to the Invalid Corps in 1864.[1] Following the war, Holland entered the University of Virginia where he received a Law Degree in 1866. He practiced law for two years and entered the ministry in 1868. The served as VP of Roanoke College from 1878-1881. He served parishes in West Virginia, Virginia, South Carolina and North Carolina. He was appointed a member of the Board of Trustees of NC College in 1908 while serving as the minister at St. Mark's Lutheran Church in Charlotte, NC. He later served on the Lutheran Board of Foreign Missions and the Board of Lutheran Seminary. Rev. Holland died in 1915 in Columbia, SC and is buried in Salem, VA.[2]

[1] "Compiled Service Records of Confederate Soldiers Who Served in Organizations Raised Directly by the Confederate Government." Database. *Fold3.com.* https://www.fold3.com: [nd] Citing NARA microfilm publication M258. Washington, D. C.: National Archives and Records Administration, 1963.

[2] "Holland, Robert C.," *Life Sketches of Lutheran Minsters, North Carolina & Tennessee Synods, 1773- 1965*, (North Carolina Evangelical Lutheran Synod, The State Printing Co., Columbia, SC, 1966), p. 95.

649 *NCC Catalogue, Year, Ending July 1861,* https://archive.org.

650 *The Raleigh Register,* Raleigh, NC, August 14, 1861, p. 2, www. newspapers.com.

651 *Minutes of the Fifty-Ninth Lutheran Synod,* 1862,. p. 18.

652 *Minutes of the Evangelical Lutheran Synod,* 1867, p. 22.

653 "Prospectus of North Carolina College at Mt. Pleasant, North Carolina, 1867," (n.p., n.p.p.), MS, ECHS Library, Mt. Pleasant, NC.

654 *NCC Catalogue, 1871-72,* pp. 4-5, https://archive.org.

655 Bansemer Papers.

656 *The Charlotte Democrat,* Charlotte, NC, June 1868, p. 3, www. newspapers. com.

Robert P. Waring was a Civil War veteran who had served in the 43rd NC Regt. and participated in the Battle of Gettysburg. He resigned his commission in November, 1863 due to sickness, but later served as Adjutant of the 4th NC Senior Reserves.[1] He was an Attorney and former editor of the Charlotte Times. In 1866 he had been found guilty and fined by a military court of making statements in his newspaper that *"were calculated and intended to produce hostility toward the government of the United States."*[2]

[1] htpps://www.civilwardata.com

[2] *The Daily Standard,* Raleigh, NC, January 20, 1866, p. 1, www.newspapers.com.

657 *NCC Catalogue,* 1869, MS, ECHS Library, Mt. Pleasant, NC.

658 *North Carolina Argus,* Wadesboro, NC, December 1868, p. 1, www.newspapers.com.

659 *NCC Catalogue,* 1869.

660 Ibid.

661 Minutes NCC, September, 1870.

662 *NCC Catalogue for the Year ending May 16, 1870,* hptts://archive.org.

663 *Minutes of the Sixty-Seventh Annual Meeting of the Evangelical Lutheran Synod & Ministerium of North Carolina, convened at Lutheran Chapel, Rowan County, NC on August 25, 1870,* (J. J. Bruner, Printer, Salisbury, NC), p. 15.

664 *NCC Catalogue for the Year ending May 25, 1871.* https://archive.org.

665 *The Old North State,* Salisbury, NC, December 30, 1870, p. 2, www.newspapers.com.

666 *NC Catalogue for the Year ending May 25, 1871,* hptts://archive.org.

John Monroe Reid was the son of William W. Reid and Julia Ann Melchor, and the grandson of Christopher Melchor, the first Chairman of the Board of Trustees of the Western Carolina Academy and NC College. He died in August 1871, only three months after graduating.[1]

[1] https://www.ancestry.com.

667 *Minutes of the Sixty-Eighth Annual Meeting of the Evangelical Lutheran Synod & Ministerium of North Carolina, convened at Pilgrim Church, Davidson Co, NC August 1871.* (J. J. Bruner, Printer, Salisbury, NC), p. 6.

Rev. William Effiah Hubbert was born in Roanoke,VA in 1844. He was a Civil War veteran serving as a Corporal with Co. B., Griffin's Salem Artillery, 1st Battalion VA Light Artillery. He graduated from Roanoke College in 1867 and received his AM Degree from Philadelphia Seminary in 1871. He was ordained by the Southwest Virginia Synod in 1870. He joined the NC Synod in 1871 when he was hired at NC College. He returned to Virginia in 1877 where he served as Editor of The Lutheran Visitor and Secretary of the Southwest Synod. His second wife, Virginia Ribble, was the Principal of Mont Amonea Seminary at the time of their marriage. He died in 1915.

[1] "Hubbert, William E," *Life Sketches of Lutheran Minsters, North Carolina & Tennessee Synods, 1773- 1965,* (North Carolina Evangelical Lutheran Synod, The State Printing Co., Columbia, SC, 1966), p. 98.

668 *NCC Catalogue*, 1871-72. ECHS Library, Mt. Pleasant, NC.

669 Ibid.

670 "Commencement at N. C. College, Mt. Pleasant, N. C." *The Charlotte Democrat,* Charlotte, NC, June 11, 1872. p. 3, www. newspapers.com.

671 Minutes NCC, October, 1872.

672 "President's Report to Board of Trustees," NCC Minutes, May 28, 1873.

673 "Faculty Minutes for April 15, 1874," Records of North Carolina College, MS, Eastern Cabarrus Historical Society Library, Mt. Pleasant. NC, (hereafter cited as Faculty Minutes).

674 Ibid.

675 Ibid., May 20, 1874.

676 Ibid.

Joseph Adolphus Linn was the son of Rev. J. A. Linn, who, as President of the Lutheran Synod in 1852, had proposed the creation of the school which became NC College.

677 *Minutes of the Seventy-Second Annual Meeting of the Evangelical Lutheran Synod & Ministerium of North Carolina, convened at St. John's Evangelical Lutheran Church, Cabarrus County, NC on August 28, 1875,* (Henkel & Co. Printers, New Market, VA). p. 12-13.

678 Faculty Minutes.

679 *The Concord Register*, Concord, NC, May 27, 1876. p. 4, www. newspapers.com.

680 Ibid.

681 Faculty Minutes.

682 Faculty Minutes, Feb 7, 1877.

683 *The Charlotte Democrat*, June 29, 1877, p. 3, www. newspapers.com.

684 *Minutes of the Seventy-Fifth Annual Meeting of the Evangelical Lutheran Synod & Ministerium of North Carolina, convened at Frieden's Church, Guilford County, NC on May 1, 1878*, (Henkel & Co. Printers, New Market, VA), pp. 15-16.

685 *The Charlotte Democrat*, Charlotte, NC, May 23, 1878, p. 4, www. newspapers.com.

686 *Minutes of the Seventy-Sixth Annual Meeting of the Evangelical Lutheran Synod & Ministerium of North Carolina, convened at Bethel Church, Stanly County, NC on April 30, 1879*, (J. J. Bruner, Printer, Salisbury, NC), pp. 8-9.

687 *The Carolina Watchman*, Salisbury, NC, August, 15, 1878, p. 3, www. newspapers.com.

688 *The Wilmington Sun*, Wilmington, NC, January, 28, 1879, p. 1, www. newspapers.com.

689 *The Carolina Watchman*, Salisbury, NC, May 8, 1879, p. 2, www. newspapers.com.

690 *NCC Catalogue, 1879-80.*

691 Ibid.

692 Ibid.

693 *The Charlotte Democrat*, June 4, 1880, p. 3, www. newspapers.com.

694 *Minutes of the Seventy-Eighth Annual Convention of Evangelical Lutheran Synod & Ministerium of North Carolina. convened at Sandy Creek Lutheran Church,*

Davidson, Co. NC, April 27, 1881, (Henkel & Co. Printers & Publishers, New Market, VA), p. 17.

695 NC College Records, MS, ECHS Library, Mt. Pleasant, NC.

696 Minutes NCC, May 23, 1882.

697 *The Charlotte Observer*, Charlotte, NC May 13, 1882. p. 3, www.newspapers.com.

Henry S. "Hal" Puryear was a prominent Attorney and Democrat from Concord, NC. He was also an advocate for the railroad which may have been the reason for his being invited to speak at the NC College commencement.

698 *NCC Catalogue, 1881-1882.*

699 *The Wilmington Morning Star*, Wilmington, NC, June 16, 1882, p. 1, www.newspapers.com. and https://www. Ancestry.com. United States Federal Census [database on-line].

700 NC College Records, MS, ECHS Library, Mt. Pleasant, NC.

701 Minutes NCC, 1884.

Luther Hazelius Rothrock was the son of Rev. Samuel Rothrock, a member of the original Board of Trustees of the Western Carolina Academy, and in 1884, the Chairman of the NC College Board of Trustees. After serving as an Officer in the Civil War, L. H. returned to North Carolina and began teaching school. He served as the Principal of the Mt. Pleasant Female Academy from 1876-1882 and received his A. M. Degree from NC College in 1884. He served on the Mt. Pleasant Town Board in 1886. In the 1890's he moved to Gold Hill in Rowan County where he served on the Town Board and as Principal in the local schools.[1]

[1] Ben F. Callahan, "Rothrock Family Genealogy," unpublished research manuscript, Gold Hill, NC.

James Philmore Cook was the brother of Jonas Cook, the Treasurer of the Board of Trustees. He graduated from NC College in 1885 and was elected Superintendent of Cabarrus County, NC schools in 1886. He was elected Chairman of the County Board of Education in 1893 and remained in that position until 1912. He was elected to the NC State Senate in 1912. In 1887, Cook established the Concord Standard newspaper and he served as the Editor and Publisher of the paper until 1896. In 1907, Cook began a campaign to establish a school for underprivileged boys and in 1909, he oversaw the opening of the Stonewall Jackson Training School in Cabarrus Co. NC, a facility to which he dedicated much of his time and energy until his death in 1928.[1]

[1] Ben F. Callahan, "Cook Family Genealogy," unpublished research manuscript, Gold Hill, NC.

702 *NCC Catalogue, 1883-84.*

703 *The Charlotte Observer*, Charlotte, NC, April 25, 1884, p. 2, www.newspapers.com.

704 *The Wilmington Star*, Wilmington, NC, May 27, 1884, p. 1, www. newspapers. com. and NC College Records.
705 *North Carolina College Catalogue, 1884-85*. ECHS Library, Mt. Pleasant, NC.
706 *NCC Catalogue, 1884-85.*
707 NC College Records.
708 *NCC Catalogue, 1885-1886.*
709 Ibid.
710 *The Concord Times*, Concord, NC, May 20, 1886, p. 3, www. newspapers.com.
711 *NCC Catalogue, 1886-1887.*

The report of the NC Synod stated that of the 53 students enrolled, only 33 were in actual attendance.

712 *The Concord Times*, Concord, NC, June 9, 1887, p. 3, www. newspapers.com.
713 *NCC Catalogue, 1887-1888.*

Eighteen of the students enrolled in the College Department, eight were from Mt. Pleasant, and of the thirty-seven enrolled in the Sub-Freshman and Academics Departments, twenty-one listed Mt. Pleasant as their home town.

714 Ibid.
715 *NCC Catalogue,1888-1889.*
716 Ibid.
717 *The Concord Standard*, Concord, NC, June 7, 1889, p. 2, www.newspapers.com.
718 *North Carolina College Catalogue,1888-1889.* ECHS Library, Mt. Pleasant, NC. and *Life Sketches of Lutheran Ministers*, pp. & 56.
719 *Minutes of the Eighty-Eighth Synod, 1891,* p. 24.
720 *NC College Advance*. Mt. Pleasant, NC, Vol. 1, #8, June 1890. ECHS Library, Mt. Pleasant, NC. and *North Carolina College Catalogue, 1889-1890.* ECHS Library, Mt. Pleasant, NC.
721 *The The Concord Times*, Concord, NC, June 6, 1890, p. 2. www. newspapers.com.
722 *NCC Catalogue, 1890-1891.*
723 Ibid.

The Volapuk language was an artificial language created in 1879-1880 by a Roman Catholic priest, Johann M. Schleyer. Schleyer claimed he had been inspired by God to create an international language and by 1889 there were over 280 clubs and twenty-five periodicals in or about Volapuk. At its peak, the language had almost one million adherents.

[1] https://en.wikipedia.org/wiki/Volapük.

724 *NCC Catalogue, 1890-1891.*
725 *The Concord Standard*, Concord, NC, June 11, 1891, p. 2, www. newspapers.com.
726 Minutes NCC, May 1891.
727 *NCC Catalogue, 1891-1892.*

728 Ibid.

729 Minutes NCC, May 31, 1892.

730 *NCC Catalogue, 1892-93.*

Edwin Boines Setzler was born in Pomaria, SC in 1871. He graduated from Newberry College in Newberry, SC in 1892 (valedictorian) and taught in Lindale, TX before coming to NC College. He taught at NC College until 1897 before moving to his alma mater in Newberry. He received his M. A. Degree from Newberry College and his PhD from the University of Virginia in 1902. The taught at The University of Virginia in 1906-'07 and in 1911 he was the Chairman of the English Department of Newberry College. He wrote several books, including "Notes on English Grammar" and "On Anglo-Saxon Verification," which were used extensively as reference texts by college English Departments. He died in 1939 in Newberry, SC.[1]

Setzler was also an early organizer of the Newberry College Athletic Department, and Setzler Field, the Football Stadium at Newberry College, is named in his honor.[2]

[1] *University of Virginia Alumni Bulletin*, Vol. 4, 1911,(University of Virginia Press, Charlottesville, VA), p. 286.

[2] htpps:// Newberrywolves.com.

731 *NCC Catalogue, 1892-93.*

732 Ibid.

733 NCC Minutes, June 1, and *The Concord Standard.* Concord, NC. June 1, 1893, p. 1, www.newspapers.com.

734 *NCC Catalogue, 1893-94.*

735 *NCC Catalogue, 1894-95.*

736 *NCC Catalogue, 1895-96.*

737 Ibid. and "Commencement at Mt. Pleasant," *The Concord Times, Concord, NC,* May 30, 1895, p. 3. www. newspapers.com.

738 *NCC Catalogue, 1896-97.*

739 Ibid. and McAllister Papers, ECHS.

740 Ibid.

Samuel Thomas Hallman was born in Lexington, SC in 1844. He attended Newberry College and was a Civil War veteran. After the war he attended Southern Seminary in Newberry, SC and was ordained by the South Carolina Synod in 1869. He transferred to the NC Synod in 1880 and served two congregations in Cabarrus County. His second wife was Lillie L. Brown, niece of Rev. Samuel Rothrock. He was a member of the Board of Trustees of NC College from 1881-1883 and President of the NC Lutheran Synod in 1882-1883. He transferred back to the SC Synod in 1883. He was President of the SC Synod and a member of the Board of Trustees of Newberry College for 43 years until his death in 1927.[1]

[1] "Hallman, Samuel Thomas." *Life Sketches of Lutheran Minsters, North Carolina & Tennessee Synods, 1773- 1965,* (North Carolina Evangelical Lutheran Synod,The State Printing Co., Columbia, SC, 1966), pp. 81-82.

741 *NCC Catalogue, 1897-98.*

742 Minutes NCC, May 31, 1898.

743 *NCC Catalogue, 1898-99.*

744 Ibid. and *The Concord Standard*, Concord, NC, June 12, 1899, p. 1, www. newspapers.com.

745 *The Concord Standard*, Concord, NC, June 12, 1899, p. 1, www. newspapers.com.

746 *NCC Catalogue, 1898-99.*

747 McAllister Papers, ECHS.

748 *NCC Catalogue, 1899-1900.*

749 *NCC Catalogue, 1900-1901.*

750 NCC Minutes, 1900.

751 *NCC Catalogue, 1900-1901.*

752 NCC Minutes, 1901.

753 *NCC Catalogue, 1900-1901.*

754 NCC Minutes, 1902.

755 *The Carolina English & Classical School*, Pamphlet, (The Times Presses-Printers, Concord, NC), 1902. p. 1, ECHS Library, Mt. Pleasant, NC.

756 Ibid., pp. 1-3.

757 McAllister Class Register, MS, December.1902, McAllister Papers, ECHS.

758 "Opening of Mt. Pleasant Collegiate Institute," *The Concord Tribune*, Concord, NC, September 22, 1904, p. 3. www. newspapers.com.

759 "Principals' Report to Board of Trustees,": Minutes NCC, 1904.

760 *Mt. Pleasant Collegiate Institute*, Pamphlet, MS, p. 1, ECHS Library, Mt. Pleasant, NC.

761 McAllister Class Register, September. 1903, McAllister Papers, ECHS.

762 McAllister Papers, ECHS.

763 Ibid.

764 "From Mt. Pleasant," *The Concord Tribune*, Concord, NC, December 19, 1904, p. 1, www.newspapers.com.

765 McAllister Papers, ECHS.

766 "At Mt. Pleasant Institute," *The Charlotte Observer*, Charlotte, NC, December 25, 1904, p. 3, www. newspapers.com.

767 "Invitations to the Commencement Exercises at Mt. Pleasant- Program of Events," *The Concord Daily Tribune*, Concord, NC, May 12, 1905, p. 4, www. newspapers.com.

768 *The Concord Daily Tribune*, Concord, NC, August 3, 1905, p. 3, www. newspapers.com.

769 "The Mt. Pleasant Schools," *The Concord Times*, Concord, NC, September 22, 1905, p. 5, www.newspapers.com.

770 *MPCI Catalogue, 1905.*

771 *MPCI Catalogue, 1906.*

772 Ibid.

773 "Commencement at Mt. Pleasant." *The Concord Daily Tribune*, Concord, NC, May 1906, p. 1, www.newspapers.com.

774 McAllister Papers, ECHS.

Roy Webster, was born in Cherokee Co SC, the son of Judge James E. Webster and Rachael C. Littlejohn. He graduated from Wofford College, SC in 1906 with "high honors" and received an AM Degree in 1907. He taught for one session at the Mt. Pleasant Collegiate Institute in 1907 as Professor of Latin & Greek before entering Law School at the University of South Carolina. He received his LLB Degree from USC in 1909 and practiced law in Spartanburg, SC. During the next four years, he was a frequent visitor to Mt. Pleasant where he was courting his future wife. [An article in the Concord Standard on 28 Dec 1910 stated, *"Prof. Roy Webster, formerly in charge of ancient languages at the Collegiate Institute, but at present engaged in the practice of law in Spartanburg, is shaking hands with old friends here this week. Though the genial professor denies the Mecklenburg Declaration, disputes the birthplace of Andrew Jackson, and is an anti-North Carolinian in toto, still we are glad to have him call around. A few years additional residence in the Old North State and he will believe he was born in NC along with other noted men."]* On 2 Jul 1913, Webster married Elma Rushing Welsh in Mt. Pleasant. Elma Welsh was born in Lancaster Co. SC in 1885 and was the daughter of Benjamin F. Welsh and Mary Ella Barrier. Benjamin Welsh was a former student at NC College and Ella Barrier was the daughter of Daniel Dixon Barrier & Margaret M. Boger of Mt. Pleasant. Following their marriage, the Websters moved to Gaffney, SC where Roy continued to practice law. Sometime before 1918, the Websters moved to Hendersonville, NC where Roy practiced law.

Webster was drafted into the US Army in July 1918 and served in US Chemical Warfare Unit in Washington, DC during World War I.

While her husband served in the Army, Emma Webster returned to Mt. Pleasant where she taught school and served as Principal of the MP Graded School in December of 1918 after it reopened following an influenza epidemic.

From 1919 through 1921 Roy Webster was a teacher at the Carlisle Military School in Bamberg, SC, and from 1921 through 1923 he was the Superintendent of Schools in Martinsville, VA. Also, from 1919 through 1922 he attended summer Graduate School at Columbia University, NY, receiving his second AM Degree from Columbia in 1922.

In 1923, he was employed as a Professor of History & Greek at MPCI. He left MPCI in 1924 and re-entered Columbia University where he was a resident student until 1926. In 1926, Webster returned to MPCI where he was Professor of History and Bible. Webster served as the Mayor Mt. Pleasant in 1927. In 1932 he was an Instructor of Government and History at MPCI, and in 1933 he taught Government, Bible, Economics and History. Following the closing of MPCI, Webster taught at Mt. Pleasant High School where he served as Principal from 1934-1937. He retired in 1955. He was a member of the Mt. Pleasant American Legion and the first President of the Mt. Pleasant Lion's Club in 1944, serving in that position until 1946.[1]

[1] Ben F. Callahan, "Barrier Family Genealogy," unpublished research manuscript, Gold Hill, NC.

775 *Minutes of the One Hundred-Fourth Annual Meeting of the Evangelical Lutheran Synod & Ministerium of North Carolina, held in Salem Church, Rowan Co. NC beginning on May 1, 1907,* (Henkel & Co. Lutheran Publication Establishment, New Market, VA), p. 36.

776 *MPCI Catalogue, 1908*; Minutes NCC, 1908, and "Commencements Over," *The Concord Daily Tribune*, Concord, NC, May 23, 1907, p. 1, www.newspapers.com.

777 *Minutes of the One Hundred-Fifth Annual Meeting of the Evangelical Lutheran Synod & Ministerium of North Carolina, held in Lutheran Chapel Church, China Grove, NC beginning on April 29, 1908*, (Henkel & Co. Lutheran Publication Establishment, New Market, VA). p. 44.

778 *Minutes of the One Hundred-Eighth Annual Meeting of the Evangelical Lutheran Synod & Ministerium of North Carolina, held in St. Paul's Church, Wilmington, NC, beginning on May 10, 1911*, (Lutheran Board of Publication, Columbia, SC), p. 40.

Jefferson Polycarp Miller was born in Catawba County, North Carolina in 1866He attended Concordia College in Conover, Catawba Co. NC, graduating in 1889. He was ordained by the Tennessee Synod in 1889.

From 1891-1902 he served the congregations in North Carolina. In 1902 he moved to Orangeburg, SC and in 1905 to Virginia.

In 1907, Rev. Miller moved back to North Carolina where he was the Minister at Holy Trinity Lutheran Church in Mt. Pleasant, NC. While at Holy Trinity, he served as an Instructor at Mont Amoena Female Seminary and as Co-Principal of the Mt. Pleasant Collegiate Institute. He resigned his position as Co-Principal at MPCI in 1909 but continued to teach there and at Mont Amoena, while still serving Holy Trinity until 1911.

Rev. Miller moved to back to Virginia in 1911 and served as the President of Marion College in Marion, VA until 1913. He was the "Field Representative" for Elizabeth College in Charlotte, NC from 1914-1915. He moved to Tyrone,

Blair Co. PA, in 1915 and served as Minister at First Lutheran Church in Tyrone from 1915-1920.

From 1928–1931 Rev. Miller served Holy Trinity Lutheran Church in Wytheville, Wythe Co. VA. He retired to Radford, VA after 1931. Rev. Miller died in Radford, VA on May 11, 1939. He is buried at Sunset Cemetery, Christiansburg, Montgomery Co. VA.[1]

[1] "Miller, Jefferson Polycarp,." *Life Sketches of Lutheran Minsters, North Carolina & Tennessee Synods, 1773- 1965,* (North Carolina Evangelical Lutheran Synod, The State Printing Co., Columbia, SC, 1966), pp. 81-137.

779 *Minutes of 108th Lutheran Synod Convention,* and *The Statesville Landmark*, Statesville, NC, Aug 1907, p. 3,www.newspapers.com.

780 *The Concord Times,* Concord, NC, July 3, 1907, p. 4, www. newspapers.com.

781 "Commencement at Mt. Pleasant, *The Concord Times*, Concord, NC, May 22, 1908, p. 3, www.newspapers.com.

782 Ibid.

783 McAllister Papers, ECHS.

784 *MPCI Catalogue, 1908-1909.*

785 "Mt. Pleasant Commencement," *The Concord Times*, Concord, NC, May 20, 1909, p. 3, www.newspapers.com.

786 Minutes NCC, 1909.

787 *Minutes of 107th Lutheran Synod Convention, 1910*, pp. 36-37.

788 Minutes NCC,1910.

789 Ibid.

790 *MPCI Catlogue, 1910-1911*, pp. 31-33.

791 Ibid.

792 *Minutes of the One Hundred-Eighth Lutheran Synod*, p. 40.

793 *MPCI Catalogue, 1910-1911*, p. 37.

794 Ibid., pp. 28-30.

795 "Last Day of Commencement at Mt. Pleasant," *The Concord Times*, Concord, May 18, 1911, p. 2, www.newspapers.com.

796 Ibid.

797 "Principal's Report to Synod," Apr 1912, McAllister Papers.

798 *MPCI Catalogue, 1911-1912.* p. 2.

799 Gurley Moose graduated number one in his class from the School of Pharmacy at Maryland College in and received his medical degree from the University of Maryland at the age of 23. He returned to Mt. Pleasant and began his medical practice, but remained for only a short time, as he contracted tuberculosis and died in at the age of 30.

800 *MPCI Catalogue, 1911-1912.* p. 2.

801 Ibid.

802 Ibid., p. 20.

803 *The Concord Times*, Concord, NC, May 23, 1912, p. and *The Concord Daily Tribune*, Concord, NC, May 6, 1912, p. 1, www.newspapers.com.

804 *Minutes of the One Hundred-Tenth Annual Meeting of the Evangelical Lutheran Synod & Ministerium of North Carolina, held at St. John's Church, Cabarrus Co., NC beginning on May 7, 1913*, (Henkel & Co. Lutheran Publication Establishment, New Market, VA), pp. 35-36.

805 Minutes NCC, 1913.

806 "Commencement at Mt. Pleasant," *The Charlotte Observer*, Charlotte, NC, May 31, 1913, p.3, www.newspapers.com.

Edward K. Graham was Dean of the UNC College of Arts and Sciences and was acting President of UNC in 1913. He became the President in 1914. He died in the Influenza Epidemic in 1918.[1]

[1] Dennis, Helen Oldham, "Graham, Edward Kidder," ncpedia.org.

807 Minutes NCC, 1913.

808 *The Progressive Farmer*, Raleigh, NC, July 5, 1913, p. 3, www.newspapers.com.

809 "Institute Opens," *The Concord Daily Tribune*, Concord, NC. September 19, 1913, p. 1, www.newspapers.com.

810 MPCI Catalogue of Mt. Pleasant, 1913-1914.

811 "School Notes," *The Concord Times*, Concord, NC. March 26, 1914, p. 6, www.newspapers.com.

812 *MPCI Catalogue, 1913-1914.*

813 "Final Exercises at Mt. Pleasant," *The Concord Daily Tribune*, Concord, NC, May 28, 1914, p. 1, www.newspapers.com.

814 Ibid.

815 Principal's Report to Board of Trustees, Apr 1915, McAllister Papers. ECHS Library, Mt. Pleasant, NC.

816 "MPCI Commencement," *The Concord Daily Tribune*, Concord, NC, May 1915, p. 1, https.www. newspapers.com.

817 Ibid. and *MPCI Catalogue, 1914-191.5*

818 *MPCI Catalogue, 1915-1916.*

819 Ibid., p. 18.

820 Ibid., p. 28.

821 Walker Family Documents. ECHS Library, Mt. Pleasant, NC.

822 *MPCI Catalogue, 1916*-and McAllister Papers, ECHS.

823 *MPCI Catalogue, 1916-1917*, p. 18.

824 McAllister Papers, ECHS.

825 Ibid.

826 "The Commencement at Mt. Pleasant," *The Concord Daily Tribune*, Concord, NC, May 21, 1917, www. newspapers. com.

827 MPCI Catalogue, 1917-1918.

828 McAllister Papers, ECHS.
829 Ibid.
830 McAllister Papers, ECHS. and *MPCI Catalogue, 1917-1918.*
831 McAllister Papers, ECHS.
832 *MPCI Catalogue, 1918-1919*, p. 43.
833 *The Concord Times*, Concord, NC. July 25, 1918, p. 4, www. newspapers.com.

Schenck had been selected to attend the "Plattsburg Camp" in compliance with a new system inaugurated by the Secretary of War to provide assistant military instructors to schools and Colleges with a military department.

834 MPCI Catalogue, 1919-1920, p. 4.
835 MPCI Catalogue, 1919-1920, pp. & 46.
836 McAllister Papers, ECHS.
837 *The Concord Times*, Concord, NC, May 17, 1920, p. 4, www. newspapers.com.
838 *MPCI Catalogue, 1920-1921*, pp. & 49.
839 McAllister Papers, ECHS.
840 *MPCI Catalogue,1921-'22*, pp, 41, 45-and *The Concord Daily Tribune*, Concord, NC, May 26,1921, pp. & 3, www.newspapers.com.
841 *MPCI Catalogue,1921-'22*, p. 4.
842 *MPCI Catalogues, 1906-1920.*
843 Letter from G. F. McAllister to H. E. Isenhour, February 6, 1932, McAllister Papers, ECHS.
844 *The Concord Daily Tribune*, Concord, NC, May 24, 1922, p. 4, www. newspapers.com.
845 *MPCI Catalogue,1921-'22,* pp. & 44.
846 *MPCI Catalogue,1922-'23*, pp. & 52.
847 *MPCI Catalogue,1923-'24*, pp. & 56.
848 Ibid., p. 4.
849 McAllister Papers, ECHS.
850 *MPCI Catalogue,1924-'25*, pp. & 46.
851 *The Tour Path*, Mt. Pleasant Collegiate Institute Yearbook-1925, Charles MacLaughlin, (ed.), (Published by the Senior Class of Mt. Pleasant Collegiate Institute, The Observer Printing House, Inc., Charlotte, NC), 1925.
852 MPCI Catalogue,1925-'26, pp. 42, 46-47; *The Institute News*, Nov, 1925, Vol. IV, No. 1, and *The Tour Path.*
853 McAllister Papers, ECHS.
854 *MPCI Catalogue, 1925-'26*. p. 4.
855 *MPCI Catalogue,1926-'27*, pp. & 33.
856 Ibid., pp. 53-56.

College Catalogue lists 118 students.

857 Ibid., pp. 4-5.
[MPCI Examination Questions]

Civics Examination, November 30, 1926

Tell what difference climate has upon people and countries. Illustrate.

Why do we have schools and colleges? Mention various kinds of schools.

Of what importance is the church to a community? Name as many kinds of churches as you can.

In what three ways may a nation increase its population?

What problems does the immigrant cause in the United States?

How can one continue to gain intelligence after his school days are ended?

What are the benefits of prohibition?

What is Security? Explain fully.

Government Examination, November 30, 1926

What is Proportional Representation? Explain Fully.

What is the importance of the Budget in government?

In what respects has the Constitution proven superior to the Articles of Confederation?

Describe the ways in which the Constitution can be amended, and give briefly an outline of the various amendments.

Trace the growth of various political parties in our history down to the present and tell something of the origin of each.

What are the roots and sources of party strength?

Give complete details concerning the nomination and election of the President of the United States.

Contrast the American Cabinet with the Cabinet system in England.

Classify the various powers of the President and give detail concerning them.

Sophomore History Examination, December 2, 1926

What do you know about the Divine Right of Kings

Tell what you known about the Reign of Louis XIV.

What caused the revolt of the American Colonies?

What was the Old Regime?

Mention at least four great reformers, and tell what each attempted to do.

Who were the enlightened despots, and what did they try to do?

Point out specific abuses in France prior to the French Revolution.

Junior History Examination, December 1, 1926

Contrast the system of land-owning in Virginia, Massachusetts, Maryland, and New York.

What was the nature and purpose of the Navigation Acts?

Mention those features of English policy which let to the Revolution.

Tell something about the following men: Pitt, Burke, Franklin, Dickinson, Paine.

Describe the weaknesses of the Articles of Confederation. Illustrate.

What were the main features of the Ordinance of 1787?

Name the leading members of the Constitutional Convention; describe the principal plans proposed for union, and the compromises adopted.[1]

[1] McAllister Papers, ECHS, November 30 – December 2, 1926.

858 "President's Report to Board of Trustees," April 26. 1927,. McAllister Papers, ECHS.

859 *MPCI Catalogue, 1928-29.*

860 *The Sabre,* Mt. Pleasant Collegiate Institute Yearbook, 1928, Carl A. Honeycutt, (ed), (Queen City Printing Co., Charlotte, NC), 1928; McAllister Papers, ECHS;, and MPCI Catalogue,1927-'28.

861 *The Institute News*, Mt. Pleasant, NC, Sept. 1927, Vol. V, No. 1. p. 1.

862 Ibid.

863 *MPCI Catalogue,1927-'28.*

864 McAllister Papers, ECHS.

865 Ibid.

866 Ibid.

867 *The Sabre.,* pp.8, & 64.

868 Ibid.

869 Ibid., p. 15.

870 *MPCI Catalogue, 1929-30*, p. 41.; *The Sabre*, pp. 17, 34, 41, 44, & 46, and *The Institute News*, Vol. 4, No. 3. April 1928, pp. & 5.

871 McAllister Papers, ECHS and "Military Training," *The Twin City Sentinel*, Winston-Salem, NC, July 5, 1928, www.newspapers.com.

872 *MPCI Catalogue,1928-'29*, pp. 64-67.

873 Ibid. and https://tigerprints. clemson.edu.

874 *MPCI Catalogue,1928-'29.*

875 *MPCI Catalogue,1929-'30*, pp. 41& 44.

876 Ibid., pp. 67-and "Principal's Report to Board of Trustees," October 17, 1929, McAllister Papers, ECHS.

877 Ibid., p. and *MPCI Catalogue,1929-'30*, pp. 41& 44.

878 https://www.findagrave.com/memorial/138392705/theodore-patton.

879 https://www.newberrywolves.com.

880 *The Institute News*, April 1930, Special Edition, p. 6.

881 *MPCI Catalogue,1930-'31,* p. 66.

882 Ibid.

883 Ibid.

884 *MPCI Catalogue,1931-'32*, p. 45.

885 Ibid., p. 3.

886 *MPCI Catalogue,1930-31,* pp. 3-4,

887 Ibid.

888 Ibid., pp. 50, 55, 57, & 70.

889 *MPCI Catalogue,1931-32*, p. and *The Recall*, MPCI Yearbook, 1932, pp. 12-13.

890 *MPCI Catalogue,1931-32,* p. 3.
891 *The Recall*, pp. 4-5.
892 *MPCI Catalogue,1931-32,* p. 39.
893 Hilbert A. Fisher was a graduate of Mt. Pleasant Collegiate Institute. He attended the United States Naval Academy, graduating in 1915. At both MPCI and the Naval Academy he was an excellent athlete, earning his athletic letter at Annapolis for all four of his years of attendance. He was the leading hitter on the baseball team for his last three yers. During World War I he was in transport service and made round trips to Europe convoying troops. He served on the dreadnought (battleship) *U. S. S. New Hampshire* for two years and was Executive Engineering Officer for one year. In and Fisher was employed as an instructor at NC State College in the Department of Mathematics. In Prof. Fisher accepted an offer to be co-principal of the Mount Amoena Seminary at Mount Pleasant. He returned to State College in 1924. In Fisher received a Master of Science in Physics Degree from State College. He also received an honorary doctorate from Lenoir-Rhyne College. He was the author of several textbooks in solid geometry and algebra.[1]

[1] McLain, *Memories of Mont Amonea Female Seminary.*

894 *The Concord Tribune*, Concord, NC, May 21, 1932, pp. 1-and MPCI Catalogue,1932-33, p 58.
895 Minutes NCC, 1932, McAllister Papers, ECHS.
896 Letter to Cadets, Aug 1932, McAllister Papers, ECHS.
897 *The Falcon*, MPCI Year Book, and "Principal's Report to Board of Directors," May 1933, McAllister Papers, ECHS.
898 *MPCI Catalogue,1932-33.*
899 Ibid., p. 3.
900 *The Concord Tribune*, Concord, NC, May & 23, 1933, pp. & 6.
901 *The Concord Tribune*, Concord, NC, May 23, 1933, p. 1.

Part III Campus Life

902 *Minutes of The Forty-ninth Meeting of Evangelical Lutheran Synod,* 1852, p. 16.
903 "Western Carolina Male Academy," *The Republican Banner*, Salisbury, NC, October 2, 1855), p. 3, www. newspapers.com.
904 *WCMA Catalogue, 1857*, p. 12.
905 Ibid.
906 Ibid.
907 *NCC Catalogue, 1861*, p. 12.
908 *NCC Catalogue, 1867*, p. 7.
909 Minutes NCC, October 15, 1873.
910 Faculty Minutes. North Carolina College, March 25, 1874.

911 Faculty Minutes. February 10, 1875.
912 *NCC Catalogue, 1878-1879*, pp, 12-13.
913 *NCC Catalogue, 1886,* pp. 14-15.
914 *NCC Catalogue, 1901,* p. 57.
915 *Minutes of the One Hundred-Second Lutheran Synod*, 1905, p. 26.
916 MPCI Catalogue, 1907, p. and McDaniel, *George Franklin McAllister, 1874-1938.*
917 *Regulations of Mount Pleasant Collegiate Institute*, Pamphlet. ECHS Library, Mt. Pleasant, NC, (The Times Printing, Concord., NC). [See Appendix 10].
918 *NCC Catalogue, 1916,* p. 23.
919 McAllister Papers, ECHS, Dec 1930.
920 *NCC Catalogue*, January 1856.
921 Minutes NCC, March, 1856.
922 "Report to Board of Directors of North Carolina College," Minutes NCC, August 1, 1856.
923 "President's Report to Board of Trustees of North Carolina College," Bansemer Papers.
924 *Minutes of the Fifty-Eighth Annual Meeting of the Evangelical Lutheran Synod*, 1861. p. 15.
925 Faculty Minutes, March 19, 1873,ECHS Library.
926 Faculty Minutes, February 2, 1875.
927 Faculty Minutes, March 16, 1876.
928 Faculty Minutes, April 20, 1876.
929 Faculty Minutes, September 2, 1875.
930 Faculty Minutes, October 20, 1875.

Daniel Burton "Burt" Tucker was expelled from NC College for gambling. He returned home to Stanly County and married Sophia Morton and had several children. He was employed as a school teacher but continued his gambling and "his associations brought him into evil repute." Sometime in 1891Tucker moved to Clark Co. AR where he met a former Stanly County neighbor, AlexWhitley. In February, 1892, Tucker was killed while gambling at Whitley's home. His body was dismembered and thrown into a nearby river. Whitley denied involvement in the murder, but fled authorities back to North Carolina. The Clark Co. Sheriff notified the Stanly Co. Sheriff and Whitley was arrested, pending extradition back to Arkansas. While he was being held in the Stanly Co. jail, a "mob" broke in and took Whitley to a nearby tree where he was hanged.[1]

[1] David D. Almond, *The Lynching of Alex Whitley, (*Concord Printing Co., Concord, NC), 1978.

931 Faculty Minutes, April 20, 1876.

After being expelled from NC College, Benjamin Franklin Welch, returned to his home in Lancaster, SC and became the owner/editor of a local newspaper, The Lancaster Review. He sold the paper in 1881, the same year he married Mary Ella Barrier, daughter of Daniel Barrier of Mt. Pleasant. Welch and his wife had two children by 1885 when he was arrested for shooting and killing a man during an argument. At the time of the killing Welch was noted as a "respectably connected" merchant in Lancaster. He was not convicted of the crime and in 1886, he took the South Carolina Bar examination but failed to pass. Either in response to his failure or for some other reason, Welch threatened the Chief Justice of the South Carolina Supreme Court, William D. Simpson. Simpson was placed under guard and an attempt to find and arrest Welch. According to a local newspaper account, "The matter was kept quite and known to but a few in the city."[1]

In 1888 the Manning, SC Times, described Welch as a "desparado and outlaw who has killed two men and implicated in the murder of another." According to the newpaper, Welsh was a member of "gang of lawless roughs," who two years before had attempted to kill the state Chief Justice, Welsh had thus far escaped justice de to cowardly juries. He was at this time in custody on the basis or a "peace warrant" sworn out by D. D. Barrier, of Cabarrus Co. NC on behalf of his (Barrier's) sister, Mary E. Barrier, wife of Welsh. The warrant had been issued after Mary had sent a message to her brother that Welsh had attacked and assaulted her and he had in the past, beat her and threatened her with a knife and a gun. Welsh was arrested on the warrant and placed in jail under $5,000 bond. The bond was later reduced to $1,000 and Welch was released a short time afterwards, pending a trial which had been postponed due to the absence of "a key witness."[2]

On November 19, 1890 Welch was arrested for the theft of a watch in Lancaster, SC. He died of delirium tremors after being transferred to the Columbia, SC.[3]

[1] "Lancaster Letter," *The Watchman & Southron*, Sumter, SC, August 25, 1885. p. 3, www. newspapers.com and *Yorkville Enquirer*, York, SC, December 22, 1886. p. 2, https:// www. newspapers.com.

[2] "A Brutal Husband Committed to Jail," The Manning Times, Manning, SC, February 29, 1888, p. 6, www. newspapers.com.

[3] "A Sad Story," *Yorkville Enquirer*, York, SC, November 19, 1890, p. 2, www.newspapers.com.

932 Faculty Minutes, 1874, ECHS Library.

933 Faculty Minutes, March 23, 1974.

It seems that John Burkhead was somewhat of a discipline problem. A year earlier he had been involved in "a difficulty" with another student, Addison Crowell, and had been given five demerits.[1]

[1] Faculty Minutes, March 19, 1873.

934 Faculty Minutes, March 24, 1874.

935 "Principal's Report to Board of Trustees", Minutes NCC, August 1858.

936 Faculty Minutes.

937 Faculty Minutes, Apr 1874.

938 Minutes NCC, 1876.

939 "Letter form Mayor of Mt. Pleasant." Minutes NCC, 1901.

940 McAllister Papers, ECHS, 1915.

941 McAllister Papers, ECHS, January 23, 1927.

942 Ibid.

943 McAllister Papers, ECHS, March 21, 1928.

944 McAllister Papers, ECHS, 1928-1930.

945 Ibid.

946 McAllister Papers, ECHS, May 30, 1930.

947 "The Western Carolina Male Academy," *The Concord Weekly Gazette*, Concord, NC, October 13, 1855, p. 3, www.newspapers.com.

948 Minutes WCMA, May, 1856.

949 Ibid.

950 *WCMA Catalogue, 1857.* pp. 15-16.

951 Minutes NCC, 1860.

952 *WCMA Catalogue, 1857.* pp. 15-16.

953 Bansemer Papers, 1830-1866.

954 Ibid.

955 Ibid.

956 *NCC Catalogue, 1870.* p. 14.

957 *NCC Catalogue, 1871.* pp. 13-14.

958 *NCC Catalogue, 1872.* pp. 14.

959 *NCC Catalogue, 1884.* p. 13.

960 *NCC Catalogue, NC,1885.* p. 14.

961 *NCC Catalogue,1889-1890.* p. 34.

962 *NCC Catalogue, 1890-1891.* p. 26.

963 *NCC Catalogue, 1891-1900.* p. 27.

964 *NCC Catalogue, 1885-1886.* p. 20.

The rooms which were furnished were provided by: St. John's, Rev. R. W. Petrea, pastor, 2 rooms; Lutheran Chapel, Rev. B. S. Brown, pastor; Centre Grove, Rev. B. S. Brown, Pastor; Merchants of Concord; Concordia, Rev. W. Kimball, Pastor, in part; Trinity, Rev. W. A. Lutz, Pastor, in part; St. Enoch's, Rev. W. A. Lutz, Pastor, in part; St. Peter's, Rev. T. H. Strohecker, pastor, in part; Mt. Olive, Rev. J. B. Davis, pastor, in part; Ebenezer, Rev. S. Rothrock, pastor, in part; The Young People's Association.[1]

[1] Minutes NCC, 1886.

965 *NCC Catalogue, 1889-1890*. p. 24.
966 *NCC Catalogue, 1890-1891*. p. 26.
967 *NCC Catalogue, 1891-1901.*
968 "Wants & Needs," NCC Catalogue, 1900-1901. pp. 30-31.
969 Pamphlet, Mt. Pleasant Collegiate Institute, 1903.
970 Ibid.
971 Pamphlet, Mt. Pleasant Collegiate Institute, 1905, ECHS Library, Mt. Pleasant, NC. pp. 1-4.
972 *MPCI Catalogue, 1906.*
973 *MPCI Catalogue, 1909-1910*, 14, 38, 39.
974 *MPCI Catalogue, 1910-1911*, pp. 6, 34, 35.
975 "Letter to incoming students, dated July 10th, 1917." McAllister Papers, ECHS.
976 *MPCI Catalogue, 1917-1918*, pp. 38-39.
977 *MPCI Catalogue, 1918-1919.*
978 Ibid. p. 26.
979 *MPCI Catalogue, 1919-1920.*
980 *MPCI Catalogue,1920-1921.*
981 *MPCI Catalogue,1924-1925.*
982 "Principal's Report to Board of Trustees," 1925, McAllister Papers, ECHS.
983 *MPCI Catalogue,1926-1927, pp. & 50.*
984 *MPCI Catalogue, 1927-1928, pp. 46-47.*
985 Ibid.
986 *MPCI Catalogue,1929-1930*, pp. 48, 53, & 55.
987 *MPCI Catalogue,1931-1932.*
988 *WCMA Catalogue, 1857,* pp. 14-15.
989 Ibid.
990 *Constitution of Phililaethian Literary Society, MS,* ECHS Library, Mt. Pleasant, NC.
991 *NCC* Catalogue, 1899-1900, p. 23.
992 *MPCI Catalogue,1926-1927.*
993 "Principal's Report to Board of Trustees, 1921," McAllister Papers, ECHS.
994 George F. Hahn, *The First Eight Graduating Classes of MPHS*, unpublished pamphlet at ECHS Library, Mt. Pleasant, NC.
995 Papers of the Mt. Pleasant Collegiate Institute. ECHS Library, Mt. Pleasant, NC.
996 *The Concord Daily Tribune*, Concord, NC, June 12, 1911. p. 1, www.newspapers.com.
997 *The Hickory Democrat*, Hickory, NC, March 4, 1915, p. 1, www.newspapers.com.

The question for the debate was "Resolved, That the United States should adopt the policy of subsidizing its Merchant Marine engaged in Foreign Trade."

998 "Principal's Report to Board of Trustees, 1915," McAllister Papers, ECHS.

999 "Principal's Report to Board of Trustees, 1921," Mcallister Paper, ECHS and *The Charlotte News*, Charlotte, NC, March 27, 1921, p. 6.

1000 McAllister Papers, ECHS.
19 Feb 1922
Oath of "Beta Mu" Fraternity

I, a candidate for membership in the "Beta Mu" Fraternity organization on an unknown date at Trinity Park School, Durham, NC for the purpose of creating a closer fellowship among the best students in the school, do hereby swear by the Supreme Being that rules over me, and on my honor that;

First – I will never under any circumstances, reveal or let it be known in any way anything concerning said "Fraternity.

Second – I will conduct myself toward other members as members of a common "Fraternity" should: Furthermore I will not bear malice toward any fellow member.

Third – I will from this date until death assist any fellow member in any matter where my assistance is needed to the best of my ability.

Fourth – I furthermore understand the seriousness of belonging to an order of this kind and know that should I reveal any of its secrets that I will automatically sever my relations with the Fraternity and my friendship with to its members.

Minutes from the Beta Mu Fraternity (no date but names of members were students at MPCI 1919-1923)]

Members included - [???] "Stonewall" Smithdeal, High Beta Mu; [???] "Toe" Smithdeal, Vice High Beta Mu (four Smithdeals attended MPCI from 1919-1923 so it is unclear who the two frat brothers actually were); [Hal] "Obie" O'Brien, Sec & Treas; [Robert] "Pop" Seahorn; [Ernest] "Reno" Sechler; [Albert] "Polo" Vestal; [???] "Pluto" Goodman; [James] "Hoodoo" Buchanon, [George] "Hobo" Petrea, and [Ralph] "Cleo" Rutledge.

Nov 22 This meeting was called to order by the High B. M. Buchanon was initiated and given the oath. Plans were discussed for another "party" to take place some time soon.

Dec 11 Meeting called to order by the High B. M. Plans were discussed for a "party" but it was decided to wait until after xmas as several of the fellows would be away on a basketball trip. The meeting was then turned into a kangaroo kourt and several of the fellows were tried for different things. Brother Smithdeal W. F. was tried for not paying his dues and sentenced to ten licks if they were not payed by the first meeting after xmas and ten licks for each additional week.

Jan 12 Meeting called to order by High B. M. Plans for the Easter trip to be held in Charlotte. It was decided at this meeting that the initiation fee be raised from $1 to $5

Feb 7 At this meeting several names were put up as candidates for membership in the Beta Mu. G. L. Petrea and Ralph Rutledge were voted in. It was also decided to have some pennants made in the fraternity colors.

??? This meeting called for purpose of initiating Petrea and Rutledge. After undergoing [page torn] … given the oath and welcomed into the fraternity.

Feb 13 The only business transacted at this meet was the selection of a design for a pennant. The colors adopted were purple and gray.

Feb 20 The only business discussed at this meeting was the trip to Charlotte Easter. It was definitely decided to go over on Thurs and then most of the fellows are going up to Winston the next day.

Mar 15 At this meeting several of the fellows made short talks about payment of dues and all agreed to pay up before Easter. The trip was discussed and then it was decided that Rutledge and Petrea must have "frat" names. Those selected were "Cleo" & "Hobo" respectively. It was decided to have a "Kangaroo Kourt" and mock trial at next meeting and various charges were brought against some of the boys.

Mar 28 [This entry is in a different handwriting than previous notes] The meeting ws called to order by the High B. M. at the regular meeting time in Polo & Pop's room at which time definite plans were made for our trip to Charlotte during the Easter Holidays. It was [page cut off]

[New Pages] Ritual for Initiates:

Initiation to take place in some secluded spot in a darkened room. Initiates to be blindfolded before entering room. In blindfolding initiate first place cotton over his eyes. Then apply a towel and fasten with adhesive tape.

Materials necessary for initiation:

I. 1 Tablet of methylene Blue to be give internally to each initiate

II. [Blank]

III. Fruit of some kind on which to apply fluid extract of capsicum. Ask druggist how much to apply. (Bananas are preferable).

IV. Ether

V. Soap

VI. Bucket of Water

VII. Basin filled with water

VIII. Electric extension cord with one end of wires bare

IX. Oysters (raw)

The high B. M. shall ask the candidates if they realize how serious a thing this initiation is and shall instruct them to do promptly and without a word of comment everything that they are told to do. All questions to be answered by yes sir or no sir. Acquaint the candidates with NC Law which prohibits fraternities in Military Schools. [Pages missing]

[New Page] Some things to be Done

1st give the candidate a methylene blue tablet and force him to drink a large glass of water. This tablet is harmless and will color urine blue. Do not in any way allow candidate to know what was given him.

2nd apply some fluid extract of capsicum on a piece of fruit. This is harmless and merely causes a burning feeling in the mouth.

3rd Apply a small quantity of ether to his penis and quickly close his pants up. This causes a feeling of freezing.

4th Brand B. M. on candidate with electric current. This is merely a shocking trick and is very effective.

5th Secure a piece of wood and piece of soap of about the same size and tell candidate that you are testing his biting power. Give him three trials substituting the soap for the wood on the 3rd bite. Immediately force candidate to take a drink of water after this.

6th Oyster trick. Have candidate open mouth and bend head back. Then have a member clear his throat and pretend to spit in his mouth except that the same time he spits throw oyster in mouth. Make him swallow it.

7th Kissing King's Ass

8th Tell them that initiation is half over and give them a chance to drop out or ask them if they want to go thru with it.

9th Trick of talking about them some running them down while others defend them.

10th Have a candidate execute a reville exercise hands over head and bending over touch the floor without bending knees. Hit with paddle at unexpected times.

11th Kill constitution. Have candidate kiss constitution 3 times by bending way over and on the 3rd time substituting basin of water

12th Branding on BM with iodine

13th Read oath of BM's and if the candidates accepts oath remove blindfold and have him take pledge. Then read the constitution and show him the grip – each brother welcoming him as a full fledged brother.

[FIND FIRST PORTION OF OATH]

… be known in any way anything concerning said "Fraternity."

Second:

I will conduct myself toward other members as members of a common "Fraternity" should: Furthermore I will not bear malice toward any fellow member.

Third:

I will from this date until death assist any fellow member in any matter where my assistance is needed to the best of my ability.

Fourth:

I furthermore understand the seriousness of belonging to an order of this kind and known that should I reveal any of its secrets that I will automatically sever my relations with the Fraternity and my friendship to its members.

Candidate must hold hand on Bible during reading of Oath and then say: "I swear to carry out this Oath to the best of my ability."

On Friday the fraternity met in Charlotte where a banquet was given at the Myers Park Club. There were several girls invited and everybody had a big time. The next morning everybody went to Winston-Salem and spent the Easter Holidays there returning to school on Monday.

Meeting called to order by H. B. M. There was no special business to attend to so after a great deal of foolishness the meeting was adjourned.

This the last meeting for this year was called to order by the High BM all of the fellows agreed to keep in touch with each other as much as possible during the summer and the ones that return next year, to keep the "frat" going and up to a high standard"

1001 North Carolina College Papers, ECHS Library, Mt. Pleasant, NC.
1002 McDaniel, *Brief History of North Carolina College, Mt. Pleasant, NC 1859-1901.*
1003 *The Advance*, Vol 1, Feb 1890, p. 5.
1004 *MPCI Catalogue, 1911-1912, p.* 19.
1005 MPCI Student Handbook, 1923-1924, MS, ECHS Library. Mt. Pleasant, NC.
1006 *MPCI Catalogue,1928-1929.*
1007 *The Institute News*, December, 1928, Vol VI, #3.
1008 MPCI Student Handbook, 1923-1924, p. 10.
1009 *The Tour Path.*
1010 Mt. Pleasant Collegiate Institute Reunion Program, September 9, 1978, ECHS Library.
1011 *MPCI Catalogue,1932-1933.*
1012 Ibid.
1013 Ibid.
1014 Papers of The Mt. Pleasant Collegiate Institute.
1015 *The Concord Times*, May 15,1922, p. 4, www.newspapers.com.
1016 Papers of The Mt. Pleasant Collegiate Institute.
1017 Ibid.
1018 *MPCI Catalogue,1911-1912.*
1019 *The Concord Times,* September 29, 1910, p. 2, www. newspapers. com.
1020 *The Concord Daily Tribune,* January 24, 1911, p. 1, www. newspapers.com.
1021 *The Concord Times,* January 8, 1917, p. 6, www.newspapers.com.

1022 *NCC Catalogues, 1871-1884.*

In 1885 this paragraph was removed and replaced with a short sentence stating that, *"no place in the state surpasses Mt. Pleasant in healthfulness."*[1]

[1] *NC Catalogue, 1885*, p. 20.

1023 McDaniel, *Brief History of North Carolina College.*

Bandy appears to have been an activity similar to field hockey or, possibly, a kind of stickball.

1024 "Faculty Minutes," October 16, 1874.

1025 Minutes NCC, October, 1875.

1026 *The Daily Standard*, Concord, NC, April 8, 1893. p. 2, www. newspapers.com.

1027 Minutes NCC. October 1893.

1028 *The Daily Standard,* Concord, NC,. April 27, 1899, p. 2, www. newspapers.com.

1029 *The Concord Times,* Concord, NC. March 7, 1900, p. 3, www. newspapers.com.

1030 Hahn, *History of Eastern Cabarrus County,* p. 246.

1031 *The Concord Times,* Concord, NC, February 5, 1907, p.1, www.newspapers.com.

1032 MPCI Catalogue, 1911-1912.

1033 MPCI Student Handbook, 1923-1924.

1034 MPCI Catalogue, 1929-1930.

1035 "Herman Fink," https://www.baseball-reference.com/players.

1036 *The Concord Daily Tribune*, Concord, NC, September 21, 1911, p. 1, www. newspapers.com.

1037 *The Concord Times,* Concord, NC, October 12, 1911, p 1, www. newspapers.com.

1038 *The Charlotte Observer*, Charlotte, NC,. October 3, 1911, p. 3, www. newspapers.com.

The line-up for the first game was – Cecil B. Lentz, Left End; G. F. Conrad, Left Tackle; H. Ritchie, Left Guard; Paul R. Moose, Center; Fred L. Harkey, Right Guard; C. H. Crane, Right Tackle; F. Auten, Right End; E. Murray, Quarterback; F. Broad, Right Halfback; P. H. Moose, Right Halfback; Benjamin T. Cripps, Left Halfback, and Zeno Edwards, Left Halfback.

1039 *The Charlotte Observer*, Charlotte, NC, October 12, 1912, p. 7, www. newspapers.com.

1040 *The Concord Daily Tribune*, Concord, NC, October 22, 1912, p. and *The Asheville Citizen-Times*, Asheville, NC, October 31, 1912, p, 3. www. newspapers.com

1041 MPCI Student Handbook, 1923-1924.

1042 *The Institute News,* November 1928, p. 6.

1043 *The Tour Path,* p. 66.

1044 *The Institute News,*October 1928, p. 1.

1045 *The Asheville Citizen-Times*, Asheville, NC, November 3, 1929, p. 25, www. newspapers.com.

1046 *The Recall,* MPCI Yearbook.
1047 *The Concord Daily Tribune,* Concord, NC. September 29, 1916, p. 1, www.newspapers.com.
1048 *The Charlotte Observer,* Charlotte, NC, December 12, 1916, p. 2, www.newspapers.com.
1049 *The Concord Times,* Concord, NC, January 29, 1917, p. 1, www. newspapers.com.
1050 *The Charlotte Observer,* Charlotte, NC, December 12, 1916. p. 2, www.newspapers.com.
1051 *The Concord Times,* Concord, NC, December 18, 1916,. p. 6, www.newspapers.com.
1052 *The Concord Times,* Concord, NC, January 29, 1917, p. 1, www. newspapers.com.
1053 Ibid.
1054 Ibid.
1055 *The Concord Times,* Concord, NC. February 26,1917, p. 6, www.newspapers.com.
1056 Ibid.
1057 *The Concord Times*, Concord, NC, March 12,1917, p. 3, www. newspapers.com.
1058 *The Concord Times*, Concord, NC, March 19,1917, p. 6, www. newspapers.com.
1059 *The Institute News*, March 1924, Volume II, #5.
1060 *The Tour Path*, p. 76.
1061 *The Daily Tar Heel*, Chapel Hill, NC, February 7, 1925, p. 1, www.newspapers.com.
1062 *The Tour Path,* p. 81.
1063 *The Institute News*, October, 1928, Volume 6, No. 1, p. 1.
1064 *The Falcon*, p. 55.
1065 *The Sabre.*
1066 *MPCI Catalogue, 1909-1910,* p. 14.
1067 *MPCI Catalogue, 1915-1916,* pp. 13-14.
1068 *MPCI Catalogue*, *1919-1920*, p. 21.
1069 *MPCI Catalogues*, *1923*-and *1927-1928.*
1070 *MPCI Catalogue, 1927-1928*, p. 43.
1071 MPCI Records, ECHS Library, Mt. Pleasant, NC.
1072 McAllister Papers, ECHS.
1073 *MPCI Catalogue, 1917-1918*, p. 13.
1074 *MPCI Catalogue, 1927-1928,*. p. 16.
1075 *MPCI Catalogue, 1917-1918,* p. 20.
1076 Ibid.
1077 McEntyre, *Service Cards for Mount Pleasant Collegiate Students Known to have Served in the First World War.*
1078 Ibid.
1079 *NCC Catalogue*, 1900.

1080 Callahan, *Mt. Pleasant By the Minutes.*

1081 Jonas Cook Account Book, ECHS Library.

1082 *The Institute News*, December 1928, p. 1.

1083 Ibid.

1084 "Minutes of the Mt. Pleasant Board of Commissioners, Mt. Pleasant, NC," December 15, 1899, MS, ECHS Library, Mt. Pleasant, NC.

1085 "Negro Has Trouble with Student at Mt. Pleasant," *The Charlotte Observer*, Charlotte, NC, February 10, 1921,. p 4,. www.newspapers.com.

1086 *MPCI Catalogue, 1917-1918*. p. 3.

1087 "B. M. Club Dinner Party," *The Charlotte Observer,* Charlotte, NC, Apr 1922, p. 15, www.newspapers.com.

1088 *MPCI Catalogue, 1923-1924*, p. 14.

1089 "Football Program." MPCI Papers, MS, ECHS Library, Mt. Pleasant, NC.

1090 Hahn, *Eastern Cabarrus History, 1986,* p. 232.

1091 NC College/MPCI & Mont Amoena Records and Family Histories, ECHS Library.

SOURCES

"A Joyous Occasion- The Illumination of Mt. Pleasant." Unattributed manuscript located at Eastern Cabarrus Historical Society, Mt. Pleasant, NC.

Abstracts of the Lutheran Visitor, 1866-1868 and 1870-188, Abstracted and contributed by Edith Greisser, South Carolina Genealogy Trails. www.genealogytrails.com/scar/ Lutheranvisitor

Bernheim, Gotthardt D., DD and George H. Cox, DD. *The History of The Evangelical Lutheran Synod and Ministerium of North Carolina.* Philadelphia: Lutheran Publication Society, 1902.

"Bittle, Daniel Howard, Dd." McClintock, John, H., DD & James Strong, STD (eds). *Cyclopedia of Biblical, Theological and Ecclesiastical Literature,* Harper & Brothers, New York, 1891, Vol. 11, p. 514. https://www.biblicalcyclopedia.com /B/bittle-daniel-howard-dd.html.

Boyd, William K. and Charles A. Krummel, (eds.). "German Tracts Concerning the Lutheran Church in North Carolina During the Eighteenth Century." North Carolina Historical Review, Vol. VII, No. 1, (Jan 1930).

Brown, Bachman S. DD, et al. (eds). Life Sketches of Lutheran Ministers: North Carolina & Tennessee Synods – 1773-1965. Columbia, SC., North Carolina Synod of the Lutheran Church in America. The State Printing Co., 1966.

C. F. Bansemer Papers, 1830-1866. Collection #03688. Chapel Hill, NC. The Southern Historical Collection, Wilson Library, University of North Carolina at Chapel Hill.

Cabarrus County Deed Books. Cabarrus County Register of Deeds, Concord, NC.

Callahan, Ben F. The Founders & Associated Families of St. Stephen's Lutheran Church. Unpublished manuscript. 2011.

Callahan, Ben F. Mt. Pleasant by the Minutes, 2016. Published by Ben F. Callahan, 2016.

Carolina English and Classical School [Pamphlet]. Concord, NC. The Times Presses, 1902. MS. Eastern Cabarrus Historical Society Library, Mt. Pleasant, N. C.

Catalogues of The Collegiate Institute, Mt. Pleasant, NC. 1903-1933, Eastern Cabarrus Historical Society Library, Mt. Pleasant, NC.

Catalogues of the Officers and Students of North Carolina College, Mt. Pleasant, NC. 1869-1901. Eastern Cabarrus Historical Society Library, Mt. Pleasant, NC.

Catalogue of the Officers and Students of Roanoke College, Salem, VA. Thirty-Seventh Session. 1888-1889. New Market, VA. Henkel & Company, Steam Printing, 1888.

Catalogue of the Officers and Students of Western Carolina Academy at Mt. Pleasant, Cabarrus County, NC. Salisbury, NC. J. J. Bruner, Book and Job Printer, 1857. MS. Eastern Cabarrus Historical Society Library, Mt. Pleasant, NC.

Civil War Poster, MS. Eastern Cabarrus Historical Society Museum, Mt. Pleasant, NC.

"Collegiate Institute Appeal– A Handbook, of Facts and Plans" [Pamphlet]. 1 Apr 1924. *North Carolina College Papers.* North Carolina Collection, University of North Carolina, Chapel Hill, NC.

"Compiled Service Records of Confederate Soldiers Who Served in Organizations Raised Directly by the Confederate Government." Database. *Fold3.com. http://www.fold3.com:* [nd] Citing NARA microfilm publication M258. Washington, D. C.: National Archives and Records Administration, 1963.

"Constitution and By-Laws of the Phililaethian Literary Society, 1857." MS. Eastern Cabarrus Historical Society Library, Mt. Pleasant, NC.

"Curriculum." Indiana University Bloomington. www.Collections.Libraries.indiana.edu.

Cruse, Bernard W., Jr. *Union Churches in North Carolina During the Eighteenth & Nineteenth Century.* Published by Bernard W. Cruse, Jr., 2001.

Dobbs, Arthur, "Letter to the Board of Trade of Great Britain, 24 Aug 1755." *The Colonial Records of North Carolina,* edited by William L. Saunders. Vol. V. Raleigh, NC, Josephus Daniels, Printer for the State, 1887. http://docsouth.unc.edu.

Eichelberger, Abdiel W. *Historical Sketch of Philip Frederick Eichelberger*, Hanover, PA. Hanover Herald Print, 1901.

Hahn, George Franklin. *Eastern Cabarrus History, 1986*. Concord, NC. Mitchell Sherrill, Publisher, Cabarrus County Graphics, 1986.

Henkel, Socrates, DD, *History of the Evangelical Tennessee Lutheran Synod*. New Market, VA, Henkel & Co., 1890.

Historical Data Systems. "American Civil War Research Database," civilwardata.com

History of Concordia College.school.concordianc.org

Horton, Clarence E., Jr. and Katherine L. Bridges, (eds). *Piedmont Neighbors*. Concord NC. Historic Cabarrus, Inc., 1999.

https://civilwardata.com.

htpps:// Newberrywolves.com.

https://tigerprints.clemson.edu.

https://www.findagrave.com.

hptts://Wikipedia.org. "Lutheran Theological Seminary," Wikipedia contributors.

https://www.Ancestry.com. United States Federal Census [database on-line]. Provo, UT, USA: Ancestry.com Operations, Inc., 2009. Images reproduced by FamilySearch.

Lenoir Rhyne University, "History and Traditions." https://www.lr.edu.

"McAllister Papers, ECHS." MS. Eastern Cabarrus Historical Society Library, Mt. Pleasant, NC.

McDaniel, Michael C. D. *A Brief History of North Carolina College, Mt. Pleasant, NC 1859-1901*. Unpublished manuscript written as part of the requirements for English 52, at UNC-CH, March 10, 1951.

McDaniel, Michael C. D. *George Franklin McAllister, 1874-1938, Lutheran Educator*. Unpublished manuscript written as partial fulfillment of the requirements of the course in American Christianity, Hamma Divinity School, January 21, 1954.

McEntyre, Nick. *Service Cards for Mount Pleasant Collegiate Students Known to have Served in the First World War*. Unpublished manuscript. Eastern Cabarrus Historical Society Library, Mt. Pleasant, NC, 2018.

McLain, Denise Melanie. *Memories of Mont Amonea Female Seminary: An Island of Culture in the Difficult Years, 1859-1927*. Master's Thesis. UNC-Charlotte, Charlotte, NC, 2017.

"Minutes of the Board of Directors of Western Carolina Male Academy." MS. Carl A. Rudisill Library, Lenoir-Rhyne University, Hickory, NC.
"Minutes of the Board of Trustees of North Carolina College." MS, Carl A. Rudisill Library, Lenoir-Rhyne University, Hickory, NC.
"Minutes of The Board of Directors of Mt. Pleasant Collegiate Institute. MS. Eastern Cabarrus Historical Society Library, Mt. Pleasant, NC.
"Minutes of the NC College Faculty." MS. Eastern Cabarrus Historical Society Library, Mt. Pleasant, NC.
Minutes of the Evangelical Lutheran Synod & Ministerium of North Carolina. 1852-1942.
Morgan, Jacob L, DD; Bachman, Brown, Jr., DD, and John Hall, DD (eds.). *History of the Lutheran Church in North Carolina, 1803-1853*, United Evangelical Lutheran Church of North Carolina, 1953.
Morris, Jeff L. & Ellis G. Boatmon. *A Centennial History of Lenoir Rhyne College*. Downing and Company, Virginia Beach, VA.
Mt. Pleasant Collegiate Institute, Pamphlet, 1903 & 1904. MS. Eastern Cabarrus Historical Society Library, Mt. Pleasant, NC.
North Carolina College Advance. Mt. Pleasant, NC. MS. Eastern Cabarrus Historical Society Library, Mt. Pleasant, NC.
North Carolina State Troops, 1861-1865, A Roster, Vol. IV. published by the North Carolina State Archives & History, Raleigh, NC, 1973.
Phillips, Kenneth E. *James Henry Lane and the War for Southern Independence*. Master's Thesis, Auburn University, 1982 Wallace Community College. Article at *www. encyclopediaofalabama.org.*
Powell, William S. [ed]. "Daniel Efird Rhyne" *Dictionary of North Carolina Biography*. University of North Carolina Press, Chapel Hill, NC 1994.
Powell, William S. [ed]. "John Solomon Melanchthon Efird" *Dictionary of North Carolina Biography*. University of North Carolina Press, Chapel Hill, NC, 1979.
Private Laws of the State of North Carolina Passed by the General Assembly at its Session begun on January 6, 1909, Raleigh, NC. "An Act to Revise the Charter of the Trustees of North Carolina College, Mt. Pleasant, NC." Raleigh, NC. E. M. Uzzell & Co., Printer & Binders, 1909.
Private Laws of the State of North Carolina Enacted by the General Assembly at its Extra of 1921 Session begun on December 6, 1921, Raleigh, NC. "An Act To Amend Chapter 357 of Private Laws of 1909, Raleigh

8th Day of March 1909. Amending the Charter of North Carolina College, Mt. Pleasant, NC." Raleigh, NC. Mitchell Printing Co., State Printers, 1922.

Suther, John A. *The Heritage of St. John's*. St. John's Lutheran Church, Concord, NC. www. stjohnslutheranchurch.net.

"Records of Mont Amoena Seminary." MS. Eastern Cabarrus Historical Society Library, Mt. Pleasant, NC.

"Records of Mt. Pleasant Collegiate Institute." MS. Eastern Cabarrus Historical Society Library, Mt. Pleasant, NC.

"Records of North Carolina College." MS. Eastern Cabarrus Historical Society Library, Mt. Pleasant, NC.

Rules & Regulations of Mt. Pleasant Collegiate Institute. Pamphlet at ECHS Library, MP. Nd. The Times Printing, Concord., NC.

The Institute News, MPCI Alumni Association Newsletter. MS. Eastern Cabarrus Historical Library, Mt. Pleasant, NC.

The Falcon. Mt. Pleasant Collegiate Institute Yearbook, 1933. Published by the Senior Class of Mt. Pleasant Collegiate Institute, Mt. Pleasant, NC. Charlotte, NC. Press of the Observer Printing House of North Carolina. 1933.

The Sabre. Mt. Pleasant Collegiate Institute Yearbook, 1928. Published by the Senior Class of Mt. Pleasant Collegiate Institute, Mt. Pleasant, NC. [npp].

The Recall. Mt. Pleasant Collegiate Institute Yearbook, 1932. The Collegiate Institute, Mt. Pleasant, NC. [np] [npp].

The Tour Path. Mt. Pleasant Collegiate Institute Yearbook, 1925. Published by the Senior Class of Mt. Pleasant Collegiate Institute, Mt. Pleasant, NC. Charlotte, NC. Press of the Observer Printing House of North Carolina, 1925.

The Weddington Webpage. http://Millenium.Fortunecity.com [No longer active.]

University of Virginia Alumni Bulletin, Volume 4, 1911. University of Virginia Press, Charlottesville, VA.

Wallace, Carolyn A., "Daniel Moreau Barringer," www.ncpedia.org/biography/barringer-daniel-moreau.

Wills, 1757-1959, North Carolina Superior Court, Rowan County, NC at Ancestry.com. North Carolina, Wills and Probate Records, 1665-1998 [database on-line]. Provo, UT, USA: Ancestry.com Operations, Inc., 2015.

NEWSPAPERS

The Albemarle Press, Albemarle, NC. 1923 & 1925. www.newspapers.com.
The Burlington Daily Times, Burlington, NC. 1930-1935. www. newspapers. com.
The Carolina Watchman, Salisbury, NC. 1886 -1889. www.newspapers.com.
The Charlotte Democrat, Charlotte, NC. 1859-1876. www.newspapers.com.
The Charlotte Observer, Charlotte, NC, 1882-1922. https:www. newspapers. com.
The Concord Daily Tribune, Concord, NC, 1905-1923. www. newspapers. com.
The Concord Register, Concord, NC. 1876. www.newspapers.com.
The Concord Times, Concord, NC, 1886 -1942. www.newspapers.com.
The Concord Weekly Gazette, Concord, NC, 1855. www.newspapers.com.
The Daily Standard, Concord, NC, 1899. www.newspapers.com.
The Dispatch, Lexington, NC, 1920. www.newspapers.com.
The Goldsboro Messenger, Goldsboro, NC, 1885. www.newspapers.com
The Herald & News, Newberry, SC, 1922. www.newspapers.com.
The Hickory Record, Hickory, NC, 1920-1922. www.newspapers.com.
The Manning Times, Manning, SC, 1888. www.newspapers.com.
The Morning Newbernian, New Bern, NC, 1923. www.newspapers.com.
The North Carolina Argus, Wadesboro, NC, 1868. www.newspapers.com.
The Old North State, Salisbury, NC, 1870. www.newspapers.com.
The Progressive Farmer, Raleigh, NC, 1922. www.newspapers.com.
The Republican Banner, Salisbury, NC, 1852. www.newspapers.com.
The Rocky Mount Telegram, Rocky Mount, NC, 1941. www. newspapers.com.
The Salisbury Evening Post, Salisbury, NC, 1918. www.newspapers.com.
The Statesville Record & Landmark, Statesville, NC, 1941. www. newspapers. com.
The Weekly Raleigh Register, Raleigh, NC, 1859-1861. www.newspapers.com.
The Watchman & Southron, Sumter, SC, 1888. www.newspapers.com.
The Western Democrat. Charlotte, NC, 1869. www.newspapers.com.

The Wilmington Messenger, Wilmington, NC, 1890. www.newspapers.com.
The Wilmington Morning Star, Wilmington, NC, 1921. www.newspapers. com.
The Wilmington Post, Wilmington, NC, 1881. www.newspapers.com.
The Wilmington Sun, Wilmington, NC, 1879. www.newspapers.com.
The Yorkville Enquirer, York, SC, 1886 & 1890. www.newspapers.com.